*The Making
of Modern Ireland
1603-1923*

THE MAKING
OF MODERN IRELAND
1603-1923

by

J. C. BECKETT
*Professor of Irish History
in the Queen's University
of Belfast*

FABER AND FABER

3 Queen Square

London

First published in 1966
by Faber and Faber Limited
First published in this edition 1969
Reprinted 1971
Printed in Great Britain by
R. MacLehose and Company Limited
The University Press Glasgow
All rights reserved

ISBN 0 571 09267 5 (Faber Paper Covered Edition)
ISBN 0 571 06654 2 (Hard Bound Edition)

Contents

MAPS *(at end of book)*

ULSTER IN THE EARLY SEVENTEENTH
CENTURY

IRELAND

PARLIAMENTARY CITIES AND
BOROUGHS

Preface

THE historian who sets out to cover more than three centuries in the life of a country must, of necessity, lean heavily upon his predecessors and colleagues, and the bibliography indicates the extent of my indebtedness to the published work of other scholars. Some more direct and personal obligations must be acknowledged here. Professor Michael Roberts read the book in typescript and Mr J. L. Lord, M.A., read it in proof; it owes more than I can easily calculate to their comment and criticism. I am indebted also to Dr R. E. Glasscock, and to the Geography Department of Queen's University, for preparing the maps; to Mr David Kennedy, M.Sc., for the extract from the unpublished diary of John Black, quoted in Chapter VII; to Mrs Anthea Orr, of the Queen's University History Department, who cheerfully undertook the laborious task of typing and re-typing the whole work.

Finally, I must confess that I entered upon the writing of this book almost by accident. I continued it, despite a growing conviction of my own incompetence, because I felt that the work should be done. My feelings on its completion can most appropriately be expressed in the words of that gentle and modest author, Izaak Walton: 'if I have prevented any abler person, I beg pardon of him, and my reader.'

J. C. BECKETT

Queen's University
Belfast
August 1965

*Commouisti terram et conturbasti eam: sana contritiones eius
quia commota est*

I

Pacata Hibernia

An English civil servant of the sixteenth century, writing gloomily about the state of Ireland, found support for his pessimism in a proverb: 'It is a proverb of old date, that the pride of France, the treason of England, and the war of Ireland, shall never have end. Which proverb, touching the war of Ireland, is like alway to continue, without God set it in men's breasts to find some new remedy that never was found before'. One reason why the year 1603 is so significant in Irish history is that then 'the war of Ireland' was, for a time, ended, and the country entered on a period of unwonted peace, united for the first time under a central administration. It is true that the peace lasted hardly more than a generation, but it was long enough to give a new character to the political and economic life of the kingdom. The Ireland of the 'protestant ascendancy', out of which the Ireland of to-day has arisen, took form during the first four decades of the seventeenth century.

Though the peace and unity of 1603 were the outcome of Tudor policy, that policy was essentially defensive rather than aggressive: its great end was the safety of England, not the subjugation of Ireland. The Tudor sovereigns sought this end by many means: 'sober ways, politic drifts and amiable persuasions'; flattery and fraud; repression and conciliation. It was only slowly and with reluctance that Elizabeth finally embarked on a war of conquest. But the shifting policies and varied expedients of the previous hundred years had left an inescapable legacy: the conquered Ireland — the 'Pacata Hibernia' — of 1603 was the creation of the Tudors; and their influence went far to determine the character of the new Ireland that was to emerge under the rule of the Stuarts.

(2)

When Henry Tudor seized the crown in 1485 Ireland was still remote from the main currents of European life. Without either political strength or material resources to counter the influence of physical isolation, she lay, as it were, on the outer edge of the world, culturally no less than geographically — *la divisa dal mondo ultima Irlanda*. At one time a different development had seemed possible. In the twelfth century Henry II's assumption of the 'lordship of Ireland' had opened the prospect of an Anglo-Norman conquest, transforming the loose congeries of tribal kingdoms that constituted the Gaelic political system into a strong feudal state. But the conquerors were not numerous enough to colonize effectively the territories they had overrun; the English kings, absorbed in Scottish, French and Welsh wars, paid scant attention to their new province; the native Irish, at first overawed by the superior equipment and organization of their enemies, were able gradually to check and then to turn back the tide of conquest. The Bruce invasion in the early fourteenth century, though eventually defeated, hastened the decline of English influence and encouraged native resistance.

From this point, Irish politics assumed a pattern that was to survive until the reign of Elizabeth. The authority of the royal government, with its capital at Dublin, extended nominally over the whole country, but was effective only within a relatively small area, significantly referred to as 'the land of peace', 'the obedient shires', and, later, 'the English Pale'. During the later middle ages it was this area alone that was regularly represented in parliament and contributed to parliamentary subsidies. In territories beyond the Pale, and especially in the towns, royal authority could sometimes be enforced and royal revenues sometimes collected; but the greater part of the country was divided into some fifty or sixty regions, each of which was virtually an independent state, ruled over by a native chief or *rí* (king) or by an Anglo-Norman noble. By the fourteenth century many of the latter had adopted native names and customs and were hardly distinguishable from their Irish neighbours. Both native and Norman were ready, when interest or necessity impelled them, to make formal submission to the crown; but for the most part they lived as independent rulers, each one of whom, to quote a sixteenth century writer, 'maketh war and peace for himself . . . and obeyeth to no other person, English or Irish, except only to such persons as may subdue him by the sword'.

With little support from England, and with scanty resources of its own, the Dublin government had a hard struggle to maintain itself. Despite the effort made in the Statutes of Kilkenny (1366) to set a permanent barrier between the colonists and the native Irish, the Gaelic influence increased, and the 'Old English' (as the colonists were commonly, if erroneously, called)[1] tended more and more to fall into the native way of life. The boundaries of 'the land of peace' were gradually pushed back; by the end of the fifteenth century the Pale comprised only a narrow coastal strip, stretching from Dundalk to a few miles south of Dublin, and even this small area could with difficulty be defended against the depredations of the Irish.

Political instability and endemic warfare hampered the development of Ireland's economy. There was no manufacture of importance, and agriculture was backward by contemporary English standards. Overseas trade brought prosperity to a few seaport towns, but was not extensive enough to produce a substantial middle class. The social and intellectual developments that in other parts of western Europe were linked with industrial and mercantile expansion had little effect on medieval Ireland. Nothing, perhaps, is more expressive of the poverty, backwardness and isolation of the country than the failure of all efforts to establish a university. The merchant and the university scholar were two of the agents by which the life of Europe was welded into a unity, and neither played much part in Irish society. It is true that the tradition of Gaelic learning was kept alive in the bardic schools and in some monastic houses; but the bardic schools had little or no contact with literary movements outside Ireland, and by the later middle ages the Gaelic tradition where it survived among the religious orders had become almost entirely self-contained.

In the ecclesiastical sphere, the isolation of Ireland was less strongly marked. Henry II's assumption of the lordship had been preceded and accompanied by measures of reform designed to remodel the Irish church on the common pattern of western Christendom, and papal support for his venture arose from the desire to see this effectively accomplished. But the incompleteness of the Anglo-Norman conquest left the church, as well as the country, divided into spheres of influence. In the conquered and colonized territories (*inter Anglos*) the clergy, both secular and regular, were English or Anglo-Norman by birth or descent; in the areas under Irish control (*inter Hibernicos*) they were for the most part native Irish; and there was little co-operation between the two groups. Among the native Irish clergy the administrative reforms of the twelfth century were only partially effective, and they were much less closely influenced than the English clergy by the ecclesiastical life of the continent.

[1] The term 'Anglo-Irish' does not seem to have come into general use until the eighteenth century, when it was used to denote the protestant ruling class.

(3)

Though the English king, as lord of Ireland, exercised a nominal authority over the whole country, and a more effective control within the Pale, Irish politics in the later fifteenth century were in large measure self-contained. While England was distracted by civil conflict a great Anglo-Norman family, the FitzGeralds of Kildare, had established an unrivalled supremacy. Their vast estates gave them a dominant position in eastern and south-eastern Ireland; they had built up a widespread network of alliances among Anglo-Norman and Gaelic magnates; and they had acquired, in the 1470s, almost a monopoly of the office of lord deputy, or king's representative in Ireland, which carried with it control of the Dublin administration and of the military forces of the Pale. This Kildare supremacy reached its height in the career of Gerald, the eighth earl — Garret Mór, or 'Gerald the Great', to the Irish. In 1477 he succeeded his father in the deputyship almost as naturally as in the earldom of Kildare; he held it, with brief intermissions, for the rest of his life; and on his death in 1513 it passed to his son.

To the historian it might seem that a family power of this sort represented the very antithesis of all that the Tudor monarchy stood for; but the Tudors were, in fact, guided by expediency, not by principle, and their policy towards Ireland rested on practical considerations of economy and security: Ireland must not become a drain on English resources, nor be left as a base for the foreign enemies of England. It was these considerations that governed Henry VII's treatment of Kildare. He knew that Kildare was a Yorkist; but he could rule Ireland cheaply, whereas any other deputy would require men and money from England. Henry therefore left Kildare in office, save for one brief period between 1494 and 1496 when Ireland was a centre of Yorkist conspiracy backed by foreign aid. Then, indeed, Henry acted firmly. He removed Kildare from the deputyship, appointed in his place an English official, Sir Edward Poynings, and sent over a well-equipped English army to support the new deputy's authority. But once the danger had shifted from Ireland to the Scottish border, Poynings was recalled, Kildare restored, and things left to go on as before.

Though Henry VIII was somewhat less cautious than his father, his policy was based on the same considerations. It was, perhaps, Wolsey who taught him to look jealously on the great Kildare power, and a few years after Garret Mór's death he removed his son, the ninth earl, temporarily from office. But he found the only viable alternative, government

by an English deputy backed by English arms, so costly that he soon
abandoned it, and tried instead to counter the influence of Kildare by
encouraging the power of a rival family, the Butlers of Ormond. In the
end, like Henry VII, he was not prepared to act decisively in Ireland until
threatened by a foreign danger.

The danger, when it came, was largely of his own making. His aggressive foreign policy and his quarrel with the pope raised up enemies who
were ready to take advantage of every weakness in his position; and by the
early 1530s Spanish agents had drawn the discontented magnates of
Munster, headed by the earl of Desmond, into alliance with Charles V.
Though this alliance came to nothing, the threat of insurrection backed
by foreign help was enough to outweigh considerations of economy; the
king resolved on active intervention in Ireland; and by the summer of
1534 the necessary forces had been collected. But at this point, events in
Ireland took an unexpected turn. Kildare, who had been restored to office
two years earlier, had been called over to London in February 1534; and
though he remained deputy in name, it was known that he would soon be
removed: the new policy demanded an English deputy, and in any case
Kildare's loyalty was under suspicion. His son, Lord Offaly ('Silken
Thomas'), young, proud, impetuous, and chafing under this threat to the
family power, was roused to fury by reports that the earl had been put to
death. In June, he broke into sudden insurrection, and within a few weeks
had overrun the greater part of the Pale. Henry thus found himself forced
into a major campaign, and launched, without any deliberate design, on a
course of policy from which retreat would be impossible.

The war lasted, with some intervals, until 1540. Though it was
preached up by the friars as a crusade against a schismatical king, and
though the rebels were in constant expectation of aid from the pope's
allies on the continent, religion played, in fact, very little part either in
provoking the war or in maintaining it; and neither the pope nor his allies
took part. But the hope of enlisting foreign aid in a crusade against the
English had been born, and was to remain a potent force in Irish politics
until the end of the seventeenth century.

By 1540 the Kildare power had been broken. The earl himself had died
in prison; five of his brothers, and his elder son, Thomas, had been
executed at Tyburn. A great 'Geraldine League', formed to support the
claims of his younger son, Gerald, and including many of the most powerful Irish chiefs and Old English nobles throughout the country, had
collapsed, and its members had submitted to the crown. This military
success had been paralleled in the political field. A parliament held in
1536–7, during an interval of comparative peace, had obediently enacted

for Ireland the ecclesiastical legislation of the English Reformation Parliament; the dissolution of the religious houses had begun, and the distribution of the spoil helped to bind the magnates, for a time at least, more closely to the crown. The country was now quiet, there was no centre of opposition, and the prestige of the crown stood high. Henry was determined to use this opportunity to extend royal authority over all Ireland.

To this end, every important ruler, whether of native Irish or of Old English descent, was induced to make a formal agreement with the crown, by which he promised to observe English law, to maintain no forces without the consent of the deputy, to surrender his lands to the king and receive them back to be held by knight-service. This 'surrender and re-grant' of lands was the essence of Henry's policy, for it established a defined feudal relationship between the crown and the magnates, in place of the existing vague suzerainty. So far as the Old English were concerned this was no more than a re-assertion of their original position; but for the native Irish it meant a fundamental change. Under Gaelic law, a chief's right in the lands that he ruled was a limited life-interest, and there was no succession by primogeniture; his surrender of lands was therefore, from the Irish standpoint, invalid, and to turn him into a tenant-in-chief of the crown was to ignore the rights of his clansmen. But though the clash between the two legal systems was later to produce trouble, all went well at first; the chiefs themselves were anxious to extend their personal authority and to establish direct succession in their own families by primogeniture, and the most important of them were flattered by being granted titles of nobility. The approval with which the ruling class in general regarded Henry's policy appeared in June 1541, when a well-attended parliament 'most willingly and joyously consented and agreed to' a bill conferring on him the title 'king of Ireland', in place of the title 'lord' granted by the papacy to Henry II. It was significant that the bill had to be read and explained in Irish as well as in English.

Henry's Irish policy won the admiration of contemporaries in England; but it was based on a misjudgement of the position, and its success was short-lived. Within a few years of his death Ireland was plunged into war, the authority of the crown was being widely defied, and the defence of the Pale was once more a serious problem. Many causes contributed to the failure, but the basic factor was this, that the fall of Kildare power and the break-up of the Geraldine League had made much less difference in reality than on the surface; outside the Pale there had been very little change, the magnates had not been permanently weakened, their submission to the crown was hardly more than a formality, and would last no longer than they chose to remain loyal. Henry had tried to impose peace on a country long divided among petty rulers accustomed to make war at will, and he had attempted to do it by means of paper agreements and acts of parliament; the next half-century was to show that these were of no avail unless backed by dominant military force. Yet the reign marked a step towards the military conquest that Henry himself thought to avoid. It was too late now to go back to the policy of ruling Ireland through an Irish-born nobleman; there was no one to take Kildare's place, no one else whose territorial power, personal prestige and family alliances would enable him to govern cheaply, protect the Pale, and maintain contact with the Old English and native Irish magnates. Henceforth, the deputy was to be an Englishman, supported by an English army; and the Pale became in fact, what it had always been potentially, a bridgehead from which the royal forces would, sooner or later, advance to the subjugation of the whole kingdom.

(4)

The religious divisions that took their rise in the reign of Henry VIII have played a great and probably dominant part in Irish politics since the early Stuart period; but the issue had not become clear-cut even at the end of the sixteenth century. Bishops and laymen alike had accepted Henry's act of supremacy with few qualms. The doctrinal changes under Edward VI were very unpopular; but no serious attempt was made to enforce them, even within the Pale, and they contributed little to the growing political unrest that marked the reign. Under Mary, though the restoration of papal authority was generally welcomed, the political situation rapidly deteriorated, and the hollowness of Henry's pacification became evident. In Elizabeth's reign, opposition to English power became allied to support for the pope; but even in Elizabeth's reign the bulk of the Old English, and especially those of the Pale, remained loyal to the crown, while refusing to accept its ecclesiastical settlement.

This uneasy situation forced Elizabeth to be cautious. Her Irish church settlement followed the English model, and was based on acts of supremacy and uniformity passed by the Irish parliament in 1560. But these acts were not rigidly enforced, even in Dublin itself. The recusants (i.e. those who refused the oath of supremacy) were rarely disturbed while their political loyalty could be counted on; and, despite the law, recusancy was not a barrier to municipal office, or even to a seat on the judicial bench. Elizabeth had no missionary zeal for the spread of protestantism, and her concern for Ireland sprang solely from her interest in the safety of England. Her policy was that of her grandfather, Henry VII, modified by circumstances: Ireland could no longer be governed without the expenditure of English money to maintain the garrison of the Pale; but Elizabeth strove to keep that expenditure as low as possible, and nothing but the risk of leaving an opening for Spanish intrigue would induce her to face the cost of campaigns in the more remote parts of the country. When such a campaign had achieved its immediate object she was prompt to reduce her forces, and tried to keep what had been gained, if it could be kept at all, by less expensive means.

Cautious and parsimonious as this policy was, it involved a fairly steady expansion of royal authority. The motive behind this expansion was essentially defensive, for it was inspired by fear of Spain; but it was none the less a threat to the age-old independence of chiefs and nobles, an independence that had been only superficially affected by Henry VIII's policy of 'surrender and re-grant'. This encroachment on local independence naturally provoked discontent, which could easily be fanned into insurrection, and this in turn led to a tightening of royal control. The process can be seen in Munster, which was, by its geographical position, particularly open to Spanish influence. For this reason the government watched the province carefully, and during the 1560s endeavoured to extend the influence of the crown, though rather by negotiation and intrigue than by direct military force. Even this cautious advance provoked an insurrection in 1569; and the government, now compelled to act more vigorously, applied a new system of administration, placing the whole province under a president, who was virtually a military governor. But once the insurrection had been crushed Elizabeth, after her manner, cut down the army, released the captured rebel leaders on promise of good behaviour, and left the president to do what he could with the meagre forces at his disposal. The inevitable result followed. The president was not strong enough to keep the province in peace, but his attempts to do so provoked another insurrection in 1579. This time the rebels received arms, men and money from Spain, and their religious ardour was sustained by the presence of a papal nuncio; but they had no effective leadership, their alliance fell to pieces, and by 1583 the last of them had submitted.

Anxious, as ever, to attain her end by the cheapest possible means, Elizabeth resolved to secure royal authority in Munster by establishing a 'plantation', or colony. Such projects were popular at the time, and twice already, during the previous thirty years, had been attempted in Ireland, though without much success. In Mary's reign the Irish territories of Leix and Offaly, on the borders of the Pale, had been re-organized as Queen's County and King's County and granted out to loyal Old English to be

settled in the English fashion. In the 1570s attempts to establish a plantation in north-east Ulster by bringing in new settlers from England had
failed completely. But the prospects in Munster seemed more promising,
for here there had been an effective conquest, whereas in Leix and Offaly
the plantation had been imposed on a territory only half pacified, and
in Ulster the settlers had had to fight for the lands they hoped to occupy.
A comprehensive scheme for the Munster plantation was drawn up by
Burghley and Walsingham. It was based partly on Raleigh's proposals for
Virginia, and both Raleigh himself and his half-brother, Sir Humphrey
Gilbert, took part in the project. But it proved very difficult to attract
colonists from England, and the 'undertakers' to whom lands were let on
condition that they should bring in English families found it easier and
more profitable to take Irish tenants, so that the main purpose of the
plantation was foiled.

The suppression of the Munster rebellion, and the subsequent plantation, imperfectly executed though it was, marked a great advance of royal
authority. And about the same time advances were being made in other
directions also, though by more peaceful means. Government by a president was established in Connaught as well as in Munster; and a settlement
of the landed estates of the province (the so-called 'composition of Connaught') substituted money rents and English land-titles for the existing
mixture of Gaelic and feudal tenures. Another indication of the growth
of royal authority was the extension of the shire system. By 1585 the whole
of Ireland had been divided into counties; and though these divisions
could not everywhere be made immediately effective, there was a general
tightening up of royal authority in local affairs, and twenty-seven
counties sent members to the parliament of 1585.

(5)

Over much of the country this expanded royal power rested on a precarious basis; but in the 1580s and 1590s it seemed to be growing stronger,
and the only obvious barrier to its extension throughout the whole
kingdom was the province of Ulster. There, behind a formidable frontier
of mountain and lake, the Gaelic social and political system remained
almost intact. In Ulster, as elsewhere, Henry VIII had applied his policy of
'surrender and re-grant'; and in 1542 Conn O'Neill, head of the greatest
ruling family in the north, had accepted a royal grant of his lands, with the
title of earl of Tyrone. But this settlement had made no practical difference
in the administration of the province; and, so far from bringing peace, it
had led to a fierce struggle over the O'Neill succession, in which the domi-

nant figure was Conn's younger son, Shane. When Conn died in 1559, a
helpless refugee in the Pale, Shane assumed the traditional title of 'The
O'Neill', and made it clear that he intended to maintain virtual independence, while professing a formal allegiance to the crown. Elizabeth had
neither men nor money to spare for a difficult campaign, and was obliged
to accept the situation; but Shane's restless ambition led him to ruin. His
most powerful neighbours were the O'Donnells of Tyrconnell, on the
west, and on the east a branch of the Scottish MacDonnells, who had
established a strong colony in north Antrim. Unable to brook any equal,
he quarrelled with both, and after some initial successes was defeated and
killed in 1567.

After this, Ulster had more than twenty years of comparative tranquillity, marked by the gradual rise to power of Conn's grandson and
legitimate successor in the earldom, Hugh O'Neill. Hugh had been brought
up in England as a protégé of the crown, and after Shane's death had
been established in part of the O'Neill lands with the title of baron of
Dungannon. He showed himself consistently loyal, supporting the
deputy's authority in Ulster and serving in person against the Munster
rebels; in the parliament of 1585 his claim to the earldom of Tyrone was
formally recognized.

Ten years later Hugh O'Neill was to appear as the champion of Gaelic
separatism, the ally of the pope and Philip II against the queen of England;
but it is not necessary to suppose that his earlier loyalty was hypocritical,
that for a quarter of a century he was playing a part, and secretly preparing for rebellion. The great object of his ambition was to make himself
head of the O'Neills, 'the chief of his name and nation', a position in
which Shane had been succeeded by his cousin Turlough; and he thought
that the support of the government might help him to attain this end. In
spite of his English education he understood very clearly the character
of the power at which he aimed, and its dependence on tradition; he saw
that the spread of English law and English administration in Munster and
Connaught had undermined the basis of local independence there; but he
seems to have thought that Ulster might be allowed to remain Gaelic.
Only when he came to realize that the process of Anglicization threatened
Ulster also did he prepare for armed resistance. His fears were not groundless. The government had no settled plan for a conquest of Ulster, but it
certainly hoped to establish firmer control over the province by less direct
means; it was becoming alarmed at the growth of O'Neill's power, and it
could not ignore the possibility of a new Spanish attack, with Ulster
instead of Munster as the first object.

In these circumstances, a clash was probably inevitable, though neither side was in a hurry to provoke it. By the early 1590s Hugh was making careful preparations for war: he allied himself with Hugh Roe O'Donnell of Tyrconnell and with other Ulster chieftains, he accumulated military stores, he trained his followers in the use of musket and pike in place of the old-fashioned bow and halberd; and in 1593 he greatly strengthened his political position by persuading Turlough to cede to him the headship of the O'Neills. But for two years more he maintained his outward loyalty, even helping the deputy to suppress a local insurrection in Monaghan; and it was not until the spring of 1595 that he appeared openly against the crown.

If Hugh had been slow to rebel, the government was even slower to recognize how serious was the threat to royal authority when he did so; three years were frittered away in futile attempts to make peace by negotiation, and to break Hugh's power by winning over his allies. But in August 1598 the whole situation was changed by Hugh's great victory over the English at the battle of the Yellow Ford. This was a startling blow to royal prestige; rebellion, hitherto confined to the north, spread over the whole country; and Hugh found himself at the head of a national movement that seemed to threaten the complete destruction of English power in Ireland. Now at last Elizabeth realized that the time for compromise had gone by, that the rebellion must be crushed, at whatever cost, and Ulster effectively conquered.

Hugh's very success had thus ensured his ultimate overthrow, for against the forces that the crown could put in the field he had no chance of lasting victory. His one hope lay in help from abroad; but that help was late in coming and ineffective when it came. In September 1601 four thousand Spanish troops landed at Kinsale, where they allowed themselves to be besieged by the English; an Irish attempt to relieve the town was heavily defeated, and the Spaniards sailed home again. After this, the end could not be long delayed. Hugh Roe O'Donnell gave up the struggle at once and retired to Spain. His brother Rory took his place, and he and O'Neill held out longer; but they were forced back into Ulster, where garrisons established by the deputy, Mountjoy, harried and wore down their forces. In December 1602 O'Donnell surrendered at Athlone, and in the following March O'Neill let the deputy know that he too was ready to make submission. Mountjoy came to Mellifont, in County Louth, to receive him, and while waiting there received unofficial news that Elizabeth had died on 24 March; but this news he carefully concealed, and it was to Elizabeth, and to Mountjoy as her deputy, that O'Neill made abject submission on his knees on 30 March. The Tudor conquest was complete, six days after the last of the Tudors had died.

(6)

Fynes Moryson, who was Mountjoy's secretary, records that when O'Neill learnt of Elizabeth's death he could not conceal his tears, 'for no doubt, the most humble submission he had made to the queen he had so highly and proudly offended, much eclipsed the vain glory his actions might have carried, if he had held out till her death'. But in fact the terms of the settlement were so generous that it is hard to see how O'Neill could have improved his position by longer resistance. All those who had been engaged in the rebellion received pardon. O'Neill himself was confirmed in the earldom of Tyrone and in almost all the vast estates granted in 1542 to his grandfather, Conn; Rory O'Donnell was likewise confirmed in his lands, which comprised most of the county of Donegal, and was created earl of Tyrconnell; and the lesser leaders received similar treatment.

These generous terms aroused much discontent among English officers who had fought in the long struggle. In England itself there was some bitter feeling, for casualties in the Irish wars had been heavy; when O'Neill and O'Donnell visited England in the summer of 1603 they had to be protected from angry crowds on their way to London. But James received them gladly, and Mountjoy supported the cause of his beaten foes. He, who was in the best position to judge, knew that generosity was now a perfectly safe policy: the Gaelic independence of Ulster was broken; the earls of Tyrone and Tyrconnell might be wealthy and influential noblemen, but what they held they held by grace of the king, and not in their own strength.

It was left to James I to reap the victory of 1603, to settle the terms of peace, and to direct the course of the newly-conquered kingdom. But the conquest itself had been the work of the Tudors, and above all of Elizabeth. Well might Sir Thomas Stafford write, a generation later, 'The queen did seal up the rest of all her worthy acts with this accomplishment, as if she had thought that her task would be unfinished, and her tomb unfurnished, if there could not deservedly be engraven thereon, *PACATA HIBERNIA*'.

II

Ireland in the Early Seventeenth Century

----

(1)

'That it may please her excellent majesty to conceive of this her kingdom of Ireland', wrote Mountjoy in 1601, 'that it is one of the goodliest provinces of the world, being in itself either in quantity or quality little inferior to her realm of England . . . abounding with all the sustenance of life, as corn, cattle, fish and fowl'. But he was speaking of what might be, rather than of what actually was; and Ireland in 1603, after nine years of warfare, bore little resemblance to this glowing picture. Whole counties had been devastated; cattle slaughtered; crops burnt; churches and castles laid in ruin. And war had scarcely ended when the country was swept by plague. About Michaelmas 1603 it appeared in Dublin, where it brought administrative and judicial business almost to a stand-still; for councillors and judges were unwilling to live, or even to meet, in the city. A year later it drove the president of Munster from Cork to Mallow; and another year was to pass before it had slackened sufficiently for things to return to normal. The country generally was in a desperate condition. Ulster was said to be a very desert or wilderness; for sixty miles westward from Cork the country was almost uninhabited, and lands formerly cultivated had been allowed to fall out of tillage for ten or twelve years at a stretch; in Roscommon the scarcity of labourers had forced wages up to an almost prohibitive level; in the 'waste and desert places' of Munster 'those pestiferous wild beasts the wolves' showed a frightening increase, and in seventeenth-century Ireland the wolf was a kind of barometer of human population. What that population was at the opening of the century we have no means of assessing. In 1672 Sir William Petty put it at 1,100,000; but there had been a large influx of English and Scottish settlers during the interval, and in 1603 it cannot greatly have exceeded half that figure.

But though Ireland as a whole suffered from depopulation and consequent shortage of labour, communications were so bad and intercourse between one part of the country and another so scanty, that some areas suffered from over-population and unemployment. In the early years of James's reign large numbers of Irish paupers, with their wives and children, drifted over to England, where they were complained of both as a charge on the country and as a source of infection. Some even got as far afield as France, where the government made similar complaints, and ordered them to be shipped home again.

The establishment of peace in 1603 soon brought a measure of economic recovery, for the simplicity of the Irish economy made it resilient. There were no centres of manufacturing industry; the bulk of the population depended directly on the land; and once the depredations of rival armies had ended it was not long before wealth began to increase. In Ulster, barely touched so far by the process of Anglicization, this wealth consisted almost wholly in herds of cattle, which were driven from one place to another as pasture became exhausted, a practice known as 'creaghting'; there was little use of money, rents were paid in kind, and internal trade hardly existed. In those parts of Leinster, Munster and Connaught that had long been under English influence the agricultural system was more settled, though still backward; for example, the primitive practice of 'ploughing by the tail' was still common, and, indeed, survived into the eighteenth century. Farming was generally carried on for subsistence rather than for the market, and internal trade, though more considerable than in Ulster, was of small extent. But Irish agriculture, underdeveloped though it was, produced an exportable surplus; and this, with a few other commodities, formed the basis of a foreign trade, limited and fluctuating, but by no means unimportant.

A barrier to commercial development, though one not peculiar to Ireland, was the wretched state of the currency. A debased silver coinage had been issued at the end of Elizabeth's reign, and this 'base' or 'mixed' money was so unpopular that the merchants either refused it altogether, or only accepted it at far below its face value. To remedy this state of affairs James authorized (August 1603) the minting of new silver coins for Ireland, and the 'calling down' of the Elizabethan coinage to one-third of its face value. This brought some improvement; but even the new Irish currency was inferior to the English — the Irish (or 'Harp') shilling was worth only ninepence in English money. There were thus three standards of coinage: English coins, which were regularly current in Ireland, and the Irish coins of Elizabeth and of James. But though this state of affairs produced uncertainty and confusion, it was probably a less serious hindrance to trade than the general shortage of currency, which made the accumulation of capital very difficult and forced up the rate of interest on credit transactions to thirty, or even forty, per cent. Proposals for solving these difficulties, either by establishing a mint in Ireland, or by putting the Irish coinage on the same basis as the English, came to nothing; and the economic development of Ireland long continued to be hampered by an inadequate and inefficient currency system.

One serious hindrance to overseas trade under which Ireland at this time laboured was the prevalence of piracy on the southern and south-western coasts. In summer, when the royal galleys of France and Spain patrolled the seas further south, the pirates took refuge in the long inlets of Munster. They would arrive in regular fleets of ten or twelve sail apiece, each under its own admiral; and neither merchant nor fisherman was safe from their depredations. The government, with no forces available to deal with such powerful combinations, was obliged to negotiate, offering pardon on easy terms, in the hope of setting one pirate leader against another. Such intrigues produced no more than temporary relief; and sometimes they led to trouble with the French, the Spanish or the Dutch, who were all menaced by the virtual freedom of the Irish coast that the pirates enjoyed. In 1611 the Dutch, tired of waiting for the English government to take action, fitted out a fleet of their own, and scattered the pirates for the time being. But it was not until the 1630s, when Ireland was under the firm hand of Wentworth, that a sustained, and largely successful, effort was made to stamp out piracy in the Irish seas.

(2)

Manufactures contributed little to Ireland's trade. An Elizabethan statute had restricted the free export of certain commodities, including wool, flax, and yarn, partly to encourage industry, but mainly to increase royal revenue. Licences for the export of the prohibited commodities were granted regularly to the ports, and frequently to individuals; and even apart from this draining away of raw materials Ireland did not possess the resources necessary to develop textile manufactures on a large scale. Some very narrow linen cloth was woven for home use, but linen does not figure at all among the exports of the period except in the form of yarn. The only woollen cloths woven in Ireland were coarse friezes and ruggs', the export of which was not very considerable. In 1617 an attempt to establish a woollen manufacture at Bandon, where raw wool was readily available, and where there were many English settlers familiar with the technical processes, broke down for lack of capital.

The great bulk of Irish exports was made up of agricultural commodities, sheep-skins, wool, cattle, and cattle products — hides, tallow, and beef. There was some export of grain, but the quantity varied considerably from year to year; in 1608, for example, the export had to be prohibited altogether, in order to ensure an adequate supply of bread for the army. Apart from this trade in agricultural produce, there was a long-established export trade in fish; herrings were the most important item, but Derry was already known for its salmon, and Barnaby Rich thought the eel-fishery on the river Bann the best in Europe. The export of pipe-staves,[1] begun towards the end of the Tudor period, was to increase very rapidly in the early seventeenth century. The chief markets for these Irish exports were England, France, and Spain, which sent in return fine cloths and hardware, salt and wine, and various other luxury and semi-luxury goods.

(3)

One feature of the economic revival of the early seventeenth century was the rapid exploitation of the woodlands. During the Tudor period the destruction of the woods had already begun, though mainly for military reasons: they blocked the passage of the royal armies, and afforded secure fastnesses into which the more lightly-equipped Irish troops could easily retreat. It was therefore a constant policy of the government to open up passes; and during the later Elizabethan wars this was extended to a general clearance of large areas. Fynes Moryson, who travelled extensively in Ireland at the end of Elizabeth's reign, declared that he had 'been deceived in the common fame that all Ireland is woody', for in the course of a journey from Armagh to Kinsale he found, except in Offaly, no woods at all, beyond 'some low shrubby places which they call glens'. But Moryson's description cannot be applied to the whole country. At the beginning of the seventeenth century there were still extensive woodlands in Munster; the great wood of Glenconkeyne in Ulster was reckoned by Sir John Davies to be as big as the New Forest in Hampshire; and even beyond these areas, the country was at this time fairly heavily timbered. But the process of destruction was soon to be speeded up.

One cause of this more rapid destruction was the increase in the export of pipe-staves. They required little capital to produce, they found a ready market, and the profits were good. The price seems to have remained

[1] Pipe-staves: the narrow pieces of wood from which pipes (large casks, commonly used for wine) were made.

fairly constant during the first thirty years of the century at £5 per thousand in the northern ports and £6 per thousand in the southern. The cost of cutting was reckoned at thirty shillings per thousand, and where suitable rivers were available the cost of transport to the coast was not great; even after an export duty of 6s 8d per thousand had been imposed in 1611 there remained a tempting margin of profit. When Christopher Hampton became bishop of Derry in 1612 he found that though his predecessor had held the see for barely two years, one of his lessees had already cut down 3,000 trees on the episcopal estates and turned them into pipe-staves for export to Spain. In 1619 the earl of Cork had 400,000 pipe-staves lying at Youghal, 'which merchants of London daily send ships hither for, to transport beyond seas'.

The destruction of the woods was also hastened by the development of the iron industry. Ironware had been manufactured in Ireland for centuries; but the first large-scale iron-works seem to have been those set up in Munster by Sir Richard Boyle, afterwards earl of Cork. His example was followed by others, both in Munster and elsewhere, and bar-iron became an important Irish export. To begin with, the industry depended on ore mined in Ireland; later, the plentiful supply of timber made it profitable to import ore or half-worked iron from Bristol, and re-export it in the form of bar-iron. But the industry developed locally and unevenly; as late as 1611 all the iron used in Youghal, one of Boyle's principal towns, had to be imported from England.

The widespread destruction of woodlands did not pass without notice. Luke Gernon, writing in 1620, remarked that Ireland 'hath had goodly tresses of hair ... but the iron-mills, like a sharp-toothed comb, have notted and polled her much, and in her champion [champain] parts she hath not so much as will cover her nakedness'. Even earlier than this, the government had become alarmed; in 1608 Salisbury had sent over an agent to see what timber Ireland might yield for naval construction. But though surveys were made, and some trees were felled by royal officials, very little was accomplished; partly because the owners of woods found such profitable sale for their pipe-staves that it was impossible to restrain them, partly because the cost of transporting timber from Ireland to naval dockyards in England was considered prohibitive. The lord deputy, Chichester, suggested that the latter difficulty might be overcome by building ships in Ireland, or at Milford in South Wales. The government did nothing about this, but the experiment was tried by the East India Company. In 1611 they took land on the coast of Cork, planted an English settlement, built a dock, and set up iron-works. By 1613, despite trouble with the agents of the navy, who tried to seize their timber, and in face of some obstruction from the local inhabitants, they had launched two ships, one of 400 and one of 500 tons. But at that point the experiment ended, presumably because the disadvantages of building in Ireland more than outweighed the convenience of a ready supply of moderately-priced timber.

(4)

In a country with few manufactures the development of urban life depended on trade, and the only large cities and towns in Ireland were sea-ports. Inland towns counted for little; apart from Kilkenny, which had a special position as the headquarters of the powerful Butler interest, they were hardly more than local markets or military garrisons. The ports were mostly of Norse or Anglo-Norman foundation; and, with the single exception of Galway, those of any importance were situated in Leinster and Munster, whose rich lands had long been exploited by Anglo-Norman and English settlers.

The greatest of these sea-ports was Dublin, which in size and wealth far exceeded any other city or town of Ireland. Its importance, however, did not depend solely on trade. As the centre of royal government since the twelfth century, the headquarters of the judicial system, and the usual meeting-place of parliament, it had sources of wealth and growth that more than outweighed its serious geographical disadvantages. As a port, indeed, it had little to commend it. The approach was blocked by a bar; and large ships, even when they had crossed the bar, could not reach the quay, but must lie at Ring's End, where they were exposed to dangerous storms. But the presence of the chief governor and council, with all the officials and hangers-on of government, meant that there was a ready market for imported wares; and the economic as well as the political importance of Dublin grew with the expansion of central authority, so that it became the principal inlet of goods not only for Leinster but, in time of peace, for Ulster also. At the beginning of the seventeenth century it was spreading rapidly, and the cage-work houses of the Tudor period were giving way to buildings of stone and brick. In appearance and character it was the most English city in Ireland; its economic and political importance depended almost wholly on the English connection, and its trade was mainly with London, whose fashions the nobility and leading citizens were always eager to follow. It was for their amusement that a theatre was opened in Werburgh Street, in 1637, the first to be established anywhere in the British Isles outside London.

Galway, at this time reckoned the second city of the kingdom, had, because of its remoteness, developed a more independent tradition. Its citizens had little sympathy with the native Irish — a civic ordinance of 1581 enacted that 'neither O nor Mac shall strut nor swagger through the streets of Galway' — but they were almost equally opposed to the centralizing policy of Tudor government. Their intercourse was mainly with Spain, and something of Spanish influence appeared in their architecture and also, perhaps, in their attachment to municipal independence. The wealth of Galway depended on its virtual monopoly of the overseas trade of Connaught. But Connaught was much poorer than Leinster or Munster, and was soon to be surpassed by Ulster, at this time the least developed part of the country. The great days of Galway were already passing, and by the middle of the century it had entered on its long decline.

Waterford, the largest city in Munster, had the advantage of a fine natural harbour, and large ships could approach its quays, even at low tide. Like Dublin, it was English in appearance and character. By its charter it enjoyed the liberties of Bristol, with which it maintained a close connection, sending a fleet there every July for St James's fair. It had a continental trade also, especially with France and Spain, which provided the best markets for pipe-staves.

The two other principal ports of Munster were Cork and Limerick. Both were strongly built, in a castellated style; Limerick especially was noted for the thickness of its walls, which some travellers asserted (no doubt with exaggeration) to be broader than those of any city in Europe. Both cities had suffered in the wars at the end of Elizabeth's reign, when their trade had been interrupted both by land and sea. Cork had recovered fairly rapidly, partly because of its political importance as the seat of the president of Munster; but Limerick, despite the advantages of its position on the estuary of the Shannon, seemed to have sunk into poverty, though it retained the external appearance of its former wealth. Sir John Davies in 1606, Luke Gernon in 1620, both remark on the contrast between its fine buildings and the decay and slovenliness within; the latter found the high street 'so magnificent that at my first entry it did amaze me' and goes on, '*sed intus cadavera*, noisome and stinking houses'.

Dublin, Waterford, Cork and Limerick between them engrossed most of the trade of Leinster and Munster; but there were many smaller ports, of which Dundalk, Drogheda, Wexford and Youghal were the most considerable. The prosperity of Wexford depended mainly on its fisheries; but in the early years of the seventeenth century the herring-shoals deserted the coast, and by the 1630s the town was impoverished and decayed, and the quays going to ruin; such importance as it still possessed rested mainly on the export of pipe-staves. Drogheda, in contrast, was growing, partly because the extension of royal authority in the north had increased the area that it could serve, partly because the pacification of North Wales had encouraged the development of Chester as a port, and had diverted some portion of Anglo-Irish trade northwards from the older Bristol–Waterford route. Drogheda, unlike most other Irish ports, had a greater volume of outward than of inward trade, which meant that there was a regular return of money, mainly from England, in exchange for commodities.

Ulster had few towns of any sort. It was still the most thoroughly Gaelic part of the country, and the Gaelic social system did not conduce to urban life or commercial activity. Besides this, the province had suffered severely during the later stages of the Elizabethan wars. Inland towns could hardly be said to exist. When the deputy and his train toured the inland parts of Ulster in 1606 they found no settled lodging; even when they stopped in the neighbourhood of what passed for a town (as, for example, at Cavan) they slept in their tents; and in the whole of the county of Fermanagh they could find nowhere to hold the assizes but a ruined monastery, temporarily fitted up for the purpose. External trade amounted to very little. There was, and had long been, some intercourse between the north-western coast and Spain, fish being exported in exchange for wine; but the trade was not great enough for the development of sea-ports. The old ports of the north-east, relics of Anglo-Norman settlement in the twelfth century, had only a local importance; the chief of them, Carrickfergus, had little to boast of save its antiquity, its castle, and its unswerving allegiance to the crown. Two of the garrisons planted during the Tudor period, Newry and Derry, were well-placed for trade; and though of small account in the opening years of the century, they soon shared in the economic development that followed the establishment of peace.

Since the main centres of population lay along the coast communication between them could be maintained by sea; but inland communication was slow and difficult. The rivers, though interrupted by fords, weirs and cataracts, provided the best means of transport for heavy goods; it was, for example, the woodlands lying along the great rivers of Munster that were most quickly and profitably exploited. But there were few roads capable of taking wheeled traffic, and in many areas there were no roads at all: rural Ireland was much more self-contained than rural England. The English or continental traveller found that Irish urban life followed, though with sharp local variations, the general pattern to which he was accustomed; but if he ventured beyond the towns he was in a strange land indeed. The dwellings of the people — little villages of round, wattled huts without chimneys, like 'so many hives of bees about a farm'; their costume; their diet, which contained little bread and no beer, but great quantities of curdled milk — in all this he could find matter for astonishment, or even for disgust. But traveller after traveller remarks on the richness of the soil and the possibility of development; and the ruins with which the countryside was dotted — churches, abbeys, castles — bore witness to a greater prosperity in the past. Before the end of James I's reign the first signs of recovery had begun to appear.

(5)

Peace and unity had their effect on the constitutional as well as on the economic life of Ireland. The central administration was now for the first time effective over the whole country, and it was no longer, as it had commonly been in the past, mainly concerned with military problems — the defence of the Pale, or the suppression of rebellion. The 'kingdom of Ireland' had at last become a reality, and all the benefits of 'civil rule', so long promised by English statesmen, were now to be made available to the Irish people.

From the twelfth century onwards the royal government in Ireland had been modelled on that in England. The crown was represented by a chief governor; and council, parliament and law-courts all followed the English pattern in their composition and powers, modified by the fact that Ireland was a dependent state. The crown's representative might be either a lord lieutenant or a lord deputy. In the sixteenth and seventeenth centuries the office of lord lieutenant was often either vacant, or held by an absentee nobleman, and the actual government was entrusted to a lord deputy, usually chosen for experience and ability rather than for rank. The office of chief governor might also be put in commission, and held by two or more lords justices; but though this was to become a regular practice in the eighteenth century, it was unusual in the seventeenth. The chief governor, even if he was the deputy of an absentee lord lieutenant, was always appointed directly by the crown; but the Irish council claimed the right to fill a sudden vacancy by electing a justiciar or lord justice to hold office until the crown's pleasure should be known, a claim based on an alleged enactment of Henry II commonly referred to as 'the statute of FitzEmpress'. The chief governor, whatever his title, was the active as well as the nominal head of the administration and, normally, commander-in-chief of the army. The extent of his influence depended very much on circumstances. Policy was decided in the English council, and its execution was supervised by the council itself and by its Irish committee — the

B

commissioners of Irish affairs. But communication was so slow and uncertain that the chief governor had to be left a good deal of freedom in
interpreting his instructions; and a strong-minded man, provided he had
influential friends in the English council to defend his views, and provided
he could keep the royal favour, might go far towards shaping the government's Irish policy. Commonly, however, the chief governor was satisfied to be an executive official, supplying king and council with information and advice, but making no sustained effort to influence their
decisions.

The chief governor was assisted and in some measure controlled by a
council nominated by the crown. It was composed mainly of officials
resident in or near Dublin, together with two or three ecclesiastics, usually
the archbishops of Armagh and Dublin and the bishop of Meath. The
powers of the council were not closely defined, but its concurrence was
normally necessary for the issue of proclamations and in other acts of
state. The council also enjoyed statutory powers in preparing measures
to be laid before parliament; but parliaments in Ireland had fallen into
temporary disuse, and between 1586 and 1613 there was no occasion for
the exercise of these powers.

The Irish legal system, which, according to tradition, had been established by King John, was an almost exact reproduction of the English.
There were courts of king's bench, common pleas, chancery and exchequer, with the same division of jurisdiction as in England; and there
was the same system of itinerant justices and county courts. Since Elizabeth's reign Ireland had also had a special court, the court of Castle
Chamber, guided by the same principles and dealing with the same sort of
cases as the court of Star Chamber in England. The extension of this legal
system over the whole country followed hard on the completion of the
conquest. Before the end of 1603 Chief Baron Pelham conducted the first
assizes ever to be held in the county of Donegal; and within a few years
Sir John Davies, then attorney-general, could write complacently that the
judges 'do now every half year (like good planets in their several spheres
or circles) carry the light and influence of justice round the kingdom;
whereas the circuits in former times went but about the Pale, like the
circuit of the Cinosura about the Pole'. The justice that they carried was,
of course, that of the common law, and any doubt about the status of the
Gaelic system was speedily brought to an end. A proclamation of March
1605 abolished the authority hitherto exercised by Irish chiefs and lords
over their tenants, and declared the latter to be 'the free, natural, and immediate subjects of his majesty' and not 'the natives or natural followers of
any lord or chieftain whatsoever'. In judicial decisions of 1606 and 1608

the customs of gavelkind and tanistry,[1] which were essential parts of the Gaelic social and political system, were found by the judges to be void in law. Henceforth all Ireland was to be governed according to the common law of England and the statutes of force within the realm.

(6)

With the submission of Hugh O'Neill in 1603 open warfare in Ireland came to an end; but local disorder remained. The lawlessness bred during the long wars could not be stamped out at once; brigandage was endemic in many parts of the country; and a leader of ancient family, such as Donal Kavanagh of Carlow ('Don Espagne' or 'Spaniagh' — the Spaniard), found it easy to gather a large body of outlawed wood-kerne, whose thirst for plunder was quickened by the anti-English feeling strong among the Gaelic population. This political element in Irish brigandage, which survived until the eighteenth century, was alarming to a government that could never ignore the possibility of renewed insurrection; and even after peace had been made with Spain in 1604 the government's anxiety was kept alive by constant rumours of Spanish intrigues with the discontented Irish. The sudden insurrection of Sir Cahir O'Doherty in 1608[2] showed that this anxiety was not altogether groundless, and the ease with which he seized Derry was a sharp warning of the need to be prepared.

The difficulty of keeping order was increased by the practice, prevalent among both Irish and Old English magnates, of maintaining large bodies of armed followers or 'swordsmen'. Their former habit of settling disputes by force was restrained by the greater efficacy of the law-courts; but the importance of a great man was still commonly judged by the length of his retinue on public occasions. In 1609 it was reckoned that there were some 10,000 or 12,000 swordsmen in the country, without house, land, or trade, and wholly dependent on the lords and gentlemen whom they followed. A few years later Chichester, the lord deputy, took credit for having shipped off 6,000 of them to Sweden; but this was almost certainly an exaggeration, and in any case enough remained behind to threaten the peace of the country. It would be a mistake to regard this state of affairs as peculiar to Ireland, for throughout much of Scotland

---

[1] English lawyers commonly applied the Anglo-Saxon term 'gavelkind' to the Gaelic practice whereby the lands of a family group were redistributed on the death of one of its landholding members. 'Tanistry' was the practice whereby, during the life-time of a king or chief, his successor was chosen from among his kindred within a certain degree of consanguinity.

[2] See below, chap. III.

and in outlying parts of England the crown had similar difficulties in maintaining law and order. The Grahames of Cumberland, for example, proved such a threat to the peace of the borders that early in James's reign an attempt was made to transport some hundreds of them out of the kingdom. But England, and even Scotland, had a solid core of peaceful and prosperous life such as Ireland did not yet possess. The government in London or Edinburgh was not likely to be shaken by lawlessness on the periphery of the kingdom; the government in Dublin could have no such sense of security.

The chaotic state of Irish finance increased the difficulty of government. The war had been a heavy burden on the English exchequer, and James hoped that with the return of peace Ireland would become self-supporting. But the prospects were not very hopeful. Some branches of royal revenue had been leased to individuals at easy rates; all the great ports claimed privileges and exemptions that reduced the king's revenue from customs to a mere trifle; above all, the unsettled state of the country through so many centuries had left a legacy of confusion, inefficiency and corruption in the financial administration. Early in James's reign great efforts were made to re-assert royal rights and to restore order. From 1613, when a farm of the customs on the English model was established, there was some improvement, and the gap between income and expenditure was narrowed. But during most of the reign the Irish government lived from hand to mouth, depending upon grants from the English exchequer, which had no sooner arrived than they were almost wholly swallowed up in meeting accumulated debts.

It was the cost of the army that kept the government in such continuous poverty. But an army was absolutely indispensable, for Ireland had to be governed as a conquered country. The large forces maintained during the later stages of the war were, of course, cut down once peace had been made: at the end of 1603 there were still some 9,000 troops in the country; within a few months more than half of these had been disbanded, and by the spring of 1606 the regular establishment had been reduced to 880 foot and 234 horse. It was recognized, however, that this was barely sufficient: the deputy was authorized, in case of emergency, to raise a further 2,000 men without waiting for instructions from England, and later in the reign the standing army was somewhat increased.

The first duty of this army was not to repel foreign invasion but to maintain order at home, and it was scattered over the country in small garrisons, mainly in Ulster, where the danger of an insurrection among the native Irish was thought to be greatest. Even the Old English, however, were regarded as only doubtfully loyal. Chichester questioned the wisdom of pressing the sea-ports in the matter of customs duties, lest their discontent should endanger the safety of the kingdom; and he was almost constantly alarmed lest the influence of Jesuits and seminary priests from the continent should weaken the traditional attachment of the lords and gentry of the Pale to the English crown. While racial and religious antipathies remained so strong there could be no permanent security; Ireland would never, in English opinion, be safe or happy until the long and halting process of Anglicization had been completed, and the Irish (as Sir John Davies prophesied hopefully in 1612) 'in tongue and heart and everyway else become English, so as there will be no difference or distinction but the Irish Sea betwixt us'.

(7)

The Anglicization of the upper classes of Gaelic society, so far as language and dress were concerned, had already made some progress by the end of the sixteenth century. They had abandoned the use of the *braccae* or trews — a long stock of frieze, close to the thighs, and drawn on almost to the waist, 'but very scant' — and they now began to dress completely in the English fashion, at least on formal public occasions. In 1606 Sir John Davies noted with satisfaction that the principal gentlemen and freeholders of Wicklow, predominantly of native descent, attended the assizes in English dress. Very often, however, the natives continued to wear the characteristic Irish cloak or fringed mantle over clothes otherwise in the English fashion. Among the upper classes, also, the use of the English language made great progress; and though they no doubt remained more at home in Irish, it is probable that by the end of James's reign most of them spoke English as well. But there must have been many exceptions. Even in the parliament of 1613–15 there were said to be some members who could not speak English; and as late as 1628 a group of Irish nobles and gentry asked for the appointment of at least one Irish-speaking judge, 'many of the subjects hazarding their causes and sometimes their lives because they are not understood by the judges without interpreters'. Though this request may, of course, reflect their concern for the lower classes, among whom English was much less common, the context rather suggests that they were thinking of members of their own order. But fourteen years later, when the native Irish combined with the Old English in the Confederation of Kilkenny, they conducted their public business in English; and there is no evidence to suggest that this either created difficulty or caused jealousy.

Among the lower classes of the Gaelic population the process of

Anglicization made slower headway. Down to the 1640s they continued to wear the *braccae*, at least in Ulster, despite the threats of the civil power and the exhortations of their own clergy, who denounced the dress as immodest. And in the face of all discouragements they clung to the Irish language, which remained until the nineteenth century the strongest bulwark of the native tradition.

The Anglicization of the Gaelic gentry in dress and language was no doubt aided by their intermingling with the Old English. But this inter-mingling, though it thus tended to promote government policy in one respect, strengthened both groups in their refusal to conform in matters of religion. This refusal, and their common anxiety about the govern-ment's reaction to it, prepared the way for their future co-operation in politics. Religion, not race, was to be the great dividing line in Irish life.

(8)

Elizabeth had, in practice, tolerated the recusants so long as they remained loyal to the crown; and in the troubled conditions of her reign this policy had answered its purpose of conciliating the Old English; but it could hardly provide the basis of a permanent peace-time settlement, if only because the recusants themselves were unlikely to be content with it for long. The failure of the early Stuarts to work out a satisfactory alternative was due as much to the intractable nature of the problem as to the government's inefficiency and lack of consistent purpose. On the one hand, open and formal toleration was out of keeping with the spirit of the age; and in any case it would have been strongly resented by the growing protestant interest in Ireland, on which the crown had in the long run to rely, and it would have alienated public opinion in England. On the other hand, any attempt to enforce general conformity was unlikely to succeed and sure to be dangerous.

Any hope of winning over the recusants by persuasion must rest with the established church, which was still, at the opening of the seventeenth century, in a state of confusion, inefficiency and neglect. At Elizabeth's death, many sees had been vacant for years and many were held in plurality. The bishops, appointed mainly on political grounds, were generally more concerned to enrich themselves and their families than to further the cause of religion, and often combined with laymen to alienate the property of the church. The parish clergy were for the most part poor, careless and ignorant, though the foundation of a university (Trinity College, on the outskirts of Dublin) in 1591 promised some improvement in their educational standard. Church buildings were everywhere in ruins, and parochial duties neglected. So late as 1632 Lord Cork, whose greed for ecclesiastical lands was tempered by a streak of piety, found that the parish church of Maynooth 'had been, God forgive the doers thereof, misapplied to the keeping of cattle and making of malt and other base uses'. He rebuilt it at a cost of £120, and the sermon preached by his chaplain in the restored building 'for aught I could hear, was the first sermon made by a protestant minister in any man's memory herein'.

There were doubtless some exceptions to this gloomy state of affairs. At Limerick, for example, the cathedral was 'by the providence of the bishop fairly beautified within, and as gloriously served with singing and organs'. But in the country generally the whole fabric of ecclesiastical life was in decay. There was little zeal for the spread of the reformed faith, and no one to direct such zeal as there was. Tardy and half-hearted efforts to reach the native Irish through their own language had so far produced little result. Neither Irish Bible nor Irish prayer-book had been published, though an Irish translation of the New Testament, undertaken more than a generation earlier, was at last published in 1603. Even preaching in Irish was unusual. In 1604 the diocese of Meath had twenty-nine clergy with livings worth at least £30 a year — the income generally reckoned adequate to support a 'learned minister' — and of the twenty-nine only three could preach in Irish.

In contrast with all this, the Roman Catholic clergy were numerous, zealous and efficient. Their main task was to restore discipline and maintain the ecclesiastical framework; and this they did so effectively that whatever chance the reformed church may have had of capturing the Irish people was, by the beginning of James's reign, irretrievably lost. The vast bulk of them, natives and Old English alike, were determined recusants, and the protestant population, though growing slowly, consisted of little more than a handful of officials and a few recent settlers. The struggle between these two religious groups was to dominate Irish history throughout the seventeenth century, and beyond.

III

Protestant and Recusant: The Constitutional Struggle, 1603-1641

(1)

On 5 April 1603 Queen Elizabeth's death was formally announced in Dublin, and James VI of Scotland proclaimed as her successor. 'The Irish at once submitted heartily to a prince descended from the ancient line of their own native monarchs, and joyfully hailed the revival of the long-suppressed dynasty of their first king, Eireamon, in the person of one of his descendants.'

Thus wrote John Lynch, titular archdeacon of Tuam, some sixty years later. One may reasonably doubt if Irishmen in general paid much attention to James's early ancestry, which Lynch traces up to Adam in a threefold line, taking in the principal families of Gaelic Ireland on the way. What mattered much more in 1603 was that the new king was the son of Mary Stuart: it was in expectation that he would show himself well-disposed towards his mother's faith that Irish recusants looked forward hopefully to his reign, and it was among the Old English, not among the natives, that this expectation ran highest. They were still strongly established in local administration, and once the news of the queen's death became public they had the strength and the confidence to act without delay. In all the principal towns of Munster, and in Wexford, Kilkenny and some other towns of Leinster, the recusant clergy, with the support of the magistrates, took possession of the churches and restored the old services.

Though the recusants had protested their loyalty to the crown, the Dublin government was thoroughly alarmed, and suspected that they were plotting a general insurrection, to be backed by the power of Spain. But if there was any such plan, which seems highly unlikely, it was frustrated by the swift action of Mountjoy, who was still at the head of the government. His commission had determined with the queen's death; but the council, exercising its traditional right, had elected him lord justice on 9 April. Within a few weeks two royal commissions arrived from England, the first appointing him lord deputy, the second raising him to the more dignified rank of lord lieutenant; but without awaiting this confirmation of his authority Mountjoy had collected every man that could be spared, even withdrawing some troops from the newly-conquered north, and marched into Munster. The strength of his army made effective resistance impossible, and in most places the magistrates made instant submission. Waterford tried to argue that the charter granted by King John freed the city from any obligation to admit royal troops; but Mountjoy's curt reply that he would cut King John's charter with King James's sword soon brought the citizens to their senses. In Cork the situation was more serious, for there had been a breach between the city and the commander of the garrison; but here too Mountjoy's arrival brought submission and peace. Before the end of May, government authority had been restored throughout Munster.

The recusants had failed to gain what they wanted by direct action; but they still believed that they could count on royal favour, and in June they sent agents to court to lay their grievances before the king. James was in no hurry to make a declaration of policy, and for two years his delay kept Ireland in a state of suspense. The government in Dublin, ignorant of his intentions, hesitated to enforce the law strictly, and found its authority flouted by the recusant clergy. Mountjoy might have taken a stronger line; but he had been recalled to England in May 1603, and though he retained the title of lord lieutenant until his death in 1606 and continued to exercise great influence in Irish affairs, immediate responsibility rested on the deputy and council in Dublin. Sir George Carey, the vice-treasurer, who had become deputy on Mountjoy's departure for England, was content to await royal instructions on the recusancy question and in the meantime to let things take their course; but in February 1605 he was succeeded by Sir Arthur Chichester, governor of Carrickfergus, a man of strong character, and one not likely to tolerate defiance of the law. For the next ten years he remained at the head of the Irish administration, and sought by every means to strengthen its hold upon the country.

To Chichester the open activity of the recusants, and especially of the recusant clergy, seemed to threaten the very basis of government. He urged the king to authorize strong measures against them, and it was, perhaps, in response to this appeal that James at last declared his policy in July 1605: there was to be no toleration contrary to law; attendance at church was to be enforced; Jesuits and seminary priests were to leave the kingdom by 10 December. With this encouragement Chichester set to work, assisted by Sir John Davies,[1] the solicitor-general and his most active colleague in the government. They were convinced that if prominent recusants could be made to conform the rank and file would follow their example. Since the shilling fine for non-attendance at church, the only penalty provided by the law, was insufficient for their purpose, another method was devised. 'Mandates' were issued to several aldermen and other prominent citizens of Dublin, requiring them to accompany the deputy to church; and when they refused they were brought before the court of Castle Chamber, which ordered them to be fined, and imprisoned during pleasure. But Chichester had misjudged the attitude of the English government. James would not formally tolerate recusancy, but neither would he allow persecution. The recusants had responded to Chichester's action by despatching protestations of loyalty and appeals for relief to London; the king and council, fearful of a new insurrection in Ireland, urged Chichester to proceed with caution. They did not explicitly condemn what he had done and they admitted that open flouting of the law must be punished, but they recommended him to rely on time and persuasion to bring about conformity, rather than on any sudden and violent courses. In particular, they queried the legality of the mandates, and though Chichester claimed that they were justified by precedent, they were in fact abandoned in 1607.

This was a victory for the recusants, and about the same time the strength of their influence was further shown by events in Munster. There, Sir Henry Brouncker, the president, without waiting for royal guidance, had issued a proclamation in August 1604, ordering all Jesuits and seminary priests to leave the province before the end of September, and threatening punishment against all who should receive them thereafter. He followed this up by an energetic search for recusant clergy, he encouraged the settlement of 'teachers of God's most holy and true word', and he tried to force uniformity on the towns by deposing recusant mayors and by fining the citizens for non-attendance at church. Brouncker claimed that his methods were successful; but the recusant gentry and citizens made their complaints heard not only in Dublin, where Chichester ignored them, but in London, where James and the English council were so alarmed that they urged Brouncker to moderate his policy; and when in June 1607 he died (according to recusant accounts in a fury of remorse and gnawing the flesh from his arms) his policy died with him. 'His zeal',

---

[1] Solicitor-general, 1603–6; attorney-general, 1606–19.

wrote James to Chichester, 'was more than was required in a governor, however allowable in a private man'.

The position that emerged during the early years of James I remained basically unchanged down to 1641. The recusants failed to secure a formal toleration, but they did not give up hope of it, and their political strength made it difficult, if not dangerous, to enforce the laws against them strictly. The Dublin government, conscious that its own prestige was involved, and under pressure from Irish protestant interests, ecclesiastical and secular, would have been prepared to take the risk. But the crown and the English council, anxious that Ireland should be governed as quietly and as cheaply as possible, insisted on caution. As a result, the recusants were neither conciliated nor crushed; occasional attempts at persecution kept alive their sense of grievance; and the efforts to undermine their position by building up a protestant population of English and Scottish settlers helped in the long run to force them into rebellion.

(2)

The Elizabethan attempts to establish new English colonies in Ireland had come to very little, but with the completion of the conquest the policy was resumed. Lord Deputy Chichester, who thought it an absurd folly that men should run after Virginia and Guiana and other remote lands while Ireland lay waste and desolate, was mainly concerned about Ulster. In 1605 he proposed the establishment of English and Scottish settlements at strategic points throughout the province; in 1606 he put forward a scheme for the whole county of Cavan, by which land was to be found for new colonists without any injustice to the native proprietors; and he gave official encouragement to the Scottish adventurers who were at this time establishing themselves in north Down. But the events of the next few years overshadowed these plans for local and piecemeal settlement and opened the way for a comprehensive scheme covering most of the province of Ulster.

At James's accession Ulster still remained the most thoroughly Gaelic part of Ireland. But the influence of the newly-established English supremacy was felt almost at once: county divisions, drawn out on paper in 1585, were made effective; assizes were held; the power of the great Irish lords was curtailed; a new class of native freeholders, dependent directly on the crown, was brought into existence. The progress of these changes helped to precipitate a crisis that had only been postponed by the settlement of 1603. Tyrone and Tyrconnell had never become reconciled to their new positions, and each advance of the central power added to their discontent. The loss of their ancient authority, temporarily disguised by the return of their lands, became more and more evident; and a proposal by Chichester, in 1606, to establish in Ulster a presidency on the Munster model threatened to destroy what was left of it.

The earls had another and more urgent cause for anxiety. They were, perhaps inevitably, suspected of planning a new insurrection; their every move was watched; and they knew, or believed, that they had enemies in Dublin and London who would make the most of any unfavourable report. It is impossible to tell how far this suspicion of their loyalty was well-founded. Though Tyrconnell may have talked treason from time to time, and though Tyrone certainly took the law into his own hands in a quarrel with his neighbour O'Cahan, there is no evidence of any organized plot against the state; and Tyrone, at least, seems to have realized the hopelessness of rebellion. But faced with the prospect of a steady decline in their influence, and the possibility of arrest on a charge, whether justified or not, of treason, they decided to leave the country. In August 1607 Tyrone was summoned to London, that his quarrel with O'Cahan might be settled by the king. He may well have feared that if he obeyed he would never be allowed to return, and this fear may have hastened his final decision to fly; but the causes of his flight lay deeper, and long befor the summons to London arrived he had already made his preparations. A ship secretly hired in France arrived in Lough Swilly towards the end of August. Tyrone received the news at Slane (Co. Meath) where he had just concluded an apparently friendly conference with Chichester; he set out at once and by travelling hard reached Lough Swilly just over a week later; Tyrconnell was awaiting him, and the two earls, with almost 100 followers, embarked at once. They had intended to make for Spain, but after a stormy passage of three weeks they were forced to land in Normandy, and passed on quickly to the Spanish Netherlands, whence, by a slow and circuitous journey, they arrived in Rome at the end of April 1608. Here at length they found asylum; but the pope was unable, and the king of Spain unwilling, to support any project for their restoration.

The departure of Tyrone and Tyrconnell for the continent was a belated and despairing recognition that they could never undo the effect of their surrender to the crown. But to Gaelic Ulster 'the flight of the earls', rather than Mountjoy's victory in 1603, marked the end of the old order; and it soon came to be regarded as a national disaster:

'Woe to the heart that meditated, woe to the mind that conceived, woe to the council that decided on, the project of their setting out on this voyage, without knowing whether they should ever return to their native principalities or patrimonies to the end of the world.'

It is doubtful if the distinctively Gaelic character of Ulster could in any case have long resisted the processes already at work; but the events of 1607 certainly opened to the government an opportunity of Anglicizing the province by more speedy and direct methods. The secret and unauthorized departure of the earls was treated as confession of treason, their estates were declared forfeit to the crown, and plans were drawn up for planting them with English and Scottish settlers. This project affected the greater part of Ulster, for the government treated as liable to confiscation the whole area over which the earls had exercised any authority, though this was hardly consistent with the earlier policy of granting their dependants freeholds with right of inheritance. The claims of the crown were pressed to the utmost, and six of the nine Ulster counties — Armagh, Cavan, Coleraine (later renamed Londonderry), Donegal, Fermanagh, Tyrone — were found to be in the king's hands and open to colonization.

Chichester was quick to recognize the opportunity presented by the new situation in Ulster. On receiving news of the flight of Tyrone and Tyrconnell he wrote to the English council, setting out in some detail a scheme for the settlement of their lands. This was similar to his earlier scheme for Cavan and provided, in the first place, for the natives; when they had been granted as much land as they could profitably develop, there would still remain, in Chichester's opinion, sufficient for a strong settlement of English and Scots.

Whatever chance of acceptance these modest proposals might have had was ruined by an unexpected turn of events in the spring of 1608. Sir Cahir O'Doherty of Inishowen, chafing under an insult received from the governor of Derry, and also, perhaps, uneasy at the steady growth of royal authority, broke into sudden insurrection on 18 April, seized Culmore fort, on Lough Foyle, by a stratagem, and next day captured and burnt Derry. This, however, was all that he could do: the rising received no general support, he had no plan of campaign, and no means of maintaining a long struggle. By the end of July he himself had been killed and his followers scattered, to be tracked down and destroyed in isolated groups, the last of them on Tory Island in September.

Though the rising was quickly crushed, its early success had frightened the government into a belief that strong measures were necessary; and the scheme for the plantation of the six escheated counties, published in 1609 and modified in 1610, treated the native landholders much less favourably than Chichester had proposed. In each county a comparatively small area was assigned to 'deserving' natives, who were to grant leases to their tenants, build houses and follow English methods of husbandry. The rest of the territory, apart from the extensive church lands, was set aside for colonization. The main work was to be entrusted to 'undertakers'. They were required to bring over English or Scottish settlers and establish them close together in villages and townships; to build stone or brick houses with fortified enclosures or 'bawns', and to keep arms for their defence. Lands were also to be granted to 'servitors' (men who had served the crown in Ireland); they were under similar obligations as to building and defence, but were allowed to take native Irish tenants, though they were encouraged to plant with English or Scots.

This scheme was put into operation slowly and imperfectly but it left a permanent mark on the province; and the long traditions of Gaelic Ulster were gradually overlaid, though not extinguished, by those of a new Anglo-Scottish population. The change in population, however, was neither so rapid nor so extensive as the government had intended. According to the scheme, the natives were to be completely removed from the lands assigned to undertakers, though they were allowed to remain as tenants on church lands, as well as on lands assigned to servitors and native proprietors. But the undertakers, anxious for quick profits, readily accepted Irish tenants; and the difficulty of bringing over a sufficient number of settlers was, in fact, so great that the government was unable to compel them to fulfil their obligations. One main purpose of the plantation was thus foiled; for such settlers as came, instead of forming compact islands of 'civility', were scattered through a population still predominantly Gaelic.

The whole plantation was not left to individual undertakers and servitors. In May 1609 a proposal was put before the city of London, showing the advantages to the city of taking a share in the work; and, after receiving a report from agents whom they had sent over to investigate the prospects, the Londoners entered into an engagement with the crown in January 1610. By this, they undertook to plant the county of Coleraine, and to rebuild, enlarge and fortify its two main towns, Coleraine and Derry. In return, they were to receive extensive privileges, including the patronage of all churches within their territory, the fisheries of the Foyle and the Bann, and a long lease of the customs at a nominal rent.

The Londoners organized their undertaking as a joint-stock enterprise, to which the various city companies contributed, and by April 1610 they had sent 200 workmen to start building in Coleraine and Derry. But this energetic opening was not followed up in the same manner, and even ten years later neither town had been completed or fortified in accordance with the plans originally laid down. Some progress was made with the bringing over of colonists, but the Londoners, like the other undertakers, were ready to take Irish tenants; and apart from Coleraine and Derry their towns were weak and precarious settlements, dangerously exposed to attack from a potentially hostile population. Incomplete as it was, however, the work of the Londoners was the most important contribution to the plantation of the six escheated counties during the reign of James I; and its permanent character is significantly commemorated in place-names. Derry was renamed Londonderry, and gave its name to the whole county; Draperstown and Salterstown owe their foundation to two of the city companies concerned in the work of colonization.

In the Ulster plantation no distinction was made between English and lowland Scots. The latter came over in considerable numbers, and proved themselves in some ways the more efficient colonists; for they were readier than the English to sink labour and capital in tillage. Scots took a large share in the plantation of Donegal, and made up a high proportion of the new tenantry brought in by the London companies, but it was in Antrim and Down, which did not form part of the territory confiscated in 1607, that they made their main contribution to the re-peopling of Ulster.

These counties were conveniently situated for Scottish exploitation; and the accession of James VI to the throne of England provided an opportunity that was not likely to be missed. The two men most forward in pushing their fortunes were Hugh Montgomery, laird of Braidstane in Ayrshire, and James Hamilton, who had served the king usefully as a secret agent in Dublin during the later years of Elizabeth. Montgomery, who was well-informed of what was happening in Ulster, knew that Con O'Neill of Clandeboye, the somewhat shiftless proprietor of 60,000 acres in north Down, lay a prisoner in Carrickfergus Castle on suspicion of treason, and undertook to secure his pardon in return for a share of his lands. Hamilton, by some means, got himself included in the transaction; and in 1605 the king made a triple division of the Clandeboye estate — one-third to Con O'Neill, and one-third to each of the two Scots. Con proved no match for his new neighbours, and within a few years they had got possession of almost all that the royal settlement had left him. But if Montgomery and Hamilton were not always scrupulous in their methods, they were able and energetic colonizers. Their lands, which were waste and depopulated when they took possession of them, soon flourished. They brought in stock, they planted settlers, they built houses, they refounded old towns and founded new ones. The prosperity of north Down, as well as its strongly Scottish character, had its origin in their labours. Their example was soon followed by other Scots, in Antrim as well as in Down; and within a generation a great part of both counties had been transformed, in population and way of life, into a sort of extension of the Scottish lowlands.

The settlement of the Scots in the north-east introduced a new compli-
cation into the pattern of Irish ecclesiastical life. Some of their own
ministers accompanied or followed them; and through the easy-going
tolerance of a few Ulster bishops, Scots like themselves, these ministers
were soon able to get possession of benefices without much regard to the
law of the church. For more than twenty years they were allowed to live
inside the establishment, and draw their incomes from its property, while
maintaining their own form of worship and their own views on church
discipline. When an effort was at length made to end this anomalous
position and bring them to conformity, they not unnaturally regarded
it as an act of tyranny.

(3)

While the Ulster plantation was still in its early stages preparations
were begun for a meeting of parliament. There had been no parliament
in Ireland since that of 1585–6, and the great changes that had taken place
in the interval — the completion of the conquest, the extension of English
law over the whole kingdom — made new legislation necessary, or at
least very desirable. Since the beginning of the reign, indeed, the calling
of a parliament had been under discussion; but it was not until 1610 that
James issued definite instructions, and the preparatory work took so long
that it was not until May 1613 that parliament actually met. The delay
was due in part to technical difficulties: the records of the Irish parliament
had been imperfectly kept, and after a gap of almost thirty years there was
much doubt about rules of procedure. The main reason for the delay,
however, was the government's determination that the elections should
produce a protestant majority, a result that could be attained only by
very careful management, but a result that was essential if the government's whole programme was to be carried out. It is true that much of the
proposed legislation was likely to pass without controversy; bills for the
formal recognition of the king's title, for the attainder of Tyrone and
Tyrconnell, for the suppression of piracy, would be accepted by recusants
as readily as by protestants. But the government had other measures in
mind which the recusants were certain to oppose with all their strength.

In their efforts to enforce religious conformity Chichester and Davies
had found the existing recusancy laws, which were much less severe than
those in England, insufficient for the purpose, and attempts at extra-legal
action had been so strongly opposed that they had had to be abandoned. It
was now intended to remedy this state of affairs by fresh legislation, and
accordingly three bills were prepared; one against Jesuits and seminary
priests, their receivers and relievers; one to restrain Irish gentlemen from

sending their children abroad to be educated; one to make English recusants resident in Ireland subject to the English recusancy laws. Such
bills could have no chance of passing unless there was a protestant
majority in both houses.

In the upper house there was nothing to fear; for though most of the
temporal lords were Roman Catholics, the episcopal vote would ensure
government control, even without any fresh creations. In the house of
commons it was otherwise. Here the recusants had had a substantial
majority in the parliaments of Elizabeth's reign; and no amount of government pressure was likely to make any decisive difference in the existing
constituencies. There were now, since the shiring of Ulster, thirty-three
counties,[1] each returning two members; even allowing for the influence of
the new protestant settlers in the north, the county members as a whole
were sure to be predominantly Roman Catholic. The boroughs entitled to
return members to parliament numbered forty-one, including four created
by James I, and most of them were firmly in the hands of the Old English
recusants. In these circumstances, there was no way of securing protestant
control of the house of commons save by increasing its size; and this was
the policy on which the government resolved. Between December 1612
and May 1613 charters of incorporation were issued to forty new boroughs,
eighteen of them in Ulster; in each of these new boroughs the power of
electing the parliamentary representatives was entrusted to the corporation,
and the corporations, named in the charters, were exclusively protestant.

From one point of view, the creation of new boroughs was not
unreasonable; for of those already existing only four were in Ulster and
only two in Connaught. But the government's concern was not at all to
distribute representation more fairly. The timing of its action, the choice
of new boroughs, many of them places of very little importance,[2] the
number created, and the protestant character of their corporations, were
all directed to one end only — the manufacture of a protestant majority
in the commons. The recusant leaders had good reason for anxiety when
they expressed to the king 'a fearful suspicion that the project of creating
so many corporations in places that can scantly pass the rank of the poorest
villages, in the poorest country of Christendom, do tend to naught else

---

[1] Tipperary at this time formed two counties, the church lands being grouped
separately to form the County of the Cross of Tipperary ('Cross Tipperary').
The two were united by letters patent in 1637.

[2] Most of the new Ulster boroughs, for example, were little more than
villages in 1613. But they were chosen with an eye to their future development;
and before the end of the century many of them had become substantial towns.
They included Belfast, Coleraine, Enniskillen, Londonderry and Newry.

at this time, but that by the voices of a few selected for the purpose, under the name of burgesses, extreme penal laws should be imposed upon your subjects here'. But their protest went unheeded; elections were held; and on 18 May 1613 parliament assembled in Dublin Castle. In the house of lords the protestant majority was 24 to 12, in the commons, 132 to 100.

The recusants had no intention of submitting tamely; and on the first day of the session the minority in the commons, styling themselves (as indeed they were) 'the knights and burgesses of the ancient shires and corporations', impugned the conduct of the elections and demanded an examination of returns before any other business was done. This being rejected, they opposed the government candidate for the speakership, Sir John Davies, and put up Sir John Everard, formerly a justice of the king's bench, who had resigned his post in return for a pension, rather than take the oath of supremacy. When they failed in this also, they withdrew from the house in a body, declaring that 'those within the house are no house', and refused to return. A few days later the recusant minority in the house of lords followed this example; and both groups, in a series of letters to Chichester and to the English council, set out their grievances in detail. These withdrawals, though they left the protestants in undisputed control, so weakened the moral authority of parliament that the government dared not proceed. On 22 May parliament was prorogued, and the prorogation was continued from time to time until October 1614.

During the interval the complaints of the recusants, not only in relation to parliament but in relation to their general treatment by the government, were considered by the English council; and James, who had followed the whole dispute, delivered his final judgement in August 1614. He had already declared that the recusants had no legitimate ground of complaint against Chichester's government, in which he affirmed his full confidence; but his decision in relation to the parliament was something of a compromise. Eight boroughs, which had not received their charters until after the issue of the writs for the election, were deprived of representation in the present parliament; three others were declared to have no right to return members at all; in two boroughs the elections were reversed on the ground that the sheriffs had made false returns. The net result of these changes was that the total membership of the house of commons was reduced to 210, of whom 108 were protestants and 102 recusants.

With the protestant majority so reduced, the government did not dare to bring in its bills against recusancy; and though two more sessions were held (October–November 1614 and April–May 1615), only ten acts in all were passed. The acts for the recognition of the king's title, for the attainder of the northern earls, and for the suppression of piracy went through without any trouble; but a subsidy act, though eventually passed, was criticized because it changed the method of assessment so as to bring it into line with English practice. Even so, the subsidy yielded only about £26,000, a very small contribution towards clearing the deficit on the Irish accounts.

The significance of this parliament did not depend only on its output of legislation: it saw a significant development in constitutional procedure; and it marked a stage in the rising conflict between the recusants and the government. Since the end of the fifteenth century procedure in relation to bills had been regulated by Poynings' Law, an act passed by the Irish parliament in 1494, and amended in the reign of Philip and Mary.[1] By the terms of this act, as amended, all Irish bills had to be submitted by the chief governor and council in Ireland to the king and council in England, where they might be approved, with or without modification, or suppressed altogether. Only those bills which had been approved by the king and council in England and returned to Ireland under the great seal of England were presented to the Irish parliament, which might accept or reject them as they stood. A bill might be amended in parliament; but if it was so amended it reverted to the status of a new bill, and had to go through the whole process again. The original purpose of Poynings' Law had been to curb the independence of the chief governor; but its effect on parliamentary initiative, which had been of little importance in the fifteenth century, was beginning to be felt as a grievance in the seventeenth. In the parliament of 1613–15 the commons tried to win some share in the initiation of legislation, not only by suggesting subjects on which bills should be prepared by the council, but by drawing up bills of their own and requesting permission to send delegates to England to present them to the king. This permission was refused; but later parliaments took up the struggle; and by the end of the century it had become a normal, though not invariable, practice for bills to take their rise in one or other house of parliament.

The events of 1613–15 displayed both the strength and weakness of the recusants' position. Though reduced to a minority in parliament, they had compelled the government to abandon its proposed legislation against them, and the degree of practical toleration that they enjoyed was as great after the parliament as it had been before. But their security for

[1] In its original form Poynings' Law required that all proposed bills should be submitted before a licence was issued. The amendment made possible the introduction of new bills after parliament had met.

the future was at best doubtful. The eight boroughs that had been temporarily deprived of representation would send members to future parliaments, so that there was almost certain to be a permanent protestant majority, and it was very improbable that the tactics of 1613 could be successfully repeated. There seemed to be no hope of escape from the position of constitutional inferiority against which the recusants had been struggling since the beginning of the reign.

The recusants concerned in this struggle were almost exclusively the Old English nobility, gentry and townsmen, whose main strength lay in Leinster and Munster; the native Irish recusants scarcely came into the constitutional pattern. So far as surnames are a guide to nationality, it would seem that only some eighteen native Irish were elected to the parliament of 1613; some others had contested seats in Ulster (an O'Neill in Armagh, a Magennis in Down, a MacMahon in Fermanagh) but none had been successful. While the Old English could hope to defend their rights by constitutional methods, their traditional loyalty to the crown might hold them apart from the native Irish, who were, after all, their ancient enemies. But if this hope were seriously weakened, or destroyed altogether, the identity of interests between the two groups of recusants, both alike threatened by the expanding power of protestantism, would almost inevitably produce an alliance. The government's treatment of the recusants in the parliament of 1613 marks a step towards the fusion of Old English and native Irish in the Confederation of Kilkenny.

From the government's viewpoint the parliament had been an almost complete failure; the recusancy laws had not been strengthened, and the subsidy act went a very short way towards solving the financial problem. Since the beginning of the reign the army had been steadily cut down, and great efforts had been made to increase income by better administration and by inducing the ports to surrender their claims to the customs duties; but even so, the total annual revenue amounted to less than half the cost of the civil and military establishments. The difference had to be made up by payments from England; and James, already in financial difficulties there, was anxious that Ireland should be made as nearly as possible self-supporting. The smallness of parliament's contribution to this end helps to explain why twenty years elapsed before it was summoned again.

Perhaps the one event connected with this parliament that might give even moderate satisfaction to the government, and to the protestant interest in general, was the meeting of the Irish convocation, which took place at the same time. During the medieval period the Irish convocation had not developed on the same lines as the English, for down to the reign of Henry VIII clerical proctors from the dioceses under English control formed a regular part of parliament. They were finally expelled in 1537, but the practice of holding a separate clerical assembly, concurrently with parliament, had not been established. The calling of a convocation along with the parliament in 1613 was therefore a new departure; and, though no doubt this was based on English example, the Irish convocation differed from the English in that it was a national and not a provincial synod. The main work of this convocation was to draw up articles of religion for the Church of Ireland; and these were agreed upon in 1615. Their explicit Calvinism reflects the puritan outlook of many of the leading Irish clergy, and was later a cause of offence to the Laudian party in the Church of England. They have a dual connection with the history of English theology, for they virtually incorporated the rejected Lambeth articles of 1595, and they were themselves to form the basis of the Westminster confession of faith of 1643.

The conclusion of the parliament was the last important event of Chichester's government, for he was recalled in November 1615, after more than ten years as deputy. His early training had been military, but he proved himself an efficient, as he was certainly an honest, administrator. Had his proposals for plantation of the escheated lands in Ulster been acted upon that great undertaking might have been carried through without the bitter resentment that marked its execution and dogged its subsequent history. In his attitude towards the recusants he was no more of a persecutor than one would expect from a man of his time, and he acted from the belief that his policy would promote the peace and security of the kingdom. Though English by birth and education, he established permanent roots in Ireland, and he may be regarded as a distinguished example of that numerous class of soldiers and officials from whom sprang the new protestant population that was to contribute so much to the life of Ireland during the next three centuries.

Chichester had held office for an unusually long time; and this, rather than loss of royal favour, accounts for his removal. There is nothing to suggest that any change of policy was intended: the new deputy, Sir Oliver St John,[1] formerly master of the ordnance in Ireland, had been his colleague for many years, and in his attempts to enforce religious conformity and to extend plantations he followed his predecessor's example.

(4)

Disappointed at what it had achieved in parliament, the government turned with renewed energy to the policy of plantation. The settlement

[1] St John was created Viscount Grandison in 1621.

in Ulster had not been an isolated venture. Similar projects, though on a smaller scale and on a somewhat different basis, had been under discussion since the beginning of the reign; but down to 1615 little had been accomplished outside the north. Now, however, the government was convinced that something must be done at once to strengthen the protestant interest; and plantation schemes that had been languishing for years were revived and completed.

These schemes could not be based on outright confiscation, such as the 'flight of the earls' had made possible in Ulster; but the confused and troubled course of Irish history had left many openings for unscrupulous crown lawyers to revive half-forgotten royal claims to vast estates. Longford provides a typical example. The county was occupied by the O'Ferralls, who had been confirmed in possession by Queen Elizabeth; but it had once formed part of the Irish lands of the earls of Shrewsbury, which had been vested in the crown under a statute of absentees of 1537, and this old claim was now revived and enforced. In Wexford the royal claim was carried back to the fourteenth century, and a title established on the basis of surrenders alleged to have been made to Richard II. By similar means a royal claim was made good to the county of Leitrim and to the territory of Ely O'Carroll in King's County. In areas where a royal title was thus established, it was not the king's intention to dispossess the existing proprietors completely; they were to be confirmed in the greater part of their lands, with new and secure titles, and the remainder, usually about one-fourth, was to be set aside for plantation.

James, convinced that he was acting within his rights, was anxious that these schemes should be carried through without leaving any sense of injustice; and for a time he gave serious consideration to the complaints that inevitably poured in from the areas affected. A detailed plan for the settlement of Wexford, which had been approved in 1611, was twice suspended on account of objections raised by the landlords of the county, and in 1614 was modified in the hope of satisfying them. But it was very shortly after this that the government resolved to press on vigorously with new plantations; and in March 1615 Chichester was directed to imprison the leader of the Wexford opposition, to proceed against other recalcitrant persons in the county, and to put the plan for settlement into immediate execution. A few months later, however, Chichester was removed from office; and it was left to his successor, St John, to complete the work. There were still many difficulties, arising partly from the dishonesty and incompetence of royal officials, partly from strenuous opposition among the smaller proprietors, who stood to lose most by the plantation and many of whom took to brigandage, attacking and terrorizing the new colonists. But by 1620, order had been established; and the deputy could report that Wexford was one of the best-settled areas in the kingdom.

Elsewhere the plantation policy met with less success. Francis Bacon, who was one of its strongest advocates, saw where the danger lay. 'Take it from me', he declared in 1617, 'that the bane of a plantation is, when the undertakers or planters make such haste to a little mechanical present profit, as disturbeth the whole frame and nobleness of the work for times to come. Therefore hold them to their covenants, and the strict ordinances of plantation.' But in Leitrim and Longford, which were settled on the same principles as Wexford, it proved impossible to enforce this salutary rule. The undertakers were for the most part content to receive their rents; few of them appeared in person; and fewer still made any serious attempt at building, or at bringing in English settlers. The plantation of Ely O'Carroll, which at first was equally unsuccessful, was eventually saved by the energy and persistence of Sir William Parsons and his successors; and Parsonstown long remained a strong centre of English influence.

The general effect of this attempt to extend the plantation policy out-side Ulster was discouraging. There was some increase in royal revenue, for a crown rent had been reserved on all lands, whether granted to new undertakers or regranted to old proprietors; and there had been some expansion of the area in protestant ownership; but the main purpose of building up a strong protestant population, though it met with some success in Wexford and Ely O'Carroll, had been largely frustrated. And even such minor advantages as had been gained were dearly bought. The recusant nobles and gentry felt that their long-standing suspicion of government policy was now fully confirmed; and the chance of attaching them firmly to the crown became more remote than ever. So far, it was the natives who had suffered most, both in Ulster and in the other planted areas; but the practice of raking up dormant royal claims was capable of a wide extension, and the Old English saw with alarm that the very basis of their power and influence was threatened. They had been pushed one step nearer that alliance with the natives, which in the 1640s was to shatter royal power in Ireland and open the way for the climacteric advent of Cromwell.

(5)

The government's desire to strengthen the protestant interest, which inspired both its conduct of parliament and its plantation policy, was closely associated with the constant poverty that hampered it at every turn: while the recusants remained so powerful in number and influence the safety of the state required the maintenance of a standing army; and it was the cost of the army that ate up the revenues of the crown. To the complicated problem created by this state of affairs there was no obvious solution. A policy of stern and consistent repression would require a stronger army than the government could afford to support, and would create unrest that would be very damaging to the economy. A policy of conciliation, if sincerely followed, would fatally discourage the small and slowly-growing protestant population on which the government placed its hopes for the future. To steer a safe course between repression and conciliation, to encourage the protestants without driving the recusants to the edge of revolt, to maintain a strong army and at the same time preserve financial stability, called for a combination of strength and subtlety such as no Irish governor before Wentworth displayed; and it is at best doubtful if Wentworth's success would have proved lasting, even if his Irish policy had not been interrupted by the course of events in Britain.

From 1615 onwards the means by which the government tried to solve these problems of finance and of recusancy tended to link them still more closely together. As the crown's financial difficulties in England became more urgent, it was natural to seek some way of relieving the English exchequer of the recurrent necessity for subsidizing Irish administration; and as a step towards increasing Irish revenue a committee was appointed in 1615 to investigate the management of wardships in Ireland. By feudal law the king had the wardship of both the bodies and the lands of minors whose estates were held of the crown by knight service; the heirs of such estates, on coming into their inheritance, had to go through the legal process of suing out their liveries; and no lands so held could be alienated without royal licence. Here was a wide field to be exploited for revenue purposes; and in England the court of wards and liveries had long yielded a large income to the crown. But in Ireland, though the rights of the crown were the same as in England, the income from this source was negligible. As a result of the committee's investigation a temporary commission of wardships was appointed in 1616, and almost at once the income began to rise.

But piecemeal reforms of this sort were not sufficient to make Ireland self-supporting. What was needed was a comprehensive survey and over-haul of the whole administrative system, and within a few years this was actually undertaken. The driving force behind the inquiry was Lionel Cranfield, earl of Middlesex, who became master of the English court of wards in 1619 and lord high treasurer of England in 1621. Middlesex had already had close connections with Ireland as a farmer of the Irish customs, as a member of a committee set up in 1616 to establish an Irish wool staple, and as a speculator in Irish land. On the strength of this experience he assured Buckingham, under whose patronage he had risen to power, that the need for subsidizing Ireland from England could be brought to an end; and when a commission of inquiry into Irish affairs was appointed his advice was followed both in its terms of reference and in its composition.

The commission began work in March 1622 and dealt with almost every aspect of Irish life — the church, trade, industry, revenue, plantations. But Middlesex fell from power in 1624 before his Irish policy had been given a fair trial, and almost the only significant result of the commission's work was the establishment of a permanent court of wards and liveries on the English model to replace the temporary commission of 1616. The change brought a further increase in revenue from this source, but it had the serious disadvantage of offending the Old English recusants, who regarded the court of wards as directed especially against themselves.

It is easy to understand their attitude. In the first place, it was they who had to bear the financial burden, for the estates of the new settlers had been granted in common socage, a form of tenure that was free from almost all feudal incidents. Secondly, the crown frequently used its right of wardship to have recusant minors brought up in the protestant faith: it was thus, for example, that James Butler, afterwards twelfth earl and first duke of Ormond, became a protestant while most of his relations remained recusants. Thirdly, an heir in suing out his livery was required by statute to take the oath of supremacy, and from 1622 onwards this requirement, previously neglected, was more strictly enforced; a recusant heir must either conform, or else, by failing to sue out his livery, leave himself virtually at the mercy of the court of wards. Thus the crown's effort to enlarge its revenue resulted in another threat to the security of the Old English, and one that was, at least in appearance, even more direct and dangerous than the policy of plantation. But within a few years they were able, by a bargain with the crown, to counter this threat effectively; and though the court of wards remained as an important source of royal income, it ceased to be an instrument of persecution or proselytism.

The course of events leading up to this bargain, and the terms of the bargain itself, illustrate very clearly the uncertainty that characterized the government's attitude towards recusancy at this period. Generally speaking, those in authority in Ireland favoured an active policy, while the king and council in England, nervous about the possibility of a new insurrection, were more inclined to be cautious. Lord Deputy St John, for example, 'behaved briskly against the papists', tried to compel civic officials to conform, and broke up a Franciscan friary that had been established at Multyfarnham in Westmeath. But the complaints that the recusants sent into England were sympathetically received, and St John was obliged to moderate his zeal. Yet the king had no positive policy of toleration; and when St John was recalled in 1622 his successor, Henry Cary, Lord Falkland, was certainly not chosen in order to conciliate the recusants, whose clergy he regarded with intense suspicion — 'the locusts of Rome, whose doctrines are as full of horrid treasons as many of their lives full of horrible impieties'.

At this point the king's foreign policy introduced a new element of instability. James's long-cherished project of a Spanish marriage had already, no doubt, affected his attitude towards recusancy in Ireland as well as in England; but it was in 1622, when the project seemed within sight of being accomplished, that it began to have a significant influence on Irish affairs; and during 1623, while Charles and Buckingham were on their romantic excursion to Madrid, recusants throughout Ireland were openly jubilant at the prospect of a speedy release from their troubles. The abandonment of the marriage project at the end of the year and the reversal of policy that followed proved no less significant for Ireland. Charles and Buckingham were soon as eager for war with Spain as they had formerly been for an alliance; and the English government, aware that pro-Spanish feeling was strong among the Irish recusants and fearful of their attitude if war should break out, resolved on a policy of repression. A proclamation issued in January 1624 ordered all titular archbishops and bishops, Jesuits and seminary priests to leave the kingdom within forty days.

At first the recusants were greatly alarmed. Their high hopes of religious freedom were now turned, as one of them wrote, 'into terror and despair'. But the government lacked any means of making the proclamation effective; there was hardly even an attempt at enforcing it strictly; and the breach between England and Spain, which developed into open hostility in 1625, soon provided the recusants with an opportunity of improving their position.

On his accession in March 1625 Charles I had found himself saddled with a war which he had no money to maintain, and parliament gave him little assistance. Ireland, exposed to the twin dangers of invasion and insurrection, was in no state to meet either: the forts were ruinous, the arsenals half-empty, the army unpaid. And at a time when money was more necessary than ever royal revenue was shrinking, for overseas trade had been disrupted by the war. Falkland was in desperation; the troops were, he reported, more ready to mutiny than to fight, yet he had no resource but to quarter them on the country, where their disorderly conduct stirred up constant complaints. In these circumstances Charles abandoned any thought of a repressive policy against the recusants, and turned instead to consider how they might be persuaded to contribute to the support of the government.

In the summer of 1625 Falkland was authorized by the English council to hold informal discussions with the lords and gentry of the Pale. No open bargain was proposed; but in October the levying of fines for failure to attend church, never very widely enforced, was dropped altogether, and in November the lords and gentry promised a voluntary contribution of £3,000 to be levied on the counties of the Pale, an example that was followed a few months later by the province of Munster. The Old English would gladly have given help of another sort, and welcomed a proposal put forward early in 1626, and provisionally approved by the king and council in England, for the raising of train-bands after the English fashion. But the proposal was soon dropped, mainly because of the opposition from Irish protestants, who shrank from putting arms 'into their hands of whose hearts we rest not well assured'. The difficulty of winning support from recusants without undermining the confidence of protestants was to recur with greater urgency in the 1640s.

The contributions promised by the Pale and by Munster were too small to relieve the government's difficulties, but they encouraged Charles to hope that more might be got by the same method. In September 1626, when fear of invasion was high and the need for strengthening the Irish defences urgent, Falkland was instructed to re-open negotiations. This time a definite bargain was put forward: the country was to support an enlarged army of 5,000 foot and 500 horse, and in return the king would make numerous concessions, which were set out in detail — 'matters of grace and bounty', commonly referred to, in their later modified form, simply as the 'Graces'. In November Falkland discussed these proposals with the Irish nobility, but could not bring them to agree. A larger assembly including representatives of the commons met in April 1627, but was no more amenable; and Falkland was then obliged, rather against his will, to allow agents selected by the four provinces to cross over to England to negotiate directly with the king. Here at last a settlement was reached in May 1628. The king was to receive three annual subsidies of £40,000 each; in return, he agreed to the Graces, and promised that a parliament should be summoned to confirm them.

The Graces, as approved in 1628, were set out in fifty-one sections, and covered a wide field. They provided protection for the titles of under-takers in the plantation areas, including Ulster, and of the landlords of Connaught and Clare, who were exposed to some danger because the settlement of their tenures by the 'composition of Connaught' in Eliza-beth's reign had never been formally confirmed. An English act of James I's reign, by which a title of sixty years barred any royal claim to an estate, was to be extended to Ireland. The army was to be kept in garrisons, and not quartered on the country save in case of necessity. Court fees were to be reduced, and the activities of court officials, especially those of the court of wards, were to be curtailed. Restrictions on exports were to be relaxed and certain monopolies abolished or modified. But probably the most significant provisions were those directly affecting the recusants: in future, they might sue out their liveries, and other grants of the court of wards, taking only an oath of allegiance, instead of the oath of supremacy; and those who were duly qualified might practise law on the same terms.

The fact that the Graces were particularly valuable to the Roman Catholics did not escape the notice of the protestants, who, though a tiny fraction of the population, already owned more than one-fourth of the land, and would have to bear a corresponding proportion of the promised subsidies. It was probably in deference to them that a proposal, included in the king's original offer, to remit the fines for failure to attend church did not form part of the final version. The proposal had been publicly condemned by the bishops, on the ground that toleration of heresy was sinful, and the sale of toleration for money immoral. But this opinion (which would certainly have been endorsed *mutatis mutandis* by any assembly of theologians in any country of Christendom) was less signifi-cant than its reception by the protestant laity. On Sunday, 22 April 1627, George Downham, bishop of Derry, read the bishops' declaration publicly in Christ Church cathedral in Dublin, when he preached before the lord deputy and council from the text 'That we being delivered out of the hand of our enemies might serve him without fear'; he then called on all present to say 'Amen', and 'suddenly the whole church almost shaked with the great sound their loud Amens made'. The 'protestant interest', which had been gradually growing up into self-consciousness since the reign of Elizabeth, thus proclaimed itself — an interest, now, not merely of government officials concerned mainly about present security and a speedy return home, but of men who had come to Ireland to settle down, who had established a stake in the country and meant to defend it to the death. The thunderous Amen that rang out in Christ Church that April Sunday was to echo through the seventeenth century, in battle and siege, in victory and defeat, until the day, more than sixty years later, when protestant Ireland sang a *Te Deum* in nearby St Patrick's for its delivery from popery, brass money, and wooden shoes.

The Graces had included the promise of a parliament to meet in November 1628, and Falkland accordingly issued writs for elections. But he had omitted to follow the procedure laid down by Poynings' Law, requiring that proposed legislation should first be submitted to the king and council in England, and a licence under the great seal of England obtained, before the writs were issued; and the English judges, whose opinion was taken in September, reported that the parliament, if it met, would be invalid. The elections were accordingly suspended, and the plan for holding a parliament allowed to lapse. This failure to give statutory confirmation to the Graces long remained a source of grievance, the more so as there were complaints, almost from the beginning, that the Graces were not being observed. But though the evidence is conflicting, there can be no doubt that the position of the recusants in general was substantially improved. There was, for example, a sharp rise in the number of heirs suing out livery in the court of wards, which suggests that the oath of supremacy was no longer being exacted.

The three subsidies agreed upon in May 1628 did something to relieve Falkland's financial difficulties; but in other respects the closing years of his administration were uneasy. The economic depression produced by war was made worse by a great scarcity of corn in the winter of 1628–9, and thousands of poor Irish flocked across the channel to Wales and western England, where their presence aroused a good deal of local resentment. The recusant bishops and regular clergy, no doubt encouraged by the negotiations of 1627–8, were more openly active than ever; and though the English council, to whom Falkland turned for advice, promised full support in enforcing the law, they made it clear that they held the Irish government responsible for allowing things to come to such a pass. Falkland's quarrels with the lord chancellor, Adam Loftus, and the part he took in an attempt to dispossess the O'Byrnes of Wicklow, affected his prestige in Ireland and aroused some hostile criticism in England. Whether or not Falkland was guilty of all that was alleged against him in the O'Byrne affair, the intemperate language in which he defended himself drew a sharp rebuke from the English council: '... we would adminish your lordship to forbear such taunts and invectives which we cannot interpret to stand with the honour due to this board'. In the political manœuvres that followed the assassination of Buckingham in August 1628 Falkland's enemies gained the upper hand. In April 1629 his removal from the government of Ireland was decided on, though the formal letter of recall was not sent until August, and he did not finally leave the country until October. His removal was accompanied by expressions of royal confidence, and he was sworn of the English privy council almost immediately on his arrival in London; but this could not disguise the fact, of which Falkland himself was well aware, that the king had been persuaded to remove him on grounds of injustice and inefficiency.

(6)

On Falkland's recall the deputyship was left vacant and the government entrusted to two lords justices, Loftus and Boyle. They were men of ability and experience. Adam Loftus, Viscount Ely, who had been early pushed forward by the influence of his uncle, the archbishop of Dublin, had held a succession of public offices and had been chancellor since 1619. Richard Boyle, earl of Cork, was an English adventurer who had arrived in Dublin more than forty years earlier, well-dressed, well-recommended, but almost penniless; by energy and thrift, and by a not very scrupulous use of every opportunity of profit, he had built up a vast estate in Munster, had married his numerous children into some of the best families of England and Ireland, and, at the same time, done a good deal to strengthen the English interest and promote the prosperity of the country. Either of these men by himself might have managed affairs tolerably well, but long-standing enmity between them made it almost impossible that they should work comfortably together. A formal reconciliation was brought about by Lord Wilmot, president of Connaught, who had been appointed commander-in-chief; but Cork's pious resolve, noted in his diary, to observe this agreement was qualified by the ominous condition 'if new provocations enforce me not to alter my resolutions'. Though open quarrel was averted, the two men never really trusted one another, and the efficiency of government suffered accordingly. Cork seems to have undertaken most of the work, for the chancellor was so continuously busy in his court that the two rarely met; one reason, perhaps, why outward peace was kept between them.

In one way the lords justices had an easier task than Falkland had had, since peace with France, in April 1629, and with Spain, in November 1630, re-opened those markets to Irish goods. But trade recovered very slowly. for piracy, stimulated by the war, had become more serious than ever, English, French and Spanish were all active, but the most dreaded were the Algerines. Their raid on Baltimore in June 1631, when they carried off more than 100 prisoners, startled the English government into a flurry of letters and reports, but not into effective action; and in the following year a rumour that the attack was to be repeated along the whole southern coast brought trade in the area almost to a stand-still. Nor did peace with Spain put an immediate end to fear of invasion: at the very time when the treaty was being concluded the English council was alarmed by great naval and military preparations on the Portuguese coast, which they thought might be intended against Ireland.

Cork did not think the Spaniards likely to act unless there were a serious rising in Ireland; for this reason he was anxious that peace with Spain should not be made an excuse for any further reduction of the Irish army, which in 1629 had been cut down to 400 horse and 1,250 foot. He regarded a strong army as the only guarantee of government authority; and he believed that if the revenue were properly managed he could now pay this force regularly, and keep the king clear of future debts. His attempt to apply to the administration of the country the business-like methods by which he had built up his own fortune was hampered by bad relations with the vice-treasurer, Francis Annesley, Lord Mountnorris, against whom he lodged fruitless complaints in England; but at least the army was maintained at its existing strength, and apparently without any increase in arrears of pay.

Cork thought that the main danger to government came from the recusants, and in this view he was supported by most of the protestant official class. But the policy dictated from England was an ineffective mixture of conciliation and repression. Recusant gentry and lawyers benefited from the terms of the Graces; the secular clergy were, in general, left alone; and the Sunday fines were not collected. But the public celebra-tion of Roman Catholic worship and the open exercise of ecclesiastical jurisdiction were suppressed; throughout the country 'mass-houses' were pulled down; conventual establishments were seized and turned to other uses, and their occupants forced into hiding. Popular resentment at such proceedings was inevitable; in Dublin, on St Stephen's Day 1629, the arrest of some friars caused a dangerous riot, and further operations against recusants in the capital had to be suspended until fresh troops were brought in. There was no concerted resistance, nor any other local disturbance on such a scale; and Cork's declaration, in December 1630, that he had never seen Ireland so quiet in the forty-three years he had known it, seemed to be justified. But Cork himself admitted that the cleavage between the protestant minority and the mass of the population was so deep that he could not speak with confidence; and the peace that he described was in fact only superficial.

One source of constant anxiety to the government, even when the country was comparatively quiet, was the large number of idle men, many of them accustomed to the use of arms, still to be found in every district.

The brigandage endemic in Ireland in the early years of the century had never been effectively stamped out, and it increased with the depression of trade and scarcity of corn: Lord Esmonde, in May 1630, marked the connection between poverty and cattle-thieving. A year later the government tried to revive Chichester's policy of shipping the swordsmen abroad by authorizing Sir Piers Crosbie, a protestant landlord, to raise 3,500 troops for the Swedish service; but Gustavus Adolphus had no faith in Irish soldiers, and the project fell through.

The failure of the Swedish plan was a great disappointment to the lord justices, but they were much more concerned about the approach of a new financial crisis, for the three subsidies promised in May 1628 were now coming to an end. The rate of payment originally agreed on was £10,000 a quarter; but from September 1629 this was reduced to £5,000, though the total to be paid remained unchanged; thus by the end of 1632 the whole amount would have been collected, and some new source of income would have to be found. It might seem natural to summon a parliament, which, indeed, the government was under promise to do; but a parliament could not be relied on to grant supplies, and it was certain to put forward demands that the crown would find it inconvenient to concede. Charles hoped for a continuation of the voluntary contribution; but the lords justices considered this impracticable, and suggested that the best way of raising money would be to re-impose the Sunday recusancy fines, and to this proposal Charles gave rather reluctant approval in April 1632. By this time, however, he had already resolved to put the deputyship into the hands of Thomas, Viscount Wentworth, who, as president of the council of the north, had governed northern England since 1628. The king's decision had been taken in the summer of 1631, but the formal appointment was not made until January 1632, and it was not until the July of the following year that Wentworth arrived in Dublin.

(7)

The appointment of Wentworth was a departure from precedent, for he had had no previous connection with Ireland, nor any experience of Irish affairs. But he had shown great administrative ability and an unhesitating devotion to the royal service — a devotion that his enemies, recalling his former share in the parliamentary opposition, were ready to stigmatize as the zeal of a renegade. It was natural enough for Charles to hope that such a loyal and efficient servant might make Ireland a source of security and profit to the crown instead of a burden and liability.

Wentworth set to work at once, even before his arrival in Ireland; and until his final departure, in April 1640, his hand was felt in almost every field of Irish life. But his personal influence was not so great as his contemporaries tended to think. 'A most cursed man to all Ireland, and to me in particular', noted the earl of Cork in his diary; and the Irish parliament, when freed from his overaweing presence, was ready to make him directly responsible for every grievance of which it complained. Historians, too, whether they regard him as a tyrannical oppressor or as a strong man giving Ireland the firm government she needed, have often attributed to him a greater degree of originality and independence than he actually possessed. For in Wentworth's time, as before, the springs of Irish policy lay in England, and such freedom as a deputy had was in the method of its application. Wentworth, strengthened by his alliance with Laud, stretched this freedom to the utmost; but it remains true that what distinguished his government from that of his predecessors was not the policy that he followed, but the thoroughness with which he carried it out.

At the time of Wentworth's appointment the overriding problem was that of finance. Despite the lords justices' advice to the contrary, Wentworth believed that the voluntary contribution could be renewed. He played on the recusants' fears that the Sunday fines would once more be exacted, taking care that they should know that the proposal came not from him but from the lords justices, and so brought them to consent to a continuation of the quarterly payment of £5,000 for a further year. The protestants were not under any similar threat, but they were unwilling to appear less loyal than the recusants, and after some pressure from the government they agreed also. Thus, at the very outset, Wentworth established a pattern of balancing party against party in the interests of the crown; as he himself expressed it in a report to Secretary Coke in January 1633: 'The truth is, we must there bow and govern the native by the planter, and the planter by the native'.

This was the principle that Wentworth applied in his dealings with parliament, for which he began preparations soon after his arrival in Ireland. Safety required that there should be a protestant majority, and the borough creations of James's reign made it easy to secure this; but it was doubtful if the protestants would be wholly submissive to the government, and he must therefore maintain good relations with the recusants as well. Both groups, and especially the recusants, would expect legislation confirming the Graces; and since Wentworth had advised the king against this, he must face the possibility of combined opposition. To strengthen the government he tried to secure the return of reliable members, and though not all his nominees were successful, there were

c

about fifty office-holders in a house of commons numbering 256, and a protestant majority of between 30 and 40.[1] The house of lords now had an overwhelming protestant majority, for James and Charles had extended the peerage considerably; and since many of the new peers were absentees whose proxies were at Wentworth's disposal he had little to fear from any opposition.

To Wentworth, the main purpose in holding a parliament was to secure supplies, and in a speech to both houses on 15 July 1634, the day after the opening of the first session, he told them what was expected of them: to clear off the accumulated royal debt, reckoned at £100,000, and to meet the annual deficit of £20,000 on current expenditure. This would be the business of the first session; if they did their duty then, another session would be held, and 'his majesty above all you can think will go along with you in that latter session, through all the expressions of a gracious and wise king'. This speech, and Wentworth's careful preparations, produced such an effect that a few days later the commons unanimously voted six subsidies, and the necessary bills had passed both houses before the session ended on 2 August.

Though Wentworth had thus gained his main purpose, he had been unable to prevent the voicing, in both houses, of a demand that the Graces should be confirmed by statute; and in this demand protestant and recusant combined, none being more forward among the protestants than Lord Ranelagh, son of a former archbishop of Dublin and son-in-law of the earl of Cork. The matter was still undecided when the session ended, but when parliament reassembled on 4 November the commons lost no time in pressing the deputy for an answer. When this was delayed, Wentworth not having yet received final instructions from England, they showed their uneasiness by rejecting a government measure against bigamy, an action probably intended as a warning that the will of the commons could not be flouted with impunity. At length, on 27 November, Wentworth made a detailed statement of the government's intentions. Ten of the Graces were to be passed into law; but this group did not include any of first-rate importance. Of the remainder, all save two were either to continue at the king's pleasure, or to be settled by administrative action. But the exceptions were the most important of all ('their two darling

[1] Several new boroughs were created between 1615 and 1634, and four 'ancient boroughs', unrepresented in 1613, sent members in 1634. The right of the latter to sit was disputed, and the decision finally went against them, but they remained throughout most of the life of the parliament. For an analysis of the membership of the house of commons in 1634 and a comparison with the house of 1613 see H. F. Kearney, *Strafford in Ireland*, pp. 223–59.

articles', Wentworth called them), namely a statute of limitations, guaranteeing land titles of sixty years' standing, and a specific confirmation of land titles in Connaught. So indignant were the commons at this treatment of the Graces that next day they revolted against government control; 'they rejected hand over head', reported Wentworth, 'all that was offered them from his majesty and this state'. There is some exaggeration in this account; but there is no doubt about the reality of the crisis, and it lasted until 3 December.

Wentworth attributed the disturbance to 'the popish party', who had secured a temporary majority owing to the slack attendance of protestant members. But it seems certain that the recusants had at least the passive support of a number of discontented protestants; and Wentworth himself describes Sir Piers Crosbie, member for Queen's County and a protestant, as a 'ringleader' of the opposition. It was, however, natural for Wentworth to emphasize the influence of the recusants, partly to explain a state of affairs that might seem to reflect on his own ability, but mainly in order to rally protestant support. In this latter object he quickly succeeded, and from 3 December until the end of the session on 15 December, as also during the third session (January to April 1635), things moved on more quietly. The recusants maintained a fairly steady opposition, and were occasionally in control of the house; but, in general, government business went through, and Wentworth was so well satisfied that he would have kept the parliament in being by a prorogation had not the king insisted on its being dissolved.

At first sight, Wentworth had good grounds for his satisfaction. Not only had parliament voted six subsidies, but the system of assessment had been revised, so that each subsidy would bring in over £40,000, whereas the single subsidy voted by James I's parliament in 1615 had brought in only £26,000. And this had been accomplished without statutory confirmation of the Graces; so that the king was still free to press his land claims to the utmost, and in particular to make out a title to almost the whole province of Connaught. But on a longer view, things had not gone so well. In his opening speech Wentworth had warned parliament of the danger of disunion: 'Divide not between protestant and papist . . . divide not nationally, betwixt English and Irish'. Yet later on he himself had had to employ these divisions, and to appeal to protestant and English prejudices in order to recover control of the house of commons. These tactics were, perhaps, in accordance with his declared intention of playing off party against party, and they certainly brought him relief from his difficulties in December 1634; but he had applied them with a dangerous recklessness. He had, in fact, made the worst of both worlds:

he had used the protestants without conciliating them, and they were still ready, when opportunity offered, to unite with the recusants against him; while the Old English had been given fresh cause to distrust the government's sincerity, and to wonder if their religion and lands would ever be secure under protestant rule.

In 1635, however, the most immediate danger to Wentworth was within the administration itself, and arose from his determination not only to make government efficient but to bring it thoroughly under his own control. From the first there had been ill-feeling between Wentworth and Cork, and the latter had the support of a considerable group in the council, including Wilmot, the president of Connaught, who had probably hoped to become deputy himself. But even those councillors and officials who were disposed to support Wentworth were not admitted to his confidence. This was reserved for a small group of Englishmen, who depended wholly on him, and who were his instruments rather than his advisers. The most important members of this group were George Radcliffe, his secretary, and Christopher Wandesford, appointed master of the rolls in 1633; both were related to Wentworth, and both had served under him in England.

This policy inevitably produced resentment among Irish officials, which Wentworth made no effort to smooth away. He meant to crush every element of independence, and he seized any opportunity that offered to achieve this purpose. Lord Cork was forced to surrender much of his church property and to pay a fine of £15,000, under threat of proceedings in the court of Castle Chamber; and though Wentworth's treatment of Cork had some appearance of personal spite, the main object was to undermine, and if possible destroy, his political influence. Mountnorris, the vice-treasurer, suffered even more severely, for he was tried by court martial on a far-fetched charge of mutiny, and condemned to death.[1] The sentence was not carried out; but Mountnorris had to surrender his office, and this no doubt was what Wentworth had aimed at. The vice-treasurer controlled the exchequer and was also *ex officio* one of the quorum of the court of Castle Chamber, and Wentworth could not endure that so much influence should be in the hands of a man who showed some independence of judgement.

Those who felt themselves oppressed or threatened by Wentworth, though they could make no stand against him in Ireland, were able to find allies among his enemies at court. In November 1635 Laud warned him

---

[1] Mountnorris, like many other Irish officials, held a captaincy in the army but he was not really a soldier.

that there were complaints about his conduct of affairs 'as being over-full of personal prosecutions against men of quality'. Wentworth pro-fessed to scorn these complaints, but he knew how seriously they could affect his position; and in 1636 he paid a long visit to England, ostensibly to inform the king concerning the affairs of Ireland, in reality to counter the intrigues against himself. In this he was successful; and he returned to Ireland stronger than ever. The protestant official class — the Boyles, the Wilmots, the Annesleys and the rest — were forced to submit; but they neither forgot nor forgave, and in the crisis of 1640–41 they were ready to unite with Irish recusants on the one hand and with English puritans on the other to secure their revenge.

(8)

The state of Ireland in 1636 certainly seemed to entitle Wentworth to the king's continued confidence. The government had never been in such a strong financial position: accumulated debts had been cleared off, administration reformed, the farm of the customs improved, and royal revenue was rising. Wentworth used his resources to good effect. Pirates were driven from the coast, to the great advantage of trade. The army, regularly paid and properly armed and equipped, was brought under a stricter discipline than it had hitherto known in peacetime. The officers were taught that a captain's place was no longer a sinecure, and the men that they could not plunder the country at will; they are now, he wrote in 1636, 'so reformed and orderly as they dare not take a chick or anything they pay not for at the owner's price'.

With a rising revenue and a reliable army Wentworth was well placed to make Ireland a source of strength and profit to the crown. His refusal to allow the Graces to be confirmed in parliament had left the way open for a vigorous prosecution of the policy of plantation, and it was by this policy, which he had inherited from his predecessors, that he hoped to establish royal power on a firm and permanent basis throughout the kingdom. At first, however, while he had to rely on the support of the Old English, he kept his plantation schemes in the background; and it was not until after the dissolution of parliament, in April 1635, that he made them public. Then he launched an attack upon the province of Con-naught, which, except for the Leitrim plantation, had so far been left alone, though various schemes for planting it had been put forward. The essence of the royal claim was that Edward IV had inherited the de Burgo lands, including the lordship of Connaught, through the marriage of Eliza-beth de Burgo to Lionel, duke of Clarence, and that this claim, though it had never been made effective, was still good in law. At first all went well. Early in July 1635 a County Roscommon jury admitted the king's title to the whole county, and before the end of the month Mayo and Sligo had followed this example. But Galway proved more troublesome. Here the dominant influence was that of Richard Burke, fourth earl of Clanricard, who, though a recusant, stood high in favour with Charles, as he had with his father. He had served the crown loyally during O'Neill's rebellion; he was governor of the town and county of Galway (which he had made, Wentworth complained, 'little less than a county palatine'); he was earl of St Albans in the English peerage; and he had married the widow of Sir Philip Sidney. Feeling safe under such powerful protection, a Galway jury, in August 1635, refused to find for the king, and the struggle was carried into England. This check to Wentworth at the very time when his position was being threatened by his enemies in the Irish council might have proved fatal. But the king stood by him; the strong measures he had taken against the jury and against the sheriff of Galway were approved, and the agents whom the Galway landlords had sent into England were returned to Ireland as prisoners, to be dealt with at Wentworth's discretion. In April 1637 a new jury, seeing that further resistance was hopeless, admitted the king's title to the town and county of Galway, so that the whole province was now open to settlement.

The plan proposed was the same as that followed in the later plantations of James I; one-fourth of the area was to be set aside for new settlers, and the existing proprietors were to be given a good title to the remainder; Galway, however, was to be punished for its recalcitrance by losing a half instead of a quarter. In fact, though the preliminary work of survey was carried out, no plantation had been established in Connaught when Wentworth's government came to an end. But the Old English had received further evidence, if any were needed, of the insecurity of their position, and of the government's determination to extend by any means, however unscrupulous, the area of colonization. When Wentworth's power was in decline and the Irish parliament turned against him, the reversal of the plantation scheme for Connaught was one element in the temporary alliance of protestant and recusant opposition.

The failure to confirm the Graces affected the planters of Ulster as well as the proprietors of Connaught, and left them equally exposed to attack by the crown. Few of them had complied strictly with the conditions laid down in the articles of plantation; and in Falkland's time they had been obliged to renew their patents at a higher rate of rent. But Wentworth, by threatening them with fresh proceedings, compelled them to accept much less favourable terms: their rents were to be increased still further, and, what was more serious, two-thirds of their lands were to be held by knight service *in capite* instead of by the much less onerous tenure of common socage on which they had originally been granted. These new terms applied to the undertakers in Armagh, Cavan, Donegal, Fermanagh and Tyrone. The county of Londonderry, held by the city of London, was to be treated even more severely.

At the time of Wentworth's appointment to the deputyship Star Chamber proceedings had already been begun against the London companies for failure to fulfil the terms of their undertakings in Ulster; and to these proceedings he gave enthusiastic encouragement and support. When the Londoners were sentenced, in February 1635, to a fine of £70,000 and the loss of their charter, he was immediately anxious to press this advantage to the utmost, and suggested that Londonderry might make a suitable appanage for the young duke of York. In fact, only a small part of the fine was levied, and the sequestration of the estates was not completed; but the Londoners attributed their harsh treatment to Wentworth, and their resentment was to cost him dear in the end.

In economic affairs, as in his plantation schemes, Wentworth followed lines already well established, and it is probably a mistake to attribute to him any comprehensive economic policy. As things turned out, his attempts to direct or control Irish industry and commerce proved more important for their political effects than for their influence on the development of the Irish economy. He announced his determination to discourage the woollen manufacture; but in fact a previous decision of the English council to prohibit the export of fuller's earth to Ireland had already made the future of the industry precarious. In any case, it is doubtful if Ireland possessed either the capital or the skill necessary to develop a large-scale textile industry at this time. Even the English woollen industry was going through a period of depression, so that there was hardly likely to be room for Irish competition in what seemed to be a shrinking market; and Wentworth's attempt to encourage the weaving of linen had very little success. The main interest of Irish producers and merchants was in the export of raw materials. Their complaint against Wentworth was not that the manufacture of woollen cloth was discouraged, nor even that raw wool could be exported only to England, but that the export could take place only under licence, for which fees had to be paid, and that the export duties were excessive. The restriction on the export of linen yarn, intended to encourage weaving at home, was equally unpopular. Its effect was felt mainly in the north; and in the charges levelled against Wentworth in 1641 it was cited by the Ulster planters as an example of his tyranny.

It would be rash to assert that Wentworth's only concern in his management of economic affairs was to increase the royal revenue. But the powerful influence of this motive appears in the raising of the export duties and in the sale of licences for the export of wool; and is even more obvious in the establishment of a tobacco monopoly in 1637, for this was simply an expedient for raising money. Judged from a purely financial viewpoint, Wentworth's administration was successful; he made the Irish government self-supporting and a source of strength to the crown. But he ignored the political effect of his actions, and alienated every influential group in the kingdom, without showing any awareness of their power to retaliate. His confidence in the stability of the existing system appears not only in his correspondence but also, and more cogently, in his actions, for he invested large sums in the purchase of Irish lands. Wentworth, in fact, suffered from a limitation not uncommon among administrators; having made rules and enforced them, he thought his task accomplished, forgetting that the material on which government has to work is human nature, and that men who submit to force retain the will, and may acquire the ability, to resist.

(9)

Wentworth's handling of ecclesiastical affairs had the same superficial success and aroused the same sort of resentment as the rest of his administration. His love of order and his desire to extend English influence naturally disposed him to bring the Church of Ireland as closely as possible into line with the Church of England; and he was not likely to have much patience with the laxity of those Ulster bishops who had allowed Scottish presbyterian ministers to hold livings without conforming to the rules of the establishment. But the character of his policy and the vigour with which he pursued it derived their inspiration from Laud. Without Laud's steady support in the English council he could hardly have maintained his position; and in return for that support he accepted, not unwillingly, Laud's view that his great task in Ireland was to reform the abuses of the church, to rescue its patrimony out of lay hands, and to purge it of every taint of puritanism. Since men to carry out this programme could hardly be found in Ireland, clergy of the Laudian school were imported from England; and John Bramhall, a Yorkshireman appointed to the see of Derry in 1634, virtually replaced Archbishop Ussher of Armagh as the dominant figure in the government of the church.

All this antagonized the protestant official class, the 'English born in Ireland', who had always resented the appointment of Englishmen to posts that they thought should be reserved for themselves. And in any case they had little sympathy either with Laudian doctrines or with the stricter enforcement of church discipline, backed up as it was by a new 'court of high commission' established in 1635. They were even more directly affected by inquiries concerning church property in lay hands; the earl of Cork was the most distinguished of those who suffered in this way, but many another of less note had to surrender impropriate tithes, or restore ecclesiastical estates unlawfully held. As early as 1636, Wentworth claimed that he had improved the income of the church by £30,000 a year, and most of this improvement was at the expense of protestant landlords.

Meanwhile, a blow had been struck at the puritanism of the Irish church. In 1634 a convocation summoned at the same time as parliament accepted the Thirty-nine Articles of the Church of England; and the Calvinistic articles of 1615, though not formally abrogated, fell into disuse. The same convocation enacted, with some minor changes, the English canons of 1604. They had been drawn up under the influence of Archbishop Bancroft to discipline the puritans of the Church of England, and were now to perform the same function in Ireland. These measures were not carried without some opposition, especially in the lower house; but Wentworth, who knew what Laud expected of him, made his determination quite clear, and the clergy submitted. But if the ideas thus reluctantly accepted were to take root in the church, the education of its future clergy must be carefully looked to. Trinity College, Dublin, with Laud as its new chancellor, and his protégé William Chappell as provost, was subjected to extensive reform; and the puritan spirit of its earlier years gave way to a more orthodox Anglicanism.

It proved easier to overawe convocation than to enforce the Laudian policy on the church as a whole. Archbishop Ussher had reluctantly accepted the English articles and canons, but he had no mind to use them as weapons against the puritan clergy, and he asked to be excluded from the quorum of the new court of high commission. Wentworth thought Ussher 'so learned a prelate and so good a man' that he was unwilling to trouble him; and the main burden fell on Bramhall of Derry and Henry Leslie, a Scot long resident in Ireland, who was made bishop of Down and Connor in 1635. Leslie's diocese contained many Scottish ministers who lived within the pale of the establishment but had little sympathy with its principles: the most distinguished of them, Robert Blair of Bangor, when called upon to preach at the triennial visitation of 1626, had delivered in the presence of two bishops a sermon on the unscriptural character of episcopacy. Such men were little likely to accept the decisions of convocation, and when required to do so five of them refused. Leslie engaged them in a public debate on the questions at issue in the church of Belfast,[1] probably not so much in hope of convincing them as in order to show that he was not acting summarily. When they still refused to conform they were deprived of their livings. Most of them retired to Scotland; others of similar views joined them later, and their influence contributed to the mounting opposition to Laudian policy there.

Outside the north, most Irish protestants submitted to the government's ecclesiastical policy, much as they disliked it. But they saw with indignation that while puritan ministers were harried over canons and articles, the laws against recusancy were disregarded and the recusant clergy left quietly alone. It was hardly surprising that they should accuse Wentworth of favouring popery; and a few years later, when a breach between king and parliament developed in England, many of them leaned to the side of parliament, simply because it stood for a strong protestant policy.

In 1638, when the monarchy was obviously approaching a crisis, Wentworth had been at the head of the Irish government for more than five years. During that period he had failed to win the firm support of any powerful group in the country. He had done nothing to conciliate the native Irish, whose sense of grievance had been mounting since the sixteenth century. His refusal to confirm the Graces and his extension of the plantation policy had alarmed and alienated the Old English. The protestants were uneasy about the safety of the church; their leaders had suffered both in property and pride; and the whole body of the planters in the north was indignant at the new conditions that Wentworth had imposed. The Ulster Scots, faced with a demand for religious conformity, naturally decided to make common cause with their fellow-countrymen at home.

But the traditional rivalries of Irish politics — the long-standing antagonism between native Irish and Old English, between recusant and protestant — temporarily disguised the fundamental weakness of Wentworth's rule. At a time when discontent was rising in England and when Scotland was in open rebellion Ireland remained outwardly calm, apparently a safe centre of firm royal authority. When Charles found himself forced to abandon his campaign against the Scots, and submit to the treaty of Berwick, it was natural that he should turn to the one man who might enable him to re-establish his authority. On 21 September 1639

---

[1] A report of the debate, which was conducted according to the syllogistic pattern of a medieval disputation, is printed in Reid, *History of the presbyterian church in Ireland* (ed. Killen), i, 523 ff.

Wentworth arrived in London, and from then until the meeting of the Long Parliament he was the driving force behind royal policy.

(10)

By this time Irish politics had become inextricably entangled with those of Great Britain. In the resulting confusion the struggle between recusant and protestant that had dominated Ireland since 1603 seemed to fall for a time into the background; but in the closing months of 1641 it was to re-emerge more sharply than ever, and to pass beyond the field of political manœuvre into open warfare.

To begin with, however, it was the Ulster Scots who were most closely affected by the course of British politics. The bulk of them had already been alienated from the government by the attempt to make their ministers conform to the law of the church; and the rapid spread of the National Covenant in Scotland, after its renewal at Edinburgh in February 1638, naturally encouraged them in their opposition. Intercourse across the North Channel was easy and frequent; many Ulster Scots signed the covenant during visits to Scotland in the course of the year; and there was at least a possibility of more active co-operation. In face of this danger Wentworth raised fresh troops, and stationed a considerable force at Carrickfergus to overawe the north-east, and to protect the country against possible intervention from Scotland. By way of counter-propaganda he persuaded a number of prominent Ulster Scots, some of whom were genuine supporters of the royal policy and some frightened into acquiescence, to petition the government for leave to give a public demonstration of their loyalty. In response to this inspired request a form of oath was drawn up, promising the most abject submission to the king's authority, and in May 1639 a proclamation was issued imposing this on all Scottish residents in Ulster above the age of sixteen years. This 'black oath' was widely resisted; great numbers of people left their homes to escape the government agents sent to enforce it, and either took refuge in the woods and hills, or fled to Scotland. The fact that it was imposed only on protestants and that the Roman Catholic Macdonnells were left in peace increased the bitterness against Wentworth, and strengthened the conviction that he was the foe of the reformed faith.

The treaty of Berwick, in June 1639, relieved the pressure on Ulster. But Charles had no intention of accepting the treaty as a permanent settlement with the Scots, and he looked to Ireland to provide him with the means of renewing the war. Wentworth had already, in May 1639, sent 500 men to garrison Carlisle, and he thought that no more could be spared with safety. But during his visit to England later in the year it was decided to raise a new Irish army of 8,000 foot and 1,000 horse, to be available for service wherever they were required. The king promised ready money for their equipment; and the funds for their maintenance were to be provided by the Irish parliament, on whose acquiescence Wentworth felt, not without reason, that he could safely count. On his advice, a parliament was to be called in England also, for he was convinced that national antipathy to the Scots would produce a readiness to support the king's policy. Partly as a reward for past services, partly to strengthen his prestige for the work now in hand, Wentworth was made earl of Strafford, and shortly afterwards raised to the dignity of lord lieutenant. Wandesford, who had acted as one of the lords justices to whom the government of Ireland was entrusted during Wentworth's absence, was now appointed lord deputy, and instructed to prepare for a meeting of parliament in March 1640. Strafford himself was to be present during the session, and then return to England for the proposed parliament there.

The first stages of this plan went well. The Irish parliament met on 16 March, though as Strafford did not arrive until two days later the state opening was postponed. The commons readily voted the four subsidies asked for, and promised more if required. They declared their unbounded loyalty to the king, and the preamble to the subsidy bill contained an enthusiastic eulogy of Strafford himself. At the end of the month parliament was prorogued to 1 June, and Strafford hurried back to England for the opening of parliament there, leaving Wandesford as his deputy.

Preparations for raising troops now went on briskly, though somewhat hampered by the king's inability to provide the promised money; and in July the new army assembled at Carrickfergus. It contained a nucleus of protestant soldiers, drawn from the old standing army, most of the officers were protestants, and the chief command was entrusted to the earl of Ormond, the protestant head of the predominantly recusant Butler family. But a few of the officers, and the great bulk of the rank and file, were Roman Catholics. Nothing told so heavily against Strafford, or in the long run against Charles himself, as this raising of an army of 'Irish papists' for use against the king's protestant subjects. All these preparations, though politically disastrous, had no effect on the military situation in Britain. Before the new Irish army met at Carrickfergus the Short Parliament had come and gone, and the Scots were once more on the move. A few weeks later they crossed the Tweed, scattered the royal forces at Newburn-on-Tyne, and occupied the north of England. Charles had no resource but to summon the English parliament once more; and with its meeting, on 3 November 1640, he virtually lost his freedom of action. The new Irish army remained in being for some months longer, but the chance of using it as a bulwark of royal authority had passed away.

By this time it had become clear that Strafford's system of government was not likely to survive in his absence. When parliament re-assembled on 1 June 1640, the commons busied themselves about grievances — the manner of assessing the subsidies, the exactions of the clergy, the court of high commission, the failure to issue writs to seven ancient boroughs represented in former parliaments. They combined with these complaints a re-affirmation of the declaration of loyalty to the king that they had passed in March; but this did not reassure Wandesford, and after a session of less than three weeks he thought it safer to prorogue parliament until October.

This opposition in the commons was based on an alliance between Roman Catholics and protestants, arising from their common hostility to Strafford. The Roman Catholics now formed only about a quarter of the house; but many protestant office-holders were too busily engaged in organizing the new army to attend parliament, and the relative strength of the Roman Catholics was correspondingly increased. Even so, they could not have controlled the house by themselves, and their influence depended upon the co-operation of a considerable body of protestants. Inevitably, therefore, they had to keep in the background their special grievances in matters of religion and concentrate on those constitutional questions about which protestants were equally concerned.

It was, of course, the constitutional grievances that would be useful to Strafford's English enemies, and Pym and his colleagues were quite ready to collaborate with the Irish parliamentary opposition. After the meeting of the Long Parliament, in November, the Irish commons appointed commissioners to carry a remonstrance into England, and this provided Pym with a good deal of the material for the articles of impeachment against Strafford approved by the commons on 24 November. In building up the case against Strafford's Irish administration Pym also had the assistance of Sir John Clotworthy, an Ulster landlord of strong puritan sympathies, for whom a seat had been found in the English house of commons.

Despite this alliance between the opposition parties in the two kingdoms, Charles still hoped to bring Irish opinion over to his side; and the resulting competition for their support gave Irish parliamentary commissioners in London an extraordinary degree of influence. When Wandesford, worn out by the hopeless struggle to maintain government authority, died on 3 December 1640, the king appointed two lords justices, Sir William Parsons and Lord Dillon. Parsons, though master of the court of wards, had signed the commons' remonstrance of the previous month, and so was acceptable to the Irish commissioners. But they objected to Lord Dillon, who had been a close associate of Strafford, and the king at once replaced him by Sir John Borlase, master of the ordnance. Both Parsons and Borlase had a good deal of administrative experience, and they might have managed affairs well enough in normal times; but neither in ability nor in character were they suited for the difficult task that faced them on appointment, and still less for the crisis that burst upon the kingdom nine months later.

During the early months of 1641, while Pym and his party, aided by the Irish commissioners in London, were preparing their case against Strafford, the Irish commons were trying to make sure of the ground already won. In February they drew up a set of queries, covering a great range of administrative practices with which they were dissatisfied, and these queries they sent to the lords for submission to the judges, with the idea of having an authoritative pronouncement that the practices complained of were illegal. At first the two houses were in substantial agreement; but whereas the lords accepted the rather cautious answer returned by the judges, the commons rejected it; and a long and inconclusive wrangle between lords and commons ensued. But the episode was significant for the future: the constitutional principle implied in the first of the queries was the basis on which every movement for Irish independence, whether led by Roman Catholics or by protestants, was to rest for more than a century to come: 'Whether the subjects of this kingdom be a free people, and to be governed only by the common laws of England, and the statutes of force in this kingdom?'.

There is some indication that at this time the recusants had a temporary majority in the commons, and they certainly took a leading part in pressing the 'queries'. But they still retained the co-operation of a substantial group of protestant members, and it was a protestant, Audley Mervyn, who took the lead in a committee that prepared articles of impeachment against four members of the administration: Sir Richard Bolton, the lord chancellor; John Bramhall, bishop of Derry; Sir Gerard Lowther, chief justice of the common pleas; Sir George Radcliffe, Strafford's former secretary, who was, however, already a prisoner in London, having been impeached by the English house of commons.

A prorogation of parliament early in March 1641 held up the impeachment proceedings, and during the recess the main interest centred on legislation to confirm the Graces, for which the Irish commissioners in

London had been pressing. Charles was now in no position to resist, and in April he instructed the lords justices and council to prepare the necessary bills. A committee of the Irish lords and commons, appointed before the prorogation, kept a close watch on what was being done, and even drew up some of the bills themselves. The lords justices considered that these went beyond what the king ought to grant; but they dared not make any alteration, and transmitted the bills to London in May. The part played in this affair by the committee of lords and commons was particularly significant; for almost at the same time the Irish commissioners in London were proposing, though unsuccessfully, a change in the operation of Poynings' Law, by which the Irish parliament would be regularly consulted in the drawing up of bills.

When the Irish parliament re-assembled on 11 May the dominant party in the commons were as determined as ever to press their grievances and demands. But the political situation was changing. The fate of Strafford had been decided by an act of attainder and he was executed on 12 May. Before the end of the month his Irish army had been quietly disbanded. With Strafford out of the way, Pym and his friends no longer needed the co-operation of the Irish parliament, and so were less ready than they had been to receive and support Irish complaints. In Ireland, also, the alliance between recusants and discontented protestants, originally based on their common enmity to Strafford, was weakened by his death. The alliance, indeed, still had a small majority in the house of commons, which continued to discuss grievances, and rejected a proposal from the lords justices that the impeachment proceedings should be dropped. But their resolutions and declarations, unsupported by a powerful party in England, carried little weight, and when parliament was adjourned on 7 August they had accomplished very little. Even the bills for confirming the Graces had not yet returned from England.

The activities of parliament and administration were not the only, nor perhaps the most important, aspect of Irish politics at this time. Other interests were at work, hoping to pluck advantage from the unsettled state of the kingdom. Charles had not given up the idea of getting military help from Ireland; he hoped that it might be possible to re-assemble, and even enlarge, Strafford's disbanded army, and during the summer of 1641 he entered into secret negotiations with its former commander, Ormond, and with the earl of Antrim, head of the Irish branch of the MacDonnells. The details of the plan are obscure; but the outline is clear enough — they were to declare for the king against the parliament of England, and the support of the Roman Catholics was to be secured by a promise of toleration. This plan came to nothing; but its existence became known to a group of conspirators who were working to a very different end, and encouraged them to proceed in their design.

The recusant party in parliament was almost exclusively Old English, and the policy they followed promised little direct advantage to the native Irish. But the natives were not disposed to let slip an opportunity of striking a blow for their lost estates; they were encouraged by the success of the Scots; and they feared that the rising hostility of the English parliament to Roman Catholicism would endanger the practical toleration enjoyed by Irish recusants. This feeling was strongest among the Ulster Irish; but it was a Leinsterman, Rory O'More, who first brought them together in an organized conspiracy against the state. Through Lord Maguire, a young, rash and spendthrift peer from County Fermanagh, he got in touch with some of the leading native gentry of the north, and by playing on their hopes and fears induced them to join in a plot for the overthrow of the government. Negotiations with their countrymen in the Spanish service, and especially with Owen Roe O'Neill, nephew of the great earl of Tyrone, encouraged them to count on foreign help; O'More assured them, falsely, that he already had promise of support from the lords and gentry of the Pale; and their discovery, through Antrim's indiscretion, that Charles himself proposed to arm his Irish Roman Catholic subjects against his English parliament removed any remaining doubts. By August, their plans had been made for a rising on 5 October. Even when they found, as they did in September, that Charles's plan had fallen through, they still went ahead with their own, though they postponed the date of action. Dublin Castle was to be seized on 23 October, and there was to be a rising throughout Ulster on the same day.

Widespread as the conspiracy was, the government seems to have known nothing about it. Early in the year Sir Henry Vane, the English secretary of state, had passed on to the lords justices a report about the great number of Irish recusant clergy returning from the continent to the British Isles; but no one in authority seems to have known, or even suspected, that an insurrection was being planned, and even the gathering of the conspirators in Dublin had escaped notice. When a somewhat drunken Irishman named Owen O'Connolly turned up at Parsons's house at nine o'clock in the evening of Friday, 22 October, with a story about a plot to seize Dublin Castle the next day, the lord justice was more than half-inclined to disbelieve him. He did, however, take the obvious precautions, and Dublin Castle and the capital were saved. But on the Saturday all Ulster was ablaze with insurrection.

Though the Old English recusants were not directly involved in the insurrection, its outbreak affected their position profoundly. They at once found themselves isolated from their protestant allies, who now thought of nothing but the defence of the English and protestant interest against popish rebels. The parliamentary struggles of the past twelve months had become irrelevant overnight. The constitutional grounds on which the recusant lords and gentry of the Pale had hitherto based their effort to maintain and improve their position had crumbled away; they must fight or perish.

IV

The War of the Three Kingdoms

---

(1)

About six o'clock in the evening, on Saturday, 23 October 1641, Bishop Leslie of Down, then in his house at Lisburn, received the alarming intelligence that the Irish had broken into sudden insurrection and seized Charlemont and Dungannon, the two key points of central Ulster. Four hours later the news was even worse. The insurrection had spread to County Down, the rebels had taken Newry, and might be expected in Lisburn before morning. From nearby Belfast the startled inhabitants could already see the great fires that the Irish had lit to guide their supporters to the points of rendezvous. So began the famous Ulster rising of 1641, soon to be merged in that 'war of the three kingdoms' which was to subvert the Stuart monarchy, and expose Ireland to a new and more devastating English conquest.

In its origins and effects the rising was closely linked with the course of events in Great Britain: the king's difficulties in England and Scotland provided both stimulus and opportunity for the outbreak, and the rising itself helped to precipitate the civil war towards which Great Britain was already moving. For Charles, the rising was a political disaster. Sir Phelim O'Neill, who took the lead during the first few months, claimed to be acting by his authority, and displayed a commission under the great seal of England. Charles denounced this as a forgery, which it undoubtedly was; but English puritans and Scottish presbyterians, already suspicious of the king's dealings with Ireland, were not easily convinced; and repeated declarations by the rebels that they were loyal to the crown and determined to defend its prerogatives against the encroachments of the 'puritan faction' seemed| to give some colour to their suspicions. To the day of his death Charles was never able to shake off completely the imputation of complicity in the rising, and nothing was more damaging to his cause in England and Scotland.

Protestant opinion in general regarded 'Irish papists' with mingled contempt and fear; and even the most improbable of the numerous atrocity stories that were soon in circulation found ready acceptance. There can, indeed, be no doubt that great brutalities were committed. Many English settlers were slaughtered in the first heat of the rising; others, after being held as prisoners for a time, were deliberately murdered, sometimes by scores together. Thousands more, driven from their homes, plundered of their goods, stripped almost naked, were left to find their way to some place of refuge, or perish in the attempt. These excesses sprang from the undisciplined fury of the Irish, chafing under a thousand grievances, not from the settled policy of their leaders. Sir Con Magennis, when he marched into Down, explained that policy in a brief but business-like letter to the government commanders in the county: 'We are for our lives and liberties . . . we desire no blood to be shed, but if you mean to shed our blood be sure we will be as ready as you for the purpose'. But in popular propaganda the cruelties inflicted on the settlers, dwelt upon and exaggerated, became irrefutable proof of a preconceived plan to massacre the entire protestant population; and they amply account for the horror with which protestants throughout the British Isles looked upon the rebellion and all connected with it. Almost a decade later, Cromwell could justify the slaughter of the garrison of Drogheda as a divine judgement on 'barbarous wretches who have imbrued their hands in so much innocent blood'.

Though the leaders of the insurrection must be held in some measure responsible for the excesses that accompanied its outbreak, their declared policy was a moderate one. They aimed at getting control of the province and then, in alliance with the Old English of the Pale, on whose support they counted, exacting from the government a guarantee of religious liberty. Whether, in fact, they could ever have been satisfied without some restitution of forfeited estates may well be doubted; in any case, the rapid development of military and political events both in Ireland and in Great Britain soon made their original programme irrelevant.

(2)

The Ulster leaders had begun the insurrection in the belief that Dublin Castle had already fallen to their allies, and that they would have the immediate support of the lords and gentry of the Pale. By the time they discovered their mistake they had gone too far to withdraw, and their own early successes had increased their confidence. But their position was not so strong as it seemed, and they could have no hope of ultimate victory without the alliance of the Old English. They were ill-equipped for a regular campaign: they had few arms, except what they had captured; their men were almost wholly untrained; and the leaders themselves had little military experience. The advantage of surprise had enabled them to capture many towns, including Charlemont, Dungannon, Mountjoy and Newry, on the very day of the outbreak; and they dominated the open country over the greater part of the province. But after this they were almost at a stand; though they captured and burnt Strabane in December, they accomplished little else beyond the reduction of some isolated castles and fortified houses. Their attack on Enniskillen, where hundreds of refugees had found shelter, failed completely; and Coleraine and Londonderry both held out against them. Despite their numbers, they proved no match in the field for the forces that the protestants speedily assembled. In north Donegal, where there was a strong plantation of Scots, Sir Robert Stewart, a veteran of the Thirty Years' War, not only defended his own area successfully, but was able to send relief to garrisons in Tyrone. Towards the end of November, when the insurgents after long delay attacked Lisburn in strength, Sir Con Magennis, at the head of some three or four thousand men, was repulsed with great slaughter by a handful of regular troops and a few companies of hastily-raised volunteers.

Meanwhile, the Pale was in a state of growing confusion. Borlase and Parsons, once convinced that the danger was genuine, had acted promptly, and had put the Castle in a state of defence. But they hardly knew what to do next; for though they had a good supply of arms, they had few troops and no money. News of the rising had reached the king, who was at Edinburgh, on 27 October, and the English parliament four days later. Both at once promised reinforcements, but weeks must elapse before they could arrive, and in the meantime the lords justices were almost at their wits' end. They sent off post-haste for Ormond to take command of what troops there were, and he reached Dublin early in November. But though he was appointed lieutenant-general of the army, on instructions from the king, the lords justices were too nervous about the safety of the capital to let him take the offensive. Ormond himself had immediately set about raising fresh troops from among the refugees who flocked into Dublin; and since there was a plentiful supply of arms he soon had a considerable force ready, with which he was eager to march against the rebels. But the lords justices shrank from such bold measures; they contented themselves with despatching some reinforcements to Sir Henry Tichborne, who was in command at Drogheda, and then waited anxiously for the expected help from England.

The cautious conduct of the lords justices was due partly to the weakness of their forces, but partly also to their suspicion of the Old English recusants. They shared the common protestant view that all papists were potential traitors, and they feared that the Old English, despite their traditional loyalty, might be drawn into alliance with the Ulster rebels on the basis of a common faith. Though they tried to disguise their suspicion, and even issued arms and military commissions to some of the leading Old English nobles and gentry, they were unable to establish confidence. It has sometimes been asserted that the suspicious attitude of the lords justices was responsible for driving the Old English into rebellion; but this is to oversimplify the issue, which depended on military as well as political considerations. When the Old English finally joined the Ulster insurgents at the end of 1641 it was not just because they felt themselves distrusted by the government, but also because the Pale had by that time sunk into a state of such disorder that they could see no other way in which to preserve their property and their influence.

The disturbed state of the Pale resulted from the weakness of government and from the encouragement that the rebels' early success had given to discontented elements throughout the country. By mid-November the O'Byrnes of Wicklow were in revolt and were carrying their depredations to within a few miles of Dublin; their example was soon followed in Wexford; inside the Pale local disorders broke out, protestant settlers were driven from their homes, and bands of armed men ranged through the countryside. When, later in the month, some of the Ulster forces marched into Louth, took Dundalk and threatened Drogheda, they received a good deal of popular support. The lords and gentry of the Pale were now in a quandary. Many of their tenants and followers were in arms for the rebels, and they themselves might be held responsible by the government; but they doubted both their own power to restore law and order and the government's power to help them if they attempted to do so. They had no affection for the Ulster Irish, but they sympathized with their demand for religious liberty; and they feared that if, as seemed likely, the English parliament had its way, the practical toleration they already enjoyed would be drastically curtailed. Nevertheless, they would probably have remained loyal if reinforcements had reached Dublin in time to give the government secure control of the Pale; but at the end of November, with reinforcements as far off as ever, they received a striking demonstration of the government's weakness and of their own danger. On 29 November a force of 600 men, sent from Dublin to strengthen the garrison of Drogheda, was scattered by a large body of rebels at Julianstown, a few miles south of their destination. The effects of the engagement were instantly felt. The captured arms went to equip the rebels; their victory over a government force added immensely to their confidence and prestige; more recruits joined them; and with this addition to their strength they were able to complete the investment of Drogheda, which was now cut off from all communication with Dublin, except by sea.

The engagement at Julianstown finally convinced the lords and gentry of the Pale that it was useless to resist the rebels and that they must either combine with them or suffer their estates to be overrun. Under the leadership of Lord Gormanston they demanded and received from the Ulster leaders a formal public declaration of loyalty to the crown; and having thus asserted their principles before the world, they joined forces with the army besieging Drogheda.

(3)

The promised help from England was delayed, not just because it was difficult to raise and equip the necessary forces at short notice, but also because of the political situation. Pym and his friends had seized eagerly on the news from Ireland as a means of discrediting Charles still further; without openly accusing him of complicity in the insurrection, they attributed its outbreak to the influence of evil counsellors, and declared that unless the king would consent to be guided by ministers approved by parliament, then parliament itself must have control of any forces raised for service in Ireland. At the same time they took advantage of the anti-popish feeling stimulated by the insurrection to press on with their 'Grand Remonstrance', and in particular to intensify their attack upon the church. But although they managed to retain the support of a majority in the house of commons, their conduct alarmed the moderates, a royalist party began to emerge, and the danger of civil war came closer. In these circumstances, the defence of the Irish protestants became a matter for negotiation and propaganda, rather than for immediate action. The king, while still at Edinburgh, had issued to some leading Ulster protestants commissions for the raising of troops; but he placed reponsibility for further action on the parliament of England, partly because he himself had no means at his disposal, partly to counter the suspicion that he was in league with the rebels. The parliament had already voted money and men, but was in no hurry to make its votes effective, and only a small part of the proposed force was actually raised.

Scotland, closely linked to Ulster by the Scottish colony there, felt the impact of the insurrection even more sharply than England. The rebels had at first declared their intention of attacking only the English and

leaving the Ulster Scots alone; but this distinction was not long maintained, partly because of the attitude of the Scots themselves; and within
a few weeks of the outbreak swarms of refugees arrived in Scotland,
exciting the anger and sympathy of their fellow-countrymen. The
Scottish parliament was very willing to assist in suppressing the rebellion,
and offered to send 10,000 men to Ulster, provided that they were maintained at English expense. Scotland was well placed for the despatch of
speedy help, and with the disbanding of a great part of the Scottish army
after the treaty of Ripon there were plenty of men available. But on the
English side, and especially in the house of lords, there were doubts about
the wisdom of allowing the Scots to acquire such a powerful interest in
Ireland as the presence of 10,000 troops would necessarily give them;
and it was April 1642 before the first Scottish contingent, 2,500 strong,
landed at Carrickfergus under Major-General Robert Monro. Meanwhile,
help from England had already reached Dublin, where 1,100 troops had
landed at the end of December.

Though the English parliament voted money for these expeditions, it
was resolved that the cost of the war should fall ultimately on Ireland
itself. Almost every Irish rebellion in the past had been followed by confiscation; and this rebellion was so extensive that it might be expected to
result in the forfeiture of vast estates to the crown. It was on the credit of
these prospective forfeitures that parliament proposed to raise the funds
immediately required. An act to which Charles gave his assent in March
1642 promised repayment in Irish land to those who advanced
money for the war, and set aside 2,500,000 acres out of the expected
confiscations to meet this liability. Much of the money so raised was, in
fact, diverted by parliament to finance its war against the king; but those
who had advanced it (the 'Adventurers', as they were called) retained
their claim to compensation in Irish land; they formed an influential
group, with a strong interest in the suppression of the rebellion and in
the settlement that followed.

(4)

The defection of the Old English of the Pale turned the rebellion into a
national movement, for their example was soon followed throughout the
country. In the south, the recusant nobles and gentry, who were at first
inclined to remain loyal, were alienated by the harsh methods and suspicious attitude of the president of Munster, Sir William St Leger. Under
the leadership of Lord Mountgarret, an uncle of the earl of Ormond, they
took possession of Kilkenny, and overran most of Munster. In Connaught,
the position was more complicated. Leitrim, lying along the Ulster

border, and disturbed by the recent plantation, quickly followed the Ulster example. In the rest of the province, however, the marquis of Clanricard used his immense influence to prevent an open breach with the government. But the lords justices could send no help, the lords and gentry of Connaught were under strong pressure to join with those of Leinster and Munster, and within a few months they too were in rebellion. For some time longer Clanricard was able to keep the city of Galway in a state of uneasy neutrality, and its fort was still held by government troops; but most of the province was soon under the control of the insurgents.

By February 1642 only a few scattered areas remained in protestant hands. The lords justices exercised a precarious authority in the immediate neighbourhood of Dublin; Drogheda was still besieged; the Ulster Scots maintained control of a considerable area in north Down and south Antrim, including the town of Belfast and the walled city of Carrick-fergus, and of a smaller area in north Donegal; Coleraine, Londonderry and Enniskillen still held out, and were never seriously attacked; the president of Munster held the city and part of the county of Cork. Else-where, isolated towns and forts were still in the hands of government troops, who were sometimes strong enough to control the surrounding country. All the rest of Ireland was now held by the recusant forces.

The fighting, as might be expected from this state of affairs, was local and desultory. On the whole, the government had the best of it, for the recusants were poorly armed and their leaders had no united plan of campaign. St Leger held his ground in Cork, and when the recusants attempted to besiege the city he drove them back in disorder. Ormond relieved and reinforced Drogheda in March, and in April made a successful expedition into Kildare, supplying and reinforcing many of the scattered government garrisons. Mountgarret, with a considerable army, tried to intercept his return, but was easily routed at Kilrush on 15 April 1642. But the effect of these government successes was merely negative. The insurgents lost whatever chance they may have had of speedily completing their occupation of the country; but the government had not the means of establishing permanent control over the territory from which it had driven them, and the military position remained essentially unchanged.

The political developments during 1642 were more significant, for the insurgents now acquired the nucleus of a central organization, largely as a result of clerical initiative. In March, Archbishop O'Reilly of Armagh held a provincial synod at Kells which gave ecclesiastical approval to the war, laid down some rules for its conduct, and advocated the establish-ment of a council of clergy and laymen to maintain order. In accordance

The Catholic Confederacy 89

with this proposal, a national congregation of the clergy met at Kilkenny
in May, and was joined by the leading nobility and gentry; together they
set up a provisional government under a 'supreme council', and arranged
for the election of a 'general assembly' representing the parliamentary
constituencies. The assembly met at Kilkenny in October 1642; it
assumed the powers, though not the name or form, of a parliament, and
established the government on a regular basis. From this time onwards
the insurgents generally described themselves as 'the Confederate
Catholics of Ireland', and they drew up an oath of association, to be taken
throughout the kingdom on pain of excommunication. By the terms of
this oath they were to restore the rights of the church, maintain the pre-
rogatives of the crown, and defend the liberties of the nation, a policy
tersely expressed in the motto on the Confederate seal — *Pro Deo, pro
rege, pro patria Hibernia unanimis.*

This 'Confederation of Kilkenny', as historians have called it, was
meant to be an effective union of the whole Irish nation, except, of course,
for the protestants. Distinctions between Old English and native Irish,
between province and province, between townsmen and countrymen,
were to be swept away, and all were to unite in a common cause. But in
fact this unity was never achieved. Though the supreme council was
supposed to have direction of the war, there was a separate military
organization and a separate commander for each province, and inter-
provincial jealousies made successful co-operation between them impossible. The long-standing distrust between Old English and native Irish,
temporarily overcome in the early stages of the insurrection, soon re-
asserted itself. The Old English dominated the supreme council, of which
Mountgarret was president, and in the conduct of affairs they were
influenced by their own traditions and interests rather than by those of
the native Irish. They were anxious for a speedy settlement with the king,
even if it meant compromise, for their loyalty, though not unconditional,
was genuine; and after the outbreak of civil war in England they saw that
a parliamentary victory there would mean a new conquest of Ireland and
the confiscation of their estates. The native Irish, for the most part, had
lost their lands already in earlier confiscations, and having less at stake
were ready to continue the war. This diversity of interest between the
two groups made the nominal unity of the Confederates ineffective, but
it does not, by itself, account for their military failure. Their lack of
supplies, lack of training, lack of leadership appeared in almost every stage
of the war; and though these weaknesses were certainly accentuated by
the distrust between Old English and native Irish, they were probably
sufficient in themselves to make ultimate victory impossible.

(5)

While the Confederates were establishing their system of government the war in the south had languished. But in the north the landing of Monro's army at Carrickfergus in April 1642 had put fresh heart into the protestants. In co-operation with Monro they took the offensive in June, drove back the Irish, and recaptured and garrisoned Newry, Mountjoy and Dungannon. The Ulster insurgents were so discouraged that they had almost resolved to give up the struggle when their hopes were re-kindled by the arrival of Owen Roe O'Neill in Lough Swilly at the end of July. He brought only a few soldiers and a small supply of arms, but his name and reputation were more important than this material assistance. He was nephew to the great earl of Tyrone, he had served with distinction in the Spanish Netherlands, and the Ulster Irish had long regarded him as their natural leader in a struggle against England. The supreme council soon appointed him general of the Confederate army in Ulster, but he was held up by lack of equipment, and it was the following spring before he was ready to take the field. His military skill, his power of command, the glamour of his name, quickly brought him to a position of great influence, and established a fame that has survived more than three centuries.

Shortly after O'Neill had arrived in Ulster Thomas Preston, who had also made his military reputation in the Spanish Netherlands, landed at Waterford. As brother to Lord Gormanston he was well received by the Old English of the Pale, and was appointed general of the Confederate forces in Leinster. He and O'Neill had been rivals abroad, and they brought their rivalry into Ireland with them; neither would consent to serve under the other, and it was largely on this account that the Confederates were unable to have a unified command.

There was disunity among the protestants also, for they naturally tended to take sides in the dispute between the king and the English parliament. For a time the pressure of their own danger held them uneasily together; and even after the outbreak of war in England in August 1642 the lords justices continued to correspond with parliament as well as with the king; and parliament was still regarded as responsible for the conduct of the Irish war. But Ormond was a strong royalist, while Parsons and some others members of the council supported the parliamentary side, and an open rift in the government was threatened. The king's decision to negotiate with the Irish made it, in the long run, inevitable. Charles may have had in mind, even at this stage, the possibility of getting military help from the Confederates; but his immediate aim was to make peace with them, so that the forces of the Dublin government would become available for service in England. The Confederates' declarations of loyalty, in which they had expressed a desire to lay their case before the king, gave some hope that they would be ready to come to terms; and the failure of the English parliament to send adequate reinforcements provided Charles and his supporters in the Dublin government with an excuse for entering upon negotiations. In January 1643 the king issued a commission to Ormond and others to treat with the Confederates, and in April a commission to Ormond alone to arrange a cessation of arms for at least one year. In September, after months of negotiation, a cessation was at last signed.

The indecisive course of the war during the interval had strengthened the desire for a truce among leaders on both sides. It was a war of isolated sieges and scattered engagements, without strategic coherence. The government forces, penned in narrow quarters and ill-supported from England, were desperately short of food, and the half-starved and unpaid troops were often on the brink of mutiny. The only resource was a foray into enemy territory, giving support to isolated garrisons and sweeping in whatever cattle and other supplies could be found. Such forays were generally successful, for the Confederates made a poor show in the field, but they brought no lasting relief; and, as month after month passed by with no prospect of substantial help from England, opinion in favour of a truce with the Confederates grew stronger. The one considerable battle of the period showed the hopelessness of expecting a military decision. In March 1643 Ormond, anxious to employ his troops and to relieve the pressure on food-supplies in Dublin, marched south and attacked New Ross, in County Wexford. But the town had been so heavily reinforced that he saw little prospect of taking it; and when he learned that Preston was advancing against him with the army of Leinster he drew off his forces and prepared for battle. Preston had the advantage of numbers, but he chose his ground ill, Ormond's artillery did great execution, and the Irish were completely routed. The victors, led by their chaplain, expressed their jubilation in the words of the ninety-seventh psalm, 'which did meet with that glorious deliverance and victory as if it had been penned of purpose'.[1] But they had, in fact, gained nothing save an open road back to Dublin.

---

[1] They began with verse 7: 'Confounded be all they that worship carved images'. Almost certainly they used the metrical version of Sternhold and Hopkins, which had not yet been superseded in popular usage.

Though the battle of Ross hardly affected the military situation, it added to the general depression of the Confederates, for their failure in Leinster was not offset by any striking success in the other provinces. In Ulster, O'Neill was unable to stand against the Scots, and was forced to retire into Connaught in July. In Munster, though the Confederates won a cavalry action near Kilworth in June, they were unable to strengthen their general position. Only in Connaught did they make any notable progress. The fort of Galway was starved into submission in June; and the city, which Clanricard's influence had hitherto kept neutral, at length admitted the Confederate forces in August.

Despite their lack of immediate military success the Confederates seemed to have time on their side, for the government forces could hardly hold out indefinitely. But other circumstances influenced them to seek a more speedy settlement by negotiation. They had reckoned confidently on strong support from the continent; but the representatives whom they despatched to France, Spain, the Netherlands and Germany received little beyond sympathy and promises; and the French and Spanish agents who later arrived at Kilkenny were much more concerned about raising Irish troops for the service of their governments than about helping the Confederates. The pope sent an envoy, Pietro Scarampi, who arrived in Ireland in July 1643 with money and stores; but these fell far short of what was needed, and the Confederates doubted their ability to continue the war without much larger supplies of military equipment from abroad. They were concerned also about the state of affairs in England. If king and parliament should come to terms (a possibility to which the Oxford negotiations early in 1643 gave some substance), or if parliament should win the war, the Confederates would be in a very precarious position. It seemed the wisest course to help the king, and as a step in that direction to arrange a truce during which terms could be discussed.

On both sides the advocates of a truce met with strong opposition. The parliamentary party in the Dublin government feared that it would strengthen the king, and argued that the weakness of the Confederates made it indefensible on military grounds. 'The rebels', wrote Sir John Temple, a member of the Irish council, in June 1643, 'are almost starved and worn out in Ulster, beaten in Munster, and in great want of munition in Leinster'. But Ormond's influence was so powerful, especially with the troops, that Charles could afford to take strong measures. In April 1643 Parsons was removed from office, and in August he, Sir John Temple, and two other councillors known to favour parliament, were arrested; after this, Ormond could go ahead safely. On the Confederate side, the opposition to a truce was more serious, and perhaps better-founded. Its chief spokesman was Scarampi, who argued that they should press on with the war, that their military position was improving, and that they would lose rather than gain by a cessation at this stage. But the supreme council had no confidence in its ability to win the war on its own; it wanted time to organize its system of government; and some at least of its members felt that their repeated declarations of loyalty could hardly be reconciled with the rejection of the king's proposal to suspend hostilities while their grievances were discussed. Accordingly, on 15 September 1643, articles for a cessation of arms for one year were signed at Sigginstown, in County Kildare. The cessation was a truce, not a treaty, and contained no political conditions. Hostilities were to cease forthwith, each side retaining what it actually held at the time of the signature; prisoners were to be exchanged; and the Confederates were to pay the king £30,000, half in money and half in cattle, over a period of eight months.

'To what party the cessation was happy will be hard to determine', wrote an early historian of the period. The Dublin government certainly got some immediate relief; but its military position was weakened by the dispatch of 2,500 troops to England in November 1643. Their arrival there was of little advantage to the king, for they were defeated at Nantwich in January, and a great part of them subsequently joined the parliamentary army. To Ormond the cessation brought advancement to a post of little honour, no reward, and great danger; for the king at length removed the absentee lord lieutenant, the earl of Leicester, who had sided with parliament, and appointed Ormond, whom he had already raised to the marquisate, in his place. This appointment, together with the fact that the English parliament at once condemned the cessation, marked the final breach between the Dublin government and the parliamentary party, and shut off any hope of assistance from that source. To the Confederates the cessation did not even bring the advantage of peace. It was rejected by the Ulster protestants, who adhered instead to the Solemn League and Covenant concluded between parliament and the Scots just ten days after the cessation had been signed. Monro was now appointed to command all the protestant forces in the north and prepared to continue the war. In Munster, also, the cessation failed to bring peace. St Leger had died in May 1642, and since then the government cause in the province had been maintained by Murrough O'Brien, Lord Inchiquin, native Irish by race but fiercely protestant in religion. A brave and dashing commander, he held the Confederates at bay, using his scanty forces with skill and determination, and a ruthlessness that earned him a place in the long line of the O'Briens as 'Murrough of the Burnings'. Inchiquin had at first accepted the cessation; but when he was passed over for the vacant presidency of

Munster in favour of an Englishman, the earl of Portland, his natural disappointment reinforced his protestant doubts about the king's Irish policy, and led him to join the parliamentarians. By July 1644 he was ready to reopen the war with the Confederates.

(6)

The avowed purpose of the cessation had been to provide an opportunity for negotiating a final settlement, and in March 1644 delegates from the supreme council arrived in Oxford to lay the Confederates' demands before the king. In April they were followed by a delegation of Irish protestants, insisting that their demands should be heard also. A comparison of the two sets of demands shows the impossibility of arriving at any settlement that would satisfy both parties: the Confederates wanted complete freedom for the Roman Catholic church, and control of the Irish parliament; the protestants wanted a more rigid enforcement of the recusancy laws, and a firmer establishment of their own political supremacy than had in fact existed before the insurrection began. Charles acted characteristically. He gave the Confederates to understand that something might be done for them, and assured the protestants that they should not suffer by any peace of his making; he then let both delegations return home, and handed over the conduct of further negotiations to Ormond, who received a commission for the purpose in June. These negotiations dragged on for two years; and when at length a treaty was concluded, it was too late to be of service to either party; the king's fortunes had sunk too low to be restored by an Irish alliance; and the supreme council was in even worse case, for not only were the concessions granted by the king without effective force, but the unity of the Confederacy was shattered by the council's acceptance of them.

While the negotiations proceeded, Ireland was falling into ever greater confusion. Though the protestant forces in Munster and Ulster were alike committed to the parliamentary cause, there was no co-operation between them. Inchiquin and Monro each waged war on his own, and each was troubled by the presence of royalist sympathisers among his forces. The Confederates maintained a greater appearance of unity; but they too were divided, both by personal jealousies and by growing disagreement over policy. The divisions first took form at the time of the cessation. Its strongest advocates were among the Old English, while many of the native Irish viewed it with grave distrust, and some of them were ready to condemn those who had negotiated it as 'perjurers, infamous, disloyal and treacherous'. This revival of ill-feeling between Old English and native

Irish was now ominously linked with an emerging rivalry between lay and secular power. Scarampi had based his arguments against the cessation on political and military grounds, but his real motive was to secure satisfactory terms for the church, and he had had the support of some of the bishops. Defeated on that occasion, they watched the subsequent negotiations carefully, and built up a party for themselves, especially among the native Irish, who readily followed their lead. The Old English, though professing equal devotion to the cause of religion, were inclined to be suspicious of episcopal influence; and thus the way was prepared for the welter of rival factions in which the Confederate cause finally collapsed.

One result of the Confederates' internal difficulties was the weakening of their military effort. The cessation had neutralized the royalists, but they found themselves unable to make much progress against Monro and Inchiquin. Indeed, the French agent at Kilkenny reported to Mazarin in the summer of 1644 that if the cessation ended, and the Confederates had to fight Ormond as well as the parliamentarians, they would be unable to sustain the struggle without powerful foreign assistance. In June, O'Neill had been driven into Louth by what he himself called 'the invincible power and force of the Scots in the north'. The supreme council raised a large army to assist him, and entrusted the command to Lord Castlehaven, an English recusant with estates in Ireland, who had joined the Confederates in 1642. But Castlehaven and O'Neill neither trusted nor supported one another, and the campaign petered out in mutual recrimination. In the following year Castlehaven was given command of an army in Munster, where he won some initial successes, and Preston was sent to support him with the Leinster forces. But Preston, dissatisfied with being second in command, soon retired to his own province, and any chance of a decisive victory in Munster was lost.

The weakness of the Confederates enabled Ormond to take a firm line in treating with them, for he knew that they could not afford to renew the war. But he was under strong pressure from the king to conclude a treaty quickly. After Marston Moor, and even more after Naseby, Charles's hopes were fixed on securing a large Confederate army for service in England; and for the sake of this he was willing to make great concessions. The stumbling-block, however, was religion. By October 1644 the Confederate leaders were satisfied that they had already been promised 'as much as is reasonable for us to demand in temporal matters, either for the freedom of the nation or the assurance of . . . estates'; but they still held out for better terms in religion than Ormond, who believed himself to be acting in accordance with the king's wishes, was prepared to concede.

He refused to sacrifice what he regarded as vital to the interests of protestantism for the sake of political advantage, and reminded the Confederate negotiators that they were not the only people who made a
conscience of their religion. It was perhaps because he knew the strength
of Ormond's protestant convictions that Charles, at the end of 1644, found
a more pliable agent through whom to make the concessions that he had
come to regard as inevitable if any help was to be got from the Confederates.

The person chosen for this service was the earl of Glamorgan, an
English recusant, whose family had made great contributions to the royal
cause. He was authorized to treat secretly with the Confederates, and
Charles promised to ratify whatever terms he might conclude. Though
Glamorgan's real purpose was secret, Charles sent him openly to Dublin,
where he arrived at the beginning of August 1645, and recommended him
to Ormond as a man who might be useful in the negotiations with the
Confederates. Accordingly Glamorgan was well received, and allowed
to move freely between Dublin and Kilkenny. Before the end of the
month he had concluded a treaty with the supreme council by which the
Roman Catholic church in Ireland was to enjoy complete freedom, and
possession of all churches and ecclesiastical property not actually in the
hands of the protestants. In return, the Confederates were to supply an
army of 10,000 men for the king's service in England; but this was not
to be made available until the king had performed his share of the compact. The treaty was not made public; Ormond knew nothing of it; and
it would seem that the king himself was not told what had been promised
on his behalf. Whether Charles could ever have received any real advantage from this treaty may well be doubted; its accidental disclosure,
which occurred before the end of the year, certainly proved a major
disaster for the royalist cause. Charles at once repudiated the whole
transaction, and declared that Glamorgan had had no authority except
to raise troops; but this denial carried little conviction, and earlier
suspicions of the king's complicity with the Irish rebels were revived and
strengthened. Glamorgan, who was in Dublin when the disclosure of
the treaty took place, was at once arrested, and closely questioned by
the council; he generously remained silent about the king's part in the
affair, and Ormond, who probably guessed the truth, soon released him.

The open negotiations between Ormond and the Confederates had
not been interrupted by Glamorgan's secret diplomacy; but Ormond's
difficulties were greatly increased, for the Confederates were naturally
reluctant to accept any terms less favourable than those of the Glamorgan
treaty. Nevertheless, Ormond's persistence, and their own desire for a

settlement, gradually wore down their opposition, and agreement was reached in March 1646, though publication of the treaty was deferred until July. As in the Glamorgan treaty, the Confederates promised an army of 10,000 men; in return, the king made numerous concessions, including the abolition of the court of wards, the substitution of an oath of allegiance for the oath of supremacy, the admission of Roman Catholics to all civil and military offices, the removal of disabilities on Roman Catholic education. Nothing was said of ecclesiastical jurisdiction or ecclesiastical property; and though there was a vague promise of further concessions, which the Confederates hoped might include the terms of the Glamorgan treaty, it was made clear that these must depend upon 'his majesty's gracious favour'. The conclusion of peace on such moderate terms was a triumph for Ormond. But the triumph was short-lived. Six months before agreement was finally reached a new actor had arrived on the scene, who was to overthrow Ormond's work and give a new direction to the policy of the Confederates. In October 1645 Giovanni Battista Rinuccini, archbishop of Fermo and papal nuncio to Ireland, had landed at Kenmare.

(7)

Scarampi had been in Ireland as papal envoy since 1643; but the Confederates were anxious for a fully-accredited nuncio, and were gratified by the arrival of Rinuccini, the more so as he brought with him considerable supplies of money and arms. He was a man of courage, determination and zeal, but proud and rash, and he little understood the art of conciliation. His sincerity cannot be doubted; but he must bear part of the responsibility for the ignominious collapse of the Confederacy.

From the beginning, Rinuccini was suspicious of the negotiations with Ormond; but though he knew the terms of the treaty before it was published, he did not come out against it openly until August 1646, when he had it condemned in a synod at Waterford. All who accepted it were threatened with excommunication, on the ground that by failing to secure the full rights of the church they were breaking the oath of association. The supreme council, and the nobility in general, were willing to defy this threat; but the common people and the rank and file of the army were more amenable to clerical influence. The peace was formally proclaimed in Kilkenny and in a few other towns, but generally speaking popular opinion was against it, and an attempt to publish it in Limerick provoked a riot, from which the mayor barely escaped with his life.

Apart from clerical and popular support, Rinuccini's chief strength lay in the alliance of Owen Roe O'Neill, whom he had supplied with money

D

and arms; and at this point O'Neill's power and prestige were at their height, for he had just won a great victory over the Ulster Scots. In the early summer of 1646 Monro had advanced towards Armagh, with the idea of marching south and striking at the very heart of the Confederacy. The approach of O'Neill with a large army did not alarm him; the Scots, grown overbold with repeated victory, 'did not expect to be faced by Ulstermen, much less to be fought with'; and Monro was so eager to bring O'Neill to an engagement that he allowed himself to be drawn into an unfavourable position at Benburb, some seven miles from Armagh. Here, on 5 June, the armies met. 'Let your manhood be seen by your push of pike', was O'Neill's exhortation to his troops; and it was after a desperate encounter at push of pike that the Scots forces were broken, and 'the slaughter was followed until night separated them'. Monro lost not only his wig and his sword, but his artillery, his stores, and half his infantry; and O'Neill was able to send thirty-one captured colours as a triumphal offering to the nuncio. 'For aught I can understand', wrote Monro piously, 'the Lord of Hosts had a controversy with us'.

Benburb was at first hailed as a decisive victory — when the news reached Rome the pope himself attended a *Te Deum* in S. Maria Maggiore. But O'Neill failed to press his advantage; the Scots were given time to re-form their army; and very soon they were once more harrying the Irish forces in south Ulster. Instead of completing the work he had begun O'Neill marched to the support of the nuncio; and Benburb proved, in the end, a far greater disaster for the supreme council than for the protestants of the north. Rinuccini, supported by O'Neill's victorious army, entered Kilkenny in triumph in September, deposed and imprisoned the supreme council, and appointed a new one, with himself as president. Even Preston, who had formerly had the Ormond treaty proclaimed in his camp, was overawed by the nuncio and submitted to his instructions. The peace was at an end, and the Confederates, under their new government, prepared to resume hostilities.

The first object of attack was Dublin, which Ormond was desperately trying to put in a state of defence. His position was so weak that he saw little prospect of making it good against the combined forces of O'Neill and Preston, and he turned to the English parliament for help. But before he had concluded any bargain, the pressure on Dublin had been relieved by disagreement between the Confederate generals. O'Neill withdrew his forces in November, and a few weeks later Preston, temporarily re-converted to support of the treaty, made a pact with Ormond for a joint attack on the Ulster army. His fear of excommunication, however, was too strong for him; almost immediately he changed his mind again, and placed himself once more at the service of the nuncio. But the Confederates had lost their chance of taking Dublin.

This failure was a blow to Rinuccini's prestige; a natural reaction against his high-handed proceedings had already begun; and he was embarrassed by the undisciplined conduct of the Ulster army, which proclaimed itself as peculiarly under his patronage. To restore his popularity and strengthen his position he released the old supreme council from prison, and summoned a meeting of the general assembly for January 1647. This assembly, which was dominated by his supporters, rejected the peace treaty of 1646, and declared against any future treaty that did not provide for the rights of the church and the clergy. The influence of the Old English was still strong enough to prevent the complete abandonment of all negotiation with Ormond, and an uneasy truce was maintained until early April. But Ormond was now convinced that peace on any terms that he could accept would be blocked by the nuncio and the clergy; and since he could not hold Dublin indefinitely, it must pass either to the Confederates or to the English parliament. Faced with this choice between rebels, Ormond was naturally inclined to prefer the protestants to the recusants; and the more so at this time, when there seemed to be some reasonable prospect of a negotiated settlement in England. As early as February 1647 he had re-opened communications with parliament, and parliamentary forces began to arrive in April. By mid-June the conditions of transfer, which included the surrender not only of Dublin but of all the other garrisons under Ormond's command, were finally agreed on; and at the end of July Ormond left Ireland. He spent some time in England, where he was allowed to visit the king; then, fearing arrest, he passed over to France, where he joined the exiled queen and prince of Wales at Paris in March 1648.

(8)

After Ormond's departure, the political and military position in Ireland quickly reached a state of confusion that defies accurate description. Almost every party in the kingdom was divided against itself, and local commanders changed sides according to their own judgement of the situation. The appearance of unity among the Confederates, temporarily restored by the general assembly of January 1647, could not survive the military disasters that they suffered. Preston, making a rash advance against Dublin, had his forces cut to pieces at Dungan Hill by the parliamentary commander, Michael Jones. Inchiquin ranged through Munster almost unchecked. In May he had taken Dungarvan, in September he sacked Cashel, in November he all but annihilated a superior Confederate army at Knocknanuss, near Kanturk. By the end of the year, the whole province, except for a few garrison towns, was at his mercy.

It was in such gloomy circumstances that the general assembly met again in November. The meeting was poorly attended, and the Old English, finding themselves in a majority, seized the opportunity to remodel the constitution in their own interests and to appoint a new supreme council. But they did nothing to redress the military position, and were soon forced to negotiate with Inchiquin for a truce, which was concluded in May 1648. This gave Rinuccini, who was bitterly opposed to the new council, the opportunity he wanted. He at once condemned the truce, excommunicated all who adhered to it, and laid an interdict on all towns where it was received. But the council appealed to Rome against his sentence, and formally dismissed O'Neill, who supported him, from command of the Ulster army. The Confederacy was now in a state of civil war, though neither side was strong enough to do very much. O'Neill advanced against Kilkenny, but he failed to press the attack; and after a useless campaign in Munster he withdrew northwards again, so enfeebled that he offered to make a truce with Inchiquin on terms much less favourable than those already condemned by the nuncio. Rinuccini himself had retired to Galway, where he lingered for some months, though unable to exercise much influence on the course of events, and finally left Ireland in February 1649.

Among the protestants also party divisions appeared. The forces in Dublin stood firmly by parliament, but in Munster and Ulster the position was more complicated. Inchiquin became increasingly dissatisfied with his treatment by the parliament, and in April 1648 declared once more for the king. But not all the Munster protestants followed him, so that the parliamentary cause still had its adherents in the province. In Ulster, the Scots were suspicious of the parliamentary commander, George Monck, and were increasingly influenced by the contemporary royalist reaction in Scotland. Monck prevented them from taking any immediate action by seizing their principal garrisons, but the position remained an uneasy one.

The Confederates' breach with Rinuccini and Inchiquin's adherence to the king opened the way for a new royalist alliance. No one but Ormond could hope to head it effectively, and at the end of September 1648 he arrived in Cork. At first all went well. In January 1649 a new treaty was signed with the Confederates; and though its terms hardly differed from those of 1646, it received the approval of nine bishops; Rinuccini, it is true, condemned it almost on the eve of his departure, but his condemnation was ignored. The Confederacy was now formally dissolved, and the government temporarily entrusted to twelve commissioners; but the real centre of authority was Ormond himself. He hoped that the revulsion of feeling after Charles's execution would enable him to win further allies. But Owen Roe O'Neill preferred to retain his independence of action: he rejected Ormond's offers, and made an agreement of his own with the parliamentary commanders in the north, by which he was enabled to obtain military supplies. This understanding between O'Neill and the parliamentarians tied the hands of the Ulster Scots, who in any case would have been loath to enter into any alliance with the Irish, and they too refused to join Ormond. An attempt to negotiate with Michael Jones came to nothing; for Jones declared roundly that the protestant interest in Ireland depended on the English, and could never be secured in alliance with popish rebels.

Negotiations having failed, Ormond opened the campaign in June 1649. Drogheda and Dundalk quickly fell to Inchiquin; and Monck, who had commanded in Dundalk, retired to England. But the essential prize was Dublin, and here Ormond failed completely. He had advanced the main body of his army as far as Rathmines, on the southern outskirts of the city, when he was unexpectedly attacked by Jones, on 2 August; the royalist forces were shattered, and Ormond was obliged to abandon his camp, with all his stores, and escape with a few followers to Kilkenny. A fortnight later, Cromwell and 3,000 Ironsides reached Dublin, 'the great guns echoing forth their welcome, and the acclamations of the people resounding in every street'.

(9)

Cromwell's arrival changed the whole character of the war. He was as much superior to his enemies in material resources as in military genius, and he had the enormous advantage of being unhampered by political dissensions among his followers. Ormond's position still appeared a strong one, for he had superiority in numbers, and his adherents controlled the greater part of the country; but his troops had been demoralized by the defeat of Rathmines, and the alliance that he headed contained too many dissident elements to achieve much stability. For a year and a half he maintained the struggle, but within that time military disaster and political disruption had made his task impossible.

Cromwell's campaign began with one of the best-remembered events in Irish history, the storming and sack of Drogheda on 11 September 1649, after a very brief siege. Almost the entire garrison and such recusant clergy as could be found were put to death, and no doubt many of the townspeople perished also; but there seems to be no foundation for later stories of an indiscriminate slaughter of the whole civilian population. Cromwell, in his report to parliament, justified what was done as retribution for the massacres attributed to the Irish rebels; but in fact the backbone of the garrison consisted of English royalists.

The fall of Drogheda, which had been expected to make a strong resistance, showed O'Neill the danger of isolation, and in October he at length concluded an alliance with Ormond. Had he been prepared to accept the same terms in the previous January the history of the intervening months might have been very different; but his conversion came too late to affect the course of events. Already he was a sick man, and died three weeks later, protesting from his death-bed that all his actions had been directed to the service of religion, of the king, and of the nation. O'Neill was a soldier, not a statesman, and as a soldier he has perhaps been overrated; but he was the only Confederate commander to win even one important battle, and the striking if almost fruitless victory of Benburb has shed an enduring lustre on the memory of the last great representative of the Gaelic aristocracy.

Though O'Neill's army was now on Ormond's side, the parliamentary forces were soon able to dominate the north, and by the end of November the only Ulster strongholds in royalist hands were Charlemont and Enniskillen. Cromwell himself had turned south. In October he took Wexford and New Ross; in November Cork, Youghal and Kinsale, all garrisoned by protestant royalists, joined him of their own free will. Waterford was besieged in November; but Ormond managed to send in reinforcements, and the siege had to be raised at the beginning of December. This was the first serious check that Cromwell had so far met. But it made little difference, for within the next few months he had overrun almost all the south; Kilkenny fell in March, and Clonmel, after a stout resistance, in May. When Cromwell left Ireland on 26 May 1650 the work of conquest had not, indeed, been completed, but the backbone of resistance had been broken.

In spite of this, the struggle was protracted for almost two years longer; partly because Cromwell's successors in Ireland moved with caution, partly because the nature of the terrain was unfavourable to a quick decision, partly because the break-down of authority among the Irish meant that there was no one who could negotiate a general settlement on their behalf. Ormond's influence, already undermined by military failure and the attacks of the recusant clergy, was ruined by the policy of the new king. Charles II had temporarily put his faith in the Scots, and in

August 1650, under Scottish pressure, he publicly disowned and condemned Ormond's treaty of January 1649 with the Confederates. When
the news reached Ireland, Ormond did his best to persuade the Irish that
Charles had acted under duress, and that the declaration did not represent
his real opinion. But the task was impossible; and Ormond soon realised
that there was no hope of effective unity under his leadership. He already
had royal authority to leave Ireland at his discretion; and on 11 December,
having appointed Clanricard as his deputy, he sailed for France.

Ormond's departure did nothing to restore Irish unity. The clerical
party had no confidence in Clanricard, for though a Roman Catholic he
had refused the oath of association. Instead, they fixed their hopes on
Charles IV, duke of Lorraine, who had turned his adventurous mind
towards Ireland and whom they proposed to make protector of the kingdom, though without any formal repudiation of their allegiance to the
king. The duke did, in fact, send some money and arms; but if he ever had
any serious designs on Ireland he soon abandoned them. The real hope for
the Irish, had they but realized it, lay not abroad but at home, where they
still had 30,000 men in the field; and though Waterford had surrendered
in August 1650, Limerick and Galway still held out. But there was neither
unity of command nor unity of purpose. Rival factions in Limerick had
almost come to blows before the city surrendered, after a long siege, in
October 1651; Galway, split by similar dissensions, surrendered in the
following May. In the same month, the Irish forces in Leinster, who held
no fortified post and lived at large on the country, surrendered on articles
that left the officers free to take service abroad and to carry recruits with
them; in June, Lord Muskerry's forces in Munster accepted similar terms.
For some months longer isolated centres of resistance held out in Ulster
and Connaught; but by the summer of 1652 the war was over, and all
Ireland lay helpless in the hands of the English parliament.

V

Confiscation and Settlement

---

(1)

When Ormond left Dublin in the summer of 1647 he was obliged, by the terms of his agreement with the parliamentary commissioners, to surrender into their hands 'the king's sword, the mace, the royal robes . . . with all other ensigns of royalty, and all other things belonging to the lord lieutenant or lord lieutenancy of this kingdom'. But the English parliament, though it had thus assumed the traditional symbols of government, was for some years much more concerned with military than with civil affairs. Cromwell was appointed lord lieutenant as well as commander-in-chief, and when he left Ireland in May 1650 Ireton, who succeeded him in the command, was appointed lord deputy; but neither had much time to spare for the problems of civil administration. As the conquest progressed, however, it became necessary to establish a system of government on some sort of regular basis: in October 1650 four parliamentary commissioners were appointed, and in the following January they arrived in Ireland.

According to their instructions, the commissioners were to encourage the propagation of the gospel, suppress popery, make provision for education, inquire into the administration of justice, and settle the revenue. But Ireland was not yet in a state for such a programme to be executed in detail. Ten years of almost continuous warfare, during which the contending armies had lived off the country, had destroyed the framework of law and order, and reduced many areas to famine conditions; plague was rife, especially in the cities and towns; and the re-appearance of the wolf as a menace to society marked the general desolation of the countryside. The commissioners' immediate task was to establish some sort of local government; and to this end they divided the area already under parliamentary control into six 'precincts', each under a military governor, with commissioners for the collection of revenue and the administration of justice. As the conquest proceeded the system was extended, and the number of precincts for the whole country was finally settled at twelve. In this way something was done, by piecemeal, towards restoring order, establishing preaching ministers, and raising revenue.

The commissioners' responsibility was not confined to civil affairs; for shortly after Ireton's death, in November 1651, the offices of lord lieutenant and lord deputy were abolished, and the commissioners became responsible for the whole field of government, including the conduct of the war. So long as the war lasted military affairs occupied much of their attention: they had to see to the payment and provisioning of the army; and they kept a careful watch on all negotiations with Irish commanders. Thus, for example, they refused to approve the terms on which Coote had accepted the surrender of Galway, as being too favourable to the garrison, and insisted on their modification. But, though always suspicious of any lenity towards the Irish, they were acutely aware of the danger that must arise from the presence in the country of large bodies of disbanded soldiers; they readily allowed Irish commanders, on surrender, to take their troops abroad for service with any power at peace with the Commonwealth; and they did what they could to facilitate their departure. Many thousands took advantage of this opportunity, but enough remained behind to be a threat to peace and security. Even after formal hostilities had everywhere ceased, there were many areas in which the broken remnants of the Irish forces maintained a guerrilla warfare that rapidly developed into brigandage. It is at this period that the ominous name 'tory' first appears in the state papers, and until almost the end of the century the suppression of toryism remained one of the constant problems of Irish government. The tories were outlaws whose natural taste for robbery was strengthened by resentment against the new settlers and the régime that supported them. In spite of their depredations, they acquired something of a patriotic character among the native Irish; and the names that have been recorded suggest that they were themselves for the most part of native extraction — 'Blind Donough', Dermot Ryan, Hugh McBrian O'Hart, and, most famous of all, Redmond O'Hanlon, who still lives in popular tradition as a kind of Irish Robin Hood.

(2)

The commissioners held the view, widespread among Englishmen at the time, that the only hope of establishing order and good government in Ireland lay in a new and more extensive plantation, for which the rebellion and its suppression seemed to offer an unrivalled opportunity. And there were other more immediate reasons for pressing on with a policy of confiscation. The Adventurers were clamouring for a speedy settlement of their claims; the commissioners wanted lands set aside to meet the soldiers' arrears, so that they could reduce the army; and the government looked to Ireland as a source from which some of its outstanding debts could be satisfied. After long negotiations between the various interested parties, parliament passed an 'Act of Settlement' in August, 1652 and in the same month new instructions were issued to the commissioners, including a direction that this act should be published and put in force.

It was this Act of Settlement that gave force to the Adventurers' Act of 1642 and the subsequent measures of the Long Parliament modifying its terms. This earlier legislation had ensured that the war should be followed by confiscation, and prescribed the rates at which those who had adventured their money on the prospect should be repaid; the act of 1652 laid down what classes of proprietors should forfeit their estates. The preamble to the act declared that it was not the intention of parliament 'to extirpate that whole nation', but its penalties did in fact extend to virtually the whole population of Ireland above the rank of landless labourers. Four classes of persons were excepted from pardon for life and estate: all who had taken part in the first stages of the rebellion, before the establishment of the Confederate government at Kilkenny; all Roman Catholic ecclesiastics who had in any way aided or abetted the rebellion; all who had been responsible for killing civilians, or, being themselves civilians, had been responsible for killing English soldiers; all those still in arms who failed to submit within twenty-eight days of the publication of the act by the parliamentary commissioners or the commander-in-chief. To close any possible loop-hole by which the leaders, or some of them, might escape this condemnation, 104 persons were excepted from pardon by name. The list included recusants and protestants, Old English and native Irish: Bishop Bramhall and Ormond and Inchiquin, along with Clanricard and Castlehaven, Phelim O'Neill and Rory O'More. All other persons possessing real estate, except such as had, throughout the rebellion, 'manifested their constant good affection to the commonwealth of England', were to suffer partial forfeiture, losing one-fifth, one-third, or two-thirds of their estates, according to the degree of their 'delinquency'; and they might be obliged to accept, in exchange for the proportion of their estates that remained to them, other lands of equal value 'in such places in Ireland, as the parliament, for the more effectual settlement of the peace of that nation, shall think fit'. A final section slightly modified the general severity of the act: all who had surrendered on conditions, provided the parliamentary commander who made the conditions had acted within his authority in doing so, were to have the benefit of their articles of surrender, even if they were included by name among those excepted from pardon.

The Act of Settlement declared what persons or classes of persons were to forfeit the whole or part of their estates; but it prescribed neither how the forfeitures were to be enforced, nor how the lands so forfeited were to be set out to the various claimants. The execution of the act was entrusted to Fleetwood (who received his instructions as commander-in-chief in Ireland in September 1652) and to the parliamentary commissioners. They published the act in October; but there was little more that they could do, partly because of the rivalry between the claims of the Adventurers and those of the soldiers, but mainly because they felt the need of further legislation. The English parliament was, in fact, considering a bill, which the commissioners hoped would put an end to their troubles; but it made such slow progress that it had not been passed when Cromwell suddenly expelled the parliament in April 1653. In the interval that elapsed before the assembly of Barebone's parliament in July, Cromwell directed affairs himself, and a comprehensive scheme for the future settlement of Ireland began to take shape.

According to this scheme, all 'delinquent' proprietors were to be re-moved across the Shannon into Connaught (including the county of Clare), where they were to receive lands equivalent in value to the proportion of their estates that they were entitled to retain. Ten counties in the other three provinces were set aside to meet the claims of the Adventurers and soldiers, one-half of the forfeited lands in each county being assigned to the Adventurers, one-half to the soldiers. Forfeited lands in the remaining counties were to be at the government's disposal for various purposes, including the payment of debts, grants to parliamentary leaders, and the making good of possible deficiencies in the areas allocated to Adventurers and soldiers. To begin with, this scheme rested simply on Cromwell's own authority; but in September 1653 an 'Act of Satisfaction' passed by Barebone's parliament regularized the position, and gave statutory force to instructions already issued.

The execution of this scheme presented serious administrative difficulties. The transplantation to Connaught, which was regarded as the necessary first stage, progressed very slowly and was, in fact, never completed at all. It was first announced that all 'transplantable persons' should remove themselves by 1 May 1654, and that they should be liable to death if found east of the Shannon after that date. But permission to delay departure was freely given to individuals, and the time for the general removal was extended, first to December 1654, then to March 1655. The natural reluctance of the Irish to move was strengthened by the hope of a change of policy, for there was division of opinion on the English side about the wisdom of the transplantation scheme. In the end, however, the scheme was enforced; and many thousands of people, though by no means all those comprised within the Act of Satisfaction, were compelled to leave their homes and transport themselves, their families, their cattle, goods and dependants, across the Shannon. There was no attempt at uprooting the whole population. Such a plan, even if feasible, was clearly against the interest of the prospective new settlers, who would require labourers on their lands; but many tenants did, in fact, choose to follow their landlords. The officials in charge of this process of removal and re-settlement had first to assess the value of each 'delinquent' proprietor's estate, and then assign him, from forfeited lands in Connaught, an area equal to the proportion he was entitled to retain. They found the task too complicated to be performed as quickly as the circumstances required, and were reduced to the rough-and-ready expedient of settling each applicant on such land as the stock he had brought with him seemed to require.

The commissioners responsible for distributing lands in Connaught were able to use a partial survey of the province made in Wentworth's time. There was no such guide to distribution for the rest of the country, and until something of the sort was available it was impossible to proceed. In the course of 1653 the surveyor-general, Benjamin Worsley, began to prepare a descriptive list of all forfeited lands, barony by barony; but the rate of progress was very slow, and Worsley's methods were strongly criticized by William Petty, physician-general to the forces, and a man of great and wide-ranging ability. Petty proposed an alternative scheme for a survey of which the results should be noted down on maps (hence it is commonly called the 'down survey'), and this was finally accepted by the government in December 1654. On the basis of this survey, which was ready in little more than a year, the distribution went steadily forward. Some change of plan was found necessary. The soldiers' claims could not be satisfied out of their share of the ten counties set apart for the purpose, and the deficiency had to be made up in other areas, including parts of Connaught originally intended for transplanted persons. By the end of 1658 the work was substantially complete. Some lands remained unallocated, some claims were still unsatisfied, but throughout the whole country a sweeping change in the ownership of land had been effected; the old proprietors had been dispossessed and either banished or removed to Connaught, and new proprietors established in their place.

The government's purpose was not just to meet its liabilities at the expense of the Irish rebels, but to establish such a strong population of English protestants as would ensure the future loyalty and tranquillity of Ireland. But many of the difficulties that had undermined the effectiveness of previous plantations now reappeared. The Adventurers were slow to take possession, deterred by the general desolation of the country and the prevalence of tories; and they refused to bind themselves to bring in a prescribed number of English settlers within a fixed period. Much was hoped for from the settlement of the disbanded soldiers, who were expected to form a resident garrison, overaweing the Irish and protecting the other colonists. It was for this reason that their lands were interspersed with those of the Adventurers; and there was to be a belt of soldier-settlements round the borders of Connaught to contain the transplanted Irish. But some soldiers were unwilling to settle on the land; and many others, though willing to settle, could not afford to wait until they were put in actual possession. They had received debentures, stating the amount of arrears due to them and promising satisfaction 'out of the rebels' lands, houses, tenements and hereditaments in Ireland'; those in urgent need of ready money, or whose claims were for small amounts, were under strong temptation to sell their debentures; and, despite government attempts to prevent such sales, speculators did a brisk business. The result was an increase in the number of large holdings; and the rank-and-file of the army played a less important part in the settlement than had been intended. Moreover, the soldiers who did settle showed an immediate tendency, which no threats or punishments could check, to intermarry with Irish papists, and the protestant character of the settlement was thus endangered from the beginning.

Though the Cromwellian plantation was in some respects less successful than had been hoped, its importance in the later history of Ireland can hardly be over-estimated. It had a profound effect on the balance between protestant and recusant, not only in land-ownership but also in civic life. The old corporations, which had been a major element in the political power of the recusants down to 1641, now passed under protestant control. In the cities and towns that had been held by the Confederates, all property was confiscated, and granted or leased to protestants. Attempts to drive recusants out of the towns altogether had only partial success; but those who remained had no political power, and little share in trade. In town and country alike, the protestant interest that had been growing since the latter part of Elizabeth's reign had now established complete ascendancy; and this ascendancy, surviving both Restoration and Revolution, was to control the life of Ireland down to the nineteenth century.

(3)

While the land settlement went forward there was, despite all difficulties, a slow but noticeable improvement in the general condition of the country. The war had almost destroyed economic life. Export trade had languished, and Ireland had been drained of so much of her currency that there was little in circulation but clipped, debased, or counterfeit coins. Over wide areas agriculture had almost ceased; there was a general shortage of corn, and cattle had been destroyed in large numbers. It seems to have been at this period that the potato, a crop not easily seized by marauding troops, became the staple food of the rural poor. So great was the dearth in the closing years of the war that the parliamentary authorities put a prohibition on the export of provisions, and this was maintained even after the return of peace. But as agriculture revived the restrictions were gradually relaxed, and trade began to resume its normal course.

The government was concerned to increase revenue, for the army was a heavy financial burden: in 1658, after a considerable number of soldiers had been disbanded, the cost of the military establishment was still reckoned at not less than £264,000 a year. No one supposed that such a sum could be raised in Ireland; but there was a natural anxiety to reduce the gap that had to be made up from the English exchequer. By far the greater part of the Irish revenue at this time came from monthly assessments laid on each county; if trade improved not only would the income from customs and excise increase, but the country would be better able to bear the assessments and accordingly the government did what it could to hasten the economic revival. A council of trade was set up in 1655, and encouragement was given to manufacturers, especially of cloth and iron: by 1657 Sir Charles Coote's iron-works in Queen's County was giving employment to sixty families; in 1658 the customs and excise were farmed for £70,000. The country still swarmed with beggars, thousands of whom were transported to the West Indies; but the economic recovery that marked the Restoration period had its beginnings in the 1650s.

(4)

During these years, as the country gradually settled down, the civil government was established on a more regular footing. The setting up of the protectorate in 1653 brought a return to the traditional pattern; in the following year Fleetwood, who was commander-in-chief, was appointed lord deputy, and the commissioners were replaced by a council. By this time, also, a judicial system was in operation. The first courts established in Ireland by the parliamentary authorities were for the trial of Irishmen accused of murder during the rebellion. But provision had also to be made for routine cases. Commissioners for the administration of justice were appointed in 1651, and the practice of sending judges on circuit was quickly resumed. By 1655 Ireland had a lord chancellor, with a new great seal, and the traditional 'four courts' — chancery, upper bench (in place of king's bench), common pleas, and exchequer — were once more sitting in Dublin. In 1656, with the re-establishment of probate courts (including a prerogative court in Dublin)[1] and a court of admiralty, the pre-war system was virtually restored. There was the same sort of restoration in local government; for though the division into precincts remained, sheriffs and justices of the peace were appointed for every county; and towns that had forfeited their charters in the rebellion received new ones.

Despite the revolutionary character of the period, this restoration was not merely one of forms but, in some measure, of men also. Many of the Commonwealth officials in Ireland were men whose families had been established in the country before 1641, and some of them had held office under the crown. Sir Gerard Lowther, who had been chief justice of the common pleas, presided over one of the first courts established in Ireland by the parliamentary authorities; Sir Edward Bolton, one of the commissioners for the administration of justice appointed in 1651, was a son of Lord Chancellor Bolton; Sir John Temple, as master of the rolls, Sir Robert Meredith, as chancellor of the exchequer, resumed under Cromwell the offices they had held in 1641; of 21 sheriffs appointed in 1656 more than half had been settled in Ireland before the war. The English and protestant population of the pre-1641 era was reinforced, not swamped, by the Cromwellian settlers. The two groups had a common interest that proved stronger than any enmity surviving from the civil war; they readily co-operated in working the Commonwealth administration; and, when the time came, they were equally forward in bringing King Charles home again.

This gradual restoration of old forms of government during the 1650s stopped short of completion. Cromwellian Ireland had no parliament of its own, but was merged in one commonwealth with England and Scotland, and sent members to the parliament at Westminster. This principle of joint representation was first established in Barebone's

---

[1] The prerogative court dealt with probate of wills in which property had been left in each of two or more dioceses. Under the Commonwealth, diocesan divisions were ignored; and local probate courts were established for groups of counties.

Parliament, which contained six members for Ireland, all but one of them soldiers. By the Instrument of Government (December 1653) Ireland was to have thirty members, the arrangement of constituencies being left to the protector and council; and Irish members accordingly sat in the parliaments of 1654, 1656, and 1659. The forms of election seem to have been observed, at least in 1656 and 1659; but government influence was very strong, and army officers formed a high proportion of the membership. But other influences sometimes prevailed: John Davys, a Carrickfergus alderman of royalist sympathies, was one of the three members elected in 1656 for the counties of Antrim, Down and Armagh (which formed a single constituency), and his return was so distasteful to the government that he was deliberately detained in Ireland during the parliamentary session. Barebone's Parliament had passed the Act of Satisfaction; but the later parliaments of the Commonwealth played no such decisive part in Irish affairs; and it was only in the parliament of 1659 that the Irish members, as a body, seem to have exercised any significant influence. The parliamentary union had no time to establish itself; and, even while it lasted, Ireland retained a separate administration and a separate judicial system. The notion of Ireland as a distinct political entity, with a right to its own parliament, survived among the older protestant population, and was readily taken up by the new Cromwellian settlers when it suited them to do so.

(5)

The extension of English parliamentary authority to Ireland inevitably brought with it the application of puritan ecclesiastical policy. The commissioners to whom Ormond handed over Dublin in June 1647 at once prohibited the use of the book of common prayer, though they seem to have allowed those Church of Ireland clergy who accepted the prohibition to continue their functions. But this was only a temporary arrangement; and as the area under the control of parliament expanded provision was made for the appointment and payment of approved 'ministers of the gospel'. The duty of making such provision was a prominent item in the instructions issued to the commissioners who virtually governed Ireland from January 1651 to September 1654, and it was repeated in the instructions subsequently issued to the lord deputy and council. As long as the war continued, and even afterwards, while much of the country was in a disturbed condition, comparatively few ministers were appointed. In 1654 there were only 113, and most of these were either in Dublin or in Ulster. By 1656 the number had risen to over

300, and included a good many in the midlands and in the south. At first, most of the appointments were made to towns, where the protestants were more numerous, and where the authority of the government was more effective than in the rural areas. But from 1657 onwards an attempt was made to revive the parochial system and, by placing ministers in every parish or union of parishes, to provide a 'preaching ministry' throughout the country.

To begin with, the 'ministers of the gospel' were paid directly by the state, which had taken all ecclesiastical property, including tithe, into its own hands. Later on, in areas where the parochial system had been re-established, the minister received the tithe of the parish, provided it did not exceed £200 a year; if it fell short of his former stipend the government made up the difference. But over much of the country the practice of direct state payment was continued throughout the whole Commonwealth period.

The main difficulty was a shortage of suitable men. The authorities were ready to appoint such Church of Ireland clergy and presbyterian ministers as were willing to serve, provided they found them 'orthodox' in religion and reliable in politics. But they depended mainly on recruits from England, whom they tried to attract by promise of a 'comfortable subsistence'. The number who came fell far short of what was needed, and not all of them were found suitable. In February 1655, for example, one Dunbarre, who had arrived with a certificate from the English committee for the approbation of ministers, proved so unsatisfactory that he was given £20 to take him home again. The problem of supply was never solved; and down to the end of the Commonwealth period the Irish administration was still trying to attract more ministers from England, and even from the North American colonies.

The Church of Ireland was in no position to resist or counter puritan policy. Over the greater part of the country the clergy had been driven out by the Confederates in the first year of the war; most of the bishops were dead or forced into exile; there was no possibility of holding a synod or convocation; and the remaining clergy were left to decide individually what course to pursue. A considerable number, not fewer than sixty-five and probably more, accepted appointments under the Commonwealth, sometimes in or near their old parishes; others maintained an unobtrusive private ministry; and a few got into trouble with the government for using the prayer-book openly. In general, however, the suppression of 'prelacy' did not provoke in Ireland the same dangerous resentment that it provoked in England.

The government had much more reason to fear the Ulster Scots. Since

1642, when the arrival of Monro's army had greatly strengthened their links with Scotland, they had organized their ecclesiastical life on the presbyterian model, and had maintained communication with the Scottish general assembly. The movement of opinion in Scotland had, naturally, a powerful influence upon them: they had followed the example of their brethren there in condemning the execution of the king, and their ministers prayed openly for Charles II. The government, alarmed at this defiance of its authority, imprisoned some ministers and silenced others; and in 1653 it proposed, as a precautionary measure, to remove the Scottish settlers from Antrim and Down, where they were dangerously near Scotland, to other parts of the country. The establishment of the protectorate in that year, however, not only put an end to this scheme, but benefited the presbyterians in other ways also. The harsh treatment they had hitherto received was not due solely to political considerations; it sprang also from the hostility of the sectaries, and especially the ana-baptists, who hated presbytery as much as they hated prelacy. But Cromwell was more inclined towards comprehension; and his son Henry, who came to Ireland in 1655 as a member of the council and major-general of the army, checked the influence of the anabaptist Fleetwood. The presbyterians were now left in peace; ministers returned to their charges, and new recruits came from Scotland; throughout a great part of Ulster the parish churches were in their hands, and some sixty or seventy of them received stipends from the state.

Though the puritans hated prelacy and were suspicious of presby-terianism, they regarded popery as the great evil that they were called upon to extirpate at all costs. Cromwell's declaration in October 1649 set the note for what was to follow: 'If by liberty of conscience you mean a liberty to exercise the mass, I judge it best to use plain dealing, and to let you know, that where the parliament of England have power, that will not be allowed of'. Accordingly, great efforts were made to get rid of the Roman Catholic clergy. From 1649 until the end of the war they were generally excluded from the benefit of any article of surrender, and many suffered death. Thereafter, they were hunted down, with a price on their heads; and if caught were either imprisoned or forced to leave the country. But very many remained at liberty, going about in disguise, even in garrison towns; and despite the rigorous measures against them, their numbers were increasing during the later 1650s.

At least to the more enthusiastic puritans, this campaign against the clergy was a preparation for converting the popish natives to protestan-tism, for it was thought that if the influence of the clergy were once removed they would be more likely to listen to 'ministers of the gospel'.

But there were very few conversions, and those few the result rather of fear than of conviction. The parliament of 1656 passed an act by which any person above the age of sixteen might be required to take an oath abjuring the supremacy of the pope and other distinctively Roman Catholic doctrines, on penalty of losing two-thirds of his real and personal property; but though this act provoked widespread unrest in Ireland, there is no evidence that many people took the oath.

The general result of the Commonwealth's religious policy in Ireland was to deepen the gulf between protestant and recusant, and to strengthen the recusants' conviction that they could never be safe under a protestant government. And by subjecting both Old English and native Irish to a common condemnation it did more to fuse the two groups into a single body than ever the Confederates themselves had been able to do.

(6)

In Ireland as in England the closing years of the protectorate were marked by doubt and anxiety, and in both countries the army helped to shape political developments. But whereas in England the army had come to form a distinct party of its own, cut off from any clear national purpose, the army in Ireland was closely linked with the powerful new landed interest, and it was the co-operation between the two that enabled the Cromwellian land settlement to survive substantially intact.

When Oliver Cromwell died on 3 September 1658 his son Henry was lord deputy of Ireland, having succeeded Fleetwood in the previous November. His popularity with the Irish army was considered to be a source of strength to his brother Richard, the new protector; but in fact Henry played little more than a negative part in the critical events that followed. When the English army virtually deposed Richard and restored the rump of the Long Parliament in May 1659, Henry made no move to support his brother; and when, in June, he heard that parliament had resolved on his own recall and the appointment of commissioners to govern Ireland he did not wait for any formal notification, but wrote to Speaker Lenthall, resigning his post. This submission was a blow to the royalists, who had been angling for Henry's support. 'Harry of Ireland', wrote one of them bitterly, 'hath laid down the cudgels with a pusill-animity suitable to his elder brother'. Henry Cromwell had, indeed, little political ambition, and his main aim at this time was to live quietly in England; but his refusal to join with the royalists arose from principle, not from cowardice.

This change of government passed without disturbance in Ireland. The authority of the new commissioners was accepted; and when a royalist rising under Sir George Booth broke out in Cheshire in August 1654 troops were sent over from Ireland to assist in suppressing it. But the English army's new expulsion of the Rump in October altered this situation. In Scotland, General George Monck issued a declaration in favour of the parliament, and appealed to the army officers in Ireland for their co-operation. The first reaction to this was unfavourable; but within a few weeks the parliamentary cause had grown much stronger, and on 13 December a group of officers, under Sir Hardress Waller, seized and held Dublin Castle in the name of the parliament. Ten days later almost every garrison throughout the country had been similarly secured. Ireland, like Scotland, had ranged itself behind Monck's policy.

The result of this combined action was a second restoration of the Rump on 26 December, and it quickly appointed three new commissioners for the government of Ireland. The choice of men was significant. Major William Bury, 'a religious prudent gentleman', was known to favour the presbyterians; Lord Broghill and Sir Charles Coote were both ex-royalists, and though they had not yet committed themselves openly to a restoration of the monarchy, this was, in fact, the policy on which they had already resolved. Each was anxious to establish his credit with the king, and they watched one another suspiciously. By February 1660 both were in touch with the exiled court at Brussels; and Charles was so much attracted by the prospect of their support that he even proposed to come directly to Ireland. This course was abandoned at the instance of his English advisers; but he wrote to Coote, promising to fulfil whatever undertakings might be made in his name.

Meanwhile, a convention representing the parliamentary constituencies of Strafford's time had met in Dublin on 7 February. It was dominated by the army and the Cromwellian planters, whose main aim was to secure their own interests; and the royalists, under the skilful management of Broghill and Coote, were able to persuade the majority that this could best be done by restoring the king. There was, of course, some opposition. Sir Hardress Waller, who was one of the regicides and so had every reason to fear a monarchical restoration, seized Dublin Castle once more on 15 February, this time in defence of republican principles; but he got little support, and had to surrender a few days later. When the convention and the Irish army joined Monck in demanding that the Rump should re-admit the members expelled in 1649, whose influence was certain to be on the royalist side, the issue could hardly be in doubt. In March the Long

Parliament, thus reinforced, at last dissolved itself; and in April an English convention, on the Irish model, met at Westminster. It quickly came to terms with Charles, who was proclaimed king in London on 8 May and in Dublin six days later.

Though Ireland had appeared to follow the English lead during the last stages of the restoration, the attitude of the Irish army and the Irish convention had done much to force the pace in England, and had established their claim to a settlement in accordance with their interests. Some steps had already been taken towards satisfying the army, for the convention had raised money by a heavy poll-tax and had cleared off a great part of the soldiers' arrears; but the question of the land settlement still remained. After Charles's return to England the convention sent Broghill and Coote to lay certain requests before him: the appointment of a chief governor and council; the calling of a parliament of protestant peers and commoners; the issue of a general pardon and indemnity to all the protestants of Ireland, on terms to be fixed by parliament; the preparation of an act of attainder; the preparation of an act for the settling of estates; the restoration of forfeited glebes and tithes to the clergy. The core of this programme was the part relating to parliament; for a parliament elected in the existing circumstances would be dominated by Cromwellian settlers, even if recusants were not formally excluded; and this would determine the character of the settlement to be made.

Charles, unwilling to lose all liberty of action, deferred the calling of parliament; but he put the government on a regular footing by appointing a lord lieutenant. Monck, now duke of Albemarle, had acquired great estates in Ireland, and insisted on having the office; but he had no intention of coming over, and in November 1661 he resigned in favour of Ormond, whose services to the crown had already been rewarded by the title of duke and the office of lord high steward of England. Ormond did not reach Dublin until July 1662, and in the meantime Ireland was governed by lords justices: Sir Maurice Eustace, the new lord chancellor, Lord Broghill, now earl of Orrery, Sir Charles Coote, now earl of Mountrath. All three belonged to families established in Ireland before the wars, and Eustace was inclined to favour the older protestant settlers; but Orrery and Mountrath were directly interested in maintaining the Cromwellian settlement of land and property. It seemed clear that despite the change from commonwealth to monarchy the new protestant interest was going to retain the fruits of victory.

(7)

From the time of his restoration, Charles was under constant pressure
from those who had lost estates in Ireland and now hoped to recover
them. Their claims were based on various grounds. A few, mostly protestants, had been consistently loyal to the crown, and had been despoiled
first by the Confederates and then by the Commonwealth. Others, who
had fought on the Confederate side, claimed the benefit of the treaties of
1646 and 1649. Soldiers who had gone into exile had earned the king's
gratitude by their readiness to change services at his behest, for they had
thus given him a useful bargaining counter in his dealings with France
and Spain. To many of these claimants Charles issued letters instructing
the authorities in Ireland to restore their lands; but there was no machinery
for making these instructions effective, and in face of opposition by the
new planters they could seldom be executed. It was clear that the problems
created by rival claims could not be solved piecemeal, but required some
coherent and comprehensive scheme.

Such a scheme was laid down in a royal declaration, of 30 November
1660, which was to be administered by a body of commissioners. This
declaration eventually provided the basis for a settlement; but to begin
with it achieved nothing, for the Irish courts refused to enforce the
commissioners' decisions, as lacking statutory authority; and Charles
found himself obliged, however, reluctantly, to submit the land question
to the judgment of parliament.

It would, of course, have been necessary to call a parliament in any
case, if only to settle the revenue. But if the declaration of 30 November
had been effective the meeting of parliament could have been postponed;
and the settlement of the land question in advance would certainly have
influenced its composition. As it was, when parliament met on 8 May 1661,
very few of the dispossessed had been restored, apart from Ormond and
some other prominent royalists, and the Cromwellian interest dominated
an exclusively protestant house of commons. Had this parliament been
free to frame a land measure of its own, it would have paid scant attention
to Roman Catholic claims. But the operation of Poynings' Law meant that
the final form of any bill would be decided in England; and for months
the matter was debated in the English council, where delegates from both
houses of the Irish parliament and agents of the dispossessed Roman
Catholics presented their arguments for or against every proposal. In
April 1662 the council at length decided on the terms of a bill, and the
Irish parliament, though not without some complaint, accepted it in the
following month. In effect, this 'Act of Settlement' gave statutory force to

the royal declaration of 30 November; and seven commissioners, forming a 'court of claims', were appointed to administer its provisions.

By the Act of Settlement all land confiscated since 23 October 1641, by reason of rebellion, was vested in the crown, as trustee for certain specified purposes. These were: first, the confirmation to Adventurers and soldiers of lands held by them on 7 May 1659; secondly, the payment of arrears due to officers who had served under Ormond before 5 June 1649, certain lands being set aside to provide the necessary funds; thirdly, the restoration of various classes of dispossessed proprietors. The main business of the commissioners was to hear the claims of those seeking restoration. If a claim was made good, and the 'restorable person' found, as was likely to be the case, that his estate was actually in the possession of some Cromwellian settler, the latter was to be compensated (or 'reprized') with other lands of equal value, and so to give place to the former proprietor.

It was obvious that the act would work only if the land available for compensation (or 'reprizal') were equal to the demands upon it; and this in turn would depend on the number of successful claims for restoration. There were three classes of persons entitled to make such claims: those who had served the king abroad ('ensignmen'); those who had accepted, and kept, the terms of peace of 1646 or 1649 ('article men'); those who had been innocent of any part in the rebellion ('innocents'). In fact, all the claims heard by the commissioners were claims of innocency; for the terms of the act were more favourable to 'innocents' than to either of the other classes of 'restorable persons'. By August 1663, when the time prescribed by the act for hearing of claims ended, the commissioners had dealt with some 800 cases, and had issued 700 decrees of innocency. There were thousands of claimants waiting to be heard, and if they were to be declared 'innocent' in the same proportion the operation of the act would become impossible. Even as it was, by no means all those who had already made good their claims were actually restored, and their demands added to the growing unrest.

The Cromwellian planters were naturally alarmed at the decisions of the court of claims. They declared, not without justification, that many decrees of innocency had been obtained on false evidence; they knew that the stock of land for reprizal, never very large, had been seriously diminished by lavish royal grants; and they feared that the whole protestant position was being undermined. Stimulated by this fear, a group of army officers, led by the celebrated Colonel Thomas Blood, organized a conspiracy to seize Dublin Castle and overthrow the government. The attempt, made in May 1663, was a failure; but many who refused to adopt Blood's methods sympathized with his motives; and there was a strong demand among the Cromwellians that the commissioners' decisions should be reversed, and the Act of Settlement amended so as to guarantee the security of existing proprietors.

The rivalry between Cromwellians and 'innocents' revealed very clearly how impossible it was to meet all the expectations that had been aroused by the king's declaration and by the Act of Settlement. Ormond put the problem bluntly: 'There must be new discoveries made of a new Ireland', he wrote in 1662, 'for the old will not serve to satisfy these engagements'. He himself favoured a policy of compromise, and gave his strong support to a 'Bill of Explanation', intended to rectify some of the injustices in the Act of Settlement. This bill was drawn up in September 1663, and after prolonged debates in the English council received its final form in August 1665. By its terms, all decrees of innocency already issued were to be confirmed, but no more claims were to be heard; instead, certain persons, named in the bill, were to have full or partial restoration of their former estates. To provide the land necessary for this, Adventurers and soldiers were to surrender one-third of what they had received under the Act of Settlement, and the arrears of the '49 officers', were to be reduced in the same proportion. These proposals were very unpalatable to the Irish house of commons, where the debate on the bill continued for more than six weeks, often in very bitter terms, 'some being heard to say that the lands they had gotten with the hazard of their lives should not now be lost with Ayes and Noes'. But Poynings' Law made amendment impossible; and when it came to a final vote members were not prepared to risk the security that the bill promised, though at a heavy cost, and it passed safely. In its operation, it went but a small way towards meeting the claims of the dispossessed. The additional land made available for distribution was insufficient for the purpose designed; and not even all those specifically named for restoration in the act received what they had been promised.

The acts of settlement and explanation were based on expediency, not on justice. Yet it is hard to see how Charles could have acted very differently. He dared not alienate the Irish Cromwellians at a time when his throne was still insecure, when Scotland was full of unrest, and when even in England there were powerful discontented elements ready at every opportunity to conspire against him. Inclination led him to favour the Roman Catholics, but prudence compelled him to side with the protestants. The full rigour of the Cromwellian settlement was somewhat modified, but its general effect on the relative strength of protestants and recusants was not substantially changed: in 1641 the recusants had held about three-fifths of the land of Ireland, after the Act of Explanation they held a little more than one-fifth; they had been deprived of political influence in cities and towns; they had lost their control of trade; they had been excluded in practice, though not yet in law, from membership of parliament. But they did not despair of recovering what they had lost; and while there was any chance of their succeeding the protestants must feel insecure. The hopes and fears of the two groups coloured the reign of Charles II and dominated that of his brother.

VI

Restoration Ireland

(1)

The character of the convention that met in Dublin in February 1660, and its activity during the next few months, seemed to suggest that the Restoration was to be a restoration of parliament as well as of the monarchy. The convention was quick to claim that Ireland had the right to be governed by parliaments of its own; and among the requests that it laid before the king was one 'that no tax, imposition or other charge whatsoever be laid upon your majesty's subjects of Ireland, but by common consent of parliament there'. When parliament met in the following year the commons seemed disposed to stand upon their rights. They ignored the king's recommendation for the speakership, and elected Sir Audley Mervyn, who had been one of the leaders of the attack on Strafford's government twenty years earlier; and they attempted to maintain their claim to initiate legislation by presenting the lord lieutenant with proposals for new bills. But they were too much concerned about the land question to embark on a serious constitutional conflict with the crown; they had no strong tradition of independent action; they accepted readily enough the view that it was their business to settle the revenues of the kingdom on a permanent basis; and once they had done this their power to influence government had almost gone.

The new financial settlement followed the pattern of that made in England. Parliament first granted subsidies to meet the most pressing needs of government; and then, in 1662, undertook the task of establishing the permanent revenue on a satisfactory basis. The king surrendered some of his more lucrative feudal rights, including wardships, and in return his total revenue was raised to a level at which he might be expected to 'live of his own'. There were three important new sources of royal income: increased customs and excise duties; a hearth tax, specifically granted in compensation for the abolition of the court of wards; a new quit-rent, reserved on all lands forfeited since 1641 and regranted under the terms of the acts of settlement and explanation. It was reckoned that this new income, together with what remained of the old hereditary revenue of the crown after the surrender of feudal dues, would yield something over £200,000 a year. But the immediate position was not so prosperous; and it was several years before income reached this level. Economic recovery was still far from complete; between 1664 and 1667 seaborne trade was seriously injured by hostilities with the Dutch; and though parliament granted fresh subsidies in 1665, the government was so straitened for money that it had to depend on help from the English exchequer. Later on, as the economy improved, revenue rose above what had originally been expected; but, even then, mismanagement and extravagance kept the government in a state of almost continuous financial embarrassment.

In these circumstances, the king thought of turning to parliament for further assistance; and on several occasions during the 1670s and early 1680s preparations for summoning a new parliament were actually begun. But it was, in fact, doubtful if the country could bear any additional burden; the fear of parliamentary inquiry into the administration proved stronger than the uncertain hope of an increased revenue; and no second parliament was called during Charles's reign. Restoration Ireland had the form of a parliamentary constitution; but throughout most of the period its government was purely conciliar.

(2)

On the eve of the Restoration, the ecclesiastical situation in Ireland presented a conflict of interests less complicated, perhaps, than that over the land question, but one equally incapable of being settled to the satisfaction of all parties. The anabaptists were suspicious of any kind of church establishment, and were opposed to monarchical government; but though they still had some hold on the army, their politicial power was declining, and they counted for little in the events of 1659–60. Among the newly-arrived settlers, the Independents were numerous, wealthy and influential; but the very nature of their ecclesiastical polity made it almost impossible for them to act as a body, even in their own defence; many of their ministers were Church of Ireland clergy, who were ready to welcome a re-establishment of episcopacy; and in the crisis of the Restoration, Independency succumbed almost without a struggle. The presbyterians, firmly entrenched in the north, were in a much stronger position; they favoured a restoration of monarchy, hoping that it would bring with it a restoration of the covenant, which Charles himself had sworn to maintain. Their aim was not a toleration, which they already enjoyed, but the imposition of the presbyterian system on the whole country, and, indeed, on the whole British Isles. The Roman Catholics, despoiled of power and property, hated and feared by protestants of every denomination, could do little to influence events; and the best they could look forward to was that a restored monarchy might give them some protection from the full fury of their enemies. But no ecclesiastical group watched the situation so anxiously, and at the same time so hopefully, as the clergy of the Church of Ireland. By the beginning of 1660 some of the few remaining bishops and many of the parish clergy had congregated in Dublin, and were trying to build up a party among the political leaders there. Their strength lay partly in their legal position; for if the acts of the interregnum were disallowed, their church was still established, and they had firm titles to their livings. But their main reliance was on the king; and the event soon showed that this reliance was justified.

When the Irish convention first met it seemed to be dominated by a combination of Independents and presbyterians, and the latter even hoped that it might formally adhere to the solemn league and covenant. But the members were more concerned about security of property than forms of religion; and as the likelihood of a restoration increased, so did their desire to stand well with the king, and the king was expected to favour episcopacy. Patrick Adair, who was in Dublin at the time as a sort of agent for the Ulster presbyterians, remarked sadly on the convention's change of outlook: '. . . as our grandees had intelligence of the pulse of the court at Breda, they altered their course. Then they began to court the few old bishops that were in Ireland . . . all things then turned just as the king's inclination was observed to be'. But this was written many years later; at the time, the presbyterians were not so quick to sense the change in their prospects. In May 1660 the agents whom they sent to London were instructed to combine congratulations to the king on his restoration with a reminder of his former adherence to the covenant. Not surprisingly, the agents received a cool welcome, and were not allowed to present their address until all reference to the covenant had been removed. In August, any remaining doubt about royal policy was dispelled by the filling of the vacant Irish sees; and the advancement of Bramhall to the primacy seemed a clear indication that there was to be no attempt at 'comprehension'. The consecration of two new archbishops and ten new bishops in the following January was a spectacular demonstration of the triumph of the Church of Ireland; and the issue, in the same month, of a proclamation against meetings of 'papists, presbyterians,

Independents, anabaptists, quakers and other fanatical persons' was a warning to other denominations of the treatment they might expect. Independent preachers in Dublin had already been silenced, and the turn of the northern presbyterians was soon to come.

Early in 1661 many of the bishops held formal visitations; and it was in the visitation of Down and Connor, which included the greater part of the counties of Down and Antrim, that the position of the presbyterians was first put to the test. The new bishop, Jeremy Taylor, was neither a bigot nor a persecutor, but he had a somewhat pedantic reverence for order, and he resolved to enforce the law of the church strictly. There were in his diocese some 30 or 40 presbyterian ministers in actual possession of livings though without canonical induction; they wished to deal with him privately, and in a body, but he rejected their proposals; and when they failed to obey his summons to the visitation he declared their livings vacant. Other northern bishops proceeded more cautiously, but the result was the same in the end; and throughout Ulster some 70 presbyterian ministers were expelled from livings they had held under the Commonwealth. It is hard to see what else could have happened. The uneasy compromise of the early decades of the century was no longer possible: the dispossessed ministers did not want toleration within an episcopal church, but the establishment of presbytery in its place; and though the immediate issue might appear to be on points of detail, there was in fact an irreconcilable conflict of principles.

The Irish bishops, unlike the English, had not awaited parliamentary sanction before asserting their authority. But when parliament met it gave them full support: in May 1661 both houses passed a declaration requiring all persons to conform to the church as by law established, and ordered the public burning of the solemn league and covenant. This threat to enforce a general uniformity in religion increased the alarm among both presbyterians and sectaries, and brought some recruits to Blood's conspiracy. At first, indeed, the government wrongly supposed that the presbyterians were deeply involved, and after the failure of the conspiracy, in May 1663, many of their ministers were imprisoned. But within a few weeks Ormond seems to have been convinced of their innocence, though he still thought them potentially dangerous, and somewhat reluctantly set them at liberty.

This anxiety about the political activities of presbyterians and sectaries reflected an uneasiness pervading the whole British Isles. England was filled with rumours of 'fanatic' plots. In Scotland, the restoration of episcopacy had disturbed the whole country; and the covenanters seemed to be constantly on the edge of insurrection. It was the Scottish situation

that affected Ireland most closely; Galloway, the great centre of covenant-
ing activity, was within easy reach of Ulster, and unrest in one area
quickly affected the other. Throughout the Restoration period the
Irish government could never afford to ignore the possibility that
the Ulster presbyterians might be swept into insurrection by the
example and influence of their more daring co-religionists across the North
Channel.

The Roman Catholics had no share in bringing back the king, and their
claims to benefit under the treaties of 1646 and 1649, though nominally
recognized so far as the land settlement was concerned, were in other
respects completely ignored. The rigour of puritan persecution was,
however, considerably abated; as Ormond put it, the recusants were
'delivered from tyrannous confinements, causeless imprisonments, and a
continual fear of their lives'. But the laws against them, though less
strictly enforced, still remained; and in the early 1660s an attempt was
made to secure some measure of formal toleration. The basis of this was a
declaration of loyalty, the so-called 'loyal remonstrance', in which the
signatories disowned any allegiance to the papacy in temporal matters
and denied any papal right to depose sovereigns. The moving spirit
behind the remonstrance was Peter Walsh, a Franciscan, who had led the
clerical opposition to Rinuccini in the 1640s; and the fierce conflict that
had then split the Confederates now flared up again. After some hesitation,
the Irish Roman Catholic bishops condemned the remonstrance on
theological grounds; and though Walsh refused to accept their judgement,
and retained some support, especially in his own order, the remonstrance
lost all value as a basis of negotiation with the government. But despite
this failure to secure any change in the law, the position of the Roman
Catholics steadily improved; and for the greater part of the reign they
were free from fear of persecution.

Perhaps the most striking feature of the Restoration settlement, in
its ecclesiastical aspect, was the virtual abandonment of any attempt to
enforce general conformity. The Church of Ireland recovered its property
and its privileges, but its leaders were obliged to recognize that it was the
church of a minority. The presbyterians were unable to secure recognition
of the covenant, or to hold on to the benefices they had acquired; but
they were left in comparative peace to organize their own ecclesiastical
system outside the established church. The Roman Catholic church
retained the allegiance of the mass of the people, and could still hope that
royal favour might give it not only toleration but supremacy. These three
bodies between them dominated the religious life of the kingdom; they
gradually absorbed most of the Independents, anabaptists and other

sectaries of the Cromwellian era; and only the quakers retained a separate and continuous existence of their own.

(3)

The restoration of the monarchy had been quickly followed by a formal restoration of the old constitutional relationship between Ireland and England; but the character of this relationship was in some important respects different from what it had been. English politicians were now more continuously concerned about Irish affairs: the viceroyalty became an object of ambition in a way that it had hardly been before; there was a new rivalry between the officers of state for control of Irish business; parliament was much readier than in the past to assert its views on Irish policy. Charles was determined to keep the government of Ireland firmly under his own control; but he could not always resist the pressure of court factions or the importunity of the house of commons; and there was a tendency for Irish affairs to be caught up in the emerging party politics of England. The position of the viceroy was inevitably affected by this change. Though in theory he depended directly and solely on the king, he found himself almost helpless without powerful allies at court; and he had to keep a watchful eye on the course of English politics, knowing that any shift of power could affect his chance of retaining office. Difficulties of this sort, which a viceroy of the earlier seventeenth century might have had to face occasionally, had become for his successor in the Restoration period a source of almost daily anxiety.

This change in the character of Anglo-Irish relations brought a fresh element of instability into Irish government; but its basic problems remained, as before, those of finance, religion and land. The financial problem was of fundamental importance, for without an adequate revenue it was impossible to ensure the efficiency of the army, on which the authority of government must in the long run depend. 'I hope', wrote the lord lieutenant in June 1676, 'that we may get some little stock of money beforehand, for really I can never think any government safe, much less a military one, as this is, without it'. But so far from having even a 'little stock' of money in hand, the Irish administration was struggling, throughout most of the period, to make up arrears of army pay, and with so little success that the discontent among the soldiers led more than once to open mutiny.

On paper, it was possible to balance income and expenditure. The army maintained under the Commonwealth had been greatly reduced at the Restoration; and the new revenue granted by parliament should have been sufficient for all purposes of government. But Ormond found, when he took up the viceroyalty in 1662, that there were still heavy arrears to be paid off, and that the revenue did not answer expectations. It was only on the military list, which absorbed by far the greater part of the revenue, that any substantial saving could be made; but Ormond hesitated to weaken the army still further. He did, indeed, cut down the size of existing troops and companies; but he balanced this reduction by enlisting men in England, hoping that they would be more reliable than the ex-Cromwellians in Ireland. These new recruits were formed into a regiment of foot-guards, 1,200 strong; they were paid at a higher rate than the rest of the army; and they were usually quartered near Dublin, available for use in any emergency. When, for example, the garrison of Carrickfergus, unpaid for months and reduced almost to starvation, mutinied in May 1666, two companies of the guards, sent by sea from Dublin, quickly restored order.

Since it was impossible to economize safely on the army, the only alternative was to increase revenue; and this in turn depended upon an improvement in economic conditions. Ormond did what he could; he followed Commonwealth example in setting up a council of trade, and he had some success in encouraging the woollen manufacture. But these measures could not produce much immediate effect; and in any case overseas trade was hampered during the 1660s by hostilities with the Dutch. By far the most damaging blow, however, was given by the English parliament. At this time the most prosperous element in the Irish economy was the rapidly-expanding export of live cattle to England. The trade had existed, though on a smaller scale, before 1641, and had been revived almost immediately after the return of peace. For the new settlers it provided a quick and easy way of turning their estates to good account; and English graziers found it a profitable business to import Irish cattle and fatten them for the market. But in 1663 the English parliament, stimulated by the jealousy of the cattle-breeders, passed an act prohibiting the importation of cattle from Ireland between July and December, the period when the trade was most extensive; and three years later the prohibition was made absolute. This interruption of the cattle trade was, in its immediate effect, a disaster for Ireland; and though within a few years Irish merchants had replaced it by a much more profitable provision trade with the continent, the financial difficulties of Ormond's government were increased by the period of depression.

The cattle acts of the 1660s reflected a more jealous attitude towards the Irish economy, which was now becoming prevalent in England and which was to exercise an increasing influence during the next hundred years. But in 1663, and even more in 1666, there were other motives at work as well. Buckingham and his friends were hardly less hostile to Ormond than to Clarendon; and in pressing these measures through parliament they were more concerned to damage Ormond's administration than to protect English cattle-breeders. They knew that the king held Ormond in high regard; but they knew also that he was in constant need of money; and they believed that they could most readily induce him to make a change in the government of Ireland by convincing him that in other hands it would become a source of profit to the crown.

The attack that Buckingham launched against Ormond's administration was not altogether unfounded. The financial difficulties of Ireland did not arise solely from the backwardness of trade, the Dutch war and the cattle acts. Ormond, though honest and hardworking, was no financier; and the vice-treasurer, Anglesey, to whom he seems to have left most of the financial business, was careless and incompetent, if not actually corrupt. Buckingham, aided by Orrery, whom he brought over from Ireland for the purpose, was able to persuade Charles that under a different governor Ireland might be made to yield a surplus, instead of being a charge upon England. It was an attractive prospect; but Charles hesitated for a long time, and it was not until February 1669 that Ormond was removed from office. His dismissal was, perhaps, a natural sequel to Clarendon's more spectacular fall from power eighteen months earlier; for the two were close allies, and represented the old Cavalier interest, now going out of fashion. But it is at least doubtful if Charles would have made the change had he not hoped for some financial advantage. As for Ormond, though he had fought hard to defend his position, he accepted dismissal equally without rancour and without despair, as if confident that he could better do without the king's favour than the king without his service. He was now taken little notice of, but continued to attend court with such unruffled dignity that Buckingham was constrained to remark that it was difficult to tell whether Ormond was in disgrace with Charles or Charles with Ormond.

(4)

The change in the viceroyalty in 1669 did little to increase the efficiency of Irish government. Lord Robartes, appointed in March 1669, had some reputation as an honest and able man of business. But he was ill-tempered and obstinate; he resented the terms, mild though they were, in which Charles offered some confidential criticism of his rather brusque attempt to tighten up military discipline; and within a year of taking up office he was recalled at his own request. Lord Berkeley of Stratton, who succeeded him, was sent over as the instrument of Cabal policy. But he was too indiscreet to be of much service, for his ostentatious display of favour to the Roman Catholic clergy aroused protestant alarm in both kingdoms. In other respects his administration was incompetent and corrupt; and he was removed early in 1672.

Nevertheless, during these years there was a marked improvement in the financial position, though it owed little to Robartes and nothing to Berkeley. Even before Ormond's dismissal, trade had begun to recover from the effects of the Dutch war and of the cattle acts, and there was a consequent rise in revenue. In 1669–70 it fell short of expenditure by little more than £5,000; and in the following year there was actually a small surplus. The more hopeful state of affairs was reflected in the terms of a new farm of the revenue concluded in the summer of 1669 with John Forth, a London alderman, and his partners. Up to this time customs, excise and quit-rents, which between them made up almost the whole of the permanent revenue of the crown, had been farmed separately, and had yielded a total annual income of £124,000; Forth's farm included the whole revenue at an annual rent of £204,500. If the terms of this farm had been strictly enforced, it might have set Irish finances on a firm basis; but the whole position was hopelessly complicated by a speculative venture in which the notorious Lord Ranelagh served his apprenticeship in peculation.[1] Ranelagh, a nephew of Orrery, and a man of great influence at court, persuaded Charles that if the whole financial administration of Ireland were entrusted to him he would not only meet the annual charges and clear off arrears of debt, but would also make substantial cash payments to the king. An agreement to this effect was concluded in August 1671, and Ranelagh's 'undertaking' was superimposed on Forth's farm. The farmers still collected the revenue, but instead of making their payments into the exchequer they made them to Ranelagh's agents, who in turn were responsible for meeting the civil and military lists. Ranelagh's promises were very imperfectly fulfilled; existing debts were not paid off, and fresh arrears accumulated rapidly. But the considerable sums paid to the king were sufficient to ensure his favour; and though, when the 'undertaking' came to an end in 1675, with many liabilities still outstanding, Ranelagh failed to produce a satisfactory statement of accounts, Charles protected him against any effective inquiry.

The viceroy who had to endure Ranelagh's corrupt financial régime

---

[1] Ranelagh was paymaster-general in England from 1691 to 1702, and during this period his defalcations amounted to some £70,000. He was expelled from parliament, but escaped prosecution.

was Arthur Capel, earl of Essex, who succeeded Berkeley in May 1672 and held office until April 1677. His letters, year after year, are filled with fruitless complaints of an empty treasury and an unpaid army, of Ranelagh's broken promises and evasive replies, of the utter impossibility of obtaining any clear statement of the position; and even after the 'undertaking' had come to an end, Essex still had to deal with a legacy of debts for which Ranelagh, on one pretext or another, refused to accept liability. And yet, despite all this, the financial position was not unhopeful. Forth's farm had ended at the same time as the 'undertaking'; and a new farm, settled in 1676, yielded a rent of £240,000, which was increased to £300,000 in 1678. Though the new farmers were not always regular in their payments, so that the army was still sometimes in arrears, the financial position now became much easier; and for the remainder of the Restoration period finance ceased to be a major problem of Irish government.

This happier state of affairs resulted from a general improvement in the economy. Overseas trade, which had once more been interrupted by renewed war with the Dutch, expanded rapidly when peace was restored. Beef, butter, hides, tallow and grain were among the most important exports; and these were shipped not only to Europe but to the West Indies and to the North American colonies. The colonial trade, which had been growing since the Commonwealth period, had seemed to be threatened by the navigation act of 1670, which required that all imports from the colonies should first be landed in England: 'We are more undone in this poor kingdom by the late act', wrote Sir George Rawdon, a County Antrim landlord, in 1671, 'than by the cattle act'. But such fears proved to be exaggerated. Ireland was still free to export her provisions direct to the colonies, and this export was maintained and increased, despite the restrictions on return trade — restrictions which were, in practice, often evaded.

Though provisions, and especially pastoral products, made up the great bulk of Irish exports, the attempts made by Ormond and others to encourage the textile industry were not altogether ineffective. Skilled workmen were brought over from France and the Netherlands, and under their guidance the manufacture of fine woollen cloths made some progress, though at this time it contributed little to the export trade. The linen industry grew more rapidly, and both yarn and cloth were exported to England and to the plantations; but even in linen Ireland could not supply her own needs; and the total volume of textiles imported vastly exceeded the exports. The rising prosperity of the country depended on an agricultural economy; nor was it likely that there could be any fundamental change. Sir William Petty calculated that six-sevenths of the population lived at subsistence level, growing their own food and weaving their own cloth: with a home market so narrowly restricted, Ireland was hardly in a position to develop manufactures that could compete with those of England.

(5)

Essex's removal from office in April 1677 resulted partly from the intrigues of his enemies at court, partly from the king's reluctance to leave the viceroyalty too long in the hands of one man, partly from the fact that Ormond had now recovered royal favour; and though Ormond had taken no part in the various schemes by which Danby, Ranelagh and others had tried to undermine Essex's credit, he was anxious to resume the government of Ireland, and Charles was ready to meet his wishes. He was formally re-appointed in May; and in August he arrived in Dublin.

In one respect the prospects for a successful administration were good, for the financial problem had lost much of its urgency. But the problems of religion and land remained; and though the land problem lay dormant until the next reign, religion was to face Ormond with immediate and increasing difficulties. These difficulties arose from two sources: the possibility of co-operation between the Ulster presbyterians and the Scottish covenanters; and the possibility of unrest, or even of insurrection, among the Roman Catholic majority. Both dangers were present throughout the Restoration period; but in 1677 it was the presbyterians who gave more immediate cause for anxiety. The great majority of the Ulster presbyterian ministers were by this time reconciled to the Restoration settlement; at least to the extent of not wishing to endanger the quiet that they enjoyed by countenancing any violent move against the government; and since 1672 their loyalty had been strengthened by the *regium donum* from the crown of £600 a year. Most of the well-to-do presbyterians shared the outlook of their ministers; but the rank-and-file were open to more exciting influences. Despite all government·precautions, there was a constant coming and going of covenanters across the North Channel; Alexander Peden (the 'prophet') and other fiery preachers frequently took refuge in Ulster; and they seldom failed to gather great crowds at their field conventicles. They received no support from the Ulster ministers, whom they criticized for their 'defections, indifferency and lukewarmness in the cause of Christ'; but among the ordinary people they were able to keep alive some tradition of the covenant and of resistance to 'prelacy'.

It was hardly surprising, in these circumstances, that the governments in Edinburgh and London, as well as in Dublin, should keep a careful eye on Ulster. In 1674-5, and again in 1676, when the danger of an out-break in Galloway seemed acute, Essex was instructed to send troops to the north-east, both to overawe the Ulster presbyterians and to be ready, if the need should arise, to come to the aid of government of Scotland. When Ormond resumed the viceroyalty, danger was threatening again; and in September 1677 he received directions to prepare another expedi-tionary force for the north. Until the spring of 1678 it remained stationed on the shores of Belfast Lough, with shipping at hand to convey it across the channel at short notice; and in Lauderdale's opinion its readiness for action helped to prevent a rising during that critical winter. From the point of view of the Irish government, these military preparations, though made under orders from London and intended to support royal authority in Scotland, were really measures of self-defence; for any strong move by the covenanters was sure to have serious repercussions in Ulster. When at length open insurrection broke out in Galloway, in the early summer of 1679, Ormond at once moved troops into the north, without waiting for instructions from England; and the relief with which he received news of the government victory at Bothwell Bridge reflects his alarm over the potential danger to Ireland: 'It was time to send us good news out of Scotland; the brethren in all parts of this kingdom, especially in the north, were growing very bold, and ready to come in to bear a part if those of Scotland had had success'.

Even after Bothwell Bridge, the south-west of Scotland remained un-settled, and many refugees came over to Ulster. But the crisis had now passed; the Irish government's moderate and cautious policy kept the province quiet; and it was not until 1688, when protestant opinion gen-erally had turned against James II, that the Ulster presbyterians took up arms.

Before the crushing of insurrection in Scotland had relieved the government's fear of the presbyterians, the old spectre of Roman Catholic conspiracy had been revived; and Ormond found himself plunged into the whirlpool of the 'popish plot'. Oates made his first revelations at the end of September 1678, and the news reached Ormond at the beginning of October. Like most of his contemporaries, he accepted the reality of the plot, though he refused to believe all the detailed accusations; but he was not at all convinced that the design extended to Ireland. His policy throughout this troubled period was to persuade the protestants of their own strength, and of the government's readiness and ability to protect them. 'I do all I can', he wrote to his friend Sir Robert Southwell in November 1678, 'to give the protestants encouragement, not by bringing them into a belief that there can be no hurt intended to them, but that if they are vigilant there can be little or no hurt done them'. He was sure that the Roman Catholics would never risk another rebellion unless encouraged by signs of panic among the protestants, or goaded into it by the repressive measures that such panic might produce. The maintenance of this common-sense policy was not easy. Shaftesbury and his allies, determined to make the most of the plot, insisted that Ireland was in grave danger; and Orrery, until his death in October 1679, busied himself in collecting evidence of popish conspiracy. Ormond did not neglect reasonable precautions — he put the army in a state of readiness, and he revived the militia, which had not been regularly embodied for some years. Under pressure from England, he issued proclamations ordering Roman Catholic bishops and regular clergy to leave the kingdom, and ordering all papists to surrender their arms. But he refused to accept the more severe measures urged upon him: he would not attempt to disarm the Roman Catholics by force, nor would he expel them from the corporate towns; and he rejected as unjust a proposal that all dispossessed popish proprietors should be arrested, as potential leaders of rebellion.

Ormond's moderation was strongly attacked in the English parliament, and there was an attempt to have him removed from office, as an enemy of the protestant interest. Charles was resolved not to yield, for to dismiss the lord lieutenant in these circumstances would be to hand over control of Ireland to the house of commons; but he did not feel strong enough to support him openly against his enemies in the English council, and during 1679 and 1680 expectation of a change in the viceroyalty ran high. Ormond, left to fight his own battles, found comfort in 'an honest endeavour to do my duty, and a calm resignation to God's will'; and despite all difficulties he was able to maintain his cautious policy. But it was not until April 1681, when the Oxford parliament had been dissolved and a royalist reaction was beginning, that he received any firm assurance of the king's confidence; and even then it was sent privately, and almost secretly, as if Charles were still afraid to identify himself publicly with the measures taken by his viceroy in Ireland.

The comparative helplessness of both king and lord lieutenant appeared in the case of Oliver Plunket, Roman Catholic archbishop of Armagh, who had been arrested in November 1679. The English whigs were determined to implicate him in treason, and they found willing tools among his own flock; for he had made many enemies by his strict discipline, and by his co-operation with the government against the tories. Had Plunket been tried in Ireland, where his own character, and the character of the witnesses against him, were known, he would certainly have been acquitted. But Ormond could not prevent the transfer of the trial to London; and Charles, though he must have known Plunket's innocence, had not the courage to interfere. In July 1681 Plunket was condemned, and suffered the penalties of high treason. He was the last notable victim of the plot; the whigs were now losing ground steadily; and by the end of the year Charles, in receipt of a substantial pension from Louis XIV, was once more in control.

(6)

The upheaval of the 'popish plot' had hardly interrupted the gradual economic recovery that had been in progress since before the Restoration. By the 1680s Ireland was more prosperous, and apparently more peaceful, than she had been for centuries. But the prosperity was confined to a small section of the population, for the profits of the expanding provision trade went to merchants and landlords rather than to the tenants. And though the danger of insurrection had receded, there could be no general sense of security while so much of the country was infested by tories. The most dangerous of them, Redmond O'Hanlon — 'the Irish Scanderbeg' — was shot in April 1681, but there were many others, less famous but hardly less destructive, to take his place. An English traveller notes, in 1680, that most of the nobles and gentry still maintained castles or fortified houses; and the example set by Lord Conway's great mansion of Portmore, on the shore of Lough Neagh, was not to be widely followed until the next century.

The outward signs of peaceful prosperity were most evident in the capital; and for Dublin the period of the Restoration was one of continuous expansion far beyond the old city walls. Oxmanstown, to the north of the river, was developed so rapidly that four new bridges had to be built within twenty years. To the south, the great open space of St Stephen's Green was laid out as a residential square. To the east, Trinity College, once outside the city (*juxta Dublin*), was gradually surrounded by new building; and it was on College Green that many of the nobility — Lord Anglesey, Lord Charlemont, Lord Clancarty — had their town houses. All this expansion was encouraged, and in part directed, by Ormond. He wanted the seat of government to be as impressive as possible, and his long exile in France had strengthened his natural love of magnificence. The public buildings of the period, save for the Royal Hospital at Kilmainham, have now disappeared; but Ormond's influence left its mark; and the more splendid Dublin that arose in the eighteenth century owed something to the taste and care with which he had supervised the early stages of expansion.

The Dublin of this period was still very much an English city, and ready to follow the example of London. In Dublin, as in London, the stage quickly recovered its popularity after the Commonwealth restrictions had been removed. A new theatre, with movable scenery, was opened in Smock Alley in 1662; and here were performed the heroic plays in rhymed verse that French influence had brought into fashion. Dublin, like London, now had its coffee-houses, where men met to exchange the gossip of the day — it was, Clarendon complained, a very 'tattling' town. But men met for more serious purposes also. It was in a coffee-house on Cork Hill that the Philosophical Society, founded in 1683 on the model of the Royal Society, held its early sessions. With Sir William Petty as its president, and with William King, Narcissus Marsh and William Molyneux among its members, this society gave Dublin a more distinguished position in the world of learning than it had ever occupied before, or was often to occupy later.

(7)

With the royalist reaction of the early 1680s, Ormond's prestige rose higher than ever. When, in April 1682, he was summoned to London for discussions with the king and his ministers, he was received with every mark of royal favour. He was made a duke in the English peerage; and during the two years that he remained in England he was regularly consulted on general policy as well as on Irish affairs. When he came back to Dublin in the summer of 1684 it was in full confidence that he would be allowed to retain the government of Ireland until he asked to be relieved of it. He was now well over seventy years of age, and had already made up his mind 'next year to beg his majesty's leave to retire for the rest of my time, and to think with less distraction of my approaching dissolution'. But within three months of his return, and before he had made any request of this kind, he received a letter from the king, telling him that he was to be superseded by Laurence Hyde, earl of Rochester, younger son of the old chancellor.

Ormond was surprised rather than discontented at this sudden recall — 'more out of countenance than sorry', as he put it himself. But he was puzzled at the reasons put forward by the king for replacing him: it was, the king wrote, 'absolutely necessary' for his service that there should be a general change in the civil and military government of Ireland, and that many persons appointed by Ormond should now be removed, 'which, I think, would be too hard to impose upon you to be the director of'. During his visit to England, Ormond had received not the slightest hint that any such sweeping alteration was intended; but it is probable that a new Irish policy had already been decided upon, and that this policy involved his removal from office, though the time of his removal may not then have been settled.

This new policy reflected the domination of Charles by the duke of York. James was determined to proceed with the 'Catholic design', and as a step in this direction he wanted to put the government of Ireland into the hands of men who would accept all royal commands without scruple. It was useless to expect co-operation from Ormond in an attack on the established church; and even for the preliminary stages now planned, which included the admission of Roman Catholics to office, he was a very unsuitable agent. He was ready to support what he considered the just claims of Roman Catholics who had suffered in the land settlement; and he had made no opposition to a 'commission of grace', issued in March 1684, by which existing proprietors could purchase confirmation of their titles, the proceeds going to compensate the dispossessed; but he was as determined as ever to maintain the protestant constitution of the kingdom.

With the death of Charles II in February 1685 the policy already adumbrated went forward rapidly. Charles had given Ormond permission to retain office until the spring; but James, within a few days of his accession, ordered him to hand over the government to lords justices and to come immediately to London. This sudden change alarmed the Irish protestants, and their fears were increased by the news that Richard Talbot, one of the most active of the Roman Catholic leaders, had been appointed colonel of the late lord lieutenant's regiment of horse.

Ormond's departure from Ireland marks a turning-point in the history of the British Isles, for the policy that led to it contributed largely to the revolution of a few years later; but it is of particular significance in the history of Ireland. For fifty years he had played a leading, and often dominant, part in Irish affairs; and he represented a continuity of constitutional tradition and family connection that the Cromwellian settlement had threatened to destroy. He was perfectly loyal to the crown of England, as his ancestors had been for centuries, and he could not conceive of any conflict of interest between king and kingdom. His loyalty was essentially personal; he looked with suspicion upon the English parliament's meddling with Irish policy; and even in the king's council he was ready, when necessity arose, to defend the interests of Ireland against those of England. But when the welfare of the crown was involved he made no distinctions: Ireland must, if need be, suffer for the sake of the monarchy. He was neither a great statesman nor a great soldier; his notions of government were old-fashioned; as an administrator he was industrious and patient, but lacking in financial ability. His strength lay in his honesty, courage, and determination, and in a shrewdness of judgement acquired by long experience. Loyalty to the crown was the guide of his political life; but his devotion to the church was stronger still, and he had long ago decided that if the king should command anything contrary to the interests of religion he could 'obey only by suffering'. Fortunately for his peace of mind he died in July 1688, and thus escaped the crisis of the Revolution.

VII

'The Glorious Memory'

The glorious, pious, and immortal memory of William III, prince of Orange, who saved us all from popery, brass money, and wooden shoes.

Irish protestant toast

(1)

The alarm among Irish protestants at Ormond's recall might seem to be exaggerated, for the lords justices appointed to take over the government were Archbishop Boyle and Lord Granard, neither of whom could be suspected of any leaning towards popery. But in fact they were ciphers; and the true character of James's policy appeared in the influence exercised by Richard Talbot, raised to the peerage in June 1685 as earl of Tyrconnell. Though Granard retained the title of marshal of the army, Tyrconnell was really in command; and when Monmouth's rebellion provided an excuse for disarming the militia — an exclusively protestant body — the task was entrusted to him. But James was still moving cautiously; and another year was to pass before he was prepared to put the conduct of Irish affairs completely into Tyrconnell's hands.

Meanwhile Rochester, whom Charles had designed to succeed Ormond, had been made lord treasurer of England; and it was his elder brother, the second earl of Clarendon, who was nominated for the lord lieutenancy in August 1685. Rochester and Clarendon were James's brothers-in-law, and so might be expected to support him; but they were also staunch members of the Church of England, and their maintenance in office at this time was due in part to James's anxiety to conciliate protestant opinion. Clarendon's nomination was a disappointment to Irish Roman Catholics, who had hoped for Tyrconnell; but it was, in fact, Tyrconnell who dominated the whole period of Clarendon's government, from January 1686 to February 1687. He was now put formally in command of the army, which he rapidly remodelled, getting rid of protestant officers and men and filling their places with Roman Catholics. The same policy was followed in many branches of administration; and Roman Catholics were appointed as judges, admitted to corporations, and even given seats on the privy council. Clarendon offered no resistance to these measures. He believed that so long as the land settlement remained intact the English and protestant interest in the kingdom would be secure; and he put his trust in James's assurance on this point. At his first coming over, he had been instructed 'to declare upon all occasions that, whatever imaginary (for they can be called no other) apprehensions any man here may have had, his majesty hath no intention of altering the acts of settlement'. Though there was growing expectation among the Roman Catholics of great changes soon to come, the king's determination 'not to have the acts of settlement shaken' was formally repeated in April by the new lord chancellor, Sir Charles Porter.

But whatever James's intention might be, Tyrconnell made no secret of his. 'By God, my lord', he exclaimed during an interview with the lord lieutenant, 'these acts of settlement and this new interest are damned things'. It is hardly likely that he was more discreet in other company; and everyone in Ireland, friend and foe alike, knew how high his interest stood at court. All Clarendon's efforts could do little to allay the alarm among protestants; and by the summer of 1686 an exodus had begun. Most of the refugees were merchants, who felt that their capital would now be safer in England; but there were also a good many dismissed officers, who took their swords and their grievances to Prince William in Holland; and when the time came they cast their influence on the side of military intervention in English affairs.

These signs of protestant alarm had little effect on James, who was becoming more and more impatient of any delay in the execution of his 'Catholic design'. Under Sunderland's influence he abandoned all attempt at compromise; and before the end of the year he had resolved to break with the Hydes and to give up the policy of co-operation with the Church of England for which they stood. By January 1687 Rochester had ceased to be treasurer, Clarendon had been recalled from Ireland, and Tyrconnell had been chosen to succeed him. It was the appointment of Tyrconnell rather than the fall of the Hydes that caught public attention. John Evelyn noted the event in his diary: 'Lord Tyrconnell gone to succeed the lord lieutenant in Ireland, to the astonishment of all sober men, and to the evident ruin of the protestants in that kingdom'. No doubt many other 'sober men' were writing and saying much the same thing; but it was in the words of a popular song that the news spread alarm through all classes of society. *Lillibulero*, with which Thomas Wharton later claimed to have 'whistled a king out of three kingdoms', first made its appearance in the early months of 1687:

> *Ho brother Teague dost hear de decree*
> *Lillibulero bullen-a-la*
> *Dat we shall have a new deputy*
> *Lillibulero bullen-a-la.*
>
> *Ho by my soul it is a Talbot*
> *Lillibulero bullen-a-la*
> *And he will cut all de English throat*
> *Lillibulero bullen-a-la.*

Tyrconnell reached Ireland in February 1687, and at once pushed ahead with his plans. The army was greatly increased, and became almost entirely Roman Catholic. Extensive changes on the bench reduced the protestant judges to a minority. In preparation for a meeting of parliament, Roman Catholic sheriffs were appointed to almost every county; and cities and towns were compelled to surrender their charters and accept new ones, in which predominantly Roman Catholic corporations were nominated. Protestant Ireland, sufficiently alarmed before, now fell into a state of panic: Clarendon's reassurances had carried little conviction; Tyrconnell's carried none at all; and the growing throng of protestant exiles in England was a powerful influence in turning opinion there against the king.

Englishmen were still more alarmed by the arrival of Irish troops, whom James had called over to his support. Even his friends received them with suspicion, while the bulk of the population regarded them with unconcealed hatred and fear. Nothing did more to hasten his overthrow than the conviction that he meant to use Irish papists to destroy the protestant constitution. The transfer of troops had an ill effect on his position in Ireland also. In order to provide them Tyrconnell had weakened the garrisons in the north: 'It pleased God', said a contemporary, 'so to infatuate the councils of my Lord Tyrconnell that . . . he took particular care to send away the whole regiment quartered in and about Londonderry' — an action that was to be of decisive importance in the rapidly-approaching conflict.

(2)

William's landing at Torbay, in November 1688, did not produce in Ireland an immediate constitutional crisis such as it produced in England; for Tyrconnell still held the country firmly for King James. There was some revival of hope among the protestants; but in most areas they were too weak to take action. Those of Munster tried to imitate the exploits of the 1640s and seized Bandon and Kenmare, but they were soon obliged to yield; and even in Ulster, where the protestants might seem numerous enough to defend themselves, they did not at once appear against the king's government. But Tyrconnell's withdrawal of troops had weakened his hold on the north: when, early in December, Londonderry shut its gates against a new garrison, the example of resistance was soon followed. Enniskillen, also, refused to admit the royal troops; and joined with neighbouring gentry to raise a force for its defence: 'We do stand upon our guard', wrote Gustavus Hamilton, who had been elected governor of the town, 'and do resolve by the blessing of God rather to meet our danger than to expect it'. In January, protestant nobles and gentlemen throughout Ulster formed themselves into county associations, raised troops, and appointed a central committee, which sent an agent to England to report their actions to William. As soon as it was known that William and Mary had been received as king and queen in England, they were proclaimed by the protestant leaders in Ulster.

So far, Tyrconnell had made no serious effort to re-assert royal authority in the north, where his troops still held many important strongholds, including Carrickfergus and Charlemont. He hoped that the protestants might be induced to surrender, and offered favourable terms; but when it became clear that these would not be accepted he sent a strong force into Ulster. On 14 March the protestants were routed in a confused engagement, commonly known as the 'break of Dromore', and retreated northward amid scenes of great panic. More than sixty years later, John Black, a Belfast merchant, could recall the terror of the occasion:

'My father's family, by a night alarm at Belfast, left house and home furnished, on an express coming to town with a lamentable cry that after the break of Dromore the Irish were coming down, sparing neither age nor sex, putting all to the sword without mercy; myself carried aboard my father's ship the *John*, which immediately set sail.' And at Stranraer, they found the town so crowded with fugitives that even the women and children had to huddle on the beach, sheltered from the rain under up-turned boats.

In the north and west of the province those who could not escape by sea made for Londonderry or Enniskillen; and by the end of March these towns, both crowded with refugees, were the only fortified places in Ulster still in protestant hands.

On 12 March James himself had arrived in Ireland from France, and in April he advanced against Londonderry. The city had received some reinforcements from England, but it was in poor case to stand a siege, and James did not expect much resistance. He opened negotiations for surrender, and Robert Lundy, the governor, was disposed to accept terms. Lundy seems to have thought the place untenable; and though he held a commission from the new king and queen, his loyalty to them was not very deep. But popular feeling in the city was overwhelmingly in favour of resistance, Lundy's authority was overthrown, James's terms were rejected, and the most famous siege in British history began.

The besiegers were singularly ill-equipped for their task. They had no artillery heavy enough to breach the walls; they had very few trenching-tools; their soldiers — for the most part, Irish levies, badly armed, badly trained, badly officered — were quite incapable of making a general assault, and suffered heavily in the sorties made by the garrison. The only hope was to reduce the city by famine, and for a time this hope seemed likely to be fulfilled. Some 30,000 people were crowded within the walls. Supplies of food soon ran low; thousands died of starvation, and the soldiers were so weakened by hunger that they could sometimes hardly stand to their arms. But these privations did not shake the resolution of the commanders who had succeeded on Lundy's overthrow — Major Henry Baker, and George Walker, a country clergyman who had taken refuge in the city and now commanded a regiment of the garrison. They refused to consider terms, and their refusal was encouraged by the arrival of an English fleet in Lough Foyle in the middle of June. But the besiegers had blocked the approach to the city by a boom across the river, and it was six weeks before a determined effort was made to break it. At last, on 28 July, a relief ship forced its way through, and ample supplies reached the famishing city. Next day, the Jacobite army broke camp, and began a disheartened retreat to the south. The siege had lasted fifteen weeks, and its failure marked a turning-point in James's fortunes. Had Londonderry fallen, the moral as well as the military effect would have been immense; and William would have found the task of dislodging him from Ireland infinitely more difficult.

Throughout the siege of Londonderry the protestant forces based on Enniskillen had harried the Jacobite lines of communication and had carried their raids to within thirty miles of Dublin. On the very day on which the siege broke up, they defeated an Irish force with great slaughter at Newtown Butler; and the news of this disaster caused such terror that James even thought of quitting the capital. Four months earlier, all Ireland had seemed to be at his feet; now the north, except for a few scattered garrisons, was lost to him, and lay open for the landing of William's forces.

While James's military position was thus breaking down, any chance that remained to him of reconciling protestant opinion was being destroyed by the activities of the Irish parliament, which sat in Dublin between May and July. This assembly, almost entirely Roman Catholic in membership, has passed into Irish history as the 'Patriot Parliament'. But the native Irish were poorly represented; its patriotism was that of the Old English recusants, and its enactments were in line with the constitutional policy of the Confederates of the 1640s. It asserted the exclusive right of the Irish parliament to legislate for Ireland, prohibited appeals from Irish to English courts, and but for James's firm opposition would have repealed Poynings' Law; it removed all civil disabilities imposed on account of religion; it enacted that the clergy of each denomination should receive the tithe paid by their own adherents; it repealed the acts of settlement and explanation. The English and protestant interest in Ireland, which would have been seriously undermined by the enforcement of such measures, was threatened with complete extinction by an act of attainder, the effect of which was to confiscate the property of over 2,400 protestants, including almost all the protestant landowners of the kingdom. This legislation constituted a programme that could be made fully effective only by a military victory, of which the prospect was now receding; and when James and his Irish supporters had been finally overthrown, the protestants found in it a convenient justification for retaliatory measures.

(3)

A fortnight after the relief of Londonderry, Marshal Schomberg, a veteran of the Thirty Years' War, who had withdrawn from France on the revocation of the Edict of Nantes, and was now in William's service, landed on the south shore of Belfast Lough with 10,000 men. Carrickfergus, which was still held for King James, surrendered after a brief siege, and Schomberg then advanced as far as Dundalk, meeting little resistance on the way. He might, perhaps, have safely pushed on to Dublin, for the Jacobites were weak and disheartened; but his army consisted mainly of raw recruits, he knew that a defeat might be politically disastrous to William's cause, and he preferred to wait for reinforcements. When James, having reorganized his army, marched against him in September, he refused battle, and in the following month retired northwards into winter quarters at Lisburn. There were complaints in England about his inaction; but he strengthened the bridgehead he had established, he drove the Jacobites from their last Ulster stronghold, at Charlemont, and he kept the way open for a fresh advance on Dublin.

James, on his side, was no more enterprising, and accomplished less. There were recruits in plenty, but little was done towards turning them into soldiers. The most pressing problem was lack of money. The war had disorganized the economic life of the country, and royal revenue shrank. James could find no expedient but to debase the currency, and issued the notorious 'brass money' with which his name is for ever associated in the folk-memory of Irish protestants. The inevitable result of debasement was inflation, for no threats could induce people to accept the new currency at its face value, and the economic situation became worse.

Apart from all this, James himself was losing heart, and was anxious to leave Ireland. He had no confidence in his Irish supporters; and though jealous of French influence he accepted Louis's offer of French troops in exchange for Irish. Five regiments (which were to form the nucleus of the famous 'Irish Brigade') were shipped off to France; and in March 1690 Lauzun arrived in Kinsale with 7,000 French troops, well-armed and well-supplied.

With these reinforcements James might have been able to take the offensive and weaken, if not destroy, the enemy bridgehead in Ulster. But Lauzun urged caution, and he himself lacked the resolution for any bold action; when William landed at Carrickfergus, on 14 June, James was still in Dublin. Two days later he set off northward and advanced as far as Dundalk; then, having learned in the interval of William's arrival, he retreated, and finally decided to defend the line of the Boyne, 'the old Rubicon of the Pale'. It was probably the wisest decision he could have made. His army was inferior to William's both in size and quality, and for a defensive action the river provided a strong front, which was quickly made stronger by the erection of breast-works; and behind him lay an open road to Dublin. On 30 June, the Williamite forces appeared on the northern bank; and next day, Tuesday 1 July, the decisive battle of modern Ireland was fought.

James seems to have faced the day with little expectation of success. He was already preparing for a further retreat; the bulk of the artillery had been sent off towards Dublin; and he would have probably have withdrawn his whole army without an engagement if he could safely have done so. The advantage, however, was by no means wholly on William's side. Though he had a great superiority in numbers — some 36,000 troops against James's 25,000 — this was partly off-set by the strength of the Irish position; for though the river was fordable at several points, the crossing was bound to be hazardous and likely to be costly. Schomberg, impressed by the danger, strongly advised a flank attack by the bridge of Slane, three miles upstream; but William had already made up his own mind, and

ordered a direct assault along the whole front.[1] At ten o'clock on a clear
sunny morning, after a heavy bombardment of the Irish position, the
veteran Blue Dutch Guard entered the river and soon forced a passage.
The various contingents of William's widely-assorted army — English,
Danes and Brandenburgers, French Huguenots and Ulster protestants —
followed them, or crossed at other points, and established themselves firmly
on the southern bank. Once this had been accomplished, the battle was
virtually over, for the Irish infantry, ill-trained and ill-officered, quickly
broke and fled. The cavalry, headed by Berwick, Richard Hamilton and
Tyrconnell, charged again and again; but though they held up the
Williamite advance, they could not turn it back. Lauzun had hitherto kept
his forces in reserve, partly to guard the left wing against a threatened
flank attack, partly to keep open the road to Dublin; but at the close of
the day he came to the support of the Irish cavalry, and between them they
prevented the retreat from turning into a rout. James had lost a battle, but
he still had an army.

The battle of the Boyne had a European significance: it offset the contemporary French victories at Fleurus and Beachy Head, it enabled
William to return with confidence to the main seat of war, and it restored
the courage of his allies. But for the historian of Ireland the Boyne marks
the climax of a civil conflict that had grown steadily more explicit and
more intense as the century progressed. The campaign was not over, but
the result was no longer in doubt; and the result meant that in future the
protestant minority would rule Ireland. The power of the Roman Catholic
nobility and gentry, which had survived the Elizabethan conquest and
had not been wholly extinguished even by the Cromwellian settlement,
was now to be finally overthrown; and until the impact of the French
Revolution gave form and vigour to popular national feeling the 'protestant ascendancy' was to rule unchallenged.

(4)

By his defeat at the Boyne James lost at one stroke almost all Ireland
east of the Shannon. Dublin could not be defended, and James himself
ordered its evacuation. A few days later he quitted Ireland for France,
leaving Tyrconnell once more in command, with instructions to continue
the struggle or make peace at his discretion. Already, on Tyrconnell's

---

[1] It has sometimes been suggested that William rejected Schomberg's plan
because it would have threatened the Jacobite retreat to Dublin, and he did not
want to risk the political inconvenience of having his father-in-law as a prisoner
of war.

orders, all the Irish forces, except those in garrisons, were concentrating on Limerick, and here they were joined by Lauzun and his French auxiliaries. With Limerick and Athlone in their hands, they might hold the line of the Shannon until help should come from France; and William, anxious to end the war, would gladly have offered generous terms to secure a speedy settlement. But the Irish protestants were determined to have vengeance for the Jacobite act of attainder, and under their pressure William's proclamation calling for surrender was directed mainly to the rank-and-file of the Jacobites; it offered no hope of security of estates for the propertied classes, and its success was correspondingly slight.

William did not await the effect of his proclamation. Within a few days of reaching Dublin, he was on the road for Limerick, having detached another force to take Athlone. Both enterprises failed, and at the end of August he handed over the command to Ginkel, and left for England. Cork and Kinsale, the only towns east of the Shannon still held by the Jacobites, fell to Marlborough in the course of the autumn; but otherwise the war languished until the spring of 1691.

During this interval Louis recalled Lauzun and his troops, and seemed half-inclined to leave Ireland alone for the future. But the advantages of keeping the war alive were too great to be lightly abandoned. Though he would not again allow his troops to be tied up in such a remote theatre, Louis was prepared to give the Irish just so much help as would encourage them to continue their resistance; and in May 1691 he despatched a new commander, St Ruth, with arms, supplies and money. Lauzun had been so unwilling to risk his men that their withdrawal can hardly be regarded as a serious loss. What the Irish suffered from, in fact, was not lack of men but lack of unity. St Ruth and Tyrconnell were jealous of each other, and both were on bad terms with the most popular of the Irish generals, Patrick Sarsfield, who had been mainly responsible for William's failure at Limerick, and whom James had now made earl of Lucan. The intrigues and suspicions that had done so much to ruin the Confederate cause in the 1640s now reappeared among the Irish, at a time when their only hope lay in united action: ultimate defeat could hardly have been averted; but the disastrous outcome of the campaign of 1691 was certainly hastened by this lack of mutual confidence.

The campaign began with Ginkel's advance against Athlone. St Ruth was confident that the town was impregnable; but on 30 June it fell to a determined assault, and the Williamite forces were soon strongly established on the right bank of the Shannon. Tyrconnell and most of the Irish commanders were anxious to concentrate on the defence of Limerick, and to hold Ginkel at bay until the reinforcements they expected should arrive from France. But St Ruth was determined to wipe out his failure at Athlone by winning a pitched battle. He took up a strong position on Aughrim Hill, near Ballinasloe, where he could block any advance on Galway; and here, on 12 July, he met Ginkel's attack. The armies were evenly matched, and the fighting was stubborn; but the fall of St Ruth at a critical moment disheartened the Irish, their left was broken by a fierce cavalry charge under Ruvigny, a Huguenot refugee and a pupil of Turenne, and the whole Jacobite army was soon in flight towards Limerick.

After Aughrim, the war moved quickly to its end. Galway surrendered on 21 July, and the great bulk of the Irish troops gathered at Limerick, against which Ginkel now concentrated his forces. Even in these straits the Irish were divided by internal feuds, and when Tyrconnell died in mid-August it was reported that he had been poisoned by his enemies. The defenders' greatest source of strength was the inspiration of Sarsfield's courage and determination, and under his leadership the garrison resisted stoutly. But they had little to hope for. The presence of an English fleet in the Shannon estuary reduced the chance of help reaching them from France; and even if such help arrived, it could hardly be sufficient to enable them to continue the war with any prospect of ultimate success. It is not surprising, that before the end of September, Sarsfield and the other leaders had become convinced that the wisest course was to surrender while they were still strong enough to exact good terms; and after ten days' negotiation two sets of articles, military and civil, were signed on 3 October.

The military articles provided for the surrender of the city, for the release of prisoners on both sides, and for the transport to France of such of the Jacobite forces as wished to go abroad. These articles were faithfully carried out; about 5,000 troops sailed from Limerick in a French fleet that had arrived to relieve the city, just two days after the articles were signed, and some 6,000 sailed later in ships provided by the English government. The civil articles, commonly referred to as the 'treaty of Limerick', represent Sarsfield's attempt to obtain good terms for those who remained in Ireland. They were signed not only by Ginkel but also by the lords justices, and were subsequently ratified by the king and queen.

The purpose of this treaty was to secure three main conditions: a measure of religious toleration for the whole Roman Catholic population of Ireland; security of life and property for Jacobite officers and soldiers remaining in Ireland and submitting to the new government; similar security for the civil inhabitants of Limerick and other places held by the Jacobite forces and of areas under their protection.

The execution of the treaty depended upon co-operation between the crown and the Irish parliament. So far as William was concerned, he tried to administer it fairly: of almost 1,300 persons who formally claimed to benefit under its terms all but 16 had their claims allowed. But parliament took a very different line. It did not ratify the treaty until 1697, and even then in a mutilated form. In particular, the first article, which guaranteed that 'the Roman Catholics of this kingdom shall enjoy such privileges in the exercise of their religion, as are consistent with the laws of Ireland, or as they did enjoy in the reign of King Charles II', was completely ignored. The article was loosely drawn, but there could be no doubt of its intention; and the series of penal laws against the Roman Catholics, on which the Irish parliament had already embarked even before 1697, was contrary to the whole spirit of the treaty. It might be argued, of course, that parliament could not be bound in advance by an agreement of this sort; but in the circumstances it is natural that Limerick should have taken its place in Irish history as 'the city of the broken treaty'.

The treaty of Limerick, imperfectly executed as it was, protected a considerable number of Jacobite landowners from forfeiture. But a much larger number fell beyond its scope — those, for example, who were prisoners at the time the treaty was made, and those residing outside the protected areas. Not all who were officially classified as 'rebels' were formally proceeded against; but some 270 estates, comprising not far short of 1,000,000 acres, were confiscated. As a result, only about one-seventh of the kingdom was left in the hands of Roman Catholic landlords; and the pressure of the penal laws during the eighteenth century was to reduce that proportion still further. The monopoly of political power that the protestant minority had enjoyed even before the Revolution was thus reinforced by a monopoly of land, a monopoly that was to survive almost unchallenged until the middle of the nineteenth century.

The great change of fortune experienced by Irish protestants — from threatened destruction in 1689, to assurance of victory in 1690, and final triumph in the following year — left a memory that has survived until the present day. From the first, the central figure in this memory was King William himself — 'the deliverer'; and Grinling Gibbons' equestrian statue, erected on College Green in 1701 by the corporation of Dublin, became at once the focal point for an annual commemoration of the king's birthday on 4 November. Almost eighty years later, when Irish protestants had grown restive under restrictions imposed from Westminster, it was round King William's statue, and on his birthday, that they were to demonstrate their readiness to assert their rights in arms.

VIII

The Emergence
of the Protestant Nation

(1)

'Upon the whole, the Irish may justly blame themselves ... for whatever they have, or shall suffer in the issue of this matter, since it is apparent that the necessity was brought about by them, that either they or we must be ruined.'

So wrote William King, dean of St Patrick's, who had been imprisoned by the Jacobite government in 1689. He was a high churchman, brought up in the principles of divine right monarchy; and his *State of the protestants of Ireland under the late King James's government,* published in 1691, was written to justify his transfer of allegiance from James to William and Mary. But in the course of his argument he presented the whole protestant case against the Irish Roman Catholics; and in concluding that they had by their own actions brought ruin upon themselves he echoed the prevalent feeling of the victorious protestant party. King himself showed later that he did not wish to press his conclusion too far — he was, for example, ready to support the treaty of Limerick — but Irish protestants generally were impatient of all compromise; and for years to come they used the *State of the protestants* as a storehouse of facts and arguments to justify their demand for more and more stringent measures against the Roman Catholic majority.

Protestant fears did not arise solely from a sense of past danger. Even after the war was over, the condition of the country was far from reassuring. The tories of the Restoration period were succeeded by the 'rapparees' — armed bands made up mainly of ex-soldiers from the Jacobite armies — whose exploits were a dangerous combination of patriotism and brigandage. While the war with France lasted, privateers abounded on the coast, and a French landing, which might well be a signal for insurrection, was regularly expected. Papal support for the Stuart cause inevitably left the loyalty of the Roman Catholic clergy open to suspicion and kept alive the long-standing protestant uneasiness about their political influence. Even the surviving Roman Catholic gentry were still a force to be reckoned with in their own localities; and they were (at least in protestant eyes, and probably in fact also) Jacobites to a man. Naturally enough, then, Irish protestants regarded William's conciliatory policy with alarm: his readiness to admit Roman Catholics to the army seemed to undermine the very security of the state; and for most of them the treaty of Limerick was almost a direct betrayal of the protestant cause.

William could not afford to ignore this attitude, partly because it was supported by opinion in England, but mainly because the co-operation of Irish protestants was essential if Ireland was to be kept in safe subjection. The earlier Stuart policy of balancing protestant against recusant was now out of date; and the only alternative to ruling through the protestant minority was the hazardous and costly expedient of direct government from England. Such an expedient was in fact proposed in an anonymous state paper of 1690, which warned William of the danger of allowing Ireland to continue as a distinct kingdom. But the times were ill-suited to constitutional experiment; and before the end of 1690 William had shown, by the appointment of lords justices and a privy council, that he intended to maintain the traditional system of government. In this system, however carefully controlled from England, the Irish protestants were bound to exercise considerable influence; and with the meeting of a parliament, in October 1692, it immediately became clear how important that influence could be.

The exclusively protestant character of parliament had already been established, in practice, during the reign of Charles II; it was now made absolute by the application of an English act of 1691 requiring members of either house to subscribe a declaration against certain distinctively Roman Catholic doctrines. Having thus asserted a protestant monopoly of power, parliament pressed so strongly for coercive measures against Roman Catholics that Sydney, who had been sent over as lord lieutenant in September 1692, felt obliged to give way. He promised that steps should be taken to disarm them, and to prevent their entry into the army; and he abandoned altogether a bill that was being prepared for confirmation of the articles of Limerick.

This experience was not lost upon William. He saw that the co-operation of the Irish protestants was not to be had without some concession to their fears and prejudices, and he decided that the price must be paid. When a new parliament met in 1695 it was presented with two measures calculated to please protestant opinion: a bill prohibiting the sending of children abroad to be educated, and a bill for the disarming of papists, both of which were readily passed. The same parliament, in its session of 1697, passed an act banishing all Roman Catholic bishops and regular clergy. It was in this session, also, that William finally yielded to parliament over the treaty of Limerick, and allowed its confirmation in a mutilated form. Thus within a decade of the Boyne, the character of the new protestant ascendancy had declared itself. The practical toleration long enjoyed by the Roman Catholics was to come to an end, and they were to be deprived of every means by which they might threaten the position of the dominant minority. The era of the penal laws had begun.

The success of the Irish protestants in compelling William to modify his conciliatory policy towards Roman Catholics was only one indication of the political influence that they had now acquired. This influence had its strongest basis in the financial needs of the crown, which could no longer be met out of the hereditary revenue. Not only had revenue fallen off during the economic depression caused by the war, but the cost of both civil and military administration had risen; the deficiency could be made good only by parliament; and parliament was the instrument of the protestant landlords. It took the opportunity to strengthen its own position; for instead of increasing the hereditary revenue, as had been done in the 1660s, it granted additional duties for a limited period only; and when this period drew to a close the government had no resource but to appeal to parliament again.

To begin with, the additional duties brought in only a relatively small part of the total revenue, but they were none the less essential to the maintenance of government; and after the Revolution the Irish parliament became, what it had never been since the early Tudor period, a regular part of the machinery of government. The relations between this revived parliament and the parliament at Westminster form the main theme of Irish political and constitutional history from the 1690s to the end of the eighteenth century.

The vigour with which the house of commons asserted itself during the 1690s was, in the circumstances, rather surprising. Of the 300 members elected to William's first parliament, in 1692, some thirty or forty had sat in the parliament of Charles II, one or two had attended the 'patriot parliament' of 1689, and a few more had been members of the English house of commons. But the great majority consisted of new men; and Ireland had no strong tradition of parliamentary activity to make up for the lack of direct experience. But, from the beginning, this untried assembly showed a determination to stand on its rights that took Sydney, the lord lieutenant, entirely by surprise. The government had not originally intended to ask for financial assistance during the first session; but on his arrival in Dublin, in September, Sydney had reported so favourably on the prospects that two money bills had been prepared; and these were presented to the commons shortly after they met. They accepted the first, and less important, of these; but at the same time they passed a resolution that their action was not to be drawn into a precedent, as it was the undoubted right of the house of commons to originate all financial measures; and on this principle they refused to give the other money bill even a first reading. The commons were quite willing, as Sydney himself admitted, to grant money, and they did in fact promise £70,000; but their claim to the sole right of initiating money bills was contrary to previous usage, and both the Irish and English judges, to whom the government submitted the question, declared that the claim was inconsistent with Poynings' Law.

In other ways also the conduct of the commons was a disappointment to Sydney. They were inconveniently zealous for their own privileges; they showed their suspicion of the government's policy towards the Roman Catholics; they complained of the distribution of forfeited estates; they brought forward the need for an Irish *habeas corpus* act; some even suggested that Poynings' Law should be repealed; and in the meantime they neglected government business. One measure that Sydney thought of special importance was a mutiny bill; but when the commons at length came to debate this, they rejected it because it was perpetual, and demanded an annual bill instead. Not surprisingly, Sydney resolved to bring the session to an early close; and on 3 November, having obtained the king's authority, he prorogued parliament, with a formal rebuke to the house of commons for their conduct in refusing to consider the government's money bill. The prorogation was subsequently renewed; and parliament was dissolved in the summer of 1693, without having been allowed to meet again.

According to Sydney, the trouble in the house of commons was the work of agitators sent over from England for the purpose. This sounds too much like an excuse for his own failure to carry much conviction; though it is clear enough that in some of their demands the commons were trying to follow English example. In the long run, however, they were less concerned about constitutional rights than about protestant security. When it became clear, as it did from 1693 onwards, that William was prepared to modify his conciliatory policy towards the Roman Catholics, the way was open for a good understanding between him and his Irish protestant subjects, and his second parliament opened in 1695 with a comparatively quiet session. The commons did, indeed, bring forward proposals for a *habeas corpus* bill and a bill of rights, but they did not press them very hard; and they quietly dropped their claim to the sole right of initiating money bills.

Two other factors, besides William's abandonment of toleration, contributed to this result. First, the commons had come to understand, even if they still resented, the limitations imposed by Poynings' Law: they realized that supplies were urgently needed for the pay of the army, which poverty had compelled the government to quarter on the country, and that the quickest way to rid themselves of this burden was to pass the money bills presented to them without disputing the council's right to prepare such bills in advance. Secondly, Capel, who had succeeded Sydney in the government, had sought to conciliate the commons by making some popular appointments. The general effect was so satisfactory to the government that this parliament was summoned annually until its dissolution in 1698.

Though William's parliaments did not maintain the struggle for constitutional rights that marked the session of 1692, and though by the end of the reign the commons seemed to have reconciled themselves to accepting, in most respects, the direction of the court, there was nevertheless one development of great importance for the future. Since the reign of James I parliament had been in the habit of proposing, for consideration by the council, topics on which it desired legislation. In the parliament of Charles II there were a few occasions on which the commons had gone a stage further and drawn up 'heads of bills', in which the proposed legislation was set out in detail. In the 1690s this became a regular practice, though it is true that most legislation still originated with the council. At this stage the procedure was simple. The house of lords, or the house of commons, having decided that a particular piece of legislation was desirable, appointed a committee to draw up heads of a bill; these were then read over to the house and, if approved, sent to the privy council 'to be drawn into form and transmitted into England according to Poynings' Law'. Later on, in the eighteenth century, when it had become customary for almost all legislation to originate in this way, the normal procedure for bills (that is to say, first reading, second reading, consideration in committee, third reading) was applied to heads of bills also, except that each house sent its own heads of bills direct to the council. The system had, from the Irish viewpoint, serious drawbacks: heads of bills might be suppressed or altered in either the Irish or the English council; and when they returned to the Irish parliament they must be accepted or rejected as they stood. Nevertheless, parliament had virtually won the initiative in legislation; and the first decisive steps towards this victory were taken in the parliaments of William III.

In trying to assert their constitutional rights, the Irish protestants had to reckon not only with the crown but also with the English parliament, which had shown throughout the seventeenth century a growing determination to establish control over policy in Ireland. After the Revolution, when parliament was tightening its hold on all branches of government, this determination became stronger: the war in Ireland had been of direct and vital consequence to England; it had been paid for by English money; and parliament felt itself particularly called upon to secure the fruits of victory. It complained repeatedly about William's grants of lands confiscated from the defeated Irish; and finally, in 1700, it passed an act of resumption, by which all these grants were revoked and the lands handed over to parliamentary commissioners to be sold. But parliament did not confine itself to the land question, and went a considerable way towards establishing a general supervision over the whole Irish administration.

Supervision of this kind might give the English parliament some measure of indirect control over Irish legislation; but, quite apart from this, it had long claimed and occasionally exercised a right to legislate directly for Ireland. It was on this issue that the constitutional dispute between the Irish protestants and the English parliament was to turn; and the first clash came, very significantly, on economic policy.

In the 1690s, as on earlier occasions, Ireland recovered with remarkable rapidity from the devastation of war, and the recovery appeared especially in the development of the woollen manufacture. It had been growing slowly before the Revolution; but now, as the advantages of cheap raw material and cheap labour made themselves felt, the rate of expansion increased. The industry was still, as compared with that of England, on a very small scale, and it used up much less than half the wool produced in the country. In 1697–8, for example, the total value of all Irish exports amounted to almost £1,000,000, of which manufactured woollen goods, including yarn, accounted for only £130,000, while the value of raw wool exported in the same year was £168,000.[1] But even this modest trade was enough to arouse the jealousy of English manufacturers. They already found themselves undersold by Irish goods in the continental market; they feared that the competition would increase; and they saw with alarm that skilled workmen were moving from England to Ireland, where the cheapness of living more than compensated for the lower rate of wages. Urged on by their complaints the English parliament promised, in 1697, that if the danger continued it would pass legislation prohibiting

[1] These figures, taken from the customs returns, represent only the value of legitimate trade; a very large quantity of raw wool was smuggled abroad, especially to France.

altogether the export of woollen goods from Ireland to any foreign country.

This threat produced a dual response from Ireland. In 1698 parliament tried to placate English opinion by promising to encourage the linen industry, and by laying new export duties on broadcloths and serges, the woollen goods competing most directly with those of England. In the same year William Molyneux, a member of the house of commons, published a pamphlet dealing with the constitutional aspect of the question — *The case of Ireland's being bound by acts of parliament in England stated.* In this he took up again the issue that had been argued in the 1640s, and maintained that the English parliament had no right to make laws for Ireland. Neither line of action achieved any success. The English house of commons immediately condemned 'the bold and pernicious assertions' of Molyneux's pamphlet, asserted the dependence of Ireland upon England, and presented an address to the king, urging him to discourage the woollen manufacture in Ireland, and instead to encourage linen 'which would benefit both them and us'. To give effect to this policy, the English parliament did what it had threatened to do in 1697, and in 1699 passed an act prohibiting the export of woollen goods from Ireland to any country whatsoever except England, from which they were already effectively excluded by high duties.

Commercial jealousy may not have been the only motive behind this action; there may also have been fear lest revenue from a prosperous Ireland should lessen the king's dependence on the English parliament. But whatever the motive, the result was a ruinous set-back to the Irish woollen industry. The immediate effects on the Irish economy have sometimes been exaggerated: the industry was still in an early stage of growth, and it accounted for only a small proportion of total Irish exports. The really significant thing was that an Irish industry had been stifled in the interests of England, and by an act of the English parliament. This was a fatal discouragement to Irish enterprise; for there was a natural fear, which later events showed to be justified, that any Irish undertaking that seemed to threaten England would receive similar treatment. It was significant also that the woollen industry was largely in the hands of protestants, so that it was they who suffered most from the act of 1699. One of the main roots of the protestant nationalism that was to develop during the eighteenth century lay in this connection between the English parliament's claim to legislate for Ireland and the subordination of the interests of Irish protestants to those of England.

This nationalism had little in common with the romantic nationalist movements that were later to spring from the French Revolution and to affect Ireland, in common with the rest of Europe, during the nineteenth century. It was based on the claim that, both by the law of nature and by the common law, Englishmen in Ireland had a right to equality with their fellow-subjects in England. Irish protestants insisted on the rights of the Irish parliament simply because that seemed the best way of securing their equality, and not because they wanted to establish a distinct national existence. At the beginning of Anne's reign, when negotiations were going forward for a parliamentary union between England and Scotland, Irish protestants were anxious that Ireland should be included on similar terms, and the Irish house of commons passed a resolution to this effect in 1703. But the proposal met with no favour in England, and the Irish protestants found that if they were to establish their claim for equal rights it must be through their own parliament. Two generations were to pass before they acquired the unity and determination necessary for the task.

(2)

Though the rejection of their plea for a parliamentary union virtually compelled the Irish protestants to base their claim for equality on the rights of Ireland as a distinct kingdom, they were not prepared to extend those rights to all sections of the population. The 'protestant ascendancy' meant the ascendancy of the Church of Ireland; papists and protestant dissenters alike were to be kept in an inferior position. It was during Anne's reign that the character of that position was clearly defined.

The events of the 1690s had shown that the Roman Catholics were to be excluded from political power, and that they were to derive no benefit, as a body, from the treaty of Limerick; but positive legislation against them had been limited in scope, and not very effective in practice. When parliament met in 1703, after an interval of five years, it was with a firm resolve that this legislation should be strengthened and extended. The government was quite ready to co-operate; and, before parliament met, the Irish and English councils had prepared the draft of a bill 'to prevent the further growth of popery'. This, however, was laid aside, and the house of commons was left to draw up its own heads of a bill for the same purpose, with the same title, and incorporating much of the earlier draft. When the commons' bill came before the English council, in accordance with Poynings' Law, there was at first some doubt about accepting it. Members of the council now argued that such a measure might be held to infringe the treaty of Limerick, and that in any case its terms were injudiciously severe at a time when the English government was urging the emperor to treat his protestant subjects in Hungary and Silesia more favourably. Despite these arguments, the council not only approved the bill, but also, in circumstances that are far from clear, made it even stricter by the addition of a clause imposing a sacramental test on all office-holders. In this form the bill returned to Ireland, passed both houses, and received the royal assent in March 1704.

By far the most important provisions of this act were those relating to real property. Their purpose was to prevent any increase in the area held by Roman Catholic landlords. No Roman Catholic might purchase any interest in land, other than a lease for a term not exceeding thirty-one years; nor might he acquire land from a protestant by inheritance or by marriage. A Roman Catholic landlord might not bequeath his land by will: on his death it was to descend by gavelkind, that is, by equal division among all his sons. If, however, the eldest conformed to the established church he was to inherit the whole estate; and if he conformed during his father's life-time, the father became merely a life-tenant, and might not alienate any of the property.

These provisions were effectively enforced, and they almost completed the destruction of the Roman Catholic gentry. Landed families, faced with a choice between conforming to the Church of Ireland and seeing their estates dissipated by repeated subdivision in successive generations, commonly preferred to conform; and those who did not tended to sink lower and lower in the economic scale. A few families managed to preserve both faith and fortune, either by a happy succession of only sons, or by the collusion of friendly protestants; but during the first half of the century there was a fairly steady decline in the number of Roman Catholic landlords, and those who survived had no desire to attract the attention of government by engaging in any political activity.

Though it was mainly concerned with land tenure, the act also reinforced certain existing restrictions of a more general character and added new ones. Roman Catholics might not send their children to be educated abroad; they might not act as guardians to children under age; before voting at parliamentary elections they must take the oath of allegiance and an oath abjuring the pretender. The imposition of a sacramental test closed any possible loophole by which they might get into public employment.

The penal code contained in this 'act to prevent the further growth of popery' was extended by later legislation; in Anne's reign Roman Catholics were prohibited from conducting schools, and in 1728 they were deprived completely of the parliamentary franchise. But the essence of the system is already present in the act of 1704. It was not a system of religious persecution such as existed in contemporary France: there was no prohibition of religious worship; 'mass-houses' were to be found in every part of the country; and though bishops and regular clergy had been banished, the secular clergy were allowed to remain, and their status was legally recognized on certain conditions. By an act of 1703 they were to register their names and parishes, and give security for good behaviour, which more than 1,000 of them did. An act of 1709 required them also to take the oath of abjuration; but there was little response to this, and the act was not generally enforced. It is true that this toleration of the secular clergy was, in theory, a temporary measure; it applied only to those already resident in the country; none were to be admitted from abroad; and, with the bishops in banishment, there could be no new ordinations. Thus the Roman Catholic clergy might have been expected to die out in a generation. It is doubtful if many protestants really expected this to happen; and it is certain that the government had no sustained intention of pushing its policy to the logical conclusion, for it could not do so without alienating continental allies and risking popular disturbance in Ireland. And even if the government had been much more determined than it actually was, the machinery for enforcing the penal laws, in a country where public opinion would always be on the side of the offender, was hopelessly inadequate. Though they suffered some inconvenience and occasional danger, unregistered clergy were able to continue their work; and recruits from abroad, including bishops and regulars, were safely smuggled in.

The effect of the laws relating to education was more serious. These laws were not, indeed rigidly enforced: a constant stream of young men went abroad to be educated for the priesthood; there were numerous 'popish schools' in almost every part of Ireland; in the middle of the century Archbishop Butler of Cashel even established a diocesan seminary for ecclesiastical students. But for the Roman Catholic laity in general there was no higher education at home, and few could afford to seek it abroad. This state of affairs undoubtedly helped to achieve the essential purpose of the penal laws; which was not to destroy Roman Catholicism, but to make sure that its adherents were kept in a position of social, economic, and political inferiority.

The ruling class was hardly less suspicious of protestant dissent than of popery, though for different reasons. The main body of protestant dissenters, the Ulster presbyterians, contained very few landlords, and could not be suspected of sympathy with the Stuart cause. But the close-knit ecclesiastical organization of the presbyterians, and their commercial wealth, gave them considerable influence; at the beginning of the century the corporations of Londonderry and of the rapidly-growing town of Belfast were both in their hands. This was a kind of influence of which the landed classes were naturally jealous; and the established clergy were equally jealous of the pretensions and activities of the presbyterian ministers. This jealousy was not off-set by any gratitude for the presbyerians' help during the Revolution, nor by fear that, if alienated now, they would withhold their help in a future crisis; there was no reason to doubt that, if the Roman Catholic danger were renewed, self-interest would compel dissenters to join with churchmen in a common protestant resistance.

Fear of the presbyterians was strengthened by the knowledge that the English government tended to favour their cause. During William's reign the bishops and their supporters had successfully resisted proposals for a toleration act; but they could not interfere with the *regium donum*, which William had revived and increased to £1,200 a year; and their complaints about the dissenters' open exercise of ecclesiastical discipline brought little response from the government. Not surprisingly, then, they welcomed the English council's addition of a sacramental test clause to the popery act of 1704. It was realized from the first that this would make little difference to the Roman Catholics, who were already so effectively excluded from public office that the test could be no more than a final and almost unnecessary barrier against them; but it was a matter of great moment to the protestant dissenters. Since 1691, when the oath of supremacy had ceased to be enforced in Ireland, all civil and military employments had been open to them, and they bitterly resented the reversal of this position in 1704.

The action of the English council in adding the test clause to the bill aroused some surprise at the time, and has never been satisfactorily explained. It is, however, safe to connect it with the high church influence of Nottingham, then secretary of state. A few years later, when the whigs were in control, the council made an effort to have the test repealed, but had to abandon it in face of the Irish parliament's opposition. During the last few years of Queen Anne, with the high church party once more in the ascendant in England, the position of the Irish dissenters got worse: *regium donum* was suspended in 1714; and but for the queen's death the occasional conformity act would probably have been extended to Ireland. The accession of George I saved them from this, and brought also the renewal and augmentation of *regium donum*; but the sacramental test remained; for the English government, though willing, indeed anxious, to have it repealed, was not prepared to push the matter against the determined opposition of the Irish parliament.

The dissenters, and especially the presbyterians, long complained of the test as an intolerable grievance. It drove them out of the municipal corporations, and control of their old strongholds of Belfast and Londonderry passed into the hands of churchmen. But they probably exaggerated its importance in other respects, for their social and economic status would in any case have excluded them from the more lucrative public employments. Such considerations, however, could neither reconcile the presbyterians to a position of legal inferiority nor convince parliament that the sacramental test was not a necessary bulwark of the established church.

The Church of Ireland, though alert to defend its privileged position, showed at this time little pastoral zeal. There were a few ardent reformers, notably William King, who had been promoted from the deanery of St Patrick's to the bishopric of Derry and then to the archbishopric of Dublin, and Nathaniel Foy, bishop of Waterford. They, and some other like-minded bishops, tried to enforce clerical residence, reduce pluralities, and forward education; but they received little support from the church as a whole. King had hoped for something from the revival of convocation, which met again in 1704 after an interval of almost forty years; but it dissipated much of its energy in a fruitless squabble between the two houses; and after 1711 it was not allowed to reassemble. It had shown some interest in the conversion of the 'popish natives' and put forward a proposal for the establishment of schools where Roman Catholic children would be taught the English language and the protestant religion. But this came to nothing at the time, through lack of funds, though the scheme was later revived in the Charter Schools.[1] The more practicable project of using the Irish language for missionary purposes was also revived in Anne's reign, and a translation of the book of common prayer was published in 1712. But the small group of enthusiasts who advocated this method got little public support. The Church of Ireland as a whole was content to remain a dominant minority, and to leave papists and presbyterians to worship as they liked, provided they were excluded from political power.

(3)

The transition from Anne to George I caused less excitement in Ireland than in England. High church clergy in Dublin, knowing that their party could expect little favour from the new régime, showed their dislike of the Brunswick succession by preaching against consubstantiation; but both they and the small group of Irish gentry who chose to call themselves tories were much more afraid of Irish papists than of English whigs. For the protestant ascendancy as a whole, the peaceful accession of the new king was a welcome guarantee for the security of their estates; and this, for a time, outweighed all other considerations.

The strength of the ascendancy's position was strikingly shown a year later, in 1715, when both England and Scotland were disturbed by

[1] See below, p. 182.

Jacobite risings. Not only did the Irish Roman Catholics make no move, but the dissenters, laying aside their grievances, stood solidly behind the protestant cause; despite the risk of incurring the penalties attached to the sacramental test, they readily accepted commissions in the militia, and prepared to join in defending the country against invasion or rebellion. The ruling classes had thus good reason to feel safe for the future. They seemed to be in no danger from the Roman Catholics; but if such danger should arise, they could count on united protestant support to resist it. This sense of security grew into a firm belief that they could govern Ireland on their own; no shadow of a threat from the defeated Irish hung over the constitutional struggle that they were later to wage with the British government and the British parliament.

The main lines of this struggle, already foreshadowed in the 1690s, were laid down during the reign of George I. The fundamental question, stated in its simplest terms, was whether or not the British parliament had the right to legislate for Ireland; but this constitutional issue was overlaid by others having more obviously practical effects. Irishmen complained of restrictions on trade, of the appointment of Englishmen to offices in Ireland, of the charging on the Irish establishment of pensions to persons having no connection with the kingdom. All these grievances followed from the constitutional subordination of Ireland to Great Britain; but it was only by degrees that the discontent they produced acquired the strength and direction necessary to turn it into a programme of constitutional reform.

The Irish parliament, though its position and powers lay at the heart of the controversy, lagged behind public opinion, and was much less forward in defending its rights than it had been in the first enthusiasm of its revival in the reign of William III. It was, in fact, a very imperfect mouthpiece of the protestant population. In the house of lords the influence of the bishops, always important and sometimes dominant, was usually cast on the side of the government. The house of commons, considered as a representative assembly, suffered from all the defects of the contemporary English house. Most boroughs were controlled by patrons, and the county representation was virtually in the hands of the great landlords. Even apart from this, the absence of regular general elections reduced the influence of the constituencies; Ireland had no septennial act, and only the demise of the crown could force a dissolution — one parliament lasted throughout the reign of George I, and the next throughout the reign of his successor. Members were commonly more concerned about appointments or pensions for themselves or their dependants than about constitutional rights; and, as in England, the government regularly used its patronage to purchase support in the house. But it is easy to exaggerate the importance of this sort of influence, especially in the early part of the century. There were scores of independent members who regularly voted as the viceroy wished, not in the hope of reward, but because they thought it the duty of parliament to support the king's government. And place-holders and pensioners felt themselves free to oppose measures that they thought contrary to the interests of the country — it was their hostility, for example, that compelled the government, time after time, to abandon its proposals for repealing the sacramental test. But when all allowances have been made, it remains true that members in general were apt to follow government direction; and in the long run those Irishmen, inside and outside the house, who wished to establish the independent rights of the Irish parliament had, as their first and greatest task, the conversion of that parliament itself to support of its own cause.

This backwardness on the part of parliament was not, however, wholly due to the selfishness or short-sightedness of the members. The Irish house of commons was still, in relation to the lord lieutenant, in much the same position as the English house had been in relation to the crown under Elizabeth or James I. It had no control over the executive, no share in the making or unmaking of ministries; for the lord lieutenant was a member of the British administration, whose policy it was his duty to carry out. Occasionally, it is true, an unpopular policy might be modified, or an unpopular lord lieutenant recalled, in deference to Irish opinion; but this hardly affected the general pattern of government. The executive, through its agents in the house, regularly took the lead in business; and though opposition might be aroused on particular topics, it had no continuing principle. Contemporaries sometimes spoke in party terms — 'whigs' and 'tories', the 'court party' and the 'country party', the 'English interest' and the 'Irish interest'; but these terms were loosely used, and certainly did not indicate standing party divisions.

This absence of party divisions was, on the whole, a source of strength to the government. It meant, of course, that constant labour and vigilance were needed to hold together a majority of members in support of government policy; but it meant also that the formation of a coherent opposition, even on a temporary basis, was extremely difficult. And it was not until past the middle of the century that even the nucleus of a continuing opposition, organized in support of a specific programme, made its appearance.

(4)

Parliament was not summoned for more than a year after the accession of George I. The elections, in October 1715, went off to the government's satisfaction; and when the house of commons met in November it proved readily amenable to the direction of the court. Within a few years, however, the atmosphere had changed. Between 1719 and 1725 constitutional and economic issues combined to unite public opinion against England; the British parliament was provoked into a formal assertion of its superior authority, all elements in the Irish parliament were temporarily united in opposition to the government, and the embryonic nationalism of pro-testant Ireland had received its first popular expression.

The constitutional dispute began over a question of jurisdiction. One of the disputants in a law-suit (Sherlock *v* Annesley) had appealed successfully to the Irish house of lords, whereupon the defeated party appealed to the house of lords at Westminster, which decided in his favour. The Irish lords resisted the execution of this decision, affirmed their own right to a final jurisdiction in Ireland, and appealed to the king to support them. Precedents were cited on both sides; but the British parliament was not prepared to submit its claims to argument. Instead, it passed an 'act for the better securing the dependency of the kingdom of Ireland on the crown of Great Britain', declaring that it had full authority to make laws 'of sufficient force and validity to bind the kingdom and people of Ireland', and denying that the Irish house of lords had any appellate jurisdiction. Though the British parliament had previously claimed and exercised a right to legislate for Ireland, this formal assertion of it aroused great indignation; and the 'Sixth of George I' (as the act was commonly called) came to be one of the standing grievances of Ireland.[1]

It was while public indignation at the attitude of the British parliament was still fresh that Jonathan Swift made his first appearance as a popular pamphleteer in the Irish cause. Since his withdrawal from public life in England to his deanery of St Patrick's, at the end of Anne's reign, Swift had held himself aloof from political affairs. But he found it impossible to ignore the wretched poverty of the lower classes in Ireland. His deanery house was situated in an area occupied mainly by weavers, and he had constantly before him the miserable condition to which the depression of the woollen industry had reduced them. In 1720 he put forward his remedy, *A proposal for the universal use of Irish manufacture; . . . utterly rejecting and renouncing everything wearable that comes from England.* The pamphlet, which was published anonymously, made a thinly-veiled appeal to the prevalent anti-English sentiment; and the question that it posed, 'whether a law to bind men without their own consent be obligatory *in foro*

---

[1] The date of this act is commonly given as 1719; it was, in fact, passed in March 1720.

conscientiae', could hardly fail to be applied to the British parliament's claim to legislate for Ireland. Irishmen were slow in responding to Swift's plea that they should help themselves by using their own manufactures in place of those of England; but his attack upon England as the cause of Ireland's poverty echoed their own convictions, and they enthusiastically applauded his expression of them. The government's efforts to secure the condemnation of the printer revealed the depth of its alarm, and helped to keep the excitement alive.

Before this excitement had entirely died down, it received fresh matter to work on. In July 1722 a patent was granted to William Wood, a Wolverhampton ironmaster, empowering him to coin money for Ireland. There was nothing essentially unreasonable in this, for the shortage of small currency had been for some time a matter of complaint, and Wood's coins were to be of a higher standard than those already in circulation. But the Irish public was in a discontented and suspicious mood, and the circumstances of the grant were not likely to conciliate it. There had been no previous consultation with anyone in Ireland; both the amount to be coined and the amount of profit allowed were considered to be excessive; and it became known that Wood had obtained the patent by paying £10,000 to the king's mistress, the duchess of Kendal. It is hardly surprising that Irish opposition was immediate: the commissioners of revenue made a formal protest; indignation spread throughout the country; and when the coins began to arrive there was a widespread refusal to accept them. By the time parliament met, in September 1723, members were too full of the grievance of 'Wood's halfpence' to be pacified by any explanation that the lord lieutenant, the duke of Grafton, might offer. Both houses postponed other business till they had drawn up addresses to the king, declaring that the patent granted to William Wood was prejudicial to the revenue, destructive of trade, and dangerous to property. Members who would normally have supported the government turned against it on this issue, and parliament was completely out of control. But it was Swift's intervention a few months later that raised the agitation above a mere squabble over currency, and based it on a clear assertion of national rights.

Since the publication of the *Proposal* in 1720 Swift had almost withdrawn from Irish politics. He had, perhaps, been alarmed at the violence with which the authorities had attacked the pamphlet, and disappointed at the public's failure to follow his advice. At any rate, he did not allow the outbreak of agitation over 'Wood's halfpence' to distract his attention from work on *Gulliver's travels*; and it was not until February 1724, when *Gulliver* was more than half finished, that he published the first of the *Drapier's letters*. He continued the series during the year, maintaining throughout his assumed character of a Dublin tradesman, concerned about the effect of a debased coinage on the prosperity of the kingdom. But his real theme is the constitutional relationship between Ireland and Great Britain; and in the fourth letter, addressed 'to the whole people of Ireland', he states his position openly. He denies that the people of Ireland are 'in some state of slavery or dependence different from those of England'. Both kingdoms alike depend directly on the crown, and England has no right to make laws for Ireland. His purpose is, he declares, to show his readers 'that by the laws of God, of nature, of nations, and of your own country, you are and ought to be as free a people as your brethren in England'. This was not the first time the claim had been made; but when put forward in the 1640s it had been mainly in the interests of the Old English recusants, and its revival in the 1690s had been brief and fruitless; now Swift proclaimed it as the watchword of the protestant ascendancy.

By this time the government was already moving towards a change of policy. The total value of the currency to be issued by Wood was reduced from £108,000 to £40,000; the duke of Grafton was recalled, and Carteret sent over in his place. But Ireland wanted none of Wood's halfpence; and Carteret's efforts at conciliation were no more successful than Grafton's. Repression proved equally useless; for when the government prosecuted the printer of the fourth *Drapier's letter* the jury refused to find a true bill. At last, as the time drew near for the next meeting of parliament, complete capitulation was decided on; and in September 1725 Carteret was able to inform both houses that 'an entire end has been put to the patent formerly granted to Mr Wood'.

This victory made Swift a national hero, for his authorship of the *Drapier's letters* was an open secret, though the government could not prove it. But apart from the ending of the patent the victory brought no immediate benefit to Ireland. It had shown that government control of parliament was precarious, that when public feeling was sufficiently aroused even placemen and pensioners would swim with the tide; but public feeling quickly subsided when the immediate cause of offence was removed, parliamentary life soon resumed its normal course, and the government took steps to tighten its control of the house of commons. Yet things were never quite the same again. Swift had taught the Irish protestants that they were 'the people of Ireland', with all the rights of a distinct nation. They were not yet ready to learn the lesson fully; but it was never wholly forgotten. Protestant nationalism had been born; and however arrogant, ill-founded, or inconsistent might be the principles by which it was inspired, it had a significant contribution to make to the history of Ireland.

IX

The Economic and Social Basis of the Protestant Ascendancy

(1)

Travellers in eighteenth-century Ireland, almost without exception, noted the poverty of the country and of its inhabitants. Even the light-hearted Mrs Delany, flitting gaily from one great house to another, could not ignore it: 'The poverty of the people as I passed through the country has made my heart ache — I never saw greater appearance of misery'. The towns swarmed with beggars; and along the country roads wretched cabins, hardly better than English pig-sties, sheltered a rack-rented peasantry, who scraped a precarious living from the soil. No doubt this gloomy picture could have been matched in some parts of contemporary Europe; and the wretchedness of Ireland may have struck observers the more forcibly from its contrast to the nearby prosperity of England. But that the country was miserably poor admits of no question.

This state of affairs was not due to lack of natural resources, but to a combination of political, social and economic circumstances. The British parliament had successfully asserted its claim to dictate government policy towards Ireland; and under pressure from English merchants and manufacturers had so restricted Irish trade that the country was forced to rely upon agriculture. The landlords thus found themselves with a virtual monopoly of the means of livelihood; and it was on their use of this monopoly that the welfare of Ireland most directly depended. Over the greater part of the country they were conquerors, or descendants of conquerors, unrestrained by custom, or by traditional sympathy with their tenants, from whom they were for the most part cut off by religion and by the still-fresh memories of the seventeenth-century wars. Some of them had estates in England also, and naturally preferred to live there; but it is not surprising that many, whose whole fortune was in Irish land, nevertheless found English society more congenial.

An absentee landlord was not necessarily oppressive or grasping. His aim was generally to get a steady income with the least possible trouble; and to this end he let out his estate in large tracts, on long leases, and at reasonable rents. The men who took such leases, however, were rarely working farmers; they were middlemen, who sub-divided and sub-let their holdings, 'retailing the land which they rent in the wholesale — a practice which is the bane of this island'. There were often several sub-lettings between the original landlord and the actual tiller of the soil; and at each stage there was, of necessity, a reduction in the length of lease and an increase in the rate of rent. Thus the working farmer, on whose labour the whole top-heavy structure depended, had little security of tenure, and was burdened with a crippling rent.

It is natural to blame the gentry, landlords and middlemen alike, for the wretched condition of the peasants; but they were themselves victims of the British policy of discouraging Irish trade and manufactures and of appointing Englishmen to Irish offices. 'The whole body of the gentry', wrote Swift in 1726, are 'utterly destitute of all means to make provision for their younger sons, either in the church, the law, the revenue, or, of late, in the army; and, in the desperate condition of trade, it is equally vain to think of making them merchants. All they have left is, at the expiration of leases, to rack their tenants, which they have done to such a degree, that there is not one farmer in a hundred through the kingdom who can afford shoes or stockings to his children, or to eat flesh, or drink anything better than sour milk or water, twice in a year'. This is a one-sided statement, but it contains an important element of truth; British policy reinforced the dependence of the whole Irish economy upon land; and it was this dependence that not only put the gentry in a position to oppress their tenants but gave them a strong motive for doing so.

(2)

It is not, perhaps, very likely that, British policy apart, Ireland would ever have become an important centre of manufacturing industry. The country lacked both the capital and the reservoir of skilled labour necessary for large-scale industrial development. But the jealous watchful-ness of the British parliament ensured that these difficulties should not be overcome.

The woollen manufacture still had an outlet in the home market and in a considerable smuggling trade; but it had been disastrously weakened by the act of 1699. The promise to compensate for this by encouraging the linen manufacture was very imperfectly fulfilled; and, in the interests of the Scottish linen-weavers, Irish coloured linens were excluded from the British market. The growth of brewing in Ireland in the early eighteenth century aroused British jealousy again. The industry depended on imported hops, and a series of British acts from 1710 onwards forbade the importation into Ireland of hops from any country except Great Britain. The natural result of this monopoly was to raise the price; and down to the 1770s there was a fairly steady decline in the amount of beer brewed in Ireland, and a corresponding rise in the amount imported from England. Even stronger measures were taken against the growing Irish glass industry. An act of 1746 forbade Ireland to export glass to any country whatsoever; and as a result of this restriction the industry withered away. The Irish parliament, shackled by Poynings' Law, could neither pass retaliatory measures nor even protect Irish industries from British competition. The duties on British goods entering Ireland were low; and Irish manufacturers regularly found themselves undersold in their own home market by British competitors.

These restrictions hampered and distorted the development of the economy as a whole; but progress in certain sectors was greater than has sometimes been recognized. British policy was not wholly repressive. Ireland enjoyed, for example, a limited but profitable share of colonial trade: her linens and provisions might be exported direct to the West Indies and to North America; and from 1731 onwards some colonial products, though not either tobacco or sugar, might be shipped direct to Ireland. Between the 1730s and the 1760s the value of this colonial trade more than doubled; trade with Britain and with Europe expanded during the same period; and there seems little reason to doubt Arthur Young's statement that from the mid-century Ireland was becoming much more prosperous. But this prosperity, which rested mainly on the export of linen and provisions, brought little benefit to the great mass of the population: the linen-weavers of Ulster, it is true, had the advantage of alternative employment, and were able to maintain a somewhat higher standard of living than small-holders in the other provinces; but most of the profits of their labours, and virtually all the profits of the provision trade, went into the pockets of landlords, middlemen and merchants.

The linen industry owed a good deal to the energy and skill of Huguenot refugees who had settled in Ireland after the revocation of the Edict of Nantes. The Irish parliament voted considerable sums to encourage them, and granted bounties on the import of flax-seed and on the export of canvas and sail-cloth; and in 1710 a board of trustees (the Linen Board) was set up to supervise the industry. The linen manufacture was strongest in Ulster, for Louis Crommelin, whom William III had appointed 'overseer of the royal linen manufacture of Ireland', had made his head-quarters at Lisburn, in County Antrim; but it was to be found in many other parts of Ireland also, and until after the middle of the century most of the exports passed through Dublin. By the 1770s the total value of the linen cloth and yarn produced annually was reckoned at £2 million, and about nine-tenths of this was exported. Linen was at this time a domestic industry. The organization was generally in the hands of the bleachers, who bought yarn, gave it out to be woven, and marketed the cloth; but much of the spinning, and most of the weaving, was done in the homes of cottiers and small farmers. It was thus an auxiliary to agriculture, not a substitute for it, and had little effect on the dominant position of the landlords in the economic life of the country.

The export of cattle-products — beef, butter, tallow, hides — was even more extensive and more profitable than that of linen, and was the main basis of the prosperity of the southern ports. Cork, in particular, made a great profit from the provisioning of ships, and had grown so rapidly in size as well as in wealth that from ranking fifth among the cities of the kingdom at the beginning of the century it ranked second by the 1770s. The graziers and merchants who controlled the provision trade contained a high proportion of Roman Catholics, who found there an outlet for the skill and energy that they were forbidden to employ in the public service or in the practice of the law. This growing class of wealthy Roman Catholics could not participate directly in politics; but the command of ready money, rare in eighteenth-century Ireland, inevitably gave it social and economic influence, and helped, in time, to break down the restrictions imposed by the penal laws.

One very important branch of Irish overseas trade in the eighteenth century was the clandestine export of wool to France. This trade had existed in the seventeenth century, but it grew rapidly after 1699, as the quantity of woollen goods manufactured in Ireland declined. By law, wool might not be exported from Ireland to any country except England; but the price offered by French merchants was four or five times that paid in the legal market, so that the profits of a smuggling trade were temptingly high; and there was ready sale in Ireland for the French brandy, claret and silks that the smugglers brought in return. Public opinion was generally on the side of the smugglers; the Irish coast was well-suited for their activities; and all the government's efforts at enforcing the law failed. It was not until after 1739, when the removal of the duties on Irish woollen yarns entering England diverted some of the export into a legiti-mate channel, that the smuggling trade with France received any check; and even thirty years later it remained an important branch of Irish commerce.

(3)

The greatest weakness of the Irish economy was lack of capital; and the steady drain of payments to absentees — pensioners, officials, landlords — made the situation worse. In the seventeenth century the crown had occasionally found it convenient to reward service in England or abroad by a pension on the Irish establishment; but in the eighteenth century the practice was greatly extended, and the first two Georges used the Irish pension-list to provide for their mistresses, their bastards, and their German relations and dependants. Sinecure offices in the Irish administration were regularly used to bribe or reward English politicians, and were even kept alive for that purpose. Revenue business, for example, had been managed, since the reign of Charles II, by a board of commissioners; but all the old posts were still filled — there were three vice-treasurers, a chancellor of the exchequer, a clerk of the pells, and a host of minor officials, who drew their salaries, lived where they chose, and discharged by deputy such duties as might still attach to their offices. By the 1770s absentee pensioners and holders of sinecures probably cost the country not far short of £100,000 a year. This burden on the establishment was one of the standing grievances of the house of commons; but it was far less serious than the drain of rents by absentee landlords. According to Arthur Young this amounted to £732,000 a year in 1779, an enormous sum at a time when the total annual revenue of the kingdom was little more than one million.

An attempt to reduce this loss of capital by a tax on absentees proved unsuccessful, mainly because of English opposition. And though the establishment of legislative independence brought some decline in absenteeism during the last two decades of the century, the rise in rents during the same period meant that the amount of money being sent out of the country actually increased.

The loss of capital to agriculture through payment of absentee rents was only partly compensated for by the profits of the provision trade. Its very success, indeed, operated against the extension and improvement of tillage, which was the greatest need of the Irish rural economy; and the Roman Catholics who controlled a great part of the trade had no inducement to invest their profits in agriculture, since they were precluded by law from acquiring any permanent interest in land, a restriction that was not finally removed until 1782.

The general scarcity of capital meant, naturally, that credit was restricted, and rates of interest high. And the financial position was made worse by the confusion of the currency. The ratio in value between Irish and English currency had been fixed at the beginning of the century at 13:12; that is to say, one guinea, English, was worth £1 2s 9d, Irish. But there was no Irish mint, and the only coins specially struck for Ireland were copper pence, halfpence and farthings. Irish money was, in fact, merely money of account; actual payments, except of very small sums, were made in English coins, or in the various foreign coins that were also legally current at rates fixed from time to time by proclamation. A high proportion of these coins were counterfeit, and even those that were genuine were often light-weight; so that every transaction was a clumsy and hazardous affair.

The position would have been greatly improved by an adequate banking system; but though England and Scotland had established national banks in the 1690s, almost a century was to pass before Ireland followed their example. In the interval, Irish banking was entirely a matter of private enterprise. Some of the banks established during this period were sound and successful undertakings, notably the firm of La Touche, which was for three generations the most important banking concern in the country. But many were short-lived and unreliable; and as all enjoyed an unrestricted liberty to issue notes, there was a flood of often worthless paper money. The hardships caused by frequent bank-failures bred a suspicion of banking in general, which may help to explain the strong public opposition to a proposal put forward in 1720-1 for establishing a national bank by act of parliament, though the rejection of the proposal was probably due, in the long run, mainly to fear lest such a bank should increase still further English control over the Irish economy. It was not until 1780 that the proposal was renewed, and not until 1783 that parliament established the Bank of Ireland, with a virtual monopoly of joint-stock banking.

(4)

Though the Irish economy was forced to depend almost entirely on the land, there was little attempt at the systematic development of agriculture. And lack of capital was not the only, nor perhaps the main, reason for this failure: the great improvements made by some landlords could have been made by many more. But the landlords in general, whether resident or absentee, and the middlemen who held under them, were concerned with little more than immediate profit; and they could always be sure of tenants, even on the hardest conditions, for to the mass of the population land was the only means of livelihood. In return for his rent, the working farmer rarely got more than the bare land; and even if he possessed the skill and capital necessary to make the most of it he had little inducement to do so. His lease was generally a short one — no Roman Catholic could hold a lease of more than thirty-one years — and when it fell in he could not hope for renewal on favourable terms. If he improved the value of the farm, indeed, he might be evicted to make way for some one else; for on many estates it was the practice, on the expiry of a lease, to put the farm up to auction, and to let it to the tenant who offered the highest rent. It was no unusual thing for a tenant, when the end of his lease was approaching, deliberately to waste his farm, so as to make it less attractive to possible competitors.

For a tenant in these circumstances, with little capital and no security, pasture farming was obviously more attractive than tillage. The existence of good markets for provisions and wool was another influence in the same direction; and during the first half of the century there was a fairly steady increase in the proportion of land under pasture. From one point of view this was not an unreasonable development; Ireland was particularly suited to the raising of cattle, and the provision trade was one of the chief sources of national wealth. But against this must be set the facts that Ireland suffered from under-employment; that the profits of pasture went into a few pockets only; and that, as pasture expanded, more and more people had to depend for their subsistence on the produce of an ever-decreasing area of tillage. 'Go and preach to your own tenants to fall to the plough as fast as they can', was Swift's advice to a country gentleman, 'and prevail with your neighbouring squires to do the same with theirs; or else die with the guilt of having driven away half the inhabitants, and starving the rest'.

The situation was made worse by a rise in population. Eighteenth-century statistics are, at best, approximate; but it seems likely that the population was around two-and-a-half million at the beginning of the century, that it had risen to three million by the 1750s and to four million by the 1780s. Inevitably, the pressure on land increased; and since there was little decline in the number or size of the grazing farm, the pressure fell on the smaller holdings; there was a steady tendency for them to be subdivided to meet the demand; and as the century progressed an ever greater proportion of the population sank to the position of mere cottiers, holding a few acres of land from year to year, and dependent upon their wages to make up the rent. Wages were low and rents high, and the cottier lived at bare subsistence level. His normal diet was potatoes and butter-milk, with, on rare occasions, a salt herring or a piece of bacon; and if his potatoes failed or fell short he had no money to buy other food, but must beg or starve until the next crop was ready.

In these conditions a bad season brought great hardship; and when, a in 1727–30, one bad season followed another, there was absolute disaster — the old and sick 'dying and rotting by cold and famine and filth and vermin'; the younger labourers so enfeebled by lack of food that even when they could find employment they had no strength to work. The famine of these years was at its worst in the south; in 1740–1 another famine struck the whole country. From counties as far apart as Limerick and Monaghan came reports of whole villages depopulated by starvation and disease, of 'roads spread with dead and dying bodies', of corpses being 'eaten in the fields by dogs for want of people to bury them'. In some areas clergy and landlords spent large sums in feeding the poor, but the disaster was too serious to be remedied by private benevolence. Though the mortality cannot be accurately estimated (contemporary accounts vary from 80,000 to 400,000), it was undoubtedly very high: in Kerry, for example, where more than 14,000 families had paid hearth-tax in 1733, the number had sunk to less than 10,000 by 1744. 'The nation probably will not recover this loss in a century', wrote Bishop Berkeley of Cloyne, in May 1741. But, in fact, this famine proved to be the last of a series; though poverty and hardship continued, and though there were occasional periods of scarcity, population increased rapidly, and the production of potatoes kept pace with its needs. In the 1770s Arthur Young expressed the opinion that, so far as mere quantity of food was concerned, the Irish labourer was better off than the English: 'I will not assert that potatoes are a better food than bread and cheese; but I have no doubt of a bellyful of the one being much better than half a bellyful of the other'. It was left for the nineteenth century to show how dangerous this dependence on the potato could be.

The famines of 1727–30 and 1740–1 served as sharp reminders of what was, in any case, obvious enough, that the agriculture of the kingdom was dangerously unbalanced. From the reign of Queen Anne, the Irish parliament had shown concern at the extension of pasture-land and professed its determination to encourage the growth of corn. This, as might be expected, had aroused some jealousy in England lest Irish grain should compete seriously with English; and though the Irish parliament was allowed to pass acts for the encouragement of tillage in 1707 and again in 1727, they were too feeble to be effective. It may, indeed, be doubted if parliament was sincere in its professions. The landlord class, of which it was the mouthpiece, could have done a great deal more than it did for agriculture, without waiting for fresh legislation. And the house of commons itself gave direct discouragement to tillage by passing, in 1735, a resolution against the payment of tithe of agistment, that is, tithe on pasture-land. This resolution had no legal force; but from this time onward, tithe of agistment was not, in fact, paid; so that there was an additional inducement to raise cattle and sheep rather than till the soil.

The decline in tillage was so great that for a period of thirty years, from the mid-1740s, Ireland actually imported more grain than she exported. In the north, where the labouring poor depended on oatmeal as much as on potatoes, there were periods of severe distress; and even in the capital the supply of flour was precarious. In face of this situation, parliament at length made a serious attempt to encourage the growth of corn; and British jealousy now raised no impediment. An act of 1758 granted a bounty on grain and flour brought to Dublin by land; and this was followed, in 1765 and 1773, by increases in the small bounty hitherto paid on exported grain. These measures did something to check the expansion of pasture; but it was not until 1784, after the Irish parliament had established its independence, that a really effective corn law was passed. This act, together with a growing English demand for imported grain, led to a substantial increase in the area under tillage,[1] and helped to compensate for the continued subdivision of holdings by enabling the peasant to maintain himself on a very few acres of land. But he derived little other benefit from the change. There was no marked improvement in his standard of living: he sold his corn to pay the rent; and he and his family continued to live on potatoes while the landlord and the merchant divided the profits of his labour.

A great deal of the poverty of rural Ireland in the eighteenth century can be traced to the attitude and conduct of the landlords; but not all of them were oppressors of their tenants, and neglectful of the public good. It was a group of landlords, aided by some well-to-do Church of Ireland clergy, who established the Dublin Society in 1731. The object of the society was 'the improvement of agriculture and other useful arts', and it was one of the first and most successful undertakings of the kind in Europe. It set up a model farm, published instructive pamphlets, imported and distributed better implements than those in common use, and offered prizes to encourage more careful cultivation. At first it depended entirely on voluntary subscription, but later it received substantial parliamentary grants, which were devoted to the encouragement of manufactures and fisheries as well as of agriculture. Apart from this corporate effort, much was done locally by 'improving' landlords. Colonel Hugh Boyd established a brewery, a soap factory and other industries at Ballycastle in County Antrim; Sir William Osborne, in County Tipperary,

---

[1] See below, pp. 243–4.

advanced capital for the reclamation of waste land, so as to provide holdings for landless labourers; Robert Gregory in County Galway and Lord Shannon in County Cork tried by example and precept to raise the standard of husbandry among their tenants; Bishop Berkeley, of Cloyne, set himself 'to feed the hungry and clothe the naked by promoting an honest industry', and endeavoured by his writings to promote a reform of the economy. Even among the absentees there were those who felt it a duty to do something for the country from which they drew their incomes: Lord Shelbourne, for example, introduced English methods of agriculture on his vast estates in County Kerry.

But all these efforts, though they undoubtedly accomplished some good, go only a short way towards redeeming the general character of the Irish landlords of the period. As a class, they seem to have deserved Arthur Young's slashing condemnation — 'lazy, trifling, inattentive, negligent, *slobbering*, profligate'. His anger was aroused by their failure to improve their lands, but the description might not unfairly be extended to other aspects of their lives also.

(5)

The conduct of the landlords and the condition of the peasantry in eighteenth-century Ireland might seem certain to produce agrarian crime; but for the first sixty years of the century the greater part of the country was free from disturbance. There were, it is true, wide areas of mountain and bogland in the south-west and in Connaught, where the rapparee tradition survived, where the smuggling trade was particularly strong, and which lay virtually beyond the normal administration of the law. But these conditions could have been paralleled in Great Britain at the same time. And it is significant that in only one instance can unrest in these areas be traced directly to an agrarian grievance: between 1711 and 1713 the whole province of Connaught was terrorized by the activities of the 'Houghers', a skilfully-organized body of men, who destroyed cattle and sheep in protest against the expansion of pasture. The movement ended as suddenly as it had begun; and it is at least possible that its professed motive was a cloak for political designs. It was not until the 1760s that Ireland was troubled by widespread agrarian crime; and then it took its rise, not in the traditionally unruly west, but in the hitherto peaceful county of Tipperary.

In 1759 the restrictions imposed almost a century earlier on the import of Irish cattle into England were removed, and the immediate effect of this was a further extension of pasture; in Tipperary especially whole villages were swept away and commons were enclosed. In protest against these enclosures bands of men roamed the countryside at night, wearing white smocks over their clothes — whence they were commonly called 'Whiteboys' — throwing down fences and destroying cattle. They soon turned their attention to other sources of discontent also. Tithe has been unpopular wherever it has existed; but it was particularly so in Ireland, where the great bulk of those who paid regarded the clergy whom they were obliged to support as heretical and alien. The method of collection was an added grievance, for this was generally in the hands of tithe-proctors, who acted as the agents of the clergy, or of tithe-farmers, who bought the right of collection and made what profit they could. Both classes were noted for their extortionate methods, against which the cottier or small farmer could do little to protect himself; and his sense of injustice was increased when he saw the wide pasture-lands of the grazier go free (since the tithe of agistment had been abandoned), while his own potato-garden and patch of corn had still to bear the burden. The White-boys did not propose to abolish tithe altogether, but they attempted to settle the rate at which it should be levied. And also, since they were almost all Roman Catholics, they tried to impose on the Roman Catholic clergy a scale of charges for their services. It was more difficult for them to do anything about rents and conditions of tenure, for the most important landlords were absentees who lived beyond their reach; but by attacking unpopular tenants they acquired a real, though indirect, influence over landlord policy.

The Whiteboys committed few murders, but they subjected those who fell under their displeasure to cruel tortures, and they destroyed an immense amount of property. The government was at first almost helpless. The whole rural population seemed bound, either by sympathy or terror, in a conspiracy of silence. No one would assist the magistrates; and even when arrests were made it was impossible to get evidence. The ruling class did not long tolerate such a situation. Parliament passed a series of repressive measures, extending the powers of the magistrates, and making any participation in Whiteboy activities a capital offence; and in some areas the landlords took the law into their own hands, arming their more reliable tenants and forming them into troops of horse to patrol the countryside. But, wrote Arthur Young, 'the gentlemen of Ireland never thought of a radical cure, from overlooking the real cause of the disease, which in fact lay in themselves, and not in the wretches they doomed to the gallows'. Though stern measures brought the Whiteboy movement under some sort of control, the grievances that had given rise to it were too serious, too deeply-felt and too enduring to yield to mere repression; and it survived, in various forms, into the nineteenth century.

Though the Whiteboys appeared first in Tipperary, they soon spread over most of Munster and over parts of Leinster and Connaught. Only Ulster remained free from them; and even in Ulster there were two brief outbreaks of agrarian crime. The first, in 1763, was largely confined to the counties of Armagh, Tyrone and Londonderry, and was occasioned partly by a more rigorous exaction of tithe by some of the local clergy and partly by the conduct of the grand juries. The grand jury, consisting of the principal landlords of the county, was the organ of county administration, and by a recent act had been empowered to require the personal labour of all householders in the construction and repair of roads. The peasantry of Armagh and Londonderry complained that the grand juries had administered the act harshly and in the selfish interests of the landlords; and it was principally this grievance that bands of them set out to redress, styling themselves 'Hearts of Oak', or 'Oakboys', from the sprigs of oak that they wore in their hats as a badge. They committed few acts of violence; and when the law relating to road construction was modified the movement quickly disappeared.

A more serious agitation began in 1770, when Lord Donegall demanded heavy fines for renewal of leases on his County Antrim estates. A great many of the tenants were unable to pay these fines, and their lands were taken over by others, including a number of merchants from Belfast. But, to quote a local poet of the time,

> *Some of the tenants still remain that feel*
> *Their wrongs, and can resent with Hearts of Steel,*
> *Bravely resolved in mutual league unite*
> *To keep possession, and support their right.*

The 'Hearts of Steel', or 'Steelboys', attacked the cattle and property of those who had taken over their farms; and the movement extended into some neighbouring areas. But it was neither widespread nor longlived, and by 1773 it was extinct; mainly, it would seem, because those most deeply involved had emigrated to North America. There, they were soon to have an opportunity of showing their resentment in a more effective manner.

The agitation attracted a great deal of attention at the time, and Lord Donegall was widely blamed for his conduct. Even John Wesley, who visited Belfast in 1773, so far forgot his usual respect for authority as to express sympathy with the agitators and surprise at their moderation. But the Hearts of Steel movement left little permanent mark; and perhaps its main importance is as a reminder that the protection given by the

'Ulster custom'[1] was precarious, and that the presbyterian tenants of the north were, when aroused, just as ready as the Roman Catholic tenants of the south to defend their position by violence.

(6)

Ulster's comparative freedom from agrarian unrest was a result of the happier conditions generally prevailing in the province. Its prosperity was frequently noted by contemporaries. Swift, in 1726, specifically exempted the north from his gloomy picture of Ireland at the time: 'the whole country, except the Scottish plantation in the north, is a scene of misery and desolation, hardly to be matched on this side Lapland'. The reference to the 'plantation' is significant, though it was not so exclusively Scottish as Swift seems to have supposed; for the presence of a strong protestant population, descended from the settlers of the seventeenth century, was what marked Ulster off most sharply from the rest of the country. It is unlikely that the protestants ever formed more than about half the total population of the province; but they were spread through all grades of society, and in some areas, especially in the east, they were locally dominant in numbers. Thus the numbing effect of the penal laws was less widely felt in Ulster than elsewhere, and there was some community of feeling between landlord and tenant.

It was even more important that Ulster farmers had succeeded in establishing and maintaining some degree of security in their holdings. The 'Ulster custom', on which this security depended, had no legal basis, and it could not be enforced in the courts; but it was generally recognized throughout the province, and few landlords cared to defy it openly. The custom was never authoritatively defined, and it varied somewhat in detail from area to area, but its essential characteristic was that the tenant was deemed to possess a saleable interest in his holding. This interest, or 'tenant right', was, basically, the right of occupancy; and a tenant who wished to give up his farm could sell the right to the highest bidder, subject to the landlord's approval of the purchaser. If a landlord wished to evict a tenant, he must either allow him to sell his tenant right, or must purchase it himself at the full market value. The Ulster custom thus conferred two great benefits on the tenant: he could not be evicted without reasonable compensation; and he had some guarantee of a fair return for any improvements he might make, for either he would continue to occupy the farm himself, or, if he left, his improvements would add to the selling-price of the tenant right. But the custom was, at least indirectly,

[1] See below.

advantageous to the landlord also: generally speaking, rents were more regularly paid in Ulster than in the other provinces; and the value of the tenant right was a security against arrears.

Another reason for the comparative prosperity of the north was the fact that the linen industry was concentrated there. This concentration was originally due to Crommelin's choice of Lisburn as his headquarters; it continued partly because the local population took up new techniques with skill and energy, partly because the operation of the Ulster custom, giving the tenant a right of sale, meant that there was some capital in circulation, which naturally eased the way for industrial development.

The linen industry provided additional employment for cottiers and small farmers and their families, and made them less completely dependent on the land. According to Arthur Young, this division of interests had a bad effect on the quality of farming in Ulster: 'Agriculture is there in ruins; it is cut up by the root, extirpated, annihilated; the whole region is the disgrace of the kingdom'. But some allowance must be made for the exaggeration of an enthusiast; and there can be no doubt that the general standard of living was much higher in the north than elsewhere. Other travellers, less concerned about agricultural techniques, were impressed by the signs of comfort, security, and independence among the Ulster peasantry.

But though Ulster was prosperous in comparison with the rest of Ireland, the majority of the population were poorly enough off by contemporary English standards. And the linen industry was a precarious support: though the general picture is one of continuing expansion, the demand fluctuated considerably from time to time, and even a temporary decline could cause widespread hardship. Perhaps nothing indicates so clearly the unsatisfactory and uncertain basis of Ulster economic life as the stream of emigration to North America, which began about 1717 and continued unchecked until the outbreak of the American Revolution. The immediate occasion of this emigration was probably a general rise in rents, as the favourable leases granted after the Williamite wars began to fall in. It was stimulated also by the resentment of the presbyterians, who formed the bulk of the emigrants, at the legal disabilities under which they suffered. Once started, the process was self-perpetuating: those who had done well in the colonies urged their friends to follow; and the captains of trans-Atlantic ships, who had a vested interest in the 'passenger trade', conducted steady propaganda. All this, however, would probably have counted for little if conditions at home had been more comfortable. In fact, the Ulster peasant was just sufficiently better-off than his fellow in the other provinces to realize the possibility of escape. He could raise some capital by the sale of his tenant right; and even if he could not afford to pay his way, he could get a passage as an indentured servant. By the early 1770's it was reckoned that Ulster emigrants were reaching North America at the rate of 12,000 a year. They played an important part in the extension of the frontier; and since they brought with them a sense of grievance against the government their influence strengthened the growing anti-British feeling among the colonists.

The effect of emigration on Ulster itself was, in some respects as least, beneficial. It reduced the pressure on land, and it acted as a kind of safety-valve, drawing off some of the discontented elements in the population; in this way it was one of the factors that helped to keep Ulster comparatively free from agrarian disturbance.

One thing that marked Ulster off from the other provinces was the growth of a distinctive middle class. At least from the beginning of the century there was a professional nucleus for such a class in the presbyterian ministers, who had generally a much stronger local connection than the clergy of the Church of Ireland; and as the century progressed there was an increasing number of medical practitioners. The majority of both these groups went to Scotland for university education; both Glasgow and Edinburgh had large bodies of Irish students at this period, most of them Ulster presbyterians. But the professional element in the Ulster middle class soon became less important, at least numerically, than the mercantile element. The expansion of the linen industry and of the provision trade led naturally to the rise of merchants and ship-owners, and it was they who gave Ulster society its distinctive quality. This middle class was almost exclusively protestant; for though Roman Catholics formed about half the population of Ulster, they had little share in its growing prosperity. Belfast, which was rapidly rising in importance as the commercial capital of the north, contained only seven Roman Catholics in 1708; and though their numbers grew fairly quickly, they formed barely six per cent of the population of the town fifty years later. This protestant middle class of the north, unlike the Roman Catholic middle class of the south, was free to engage in politics. Its influence, which was felt both by the peasantry and by the landlords, goes far to explain the leading part taken by Ulster in the political movements of the later eighteenth century.

(7)

The country gentry of eighteenth-century Ireland have passed into popular history as they are portrayed in the pages of Sir Jonah Barrington and Miss Edgeworth; and the picture as generally received is at least as true as such pictures commonly are. Hundreds of gentlemen and half-gentlemen, however impecunious themselves, however wretched their tenants, lived lavish and riotous lives. The resident gentry, wrote a critical observer in the 1770s 'enjoy their possessions so thoroughly, and in a manner so truly Irish, that they generally become beggars in a few years' time, by dint of hospitality and inadvertence'. But even 'beggary' did not necessarily bring this gay life to an end; for the cost, in terms of money, was inconsiderable. Servants' wages were a mere trifle; provisions were produced on their own lands or obtained on credit; the universal practice of illicit distillation meant that whiskey was plentiful and cheap; smuggled brandy and claret were easily come by. To entertain their neighbours, and be entertained by them, at drinking and field-sports was almost the sum-total of their activities, and probably formed a fair index of their notions of social responsibility and public duty. But the number of those who had some more serious purpose in life was greater than the popular estimate allows. They were, for the most part, selfish and improvident landlords; their political principles were based on a determination to maintain their own rights and the protestant ascendancy; but they had some conception of a national interest, and they could occasionally be stirred to public activity that was not wholly or narrowly selfish. Left to themselves, these men would have done little for the good of the country; but it was their readiness to follow, however half-heartedly, the lead of others more public-spirited than themselves that made possible even the few feeble attempts at social reform that do something to redeem the character of the eighteenth-century gentry.

The most important of such attempts were those made in the fields of education and public health, though in neither was much success achieved. In 1733 a society was established to provide schools where the children of poor Roman Catholics would receive an industrial education and be brought up in the protestant faith. The society was at first dependent on private charity, but later received considerable state support, and its 'Charter Schools' were to be found in every part of the country. Their proselytizing purpose, however, made them hateful to the people for whose children they were intended; and though the central authorities of the society were no doubt honest and sincere, the actual management of the schools was inefficient and corrupt. The total number of pupils was never very great, and it may reasonably be doubted if such pupils as there were derived much benefit — a parliamentary inquiry of 1788 revealed that there were schools at which children had passed ten or twelve years without even learning to read.

The attempt to set up some kind of public health service, though not

particularly successful, was at least free from the grosser abuses of the
Charter Schools. Until past the middle of the century, Ireland had no provision for the sick poor, except for a small number of privately-endowed
hospitals, most of them in Dublin. An act of 1765 outlined a scheme for
the establishment of a hospital (or 'county infirmary') in every county;
the act was merely permissive, but when a county infirmary had been
established by private enterprise the government would pay £100 a year
for the salary of a surgeon, and the grand jury of the county was to make
an annual grant of not less than £50 or more than £100. Within ten
years there was an infirmary in every county except Leitrim and Waterford. Few of these infirmaries were in buildings specially erected for the
purpose; and John Howard, who visited Ireland in 1787 and 1788, gives
a miserable account of the state of some of them. But he is no less critical
of some of the English hospitals that he visited about the same time; and
at least a few of the Irish county infirmaries won his praise. Even at their
best, however, the infirmaries benefited no more than a tiny fraction of
the population: they were open only to the tenants and servants of
subscribers; they made no provision for the treatment of infectious fevers,
which were endemic in the country; and they could serve only their own
immediate neighbourhoods, for it was impracticable to convey patients
over long distances. It was not until the establishment of a dispensary
system that medical attention was made available for the population at
large; and though this system had its beginnings in the eighteenth century,
it was not organized on a national basis until the nineteenth.

   The comparative failure of these enterprises arose largely from lack of
co-operation by the country gentry, who were undoubtedly more selfish,
more negligent and more ignorant than their contemporaries in England,
or even in Scotland. But the country gentry, though they formed the
backbone of the 'protestant nation', were not the whole of it; and
eighteenth-century Ireland was not altogether lacking in social and cultural
activities of a higher order than sporting, drinking and duelling.

   These activities had their natural centre in Dublin, which now began to
take on its modern appearance. To this period belong most of the
buildings that give the city its distinctive architectural character: the
Parliament House, the Custom House, the Four Courts, much of Trinity
College, the mansions of the nobility, many of the most graceful of the
parish churches. Trinity College provided a focal point for intellectual
life; but it had no monopoly. The Philosophical Society of the 1680s had
been broken up during the Jacobite wars, and was not replaced until the
founding of the Royal Irish Academy in 1785; but many less formal
groups of scholars and dilettanti flourished during the interval; and some

of them owed little or nothing to any college connection. Francis Hutcheson, for example, the most distinguished figure in a circle of philosophers that included Lord Molesworth and Archbishop King, was the master of a dissenting academy until his appointment to the chair of moral philosophy at Glasgow in 1729. It was, however, for its interest in music and drama, rather than in the more severe intellectual disciplines, that Dublin was chiefly distinguished. The patronage of the viceregal court and of the nobility was sufficiently generous to attract many eminent musicians; Handel, for example, paid an extended visit to Dublin in 1741–2, and his 'Messiah' was first performed in the Music Hall in Fishamble Street, under his own direction, in April 1742. The theatres in Smock Alley, Aungier Street and Crow Street, though they had their ups and downs, maintained a high standard of performance; and this did not depend wholly on imported talent, for they produced many competent actors of their own, and a few of real distinction.

Yet, despite the elegance and brilliance of its society, eighteenth-century Dublin was lacking in national distinctiveness. The architect to whom it owed most, James Gandon, was an Englishman; English dramatists provided the staple of its theatre; its printing-presses were kept busy with pirated editions of English authors;[1] its concerts depended on imported musicians, and the works that they performed were those of foreign composers. In large part, no doubt, this state of affairs is to be explained by the dependence of Ireland upon England; but Dublin ranked far below Edinburgh, with which it seems fair to compare it, as a literary and intellectual centre, and Trinity College, though not without academic distinction, never enjoyed the great prestige of Edinburgh University. Ireland seems to have suffered even more than Scotland from the attractive power of England. Just as men of fortune were drawn across the channel by the superiority of English society, so also men of ability, with their fortunes to make, were drawn by the greater opportunities of London. Burke and Goldsmith are only the most famous of a long line of Irish writers who saw no prospect of pushing their fortunes at home; and there were many actors as well as Peg Woffington and James Quin who laid the foundations of a reputation in Smock Alley and then sought the greater glories of Drury Lane. There was at least some basis for Dr Johnson's rather contemptuous comment that Dublin was only an inferior London.

Outside Dublin, the cultural life of the 'protestant nation' found expression in country houses and provincial towns. Though so many of the resident gentry were ignorant and brutal, there were among the great

---

[1] The English copyright laws did not extend to Ireland.

landlords and the higher clergy some men of cultivated taste who wished to reproduce at home the style of living with which they had become familiar in England or on the continent. Castletown House, begun in 1722 by William Conolly, speaker of the house of commons and one of the richest men in Ireland, set an example of magnificence that was followed in many parts of the country. The duke of Leinster's seat at Carton, the marquis of Waterford's at Curraghmore, Lord Belmore's at Castle Coole, and many others, could vie with the great country houses of the English nobility; and their owners lived much the same sort of life — they made the Grand Tour, they collected books, pictures and sculpture, they organized private theatricals. But though some of them took an interest in Irish antiquities, and patronized the few remaining Gaelic bards and harpers, their connection with the life of the countryside was even more tenuous than that of the corresponding class in England.

The culture of the provincial towns, though more genuinely rooted in local society, was a feeble enough growth. Cork, Galway, Kilkenny and Limerick had permanent theatres, and other towns were visited from time to time by companies of players on tour. Most towns of any size had 'assembly rooms', where there were regular dances and occasional concerts. There were numerous spas — Mallow (the 'Irish Bath'), Lucan, Swanlinbar, Ballynahinch and others — frequented by those who did not choose, or could not afford, to make a journey to England. Local newspapers began to appear early in the century, and by 1750 there was a flourishing provincial press. But it was only in the north, where the Scottish and presbyterian influence was strong, that there was much sign of intellectual life. Belfast, the capital of Ulster presbyterianism, had a printing-press as early as the 1690s, at a time when there was hardly a printer in England north of the Trent, and the volume of production grew during the eighteenth century. The Belfast printers were mainly employed on religious works — Bibles (by arrangement with the king's printers in Dublin), presbyterian catechisms, psalm-books and sermons. But they produced also a great many controversial pamphlets, a few short-lived periodicals (other than newspapers) and occasionally works of literature — in 1714, for example, James Blow, most famous of early Belfast printers, published an edition of the works of David Lindsay.

Ulster's close connection with the universities of Glasgow and Edinburgh no doubt helped to keep intellectual activity alive. But the presbyterian leaders were dissatisfied that candidates for the ministry could not receive their training at home, and tried to provide at least part of it in 'philosophy schools', the earliest of which was one established at Killyleagh, County Down, in the 1690s. Before the end of the eighteenth century the desire for a centre of clerical education had broadened into a demand for a university in the north; and though this demand was not to be satisfied, even in part, until the following century, it indicates the growing influence of an intelligent middle class whose interests were not confined to agriculture and commerce.

Though there were some protestant landlords and protestant scholars who interested themselves in Irish antiquities and the Irish language, it was among the Roman Catholic masses that the tradition of Gaelic culture survived. But though it survived, it underwent a transformation, for it lost the aristocratic patronage on which it had formerly flourished. The older nobility and gentry, Gaelic and Anglo-Norman, had been almost extinguished by the Revolution settlement. Of those that remained, some sank under the pressure of the penal laws; some conformed to the established church and became merged with the new English aristocracy; the most enterprising, unable to make a career at home, took service abroad. For a century after the treaty of Limerick the 'flight of the Wild Geese' carried off from Ireland hundreds of men of birth and ability, to fight for France, or for Spain, or for the emperor, and to maintain on many a foreign field the struggle against England that had been so disastrously lost at home. Deprived of their traditional patrons, the Gaelic poets gradually abandoned the older and more complicated forms of courtly verse; and the characteristic poems of the eighteenth century are popular in form and content. But they still kept alive the memory of past struggles, and nourished the hope of a future resurrection of vanished glories. Even under the triumphant and arrogant sway of the protestant Anglo-Irish, there survived a 'hidden Ireland' of Gaelic legend and folk-lore, resentful of an alien culture, and filled with half-understood aspirations that were yet to exercise a potent influence on the course of Irish history.

X

The Rise of the Patriots

(1)

The violence and extent of the opposition to Wood's patent had startled the British ministers, but nothing had alarmed them so much as the reluctance of highly-placed officials, including even the lords justices, to support government policy. The fact that these recalcitrant officials were men of Irish birth gave force to a complaint made by the lord lieutenant, Grafton, in 1723, that too many 'natives' had been appointed to high office, 'which has been attended with very mischievous consequences to the English interest'. When an opportunity occurred, in the following year, of strengthening English influence, it was eagerly taken. In July 1724 the archbishopric of Armagh fell vacant by the death of Thomas Lindsay, a charitable nonentity; and before the end of the month Hugh Boulter, bishop of Bristol, had been chosen, at Townshend's suggestion, to succeed him. In one sense, there was nothing new or startling in this appointment; Lindsay and his immediate predecessor had both been Englishmen, though they had resided a long time in Ireland and had held other offices before being appointed to Armagh. But in 1724 Irish opinion was strongly convinced that the primacy should and would be offered to William King, archbishop of Dublin, an Irishman and a stalwart supporter of the Irish interest; and the fact that King was passed over in favour of an Englishman made the government more unpopular than ever.

Boulter had accepted the primacy with reluctance; but he amply fulfilled the purpose for which he had been sent to Ireland. From the time of his arrival, in November 1724, he set himself 'to serve his majesty and my country' by a relentless subordination of all other considerations to the strengthening of English influence. In this he proved so efficient that the British ministers came to rely more and more on his judgement; and after Carteret's recall in 1730 he was the principal agent of their Irish policy.

Boulter himself originated little; but within the limits imposed by his belief that the interests of Ireland must always be postponed to those of England he tried to see that the kingdom was well governed. He had a genuine sympathy for the sufferings of the poor; he expended large sums in private charity, especially during the famine years 1740–1; and he promoted legislation for the increase of tillage. His most constant concern, however, was to maintain the English interest by securing the appointment of Englishmen to influential posts. In January 1725, before he had been two months in the country, he wrote to inform Newcastle that the archbishop of Dublin was very ill, and to insist that 'his majesty's service absolutely requires that, whenever he drops, the place be filled with an Englishman, and one with whom I may hope to have a very good agreement'. The letter is typical of the voluminous correspondence that Boulter maintained with British ministers for almost twenty years. Upon the mere rumour that a bishop or a judge was ill he would write hastily into England, warning the government there of the danger of appointing a 'native', and suggesting suitable candidates. In the choice of bishops, it was not enough that they should be Englishmen, they must be such Englishmen as would follow Boulter's lead; for his control of the house of lords depended on having a solid body of episcopal votes. Public opinion could not be completely ignored; some promotion had to be left open to Irishmen; and at the time of Boulter's death, in 1742, they still occupied eleven of the twenty-two sees. But the English influence on the bench was stronger than these figures would suggest: the essential condition of further promotion was submission to court leadership, and few of the Irish-born bishops were prepared to risk their chances by going into opposition.

(2)

The practice of bringing over Englishmen to fill important posts, though it gradually strengthened the English interest in the general administration of the kingdom, did nothing to assist in the management of the house of commons, which was the government's most urgent problem in the 1720s. It even made the problem more difficult, for the commons were apt to grumble when Irishmen were passed over for appointments. In time, Boulter himself came to realize the need for caution and conciliation; on at least one occasion he modified his proposals about a vacant bishopric to avoid complaints in the house; and in distributing minor church patronage he had an eye to placating influential members. But the more immediate effect of his appointment and his policy was to give the opposition fresh ground for complaint.

It was an opposition that, in any case, was in no mood to be easily conciliated. Carteret soon found that the government's surrender over Wood's patent, in September 1725, did not mean the end of his parliamentary troubles. Suspicion and unrest survived; and during the remainder of the session he was unable to command a majority. But the dissolution on the death of George I, in June 1727, brought him some relief. The fragmentary groups that made up the opposition had no leader able to take advantage of the general election that followed; and the first session of the new parliament (November–December 1727) passed off to the government's satisfaction. The former speaker, William Conolly, had been unanimously re-elected; and the success of the session was very largely due to the fact that Carteret had trusted him with the management of the house. Conolly had a strong parliamentary following of his own, and was able to extend his influence by means of the considerable share of patronage that was put in his hands; attempts to build up an opposition got little support, and government control of the house was never in doubt.

Conolly's importance was strikingly shown by the difficulties that followed his sudden illness and death at the beginning of the autumn session of 1729. The new speaker, Sir Ralph Gore, was the lord lieutenant's candidate; but he was not at once able to fill Conolly's place as a parliamentary manager. The result was an immediate increase in the strength of the opposition; and when a storm blew up in December over a money bill that had been altered in England, it took all Carteret's efforts to avoid defeat. Gore's influence became stronger as time went on, but he died in February 1733, before he had time to establish himself firmly; and Dorset, who had succeeded Carteret as lord lieutenant in 1730, had to make fresh provision for the management of the house.

The two main candidates for the speakership were Henry Boyle and Henry Singleton, and it was generally believed that whichever could win the support of the lord lieutenant would prevail. Singleton, who was prime serjeant,[1] and a steady supporter of the government, seemed to have a better claim than Boyle, who had hitherto acted with the opposition. But Boyle had a numerous following of his own, and powerful allies in the house; and he was prepared to come to terms with the lord lieutenant. Dorset decided, after some hesitation, that he was the more likely of the two to control the house effectively, and declared in his favour. Singleton

---

[1] In Ireland, as in England, the serjeants-at-law formed a superior order of barristers. The title 'prime serjeant', given to the first in rank among them, was peculiar to Ireland.

thereupon withdrew his candidature; Boyle was elected unopposed; and shortly afterwards his alliance with the government was sealed by his appointment as chancellor of the exchequer.[1] His influence, temporarily shaken by this change of front, soon revived and increased; for the next twenty years he and his allies dominated the house of commons and played a considerable part in the government of the country.

This practice of entrusting the management of the house of commons to a group of politicians, who were rewarded with lucrative offices and a share of patronage, was continued by successive lord lieutenants down to the late 1760s. As a method of government it developed almost necessarily from the fact that the lord lieutenant was normally non-resident. Coming over, as he did, only for sessions of parliament, he lacked both the knowledge and the personal connections that he would have needed if he were to manage the house of commons himself; and he had to rely very much on the advice and assistance of others in collecting a government party, which was generally his first task on arrival. During the first two decades of the century, though there were occasional crises, this *ad hoc* method of dealing with parliament worked fairly well; but by the late 1720s it was clear that some more permanent arrangement was called for. The struggle over Wood's patent showed the instability of the executive's control of the commons — and this at the very time when circumstances were making it more dependent on parliamentary supply, partly because of the increased cost of administration, partly because the accumulation of a national debt brought with it the necessity for imposing regular 'loan duties', beginning in 1729, to meet the interest. Thus parliament was acquiring greater importance — an importance of which the magnificent new parliament house, opened in 1729, was an outward symbol.

It was this growing importance of parliament that produced the necessity for more effective government control of the house of commons; but it would be wrong to suppose that there was any deliberate or conscious adoption of a new policy. The speaker had always been expected to support the government (though he had not always done so), and Carteret certainly did not regard his arrangements with Conolly and Gore as departures from precedent. Dorset's understanding with Boyle was rather different; but to contemporaries it seemed just another example of the traditional practice of buying off an opposition leader by appointing him to office. The significant thing was that the relationship, once established, was allowed to continue. Neither Conolly nor Gore

---

[1] The post was at this time a sinecure, and Boyle held it along with the speakership.

had lived long enough to establish his power fully, but Boyle and his friends became the permanent managers of the house of commons; and since the speaker was always included in the commission of lords justices (a practice that Boulter thought dangerous), their power was not confined to the parliamentary session.

The influence of these parliamentary managers (nicknamed 'undertakers' since they 'undertook' to see government business through the house of commons) was partly personal, based on borough interest and family connections, and partly derived from their control of patronage. By the end of Dorset's viceroyalty, in 1737, they had made themselves almost indispensable; and in time they became so powerful that instead of being the agents of the lord lieutenant they were able to dictate to him. This paradoxical state of affairs was possible only because of the attitude of British ministers, who cared little about the government of Ireland provided it went on quietly. The lord lieutenancy, though a post of dignity and profit, was regarded as of small political significance, and was commonly used as a means of shelving a discarded colleague who could not be dropped completely, or of giving some impecunious nobleman a chance to repair his fortunes. 'The indigence of Ireland', wrote Lord Charlemont in his memoirs, 'was considered as the appropriated fund to compensate the losses of the gaming-table'. A lord lieutenant so appointed could not count on any backing from England if he quarrelled with the undertakers, whose agents and allies in London were always alert to warn the government there of the danger of stirring up trouble in the Irish parliament. Boulter, who might, perhaps, have curbed the rising power of the undertakers, did not concern himself directly with the management of the house of commons, nor did they constitute an obvious threat to the English interest until after his death. Chesterfield, the only lord lieutenant of the period who had the vigour and the courage to try to keep the undertakers in their place, held office for only a year and a half, and spent less than eight months in Ireland. Boyle was thus left free to consolidate his position, and the possibility of challenging him successfully diminished with every year that passed.

(3)

The main business of the undertakers was to ensure the passage of money bills and to stifle complaints about the expenditure of previous grants, and in this way they were generally successful. But they did not eliminate all opposition in the house of commons. Indeed, the very fact that the conduct of government business, with the accompanying rewards, had been handed over to one group of politicians meant that other groups were excluded; these groups naturally showed their resentment by opposition, and sometimes so effectively that one or more of them had to be taken into partnership.

Among the opposition members were some who particularly distinguished themselves by their insistence on the constitutional rights of Ireland and their denunciation of what they regarded as English encroachments. They were commonly called the 'patriots', a term that occurs in this sense at least as early as the 1720s. The patriots did not form a coherent group, they had no regular leader, and no fixed policy. The number of members who appeared as active patriots, never very large, fluctuated from session to session: they might be joined by a disappointed aspirant for office, or deserted by a former supporter who now wanted a deanery for his son-in-law or a pair of colours for his nephew. Their importance was, however, greater than their numbers would suggest: they kept alive the tradition of constitutional resistance to the British ministry; and on specific issues they could sometimes attract widespread support in the house. When this happened the undertakers might find their control seriously threatened; but such occasions were infrequent, and until the 1750s the patriots made little progress in parliament.

In the meantime, however, the principles professed by the patriots were beginning to gain wider currency among the protestant population as a whole. The most important figure in this movement was Charles Lucas — the 'Wilkes of Ireland' — a Dublin apothecary, who first acquired fame by his attacks on the administration of the city, and then turned to national politics. In 1747 he began publication of a weekly paper, the *Citizen's Journal*, in which he denounced English restrictions on Irish trade and asserted the constitutional rights of Ireland as a separate kingdom. Two years later he offered himself as a candidate for parliament at a Dublin by-election, and would probably have been successful; but before the election took place, the house of commons was induced to declare him an enemy of the country, and he went into exile to avoid arrest. But his ideas could not be banished with him; and it was not long before the growing patriot sentiment in the country had its effect in parliament also.

This development was hastened by rivalries among the undertakers themselves. By the 1740s they were divided into two main groups, which, though they combined to keep control of affairs, were bitterly jealous of each other. The more important of the two was that led by the speaker, Henry Boyle, who still had chief responsibility for the management of government business in the house of commons; but the other, led by John Ponsonby, son of Lord Bessborough, was steadily increasing its influence; and a change in the primacy made it more powerful still. John

Hoadly, who had succeeded Boulter in 1742, had favoured Boyle, with whom he was allied by marriage; but when Hoadly died in 1747 he was succeeded by George Stone, a firm ally of Ponsonby. Stone had come to Ireland as a protégé of Dorset, and had been advanced so rapidly in the church that he was barely forty when he attained the primacy. He was not content to be, like Boulter, the agent and adviser of the British government, but wanted political power for himself; to this end he bent all his very considerable abilities, and his chance of success was increased by the fact that his brother, Andrew, was under-secretary of state in England and the confidant of the duke of Newcastle. By joining his own influence with that of the Ponsonby faction he hoped to oust Boyle from the speakership, instal Ponsonby in his place, and then, in alliance with him, take over the management of the house of commons.

Stone did not at once reveal his ambitions, and he maintained outward friendship with Boyle. But in 1751 the time for decisive action seemed to have come: Dorset, Stone's old patron, was reappointed lord lieutenant, and brought as secretary his third son, Lord George Sackville, who was tone's closest friend. Dorset had been instructed by the English ministers 'to bring back the administration to the Castle' — that is, to re-establish the direct influence of the lord lieutenant in place of that of the undertakers. Later events suggest that this instruction was not very seriously intended; but it opened the way for Stone to represent his attack upon Boyle as a defence of the English interest and the rights of the lord lieutenant. Boyle now realized his danger, and saw that the only way to defend his position was to show that even against the combined forces of Stone and Ponsonby, even against the influence of the lord lieutenant himself, he could still command a majority in the house of commons. The clash did not come at once, for both sides were feeling their way; the session of 1751–2 ended peacefully; and when, in May, Dorset left for England, Boyle was, as usual, appointed one of the lords justices. But by September 1753, when Dorset returned, Boyle had chosen his ground and was ready to fight.

He had deliberately decided to stand on an issue that was bound to arouse popular enthusiasm, for it involved the commons' control over finance. In 1751 there had been a surplus in the treasury, and the commons had prepared heads of a bill applying it to the reduction of the national debt; when the bill came back from England it was found that a clause had been inserted in the preamble, declaring the king's previous consent to this allocation, thus maintaining the argument of the British ministers that the surplus belonged not to the nation but to the crown. Despite this alteration, the bill passed quietly; but now, in 1753, when there was again a surplus, Boyle and his party resolved to assert the rights of the house of commons. As before, heads of a bill were drawn up, applying the surplus to the reduction of the national debt; the lord lieutenant's demand that the king's previous consent should be mentioned in the preamble was rejected; and when the bill came back from England with the consent clause inserted it was, after a great struggle, defeated.

To begin with, the British ministry seemed determined to support the authority of the lord lieutenant; and leading place-holders who had helped to defeat the bill were dismissed, Boyle himself being deprived of the chancellorship of the exchequer. It now seemed almost inevitable that Stone and Ponsonby, though defeated in the commons, should succeed to the influence with government that Boyle and his allies had forfeited. But their position was not so strong as might appear. Dublin had gone mad with delight at the defeat of the money bill: 'The ladies made balls, the mobs bonfires, the poets joyous odes'; and the dismissal from office of those who had voted against the bill turned them into martyrs, who were toasted in popular assemblies from one end of the country to the other. In face of these demonstrations, opinion in England began to waver. George II wanted to be assured that the policy of dismissals would result in a parliamentary majority for government; Pelham's death, in 1754, meant the temporary ascendancy of Newcastle, who had always doubted the wisdom of strong measures; and Henry Fox, who now entered the cabinet as secretary of state, had close associations with the Boyle party, and was deeply suspicious of Stone — 'a false, artful, meddling priest'.

It was not long before the new ministry resolved on conciliation. In April 1755 Hartington (who became fourth duke of Devonshire before the end of the year) replaced Dorset as lord lieutenant, and a few weeks later he arrived in Ireland, with instructions to make peace. Terms were soon arranged. Boyle agreed to give up the speakership in return for a pension and an earldom, and the other dismissed office-holders were suitably compensated. Ponsonby succeeded Boyle as speaker; but feeling against Stone was so strong that it was thought wiser to drop him for the time being, and when Devonshire returned to England in May 1756 he was not included in the commission of lords justices.

It was supposed in England that this settlement had restored the authority of the lord lieutenant; but in fact the position was not essentially different from what it had been before the crisis over the money bill arose. Boyle (or Lord Shannon, as he now was) still controlled a large party in the house of commons. Ponsonby's influence had been increased by his appointment as speaker. Stone was too able to be long excluded from political power. In the viceroyalty of Bedford, who succeeded Devonshire in January 1757, these three made up their quarrel and once more combined their forces; having thus gained control of the house of commons they were able to impose their will on the lord lieutenant, who found (in the words of Chief Justice Bowes) that 'he may parade, but must submit'. Despite the vigour of Dorset and the diplomacy of Devonshire, it was clear that, without a resident lord lieutenant, government could not be carried on except through parliamentary undertakers.

The popular enthusiasm for Boyle and his friends changed to execration when it was known that they had made terms with the government. But the dispute that they had precipitated for their own selfish ends is nevertheless a landmark in the development of a more genuine patriot movement. The principles laid down in 1753, though soon deserted by many of those who professed them, made a permanent impression on the public mind. Dubliners burned Boyle in effigy, but they did not abandon their attachment to the rights of the Irish parliament; when a rumour circulated in 1759 that there was to be a parliamentary union with Great Britain, a furious crowd invaded the house of commons and compelled members to swear that they would oppose any such measure. The views of the Dublin mob were less violently, but no less strongly, held by an increasing body of responsible citizens throughout the country. The money-bill dispute had, as Lord Charlemont put it, taught Irishmen to think; it had taught them that 'Ireland had, or ought to have, a constitution'; it had taught them that it was possible to defeat the government. And these were lessons that they did not forget.

The house of commons, unrepresentative though it was, could not be wholly uninfluenced by the state of feeling in the country. The claim to dispose of surplus revenue was allowed to lapse; but it was not formally abandoned, and the house made sure that the issue did not arise again by increasing its grants to public bodies to such an extent that any possible surplus was absorbed in advance. Members were increasingly reluctant to identify themselves with unpopular causes; and though the undertakers remained in control, they found themselves obliged to take note of opinion outside as well as inside parliament. Thus, conditions were more favourable than ever before for the emergence of a patriot party, genuinely devoted to the establishment of Ireland's constitutional rights.

(4)

The spread of patriot sentiment through the country at large was not due to the emergence of any new issues, for the constitutional position had not changed. It resulted rather from the growth, slow as it was, of a commercial middle class, among whom political information and political ideas were diffused by an increasing stream of pamphlets and newspapers. The Irish economy was still precarious. The revenue-surpluses of 1751 and 1753 were followed by a period of scarcity and depression. In the summer of 1756 Belfast was disturbed by a starving mob in search of meal; in 1757 the government had to make an extraordinary grant of £20,000 for the relief of poverty; in 1759 three of the principal banks in Dublin stopped payment. But despite such set-backs, some branches of trade, in particular the export of linen and provisions, were expanding; and those engaged in them, as their wealth increased, became more anxious for a share in the political life of the country. It was natural that they should favour the patriots, whose attempts to weaken the dependence of Ireland upon England had often been associated with attacks on the commercial restrictions under which Irish manufacturers and merchants had so long suffered.

This interest in politics was most active among protestants; for the Roman Catholics, who formed an important element in the new middle class, could not hope for any immediate share of political power. But their position was in other respects improving. The laws against Roman Catholic education, against bishops and regular clergy, against unregistered priests, were increasingly ignored. Protestants in general were not yet ready to have these laws repealed, but neither did they want to see them strictly enforced. This more tolerant attitude no doubt reflected the spirit of the age; but it reflected also the protestants' growing sense of security; the Roman Catholics now seemed reconciled to the existing régime: in 1715 and 1745 they had remained passive; in 1759, at the height of the Seven Years' War, they had shown their positive sympathy with the British cause by addresses to the lord lieutenant expressing their loyalty to the crown; and on the outbreak of war with Spain, a few years later, the bishops instructed their people to pray for a British victory.

This reassurance was all the more welcome as it coincided with a projected French invasion. Hawke's victory at Quiberon Bay, in November 1759, frustrated the main design; but Thurot, with a small expeditionary force, escaped the vigilance of the British fleet, and captured Carrickfergus in February 1760. The countryside at once rose in arms against him, and thousands of volunteers flocked to defend Belfast. Thurot, seeing that the position was hopeless, withdrew his forces; only to be met and defeated by a British squadron. Throughout the whole of Ireland, not the slightest sign of sympathy with the invader appeared.

Considering all these circumstances, it is hardly surprising that protestants, having ceased to consider the Roman Catholics as dangerous, should come to regard them as fellow-countrymen, necessarily excluded, indeed, from full rights of citizenship, but nevertheless sharing a common interest in the welfare of Ireland. Thus old divisions based on religious differences tended to fall into the background, and the test of a man's political allegiance was now to be found in the issues brought forward by the patriots. It was a development that might well seem ominous to the English interest: in February 1761 Lord Chancellor Bowes wrote apprehensively to George Dodington, 'formerly protestant or papist were the key words; they are now court or country, referring still to constitutional grievances'.

(5)

For more than ten years after Devonshire's settlement of the money-bill dispute in 1756 the house of commons continued to be managed by undertakers. But during this period there was a gradual change in the character of Irish political life, due largely to the growing influence of public opinion. This was strikingly shown in the general election that followed the dissolution of parliament brought about by George II's death in October 1760. It was more than thirty years since there had been a general election in Ireland, and all over the country supporters of the patriots seized the opportunity of expressing their political views. There was no revolt against the traditional influence of patrons in boroughs or of the great landlords in the counties; but associations of voters passed resolutions and presented addresses in favour of popular measures, and in many constituencies were strong enough to oblige candidates to pledge their support for them. If the house of commons that assembled in October 1761 differed little in character from its predecessor, it was at least much more actively aware of the temper of the country.

It was in this parliament that Henry Flood established himself as leader of the patriots, for though first elected in 1759 he had kept in the background until he should grow familiar with the procedure of the house and accustomed to its tone. Flood was the eldest son of the chief justice of the king's bench, he was heir to great estates in County Kilkenny, where his family had been established since the seventeenth century, and by his marriage with Lady Frances Beresford he enlarged his fortune and allied himself with one of the most powerful connections in Ireland; he had the advantage, also, of some acquaintance with the leading political figures in England, where he spent much of his time between his twentieth and twenty-seventh years. These were ample qualifications for a parliamentary career; but it was his natural eloquence, corrected by a patient study of the

Greek and Roman orators, and attuned to the mood of the audience by his experience as an amateur actor, that gave Flood a dominant position in the house of commons. In such an assembly, so little subject to the discipline of regular party divisions, oratory was an important weapon; and though a powerful opposition speech might not often lead to a government defeat, it could greatly increase the labour of holding the majority together. Flood lacked the lighter oratorical graces; but his mastery of constitutional and financial detail and his power of sustaining an elaborate argument made him a formidable opponent. His eloquent championship of the patriot cause, supported as it was by popular feeling in the country, greatly enhanced its prestige, and helped to prepare the way for a spectacular if delusive victory. Though it can hardly be doubted that Flood's patriotism was genuine, there was in his character a strong admixture of vanity, which sometimes impaired his judgement, and was later to lead him into an apparent desertion of his principles. But for the first fifteen years of George III's reign he was the popular hero of the patriots, both inside and outside parliament.

Flood's principal allies in the house of commons were Charles Lucas, now returned from exile and one of the members for the city of Dublin, and Sir William Osborne, a country gentleman whose conduct as a landlord earned the rare approval of Arthur Young. In the house of lords the most enthusiastic patriot, Lord Charlemont, was an ineffective speaker, but he used all his political influence in Ireland and England on behalf of his 'dearest, dear Flood'. There was still no patriot party, properly so called, but there was at least some measure of agreement among these men, and those who supported them, as to the measures to be pressed for — limitation of the life of parliament by a septennial act, reduction of the pension list, establishment of a national militia, a *habeas corpus* act, security of tenure for the judges. And behind these detailed proposals lay the less clearly defined aim of establishing the position and rights of Ireland as a distinct kingdom.

So long as the undertakers remained in firm control of the house of commons not much of this patriot programme was likely to be achieved. But during the 1760s a new and decisive conflict between the undertakers and the British ministry broke out, and led to a permanent change in the method, though not the spirit, of parliamentary management. The beginning of this conflict can be traced to December 1764, when Primate Stone and Lord Shannon died within a few days of one another. Both were, at the time, lords justices, and by their deaths the remaining lord justice (John Ponsonby, speaker of the house of commons) was left in sole charge. It was therefore necessary to make further provision for the government of Ireland until the lord lieutenant should return; and this was done in February 1765 by the appointment of Bowes, the chancellor, as a lord justice. There may, perhaps, have been some significance in this passing over of Irish politicians in favour of an English-born official, but another decision of the British ministers, taken at the same time, was of far greater importance — they advised the king that the next lord lieutenant should be obliged to reside in Ireland throughout his term of office. This was a direct threat to the undertakers: not only would a resident lord lieutenant have much more influence in the government, but since there would no longer be any need for the regular appointment of lords justices the undertakers would lose both power and profit.

The fulfilment of this threat was, however, delayed by the difficulty of finding a suitable English nobleman who was prepared to live in Ireland. Lord Weymouth, appointed in June 1765, did not come over at all; his successor, the marquis of Hertford, was apparently appointed as a stop-gap to conduct the parliamentary session of 1765–6, after which he was allowed to return to England. The appointment of the earl of Bristol, in October 1766, seemed, at first, likely to mark the beginning of the new policy, and reports reaching Dublin that the king had instructed him to reside permanently caused alarm among the undertakers and their allies. It is indicative of the rising importance of the patriots that the British ministry tried to secure Flood's support for the new viceroy in advance, and he had an inconclusive interview with Lord Chatham at Bath. But these preparations came to nothing, for Bristol, like Weymouth, resigned before coming to Ireland. His brief tenure of office is memorable only because it enabled him to secure the appointment of his brother to the bishopric of Cloyne and then to that of Derry, thus introducing into Irish life one of the most eccentric and colourful characters of the eighteenth century. Bristol was lord lieutenant for less than a year. In August 1767 he was succeeded by Lord Townshend, elder brother of the more famous Charles, to whose influence he owed his appointment. He reached Dublin in the following October, and remained in Ireland for over five years.

Townshend was a soldier, with little experience of civil administration. But his frank manner and convivial habits made him, at first, very acceptable in Dublin society; and his popularity increased when it was known that he came authorized to promise some important concessions, including a restriction of the pension list, and bills for limiting the life of parliament and securing the tenure of the judges. It was hoped in England that these concessions, together with the effect of his continued residence, would enable him to break the power of the parliamentary managers and 'bring back the administration to the Castle'.

At this time, three men exercised between them a dominant influence in the house of commons: Ponsonby, the speaker, who controlled the extensive influence of the revenue board, the second Lord Shannon, who had inherited his father's borough interest, and John Hely-Hutchinson, prime serjeant since 1760. Hely-Hutchinson was a comparative new-comer to politics, who owed his rise to ability rather than to wealth or family connection. Even in the eighteenth century his shameless place-hunting was remarkable: 'If you gave him Great Britain and Ireland for a demesne', said Lord North, 'he would ask for the Isle of Man as a potato-garden'. But his skill as a parliamentarian made him a valuable ally and a dangerous foe.

During the first few weeks of the session Townshend's relations with these three were friendly but indefinite; though he treated them with confidence, and consulted them, along with other officials, about government business in parliament, there was no proposal, on either side, for an explicit 'undertaking'. But by early December he thought it necessary to try to come to terms with them. The commons, encouraged by his promises, had passed heads of a septennial bill, a *habeas corpus* bill, and a bill for securing the tenure of the judges, and these had been sent to England. The delay in returning them was causing great uneasiness, and there were threats of voting supplies for three months only. Besides this, Townshend had been instructed to secure parliament's consent to an augmentation of the Irish army from 12,000 to 15,235 men, a measure likely to be unpopular both because of the expense and because such a large proportion of the Irish army was habitually employed abroad.

It was in these circumstances that Townshend approached Ponsonby, Shannon and Hely-Hutchinson. In return for certain favours for themselves, and a share in the disposal of patronage, they promised to manage the ordinary business of government, but added that the passage of a bill for the augmentation of the army would require additional support, including that of some popular speakers, especially Flood and Sir William Osborne. But when Townshend submitted these terms to the British ministry they were rejected; and he had to face the prospect of having all the influence of the would-be undertakers used against him. He could still count on a section of the place-holders, who refused to follow Ponsonby and his friends into opposition, and he had some support among independent members; but when parliament re-assembled after the Christmas recess he found the opposition in control of the house, and could only report to England that 'it is impossible to be answerable for what may happen'.

His position was relieved somewhat by the return, in February 1768, of the bill for the limitation of the life of parliament. It had been altered by the council from a septennial to an octennial bill; but no exception was taken in Ireland to this change and it was readily passed by both houses. According to some contemporaries, most members of the house of commons really detested this measure, which compelled them to face the risk and expense of frequent elections, and had put it forward only because it was popular in the country, while secretly hoping that it would be quashed in England. But none of this appeared on the surface; its passage was accompanied by great public rejoicing, and the British ministry urged Townshend to take the opportunity of pressing on with the augmentation bill.

Townshend himself favoured delay. The octennial act provided for a speedy dissolution of the present parliament, and he thought that the augmentation bill would have more chance of success after the election. But the British ministry was anxious to have the matter settled at once; troops were needed for overseas garrisons, any increase of the British standing army would be very unpopular, and the most obvious resource was to put the burden on Ireland. Townshend, under instructions from England, laid the proposal before the house of commons in April; Ponsonby, Shannon and Hely-Hutchinson, with other important office-holders, exerted all their influence against it, and the proposal was rejected on 2 May.

The opposition leaders no doubt expected that the pattern of the 1750s would repeat itself, and that they would eventually be bought off with places and pensions. Townshend, fearing that this would happen, warned the ministry that such measures would be fatal, and insisted that now was the time to break the power of the oligarchy that had for so long domi-nated Irish government. But the ministry was, as always, reluctant to authorize wholesale dismissals, and preferred to keep things as they were until the new parliament should meet. Townshend set to work to build up a government party; but while so many influential posts were held by the opposition, and while the extent of the support that he could count on from England was so uncertain, his task was almost impossible. When parliament met, in October 1769, the opposition had a decided majority. But this majority was unstable; its numerical strength depended on the discontented office-holders, who still hoped to recover control of the administration; and though determined to show their power, they had no desire for a final breach with the lord lieutenant.

Their conduct during the session reflected this attitude. They rejected again, and by a greatly increased majority, the proposed augmentation of the army; they attacked the pension list; they brought in heads of a militia bill; and on 21 November they defeated a government supply bill.

As was usual when a new parliament was to meet, the Irish council had prepared a supply bill in advance; and though such a bill had been passed without difficulty in 1761, the government, knowing the temper of the house, probably expected its defeat in 1769. But the majority went further; following the example of the commons in 1692 they passed a resolution that the bill was rejected because it had not taken its rise in the house. Hely-Hutchinson, who had hitherto supported Ponsonby and Shannon, judged more accurately than they the extent to which it was safe to press the government, and changed sides on this resolution. The others, having demonstrated their power, were prepared to be conciliatory; they brought in and passed heads of a supply bill identical with that which had been rejected, and they approved the augmentation of the army. But it was now too late. The Irish commons had defied the prerogative, the dependence of Ireland upon England was threatened, and the British ministry was converted to Townshend's view that rebellious office-holders must be punished.

This decision was concealed until the supplies had been voted; but once this was done Townshend, on 26 December 1769, made a formal protest, as Sydney had done in 1692, against the commons' claim to initiate all money bills. He then prorogued parliament, which did not meet again until February 1771.

The opposition was now to feel the weight of the ministry's resentment. Ponsonby was dismissed from the revenue board, and Shannon from the mastership of the ordnance. Both of them, with half-a-dozen other opposition leaders, were removed from the privy council, and a host of their supporters lost places and pensions. The places thus vacated went to reward the friends of government, and when they proved insufficient new posts were created and new pensions granted. In this way the opposition was undermined; when parliament reassembled in February 1771 the government was clearly in control of the house of commons, and Ponsonby, quickly aware of his helplessness, resigned the speakership. As Townshend reported gleefully to England, 'Government had fairly driven him out of the field'. When Townshend gave up office in November 1772 he could claim that the power of the old oligarchy had been broken, and that direct control of the administration was now in the hands of the lord lieutenant.

Townshend's lord lieutenancy marked an epoch in the history of the patriot movement. So long as government could rely on undertakers to manage the house of commons the true nature of the constitutional conflict between Ireland and Great Britain was obscured. It was so much mixed up in the squabbles of rival groups of self-seeking politicians that the issues seldom stood out clearly. Once the Castle became the real centre of power, exercising a direct control over government supporters in the house, the way was open for a straight trial of strength. Such a trial might, however, have been long delayed, or even averted altogether, but for two other circumstances. The octennial act greatly increased the influence of public opinion, for despite all its imperfections as a representative assembly the house of commons was inevitably affected by the prospect of regularly-recurring general elections. It was even more important that these changes coincided with the opening of a decisive stage in the constitutional conflict between Great Britain and her American colonies. The parallel was too close to be missed; Irishmen, stimulated by American example and alarmed at the claims of the British parliament, resolved to assert their own rights in unmistakable fashion before it was too late.

These developments could hardly have been foreseen in 1772. For the next few years, indeed, government went on smoothly enough. Townshend's conduct had made him very unpopular, and he was violently attacked in a series of lampoons. But these expressed hatred of the man, not of the office; his successor, Harcourt, was well received; the constitutional questions so recently agitated were allowed to fall into the background; and the house of commons showed a general disposition to make things easy for the new lord lieutenant. One important issue did arise during Harcourt's first year of office — a proposal to lay a tax of two shillings in the pound on the rents of absentee proprietors. This was strongly opposed in England by a group of great landlords with estates on both sides of the channel. They enlisted the powerful support of Edmund Burke, and threatened to bring parliamentary pressure on the ministry to prohibit the imposition of any such tax. But Harcourt persuaded North that the state of popular feeling in Ireland made it essential that the decision should be left to the Irish house of commons. Here the measure was defeated, after long debate, in November 1773, partly by the influence of the absentee borough-owners, partly out of fear that it would open the way for a general land-tax, partly in the well-grounded belief that the Castle, though outwardly favourable to the proposal, was really against it. Thus a question that might have provoked a constitutional conflict between the two kingdoms was resolved as a domestic issue within the Irish parliament, and Harcourt's administration suffered little loss of popularity.

Much of Harcourt's success was due to the skill of his chief secretary, Blaquiere, in dealing with Irish politicians. Townshend had foreseen that if management through undertakers were abandoned the government would have to have 'a man of talents and weight in the house of commons

... to superintend and conduct its business through parliament'. This duty fell naturally to the chief secretary, and in Townshend's time Sir George Macartney had performed it with some success. But Blaquiere provided a model of efficiency for his successors to live up to; whether he was negotiating with an opposition member for the transfer of his vote, or deciding on the distribution of favours among constant supporters, he showed great address and an acute, if somewhat cynical, understanding of human nature. The 'jobbish power' formerly held by the undertakers now lay with the lord lieutenant, and the chief secretary exercised it on his behalf. As a means of managing parliament the jobbery of the chief secretary cost the country even more than the jobbery of the undertakers; but in Blaquiere's hands it achieved its end, and opposition in the house of commons dwindled away. In the course of 1774 Flood himself came round to the view that nothing could be gained save in co-operation with the government; Harcourt and Blaquiere worked hard to secure him; and in October 1775 he accepted the post of vice-treasurer.

The motives that govern human action are so varied and so difficult to weigh, so easily misunderstood by observers, and even by the actors themselves, that only a rash, or a prejudiced, or a stupid man will pass an unqualified judgement on the conduct of another. Flood's desertion of the patriot opposition was bitterly resented, and set in the most sordid light: there he stood, exclaimed Grattan, 'with a metaphor in his mouth and a bribe in his pocket'. But his own account of the transaction represents the position fairly enough: 'The only way anything could be effected for the country was by going along with the government and making their measures diverge towards public utility'. A man of stronger character would have preferred to remain independent. But Flood was chagrined to see his influence in the house decline as the government majority was extended and consolidated under Blaquiere's skilful management; he was flattered by Harcourt's obvious anxiety to attach him; the high value that he set on his own abilities made it easy for him to believe that he would carry real weight in the administration; the office that he insisted on having had traditionally been held by an English absentee, so that he could claim to have restored to his countrymen a long-lost right.

Whether or not Flood's change of front was justified, he was certainly unfortunate in the time of its occurrence. Less than three months after he accepted office, Henry Grattan, a young barrister whom he himself had inspired with patriot principles and who had won some reputation as a political journalist, was brought into the house by the patronage of Lord Charlemont. Here he quickly established his reputation. As an orator, he had few external advantages. His appearance was insignificant, his voice thin and sharp, his gesture ungraceful. But the testimony of contemporaries is unanimous about the compelling force, the almost overwhelming persuasiveness, of his speeches; and even in print, even to-day, when the subject-matter has lost all its urgency, they can hold the attention of the reader and stir his imagination. It was the great age of parliamentary eloquence, but Grattan had no equal in the Irish parliament, and in the British perhaps only Lord Chatham could produce a comparable effect. The remnant of the patriots, dispirited by the loss of Flood's leadership, rallied behind him; and Flood soon had the mortification of seeing his former protégé establish all, and more than all, the popular influence that he himself had once wielded.

Meanwhile, events had taken place on the other side of the Atlantic that were to prove more fateful for the future of Ireland than Flood's acceptance of office, or even than Grattan's entry into parliament. On an April morning in 1775 a clash between British regulars and the Lexington militia had turned the growing quarrel between Great Britain and her American colonies into open war. And this war, in which the American nation took form, also enabled the 'Irish nation' of the protestant ascendancy to achieve its short-lived 'constitution of 1782'.

XI

The Winning of a Constitution

(1)

The war found Ireland in a state of economic depression. The linen trade, always subject to fluctuations, had been declining since 1771; at least one-third of the looms throughout the kingdom were idle; and within the space of three years some 10,000 weavers, unable to support themselves at home, had emigrated to North America. But while the country was in poverty fresh burdens had been laid on the establishment, and despite the imposition of new taxes expenditure regularly exceeded revenue. The deficit had to be made good by borrowing, and since money was scarce and government credit low this could be done only at an enhanced rate of interest. The national debt (regarded by contemporaries as a sort of barometer of economic health) was not far short of one million pounds in 1773, almost double what it had been ten years earlier. The closing of the American markets in the spring of 1775 seemed to threaten complete bankruptcy.

This interruption of trade would, by itself, have been enough to make the war unpopular in Ireland; but public opinion was, in any case, opposed to the government's American policy. The parallel between the position of the colonies and the position of Ireland was too close to be overlooked. As early as 1771 Benjamin Franklin, then on a visit to Dublin, had suggested the possibility of future co-operation between the Irish and the Americans, by which both might obtain 'a more equitable treatment' from Great Britain. In January 1775 a Dublin newspaper pointed out that 'by the same authority which the British parliament assumes to tax America, it may also and with equal justice presume to tax Ireland without the consent or concurrence of the Irish parliament'. And later in the year, after the war had begun, an opposition member in the Irish house of commons asserted roundly that if the Americans were crushed 'the next step would be to tax Ireland in the British parliament'.

Irish sympathy for the American cause was not based solely on this constitutional comparison. The thousands of Irish emigrants who had crossed the Atlantic during the previous fifty or sixty years had established a strong tie between the two communities. A presbyterian minister, in a sermon on 'The ruinous effects of civil war', reminded his hearers that 'there is scarcely a protestant family of the middle classes amongst us who does not reckon kindred with the inhabitants of that extensive continent'. Irishmen in America were taking a prominent part in the struggle for independence, and it was natural that Irishmen at home should sympathize with their efforts. This feeling was strongest in Ulster which had supplied the great bulk of the emigrants: 'The presbyterians in the north', wrote Harcourt, 'are in their hearts Americans'. But interest in the war was widespread throughout the country. The Dublin booksellers found it profitable to reprint English and American pamphlets; and the news-papers reported the course of events in considerable detail, and commonly with a bias in favour of the colonists. There was, indeed, almost no sign of enthusiasm for the British cause save among those whose interest attached them to the government, and among the Roman Catholics, whose ingrained dislike of republican principles was reinforced by the rising hope of relief. 'We are all Americans here', wrote a correspondent from Cork, 'except such as are attached securely to the Castle, or papists'.

The state of Ireland was a matter of direct concern to the British ministry: North did not want another America just across the channel; he knew that British opponents of the war would seize on any discontent in Ireland as an additional argument against his policy; and he wanted to make use of Irish troops and supplies. Besides these political and military considerations, the cutting off of colonial trade had made the Irish market much more important to British merchants and manufacturers; and so Ireland must be enabled to buy more British goods. In short, the pros-perity of Ireland now seemed as likely to be advantageous to Great Britain as formerly it had seemed to threaten her. North did not at once reach the logical conclusion of this line of argument, and British opinion moved even more slowly; but in the course of 1775 at least a beginning was made: the Newfoundland fisheries were opened to Irish ships; Ireland was permitted to export clothing and other equipment for troops on the Irish establishment serving abroad; to encourage the linen manufacture, a bounty, payable by the British treasury, was granted on flax-seed imported into Ireland.

These concessions mark a change in the attitude of the British govern-ment, reflecting the anxiety produced by events in America; but their practical effect was slight, and they fell far short of satisfying Irish demands. Harcourt laid great stress on them in his opening speech when parliament reassembled in October 1775, but he was nevertheless anxious about the outcome of the session. His first business was to get a declaration in favour of the ministry's American policy; and the address in reply to his speech, drawn up by a group of government supporters, included both a condemnation of the Americans as rebels, and a pledge of 'most devoted and inviolable attachment to his majesty's sacred person and government in the assertion of his just rights, and in the support of his legal authority'. The opposition brought forward two amendments, one advocating conciliation and one for the omission of the words condemning the Americans as rebels. Both were defeated after violent debate, and the original address was carried. 'I have never passed moments so happy', wrote Harcourt to North, 'as those have been since the question was determined'.

The next step was to get military aid from Ireland. The augmentation act of 1769 had provided that not fewer than 12,000 troops were to be retained for home defence, and the government now sought parliamentary authority to withdraw 4,000 of these for service in America, promising that the cost of maintaining them while out of Ireland should be borne by the British exchequer. Once again the opposition resisted fiercely, and once again it was crushed. The victory was of moral as well as of military advantage to the British ministry. It was, as Harcourt said, 'a convincing proof to America and to the whole world of the decisive part Ireland takes in the quarrel'. Edmund Burke took the same view, but with far different feelings: 'Ireland', he said, 'has chosen, instead of being the arbiter of peace, to be a feeble party in a war, waged against the principles of her own liberties'.

Despite these failures of the opposition, Harcourt found the house of commons difficult to manage. A government offer to replace the troops withdrawn by an equal number of foreign protestant mercenaries was rejected, and this rejection was undoubtedly intended to strengthen the case for a national militia. Two money bills, which had been altered in England, were on that account heavily defeated; an embargo on the export of provisions, imposed by an order in council of 3 February 1776, was sharply attacked, both as an unwarranted extension of the prerogative and as ruinous to the country's economy. In fact, the demand for provisions to supply the crown forces was so great that prices shot up, and instead of there being any glut, as prophesied by the parliamentary opposition, there was a general scarcity; but the embargo remained a popular grievance.

Faced with these difficulties, Harcourt advised a dissolution, to which the British ministry agreed. Parliament was now approaching its statutory term; those members who had any reason to feel anxious about their prospects of re-election were growing reluctant to support unpopular measures; and Harcourt thought that a general election, properly managed, would strengthen the government's control of the house of commons. The dissolution took place in March, and the administration spared no pains to secure favourable returns to the new house. The support of important borough owners was bought by a lavish distribution of honours: seventeen[1] new peers were created in a single day, seven barons became viscounts, and five viscounts became earls. Blaquiere drew up a list of the new pensions, amounting to about £10,000 a year, that would have to be granted to make sure of a favourable result. All this, he thought would guarantee '138 plumping votes, of unequivocal men', and this would be enough to make the government safe. The effectiveness of these efforts was not immediately put to the test; for though the new parliament held a brief session in June 1776, it did not meet for business until October 1777.

(2)

In the meantime, there had been a change in the Irish government, for Harcourt's conduct of affairs was not entirely satisfactory to the British ministry and he resigned in November 1776. The king and Lord North could not immediately agree on a successor; but early in December the choice fell on John Hobart, earl of Buckinghamshire,[2] who arrived in Dublin in January. Buckinghamshire seems to have been genuinely anxious for the welfare of Ireland — he thought it necessary to defend himself from the suspicion 'of ambitioning the character of an Irish patriot' — but he was ill-qualified for the very difficult task that faced him; and his chief secretary, Richard Heron,[3] had none of Blaquiere's skill as a parliamentary manager. Buckinghamshire (wrote Lord Charlemont some years later) 'was a weak man, who, to the infinite benefit of Ireland, brought with him a much weaker man for his secretary'. Even Blaquiere might have found it impossible to control the Irish parliament during the period that followed; but Heron's inefficiency certainly made things easier for the patriots.

[1] Not eighteen, as Lecky says (*Ireland*, ii. 168); see W. Hunt, *Irish parliament in 1775*, p. 90.

[2] He habitually signed himself 'Buckingham', but is not to be confused with George Nugent-Temple-Grenville, first marquis of Buckingham, lord-lieutenant, 1787–9.

[3] Created baronet in 1778.

When Buckinghamshire met his first parliament, in October 1777, the position was not yet desperate, and he could still count on a majority in the house of commons. But it was hard to tell how long the majority would hold together. Opposition members concentrated their attention on two topics on which the government was particularly vulnerable, the state of trade, and financial administration; and it was impossible to refute the statistics on which they based their arguments. No motion directly hostile to the government was carried; but the whole house was obviously uneasy about the national economy, and inclined to receive with sympathy the addresses that came in from various parts of the country complaining of the poverty and unemployment arising from restrictions on trade: even Hely-Hutchinson spoke in favour of repealing the embargo on the export of provisions.

As the difficulties of the new administration increased, the strain upon the loyalty of its supporters became almost intolerable. It was impossible to disguise the fact that the country was on the edge of bankruptcy. Revenue had shown a temporary rise in 1777, but as expenditure had risen even more there still was a heavy deficit; and for the next three years revenue sank steadily. In 1778 Buckinghamshire, at his wit's end for money, had to borrow twenty thousand pounds from Dublin bankers; but they refused to lend more and he had to appeal in desperation to England for funds to pay the army. When Robert Stewart,[1] one of the members for County Down, moved a resolution in the house of commons, on 3 February 1778, drawing attention to the excess of expenditure over income, the government was afraid to risk a division and allowed it to pass unopposed. This was, in itself, only a very modest victory for the patriots, and their attempt to follow it up by an address to the king on the state of the nation was defeated three days later; but it was indicative of the changing temper of the house. Government supporters were getting restive; and the events of the next twelve months were to sweep the bulk of them, for a time at least, into the patriot camp.

Many factors contributed to this general conversion, but by far the most important was the force of organized public opinion. Since the 1760s popular support for the patriot cause had been growing. It had expressed itself in pamphlets and newspaper articles, in resolutions passed at public meetings and toasts drunk at more convivial assemblies; but there was no regular organization through which it could make its weight felt. The development of the Volunteer movement on a national scale during 1778,

---

[1] Robert Stewart, later marquis of Londonderry, and father of Lord Castlereagh.

by providing such an organization, changed the course of Irish politics, and prepared the way for a radical re-adjustment of Anglo-Irish relations. This movement was not the creation of the popular leaders who were to use it so effectively. It sprang spontaneously from the exigencies of the military position; it became political because the Volunteers refused to subordinate the rights of the citizen to the duties of the soldier; both in its military and in its political aspects it expressed the maturing self-consciousness of the protestant nation.

Irish protestants had never forgotten their long tradition of independent military action: in the north, they had organized resistance to Thurot in 1760, and the southern gentry had raised troops of horse to defend their property against the Whiteboys. The outbreak of the American war gave a colourable excuse for further activity of the same sort. The army had been so weakened by the withdrawal of men for service in America that it was no longer adequate for the defence of the country. There was no militia; for even though a militia act was at last carried in 1778, the government had no funds to put it into execution. As early as 1776 some young men in Wexford had formed an 'independent company', and the fashion spread quickly. 'A Mr. Tottenham, who had served in the army and had an old attachment to red clothes', formed a company of light infantry in King's County, and others soon sprang up. But it was events in the north that turned these scattered efforts into a national movement.

In April 1778 the famous American privateer, Paul Jones, who had made successful raids on the coasts of England and Scotland, sailed into Belfast Lough, where he captured and carried off a king's ship. This demonstration of British naval weakness was all the more alarming as France had now entered the war; and there was general expectation of an invasion. The people of Belfast felt themselves particularly threatened, and appealed to the lord lieutenant for troops. When they found that none were available save half a troop of dismounted horse and half a company of invalids, they suddenly realized that their own volunteer company, formed in 1777, might be their only effective defence. Volunteering now became a serious business, and the call to arms sounded throughout the north. The presbyterians had sympathized with the Americans; but they hated and feared the French, 'the jealous enemies of our liberties and religion'. Presbyterian ministers were not only active recruiting agents but sometimes took up arms themselves. The Reverend William Bruce, for example, appeared before his congregation 'in a short blue coat with white facings, brass buttons, and white breeches', his uniform as an officer of the Lisburn True Blues; others led their men to church, and did not exchange the musket for the Bible until they were about to mount the pulpit. In general, however, the landlord class provided the officers, and so widespread and infectious was the enthusiasm, so potent the attraction of gay uniforms and military titles, that few of them hung back. In the south as well as in the north, in the inland counties as well as along the coast, the fever spread, and before the middle of 1779 a volunteer army had come into existence, ready to repel a French invasion, but no less ready to assert the rights of Ireland. Irish protestants had been full of their grievances before: military organization gave them a sense not only of unity but of strength. France might be the enemy against whom they had armed in the first place, but the oppression of Ireland by England formed the main theme of their discussions; and now at last they were in a position to assert themselves: 'the dragon's teeth were sown, and the fertile soil everywhere produced a plenteous crop of soldiers'.

The Volunteers were encouraged in their political activities by the conduct of the opposition in the British parliament. During 1779 Rockingham, Shelburne and their allies, willing to embarrass North, repeatedly pressed the claim of Ireland to some easing of trade restrictions. The duke of Richmond, in the lords, and his nephew Fox, in the commons, even questioned (though indirectly) the right of the British parliament to legislate for Ireland at all. North, while professing sympathy for Irish distress, refused to take immediate action; he thought that he deserved more gratitude than he had received for the concessions already made, and he feared that any attempt to go further would raise a storm of protest in Great Britain. The opposition speeches had convinced the Irish that their claims were supported by a large body of British opinion, and their hopes had been aroused by the proposals put forward. When those hopes were dashed by North's seeming intransigence they replied by following earlier American example (and the long-neglected advice of Swift) and formed 'non-importation' associations. The Volunteers had led the way by having their uniforms made of Irish cloth; and the civic magistrates, high sheriffs, and grand juries, who were mainly responsible for organizing the new associations, were for the most part identified with the Volunteer movement. Non-importation might be a dangerous weapon to use; but the enthusiasm with which it was taken up showed a degree of unanimity, a strength of purpose, and, above all, an effectiveness of organization, such as Ireland had never known before.

In the midst of these developments Buckinghamshire sat perplexed in Dublin. Non-importation and the Volunteer movement filled men's minds; but he had no control of either, nor even much knowledge of what was going on beyond what he could read in the newspapers. The autumn of 1779 must bring a new session of parliament; and then, unless great concessions were made, the storm would burst. No exercise of patronage would enable him to secure a majority; for, as he warned the ministry, 'the occasional favour of government cannot induce men to incur the odium of their country at a crisis which they deem critical for the attainment of her objects'. As he surveyed the scene, nothing impressed him so much as his own helplessness and inadequacy: 'The present situation', he wrote in May 1779, 'requires abilities of a very superior order, far beyond any idea which the most flattering partiality could conceive of mine'. From the British ministry he could get no promise of concessions, no clear guidance for his own conduct of affairs; there was nothing for him to do but wait, and hope for the best.

(3)

The Volunteers were a protestant body. Some companies admitted a few Roman Catholics surreptitiously; but the laws forbidding papists to possess arms were still in force, and not many protestants were willing to see them evaded. The Roman Catholic leaders, on their part, were keen to support the Volunteers. While maintaining the affirmations of devoted loyalty to the government that they had made at the beginning of the war, they were naturally anxious to use any opportunity of establishing a place for themselves in the public life of the country; and they were no less interested than the protestants in obtaining freedom for Irish trade. The Volunteers in general were for some time inclined to be suspicious of Roman Catholic offers of help; but from the beginning there were many who not only welcomed but forwarded a moderate relaxation of the penal code; and this more liberal attitude soon prevailed throughout the whole body.

Protestant readiness to support an easing of the penal code was due partly to the prevailing spirit of tolerance in matters of religion, which had spread in Ireland as in other parts of Europe; partly to the sense of security bred by long freedom from insurrection. But there were still many protestants who thought that the penal laws should be retained *in terrorem*, even if they were not regularly enforced; and the more generous attitude of the patriots arose, in some measure, from political calculation. Roman Catholics had long looked for favour and protection to the British government and its representatives, rather than to the Irish parliament. It was the Irish parliament that had passed the penal laws; it was British influence that had mitigated the full rigour of their execution, and had allowed those relating to the clergy and to the exercise of public worship to fall into abeyance. At one time, protestant patriots had been inclined to regard this leniency towards papists as a grievance. But by the 1770s they had come to regard the cleavage between the two great sections of Irish society as a danger to the national cause, a means by which the British grip on Ireland might be strengthened and made permanent. Grattan's famous assertion that 'the Irish protestant could never be free till the Irish Catholic had ceased to be a slave' meant, in simple terms, that the British government must not be allowed to play off one against the other.

In later years the patriots were to differ over the amount of freedom that it was necessary, or safe, to grant; but, to begin with, they were in substantial agreement. The first breaches in the penal code were not, indeed, very serious. By an act of 1771 Roman Catholics who took bogland for the purpose of reclamation were allowed to hold it on a lease of sixty-one years, instead of the thirty-one years to which they had formerly been limited. An act of 1774 provided a form of oath, which had episcopal approval, by which they could testify their allegiance to the crown without violation of conscience; and though this conferred no immediate material benefit, it was a step towards admitting them within the constitution. A much more important measure was brought forward in 1778, the effect of which was to repeal a great part of the popery act of 1704, in so far as it related to land. Roman Catholics were now to be allowed to take leases for lives, and leases for any fixed term not exceeding 999 years; and they might inherit and bequeath land on the same terms as protestants. Thus the policy of breaking up Roman Catholic estates, and of holding out inducements to conform to the Church of Ireland, was to be abandoned. One motive behind this measure was economic: a great deal of wealth was now in the hands of Roman Catholic merchants, and it was in the interests of the country, and of impecunious protestant proprietors, that they should be enabled to invest in land. The measure was sponsored by the government; but the opposition of protestant die-hards was so strong that, but for the ardent support of the patriots, and especially of Grattan, it must have been defeated. Thus, at a critical point in Anglo-Irish relations, the national cause was identified with that of religious equality.

To the greatest Irishman of the day the passage of the act seemed to mark a new era. 'You are now', wrote Edmund Burke to Pery, speaker of the Irish commons, 'beginning to have a country'. The kind of unity that Burke foresaw was never achieved; but the old divisions of Irish life had sunk temporarily into the background, and the protestant nation could face the mounting conflict with Britain confident that it had behind it the moral support of the Roman Catholics.

(4)

Throughout the summer of 1779 Buckinghamshire waited in vain for clear directions from England. Would the British government make concessions, or would it not? This was the question that all Ireland was asking. Buckinghamshire knew that a negative answer would make the house of commons unmanageable; but an answer of some sort he must have before he could even begin to frame a policy; and he could get no answer at all. To help the ministry to make up its mind he sent over reports on the situation prepared by some of the leading politicians on the government side, including Hussey Burgh, Flood and Hely-Hutchinson. All urged the necessity of relaxing restrictions on trade: only thus could Ireland achieve financial stability. 'It has come to this', wrote Hussey Burgh, 'England must either support this kingdom or allow her to support herself. Her option is to give in trade or to give in money; without one or the other the expenses cannot be supplied'. The arguments are cogent; but the labour spent in preparing them was wasted. For three months the papers lay in London unexamined, and even when an abstract was at last prepared, in the middle of September, North refused to look at it.

The ministry had not, however, altogether ignored Ireland in the interval. A suggestion had been put forward that the best solution for Irish difficulties might be a parliamentary union on the Scottish model, and Buckinghamshire was asked for his opinion. At first he was disposed to approve, though he saw that great caution would be needed; but the opposition aroused in Dublin by the mere rumour that such a proposal had been made frightened him into withdrawing his support, and the idea was dropped. The ministry may not have been very serious about a parliamentary union, but it had no alternative policy to offer. When Buckinghamshire met parliament, on 12 October 1779, he was still without an answer to the great question of Irish trade. The Volunteers and the house of commons were soon to demand one in a way that could not be ignored.

For weeks before parliament met, tension had been rising and opposition to government taking a more definite shape than ever before. All over the country, constituents urged their members to demand the removal of trade restrictions, and to enforce the demand by voting supplies for six months only. This public excitement had its effect, even on the principal office-holders. In August, the prime serjeant, Hussey Burgh, warned Buckinghamshire that he would 'no longer stand forth in parliament as the leader of the public business'. Flood was moving in the same direction; and both of them refused to attend the regular meeting of the government's confidential advisers, held on the eve of the session.

Buckinghamshire had foretold that the commons' demand for 'unlimited commerce' would be so overwhelming that any attempt to resist it directly would be like trying 'to stop the ocean with a hurdle', and he proved a true prophet. On the day parliament met, Grattan moved an amendment to the address, urging the necessity of abolishing restrictions on Irish exports. He had good reason to feel confident of success, for he had behind him not only the public opinion of Ireland but the support of the British opposition. This support was of more than moral value, for many opposition members had estates and connections in Ireland through which they could exercise influence in the house of commons. It is a matter of some significance that Charles James Fox was at this time in Ireland on a prolonged visit.

Grattan's amendment was well received. An attempt to hold things up by appointing a committee of inquiry was brushed aside; and when Hussey Burgh came out openly in support of Grattan there could be no doubt of the result. It was, however, to a suggestion made by Flood that the amendment owed its final uncompromising form:

'That it is not by temporary expedients but by a free trade alone that this nation is now to be saved from impending ruin.'

Heron tried to rally his supporters, but they were swept away by the enthusiasm of the moment. 'It was a glorious thing', reported the patriot *Freeman's Journal*, 'to see the placemen and pensioners of government come forward with their offices in their hands ready to be sacrificed for the benefit of the country'. A few faithful officials were willing, though reluctantly, to vote as Heron bid them; but he dared not risk a division, and the amendment was triumphantly carried.

The victory had been won in parliament, but it had been made possible by the pressure of public opinion. When, two days later, the speaker drove to the Castle to present the amended address to the lord lieutenant, the streets were lined by armed Volunteers; and when both houses of parliament voted the thanks of the nation to the Volunteers for 'their spirited and necessary exertions' for the defence of the country, most members probably had in mind their support of the campaign for free trade rather than their preparations to meet a French invasion. The Volunteers themselves were determined to carry the struggle to a successful conclusion. The commons accepted the king's reply to their address, though it was studiously non-committal. But the Volunteers were dissatisfied, and showed their dissatisfaction in a public demonstration on 4 November, the birthday of King William III. They paraded at King William's statue, outside the parliament house, and amid their protestant rejoicings over the 'Glorious Revolution' displayed placards demanding 'A short money bill' and bearing the ominous warning 'Free trade or else?' Stimulated (and perhaps somewhat alarmed) by these proceedings, the patriots in parliament renewed the attack; and before the end of November the house of commons had formally decided to vote supplies for six months only. The government, desperate for money on almost any terms, had no choice but to accept, and Buckinghamshire urged the ministry to grant free trade at once, lest worse disasters should befall.

The 'free trade' that Ireland now demanded was not, of course, 'free trade' in the nineteenth-century sense; it meant the removal of restrictions imposed on Irish commerce by Great Britain, and freedom for the Irish parliament to regulate Irish commerce in future. This demand was sufficiently alarming to British mercantile interests; it was even more alarming to the ministry for its claim, by implication, of parliamentary independence for Ireland. The claim had, in fact, been made openly by some speakers during the debates in the commons; and though the question had not come to a vote, there was no doubt on which side public opinion lay; and public opinion had amply demonstrated its power to influence the house. The ministry was thus in a dilemma: resistance to the Irish demand for free trade presented an obvious and immediate danger; surrender might merely open the way for more far-reaching demands in the future.

This was the position in the middle of November 1779. At that time North was still hesitating; he professed his readiness to do something for the Irish, but complained, somewhat strangely, that he did not know exactly what they wanted. Three weeks later, all his hesitation had gone, and he put forward proposals that went even beyond what most of the patriots had hoped for. The change was not produced by any new developments in Ireland; it was the response of North and his advisers to the political situation at home. The British parliament met on 25 November, and the opposition leaders, now more firmly united than before, immediately attacked the government for its neglect of Irish affairs. They dwelt on the grievances of Ireland, they praised the Volunteer movement, and they hinted that the people of Great Britain would do well to follow Irish example and compel parliament to respond to the popular will. The excited state of public feeling in England gave sinister force to this veiled threat, and North felt that it was essential to relieve the pressure somehow; if Ireland could be conciliated the opposition attack would lose much of its drive. He had never been opposed in principle to relaxing the commercial restrictions, but he was slow to make up his mind, and he was nervous about the reaction of British mercantile interests; it required this greater danger to bring him to the point of decision. On 8 December he presented his proposals to the cabinet, and five days later announced them in the house of commons.

These proposals, which were meant to do away with every commercial grievance of the Irish, aroused much less opposition in Britain than North had expected, and the legislation necessary to give them force was carried without difficulty. Before the end of the year, the acts forbidding the export of wool, woollen goods, and glass from Ireland were repealed. By an act of January 1780 the Irish were permitted to trade with British settlements in Africa and America on condition that the Irish parliament imposed duties equal to those in force in Great Britain. An act of March 1780 repealed the prohibition (dating from the reign of Henry VII) on the export of gold and silver from England to Ireland; allowed the Irish to import foreign hops; and opened the Turkey Company to Irish merchants, thus giving Ireland a direct trade with the Levant. North had introduced his proposals by asserting the proposition 'that Ireland had a free and unlimited right to trade with the whole world', but that her trade with British possessions depended on the favour of the British parliament. In fact, however, the concessions made in 1779–80 placed Ireland in almost exactly the same position as Great Britain, save that she was still excluded from the area of the East India Company's monopoly.[1] Ireland thus obtained, as it were for nothing, commercial advantages for which the Scots had been obliged to surrender their independent parliament; and twenty years later, when a parliamentary union between Great Britain and Ireland was in agitation, there was no further inducement of like value for the British government to offer.

These concessions were joyfully received in Ireland, but they did not produce the pacifying effect for which North had hoped; gratitude for admission to British colonial trade had less influence than a sense of triumph at having compelled surrender to Irish demands. Success acted as a stimulus to the national enthusiasm. The Volunteers continued their activities and improved their organization; and the patriots resolved to press on with their programme of constitutional reform. It was now, argued Grattan, more important than ever to establish the parliamentary independence of Ireland; otherwise, the newly-won freedom of trade would lie at the mercy of the British parliament, which might at any time re-impose restrictions on Irish exports. Public opinion was behind this

[1] Apart from this, the only restriction on Irish trade with British colonial possessions was that Ireland might not re-export colonial products to Great Britain.

argument; but the government, as Grattan and the patriots were soon to find, had not lost the power of resistance in parliament.

The patriot successes of 1779 had not changed the character of Irish borough-owners. They had for a time been carried along by the strength of public feeling, but they still coveted places, pensions and titles, and for these they must look to the government. Buckinghamshire made lavish promises, and by February 1780, when parliament re-assembled after the Christmas recess, he had once more built up a government majority. But he himself realized how precarious that majority was. The political atmosphere was very different from what it had been even a decade earlier; and it was impossible to calculate how far the private interests or personal convictions of individual members would withstand the force of popular opinion.

What Buckinghamshire feared most was a major clash with the opposition on the constitutional issue, and for some weeks he seemed to have averted it. But the truth was that the patriots, influenced by the example of the Yorkshire Association in England, were deliberately postponing parliamentary action while they aroused and organized public opinion throughout the country. The government tried to counter this patriot propaganda, and in the hope of conciliating the presbyterians it allowed the passage of a measure relieving protestant dissenters from the operation of the sacramental test; but these efforts came to little, and when Grattan, on 19 April 1780, brought forward his declaration of independence in the house of commons he had a united country behind him. In one of his greatest speeches he moved a resolution that embodied the essence of the patriot claim:

'That the king's most excellent majesty, and the lords and commons of Ireland, are the only power competent to enact laws to bind Ireland.'

The debate, which lasted from half-past three o'clock in the afternoon until between six and seven o'clock the following morning, turned not on the substance of the resolution but on the expediency of making such an assertion of Irish rights at that time. At last, an amendment adjourning the question indefinitely was carried by 136 votes to 97; 'but although there were 136 of opinion that such a resolution at this time was inexpedient, there was not a single member that spoke who did not declare that Ireland was not bound by British acts of parliament in any cases whatsoever'.

The adjournment of the debate brought Buckinghamshire little relief, for the patriots soon found a means of giving practical expression to their belief in Irish independence. The army in Ireland had hitherto been governed by the British mutiny acts; a magistrate of patriot sympathies now refused to convict deserters, on the ground that there was no Irish statute compelling them to obey military law, and his example was quickly and widely followed. There was a serious danger that soon Ireland would have no army at all, or an army not subject to military discipline. To meet this situation, the commons prepared heads of a mutiny bill, which the government had no choice but to accept, though by doing so it virtually admitted the principle of Grattan's resolution. The victory of the patriots was, however, a very imperfect one. The house of commons, following British example, had limited the operation of its measure to a single year; it came back from England as a perpetual mutiny bill, and in this form, despite all Grattan's efforts, it passed into law.

In refusing to accept Grattan's declaration and in passing the altered mutiny bill, the commons were acting contrary to public opinion; but it would be wrong to attribute their conduct wholly to the corrupt influence of the Castle. Most of the members were neither patriots (in the party sense), though they might be influenced by patriot ideas, nor mere tools of government, though they might hold, or hope to hold, government appointments. They were generally afraid of committing themselves too deeply: they were glad to escape a direct vote on the principle of Grattan's resolution; and when they had to choose between a perpetual mutiny bill, on the one hand, and either no bill at all or a head-on clash with government, on the other, they naturally chose what they considered the safer alternative. Such men would certainly not lead a national movement, though they might be persuaded, or frightened, into following it.

Buckinghamshire's viceroyalty was now almost at an end. For more than a year his relations with the ministry had been strained, and he would probably have been recalled much sooner had not the precarious state of British politics made the king and North reluctant to take any action so decisive as the dismissal of a lord lieutenant. But in the autumn of 1780, with the session of parliament safely over in Ireland, and preparations on foot for a general election in Britain, the change was at last made, and Buckinghamshire left Ireland in December. It is easy to criticize his administration, and one may certainly say of him, as he himself said of his chief secretary, that his abilities were 'calculated for quieter times'. But though his failure to keep in touch with events may have been due to his own ineptitude, his failure to control them can be traced directly to the indecision of the British ministry.

(5)

Buckinghamshire was succeeded as lord lieutenant by Frederick

Howard, earl of Carlisle, who brought William Eden (afterwards Lord Auckland) as chief secretary. The change of viceroys did not mean any formal change in ministerial policy towards Ireland; but there was a change in the spirit of the Irish administration. Carlisle, a young man not without whiggish sympathies, was anxious to please; Eden was a much abler manager than Heron had been, and he had some previous knowledge of Irish affairs. Together they did a good deal to restore the damaged prestige of government. Their task was made more difficult by the continuing economic depression, for Ireland had not yet derived much solid benefit from her newly-won commercial freedom; and a revived threat of invasion during 1781 added to the importance of the Volunteers, who were almost wholly beyond the scope of official influence. Nevertheless, when parliament met in October the government had a safe majority; and this did not depend, as in Buckinghamshire's last session, mainly on bribery, but rather on a genuine confidence in the good intentions of the lord lieutenant.

This confidence was not entirely misplaced. Carlisle had been instructed to resist all demands for constitutional reform, and this he did successfully. But his secret advice to the ministers was that they should allow the passage of a measure for the modification of Poynings' Law, which had now, for the first time, come under direct patriot attack in parliament; and he strongly urged them not to include Ireland in any British act, declaring that 'the independence of Irish legislation is become the creed of the kingdom'. Carlisle's advice was not followed, and the fact that he had offered it was not, of course, generally known in Ireland; but his prestige in the Irish parliament remained high. The passage of a *habeas corpus* act, the one concession that the ministry made, was of some advantage to him; and the news of the British disaster at Yorktown evoked the loyalty of the house of commons, and made even the patriots unwilling, for a time, to embarrass the government. Besides this, many members were jealous of the political power of the Volunteers; the Gordon riots in London during the summer of 1780 had shown the danger of arousing popular emotions; and the majority of the house was not only ready but anxious to believe that the government meant to be conciliatory.

But outside parliament the Volunteers, and especially those of Ulster, were determined to press on with their demands, and there was a group of patriot members ready to co-operate with them. In December 1781 a meeting of Volunteers at Armagh arranged for a convention representing all the Ulster companies to meet at Dungannon in the following February. The resolutions to be submitted to this convention were drawn up in advance by Charlemont, with the assistance of a few other patriots. These included not only Grattan but also Flood, who was now once more in open opposition, having been at last dismissed from office, to which he had clung even after he had ceased to co-operate with government. The resolutions summarized the patriot programme: they asserted the legislative independence of Ireland, declared the powers exercised by the two privy councils under Poynings' Law to be 'unconstitutional and a grievance', condemned the principle of a perpetual mutiny act, and demanded that judges should enjoy the same security of tenure in Ireland as in England. A final resolution, which seems to have been the work of Grattan, expressed a limited approval of religious equality: 'that as men and as Irishmen, as Christians and as protestants, we rejoice in the relaxation of the penal laws against our Roman Catholic fellow-subjects'.

On 15 February 1782 some 250 Volunteer delegates assembled in the parish church of Dungannon. Far more truly than the parliament in College Green they represented the spirit of the protestant nation, and they had behind them 25,000 armed men in the north, with the support of a like number in the rest of the kingdom. Having adopted, all but unanimously, the prepared resolutions, they voted an address to the patriot minority in both houses. It encouraged them to continue the parliamentary struggle, but there was an ominous note of self-reliance in the concluding sentences:

'We know our duty to our sovereign, and are loyal. We know our duty to ourselves, and are resolved to be free. We seek for our rights, and no more than our rights, and, in so just a pursuit, we should doubt the being of a Providence, if we doubted of success.'

This was the authentic language of revolution.

A week later, Grattan once more moved a declaration of independence in the house of commons; but the government party held together, and a motion postponing the question was carried by 137 votes to 68. Carlisle well knew that this was only a temporary expedient, and he warned the ministry that, without some measure of conciliation, it would soon be impossible to govern Ireland. The whole country had been aroused by the Dungannon meeting and by the parliamentary debate on Grattan's resolution. Not a single government supporter would dare to assert that Ireland could be bound by British acts. Ireland (wrote Carlisle) would no longer consent to be ruled under the authority of the British parliament, and it was impossible to compel obedience.

Affairs were still in this uneasy condition when parliament adjourned for the Easter recess, on 14 March. Ten days later the whole position had been transformed by the resignation of Lord North and the king's reluctant acceptance of Rockingham as his successor. With their allies in power at Westminster, and a new whig viceroy, the duke of Portland, in Dublin, the patriots could feel that their difficulties were at an end. On 16 April the commons met again, 'the galleries and bar being crowded with spectators, and every heart panting with expectation'. A message from Portland expressed the king's concern at the 'discontents and jealousies' prevailing among his loyal subjects of Ireland, and recommended the house to consider means of establishing 'such a final adjustment as may give mutual satisfaction to his kingdoms of Great Britain and Ireland'. Grattan, still pale from recent illness, then moved for the third time a declaration of Irish independence. His speech on this occasion was not much concerned with explaining or defending the rights of the kingdom; it was rather a hymn of triumph over a victory already won:

'I am now to address a free people: ages have passed away and this is the first moment in which you could be distinguished by such an appellation . . . I found Ireland on her knees, I watched over her with a paternal solicitude; I have traced her progress from injuries to arms, and from arms to liberty . . . Ireland is now a nation; in that new character I hail her, and bowing to her august presence, I say, *Esto perpetua.*'

Those who spoke after him did not dare even to hint at opposition. Some, who had voted with the majority on 22 February, justified their conduct on that occasion, but declared that they were now ready to assert openly the independence of their country. The resolution was unanimously approved, and an address embodying the constitutional claims of Ireland was presented to the lord lieutenant for transmission to the king.

This sudden triumph for Grattan and the patriots was not won by any fresh effort of their own, but sprang directly from the change of party fortunes in Britain. It was a kind of first-fruits of their alliance with the Rockingham whigs, and it was an indication of a new element in Anglo-Irish political relations. From this time onwards, until the end of the century, the politics of the two countries were closely intermingled; Irish politicians now found that their prospects of gaining or of keeping office were affected, as they had never been before, by the state of the parties at Westminster. Thus the old distinction between 'English interest' and 'Irish interest' was complicated and obscured: so long as the whigs retained office the patriots were the friends and advisers of government; and when the whigs were displaced, the great aim of the patriots was to assist in their restoration.

(6)

The settlement of Ireland's constitutional claims proved less simple than Grattan had expected, for the responsibility of office had damped the enthusiasm of the whigs. They were still well-disposed towards Ireland, and had showed their resolve to abandon North's policy by dismissing Carlisle with almost indecent haste, and sending over the duke of Portland in his place, with Richard Fitzpatrick, the brother of an Irish whig peer, as chief secretary. But they wanted space for reflection; they saw the dangers that might arise from having two completely independent parliaments side by side; and they thought that the patriots should be satisfied with promises of a future settlement, and co-operate heartily with the government in the meantime. They had tried hard to prevent the Irish parliament from making a formal declaration of independence; and even though they had failed in this, they still hoped to proceed by negotiation, and suggested that both parliaments should appoint commissioners to discuss the future relations between the two kingdoms. Grattan and Charlemont rejected this proposal out of hand; Ireland would accept nothing less than the rights asserted in the declaration, and until these had been secured to her there was nothing to discuss. It is easy to understand their attitude: negotiation implied compromise; delay would give the lord lieutenant time to build up a parliamentary following of his own; and none knew better than they how precarious was the unanimity that the house of commons had shown on 16 April. They had their way, but their intransigence resulted in a settlement that was largely negative in character; Pitt was not far wrong when, eighteen years later, he described it as 'the mere destruction of another system'.

Rockingham and Fox were disappointed at the attitude of the patriots, but were in no position to ignore it. The new lord lieutenant reported that the Irish thought very little of the change of government in England, and a great deal of the Volunteers; that they attributed the progress they had made to their own efforts, and believed that even if North had remained in power he would have had to yield to their demands. He was alarmed at the excited state of public feeling:

'It is no longer the parliament of Ireland that is to be managed or attended to. It is the whole of this country. It is the church, the law, the army (I fear, when I consider how it is composed), the merchant, the tradesman, the manufacturer, the farmer, the labourer, the catholic, the dissenter, the protestant, all sects, all sorts and descriptions of men, who ... unanimously and most audibly, call upon Great Britain for a full and unequivocal satisfaction.'

In spite of his alarm, Portland at first hoped that the Irish would negotiate; but he soon changed his mind, and warned the ministry that the alternatives before them were either to yield all that was demanded, or to abandon Ireland completely.

The whigs did not allow their disappointment to cloud their judge-ment; forced to give way, they did so fully and gracefully. On 17 May Fox, in the British house of commons, announced his readiness to 'meet Ireland on her own terms and give her everything she wanted in the way she herself seemed to wish for it'; and within a few weeks the legislation necessary to make this promise effective had been carried. The British parliament repealed the 'Sixth of George I', and this repeal was held to establish both the sole right of the Irish parliament to legislate for Ireland and the final jurisdiction of the Irish house of lords. In the Irish parliament Barry Yelverton, the leading constitutional lawyer among the patriots, sponsored a measure (generally known as 'Yelverton's act')[1] which com-pletely altered the operation of Poynings' Law. The chief governor and council in Ireland lost the power to originate or alter bills; they were to transmit to the king 'all such bills, and none other, as both houses of parliament shall judge expedient to be enacted in this kingdom ... with-out addition, diminution, or alteration'. Bills so transmitted, if approved by the king, were to be returned unaltered, under the great seal of Great Britain; the king thus retained the power to suppress bills, but not to alter them. During the parliamentary debate on this measure some members proposed that Poynings' Law should be repealed altogether, and others that the power of suppression — 'the silent negative' — should be taken away; but it was generally accepted that the crown must be left with an effective veto, and that this was the best way of doing it.

Other constitutional legislation was passed about the same time — the perpetual mutiny act was replaced by a biennial act, the Irish judges were granted the same tenure as the English, the final jurisdiction of the Irish courts was specifically established,[2] but it was the repeal of the 'Sixth of George I' and the modification of Poynings' Law that formed the essential basis of what is sometimes called 'the constitution of 1782'. The term, though useful, is in some ways misleading. The legislation of 1782 did indeed establish the formal independence of the Irish parliament and of the Irish judicial system; but it remained to be seen how that independence would affect the actual government of the country. Administration was still in the hands of a lord lieutenant appointed on the advice of the British ministers, and, in effect, responsible to them. For the moment, the

[1] Another act passed at this time, confirming certain classes of English and British legislation relating to Ireland, is also known as 'Yelverton's act'.
[2] Apart from the claim of the British house of lords to hear appeals from Ireland, cases had sometimes been removed from Irish to English courts by writs of error; the issue of writs for this purpose was now forbidden.

ministry was willing to comply with the demands of the Irish parliament, but what would happen when differences arose? Could the Irish parliament hope always to have its way in such disputes? Or could it use its newly-won freedom as a basis from which to capture permanent control of the executive? Could the patriots, in fact, give substantial reality to the 'constitution' they had established? Their failure to face these questions, or, indeed, to even ask them, goes far to account for the speedy collapse of all that they had achieved in 'the never-to-be-forgotten year 1782'.

XII

'Grattan's Parliament'

(1)

The Irish parliament survived the establishment of its independence by a bare eighteen years; for more than half that time the shadow of revolutionary France hung over its deliberations, and when finally it was bribed and bullied and frightened into voting itself out of existence the country was scarred by the effects of an abortive insurrection, which the intransigence of the parliamentary majority had done much to provoke. Yet this brief and troubled period of independence, though it closed in violence and corruption, had also a brighter side: there was great economic progress; there was a notable quickening of intellectual and social life; and the gentlemen of Ireland showed that they were not wholly unfit to be trusted with the management of their own affairs. Despite all its shortcomings, 'Grattan's parliament' was to be associated, in the political memory of Irishmen, with freedom, prosperity, and national dignity.

The fact that Grattan's name has become attached to this last phase in the history of the Irish parliament is natural enough, for it was under his leadership that legislative independence, the distinctive characteristic of the period, had been achieved; he was 'the man whose wisdom and virtue directed the happy circumstances of the times, and the spirit of Irishmen, to make us a nation'. But the political ascendancy that Grattan enjoyed in the spring and early summer of 1782 did not last long, and the parliament that bore his name was not often willing to submit itself to his guidance.

In the country at large, Grattan's influence sank, though only for a time, with almost dramatic suddenness. The cause of this change can be traced to the jealous rivalry of Flood, who, ever since his return to opposition, had been struggling to win back the leadership of the patriot cause. Down to the middle of 1782 he had had little success: his former services were almost forgotten; he was looked on with suspicion as a turncoat; and in the moment of patriot victory he was mortified to find himself slighted (as he thought) by patriots and government alike. Hussey Burgh was made chief baron of the exchequer; Yelverton was made attorney-general; Grattan refused office, but parliament voted him £50,000, and would have voted twice as much had he been willing to accept it; but for Flood, who had led the patriots before any of them had even entered the house of commons, there was neither government office nor popular applause. It is hardly surprising that when he saw a chance of under-mining Grattan's position and re-establishing his own he should seize it with both hands. Grattan took the view that by repealing the 'Sixth of George I', in response to the Irish declaration of independence, the British parliament had, in fact, admitted its own incompetence to legislate for Ireland, and this view was at first generally accepted by the patriots: when an Irish M.P. queried its soundness in the house of commons, only Flood supported him. But Flood, after a brief interval, raised the question again, for it gave him the opportunity he wanted. The 'Sixth of George I', he argued, was merely declaratory; the British parliament had legislated for Ireland before it was passed, and could, with the same show of right, legislate for Ireland after its repeal. Ireland would never be free until the British parliament had, in set terms, formally renounced its claim to superiority.

With this demand for 'renunciation' Flood opened his campaign against Grattan, and soon had a large popular following, especially among the Volunteers. It was never hard to convince the Irish public of the danger of oppression by England; and the Volunteers were perhaps not sorry to be told that their services were still required in the cause of free-dom. In parliament, Grattan's views prevailed; but the country supported Flood; and Grattan, who had been a national hero in June, was being lampooned in August as 'the little gentleman who received £50,000 from the unthinking generosity of the people he betrays'. The stupidity, or carelessness, of British ministers contributed to the agitation, for they allowed Ireland to be included, by name, in certain British acts for the regulation of trade; and though this was due to inadvertence, it strength-ened Flood's argument that independence had still to be won. The rising temper of the country made surrender to the popular demand a political necessity; and in January 1783 an act of the British parliament affirmed in the strongest terms that the complete legislative and judicial independence of Ireland should be 'established and ascertained for ever, and . . . at no time hereafter be questioned or questionable'.

The 'Renunciation Act' added little to the security of Irish indepen-dence, and the controversy that surrounded it had a dangerous effect on political life. By reviving a popular agitation, after the house of commons, led by Grattan, had declared itself satisfied, Flood had undermined public confidence not only in Grattan, but in parliament itself. He had by this means risen to a position of national importance, and the temptation to maintain that position by the same means was one that he was not likely to resist. He loved his country sincerely, but, more even than most political leaders, he wished that she should owe her welfare to himself; there was truth as well as harshness in Grattan's accusation that 'he implored the people to be dissatisfied with freedom because he was not the man who obtained it'. The controversy that he had provoked left behind an excited and unsettled public opinion, a readiness to defy parliament, and a bitter personal animosity between himself and Grattan. These were results of ominous consequence at a time when Ireland had to face issues of far more fundamental importance than 'renunciation'.

The substance of these issues, which were never settled, and never forgotten, while the Irish parliament lasted, can be reduced to a single question: For whom had the constitution of 1782 been won? Three groups were interested in the answer. The landlords, or the great majority of them, regarding themselves as 'the lords and commons of Ireland' whose rights had just been established, assumed that power would remain in their hands. Middle-class protestants, who formed the rank and file of the Volunteers, and whose support had made Grattan's victory possible, looked for their reward in a measure of parliamentary reform that would give them some real control of elections. Roman Catholics hoped that the reversal of the penal laws would now be carried a stage further, and that they would recover the right to vote, if not the right to sit in parliament.

These three aims were not, of necessity, conflicting. Parliament might have been reformed by destroying the absolute control of patrons over particular boroughs, without any fundamental weakening of the landlord class as a whole. Those who advocated the admission of Roman Catholics to political rights were quite confident that this would in no way imperil the protestant ascendancy. It was hardly to be expected, however, that men would consider such measures dispassionately; and those who looked to the future might well fear that moderate concessions, however reasonable in themselves, would only open the way for further demands. Proposals for parliamentary reform, brought forward in England about the same time, came to nothing; and the Irish house of commons was not likely to be more liberal than the British. And if British protestants still feared to trust a tiny Roman Catholic minority with political power, it is hardly to be wondered at that Irish protestants should be at least equally suspicious of a huge Roman Catholic majority. The discussion of these questions in Ireland, in the 1780s, was significant, not because it produced any positive result, but because it revealed and intensified the divisions in the protestant ascendancy.

The Roman Catholic question came before parliament in the summer of 1782, and two relief acts were passed repealing or modifying penal legislation on a variety of topics, including land, education, the residence of bishops and regular clergy, and the registration of priests. But the real question was whether or not Roman Catholics should be granted political rights. During the parliamentary debates on the legislation of 1782 this question arose only indirectly; but the strength of opposition was sufficiently revealed. Many members feared that if Roman Catholics could acquire property on the same terms as protestants then, even without being able to vote themselves, they would have it in their power to influence elections. 'I admit the merit of the Roman Catholics', declared Flood, 'and that merit makes me consent to enlarge their privileges; but I will not consent to their having any influence in choosing members for this house'. Grattan took the opposite view, and would have made concessions far more extensive than those then under discussion: 'As the mover of the declaration of rights, I should be ashamed of giving freedom to but 600,000 of my fellow-countrymen, when I could extend it to two million more'. But Flood's uneasiness was generally shared, and the act of 1782, which allowed Roman Catholics to purchase land as freely as protestants, excluded from the operation of this clause land situated in a parliamentary borough.

The division in the house of commons reflected a division in the protestant population at large. A section of the Volunteers favoured the admission of Roman Catholics to the parliamentary franchise, and found a prominent spokesman in Frederick Hervey, bishop of Derry, who had succeeded to the earldom of Bristol in 1774. He had taken to volunteering with all the extravagant enthusiasm that marked every activity of his singular career, and his great wealth had enabled him to indulge his love of military display, and to build up a party of his own. But Charlemont, the general of the Volunteers, had a much more solidly-based influence; and Charlemont, like Flood, thought the proposal to grant political power to Roman Catholics — 'that unaccountable frenzy' he called it — a direct threat to protestant liberty. The Volunteers, under his guidance, refused to commit themselves, and left the question open; but the clash of opinion, and the alarm of many protestants, helped to weaken their political influence.

On parliamentary reform the position was quite different. It was supported in the commons by both Grattan and Flood, and by a considerable body of members. In the country, it had the enthusiastic backing of the Volunteers. They had a strong motive for extending their political activities, for their influence was threatened by the conclusion of peace; but their attachment to reform was perfectly genuine, and was shared by a large section of protestant opinion, especially in the north. But though there was this agreement about ends, there was serious division over means. Grattan thought reform a matter for parliament itself; the Volunteers had been indispensable allies in winning national independence, but, independence won, their political task was finished. 'Having given a parliament to the people', he had declared, in moving his famous resolution of 16 April 1782, 'the Volunteers will, I doubt not, leave the people to parliament'. Flood took a totally different view: the Volunteers must complete the work they had begun, and if parliament would not reform itself, they must compel it to do so. Charlemont, though anxious to avoid extreme measures, gave him some support. When a national Volunteer convention met at Dublin, in the Rotunda, in November 1783, he took the chair, mainly, perhaps, to keep out the bishop of Derry, of whose intentions he was, not unreasonably, suspicious. The story that the bishop met Charlemont's warnings with the excited cry, 'We must have blood, my lord, we must have blood', may be apocryphal; but there was a real danger that the irresponsible violence of his language might incite some of the Volunteers to military action. The situation was a delicate one; for while the convention was meeting in the Rotunda, parliament was in session at College Green; and thus, two assemblies little more than half-a-mile apart were simultaneously debating the affairs of the nation. The future of Ireland depended on the relations to be established between them.

On Saturday, 29 November, after three weeks' deliberation, the convention agreed on a plan of reform, of which Flood was the principal author. Without delay, and still in his Volunteer uniform, he carried this plan down to the house of commons, and there moved for leave to bring in a bill 'for the more equal representation of the people in parliament'. Yelverton, the attorney-general, at once opposed the motion. 'We sit not here', he said, 'to register the edicts of another assembly, or to receive propositions at the point of the bayonet'. Flood replied that he was acting as a member of the house, and not as a delegate of the convention. But appearances were against him — at that very moment the convention was still in session, awaiting news of the reception of its reform scheme. Even those who supported the scheme in parliament could hardly deny that the influence of the Volunteers was behind it; Grattan, for example, though he thought that the scheme should be considered on its merits, was clearly uneasy about the circumstances in which it was presented. Among those who opposed it none was more bitter than John Fitzgibbon, afterwards Lord Clare. Fitzgibbon was at this time a rising barrister, with his eye on legal promotion, and he was no doubt influenced by the knowledge that the Castle was opposed to reform; but the hatred and fear of popular political action which informed his tirade against Flood were deeply felt. 'I say, that I do not think life worth holding at the will of an armed demagogue': it was on the same principle that, half a generation later, he was to suppress the United Irishmen and engineer the parliamentary union with Great Britain.

At three o'clock on Sunday morning, after a furious debate, the house refused by 157 votes to 77 to receive Flood's bill. Immediately afterwards, it passed by even larger majorities two resolutions, one declaring that it would 'maintain its just rights and privileges against all encroachments whatsoever', and one expressing its 'perfect satisfaction' with the 'present happy constitution'. It is significant that Grattan, though he had voted for receiving Flood's bill, voted also for the two subsequent resolutions.

These resolutions marked the end of the alliance between parliament and the Volunteer movement; but the breach occurred without violence; for the bulk of the Volunteers, though indignant at the commons' rejection of their proposals, were ready to submit to Charlemont's moderating influence. The bishop of Derry might perhaps have been able to gain support for a more aggressive policy, but either his good sense, or (as Charlemont thought) his pusillanimity, kept him quiet. The convention passed resolutions justifying its conduct and reiterating its support for parliamentary reform, and then quietly adjourned *sine die*. But the precarious unity of the protestant nation had been fatally undermined, and one step taken towards the revolutionary turmoil in which its independence was to be destroyed.

(2)

In 1782 the whig ministers had feared that the existence of two independent legislatures, side by side, would be a threat to the unity of the empire, and even after they had accepted Grattan's demands they still hoped that the Irish might be persuaded to recognize the 'superintending power' of the British parliament in matters of common concern. This hope was not fulfilled; but though the independence of the Irish parliament remained absolute, the danger to the unity of the empire was more apparent than real. The Irish protestants, as a body, were enthusiastically loyal to the crown and to the British connection; their leaders constantly emphasized the indissoluble nature of the link between the two kingdoms; and this sense of union received a practical expression when the Irish parliament, in gratitude for the recognition of its independence, unanimously voted £100,000 towards raising additional seamen for the British navy.

There was another, and more solid, guarantee of unity in the fact that the lord lieutenant was still nominated by, and responsible to, the British cabinet, which thus continued to control the Irish executive; and later events showed that the powers of the executive had not been essentially impaired by the constitutional changes of 1782. The weakness that it occasionally displayed during the next few years was not so much the effect of these changes as a reflection of the instability of contemporary British politics. There was a succession of weak cabinets, and a succession of viceroys whose tenure of office was hardly long enough to enable them to establish any effective influence. The death of Rockingham, in July 1782, led to the partial disruption of his ministry. Portland, unwilling to serve under Shelburne, at once resigned, after little more than three months in Ireland. Temple,[1] who succeeded him, reached Dublin in mid-September, and less than six months later Shelburne was overthrown by the coalition of Fox and North. Temple accordingly sent in his resignation, in March 1783. The political confusion in Great Britain at this juncture delayed the sending over of a successor, and he was obliged to remain in Ireland until June; but during this 'interregnum', as he called it, though he was in office, he was hardly in power. Northington, who was the nominee of the coalition ministry, survived its fall, in December 1783, by some weeks, for British politics were once more in confusion; but in February 1784 he was at length replaced.

All the cabinets and viceroys of this period, from the summer of 1782 to the end of 1783, were anxious to conciliate Irish opinion, even at the expense of unpalatable concessions: it was to this end, for example, that Temple advocated and Shelburne accepted the passage of a renunciation act; and after the general election of 1783 Northington, with the same object, persuaded his reluctant colleagues to concede the new parliament's demand for annual instead of biennial sessions. This conciliatory attitude promoted good relations between the patriots and the government, and with Northington in particular Grattan co-operated very closely. But this harmony was no substitute for a firm, consistent policy, and Britain's influence in Irish affairs seemed in danger of being undermined, not by deliberate opposition in Ireland, but by instability and weakness at home. The establishment of Pitt's ministry, and its confirmation in power by the general election of March 1784, changed the whole position. The new lord

---

[1] Afterwards marquis of Buckingham.

lieutenant, Rutland, and his chief secretary, Thomas Orde, remained in office for more than three years; they gave the Irish executive a continuity and firmness of purpose that had long been lacking, and the threat to British influence was averted.

It is possible that if the patriots had remained firmly united in 1782-3, when government in Britain was subject to rapid and confusing fluctuations, they might have done something towards establishing parliamentary control of the executive. But they seemed unaware of the need for any such change; they were distracted and divided by other matters; and the opportunity passed, never to recur: after 1782, as before, the executive remained an instrument of British control. Its position and character were not, however, wholly unaffected by the constitutional changes.

The extended powers of the Irish parliament and the institution of annual sessions increased the range and volume of legislation, and of all kinds of parliamentary business, and made the management of the house of commons, which was one of the main responsibilities of the executive, at once more important and more difficult. It was no longer possible, for example, to allow a measure that the government disliked to pass in Ireland, and leave it to be modified or suppressed in England; for the council there had lost the right to alter bills, and though it still had power to recommend the king to suppress them, this power was not, in fact, used.[1] Members were well aware that the value of their votes had been enhanced; and the cost, in terms of pensions and places, of maintaining a government majority rose steeply. But control of parliament had never been merely a matter of distributing patronage, and in the period after 1782 the degree of skill and tact required in managing the house of commons was greater than before. The members of 'Grattan's parliament' however venal they might be, had yet a sense of national dignity and independence that made them very sensitive on any question that involved, or seemed to involve, the constitutional rights of Ireland.

These circumstances made it necessary to strengthen the executive in every possible way. The means at its disposal for rewarding and purchasing support in the house of commons were extended, not so much by creating new offices and granting new pensions (methods that were liable to arouse public protest) as by attaching large salaries to existing offices, often of very little importance in themselves. Besides this, several lucrative

---

[1] The council occasionally expressed uneasiness about bills transmitted from Ireland; but it would seem that throughout the whole period between 1782 and 1800 only two were suppressed, both of them in August 1785.

offices formerly held by English absentees were now restored to Ireland. In 1784, for example, John Foster was appointed to the chancellorship of the exchequer, which for more than twenty years had been held as a sinecure by 'single-speech' Hamilton.

Foster, who had been chairman of the committee of ways and means, was probably the ablest financier in the house of commons; and in his hands the chancellorship quickly became a post of real importance, whereas formerly it had been treated simply as a piece of patronage, to be bestowed in reward for political services, and without regard to the fitness of the person to be appointed. This change of policy resulted from a new state of affairs. The administration of Ireland had become too onerous, too complicated, too important, to be managed by the lord lieutenant and chief secretary with no better aid than that of subservient office-holders and parliamentary hacks; it was now necessary to have in the government Irishmen of standing and ability, familiar with the political and economic life of the country. Such men, though acting under the general direction of the British cabinet, were not willing to be its mere agents, but had to be given some share in the making as well as the execution of policy. Foster's brief tenure of the exchequer (1784–5)[1] reflected strongly his own views on the Irish economy; and his successor, Sir John Parnell, though his fiscal policy left no such notable mark as Foster's, was equally independent in his outlook. It is worth noticing that both men resisted to the very end the parliamentary union between Great Britain and Ireland.[2]

Two other Irishmen, John Beresford and John Fitzgibbon, had an important share in government during this period. Beresford was first commissioner of revenue; and the patronage attached to his office, combined with great wealth and an extensive family connection, made him so powerful that he was sometimes called, half in envy, half in derision, the 'king of Ireland'. The title might, with more reason, have been applied to Fitzgibbon, whose influence on government policy was far greater. Fitzgibbon had supported, though belatedly and without enthusiasm, the demand for legislative independence; but he thought that the legislation of 1782 marked the extreme limit to which constitutional change should go, and he resisted all proposals for parliamentary reform and for the admission of Roman Catholics to political power. In spite of this conservative attitude he long remained on friendly terms with Grattan, who fully approved his appointment as attorney-general in 1783, during Northington's administration. Fitzgibbon's ability, industry and courage

[1] In 1785 Foster was elected speaker of the house of commons.
[2] See below, p. 270.

soon made him indispensable to the government; in 1789 he became lord chancellor, the first Irishman to hold the office for over sixty years; and for the last decade of the century he was probably the most powerful man in Ireland. The great, one might say the only, object of his policy was to maintain the protestant ascendancy; in his view, the final guarantee of that ascendancy was British power; and he dreaded any weakening of the link between the two kingdoms as likely to threaten Irish protestants with subjection to a popish democracy. He was ready to carry this argument to its logical conclusion: 'The only security for your liberty', he warned the house of commons in 1789, 'is your connection with Great Britain, and gentlemen who risk breaking the connection must make up their minds to a union. God forbid I should ever see that day; but if ever the day on which a separation shall be attempted may come, I shall not hesitate to embrace a union rather than a separation'.

This group of officials was sometimes referred to by contemporaries as the 'Irish cabinet'. But it had no collective responsibility and no independent basis of authority; when its advice was rejected by the British ministry the 'cabinet' simply remained in office and executed, however reluctantly, the policy decided in London. It was the long ascendancy of Pitt that made the maintenance of this system possible. If the fluctuation of party fortunes that marked the years between 1782 and 1784 had continued for another decade Irish government would have developed very differently. The practice, established in 1782, by which a change of ministry involved a change of viceroy strengthened the connection between political groups in the two countries; and, if such changes had continued to occur at fairly frequent intervals, the Irish cabinet must necessarily have taken on a distinctively party character. Even as it was, the Irish patriots maintained their association with Fox and his friends, and were sustained by the hope that if Pitt could be defeated at Westminster they themselves would take triumphant possession of the Castle. Throughout the whole period of 'Grattan's parliament' this cross-channel alliance of parties was a continuing factor in the politics of both countries.

(3)

The political unrest that marked the years 1782–4 probably owed something to the continued economic depression. The freeing of Irish trade had not brought the immediate prosperity that an optimistic public had looked for; bad harvests in 1782 and 1783 added to the general distress; and the excitement of victory in 1779 was succeeded by a sense of disappointment and frustration. Disappointment was keenest among the woollen manufacturers. The restriction on the export of woollen goods had been widely regarded both as a symbol of Irish subordination to England and as a main cause of Irish poverty. The restriction had now been removed; but the struggling industry that had survived since the seventeenth century seemed to be no better off.[1] The reason, it was alleged, was the domination of the Irish home market by British goods; other industries took up the same cry; and once the constitutional changes of 1782 opened the possibility of passing protective legislation through the Irish parliament, the demand for protection became widespread. During the session of 1783–4, petition after petition came before the commons, asking that the duties on British imports should be raised.

The demand seemed a not unreasonable one; for while all British goods were admitted to Ireland at moderate rates of duty, many Irish commodities were totally excluded from Britain, and, except for provisions and plain linens, which entered free, the duties imposed on the rest were so high as to be almost prohibitive. Basing themselves on this comparison, and on the argument that Irish manufacturers could not build up an export trade unless they had a secure home market, a group of M.P.s brought forward proposals for protective legislation in October 1783 and again in April 1784. But the fear of retaliation was strong. If a war of tariffs should begin, Ireland was bound to lose; for though the Irish market was valuable to Britain, the British market, which took nine-tenths of her linen and provision exports, was absolutely vital to Ireland; and rather than risk such a struggle the house of commons rejected the proposals for protection. The decision caused some popular disturbance in Dublin, the main centre of the protectionist campaign; but elsewhere it was calmly received; a good harvest in 1784 alleviated the immediate distress; and with the gradual improvement in the economic position during the succeeding years protection ceased to be an important issue.

The campaign for protection, though it proved abortive, was a clear indication that neither the trade concessions of 1779–80 nor the constitutional changes of 1782–3 had provided a permanently satisfactory basis for Anglo-Irish relations. To find such a basis was the first great object of Pitt's Irish policy, and as soon as he could spare time from the more pressing problems of British politics, he turned his attention to Ireland. His plan was to frame a commercial treaty between the two

[1] The customs returns show a sudden and substantial rise in the export of woollen goods from 1780. But the figures are misleading: there had been a long-established clandestine trade which now, with the removal of restrictions, became open.

kingdoms, so comprehensive in its scope that it would bind them indissolubly together, and remove every possibility of misunderstanding or rivalry between them — in his own words, to make 'England and Ireland one country in effect, though for local concerns under distinct legislatures, one in the communication of advantages, and, of course, in the participation of burdens'. During the latter half of 1784 the details of the proposed treaty were worked out between Pitt and Lord Sydney (the British home secretary) on one side, Rutland, Orde, Foster and Beresford, on the other. In essence, the conditions were as follows: there was to be free interchange between the two countries of foreign and colonial goods, without the imposition of additional duties; neither country was to prohibit the import of any product of the other, and the duty, if any, levied on every article should be the same in one country as in the other; where the existing duties differed, the higher was to be reduced to the level of the lower; there was to be a mutual preference for the produce of either country over foreign imports; in any year in which the hereditary revenue of Ireland exceeded a certain sum (later fixed at £656,000), the surplus was to be devoted to the maintenance of the navy.

In Pitt's opinion, this plan was much more favourable to Ireland than to Britain, for it offered Ireland the prospect of a valuable entrepôt trade, and it would open the British market to Irish manufacturers. On these grounds he justified the demand for an Irish contribution to imperial expenses; and though Rutland warned him that it would be strongly opposed in Ireland, he insisted on its inclusion as part of the bargain, pointing out that as the hereditary revenue was mainly derived from customs duties there would be no surplus, and therefore no contribution, unless there was, in fact, a substantial increase in trade.

These terms, in the form of ten 'propositions', were debated in the Irish parliament early in February 1785. Some feeble opposition from the protectionists was easily overcome; but the proposed contribution to the navy met with determined resistance, mainly on the ground that already national expenditure was regularly in excess of revenue, and that the national debt was rising. To meet this objection the government accepted an amendment, put forward by Grattan: no contribution was to be paid in any year in which the total revenue fell short of the national expenditure; but this restriction was to apply only in time of peace; during a war, the contribution was to be paid even if there was a deficit. With this addition, the 'propositions', now eleven in number, were accepted by both houses; and on 22 February Pitt introduced them in the British commons.

In Britain, the manufacturing interest offered immediate opposition, based mainly on the ground that the lower rates of wages and taxation current in Ireland would enable Irish manufacturers to flood the British market with cheap goods. The undeveloped state of the Irish economy made this, in fact, a remote and improbable danger; and the real cause of British alarm is to be found in a traditional jealousy of Ireland, rather than in any rational consideration of the actual circumstances. But the petitions against the proposed treaty that poured into Westminster from all parts of the country had a powerful effect; and it was only after weeks of debate, and with extensive modification, that the propositions, now extended to twenty, were at last, on 20 May, approved by the commons. The advantages that they offered to Ireland, though less extensive than those formerly proposed, were still considerable; but they were accompanied by a most unpalatable condition: the Irish parliament was to enact, immediately and without alteration, all measures which had been, or should be, passed in Great Britain concerning navigation, the colonial trade, and certain branches of foreign trade. In effect, this meant that Ireland was being asked to surrender a large part of the legislative independence that she had won barely three years earlier.

Whatever chance these revised propositions might have had of finding acceptance in Ireland was fatally weakened by the course of the long controversy in England. The parliamentary opposition, eager to embarrass Pitt, and not very scrupulous about means, had played simultaneously on the commercial jealousy of British merchants and the political jealousy of Irish patriots: 'I will not', said Fox, 'barter English commerce for Irish slavery'. The Irish parliament was certainly alert to the threatened encroachment on its freedom; and Pitt's efforts to reassure British manufacturers by minimizing the probable expansion of Irish industry under the proposed arrangements did nothing to reconcile it to accepting a subordinate rôle. When, on 12 August 1785, Orde laid the 'twenty propositions' before the Irish commons and moved for leave to bring in a bill based upon them, there was bitter opposition from all quarters of the house. The debate continued until nine o'clock the following morning, and though leave to bring in a bill was at length granted, the majority was so small that the government dared not proceed, and the whole project was abandoned. Its failure was due, in the long run, to the fact that in neither country was public opinion ready to recognize the interests, or allow for the prejudices, of the other. Pitt's desire to be impartial was genuine; but it was inevitable that he should be more alive to the clamorous opposition in England than to the more remote dissatisfaction in Ireland. He refused to be convinced by the repeated warnings of Rutland and Orde that any threat to its legislative independence would make the Irish parliament unmanageable; and it was this threat, rather than the commercial details of the proposed treaty, that finally wrecked the scheme.

These commercial negotiations had revived the idea of a parliamentary union, and it has sometimes been asserted that their failure convinced Pitt that such a union was essential to the safety of the empire; but this view is unsupported by contemporary evidence. He had certainly hoped that the treaty would settle the constitutional as well as the commercial relations between Great Britain and Ireland on a firm basis, and he had at one time feared lest the break-down of negotiations might lead to a new crisis, involving 'the revival of the Volunteers, the renewal of every species of confusion and a sort of commercial war between the two kingdoms'. But these fears proved groundless: Orde's prompt withdrawal in the face of opposition left Irish opinion jubilant, rather than resentful; and the Irish parliament showed no disposition to follow a commercial policy hostile to the interests of Great Britain. There was, in fact, nothing in the situation to suggest that the legislative independence of Ireland was a threat to imperial unity, nor is there any indication that Pitt so considered it. He was disappointed that his good intentions had been frustrated, but he hoped that when the excitement died down Irish opinion would come to recognize the advantage of the treaty, and accept it willingly.

A few years later, however, there arose another difference of opinion between the two parliaments which caused Pitt more anxiety. By November 1788 it had become clear that George III was, at least temporarily, out of his mind, and that a regent must be appointed. The Prince of Wales was the inevitable choice; and it was generally expected that one of his first acts would be to dismiss Pitt and call Fox to office. To avert this threat, Pitt proposed that parliament should define, in advance, the powers to be exercised by the regent; against this, Fox argued that the prince had a hereditary right to exercise full royal authority during his father's incapacity. Had the question been settled quickly, one way or the other, Ireland would have had no choice but to follow British example. But when the Irish parliament reassembled, on 5 February 1789, the debate in Britain was still going on; and the house of commons, despite all the government could do, asserted its right to decide the matter for itself. Grattan and the patriots naturally supported Fox, and were convinced that when the expected change of ministry took place the direction of Irish affairs would be put into their hands. The principal borough-owners, persuaded that the prince's power was now in the ascendant, were anxious to be on the winning side. Some members, without much considering the merits of the case, were glad of an opportunity of demonstrating the Irish parliament's independence of the British. The result was that, in face of all the influence the Castle could exert, an address was carried, calling upon the Prince of Wales to assume the regency of Ireland; and a similar address was carried in the house of lords. When the lord lieutenant, Buckingham, refused to transmit these addresses to the prince, both houses appointed commissioners to present them in person. At this point, the situation was transformed by the king's recovery; and, once it became clear that there would be no change of ministry, the government had little difficulty in re-establishing its control of parliament.

This 'regency crisis' has sometimes been cited as illustrating the way in which Irish parliamentary independence threatened the unity of the monarchy. But its real importance arose from the party position in Britain and the link between the patriots and the whigs. Those Irish M.P.s who supported the address to the prince had no thought of weakening the connection between Ireland and Great Britain; they acted from a variety of motives; but in the long run the decisive factor was the prospect of a change of ministry, and the effect that this would inevitably have on the composition of the Irish executive.

(4)

Despite the failure of the commercial propositions of 1784–5, Ireland was now entering on a period of comparative prosperity. With the return of peace the concessions of 1779–80 began to have their effect; the quickening of national life did something to discourage absenteeism among the landed classes, so that rents formerly spent abroad were now being spent at home;[1] parliament, though rejecting the protectionist policy put forward by the woollen manufacturers, was ready to use its new independence in other ways for the encouragement of industry.

This growing prosperity was reflected in an expansion of manufactures, both old and new. The linen industry quickly recovered from the depression of the 1770s, and exports jumped from 15 million yards in 1781 to 26 million yards in 1785, and to 45 million yards in 1792, on the eve of the French war. The development of the woollen industry, though important, was less spectacular. Exports rose rapidly between 1781 and 1785, and then declined fairly steadily, for Irish manufacturers found that they could not compete, either in quality of price, with their British and continental rivals. But growth of population, and a widespread rise in the standard of living, meant that there was an expanding home market,

[1] There was a general rise in rents during this period, and the value of rents paid to absentees increased; but the proportion of the total rental of the kingdom spent abroad probably declined.

especially for the coarser kinds of cloth, and this was largely supplied by home-produced goods: it is significant that during this period the export of raw wool from Ireland ceased almost completely. Though the high hopes of the early 1780s were not fulfilled, and though from time to time there were complaints of unemployment among the weavers, the woollen industry shared in the general prosperity, and reached a higher point of production than it had known since the late seventeenth century.

The spirit of enterprise in the Irish economy at this time is strikingly illustrated in the rise of the cotton industry: in the 1770s it had barely established a foothold in the country; twenty years later, it was a serious rival to linen. This expansion was due, in the first place, to the opening of direct trade with North America, the main source of raw materials, but even more to the encouragement given by parliament. Bounties were granted on home sales in 1783 and on exports in 1784; in 1794 a heavy protective tariff was established, and, contrary to the usual Irish practice, this applied to British as well as to foreign goods. The cotton industry also benefited from the application of up-to-date techniques, which the more old-fashioned linen manufacturers were slow to adopt: the first power-driven textile machinery in Ireland was a water-mill for spinning cotton twist, established at Whitehouse, on the outskirts of Belfast, in 1784. Down to the early 1790s the industry was fairly widely distributed throughout Ireland, but thereafter it tended to be concentrated in the Belfast area, where capital for development was more plentiful.

Apart from textiles, the most important manufacture to expand under the new conditions was brewing, though here the expansion was somewhat delayed. The freeing of Irish trade in 1779–80 had re-opened the supply of foreign hops; but the brewers had to face heavy competition, not only from imported British beer but also from cheap home-produced spirits, and down to the early 1790s the position of the industry was precarious. Both government and parliament were willing to assist it, partly because of the political influence exercised by the brewers, who found a powerful champion in Grattan, and partly out of concern at the enormous increase of distillation, much of it illegal; but revenue considerations, and a reluctance to discriminate against British beer, delayed decisive action. Between 1791 and 1795, however, legislation was passed which simplified the complex system of regulations under which the industry had hitherto operated, and replaced the tax on beer by a tax on malt. The immediate effect of these reforms was an increase in home production, and a corresponding decline in the amount of beer imported from Great Britain; on a longer view, they prepared the way for the emergence of brewing as a major Irish industry in the nineteenth century. But neither the encouragement of brewing, nor the imposition of heavier excise duties on spirits, did much to check the increase in distillation.

Other manufactures established or revived during the period were of minor importance. The silk industry made some progress in Dublin; but it was hampered by the fact that Great Britain, through the East India Company, controlled the supply of raw material, and by the end of the century it was in decline. The glass industry, which had been virtually destroyed by British legislation in the middle of the century, revived so rapidly in the 1780s that it was able to supply almost the whole home market; but the value of the export trade, even at its peak, was only about £14,000 a year. Attempts were made to produce other commodities — hats, gloves, carpets, soap, candles, paper, crockery; but Irish manufacturers could not compete with British imports, which were generally lower in price and better in quality. Only a policy of full-scale protection would have enabled them to establish a hold on the market.

Despite the expansion of the textile and brewing industries, the economic life of Ireland continued to depend essentially on the land. Neither the commercial concessions of 1779–80 nor the constitutional changes of 1782 had had any direct bearing on the agrarian position: tenants still suffered under rack-rents and tithes; a series of poor harvests between 1779 and 1783 produced widespread distress; and there were food riots in many areas. While such conditions prevailed, Irish prosperity could be no more than superficial, and parliament, though it had little sympathy with the peasantry's grievances, realized the gravity of the situation. Its traditional remedy for agrarian distress was the encouragement of tillage; but earlier measures for the purpose had failed of their effect, for the British privy council had refused to sanction a scale of bounties high enough to encourage the growth of grain for export, and parliament had been unwilling to apply compulsion to the landlords. After 1782 circumstances were different: not only had the privy council virtually lost the power to quash bills, but Britain, no longer a grain-exporting country, had now no reason to be jealous of Irish agriculture. In the spring of 1784 a really effective measure for the encouragement of tillage came into operation; it was largely the work of John Foster, chancellor of the exchequer, and is commonly known by his name.

The purpose of Foster's Corn Law was twofold: to encourage agriculture, and to ensure 'a regular and standing supply of corn'. There was to be an export bounty on wheat while the price did not exceed 27s a barrel, and a heavy import duty while the price was below 30s a barrel; when the price rose above 30s all export was prohibited; similar regulations, at different price-levels, applied to barley and oats.[1] This measure proved an effective encouragement to export, for the prices at which bounty was payable were above those normally prevailing — during the next decade (1784–93) wheat qualified for bounty in eight years out of the ten, barley in seven, oats in seven. The result was a rapid rise in exports, and a vast extension of tillage.

Two other factors helped to produce this change in the Irish economy. One was the expansion of the British market for grain, which Ireland was well-placed to supply. The other was a sharp rise in population, from about three and three-quarter million in the 1770s to more than four and three-quarter million by 1791. The consequent pressure on land tended to force up rents and to encourage sub-division of holdings; and tenants often found that the cultivation of grain for export was the best, if not the only, way of making ends meet on a small farm. But this does not seem to have involved any serious encroachment on pasture, and it is possible that much of the land now brought under tillage was reclaimed from bog or mountain. Certainly, there was no decline in the volume of pastoral products, and the provision trade continued to flourish. Exports of butter, pork and bacon all increased substantially; and though there was some reduction in the export of beef, this was offset by the development of an extensive trade in live cattle. Foster's Corn Law did not, as has sometimes been said, turn Ireland from a pastoral into an agricultural country; but it encouraged a more intensive use of the land, at a time when opportunity of profit and pressure of population were working in the same direction.

The development of manufactures, the spread of tillage, the general expansion of trade, all combined to increase the wealth of the country; and contemporary opinion, at home and abroad, was convinced that Ireland had never been so prosperous. Dublin, its importance as a capital enhanced by parliamentary independence, entered on a brilliant period of expansion. The building of the Custom House and the Four Courts, the institution of the Order of St Patrick, with its chapel in St Patrick's Cathedral, the establishment of the Bank of Ireland, the Royal Irish Academy, the Royal College of Surgeons, all bore witness to the wealth and activity of the new era. Provincial cities and towns also had their share of this prosperity, and throughout the country landlords and middlemen profited from high prices and increased production; even the more sub-

---

[1] British grain was exempted from the protective duties, on condition that a similar privilege was given to Irish grain in the British market; but, since Britain was no longer a grain-exporting country, the Irish producer was in no danger from British competition.

stantial tenant-farmers, despite rising rents, were able to improve their position. But to the lowest classes of society, which in Ireland formed a high proportion of the total population, the development of the national economy brought little or no benefit. The sharp contrast between wealth and poverty, which was a commonplace of urban life throughout most of western Europe at the time, seems to have been even more strongly marked in Ireland than elsewhere in the British Isles. In rural areas, the hardships of the cottier class even tended to increase, for wages did not rise in proportion to rents and the general cost of living. Their only defence against oppressive conditions lay in secret combination: over much of the country agrarian unrest was endemic, and in Munster, from the mid-1780s onwards, there was a revival of Whiteboy activity.

This restlessness among the peasantry was a constant source of alarm to the government; and in the correspondence of successive viceroys it appears again and again as one of the most urgent problems with which they were faced. But there was little idea of any solution beyond a stricter enforcement of the law. Even the more liberal members of the landed and commercial classes were too much concerned about constitutional and economic issues, about the reform of parliament, the expansion of trade, the encouragement of industries, to spare much attention for the great social questions that threatened the peace of rural Ireland. They were no less attached to the rights of property than to the rights of the nation; and the Volunteers sometimes assisted in the suppression of agrarian disturbances. The events of 1798 were to show how precarious was the basis on which they had erected their imposing structure of parliamentary independence.

XIII

The Impact of Revolution

---

(1)

While the British and Irish parliaments were squabbling over the question of the regency, events in France were moving rapidly towards that catastrophic upheaval which was to alter the current of political life throughout western Europe, and not least in Ireland. During the summer of 1789 reports from France took up more and more space in Irish newspapers; and before the end of July the term 'French Revolution' had reached the headlines. Public opinion, in general, received these reports with satisfaction; the tradition of the Volunteers, the recent establishment of the 'constitution of 1782', the widespread movement for parliamentary reform, had all prepared the way for a genuine, if somewhat naïve, enthusiasm for revolutionary principles, and four newspapers reprinted Paine's *Rights of Man*. Even when the Revolution took a much more violent turn this enthusiasm continued; during 1792 subscriptions were raised in Ulster to assist the French in repelling invasion, and in November the Belfast Volunteers welcomed the deposition of 'Louis the Last', and the establishment of a republic. From the beginning, of course, the revolution had its critics in Ireland as elsewhere, and their number was increased by the execution of the king, and, even more, by that of the queen. But Irish reformers, even if they were disappointed or alarmed at some aspects of revolutionary policy, still found much to admire in the new France — the wide extent of the electoral franchise, the abolition of tithe, the establishment of religious equality — and their admiration for this example was bound to influence their outlook on Irish affairs.

The French Revolution, and its effect on public opinion, added greatly to the difficulties of the Irish administration. The danger lay in the country, not in parliament, for the opposition leaders there had little sympathy with democratic ideas: a Whig Club, founded in 1790 by Grattan and some of his allies to press for parliamentary reform, was so moderate in outlook that it did not even include an extension of the franchise in its programme. But outside parliament the position was very different. Revolutionary enthusiasm gave new life to the declining Volunteer spirit, and it was the Volunteers who took a leading part in celebrating the victories of the Revolution, which they linked, ominously, with the American declaration of independence and the Irish 'constitution of 1782'. But the Volunteers no longer represented, as Grattan had said of them a decade earlier, the 'armed property of the nation'; they had broken loose from the control of the aristocracy and gentry; their ranks were filled with men from the lower strata of society, and their officers were radical merchants and shopkeepers, rather than members of the landed classes. They were still proud of the legislative independence that they had won for Ireland, but they were more determined than ever that that independence should be widely shared.

It was in the north, and especially among the protestant dissenters, that the Volunteer movement remained strongest, and it was here that revolutionary and republican sentiments were most loudly expressed. In all this activity perhaps the most notable development, and that most alarming to the government, was a movement towards friendly co-operation between presbyterians and Roman Catholics. Presbyterians were certainly not all of one mind on the matter; but demands for the repeal of the remaining popery laws became more frequent among them, and, as a body, they became increasingly identified with a policy of complete religious equality.

An alliance of Roman Catholics and presbyterians certainly seemed likely in the early 1790s. It is true that Roman Catholics generally did not share presbyterian enthusiasm for the Revolution. The bishops and clergy were horrified at the treatment of the French church by the new régime; the upper classes were at least as hostile to Revolutionary ideas as upper-class protestants, and were consequently anxious to avoid embarrassing the government, even to the extent of minimizing their own claims to a further relaxation of the penal laws.[1] But there was also among the Roman Catholics, especially in Dublin, a strong democratic element, which was determined to press on with the campaign for full civil rights, which favoured parliamentary reform, and which was quite prepared to ally with the presbyterians against the government. In the course of 1791 this democratic element got control of the Catholic Committee, founded some

---

[1] This aristocratic attitude is also reflected in the conduct of those Irishmen who held commissions in the Irish Brigade of the French army at the time of the Revolution. Almost all of them refused to serve under the republic, and in 1794 many of them transferred their allegiance to George III.

years earlier to forward Roman Catholic political interests, and hitherto dominated by a group of nobles and gentry. In the following year the committee appointed as its paid secretary a young protestant barrister, Theobald Wolfe Tone, who had recently attacked the penal laws in a very able pamphlet, *An argument on behalf of the Catholics of Ireland.* It was a significant appointment, for Tone's avowed aim was to bring together Irishmen of all creeds in an effort to establish complete religious equality, and to carry through a radical reform of parliament. Though not himself a presbyterian, he was in close touch with the presbyterians of Ulster, and in 1791 had helped to found at Belfast the Society of United Irishmen, as an instrument to carry out his policy. Similar societies were quickly established in Dublin and in many other places throughout the kingdom, and the basis of a democratic alliance between Roman Catholics and protestants seemed to have been firmly laid.

Events were to prove that this alliance was, in fact, precarious; but at the time its very existence was enough to frighten the authorities, both in Dublin and in London. Their reactions to the danger were different: Fitzgibbon, whose influence was dominant at the Castle, was more than ever convinced that the Roman Catholics must be excluded from all political power; Pitt believed that timely concessions would detach them from the protestant radicals, and make them firm supporters of the government. Fitzgibbon was obliged to yield; but the obvious reluctance with which he allowed Pitt's policy to be executed went far to make it ineffective, and the Roman Catholics remained unreconciled.

(2)

Pitt's desire to conciliate Roman Catholic opinion extended to Great Britain as well as to Ireland, and in 1791 much of the British penal legislation was repealed. In both countries his object was the same — to strengthen national unity in face of possible danger from revolutionary France. But in 1791 the danger was not yet acute; he was prepared to move slowly; and he refrained from pressing an unwilling Irish executive too hard. The influence of Fitzgibbon and his colleagues, therefore, was sufficient to ensure that the initiative was not taken by the government, and that the concessions made were confined within narrow limits. When the parliamentary session opened in January 1792 the lord lieutenant's speech contained no reference to Roman Catholic claims, and it was left to a private member to bring in a relief bill. Once introduced, however, the bill received government support, and passed without difficulty. By its terms, all disabilities attaching to marriages between Roman Catholics and protestants were repealed, Roman Catholics were admitted to the practice of the law, and the remaining restrictions on their education were removed. But a proposal that they should be admitted to the county franchise, though on a qualification so high as to exclude all below the upper middle class, was defeated by an overwhelming majority, and the road to any share of political power remained closed.

The Catholic Committee refused to accept this decision as final. To give greater force to its demand for political rights it followed the example of the Volunteers almost ten years earlier and summoned a representative 'Catholic Convention', with delegates from all over the kingdom, to meet at Dublin in December. This move alarmed and perplexed the executive. It would willingly have prohibited the holding of the convention; but such action might easily provoke serious rioting, or even a general insurrection, with which the government forces were ill-prepared to deal; and appeals to the British cabinet for support were coldly received. Pitt recognized the impolicy of yielding to a threat of force; but in the autumn of 1792 relations with France were getting steadily worse, and Ireland might well become a fruitful field for French intrigue; with war now a serious possibility it was urgently necessary to abolish 'the bank of discontent', as Burke called it, 'upon which every description of seditious men may draw at pleasure'. By November the British cabinet had made up its mind, and the lord lieutenant was confidentially informed that further concessions must be granted to the Roman Catholics.

This was the state of affairs when the Catholic Convention met in Dublin on 3 December.[1] Its proceedings were orderly and moderate; and the petition that it drew up for presentation to the king was so framed as to allay protestant suspicions. But the convention showed its determination to press matters as far as possible by appointing a delegation to present the petition to the king in person, instead of forwarding it, as was usual, through the lord lieutenant. The delegates travelled via Scotland, and it is noteworthy that as they passed through Belfast, on their way to take ship at Donaghadee, the protestant inhabitants lined the streets, shouting out good wishes for the success of the petition. The delegates were well received at court; but before they arrived — before, indeed, the Catholic Convention had met — the British cabinet had already resolved to insist on a further measure of relief; and the petition, though it may have confirmed this resolution, had no decisive effect on policy.

The doings of the convention aroused widespread alarm among

---

[1] The hall in which it met was situated in Back Lane; hence it was sometimes called, in derision, the 'Back Lane parliament'.

protestants. This alarm was, in some measure, deliberately stimulated by Fitzgibbon, Beresford and their supporters, who were anxious to convince Pitt of the strength of protestant opposition to any further relief for Roman Catholics; but there can be no doubt that many protestants were genuinely frightened. Barely a century had elapsed since the Williamite land settlement, its memory was still fresh, and fears that the Roman Catholics hoped to overthrow it, though they may have been unfounded, were not altogether unnatural. Yet these protestant fears were not, in fact, likely to impede Pitt's policy. Those who felt them most acutely were, for that very reason, convinced that their own safety must depend, in the long run, on the British connection; and they shrank from persistent opposition to any measure which the British ministry was determined to carry. And Pitt could count also on the support of the considerable body of protestants who were willing to admit Roman Catholics to the parliamentary franchise, either from conviction of the justice of their claim, or in the belief that this was the readiest means of tranquillizing the country.

The attitude of the British cabinet, already known to the Irish executive, and generally suspected from the reception accorded to the delegates from the Catholic Convention, was publicly declared when parliament reassembled on 10 January 1793. The lord lieutenant's speech, in a passage inserted by the British ministers, expressed the hope 'that the situation of his majesty's catholic subjects will engage your serious attention'. The full force of this became clear three weeks later, when Hobart, the chief secretary, introduced a relief bill, the terms of which had been virtually dictated from England. Roman Catholics were now to be admitted to the parliamentary and municipal franchise on the same terms as protestants; they were to have the right, subject to certain conditions, including a property qualification, to bear arms; the few remaining restrictions on their holding of land were to be removed; all civil and military posts, with some specified exceptions,[1] were to be open to them. The only substantial disability to which they were still to be subject was exclusion from membership of parliament. The opposition to this sweeping measure was surprisingly small; and, with a few unimportant amendments, it was passed by a large majority, though it is safe to assume that many who voted for it did so reluctantly. But the progress of the revolutionary armies, and the outbreak of war with France, had changed

---

[1] These included the offices of lord lieutenant, lord deputy, or other chief governor of the kingdom; lord chancellor, lord high treasurer, chancellor of the exchequer, and other high legal and administrative officers; provost or fellow of Trinity College, Dublin; commander-in-chief of the forces or general on the staff.

the situation. Many members who shared Fitzgibbon's view that the bill was 'unwise and pernicious' and that its passage would be a 'precedent fatal to all legitimate authority', nevertheless followed his example in supporting it, on the ground that it would not now be safe to disappoint the hopes that had been aroused, even though they might not have Fitzgibbon's personal motive of a desire to remain in office.

The Roman Catholics were profuse in their gratitude for the act; but, at least in its immediate effects, it did not add much to their political power. In the existing state of the Irish corporations there were only a few boroughs where they could hope to have any important influence in parliamentary elections; and the main result of the extension of the county franchise was to enlarge what Wolfe Tone described as that 'disgrace to our constitution and our country, the wretched tribe of forty-shilling freeholders, whom we see driven to their octennial market by their land-lords'. The concessions made in 1793 might seem important, but they would have very little effect on the distribution of political power unless followed by some substantial reform of the system of representation.

Some such reform might possibly have been carried in 1793, had a determined effort been made. A large proportion of the house of commons, and even some of the principal borough-owners, were willing to support it, or at least to accept it, either from desire for popularity, or from fear of revolution; and few were prepared to offer open opposition. The govern-ment, cautiously hostile, played for time, and the question was shelved until the following session; but by then the temper of the house had changed, and in March 1794 a moderate reform bill was easily defeated. The reformers did, however, win some minor successes in 1793. The hereditary revenue was at last brought fully under the control of parlia-ment. The pension list was substantially curtailed. An act 'for securing the freedom and independency of the house of commons' (commonly called the 'place act') did something to reduce government influence over members: it excluded from the house of commons all those who held pensions during pleasure, or for a term of years, and also the holders of places of profit under the crown created after the passing of the act; and it provided that a sitting member who accepted a post of profit already in existence should vacate his seat, though he might be re-elected.

The readiness of both executive and parliament to meet at least some of the popular demands arose partly from fear of revolution; and this fear expressed itself, during the session of 1793, in measures of repression as well as in measures of reform. An arms act prohibited the importation or distribution of arms, ammunition and powder, except under licence; and a convention act prohibited the holding of representative assemblies —

the government did not intend that the Catholic Convention should be followed by a convention of the United Irishmen. A militia act, though not a directly repressive measure, was intended both to strengthen the government and also, by drawing off possible recruits, to weaken the Volunteers.

The events of 1793–4, in their total effect, marked a turning-point in the history of the protestant ascendancy. The half-hearted concessions of 1793 had conciliated neither Roman Catholics nor protestant radicals, and the rejection of the reform bill of 1794 helped to strengthen the incipient alliance between them; and this at the very time when the idea of revolutionary action was spreading, and the hope of French help growing stronger. Not only had Pitt failed to bring in a policy of genuine conciliation, but his intervention, by weakening the faith of the reactionaries in the 'constitution of 1782' as a bulwark of the protestant ascendancy, had prepared the way for a fatal division within the ascendancy itself. It is never safe to regard any historical sequence as inevitable; but there is certainly a clear line of development from the events of these years to the insurrection of 1798 and the parliamentary union of 1800.

(3)

The outbreak of war with France and the prospect of a French invasion changed the political situation in Ireland: revolution was now a present danger, not just a vague possibility, and this fact gave new and critical importance to the attitude of the Roman Catholics. The threat of revolution came, most obviously, from the United Irishmen. They had included, almost from the beginning, some members whose aim was not to reform, but to destroy, the kingdom of Ireland, and to set up in its place a republic on French principles; the outbreak of war and the hope of foreign aid won new recruits for this policy, and when a government attempt to suppress the society, in May 1794, drove it underground, the influence of the revolutionaries naturally grew stronger. From the end of 1794 onwards the United Irishmen were increasingly committed to a policy of alliance with France and complete separation from England; they were already in touch with French agents, and they pressed constantly for the dispatch of an expedition to their assistance.

In 1794 the United Irishmen were still mainly protestant, and their strength lay among the northern presbyterians. This was a dangerously narrow basis on which to plan a national revolution. It had, certainly, been a protestant movement, largely dependent on Ulster support, that had won the 'constitution of 1782'; but the position in 1794 was very different, for the landlords, who had led the campaign for legislative independence, were solidly opposed to revolution. But the position had changed in another way also, and one more favourable to the United Irishmen. By 1794 the Roman Catholics, who had played an almost passive part in 1782, had acquired political consciousness, and some measure of political power, and they were no longer to be ignored. On the one hand, if they could be brought into the revolutionary movement its chances of success would be enormously increased; on the other, if the government were able to count upon their loyalty there was little reason to doubt that the protestant republicans could be easily crushed.

It was because he recognized the decisive part that the Roman Catholics might play that Tone was anxious to win the confidence of their leaders, and to this end engaged in the campaign for relief between 1791 and 1793. But it was essential to his plans that the Roman Catholics should remain discontented, and he had, in fact, no desire that the government should yield the claims he was pressing; when the Catholic Convention and Catholic Committee expressed satisfaction with the act of 1793 he was bitterly disappointed. On the whole, however, he was less concerned about the attitude of the middle classes, represented by the committee, than about the attitude of the peasants, whose smouldering resentment against landlords and tithe-proctors he hoped to turn into a political channel. There can be no doubt that at this time some vague notions of French 'equality' had penetrated the Irish countryside, and may have given an additional stimulus to the endemic agrarian unrest. But this development, hopeful from Tone's point of view, was accompanied by another that at first seemed to threaten the ruin of all his plans — the growth of sectarian strife between Roman Catholic and protestant tenants.

Such sectarian strife was not new; but in the 1790s it became particularly acute in the southern Ulster counties, and especially in Armagh. It was the product of many influences, of which the most important was a keener competition for holdings, resulting from the sharp rise in population. Protestant farmers complained that they were in danger of being ousted by Roman Catholics, whose lower standard of living enabled them to outbid protestant competitors; they formed themselves into armed bands — 'Peep o' day boys' — which raided the homes of Roman Catholics and tried to frighten them into leaving the countryside. The latter set up a counter-organization — the 'Defenders' — and clashes between the two groups were frequent and often fatal.

With the Catholic Committee apparently willing to delay any agitation for further relief, and with the peasantry over much of Ulster almost in a state of civil war, the prospects for the United Irishmen seemed bleak.

But political events in Great Britain and Ireland in 1794 and 1795 changed the position in their favour.

In July 1794 Portland and his friends at length broke with the main body of the whigs and joined Pitt. This change had an almost immediate effect on the political atmosphere in Ireland, for it was generally believed that the Portland group had been given complete control of Irish affairs, a view that was confirmed in August, when it became known that Lord Fitzwilliam,[1] one of Portland's principal allies, was to be made viceroy as soon as a suitable post could be found for Westmoreland. In Dublin, the news produced great excitement. It was generally assumed that Grattan's influence would now be re-established; and though he himself made it clear that he would not accept any government appointment, other leading members of the Whig Club, and especially the Ponsonbys, confidently expected to assume office. They were soon in touch with Portland and Fitzwilliam, urging them to dismiss Fitzgibbon and Beresford and to reform the whole system of Irish administration. And the Catholic Committee, encouraged by Fitzwilliam's known sympathy with its claims, resumed activity. But Pitt was not, in fact, willing to hand Ireland over to his new allies, though the negotiations that preceded the coalition may have justified their belief that he was. His own view was hostile to any immediate change in Irish policy, and all the advice that he received from the Castle was against further concessions either to the reformers or to the Catholic Committee. When Fitzwilliam was at last dispatched to Ireland, in January 1795, he was instructed not to make any general change in the administration, and not to bring in a relief bill; if a bill should be brought in by a private member he was to use all his influence to have it postponed; only if resistance proved unavailing, and the bill seemed likely to pass in any case, was he to give it government support.

These instructions were not formally committed to writing, and there was afterwards great dispute about both their content and their interpretation. But it is certain that Fitzwilliam felt himself free to act as he thought the situation required; when he found the Roman Catholics clamorous for immediate relief he made no attempt to discourage them, and repeatedly urged on the cabinet the absolute necessity of granting their demands. For week after week, however, the cabinet ignored these representations; and Fitzwilliam, taking silence for approval, committed the government to supporting a relief bill that Grattan had announced his intention of introducing; its terms were not at once made public, but its essential purpose was to admit Roman Catholics to membership of

[1] William Wentworth Fitzwilliam, second Earl Fitzwilliam.

parliament. This was the position in the second week of February; and it was only at this point, when he could no longer honourably withdraw his promised support, that Fitzwilliam was warned by the cabinet that he should not enter into any engagements on the Roman Catholic question. He tried to defend his action, but on 18 February he was peremptorily instructed to oppose the bill, and five days later he was recalled.

Fitzwilliam's attitude on the Roman Catholic question was naturally distasteful to the leading politicians of the Castle; and they felt their position directly threatened by his close alliance with the Irish 'Whigs', who made no effort to conceal their hopes of a general change in the administration. Pitt had, in fact, vetoed any such change in advance; but on this matter, as on the relief bill, Fitzwilliam interpreted cabinet policy in his own way: very shortly after his arrival in Dublin he dismissed John Beresford and the two under-secretaries of state; and it was known that he intended to replace the attorney-general and solicitor-general by supporters of Grattan. Beresford and his friends at once appealed to Pitt, Fitzgibbon backed them up, and all their influence in both kingdoms was used against the lord lieutenant. It was this, as much as his support of the relief bill, that led to his recall. The dismissed officials were now restored, and the control of the Beresford–Fitzgibbon group over the Irish administration was stronger than ever: it was, significantly, in this year that Fitzgibbon was raised to the earldom of Clare.

The removal of Fitzwilliam dashed the hopes not only of the Roman Catholics but of all supporters of reform. On the day of his departure Dublin was in mourning, and public bodies all over the country drew up addresses expressing approval of his policy and grief at his recall. When his successor, Lord Camden,[1] arrived at the end of March he was sullenly received, and there was some popular demonstration of hostility. But this national feeling had little effect on parliament, which was, as usual, ready to follow the lead of the executive. The house of commons did, indeed, pass unanimously a resolution of gratitude for Fitzwilliam's services; but it decisively rejected a proposal to bring pressure on the government by a short money bill; and Grattan and the Whig Club, whose influence had seemed to be in the ascendant, were soon reduced once more to an impotent opposition. Thus the events of these months revealed not only the great strength of the reactionary group in the Castle, but also the apparent hopelessness of working for reform by constitutional means. Whig

[1] John Jeffries Pratt, second Earl Camden (afterwards first Marquis Camden).

influence in the country declined, and a struggle developed between the forces of revolution on one hand, and the most intransigent section of the protestant ascendancy on the other. No doubt many moderates were frightened into the reactionary camp; but the widespread disappointment caused by Fitzwilliam's failure, especially among Roman Catholics, created an atmosphere favourable to insurrectionary activity, and brought a host of recruits to the United Irishmen.

(4)

Lord Camden entered on the viceroyalty in an optimistic spirit; but neither by character nor by experience was he fitted for the arduous task he had undertaken. His chief secretary, Thomas Pelham, was a man of considerable ability, and had some knowledge of Irish affairs, having been chief secretary for a few months in 1783–4; but his health was poor, he accepted the post reluctantly, and he spent a great part of his time in England. In the circumstances, Fitzgibbon, his influence confirmed by recent events, was able to maintain an easy ascendancy over the lord lieutenant. This ascendancy was, from the outset, reflected in the policy of the new administration: Beresford and his friends were reinstated, a measure of which Pelham strongly disapproved; and the viceroy received explicit instructions to resist all proposals for granting further relief to the Roman Catholics. The house of commons quickly responded to the change in the political atmosphere, and Grattan's relief bill, which in February 1795 had seemed likely to pass, was rejected by a great majority in May.

From this time onwards, 'Catholic Emancipation' (as the admission of Roman Catholics to parliament was now commonly called) almost ceased to be an active parliamentary question; but it continued to be agitated in the country, and the government made an effort to conciliate the Roman Catholics by a concession of a totally different sort — the foundation and partial endowment of a college for the education of their clergy. Candidates for the priesthood had formerly been sent to continental seminaries; but the French Revolution, and the Revolutionary wars, interrupted this practice: many seminaries were closed down, travel was difficult, and, in any case, the bishops feared that students educated abroad would now be exposed to the 'contagion of sedition and infidelity'. There was a strong body of opinion, among Roman Catholics and protestants alike, in favour of educating students of both denominations together within the University of Dublin, to which Roman Catholics were already being admitted in considerable numbers; but this proposal was disregarded, and the Royal College of St Patrick, at Maynooth, was established in 1795 on a strictly sectarian basis. It was to have a profound influence on the character of the Irish clergy, and on Roman Catholicism throughout the English-speaking world.

As a conciliatory measure the establishment of Maynooth was no substitute for Emancipation, and the sense of grievance among the Roman Catholics remained strong. Even among the middle and upper classes, who had long been noted for their firm attachment to the crown, there were signs of disaffection, and some of them became involved with the United Irishmen. But the main hopes of the revolutionary leaders still lay with the peasantry, and during 1796 and 1797 they made great efforts to win them over to their cause. They were aided by a development that might at first sight have seemed unpropitious — a sharpening of sectarian strife in the north. This reached a crisis in September 1795, when a pitched battle between Peep o' day boys and Defenders took place at the Diamond, in County Armagh. The Defenders, who seem to have provoked the conflict, were completely routed, and that evening the victorious protestants established an 'Orange Society'[1] to protect their own immediate interests and to maintain the protestant ascendancy. During the next few months the Roman Catholics of Armagh and the neighbouring counties were subjected to a violent persecution, which drove thousands of them to take refuge in Connaught. It is very uncertain how far the members of the new society — the 'Orangemen' — were directly involved in these outrages; but they were held responsible for them all, and stories, often exaggerated, of the cruelties that the refugees had suffered at their hands spread throughout the country. The magistrates were at first unable (and in some cases perhaps unwilling) to restrain the disorder, and it was commonly believed that the activities attributed to the Orangemen had government approval. The fact that the Orange Society was quickly taken up by men of rank and property, and that a branch of it, established in the capital, was joined by some government officials, seemed to give colour to this belief. The Roman Catholic peasants, convinced that the Orangemen were bent on their extermination and that the law would not protect them, flocked into the ranks of the Defenders. The United Irishmen, who already had adherents among the Defenders, seized this opportunity to intensify their propaganda. They still proclaimed the need for union among Irishmen of all denominations, but at the same time they warned the Roman Catholics that they would never be safe from the Orangemen until the existing régime had been completely overthrown. In the circumstances, the argument carried great weight, and a

[1] Later known as the 'Orange Order'.

large body of the Defenders was easily brought over to the revolutionary cause.

These activities, which could not be kept completely secret, naturally alarmed the government; and its anxiety was increased by the knowledge that there was considerable likelihood of foreign aid for the conspirators — a French agent had been arrested in Dublin in April 1794. It was true that this arrest, and the revelations accompanying it, had temporarily weakened the revolutionary party. Some of the United Irishmen, realizing for the first time how far they had been led on the road to rebellion, now drew back; a few fled to the continent; and Tone himself came to a bargain with the government, by which he made a written confession of his share in the conspiracy, though with conditions as to its use against other suspects, and was allowed to withdraw to America, whither he sailed in May 1795. But the United Irishmen quickly recovered from this check, and pressed on with their preparations for a rising. Tone did not remain long in America; by January 1796 he was in Paris, and the likelihood of a French expedition to Ireland grew steadily stronger.

In face of these internal and external threats the government adopted a policy of repression. An 'insurrection act', passed in February 1796, made it a capital offence to administer an unlawful oath, and empowered the lord lieutenant and privy council to proclaim any district as disturbed: in a district so proclaimed the magistrates were given extraordinary powers in searching for arms, and might, without trial, send suspected traitors and disorderly persons to serve in the fleet. Later in the same year the suspension of the *habeas corpus* act increased still further the arbitrary powers of the government. These measures went through parliament with little opposition — there was, for example, no division on the second reading of the insurrection bill; the gentlemen of Ireland were thoroughly frightened, and many who had formerly urged conciliation were now persuaded that only strong measures could maintain law and order. This attitude appeared not only in parliament but also in the conduct of the local magistrates, and in repeated and widespread demands for the establishment of a yeomanry force, demands to which Camden reluctantly yielded in September 1796. The militia, which was raised partly by conscription, contained a large proportion of Roman Catholics, and was regarded as doubtfully reliable; the new yeomanry, largely recruited by landlords among their own tenants, was mainly, though not exclusively, protestant. 'I shall be construed', wrote Camden, after compiling the first list of officers, 'as arming the protestants against the catholics'; but the needs of the French war had so drained the country of regular troops that he felt there was no alternative.

The reality of the danger appeared in December 1796, when a French expedition carrying some 6,000 or 7,000 troops, and accompanied by Wolfe Tone, arrived in Bantry Bay.[1] Unfavourable weather, and disagreement among the commanders, prevented any attempt at landing, and after a few days the French sailed harmlessly away. But the very fact that they had been able to reach the Irish coast, despite the British navy, was enough to alarm the government and encourage the United Irishmen. During the brief period of crisis the Munster peasants had shown themselves perfectly loyal; but a French advance inland, which the government had not sufficient troops on the spot to prevent, would probably have changed their attitude; and the mere report of a landing would almost certainly have precipitated an insurrection in the north.

It was the situation in the north that was most alarming to the government. During 1796 the United Irishmen had set up a military organization, which was most fully developed in Ulster, and especially in Antrim and Down. Here thousands of peasants were already armed with the muskets that had belonged to the Volunteers or with the pikes that were being steadily turned out at scores of smithies throughout the countryside. It was the example and leadership of these Ulster protestants, mainly presbyterians, that made the much more numerous Defenders potentially so dangerous; for the Defenders, left to themselves, would have been only another agrarian secret society in the tradition of the Whiteboys, at war with the Orangemen, and a menace to landlords and tithe-collectors, but not a direct threat to the state.

The centre of revolutionary activity in the north was Belfast. Only a minority of the citizens was actually involved in the conspiracy; but this minority could count on widespread sympathy, for the strong political and intellectual life characteristic of the town at this period was deeply tinged with radicalism: the *Northern Star*, founded by the Belfast United Irishmen in 1791,[2] was by far the most influential organ of radical opinion in Ireland. The Belfast radicals drew much of their inspiration from the French Revolution, but they had a quite unrevolutionary sense of tradition: they were interested in Irish antiquities and folklore, and they were prominent among the supporters of a society established to 'revive and perpetuate the ancient music and poetry of Ireland'. The idea of an 'Irish nation', indifferent to religious rivalries, rooted in history, but

[1] The force that reached Bantry Bay was only part of the whole expedition, which left Brest on 15 December with 15,000 troops. The ships carrying the military commander, Hoche, and some 8,000 troops were separated from the rest of the fleet in a fog, and never sighted the Irish coast.

The first issue appeared in January 1792.

enlightened by the Revolution, takes its rise in the Belfast of the late eighteenth century.

Convinced that the most immediate danger came from the north, the government resolved to break the United Irish organization in Ulster. Some of the principal leaders had been arrested towards the end of 1796; but this had hardly checked the spread of the conspiracy, and in March 1797 General Lake was sent to Belfast with extraordinary powers from the lord lieutenant and council. Few regular troops were available, and he had to rely mainly on militia and yeomanry. About the militia Lake felt very uneasy: 'I have every reason to apprehend', he wrote to Pelham in April, 'that all the regiments of militia have vast numbers United'. But these fears were exaggerated, for though some militiamen had succumbed to the persistent propaganda of the United Irishmen, the great majority proved dependable: it was, for example, the Monaghan militia that terrorized Belfast into at least a semblance of loyalty, destroying, in the process, the printing-press of the *Northern Star*, and bringing its brief but brilliant career to an end. Though martial law had not been proclaimed, the yeomanry and militia acted almost without restraint: in the search for arms, houses were burnt down, suspected persons were flogged or tortured to make them reveal what they might know, and hundreds were sent off to the fleet. This brutal policy achieved a substantial measure of success. Thousands of muskets and other arms were surrendered or captured, and the hold of the United Irishmen on the mass of the population was greatly weakened. Those who had joined the society or connived at its activities under pressure of popular opinion were ready enough to surrender their arms and take an oath of allegiance; others were terrified into compliance by the conduct of the military; and only a small nucleus of stalwart republicans continued to work for an insurrection.

Even before this military repression, there had been a beginning of political reaction among the Ulster presbyterians. The first flush of enthusiasm for the Revolution was passing away, to be succeeded by a conviction that it was better to await patiently the peaceful reform of the existing constitution than to risk the chaos that must accompany its violent overthrow. This reaction was stronger among the ministers than among their people, but was gradually spreading; and it was supported by the influence of an evangelical revival now stirring among Irish protestants in general. Thus, as early as the 1790s, we can trace in Ulster protestantism the first signs of a political transformation that was to influence, and at times to dominate, the course of Irish history in the nineteenth and twentieth centuries.

(5)

The policy of military repression, first systematically applied in Ulster, was soon extended to the rest of the country, and especially to Leinster and Munster, where the Defenders were becoming increasingly active. They were now closely linked with the United Irishmen, and were definitely committed to rebellion. They seized arms wherever they could find them; they engaged almost openly in military manœuvres; and their intimidation of witnesses and jurors made the law quite powerless to restrain them.

Some historians have argued that the severities practised by the troops were deliberately designed to provoke an insurrection. General Lake, who took a soldier's view of the situation, would certainly have preferred an open fight, and said so; but the object of government was to prevent an insurrection, not to provoke it. In the long run, perhaps, the efficiency of the government's spy system, and the thoroughness of its military preparations, put the United Irish leaders in a position where they must either act at once or give up any hope of acting at all; but this is a very different thing from deliberately provoking a rebellion. It is, however, true that neither government nor parliament would make any attempt to conciliate potential rebels by offering concessions, as Grattan urged them to do. In May 1797 a last effort to introduce a parliamentary reform bill was overwhelmingly defeated; and Grattan, following the example of Fox at Westminster, thereafter withdrew from the house of commons. It is indicative of the state of the country that a general election in the summer of 1797 passed without excitement: moderate reformers were in despair, and extremists now regarded parliamentary activity as irrelevant.

By the end of the year, Ireland seemed to be drifting into chaos. Ulster was outwardly quiet; but in Munster and Leinster the brutal conduct of the troops did not immediately check the activity of the United Irishmen, who continued their raids for arms and their attacks on those whom they suspected of co-operating with the government; and peaceful citizens were caught between two rival terrors. The expectation of a French invasion remained high, despite Duncan's victory at Camperdown in October; and, with this hope to encourage them, the United Irish leaders pressed on with their plans for rebellion. According to their own reckoning (which is borne out by the information of government spies) they could count on 110,000 armed men in Ulster, 100,000 in Munster, and 68,000 in Leinster. But they believed that foreign help was necessary to ensure success, and a minority that favoured an immediate rising was overruled.

In face of this situation, the government seemed to have no policy but to intensify repression; and it strenuously resisted every proposal that its measures should be modified. When Sir Ralph Abercromby, who had been appointed commander-in-chief in November 1797, tried to restore the discipline of the troops and to confine their activities within the normal constitutional limits, he was virtually compelled to resign by the furious opposition of the Castle. Lake, who succeeded him in April 1798, had no scruples about continuing and extending the policy that he had followed so vigorously in Ulster. Though many of the protestant gentry criticized this relentless repression, they found little support in parliament; the house of commons was overwhelmingly behind the government, and in this respect it probably represented ascendancy opinion in general.

The ferocity of word and deed displayed by many magistrates and M.P.s was no doubt in some cases the blind reaction of fear; but the policy of the government was deliberate, and was based on confidence in its own strength. It had the enormous advantage of being well-informed about its enemy: whatever else was inefficient in the Castle administration, the secret service worked admirably, and the government could follow almost every move in the United Irishmen's negotiations with France, and almost every debate in the 'directory' that managed their affairs.

With so much information at its disposal, the government could choose its own moment to strike: in March 1798 most of the principal conspirators were arrested in Dublin, and their papers seized. This blow threw the central organization of the United Irishmen into confusion, and a general proclamation of martial law at the end of the month threatened to paralyse the movement throughout the country. The few leaders who remained at large managed to form a new directory; but their position was almost hopeless: they had neither the knowledge nor the skill necessary to play a waiting game, and must either embark on an insurrection without French help, or else suffer their whole system to be broken up piece-meal. Their choice of the former alternative was probably inevitable; and to this extent it is true that the government's action in March was the proximate cause of the rising.

The outbreak was fixed for 23 May; but before that day arrived the United Irishmen had received another heavy blow. Lord Edward Fitzgerald, the most important of the leaders who had escaped arrest in March, was made prisoner on 19 May, after a desperate resistance, in which he was mortally wounded. Fitzgerald had supported the radical cause in parliament; and then, in 1796, despairing of constitutional reform, had joined the United Irishmen. His abilities were not of the first order, but the prestige of his name and station gave him immense influence; and had he remained at liberty to head the insurrection it would have been more dangerous and more widespread than it actually proved. Young, hand-some, generous, aristocratic, romantically married to an illegitimate daughter of the house of Orleans, he seemed cast for a hero's part; and even his enemies had to admire the gallantry with which he played it to the end: Lord Clare himself, in defiance of the viceroy's orders, brought Lord Edward's aunt and brother to visit him in prison, and 'cried like a woman when he saw him dying'.

Despite the capture of Fitzgerald, and of some other, less important, members of the directory on the following day, the insurrection broke out on 23 May. But it lacked all coherence. The original plan had been to seize the capital and thus paralyse government. This was not even attempted; and isolated risings throughout Leinster were quickly con-tained by the government forces. In the county of Wexford alone did the rebels make any headway. Here the insurrection began on 26 May; and next day the rebels, commanded by Father John Murphy, who had given the signal for the rising, defeated and almost annihilated a body of the North Cork militia.[1] This victory brought them a large accession of strength; and soon almost the whole county, including the towns of Wexford and Enniscorthy, was in their hands. But to open communica-tion with the neighbouring counties it was essential to occupy New Ross, against which they launched an attack, in great force, on 5 June. The government commander had only 1,400 troops, mostly militia, and if the rebels had pressed their first advantage they might have carried the town. But their discipline was not equal to their courage, and after twelve hours of furious fighting they were repulsed with enormous slaughter. This was the turning-point of the war in Wexford. The rebels were still formidable, but their power was declining, and they were steadily hemmed in by government troops, now being reinforced from England. On 21 June their main stronghold, at Vinegar Hill, was captured; and after this the rebellion petered out.

The early success of the Wexford rising may be attributed in part to the weakness of the government forces in the county, in part to the leadership of some of the Roman Catholic clergy. This leadership gave the rising an essentially religious character; and though the rebels had the support of a few protestant radicals, they regarded protestants in general as their enemies, to be attacked, plundered, and even slaughtered, simply for being protestants. The conduct of the troops during the months preceding the

[1] According to some accounts it was the severity of the repressive measures taken by the North Cork militia that provoked the Wexford rising.

insurrection had goaded them into fury and resentment; but those on whom they wreaked their vengeance were for the most part innocent and peaceful citizens. The military, on their side, were certainly no more scrupulous. That rebels taken in arms should be shot out of hand was perhaps to be expected in the perilous state of affairs; but in fact no one's life or property was safe: the troops behaved as if in enemy territory; houses were burnt and the inhabitants executed on the mere suspicion of having harboured rebel fugitives, and whole tracts of country were thus laid waste. Even rank and social position gave little protection: Sir Edward Crosbie, a prominent landlord and member of parliament, was hanged as a traitor, after a hasty court-martial and on the flimsiest of evidence.

In Irish history 'the boys of Wexford' often figure as the champions of national freedom. The truth is that they were moved mainly by local grievances: neither the objects that they fought for nor their conduct of the war reflected the spirit of the United Irishmen, with whom they were connected by accidents of time and circumstances, rather than by any real community of ideas. It was in the radical north-east, the cradle of the United Irish movement, that the doctrines of revolutionary republicanism found their only clear expression in 1798. But the temper of Ulster was no longer what it had been a year earlier. Many who had drawn their inspiration from France had had their faith in the French government shaken by its oppressive policy in Switzerland and by its aggressive attitude towards America, so that the prospect of independence in alliance with France lost much of its attraction. The rapid spread of the Orange movement had strengthened the loyalist element among the peasantry, and revived old jealousies between Roman Catholics and protestants. The policy of military repression, by frightening off the half-hearted and discouraging even the enthusiasts, had added force to a reaction not unnatural after the high hopes of the early 1790s. On top of all this came the news that the Leinster rising had collapsed everywhere except in Wexford, and that in Wexford it had become a crusade against the protestants.

But even in face of these discouragements a few stalwarts were found to raise the standard of revolt. On 7 June, Henry Joy McCracken, a Belfast cotton-manufacturer and one of the original founders of the United Irish movement, led 3,000 or 4,000 men against the town of Antrim; but he was driven off after a sharp encounter, and the insurrection north of the Lagan died out within a few days. In County Down it was at first more serious, for the rebels succeeded, after an indecisive engagement, in occupying Saintfield, a dozen miles from Belfast. This success brought them fresh recruits; and their general, Henry Munro, a Lisburn linen-draper, led some 7,000 men against Ballynahinch, control of which would have given them a commanding position in the centre of the county. But here, on 13 June, they were totally defeated; and within ten days of its beginning the Ulster insurrection was at an end. McCracken and Munro, with a few other leaders, were executed; but the rank and file received pardon and protection on surrender of their arms, and the vast majority were glad to go quietly home and put any thought of further rebellion out of their minds.

Though some Roman Catholics joined in the insurrection, it was essentially a protestant affair;[1] and it is perhaps for this reason that it is remembered by Ulster protestants without any of the rancour commonly associated with Irish historical events. No matter on which side their forebears fought at Antrim or Saintfield or Ballynahinch, they have long since sunk their differences in a common loyalty to the British connection. They can admire the courage, without sharing the principles, of 'the men of ninety-eight'; and to have had an ancestor 'out' in that famous year is something to be proud of, even for the most ardent unionist in the north.

(6)

Until the last desperate weeks before the insurrection, all the plans of the United Irishmen had been based on the expectation of French help, for which Wolfe Tone and other Irish agents in France were ceaselessly working. At the beginning of 1798 their hopes had been raised by Bonaparte's preparations for an invasion of Britain; but before the insurrection broke out he had changed his plans, and was already on his way to Egypt. Tone, however, continued to press the Directory for help, and though they were in no position to undertake large-scale naval operations, they agreed to send a number of small expeditions to the Irish coast. But preparations went on so slowly that the rebellion had been crushed before the first of these expeditions, consisting of three ships, with 1,100 men under General Humbert, reached Killala, in County Mayo, on 22 August. Humbert found a state of affairs very different from what he had been led to expect. Connaught had been little influenced by revolutionary propaganda and there was no general rising: the few thousand peasants who joined the French, under the impression that they had come as champions of the pope and the Blessed Virgin, had little nationalist or republican fervour, and proved unreliable auxiliaries.

[1] It may be noted that the militia, which made up a considerable part of the government forces, was largely Roman Catholic: at Ballynahinch, the principal engagement in the rising, there were certainly many more Roman Catholics on the government side than among the rebels.

Though his position was thus almost hopeless, Humbert conducted a brilliant and courageous campaign, in the course of which he completely routed a vastly superior force, mainly of militia and yeomanry, assembled at Castlebar under General Lake; and it was not until 8 September that he surrendered at Ballinamuck, after marching his little force more than 150 miles through enemy territory. Some of the Irish who had joined him continued the struggle on their own, and retained possession of Killala; but with the recapture of the town on 23 September the rising in Connaught came to an end. On the side of the French and the rebels it had been remarkably free from the plunder and slaughter that had marked the fighting in Wexford. Humbert had kept the strictest discipline among the French troops, and his authority had been sufficient to restrain the peasantry, who had not suffered under the same military tyranny as those of Leinster, from indiscriminate attack upon the lives and property of protestants; and even after the French had withdrawn from Killala the bishop and his family, though somewhat alarmed at the loss of Humbert's courteous protection, were allowed to continue peaceably in the castle. But the rebels' moderation made no difference to the government troops; and the yeomanry and militia took revenge for the 'races of Castlebar' in the blood of their unfortunate countrymen.

More than a week before the fall of Killala, another French expedition, with Wolfe Tone and about 3,000 troops, had sailed from Brest. Almost a month later, it was intercepted off the coast of Donegal by a British naval force; most of the French ships were captured, and Tone was among the prisoners. He was recognized at once, sent to Dublin, tried by court-martial, and condemned. He made no attempt to deny his complicity in rebellion, but asked that he might be shot instead of hanged; when this request was refused, he committed suicide in prison. From the beginning of the United Irish movement, Tone had been the ablest and most vigorous of its leaders. Through all his work for Catholic Emancipation and constitutional reform in the early 1790s his ultimate goal had been the complete and final separation of Ireland from Great Britain; and after he was forced into exile in 1794 he devoted all his energies to promoting a French invasion. He had embraced in early life the deistical and republican notions of the revolutionary era, and he so far misunderstood his own countrymen as to believe that they too would readily abandon long-standing animosities of creed and class. His plans were foiled not so much by the strength of England and the hesitation of France as by the deep-seated division among the people of Ireland.

Wolfe Tone had looked forward to the insurrection as a struggle by Irishmen of all denominations against the power of Britain; instead, it proved to be a struggle of Irishmen against Irishmen. Some British forces (English, Welsh and Scottish) had been sent to Ireland before the insurrection began, and many more arrived during its later stages; but it was the yeomanry and the militia, both altogether Irish and the militia largely Roman Catholic, that were mainly responsible for crushing it: Sir William Plunket was not far wrong when he asserted, a year or so later, that the gentlemen of Ireland had saved their constitution by their own efforts. But Tone's ideals, though frustrated at the time, were to exercise a profound influence on later history. He established, and later came almost to personify, a tradition of revolutionary violence that has never wholly died out of Irish politics. And in the light of this tradition the insurrection of 1798 is seen not as it was in deed but as Tone had hoped for it to be.

XIV

The End of the Irish Parliament

---

(1)

W hile the rebellion was still raging there had been a change in the viceroyalty: Camden had long wished to be relieved of his responsibilities, and in June 1798 he was replaced by Cornwallis,[1] who was to be commander-in-chief as well as lord lieutenant. In such a crisis the choice of a soldier was natural, and Cornwallis's military reputation, despite the memory of Yorktown, stood high; besides this he had had experience of war and administration in India that might well be of service in Ireland. Within a few days of his appointment he arrived in Dublin; and at once set himself to restore military discipline, to restrain the savage policy of reprisal and revenge that had hitherto dominated the executive, and to establish, as far as he could, peaceful and conciliatory government. But he was soon to be entrusted with a task of more far-reaching importance — the creation of a legislative union between the two kingdoms.

Ninety years earlier the Irish parliament itself had asked for such a union, only to have its petition rejected in England. When the suggestion was tentatively renewed, on various occasions from the 1750s onward, it came from the British side, and aroused such fierce opposition in Ireland that for a time no statesman was prepared to take it up seriously. But after the constitutional changes of 1782–3 there was in some quarters a growing fear lest the two kingdoms should drift further and further apart, and a conviction that the only way to prevent this was by complete amalgamation. The fear of disunity was increased by the failure of the commercial propositions of 1785 and by the regency crisis of 1789, though with little justification, for the Irish parliament was perfectly loyal both to the crown and to the British connection. From 1793 onwards it gave whole-hearted support to the war, readily voting supplies that the country could ill

---

[1] Charles Cornwallis, first Marquis Cornwallis.

afford; and Pitt found that his policy of unrelenting resistance to France was far more seriously endangered by the conduct of the British whigs than by any opposition or criticism in the parliament of Ireland. But he saw that the disturbed and discontented state of the country, which seemed almost to invite French invasion, was a danger to both kingdoms; and he became convinced that the best hope of conciliating the hostile elements in the population and establishing firm and peaceful government lay in legislative union, accompanied by Catholic Emancipation.

It is impossible to fix the point at which Pitt decided on this policy; but there can be no doubt that it was the rebellion of 1798 that provided both the stimulus and the opportunity for its execution. The charge that Pitt deliberately fomented rebellion in order to bring about union is too extravagant to need detailed refutation;[1] but, rebellion having broken out, he resolved to press on with his policy, in the belief that the Irish landlords, alarmed at the perils to which they were exposed, and forced to recognize their dependence on British arms, might the more easily be persuaded to surrender their separate parliament. In the presentation of the case for union there was no point to which government spokesmen returned so often as its absolute necessity for the survival of the protestant ascendancy; and it is probably true to say that without this argument from fear all the bribery and intrigue of the Castle politicians would have failed to carry the day.

Even in these circumstances, the task of converting the protestant ascendancy to the idea of legislative union was bound to tax all the resources of government, and to put a particularly heavy burden on the chief secretary, who would inevitably have the duty of building up and maintaining the necessary majority in the house of commons. The chief secretary at the time of Cornwallis's appointment was Thomas Pelham, who had served under Camden and was retained, contrary to the usual practice, under his successor. But Pelham's ill-health made his tenure of the office little more than nominal, and since March 1798 its duties had been executed by Robert Stewart, Viscount Castlereagh; in the following November, when Pelham was at last allowed to retire, Castlereagh was appointed in his place. It was on Castlereagh, therefore, more than on any other single person, that the success of Pitt's Irish policy must depend. The position in which Castlereagh thus found himself made, at first sight, a strange contrast with the opening of his political career: at the election of 1790, when barely of age, he had contested County Down in the popular interest, and had been

[1] Lecky examines the question at some length in his *History of Ireland in the eighteenth century*, v. 143–7.

returned to parliament by the presbyterian farmers and weavers against all the influence of the church, the Castle, and the marquis of Downshire. But in fact he had never had much sympathy with radical measures; and though elected as an 'independent', he easily persuaded himself that the state of affairs, at home and abroad, obliged him to support government; the appointment of his uncle, Camden, as viceroy established a close link with the Castle; and in July 1797 he accepted office as keeper of the signet. He was one of those who most feared the separation of Ireland from Great Britain, and at least as early as 1792 he had considered the possibility of a legislative union; by 1798 he was fully persuaded that it was essential.

(2)

Before the rebellion was a fortnight old, Pitt had already decided to use the opportunity to bring forward his scheme for a union. During the summer and autumn he discussed the matter confidentially with other members of the cabinet, and with the king, and found a general inclination to proceed. In Dublin, the position was very different. Cornwallis, though he does not seem to have been taken fully into Pitt's confidence at the time of his appointment, was convinced that union was necessary; and Castlereagh, as might be expected, eagerly took up a policy that fell in so closely with his own ideas. But Beresford's support was, to begin with, only lukewarm; and Foster, speaker of the house of commons, and Parnell, chancellor of the exchequer, were vehement in opposition. And besides this, the unionists were divided among themselves. It was part of Pitt's plan that union and Catholic Emancipation should go together, and with this both Cornwallis and Castlereagh were in agreement; but Clare, the lord chancellor, who was the greatest unionist of them all, was utterly opposed to the idea. He had been the first statesman in either kingdom to make a legislative union the principal object of his policy, and during the previous five years he had repeatedly urged the necessity of it upon Pitt. But he thought of union simply as a bulwark of protestant ascendancy, as the one means of saving Ireland from the danger of a 'popish democracy', to which it had been exposed by the 'fatal mistake' of admitting Roman Catholics to the parliamentary franchise in 1793; and to couple it with any measure of Catholic Emancipation would rob it of its value and destroy the whole basis of the constitution.

This double division within the executive — between unionists and anti-unionists, and among the unionists themselves — must obviously be cleared up before the new policy could be presented to the country and to parliament with any hope of success. The first step towards unity was the victory of Lord Clare. His long-established influence was too strong to be resisted, even by Pitt; and by the beginning of November it was settled that the union should be carried on a strictly protestant basis. Cornwallis was bitterly disappointed: 'I certainly wish', he had written a month earlier, 'that England could now make a union with the Irish nation, instead of making it with a party in Ireland'. But he and Castlereagh, and others who thought like them, could still hope that though Emancipation would not accompany union, it might follow soon after; in the meantime, they were prepared to acquiesce in Clare's victory, and give their whole efforts to the immediate task of getting the union itself through.

With the anti-unionist members of the executive it had been clear from the first that compromise was impossible. But in Ireland there was no tradition of collective responsibility: office-holders who differed from the viceroy on matters of policy rarely resigned on that account; nor were they invariably dismissed, even if they carried their opposition to the point of a hostile vote in parliament. But Castlereagh realized that this was a situation in which the authority of government would have to be pushed to its limits. Parliament was to meet in January, he was busily canvassing for support, and members would hardly be convinced that government was in earnest if known opponents of union were allowed to retain office. Early in the new year, therefore, Parnell, along with several other officials who had refused to support government policy, were dismissed from their posts; Foster could not, of course, be removed from the speakership, but his son, who held a post under the revenue board, was dismissed a few days later.

By these means the government was enabled to present a united front and to show its determination; but success in parliament must depend mainly on the attitude of the great borough-owners and of the independent members, and these were, for the most part, either openly hostile or ominously reserved. Nevertheless, when parliament met on 22 January 1799 Castlereagh believed that government could count on a safe majority. The matter was put to the test almost immediately. All the government wanted at this stage was that parliament should promise to consider some scheme of union: a recommendation to this effect, in very general terms, was included in the viceroy's speech; and the government supporter who moved the address in reply in the house of commons made it clear that nothing more was being asked for. But the opposition was determined to force the issue at once, and George Ponsonby moved an amendment to the address, pledging the house to maintain 'the undoubted birthright of the people of Ireland to have a free and independent legislature'. Round this amendment a furious debate raged all night, and all the next morning.

'You would have thought', wrote Beresford, now firmly on the unionist side, 'that you were in a Polish diet. Direct treason spoken, resistance to law declared, encouraged and recommended . . . I cannot bring myself to repeat what was said or done'. Early in the afternoon of the 23rd the amendment was at last put to the vote, and was lost by 106 to 105. Such a victory was useless to the government; and even this victory was short-lived. On 24 January the address, after having been formally drafted by a committee, was again before the house; the opposition, elated and excited by its own achievements and by popular applause, renewed the attack, and moved the deletion of the paragraph relating to union. This time, after another all-night debate, they carried their amendment by 111 votes to 106. The first round of the contest had gone against the government.

The most obvious element in the opposition victory was the strength of public feeling against union. Dublin, in particular, was antagonized by the threat to its position as a capital, and the influence of the great city interests—legal, financial and commercial—was felt throughout the kingdom. For weeks before parliament met, opposition pamphlets and newspapers had been stirring up national sentiment, and Castlereagh's counter-propaganda had so far had little effect. The Dublin mob, always easily aroused, played its part: after the debate of 22–23 January the Speaker's coach was drawn triumphantly home, while Lord Clare, who had easily secured the passage of a pro-union resolution in the lords, was pelted with stones. The excited state of public opinion counted for a good deal in the house of commons: members for popular constituencies felt obliged to fall in with the wishes of their constituents;[1] others were more afraid of public opprobrium than of government displeasure — even a number of placemen voted with the opposition; above all, perhaps, the tension within and without the house produced an atmosphere in which members were likely to be influenced by oratory, and almost all the oratorical power was on the side of the opposition.

An opposition so built up inevitably contained discordant and un-reliable elements. Some of its members wished to ally with the Roman Catholics, and to put forward Emancipation as a counter-policy to union; but a mere hint of this scheme was enough to arouse the protestant fears of the country gentlemen, and it had to be dropped. The Ponsonby connection, still sore from its disappointment in 1795, was anxious to

---

[1] Thus, for example, John Beresford's son, J. C. Beresford, who was one of the members for the city of Dublin, resigned the post he held under government, and voted with the opposition, though the Beresford interest as a whole was in favour of union.

turn the crisis to its own political advantage. Foster, the Speaker, was suspected of similar ambitions. And in the background was a group of borough-owning peers, whose hostility to union, largely self-interested, might be overcome by judicious management on the part of the government.

It was Castlereagh's business to take advantage of all these weaknesses, and to break down the opposition by argument, bribery, or intimidation. And to this task he devoted himself with unremitting energy during the next twelve months.

(3)

The excitement aroused by the question of a union, though it dominated Dublin, affected only the surface of society in the country at large: 'The mass of the people of Ireland', said Cornwallis, 'do not care one farthing about the union'. They had, indeed, little enough cause to love the Irish parliament, nor any reason to suppose that the laws under which they lived would be more or less oppressive if made in London instead of Dublin. The enemies that they feared were the landlord and the tithe-proctor, whom they readily identified with the whole system of protestant government; and their only notion of a political programme was to abolish rent and tithe, to put down the established church, and to set up their own in place of it. These ideas, current throughout the eighteenth century, had become more and more influential during the revolutionary period, and had played a large part in the rising of 1798. When the rising was crushed, they found expression in an outbreak of agrarian crime more violent and more widespread than Ireland had yet known. So complete was the terror under which witnesses and jurymen lived that the ordinary courts were almost powerless. An act of February 1799 established what was virtually a system of martial law, and further reinforcements of British troops were brought in; but improvement in the situation was very slow: reports of a new French invasion threatened to revive the revolutionary excitement of the previous year, and bad harvests increased the general discontent.

With the country so disturbed, with a foreign war and a threat of invasion, the time might seem very unfit for proposing a fundamental change in the constitution; and this line of argument was strongly urged by the opponents of a union. But the very dangers of the situation were of advantage to the government: the landlords and the middle classes were more likely to be frightened than persuaded into acquiescing in a union; and the possibility of French attack justified the presence of a large British army, without which, Cornwallis frankly admitted, 'all thoughts of uniting the two kingdoms must be given up'. Had there been peace abroad and stability at home, no Irish parliament would ever have consented to its own extinction.

The general state of crisis was of advantage to the government in another way also, for it helped to secure the support of the Roman Catholic bishops, who were quite as much afraid of revolution as the most reactionary protestant landlord. This support was doubly important to the government: in the first place, it would lessen the danger of an alliance between the Roman Catholics and the opposition; in the second place, it would help forward one of Pitt's main purposes in engineering a union — the hearty reconciliation of the whole people of Ireland to the British connection. He saw that a union, if it were to bring lasting peace, must be a union of peoples as well as of parliaments, and that this could be accomplished only by concession to the Roman Catholics. Out of deference to Clare he had abandoned the idea of including Emancipation in the terms of union, but he meant that it should follow soon after; and Cornwallis and Castlereagh, both of whom sympathized completely with his views, were authorized to make this clear to the Roman Catholic leaders. At the same time, however, it was also made clear that the government would resist any proposal for Emancipation made in the Irish parliament: there was to be no prospect of relief until after a legislative union. These tactics attained their immediate object, and the Roman Catholic bishops, with the bulk of their co-religionists among the landlords and the middle classes, supported union. It was, for example, the Roman Catholic vote, used under episcopal guidance, that secured the defeat of the anti-unionist candidate at a by-election in Newry in 1799 In one quarter only was there any considerable opposition: a group of Roman Catholic barristers, headed by Daniel O'Connell (now making his first entry into political life) joined with the majority of their protestant brethren in condemning the union. The Roman Catholics received no explicit promises in return for their support; but Castlereagh, acting on Pitt's instructions, had morally engaged the government to bring in a measure of Catholic Emancipation once the union was carried.

The government was anxious for presbyterian as well as for Roman Catholic support. The presbyterians of Ulster had helped to create the 'constitution of 1782', and might be expected to defend it; but reaction against revolutionary principles, experience of military rule, the character of the recent insurrection, the threat of French invasion, all combined to change their temper; and there was now little either of gratitude or of attachment in their attitude to the Irish parliament. They were easily encouraged to believe that legislative union might better their position. In particular, Castlereagh indicated that the government would be prepared to make a considerable increase in the *regium donum* paid to their ministers. This, by itself, might have had little effect; but Ulster opinion in general was also influenced by the prospect of economic development, and the linen manufacture, especially, might hope to benefit from a closer commercial connection with Great Britain. In the end, however, government propaganda and negotiation had not much positive effect on political attitudes in the north, and there was little sign of strong feeling one way or the other.

In seeking popular support for its policy, the government was acting in the conviction that without such support legislative union could neither bring internal tranquillity to Ireland nor establish Anglo-Irish relations on a harmonious basis. But it had also the more immediate object of weakening the parliamentary opposition. Castlereagh was prepared to use every possible device for the creation of a government majority; but there were limits to what could be done in this way; and the history of the previous hundred years had shown how unreliable a government majority might prove in face of strong national feeling. Besides this, Castlereagh had been obliged to promise the house of commons, in January 1799, that he would not again bring forward the question of union 'so long as it appeared repugnant to the sense of parliament and the country'. For all these reasons the government was very anxious for public demonstrations of support. Its agents were busily at work; and addresses in favour of union came in from every quarter: in February 1800 Castlereagh claimed that 'nineteen of the most considerable counties in Ireland constituting over five-sevenths of the kingdom' had expressed their approval.

The opposition was no less active than the government in organizing public opinion. Its main strength lay in Dublin, but it had supporters throughout the country, and addresses against the union were at least as numerous as those in favour. Both sides claimed to represent the national will, and it is not easy for the historian to decide between them. The mass of the people, of whom Cornwallis wrote 'they equally hate both government and opposition', were outside the struggle, which concerned only the small politically-active minority; and evidence about the division of opinion within this minority is conflicting. The actual number of addresses for or against union proves very little: sometimes there were two addresses from the same place, one on each side. Probably the addresses against union carried more signatures than those in favour; but this is a poor basis on which to make a judgement.

Much more significant is the fact that the government refused to hold a general election on the issue. So far as most of the boroughs were concerned, an election would mean very little; but in the counties, at least, it would give some indication of opinion. A large majority of the sitting county members opposed union, many of them on the ground that their constituents wished them to do so; and the government's refusal to put the matter to the test could arise only from fear of the result. This does not completely dispose of the government's claim to popular support; for county elections were decided, almost invariably, by the landlords. In some counties a single great interest was dominant, but in most the country gentlemen kept their independence, and the country gentlemen, as a body, were determined to maintain the Irish parliament. There is some evidence that among the better-off freeholders, and especially among Roman Catholics and presbyterians, there were many supporters of a union; but in a general election they would certainly be overwhelmed by the weight of landlord influence. In brief, popular support for union came mainly from sections of the population that had little political power under the existing constitutional system, while the backbone of the opposition was provided by stalwarts of the old ascendancy. There were, it is true, some anti-unionists who had long favoured Catholic Emancipation, and more would have been willing to accept it as the price of Roman Catholic support against the government; but the majority fought to retain an independent parliament as a bulwark of protestant power and privilege.

In this connection, the attitude of the Orangemen was particularly important. Their society had grown rapidly, receiving support from landlords and government officials, and they now had a central organization, directed by a 'grand lodge' in Dublin. During the last year of Camden's administration they had gained considerable influence in the Castle, and had used it to encourage a policy of repression. But the position was changed under Cornwallis, who had little sympathy with their methods, and they denounced his comparative leniency towards the rebels as a betrayal of the protestant cause. What they knew of Castlereagh's dealings with the Roman Catholics alarmed them still further; and they were very suspicious of any scheme of union propounded under such auspices. The grand lodge, being situated in Dublin, and composed in part of place-holders, could be subjected to some government pressure; but the most it would do was to recommend that the society, as a body, should be neutral on the question of a union, and that members individually should be left to act as they thought fit. Anti-unionist feeling was too strong to be shackled in this way; the recommendation was widely ignored; and many lodges and groups of lodges publicly declared themselves against the government's policy.

This hostile attitude was not unnaturally reflected among the yeomanry, where Orange influence was dominant, and more than one proposal was made that yeomen should lay down their arms, and refuse to serve under a government that was planning to destroy the constitution. Though these proposals came to nothing, they indicate the strength of anti-union feeling among reactionary protestants; and they suggest the danger in which the government might have stood but for the presence in the country of some 40,000 British troops.

During 1799 the campaign for and against union raged throughout the country; but the government was not yet prepared for a fresh trial of strength in the house of commons, and successfully resisted opposition efforts to keep the debate alive there. All this time, however, Castlereagh had been busy; and when the new session opened in January 1800 he could face the issue with confidence.

(4)

The defeat of the proposal for a union, in January 1799, had aroused a frenzy of excitement as great as that which had accompanied Grattan's declaration of independence seventeen years earlier; and it might have seemed that the forces that had succeeded in winning the 'constitution of 1782' would now succeed in its defence. But the situations were not really comparable; and in one vital respect they were totally different: in 1782 the British government had been willing — almost anxious — to yield; in 1799 it was determined to have its way at all costs and in face of all opposition. Despite the hostile vote in the Irish house of commons, similar proposals for a legislative union were laid before the British parliament, where they passed both houses without difficulty; and the government made clear its intention of renewing the proposals in Ireland and of persisting until they were accepted; in the meantime, support for union was to be an indispensable and universal test, imposed on every candidate for any kind of government office or favour. It was the public announcement of this immovable resolution on the part of the government that enabled Cornwallis and Castlereagh to build up a parliamentary majority. Their task, as Castlereagh put it, was 'to buy out, and secure to the crown for ever, the fee simple of Irish corruption'; and those who were accustomed to sell their support to government session by session would have hesitated to make such a final surrender of their influence if they had not been convinced that refusal to do so would mean their permanent exclusion from government patronage.

Yet Castlereagh's efforts might have failed but for the apparently impregnable strength of Pitt's position at Westminster. If there had been a strong and active whig opposition, Irish M.P.s might have resisted all the threats of government in the hope that the situation would be transformed by a change of ministry. The fact that there was no prospect of any such relief goes far to explain the reluctant surrender of so many opponents of the union.

Castlereagh's first step towards securing a majority was to strike a firm bargain with the principal borough-owners, for even those who had already declared in favour of a union expected to be paid. In the circumstances, the price demanded was naturally a high one; but the government was prepared to pay it, and Cornwallis and Castlereagh were authorized to promise the peerages, places and pensions necessary to meet the claims put forward. The support thus gained, however, was hardly sufficient for the purpose now in hand, partly because so many of the independent country gentlemen who normally voted with government had gone into opposition on the question of union, partly because it was thought necessary that the measure should be carried by a substantial majority. Castlereagh set himself, therefore, to win every possible vote, by threats, by promises, in a few cases even by direct purchase for cash. Some members who could not bring themselves to vote for union were nevertheless induced to vacate their seats and make way for government supporters. Other vacancies resulted from transfers of allegiance on the part of borough-owners, whose nominees refused to accept the change of policy and were obliged to resign.[1] As a result of these transactions about one-fifth of the membership of the house of commons was changed between January 1799 and January 1800, and the strength of the government was accordingly increased.

When parliament re-assembled, on 15 January 1800, several by-elections, certain to be favourable to the government, were still pending. Eager to use this advantage, the opposition immediately raised the question of union, by an amendment to the address, pledging the house to maintain an independent Irish parliament; and the debate, conducted with great violence on both sides, continued all night. Towards dawn, members were startled by the sudden entry of Grattan, dressed in Volunteer uniform, deathly pale, and hardly able to walk. Since his secession from parliament in 1797 both his reputation and his health had declined, and he had so far taken no part in the union controversy. But the opposition

---

[1] It was an accepted convention that a nominee should vote as directed by his patron, or else give up his seat. But this did not apply to a member who had acquired his seat by purchase.

leaders, hoping that his intervention would strengthen their cause, induced him to return. A seat was hastily purchased for him; his election was rushed through; and he was now come to take the oaths. All other business was suspended while he did so; then, after an interval, he addressed the house for almost two hours, and though he began feebly, his spirit soon kindled, and he spoke with all the fire and eloquence of former days. But members were no longer open to be persuaded by oratory, Castlereagh's henchmen stood firm, and at 10 o'clock in the morning the opposition amendment was defeated by 138 votes to 96.

The struggle continued for some months, but the unionist majority could not be shaken; and opposition attempts to frighten the government and influence parliament by arousing public opinion came to nothing. Petitions against union were organized all over the kingdom. The barristers, the Orangemen, the country gentry, protested and threatened. But what could they do? The national spirit of 1782 was dead; the revolutionaries of 1798 were either cowed, or indifferent to the fate of the ascendancy parliament; and the country was full of British troops. The government's supporters in the house of commons were certainly not enthusiastic — Cornwallis reckoned that about half of them detested the union in their hearts — but Castlereagh's skilful management held them to their pledges, and the measure went steadily forward. On 6 February, when the house formally agreed to take into consideration proposals for a legislative union, the government majority was 43;[1] on 17 February, when the proposals were agreed to in committee, it was 46. After this the issue could hardly be in doubt, though the continued resistance of the opposition delayed progress; and it was not until 28 March that the terms of union were finally accepted by both houses.

The terms thus approved were laid before the British parliament; and after each parliament in turn had made some comparatively minor amendments, which the other accepted, the terms, in their final form, were embodied in two identical bills. The Irish bill was violently opposed in the house of commons; but there was now no hope of success, and before the debate on the third reading concluded, the bulk of the opposition withdrew in a body. What followed was mere formality, for the passage of the measure through the house of lords was a matter of course. Even the public excitement had subsided; and it was amid general apathy that the royal assent was given, on 1 August, to the bill that was to

[1] This division is generally supposed to have been the largest in the history of the house. There were 158 votes for the government and 115 for the opposition, making, with the speaker and the tellers, an attendance of 278 members out of a total of 300.

terminate five hundred years of parliamentary life. An observer gifted with political foresight might have thought it even stranger that the British parliament should have accepted, with little discussion and almost without a qualm, a measure that was to affect so profoundly its constitution and its responsibilities.

One important element in the whole transaction, which was not included in the act of union but was legislated for separately, was the compensation of those whose interests suffered, directly or indirectly, by the extinction of the Irish parliament. These included a whole host of parliamentary officials, and, much more important, the patrons of those boroughs which would cease to send representatives to parliament after the union. The value of a borough was fixed at £15,000, and the total sum paid in compensation to patrons exceeded one and a quarter million pounds. This compensation might be regarded as a form of bribery, but it was paid irrespective of the political conduct of the recipient. The most heavily compensated official was John Foster, speaker of the house of commons; the most heavily compensated borough-owner was the marquis of Downshire; and these two had been among the strongest opponents of the union.

(5)

The terms on which the legislative union between Great Britain and Ireland was to be established were embodied in eight articles to come into force on 1 January 1801. The first four articles settled the political basis of the union; the fifth related to the church; the sixth to commerce; the seventh to finance; the eighth to law and legal procedure.

By the political articles Ireland was to be merged with Great Britain in one kingdom, to be known as 'The United Kingdom of Great Britain and Ireland'. The succession to the crown was to continue as settled by the terms of the union between England and Scotland. The parliament of the United Kingdom was to be constituted in the same way as the existing parliament of Great Britain, with the addition to each house of Irish representatives. In the upper house, Ireland was to be represented by four spiritual lords, sitting by rotation of sessions, and 28 temporal lords, elected for life by the peers of Ireland. In the lower house, there were to be 100 Irish members: two for each county; two each for the cities of Dublin and Cork; one for each of 31 other cities and boroughs; one for the university of Dublin. Until the united parliament should decide otherwise, not more than twenty of the Irish representatives in the commons might hold offices of profit under the crown in Ireland.

By the fifth article, the Church of England and the Church of Ireland were to be united; and the maintenance of this united church as the established church of England and Ireland was to be 'deemed and taken to be an essential and fundamental part of the union'.

The sixth article provided that the king's subjects in Great Britain and Ireland should be entitled to the same privileges in all matters of commerce, and that there should be free trade between the two countries, save in two respects. First, while the excise duties on certain home products and the duties on certain foreign imports continued to be levied at different rates in Great Britain and Ireland, there was to be a system of countervailing duties and drawbacks on such commodities passing from one country to the other. Secondly, for a period of twenty years customs duties were to be maintained between the two countries on a few manufactured articles, of which cotton and woollen goods were the most important.

By the seventh article the financial systems of the two countries were to remain, for the time being, distinct: each was to have its own exchequer, and to be responsible for its own national debt. They were to contribute to the expenditure of the United Kingdom in the proportion of fifteen parts for Great Britain and two parts for Ireland; that is to say, Ireland was to pay two-seventeenths of the whole. This proportion was to be reconsidered at the end of twenty years; and subsequently from time to time. This article also provided that in certain conditions (of which the most important was that the national debt of the two countries should reach a point at which they stood in the same proportion, the one to the other, as their respective contributions to the expenditure of the United Kingdom) the two debts and the two exchequers might be united, the system of distinct contributions abandoned, and the national expense 'defrayed indiscriminately by equal taxes imposed on the same articles in each country'.[1]

The eighth article laid down that all laws in force at the time of the union, and all courts of civil or ecclesiastical jurisdiction, in either kingdom, should remain as they were, subject only to such changes as might be made by the parliament of the United Kingdom. Law cases pending, at the time of the union, in either the British or the Irish house of lords, were to be decided in the house of lords of the United Kingdom.

These terms were not the result of direct negotiation between parliamentary commissions, as the terms of the Anglo-Scottish union of 1707

---

[1] The article provided, however, that there might be 'such particular exemptions or abatements in Ireland . . . as circumstances may appear from time to time to demand'.

had been. The prolonged opposition in the Irish house of commons to the very idea of a union had made such a method of procedure impracticable; and the terms were worked out, during 1799, in consultations between the Irish executive and the British cabinet, on the basis of resolutions agreed upon by the British parliament. It is unlikely, however, that Irish interests suffered as a result: if there was to be a union at all, the terms actually proposed were as favourable to Ireland as any that the British parliament was likely to accept.

So far as the size of the Irish representation at Westminster was concerned, the intention was to strike a balance between population and wealth, and the result seems not unreasonable — Ireland was to have twice as many members as Scotland in the house of lords, and more than twice as many in the commons. The commercial arrangements resembled fairly closely the propositions of 1785, which the Irish parliament of the day would have accepted, but for their constitutional implications. The temporary retention of customs duties on certain manufactured goods passing between the two countries was a direct concession to the Irish manufacturers, who demanded some protection against British competition. The division of responsibility for United Kingdom expenditure, as laid down in the seventh article, has commonly been regarded as unfair to Ireland, and it is certainly true that the burden proved greater than the country could bear. But when the article was framed no one foresaw that the war with France would continue for another fifteen years; it is impossible to tell how the arrangement might have worked out had a lasting peace been established in 1802. It seems, then, reasonable to conclude that the political, commercial and financial articles were drawn up in an honest attempt to be fair to both countries; if Ireland was worse off after 1800 than before it may well be that the cause lay in the principle rather than in the details of the union.

In the circumstances that surrounded the making of the legislative union there was little to arouse enthusiasm or excite admiration. The hopeful prospects opened by the constitutional victory of 1782 had soon been overcast. Under the impact of the French Revolution, the principles of Grattan and the patriots had become almost irrelevant. Whatever may be said for the ideals of the United Irishmen, the insurrection that they led gave little indication that those ideals were widely shared by their followers. Ireland in 1799 was politically bankrupt; and one reason for the passing of the act of union was that even those who opposed it to the end could not agree among themselves on any alternative remedy for the desperate situation of the country.

On 2 August 1800 the Irish parliament met for the last time. However unrepresentative, ineffective, or venal, it had stood for more than five hundred years as a symbol of Ireland's separate place among the nations of Europe. It borrowed its constitution and forms from England; it was the mouthpiece, throughout its whole history, of 'the English of Ireland'; it had seldom shown any friendly regard for the old native inhabitants or for their culture. But it could not escape the influence of time and circumstance; and it had developed as an Irish institution, with its own traditions and its own distinctive style of oratory. Patriots of a later day were to scorn its achievements and to deny its claim to be a national assembly; but it has left a mark on the history of Ireland that many centuries will hardly efface.

XV

From the Union to Catholic Emancipation

(1)

After the excitement and the rapid changes of the later eighteenth century — the glittering pageant of the Volunteer movement, the high sense of national achievement in the 'Constitution of 1782', the hopes and fears aroused by the United Irishmen, the courage and terror of the insurrection, the bitter controversy and fiery eloquence amid which the legislative union had at length been carried — after all this, the political life of Ireland in the early 1800s seemed drab, and, at least to outward appearance, almost meaningless. Dublin, though it remained the centre of administration and the seat of a vice-regal court, was now little more than a provincial city. One by one the mansions of the nobility were turned over to other purposes; and the parliament house itself was sold to the Bank of Ireland, with the significant stipulation that the interior should be so reconstructed as to efface every visible reminder of its original function.[1]

Transported from Dublin to Westminster, the Irish parliamentary representatives lost any sense of national cohesion; and though they were only gradually absorbed into the pattern of British politics, even those who remained outside existing parties and groups never acted together as a distinct 'Irish interest'. The anti-unionists, almost to a man, accepted their defeat as irreversible, and many of them readily took office under the government: Foster returned to his old post as chancellor of the exchequer in 1804; William Saurin, who had led the Irish bar against the union in 1799, was attorney-general from 1807 to 1822; William Plunket, after Grattan probably the most effective speaker against the union, became solicitor-general in 1803, and eventually, in 1830, lord chancellor of Ireland.

---

[1] Despite this stipulation the house of lords remained in its original form.

Even on Catholic Emancipation, though it was essentially an Irish question, and one that cut across the normal line of party division at Westminster, there was no distinctively Irish group on either side.

In Ireland itself there was no political activity on a national scale. Among the upper classes, the protestant patriotism of 'Grattan's parliament' was dead or transformed; among the people at large, resentment and unrest found expression in local agrarian agitation and crime; but there was neither leadership nor organization for a revolutionary movement: when Robert Emmet tried to revive the United Irish spirit for a new rising in 1803 his efforts ended in a scuffle in a Dublin street. For some years the government continued to be haunted by the dangers of the situation: 'We have no strength here but our army', wrote Sir Arthur Wellesley, the chief secretary, gloomily, in 1807, 'Ireland, in a view to military operations, must be considered as an enemy's country'; and in 1815 reports of popular rejoicing at the news of Napoleon's escape from Elba so alarmed the authorities in Dublin Castle that they protested against the withdrawal of troops to reinforce the British army in Flanders. But save in the unlikely event of a foreign invasion there was, in fact, hardly even the possibility of a rebellion.

One might say, indeed, that there was at this time a kind of vacuum in Irish politics. There was no national party in parliament, and no revolutionary movement in the country, though there was material for both. The demand for Catholic Emancipation, which might have provided a programme and a rallying cry, was but feebly and timorously raised. It was not until the 1820s that the genius of O'Connell transformed it into a popular movement, and so gave, for the first time since the union, a national character to Irish politics.

This temporary abeyance of national political life might have been used as an opportunity to conciliate Irish opinion, and to promote a real, as distinct from a formal, incorporation of Ireland with Great Britain in the United Kingdom. In view of the vast divergence in social and economic conditions between the two countries the task would certainly have been a formidable one; but it was hardly even attempted. The government's preoccupation with war and foreign policy, and the exigencies of party politics at Westminster, distracted attention from the new responsibilities so lightly assumed in 1800; and the general ignorance of Ireland among the British governing class obscured the very nature of the problems to be solved. Merely by continuing to exist, the union acquired strength; and within two decades of its enactment it seemed firmly and safely established. But it was established on principles that were contrary to its ostensible purpose; and this inner contradiction, which it should have been the first business of government to recognize, mitigate, and eventually remove, had been allowed to embed itself so deeply in the system of administration that it could hardly be remedied without the overthrow of the union itself.

The essence of this contradiction lay in the fact that, despite the union of the parliaments, Ireland continued to have a separate executive. After 1800, as before, Dublin Castle, with all its traditions of ascendancy rule, was the centre of an Irish government, directed by a lord lieutenant and chief secretary. It is true that this government was simply a branch of the central executive: the lord lieutenant and chief secretary were responsible for the execution of the cabinet's Irish policy, and the chief secretary had the duty of defending this policy in parliament; but neither of them had any more independent influence or control than was enjoyed by the other departmental ministers in their own spheres. Nevertheless, the very appearance of a separate Irish government suggested that Ireland was imperfectly integrated with the rest of the United Kingdom. And this appearance had some reality behind it; the very notion of an 'Irish policy' arose from a conviction that Ireland could not be governed on the same principles as Great Britain; and different principles of government required different administrative machinery. The Irish civil service was virtually distinct from the British: in many branches of government the Irish departments were independent of the corresponding departments in Britain; and even where formal unity was maintained, the Irish section of the work was, in general, separately organized.

No doubt this dualism was in part a matter of convenience, in part a reflection of bureaucratic aversion to change, in part, perhaps a rather illogical attempt to satisfy Irish pride; this last motive was certainly behind the maintenance of a vice-regal court, an institution never considered necessary in Scotland. But the survival of a separate administrative system for Ireland had another, and a deeper, significance: it was both the symbol and the instrument of a continuing protestant ascendancy. The union of the parliaments had transferred the power of legislation from Dublin to Westminster; but in all other respects, power still rested with the same people, or the same sort of people, as before. In every department of government, central and local, the protestant landlords, their allies and dependents, remained in control. It might be argued that this was part of a bargain implicit in the union itself, or that the different circumstances of Ireland made it impossible to govern the country on the same principles as England; and that in either case a separate executive was necessary. But to admit these arguments would be to admit that the union was not what it professed to be — a fusion of the two countries into one.

The example of the Scottish union had shown that such a fusion was not incompatible with the survival of distinct institutions; but it was incompatible with a totally different spirit of government. In 1800, Irish conditions differed so widely from those in Great Britain that some difference in administration could hardly be avoided. But instead of trying, by any consistent policy, to reduce this difference to a point at which Ireland could be truly incorporated with Britain in a single political unit, successive governments accepted it as a permanent characteristic of Anglo-Irish relations; and more than two generations were to pass before any British statesman thought of asking what meaning was to be attached to a union that condemned Ireland to be perpetually governed as a half-alien dependency.

The problem that British ministers refused to face at the beginning of the century was soon rendered more difficult of solution by a heightening of religious tensions. Within two decades, the Irish protestants, as a body, had become ardent supporters of the union, which they regarded as their only protection against the Roman Catholic majority. They were convinced that this support, self-interested as it was, gave them a special claim on government favour; and they tended to judge every government's Irish policy by its effect on their own position and influence. Thus one effect of the union was to strengthen and perpetuate the line of politico-religious cleavage; and any attempt to reconcile the majority to the union was almost bound to alarm the minority whose support was already secure. The political history of the union period, from the point of view of the British government, is dominated by this dilemma; and as the century progressed its influence was increasingly felt in the internal politics of Great Britain itself. Irish problems could not be kept in permanent isolation, and their influence on the British parliamentary system was, in the end, almost disastrous.

The sharpening of the religious cleavage in Ireland might seem, at first sight, no more than a development of pre-union conditions, without new significance. But this is a superficial view. Before 1800, the Irish protestants had had some direct control, however imperfect, of their own destiny and of the destiny of the country; after 1800, though they continued to exercise much influence, their power of independent action was gone. In the seventeenth and eighteenth centuries, their struggle against the threat of domination by the Roman Catholic majority had not prevented them from asserting their own rights against the constitutional encroachments of Great Britain; in the nineteenth century, they could maintain the struggle only by standing, quite openly, as an 'English garrison'. Almost inevitably, then, the mounting Roman Catholic demand for religious equality and the ending of protestant ascendancy tended to develop into an attack on the union itself. The claim to national independence, abandoned by the protestants, became almost the distinctive political characteristic of the Roman Catholics; and the age-old connection between political and religious affiliations became stronger than ever.

This development was by no means inevitable in 1800. The Roman Catholic leaders who supported the union had done so in confident expectation that it would be followed by Emancipation; and Pitt, recognizing the necessity of establishing the union on as broad a basis as possible, had regarded one as the natural corollary of the other. Lord Clare had dissuaded him from attempting to carry the two measures simultaneously, as he had at first proposed; but in his negotiations with the Roman Catholic bishops, through the medium of Castlereagh, he had not hesitated to commit himself, morally if not formally, to bringing in an Emancipation bill once the union was established. Though Pitt knew that the king was likely to oppose, on conscientious grounds, any political concession to the Roman Catholics, he did not regard that opposition as insuperable; and there were good grounds for supposing that the king would yield to an unanimous demand by the cabinet. But the cabinet, when it came to the point, was not unanimous; Pitt and some of his supporters, including Castlereagh, resigned; a new ministry was formed under Addington; and the question of Emancipation was shelved. Had Pitt used his immense influence in parliament and in the country to the full he might, even at this stage, have compelled the king to give way; but in view of the European situation he shrank from such extreme measures; and, having satisfied his conscience by resigning office, he felt free to support the new government. However historians may judge Pitt's conduct, the failure to grant Emancipation in 1801 weakened the union at its very beginning. The Roman Catholic upper classes were naturally disposed to support authority and property: their admission to full political rights would have enabled them to use their influence more effectively in favour of the established order, and would have opened the way for a gradual easing of religious tension. As it was, they felt that they had been deliberately deceived; and no later concession could efface the resentment and distrust that spread through the whole Roman Catholic population.

(2)

The failure of the union in the political sphere can be closely related to its effect on the national economy. On both sides of the channel, advocates of union seem to have been genuinely convinced that it would make

Ireland prosperous; but, at least so far as the great mass of the rural population was concerned, the situation grew worse rather than better; and the consequent agrarian unrest was the main reason why government was compelled to rely on coercive measures. These, in turn, stimulated political discontent, and helped to create a sense of insecurity very discouraging to that investment of English capital of which Ireland stood in such dire need.

From the beginning, the anti-unionists had denounced as deceptive the high hopes of prosperity held out by Castlereagh and Pitt; but it was not, at first sight, unreasonable to suppose that Ireland would benefit from being brought into contact with the wealthy and expanding economy of Great Britain. And to some extent Ireland did benefit. The trade in grain and provisions continued to flourish, and between 1800 and 1826 the average annual value of Irish exports rose from £4 millions to £8 millions. Nevertheless, over a great part of the country economic life was declining; and as the century progressed the Irish economy, in comparison with the British, became weaker rather than stronger. The union was not solely responsible for this state of affairs; but it did produce conditions in which economic weaknesses, arising from other causes, were particularly damaging to Irish prosperity.

The provision of the act of union by which Ireland was to bear two-seventeenths of the total expenditure of the United Kingdom may or may not have been an unfair assessment. What was far more important was that the war lasted much longer and cost much more than the framers of the act foresaw, and that Ireland was obliged to find a fixed proportion of a rising expenditure, the total amount of which was decided by the needs and capacity of Great Britain. Between 1795 and 1800 the average annual cost of Irish government was about £4½ millions; by 1816 Ireland's share of United Kingdom expenditure had risen to over £13 millions. The burden on Great Britain increased, of course, in the same proportion; but whereas Britain could meet her liabilities very largely out of revenue, Ireland had to raise about half the necessary amount by loans; and, since these loans were raised for the most part in England, the payment of interest drew a great part of the Irish revenue out of the country. Between 1801 and 1817 the British national debt increased by about 50 per cent, the Irish debt by about 250 per cent. As a result, one of the main conditions laid down by the act of union for the amalgamation of the exchequers was brought about not (as had been expected in 1800) by the reduction of the British national debt, but by the increase of the Irish. In 1817, accordingly, the exchequers were united; and though for a time Ireland continued to receive preferential treatment in some respects, the financial and fiscal

K

systems of the two countries were gradually assimilated. The amalgamation of the exchequers in 1817 relieved Ireland of separate responsibility
for the enormous debt incurred since the union; but the heavy financial
strain imposed during the interval had drawn much-needed capital out of
the country, and had weakened her economy at a critical period.

Money was also being drained out of Ireland, not only at this time but
throughout a great part of the century, in the form of rent; for absenteeism
among the landlord class had, not unnaturally, increased with the transference of the legislature from Dublin to Westminster. And this loss of
capital was not compensated for by any steady inflow of British invest-
ments, such as Pitt had optimistically forecast at the time of the union.
British capitalists knew little about Ireland, save that it was poor, and
frequently disturbed; they saw no prospect either of a quick return, or of
substantial profits to compensate for delay and the risk of loss; and the
capital that might have transformed the economic life of Ireland went
elsewhere.

Few Irish manufacturers, left to their own resources, could hope to
stand against the competition of the more highly-developed industries of
Great Britain, to which they were now exposed. The woollen manufacture, though it had advanced considerably during the last two decades
of the eighteenth century, was still, at the time of the union, a scattered
industry, carried on by small concerns, and based on domestic labour.
While it enjoyed a measure of protection, it continued to exist; when this
was withdrawn, in the 1820s, it rapidly collapsed, and ten years later had
almost died out. The disappearance of the cotton industry, about the
same time, was not so directly due to the removal of protective duties.
Since the 1790s it had been firmly established in and around Belfast, and
for a time it seemed likely to supersede linen as the principal manufacture
of the area. Cotton-manufacturers were more progressive than linen-
manufacturers in the development and use of machinery; rates of profit
were consequently higher; and down to the 1820s there was a tendency for
capital and labour, formerly employed in the linen industry, to be transferred to cotton. But in the mid-1820s the introduction of the wet-
spinning process speeded up the production of linen yarn, and linen began
to recover its old predominance. The withdrawal, at this point, of the
protection hitherto afforded to cotton simply encouraged a change already
in progress. The Belfast cotton industry disappeared; but it left no gap in
the economic life of the area, for the expanding linen industry took its
place both as a source of employment and as an outlet for capital.

The woollen and cotton manufactures might have survived and grown
stronger under continued protection; but it is unlikely that they would

ever have been able to meet British competition on equal terms. The fact
that Ireland was ill-supplied with coal and iron was an obvious disadvantage at a time when power-driven machinery was becoming more
and more important; but the prosperity of the linen industry shows that
this was not, by itself, decisive. There was another factor in the situation.
The whole tendency in industrial development throughout western
Europe was towards specialization and concentration. Small local manufacturers were everywhere declining, as their markets were invaded by
cheaper goods from more highly-developed areas. Irish wool and Irish
cotton could not escape this general process; and not being strong enough to
expand, they were forced out of existence altogether. But the same process
worked to the advantage of the Irish linen industry, which grew stronger
during the nineteenth century, while the linen industry of Great Britain,
at one time almost as important as that of Ireland, shrank into comparative
insignificance. The expansion of the linen manufacture in Ulster stimulated other enterprises, both industrial and commercial, in the same area;
and the social and economic differences between Ulster, especially eastern
Ulster, and the rest of Ireland became even more marked in the nineteenth
century than they had been in the eighteenth. Not unnaturally, these
differences were reflected in differing attitudes to the union — Ulster
protestants came to regard it as the essential basis of their prosperity,
while to Irishmen in general it appeared the main barrier to economic
progress.

(3)

To the peasants who formed the great mass of the population the
legislative union must have seemed remote, and very nearly irrelevant.
They were absorbed in a struggle for mere existence; and whether Irish
laws were made in Dublin or at Westminster did not seem likely to
affect the power of the landlord or the burden of tithe. During the 1790s
the propaganda of the United Irishmen had given a political colouring
to agrarian agitation; but the agitation itself was, in origin and purpose,
economic; and in this form it continued into the nineteenth century.
In almost every part of the country there existed, under various names
— Whiteboys, Carders, Threshers, Rockites, Ribbonmen[1] — peasant
secret societies, whose main purpose was to protect the tenant against
the landlord, and in particular to combat the landlord's power of eviction.

---

[1] In the early nineteenth century the term 'Whiteboys' was often applied
indiscriminately to the members of any agrarian secret society; later in the
century the term 'Ribbonmen' was used in the same way.

The main weapon of these societies was terror, enforced by assassination; and so reluctant were witnesses to come forward that even crimes committed publicly and in broad daylight frequently went unpunished: there is a grim reality behind the story of a coroner's jury whose verdict on a murdered land-agent was 'death from natural causes'. In fact, however, landlords and their agents suffered less than those unfortunate tenants who were rash enough to take farms from which others had been evicted.

It is not improbable that contemporaries tended to exaggerate the extent of agrarian crime: Englishmen, because they found the whole situation so startlingly different from that in England; Irish landlords from an anxiety to persuade the government that repressive measures were necessary. But though there might be many areas free from disturbance for long periods, and many estates on which relations between landlord and tenant were harmonious, there was no underlying sense of security. If the whole of Ireland was not exactly in a state of 'smothered war', the threat of war was never far away.

The wretched conditions that gave rise to agrarian disturbance were not due solely to the oppressive conduct of landlord and tithe-proctor, though popular opinion generally held them responsible. Rural Ireland was at this time facing an economic crisis, produced by a rapid increase in population. From about five million at the time of the union it rose to 6,800,000 in 1821, to 7,700,000 in 1831, to 8,175,000 in 1841.[1] And since opportunities for employment in manufacturing industry tended to contract rather than expand, the great bulk of this population had to find a living on the land. Even if Irish farmers had been in a much better position, if they had had security of tenure at moderate rents, and the skill and capital necessary to make the best use of their holdings, it is hard to see how so many people could have been maintained at much above a bare subsistence level. As things actually were, an increasing proportion of the population lived on the very edge of destitution. The great and seemingly inescapable evil was subdivision. Holdings already small were divided, and divided again, so that a son, on marriage, could have a scrap of ground on which to build a mud cabin and grow potatoes. For thousands upon thousands of families no other mode of life seemed possible. Casual labour might suffice to pay the rent; harvest work, in Ireland or Britain, might bring in enough to buy food during the lean

[1] These figures have been rounded off. The census returns of 1821 and 1831 are probably inaccurate, but they indicate the trend of population; the returns of 1841, when the census was taken throughout the country on one day, are generally regarded as reliable.

months when the old potatoes had been eaten and the new were not yet ready;[1] but for the greater part of the year only the potato-patch stood between them and starvation. This cottier class, though it increased fairly steadily down to the time of the famine, never amounted to more than a minority, though a large minority, of the rural population. But even among tenants who held more than a mere potato-patch, who could grow corn and raise cattle for the market, there was a high proportion whose holdings were too small to provide them with a living, and who depended on casual and seasonal labour to make ends meet. It is probably true to say that at any time between the union and the famine there was a majority of tenants who could not have made a living from their land, even had they held it free of rent and tithe. The only hope of establishing the agrarian economy on a sound basis lay in reversing the process of sub-division, and in consolidating holdings to make farms of a reasonable size. But consolidation would have to be preceded by the eviction of a great body of existing tenants, for whose future subsistence there was no ready way of making provision. Some landlords attempted to 'clear' their estates (as the phrase ran) by encouraging emigration to North America, but their efforts had little success; and it is one of the ironies of the situation that a careless and rack-renting landlord who allowed holdings to multiply freely was almost always more popular than a more conscientious neighbour who attempted to resist or reverse a process that could only end in disaster.

In face of this situation, the government had no comprehensive or consistent remedial policy. With the return of peace in 1815, Peel, then chief secretary, put forward a scheme of assisted emigration to Canada; but this was not accepted by the cabinet; and the measures actually adopted by the government were designed merely to provide local and temporary relief at periods of particular stress. In 1817, when a partial failure of the potato crop produced famine conditions in many areas, some thousands of pounds of public money were distributed through relief committees; and between 1823 and 1828 almost two and a half millions were advanced for public works, mainly in road-construction, in order to provide employment: the poverty of rural Ireland, which reflected the unhealthy state of the whole Irish economy, could not be cured by expedients such as these. But the prevailing philosophy of *laissez-faire* made it unlikely that any more fundamental remedy would be sought; and the traditional respect for property forbade even the attempt to improve the condition of the tenantry by restricting the powers of the landlord — indeed, the only land legislation

[1] A period sometimes called 'the meal months'.

of the early nineteenth century, three acts passed between 1816 and 1820, extended those powers still further by simplifying the process of eviction.

The government was much more active in dealing with symptoms than with causes; and its legislation was directed rather to the suppression of agrarian crime than to the amelioration of the conditions that produced it. Among the earliest Irish measures of the union parliament was one for the continuation of martial law; and for more than thirty years the country was almost continuously administered under special coercive legislation. In Ireland, far more directly than in England, even at the troubled period of Peterloo, government depended on military power. 'The situation of a general officer commanding in a district in Ireland is very much of the nature of a deputy governor of a county or a province. He becomes necessarily charged with the preservation of the peace of the district placed under his command; and the government must confide in his reports and opinions for the adoption of any measures relating solely to the civil administration of the country'. So wrote Sir Arthur Wellesley, then chief secretary, to the officer commanding at Limerick in 1808. He admits frankly that disorders may have their origin in genuine grievances; but this, he says, is no concern of the military:

'Provisions may be too dear, or too high a rent may be demanded for land, and there may be no poor-laws, and the magistrates may not do their duty as they ought by the poor. But these circumstances afford no reason why the general officer should not give the military aid he may have at his command to preserve the peace.'

This was obviously the only safe principle by which a soldier could guide himself; but the very fact that troops were readily available meant that they were often called upon, even where there was no organized disturbance, simply to back up the sheriff's authority in distraint for non-payment of rent or tithe, and in the enforcement of eviction orders. To the tenant it seemed that the whole machinery of the state was organized against him. It is hardly surprising that he had little respect for the law, and little confidence in the willingness of the government to protect his interests. The resulting sense of grievance and frustration went a long way towards destroying such chance of success as the union had.

Bitter as were his complaints about rack-rents and evictions, the average tenant regarded the exaction of tithe with even greater loathing. Tithe has always and everywhere been an unpopular form of taxation; but in Ireland it was particularly detested because it was paid to the clergy of a church that the vast majority of the people regarded as not only heretical but alien. In theory, tithe was a permanent charge upon land, which should have been taken into account in the assessment of an equitable rent;

in practice, most Irish landlords exacted the utmost that the land would bear, and, so far as the tenant was concerned, tithe was an unjust additional burden. He was prepared to admit his liability for rent, though he might dispute the amount; but he felt justified in resisting, when he could, the demand for tithe. At the beginning of the nineteenth century, as in earlier periods, such resistance was common in most parts of the country; but it was not until the 1830s that it was organized as a regular campaign on an almost nation-wide scale. The reason for this development is to be found in the new sense of power with which the Roman Catholic peasantry had been inspired by the victorious struggle for Emancipation.

(4)

Between 1801 and 1829 the only issue that gave any measure of unity or continuity to Irish political life was that of Catholic Emancipation. But it was not until the 1820s that the demand for Emancipation was widely organized or vigorously pressed in Ireland. For two decades after the union the struggle was concentrated at Westminster and carried on by protestant champions, who received but feeble and divided support from the Irish Roman Catholics. Grattan made the cause peculiarly his own. After a temporary withdrawal from politics he was returned to parliament for an English constituency (Malton) in 1805 and his first speech was on the political disabilities of Roman Catholics. From 1806 until his death, in 1820, he sat as one of the members for the city of Dublin, devoting himself tirelessly to the cause of Emancipation; he found increasing support among both Irish and English members, so that it seemed only a matter of time until the house of commons should be converted; and even in the house of lords the hostile majority was shrinking. But British opinion was deeply divided on the subject; George III remained inflexibly opposed to Roman Catholic claims, and his son, on assuming the regency, maintained the same attitude. It required the pressure of a popular Irish movement to break down the barrier, and until the 1820s such a movement was lacking.

When Grattan entered the united parliament in 1805, organized political activity among the Irish Roman Catholics was confined within the narrow circle of the aristocracy and landed gentry, together with a few lawyers and wealthy merchants, mainly resident in Dublin. The great majority of them shrank from anything approaching popular agitation; and their fear of antagonizing the government made them so cautious that a proposal to petition parliament for the removal of their disabilities, brought forward in 1805 by some of the more active spirits, was accepted only with difficulty. It was in support of this petition that Daniel O'Connell, the future 'Liberator', first became prominent in the cause of Emancipation. From this time onwards his influence gradually increased; but more than fifteen years were to pass before he gained unquestioned control of a great national movement; and in the meantime the Irish Roman Catholics were weakened by a divided leadership. The division was partly social in origin: the handful of nobles who traditionally regarded themselves as entitled to speak for the whole Roman Catholic body were more cautious and conservative, more deferential to the government, than members of the growing middle class of lawyers and merchants. The course of the struggle at Westminster helped to bring out and emphasize the difference in outlook between the two groups.

The union had extended the debate on Emancipation from Ireland to England, and in doing so had changed its character. The Irish protestant argument that to admit Roman Catholics to full political rights would lead to the destruction of the established church and the overthrow of the existing settlement of landed property was still heard; but English opponents of Emancipation generally based themselves on the contention that Roman Catholics, by reason of their allegiance to the papacy, could never be good subjects. To allay this fear Grattan and his allies at Westminster suggested that Emancipation should be accompanied by some measure of government control over episcopal appointments; various proposals were put forward, but the essence of them all was the same: the crown was to be empowered to veto any candidate considered politically unreliable. In May 1808 Grattan proposed Emancipation on these terms in the house of commons, declaring that he had been authorized by the Roman Catholics to do so. But he was misinformed about the state of opinion in Ireland. The aristocratic party favoured the veto, and some of the bishops were ready to accept it; but the opposition was much more powerful and much more vocal. The veto could not be condemned on theological grounds; but it was denounced as a betrayal of Irish interests, for many Irishmen regarded the freedom of their church from government control as the last remnant of national independence. Frightened by this uproar, the bishops, at a meeting in September, decided by an overwhelming majority to reject the proposed veto as 'inexpedient'. The decision was temporarily irrelevant, for the house of commons had already rejected Grattan's motion by 281 votes to 128; but the controversy helped to widen the gap between the conservative and progressive wings of the Emancipation movement in Ireland.

From this time onwards aristocratic influence in the Emancipation movement in Ireland steadily declined. It had been powerful, and sometimes dominant, in the successive committees and boards which had been formed, since the union, to promote Irish Roman Catholic interests; but in 1808 the combination of middle-class and clerical forces had been completely triumphant. A new committee, more widely representative than any of its predecessors, was set up in 1810, and reconstituted in 1811 as the Catholic Board. Though it contained some aristocratic members, it was essentially a middle-class body, dominated by the progressive wing of the Emancipation movement, and committed to opposing any scheme for a veto.

Despite the attitude of the Catholic Board, the supporters of Emancipation at Westminster still felt it wise to retain the principle of the veto, though rather in the hope of conciliating their opponents than because they themselves thought it a necessary safeguard of government authority. Their chances of success now seemed to be rapidly improving. In June 1812 the house of commons accepted, by 225 votes to 106, a motion in favour of considering Roman Catholic claims; and Liverpool, who had just succeeded in forming a ministry, decided that the question should be left an open one, 'free from all interference on the part of the government'. The hopes thus aroused were, however, doomed to disappointment; and an Emancipation bill introduced in the commons in the following February, though it received a second reading, was lost in committee by a narrow margin.[1] Irish opinion was less concerned about the fate of the bill than about the fact that it had included provision for a crown veto on episcopal appointments. The bishops, without any of the hesitation that had marked their conduct in 1808, rejected Emancipation on these terms, and the Catholic Board, now largely under O'Connell's influence, did the same. Even when the principle of a veto received formal Vatican approval, in a rescript from Quarantotti, secretary of the Propaganda, the board renewed its condemnation, and the bishops declared that the rescript had no binding force. These decisions were not unopposed. Many among the upper classes were quite ready to accept the veto; they resented its condemnation as a sacrifice of lay interests to an over-refined clerical scruple; and they were antagonized by O'Connell's domineering and aggressive attitude. All hope of harmony in the Catholic Board was now gone; and though the vetoists were defeated at every point, repeated squabbles destroyed the board's prestige: when the government, needlessly

[1] The whole bill was not defeated in committee; but the Speaker, Charles Abbot, carried an amendment deleting the section admitting Roman Catholics to membership of parliament; the remaining concessions were of comparatively little importance, and the bill was dropped.

alarmed by its activities, ordered its dissolution in June 1814, there was not even a public protest in its favour.

The decision to dissolve the Catholic Board was in accordance with the policy advocated by the chief secretary, Robert Peel, who had been appointed in 1812. Then, as later, Peel was firmly opposed to any extension of the political rights of the Roman Catholics. 'Orange Peel', O'Connell dubbed him, 'a raw youth, squeezed out of the workings of I know not what factory in England . . . sent over here before he got rid of the foppery of perfumed handkerchiefs and thin shoes'. O'Connell's gibe was singularly misdirected. Peel had no sympathy with the Orangemen; he wanted to see the law impartially administered; and, despite his youth, he worked hard and conscientiously to understand the problems of Irish government. His predecessors, since the union, had held office for comparatively short periods — some for as little as six months, only one for more than two years — but Peel remained chief secretary until 1818, thus having a longer tenure than any other chief secretary of the century; and even after he had finally left the country he retained an active interest in its affairs.

The temporary collapse of the Emancipation campaign after the suppression of the Catholic Board left Peel freer than he had been to consider other issues. But he found the cabinet little interested in legislation for Ireland, and he often had difficulty in getting parliamentary time for the discussion of his proposed measures. He had, however, one notable success, of great importance for the future. It was his persistent advocacy that procured in 1815 a state grant for elementary education, in the form of an annual subsidy to the Kildare Place Society—a non-denominational body, supported by both protestants and Roman Catholics, which maintained schools throughout the country.[1]

The great problem for Peel, as for every other Irish administrator of the century, was the maintenance of order. He saw the need for an efficient police force, and took the first step towards its establishment in 1814. But he found that Ireland could not be governed by the normal course of law; and even his reform of the police was embodied in a coercion act. Two years later, he wrote to Sir William Gregory, the under-secretary,[2] 'I believe an honest despotic government would be by far the fittest government for Ireland'. It was a confession that the union had failed.

[1] See below, pp. 312–13.
[2] The under-secretary was a permanent official, the head of the Irish civil service.

(5)

For some years after the suppression of the Catholic Board the cause of Emancipation languished in Ireland. The minority of vetoists was still strong enough to prevent real unity; and though a Catholic Association was established to replace the suppressed Catholic Board, it had no effective organization, no clear policy, and it accomplished nothing. At Westminster the prospects seemed brighter. In 1819, the year before his death, Grattan introduced a new bill, which was defeated in the commons by only two votes. In 1821 William Plunket, member for Dublin University, who had succeeded Grattan in the leadership of the Roman Catholic cause, came even nearer to success. He introduced two bills, one for Emancipation, one for the veto, which passed the house of commons, and might have passed the house of lords but for the intervention of the duke of York.

Even if these bills had passed, the settlement that they embodied would not have been acceptable to majority opinion in Ireland; but their defeat was nevertheless felt as a serious set-back. For a time, O'Connell inclined to the view that it was useless to continue the struggle until some measure of parliamentary reform should have been passed; but he soon recovered confidence, and set about re-organizing the Emancipation movement in preparation for more aggressive and self-reliant action. In May 1823 he established a new Catholic Association, whose aim was not only to win political rights for Roman Catholics but also to defend and forward their interests in all spheres of life. The Association did not receive the popular support for which O'Connell had hoped until he introduced a change in its rules early in 1824: those who could not afford the annual membership fee of one guinea might now become associates by subscribing a penny a month. The effect of this direct appeal to the people was startling. With the aid of the parochial clergy, who were members *ex officio*, penny collections were made, Sunday by Sunday, all over Ireland; and the 'Catholic rent', as it was called, which brought in £8 in the first week, had risen to £1,000 a week within a year.

The financial success of this scheme was less important than the fact that it turned Emancipation into a truly popular cause, with O'Connell as its undisputed leader. As Sir William Gregory noted with alarm, the 'Catholic rent' was 'the most efficient mode that could be devised for opening a direct communication between the Popish Parliament [i.e. the committee of the Catholic Association] and the whole mass of the popish population'. The peasant who paid a penny a month to the association felt that he was taking a real part in its work and that his own well-being was bound up with its success. At first sight, it might seem that the admission of Roman Catholics to parliament — a concession that, in the circumstances of the 1820s, could affect only a handful of landlords — would make little or no difference to the mass of the people. But in the popular mind Emancipation had come to mean far more than this. The Irish peasant saw himself as the victim of injustice in almost all the relations of life: the landlord and the parson oppressed him; the magistrate refused him justice; his protestant neighbour, simply as a protestant, had the advantage of him at every turn. Michael Collins, parish priest of Skibbereen in 1825, admitted that the denial of full political rights was not felt by the peasantry 'as a practical and immediate grievance'; but, he said, 'it is felt by them as a cause why they have not the same confidence in those in power as the favoured classes have, and why they are oppressed, because they consider themselves to be looked on as belonging to a degraded caste'. Emancipation was to put an end to all these grievances, and to give the Irish Roman Catholic the freedom, and the equality of opportunity, hitherto denied him.

This was the theme on which O'Connell laid most stress in the great popular meetings that he began to hold about this time. He understood, better perhaps than anyone else, the condition and character of the Irish peasantry; for his practice as a barrister took him regularly into the country, and he was frequently engaged in cases that involved tenant interests. Before the achievement of Emancipation won for him the title of 'Liberator', it was as 'the Counsellor' that he was most widely and affectionately known.

The rapid progress of the Catholic Association alarmed the government; and this alarm was increased, and in some measure justified, by the violent language that O'Connell regularly employed. He was exuberant and aggressive by nature, and either the enthusiastic excitement of a popular audience or the coldness of a hostile court could drive him into fierce extravagance of expression. But the habitual violence of his language was deliberate. He believed that the Roman Catholics had for so long been accustomed to accepting an inferior status that they had lost confidence in their ability to assert their rights, and that it was his duty to set them an example by fearless defiance of the ascendancy. At every opportunity, either in the conduct of a case or in a public meeting, he denounced the laws that deprived them of equality and the system of administration that denied them full enjoyment of those rights to which they had been formally admitted by the earlier relaxations of the penal code. The government, determined to break O'Connell's power, attempted to prosecute him for incitement to rebellion, and when this failed through lack of evidence the

Catholic Association was, in 1825, suppressed. But O'Connell was equal to the situation; he re-established the Association under a new name; the 'Catholic rent' continued to be collected; and the campaign went on as before.

The aggressive character of O'Connell's campaign in Ireland had temporarily weakened support for Emancipation in Britain; but the repressive policy of the government helped to revive it, especially among the radicals; and in 1825 Sir Francis Burdett, in alliance with Plunket, introduced a new relief bill. It was accompanied by two 'wings', intended to allay protestant uneasiness. The forty-shilling freehold franchise in the counties was to be abolished, and a £10 franchise established in its place; and some measure of government influence over the church was to be secured by a provision for the payment of the Roman Catholic clergy from public funds. Both these conditions would certainly have aroused opposition in Ireland, though O'Connell himself was willing, at the time, to accept them. But the question did not arise; for the bill, having passed the commons, was thrown out by the lords.

O'Connell's readiness to sacrifice the forty-shilling freeholders arose from the conviction that they were too completely under landlord control to act independently. The events of the next few years were to prove him wrong; and it was the courageous action of the forty-shilling freeholders themselves that carried the long campaign for Emancipation to its victorious conclusion. From the inspiration of O'Connell, and under the guidance of their clergy, they had begun to acquire a sense of strength and solidarity, which first appeared in the general election of 1826. The Catholic Association called on all voters to support candidates favourable to Emancipation; but it concentrated its efforts on four counties (Louth, Monaghan, Waterford, Westmeath), in each of which it succeeded in returning at least one member. The most dramatic contest was in Waterford, where the Beresfords had held almost undisputed control for generations. On this occasion their influence went down before that of the clergy, and when Lord George Beresford saw that even his own tenants were deserting him for Villiers Stuart, a staunch ally of O'Connell, he withdrew from the poll. The Louth election was, in one respect, even more significant than that in Waterford. Villiers Stuart, a man of considerable influence, and a relation of the Duke of Devonshire, one of the great landlords of the county, would in any case have been a formidable opponent; but the successful Emancipation candidate in Louth, Alexander Dawson, could never have ventured to come forward without the assurance of clerical backing.

This great victory occurred on the eve of a momentous change in

British politics. Early in 1827 the long premiership of Lord Liverpool came to an end, and with it the continuity of government that had rested on his ability to hold together diverse and conflicting interests. Canning, who succeeded him, might have maintained a broadly-based administration, but he died in August 1827; and his successor Goderich, finding himself wholly unequal to the task, gladly resigned office in January 1828. At this point the king sent for Wellington, who reconstructed Goderich's ministry, with Peel as home secretary. But the reconstructed ministry was not much more firmly united than its predecessor; and its control of the house of commons was precarious. When Lord John Russell proposed the repeal of the test and corporation acts, in so far as they affected protestant dissenters, he received so much support that the government was obliged to accept the measure, and it passed into law. The concession was merely formal, for the acts had long been inoperative; but as an indication of the growing liberalism of parliament it was both an encouragement to the Roman Catholics and a warning to the government. When Wellington took office the king had stipulated that 'the Roman Catholic question should not be made a cabinet question'; but both Wellington and Peel were, in fact, resolutely opposed to any concession; and it was very uncertain how far they would be supported, either by their colleagues or in the house of commons, if they persisted in this attitude.

It was thus a divided and doubtful ministry that had to face O'Connell's next attack. And for this attack the ministry itself unintentionally provided the opening. When Huskisson and his allies left the ministry, in May 1828, Wellington appointed as president of the board of trade Vesey Fitzgerald, one of the members for Clare, who had consequently to seek re-election. He was one of the most popular landlords in the county, and a supporter of Emancipation; and his return was regarded as a matter of course. But the successful revolt of the freeholders in 1826 had suggested to the Roman Catholic leaders an even more daring measure; and after some hesitation O'Connell decided to contest the constituency himself. If he were elected, his refusal to take the oath of supremacy would exclude him from parliament, and the question that had been agitating the country for so long would be brought to a sharp and decisive issue: 'This business', wrote Lord Eldon, of the Clare election, 'must bring the Catholic question to a crisis and conclusion'. The poll began on 30 June; five days later Fitzgerald, recognizing the hopelessness of his position, withdrew from the contest, and O'Connell was declared elected.

The triumph of O'Connell convinced the Roman Catholics of their strength. In every part of the country there were great demonstrations of a semi-military character; and though they were peacefully conducted, the determination and confidence that inspired them could not fail to alarm the government. Wellington and Peel had opposed Emancipation hitherto, and if they had had the support of a united cabinet and a united house of commons they might have continued their opposition even now; but both cabinet and commons were divided on the question, and in these circumstances even Peel, whose opposition had been more firmly rooted in principle than that of Wellington, thought it wise to yield. With some difficulty they overcame the scruples of George IV; and when parliament re-assembled in February 1829 the king's speech included a promise of Roman Catholic relief. A month later, a bill for the purpose was introduced in the commons, and having passed both houses received the royal assent in April.

Had Emancipation been granted at any time before 1823 it would have appeared as a concession to reason and justice, and the credit would have gone to the parliamentary friends of the Roman Catholic cause. Their influence was, in fact, essential to the passage of the relief act of 1829; but their share in the victory was completely overshadowed by that of O'Connell. To Irishmen it seemed, not unnaturally, that they had wrested their rights from an unwilling Britain, entirely by their own efforts; and the government itself, by its obvious alarm, did much to strengthen this view. Wellington, in introducing the bill in the house of lords, declared that civil war was the only alternative to Emancipation: 'This', he said, 'is the measure to which we must have looked, these are the means which we must have applied . . . if we had not embraced the option of bringing forward this measure'.

A concession so granted could hardly, in any case, have much conciliatory effect; the grudging and suspicious attitude of the government made it an occasion of fresh grievance. By the terms of the relief act, Roman Catholics were made eligible for all offices of state, except those of regent, lord lieutenant, and lord chancellor of either country; Roman Catholic members of either house of parliament were relieved of the obligation to take the oath of supremacy, but were to take instead a long and comprehensive oath denying that the pope had any civil authority within the kingdom, undertaking to defend the existing settlement of property, and disavowing 'any intention to subvert the present church establishment as settled by law within this realm'. Though these terms left Roman Catholics in a distinctive and, to some extent, inferior position, they were not unsatisfactory. But other measures, passed at almost the same time, seemed calculated to minimize their effect, and to weaken the political influence of Roman Catholics for the future. The Catholic

Association was suppressed, and the lord lieutenant given powers that would enable him to suppress any new association of the same sort; and the forty-shilling freehold franchise in the counties was abolished, and a £10 franchise established in its place. In this way, the very people who had contributed most to the victory were to be deprived of the fruits of it, and the anti-British feeling aroused during the previous six years remained as strong as ever.

(6)

During the debate on Emancipation in the house of lords, in April 1829, the archbishop of Armagh, Lord John George Beresford, opposed the measure with the vigour and intolerance to be expected from one who combined, in his office and in his person, the strongest traditions of protestant ascendancy. But his speech, however intolerant in spirit, contained a remarkably accurate prophecy of future developments. He saw that Emancipation was the beginning, not the end of a process; that the Roman Catholics, having won the right to sit in parliament, must inevitably use that right to gain others; that their parliamentary representatives, acting as a body, would be able to play off party against party, and so gain their ends. He saw that the power of the Roman Catholic clergy, demonstrated during O'Connell's campaign, would be confirmed and extended by success, and that they would never rest satisfied until they had overthrown the protestant establishment. He saw that Emancipation involved, in its consequences, not so much a sharing as a transfer of power:

'Are you prepared, my lords, to go the length to which you will be urged, after you have conceded all that is now demanded? Are you prepared to sacrifice the Irish church establishment and the protestant institutions connected with it — to efface the protestant character of the Irish portion of the empire — to transfer from protestants to Roman Catholics the ascendancy of Ireland?'

Events were to bear out the truth of Beresford's reading of the situation; and 1829 proved a more important turning-point in the history of modern Ireland than 1800. The political significance of Emancipation was not immediately apparent: the disfranchisement of the forty-shilling freeholders restricted its effect on parliamentary elections; and even after the reform act of 1832 the influence of property continued to outweigh that of population. But as the century progressed the balance changed, and the power of the protestant ascendancy, fatally undermined in 1829, withered away.

The effect of Emancipation was enormously increased by the circumstances in which it was granted. O'Connell had forced the government to yield by a demonstration of power — the power of mass opinion organized under clerical influence; and that power could be used again in the future. Though Roman Catholics had been admitted to parliament, Irish politics never acquired, during the period of the union, a parliamentary character. The basic condition for a parliamentary democracy is that the minority should be prepared to accept majority decisions; and this readiness arises from confidence that the majority will not abuse its power. No such confidence existed between the bulk of the Irish people and the majority in the United Kingdom as a whole; the issues between them might be debated in parliament, but they could never be settled on a purely parliamentary basis. The whole situation was complicated by the fact that there was the same lack of confidence between the Irish protestants and the majority of their fellow-countrymen: in the long run, neither of the two main parties in Ireland was willing to have its fate decided by votes.

XVI

O'Connell and the Policy of Repeal

(1)

The victory of 1829 had raised O'Connell's influence higher than ever; but how this influence was to be maintained, and what use he was to make of it, were questions to which there were no obvious answers. He himself had always declared that Emancipation was only the first stage of his programme, and that the ultimate goal was repeal of the legislative union; but in 1829 there was much to be said against launching an immediate campaign for repeal. The bulk of the people, though angry at loss of the franchise, and disappointed that Emancipation had brought no improvement in economic conditions, would no doubt follow wherever O'Connell might choose to lead. He could count also on strong sympathy among the parochial clergy. An increasing proportion of them, drawn from the class of small farmers and trained at Maynooth, shared the social and political prejudices of their people: there is some truth as well as a good deal of exaggeration in the comment of a hostile observer that they displayed 'the bitterest feelings of the partisan and the grossest habits of a peasant'. But most of the bishops still maintained the older traditions of the continental-trained clergy: they showed greater deference to the authority of government, and more lively fear of popular agitation. The Roman Catholic middle classes were equally cautious. They had fought for Emancipation as a means of gaining political power and a share of public appointments; and now they wanted to enjoy the fruits of victory, not plunge into another agitation that could only alienate the very people to whom they must look for advancement. Again, though the policy of Emancipation had been favoured by many Irish protestants, and acquiesced in by more, and had been consistently advocated by leading British statesmen, no such support could be expected for a policy of repeal.

In these circumstances, O'Connell might well pause before embarking on a repeal campaign.

The general state of the country provided another argument in favour of delay. Many reforms, social and political, were obviously and urgently necessary; and it might seem more sensible to work for these, by pressure in parliament, than to plunge the whole country into a fresh agitation. Moreover, many of these reforms, though by no means all, could command support not only among middle-class Roman Catholics but also among moderate protestants in Ireland and among whigs and radicals in Britain; and in pursuing them he could find a programme of immediate action, which might yield tangible results within a reasonable time.

Throughout the rest of his career O'Connell kept these two policies — repeal and reform — in view, without committing himself irrevocably to either. He always maintained that repeal was his real object; but this did not prevent his interrupting his repeal campaign for the sake of co-operation with a friendly government in the cause of reform. This ambiguity in O'Connell's attitude may reflect, in part, his dependence on middle-class support. Though the most obvious basis of his influence was his power to arouse the peasantry, he could not organize an effective campaign without strong backing from the Roman Catholic middle classes, whose essential interest lay in reform, and who showed little enthusiasm for repeal until the accession of a conservative government in 1841 seemed to close the door to the kind of reform they had hoped for. O'Connell's apparent inconsistency may also be associated with his failure to think out clearly the meaning and consequences of a repeal policy. Repeal, in its simplest form, meant no more than the repeal of the act of union — the restoration to Ireland of the constitutional status she had enjoyed between 1782 and 1800. But how this was to affect the executive government; how the link with Great Britain (which O'Connell always insisted must continue) was to be maintained; what part, if any, Ireland was to play in defence and in the direction of foreign policy; what were to be her relations (and especially her economic relations) with the overseas possessions of the crown — to none of these questions, nor to many others of the same sort, had O'Connell any satisfactory answer. For the purposes of popular agitation this lack of definition was an advantage: 'repeal' could be put forward as the remedy for every grievance, and the answer to every problem. But it left O'Connell's enemies equally free to interpret his policy as they chose; and it did nothing to ease the task, almost impossible in any case, of reconciling the British people to a dismemberment of the United Kingdom.

The ambiguity and uncertainty that were to mark O'Connell's later policy appeared almost immediately after Emancipation had been won. He started a repeal campaign in Ireland, but he did not press it hard, and he was very reluctant to raise the question at Westminster; there, he devoted himself mainly to attacking the government's Irish policy and to demanding reforms, especially the abolition or modification of tithe, and such changes in the Irish administrative system as would make Emancipation a reality.

O'Connell's hesitancy, at this stage, owed something to the political situation in Great Britain, where the dominant issue was now parliamentary reform. A brief experience of the house of commons had convinced him that, as things stood, there was no likelihood of winning a majority there for repeal of the union. But he hoped that a reformed house might prove more favourable; and so, despite his opposition to the whigs, he, and the thirty repealers who had been returned at the general election of 1830, supported Grey's ministry on the question of reform: in the critical division of 21 March 1831 it was the O'Connellite vote that gave the government its majority; and O'Connell's success in keeping Ireland quiet during the general election of the following summer was of immense value to the whigs. But parliamentary reform, when it came in 1832, proved disappointing. O'Connell's demand for the restoration of the forty-shilling freehold franchise in the counties was ignored; and the total representation of Ireland was increased by only five members, instead of the twenty that he had claimed in view of the great rise in population.[1] And, apart altogether from his disappointment at the treatment Ireland had received, O'Connell was soon forced to realize that the reformed house of commons was no more likely than its predecessors to favour repeal of the union. This realization is sufficient to explain why he was still unwilling to bring repeal formally before parliament. But instead of following the obvious alternative course, and throwing all his energies into a popular campaign, he continued the dual policy of maintaining the repeal movement in Ireland while working at Westminster for specific reforms.

At this time, O'Connell seems to have believed that by keeping the government under constant threat he was more likely to win concessions than by wholehearted co-operation. It was with this in mind that he rejected a suggestion, made to him by the ministry in the autumn of 1833, that he should accept the Irish attorney-generalship: 'If I went into office',

---

[1] Each of the following constituencies received an additional member: the boroughs of Belfast, Galway, Limerick, Waterford, and the university of Dublin. In the Irish boroughs, as in the English, a uniform £10 household franchise was established.

he wrote to a friend, 'I should be their servant — that is, their slave. By staying out of office I am to a considerable extent their master'. But the reforms that he went on to enumerate, in confident expectation of being able to 'command' them — the abolition of tithe, a reduction of the church establishment, great changes in the magistracy — proved to be beyond his reach; and it was not until 1835, when he began to give open and regular support to the Melbourne ministry, that he was able to exercise any effective control over the government's Irish policy.

(2)

During the early 1830s, while O'Connell was vainly endeavouring to force his reform policy on the government, Ireland seemed in danger of falling into chaos. For this state of affairs O'Connell himself was, though unintentionally, in some measure responsible. During the campaign for Emancipation he had constantly dwelt on the grievances of the peasantry, and many of his hearers naturally believed that Emancipation was to bring these grievances to an end. At the same time, the violence with which he denounced the whole system of government created the impression that any means were justified in an effort to obtain redress; and this impression was very imperfectly corrected by his frequent, and sincere, exhortations against the use of physical force. The high expectations aroused during the campaign led inevitably to angry disappointment when it was found that victory brought no immediate relief. The sense of grievance was stronger than ever; but so also was the conviction that redress could and should be won by direct action.

This aggressive feeling expressed itself particularly in resistance to tithe. A concerted and determined refusal to pay tithe, beginning in Leinster in 1830, spread rapidly over a great part of the country. The normal legal processes by which a defaulter could be compelled to pay were almost useless in face of united opposition, even when that opposition was passive; when, as commonly happened, there was a threat of violent resistance, large forces of police and military were employed, and many areas were plunged into a 'tithe war'.

This attack on the tithe system, though not the violence by which it was often accompanied, had the support of many responsible leaders, both clerical and lay, in Ireland, and aroused sympathy among English radicals. The government could not deny the need for some measure of reform; and Stanley,[1] chief secretary from 1830 to 1833, though a stalwart

---

[1] Afterwards fourteenth earl of Derby.

supporter of the established church, was responsible for the passage, in 1832, of an act making the composition of tithe for money payment compulsory. But this did little to ease the tension; and, in fact, no bill that would satisfy Irish opinion was likely to get through parliament.

Those who suffered most directly from the tithe war were the parochial clergy of the established church, and hundreds of them were reduced almost to destitution. In 1832 the government came to their relief, with an immediate grant of £60,000, on the security of the arrears of tithe, which were now to be recovered by direct state action. But the result showed the hopelessness of the situation. At the end of many months of violence and bloodshed, and at a cost of £27,000, only £12,000 had been collected, almost £1,000,000 remained outstanding and Ireland was more disturbed than ever.

The most threatening aspect of the situation was the general weakening of authority. Agrarian secret societies, which had been comparatively inactive during the fervour of the Emancipation campaign, now revived and expanded; in some areas, especially in the west, there was a refusal to pay rent, as well as tithe; the peasantry assembled in thousands to proclaim their rights, and even began to hope that they might soon divide the land equally among themselves. As one landlord put it, they were preparing 'to combine in awful array all those who have nothing to lose against all the property and respectability of the country'. This excitement was accompanied by an enormous increase in agrarian crime. During 1832, as Grey reported gloomily in the house of lords, there were 242 homicides, over 300 attempted homicides, and hundreds of assaults on persons and property. The law was very nearly helpless, for witnesses and jurors were intimidated by fear of reprisal. To counter this threat, a very stringent coercion act, to remain in operation for a year, was passed early in 1833: the lord lieutenant was empowered to suppress public meetings, and to proclaim disturbed counties as being in a state of insurrection; in counties so proclaimed the operation of the ordinary courts might be suspended, and replaced by a system of martial law.

The effect of this measure was not only to restrain agrarian crime but also to hamper legitimate political agitation, including the repeal movement; and for this reason it was fiercely denounced by O'Connell, along with the whole Irish policy of 'the base, brutal, and bloody whigs'. But it is indicative of the grave alarm aroused by the state of the country that Bishop Doyle,[1] one of the strongest critics of the tithe system, who was

---

[1] James Warren Doyle, Roman Catholic bishop of Kildare and Leighlin; noted as a pamphleteer under the initials 'J.K.L.'.

not a repealer, welcomed the coercion act, though in qualified terms: 'If we are not to have good government or wise laws — and I see no prospect of either — I prefer Lord Grey's bill to any other less despotic measure ... The honest and industrious people of this country will suffer less and prosper more under the iron rule of the constituted authorities — let these be whom they may — than under the yoke of the impious and seditious who now torment them, and drive them into all manner of folly and excess'.

Doyle was by no means alone among Irish Roman Catholics in his opposition to repeal, or in his fear of 'the brutal *canaille* composing the Trades Unions and Blackfeet confederacies'; and the best hope of making the union a success lay in winning the sincere co-operation of such men. The price of this co-operation must be radical reform, and in particular, at this point, radical reform not only of tithe but of the whole ecclesiastical system.

The case for reform of some sort was a strong one, and had long been advocated by many English whigs and radicals. To a Benthamite generation it seemed a waste of money to maintain four archbishops and eighteen bishops, with deans and chapters, and about 1,400 parochial clergy, to minister to the spiritual needs of 800,000 people (little more than one-tenth of the population), who in some areas were so thinly scattered that there were whole parishes without a single protestant inhabitant. But the attitude of Irish Roman Catholics was not determined by these utilitarian considerations; they regarded the mere existence of the established church as a standing offence to the overwhelming majority of the people; and they demanded, at the very least, an immediate and substantial measure of disendowment.

Grey's ministry was in no position to meet this demand. Though its members were agreed that the more obvious anomalies in the establishment should be removed, they were sharply divided on the vital question of secularizing church property; and even if they had been united in favour of a secularizing policy, Grey dared not risk a conflict with the opposition majority in the house of lords. After discussions that almost split the cabinet, a bill for the reform of the Irish church was drawn up, and introduced in February 1833. It provided for sweeping changes in organization: ten sees, including the archbishoprics of Cashel and Tuam, were to be suppressed when the existing occupants vacated them; the revenues of the remaining twelve sees were to be reduced; bishoprics, and benefices of £200 a year and upwards, were to be taxed on a graduated scale. The proposal to suppress the bishoprics aroused furious opposition, and was the occasion of John Keble's famous sermon on 'National apostasy'; but the real struggle turned on the question of appropriation: what use was to be made of the revenue, reckoned at £60,000 or £70,000 a year, arising from the proposed reforms? In the bill as originally presented the disposal of the money was left to parliament; English radicals regarded this modest measure of disendowment as the most important part of the scheme; to Irish Roman Catholics, it was almost the only part in which they had any interest whatsoever. But on this point opposition was much stronger than over the bishoprics. The government, divided and uneasy, gave way; the appropriation clause was withdrawn; and the surplus revenue was entrusted to a body of commissioners, to be administered for purely ecclesiastical purposes. With this modification, the bill passed into law in August 1833, as the Irish Church Temporalities Act. The changes that it effected did something to strengthen the position of the establishment, though the manner of their execution was ominous for the future; but as a gesture of conciliation to Roman Catholics the act was worse than useless; and the hope that it might serve to 'balance' the coercion act of the same year was completely unrealistic.

(3)

While the church temporalities bill was still making its way through parliament, Stanley had given up the chief secretaryship. He left Ireland without regret; for he found Irish politics uncongenial; and his relations with the lord lieutenant, Anglesey, a somewhat blundering reformer, had not always been easy. His period as chief secretary had been dominated by the 'tithe war'; but it had seen also a significant development in the government's educational policy, a development with which he himself had been very closely concerned.

The annual grant paid to the Kildare Place Society since 1815[1] had been intended for the support of non-denominational education; and for a time the system worked tolerably well. But the Roman Catholics naturally wanted schools more completely under their own control: by the 1820s the Christian Brothers, founded by Edmund Rice of Waterford, and approved by a bull of Pope Pius VII, were already at work. The Kildare Place Society, despite its non-denominational policy, remained very largely under the management of protestants; and in the exacerbation of sectarian feeling during O'Connell's campaign for Emancipation, it fell increasingly under the suspicion of proselytizing. In these circumstances, the continued payment of the grant, which had been raised to £30,000 a

---

[1] Above, p. 298.

year, inevitably became a source of grievance; and in September 1831 it was transferred to the commissioners of national education, a newly-appointed government board representative of the three main religious denominations.

A month later, in a letter to the duke of Leinster, president of the board, Stanley defined the object of government policy: the provision of 'a system of education from which should be banished even the suspicion of proselytism, and which, admitting children of all religious persuasions, should not interfere with the peculiar tenets of any'. This 'Stanley letter' became, as one of the commissioners put it, 'the *magna carta* of the Irish system of national education'. The board sought to accomplish its purpose on a basis of 'joint secular and separate religious instruction', in 'mixed'[1] schools, attended by pupils of all denominations. The system was at first welcomed, though cautiously, by most Roman Catholics, as tolerable, if not ideal; but it was strongly attacked by the presbyterians, and regarded with cold suspicion by the Church of Ireland. Concessions meant to satisfy protestant scruples helped to arouse uneasiness among Roman Catholics; and by degrees the system was modified in practice. The principle laid down in the 'Stanley letter' was never formally abandoned, and the board maintained its impartial character; but a generation later comparatively few of the schools under its supervision were 'mixed', and almost all were controlled by one or other of the major religious denominations. The 'national schools' did a great deal towards abolishing illiteracy, but almost nothing towards increasing mutual understanding between Irishmen of different faiths. One effect of the new system that was to be bitterly criticized later on was the discouragement of the use of the Irish language: in 1831 the Irish-speaking population probably numbered between 1,000,000 and 1,500,000; after fifty years of national education it had shrunk into insignificance.

(4)

The church temporalities act and the coercion act had shown O'Connell how barren were his hopes of obtaining satisfactory reforms from the Grey ministry. But the policy of repeal, despite his frequent confident assertions, did not seem likely to yield any better results. Though he had made repeal his main point in the election of 1832, when he himself was elected for the city of Dublin and almost forty of his supporters for other constituencies, it was not until April 1834 that he brought the question

---

[1] In nineteenth-century Ireland the term 'mixed', when applied to education, referred to mixture of religious denominations, not of sexes.

formally before the house of commons; and even then he acted reluctantly, under pressure from some of his constituents. The moment was hardly a propitious one; for less than three months earlier the king's speech at the opening of parliament had declared the government's 'fixed and unalterable resolution' to maintain the union inviolate. O'Connell's motion was utterly defeated; and the house resolved, by 523 votes to 38, that the union should be maintained, unimpaired and undisturbed. It was significant for the future of the repeal movement that there was only one English vote on O'Connell's side, and that a member from Belfast was among the foremost speakers in defence of the union.

In spite of this parliamentary defeat, O'Connell continued to preach repeal in Ireland; but within a year he had temporarily laid it aside in favour of a policy of co-operation with the whigs. The events that led to this change began with the break-up of Grey's ministry in the summer of 1834. A new tithe bill had revived the question of appropriating church revenue for secular purposes; Lord John Russell expressed, in parliament, his support for such appropriation; as a consequence, Stanley, with three of his colleagues, left the ministry in June. Weakened by this secession, and finding himself in difficulties over the renewal of the coercion act which was about to expire, Grey resigned in the following month; and the cabinet was reconstructed under Melbourne. With Grey and Stanley out of the way, O'Connell was more disposed to be friendly towards the whigs; and Peel's advent to office before the end of the year provided ground for common action. In the general election of 1835 he once more made 'Repeal, sink or swim' his watchword; but when the election was over he was quite ready to assist Melbourne and Russell in building up a parliamentary majority. An informal understanding (commonly called the 'Lichfield House compact') was reached in March; next month, the combination of whigs, radicals and O'Connellites forced Peel to resign; and Melbourne became prime minister again, with Lord John Russell as home secretary. In the circumstances, O'Connell could look for a great change in the whig attitude to Ireland; and he willingly allowed repeal to fall into the background, in confident expectation of immediate and extensive reforms.

The most striking change resulting from O'Connell's new policy was in the character of the administration. To the great majority of the population Dublin Castle had long stood as the symbol of alien and oppressive rule; while to the dominant minority it had been, at least since the union, an instrument for the maintenance of their ascendancy. Between 1835 and 1840 these attitudes were reversed: Roman Catholics and liberals came to regard the Castle as their ally; protestant landlords abused it with all the bitterness of men who felt themselves to have been betrayed.

The new policy in Ireland was partly inspired, and strenuously supported, by Lord John Russell, who, as home secretary, had direct responsibility for Irish affairs. Its execution, however, was mainly in the hands of three men: the lord lieutenant, Lord Mulgrave; the chief secretary, Lord Morpeth; the under-secretary, Thomas Drummond. The most influential of the three was Drummond. Neither Mulgrave nor Morpeth was a nonentity, and he could have accomplished very little without their encouragement and support; but it was his enthusiasm, his knowledge, above all his unremitting labour, that made possible the rapid transformation of the administrative system. The under-secretaryship was not normally regarded as a political appointment — Sir William Gregory, for example, had held it continuously from 1812 to 1831; but its importance was such that any lack of sympathy between the under-secretary and the political head of the administration could be a serious weakness. Mulgrave saw this at once; he recognized that Gregory's successor, Gossett, was likely to be a hindrance to the new policy; and it was he who insisted on Gossett's removal, and on the appointment of Drummond in his place. The change was fully justified in the result; though no one at the time could have foreseen that Mulgrave's reputation would be so completely overshadowed by that of his protégé that his viceroyalty would hardly be remembered save as the period of Drummond's tenure of the under-secretaryship.

Drummond was a Scotsman, but his employment on ordnance survey work had made him familiar with the Irish countryside. He had been profoundly impressed by the wretched condition in which the majority of the peasantry lived, and it was to this wretchedness that he ascribed the prevailing contempt for the law. He fully shared the distaste of English liberal opinion for government by coercion; he saw that the only feasible alternative was to create popular confidence in the impartiality of the administration; and many of his most important measures were directed to this end. Few, if any, of these measures were entirely new; but they were informed by a new spirit of tolerance and comprehension. Thus, he took up and extended Peel's tentative reform of the police; a constabulary act, which embodied his ideas, was passed in 1836, setting up a national force, under an inspector-general; and it was due to him that Roman Catholics were encouraged to enlist in it. Like Peel, also, he secured the appointment of stipendiary magistrates, who, being under the control of the Castle, were comparatively free from the social and political prejudices that dominated the landlord class as a whole. In the appointment of unpaid magistrates, he saw that fuller representation was given to Roman Catholics and to liberal protestants; and he had some of the more bigoted champions of protestant ascendancy removed from the bench. He checked, though he could not wholly eradicate, the practice of systematically excluding Roman Catholics from juries in cases in which the crown was a party. He refused to allow the use of the military in the collection of tithe, or in the enforcement of ejection orders. By these means he did much to persuade the Irish peasant that the law was not simply an instrument in the hand of his oppressors, and that he would receive justice in the courts; and it is probably true to say that during Drummond's administration Ireland was more peaceful under the ordinary course of law than it had ever been under coercion.

It was an essential part of the new policy in Ireland that Emancipation should be made a reality by the appointment of Roman Catholics to important posts. Michael O'Loghlen, who had been O'Connell's favourite junior at the bar, was made solicitor-general in 1835, attorney-general later in the same year, and a baron of the exchequer in 1836, the first appointment of a Roman Catholic to the bench since the reign of James II. Other Roman Catholic barristers were similarly promoted; and O'Connell himself was offered, but refused, the mastership of the rolls. Thus the longstanding tradition that the higher branches of the public service were to be manned exclusively by protestants was breached, if not completely broken down.

The most effective, or at least the most obvious, instrument of the old, aggressive protestant ascendancy was the Orange Order, which had been left untouched while the Catholic Association and similar bodies were being suppressed by law. It had spread widely among protestants of all classes, in Great Britain as well as in Ireland; lodges had been established in the army, where the extent of their influence was exaggerated both by friend and foe; and its 'grand master' was the king's brother, the duke of Cumberland. In 1836, after a vigorous parliamentary attack upon the order by the English radical Joseph Hume, the central governing body, the 'grand lodge', formally dissolved itself, and the movement quickly declined in Great Britain. But it continued to flourish in Ireland, especially in the north, where it exercised great political influence; and Drummond set himself to break its power. He employed against it all the resources of Castle influence, hitherto directed exclusively against repeal organizations and agrarian secret societies. Orange demonstrations were prohibited; magistrates of known Orange sympathies were dismissed, and stipendiary magistrates appointed in strongly Orange areas; and all the activities of the order were restricted as far as the law would permit. Orangeism was not eradicated, and in the 1880s it was to be revived as a weapon in the campaign against home rule; but its political influence was, for the time being, almost destroyed. Nothing in Drummond's administration won him such popularity among Roman Catholics, or such hatred among protestants, as his treatment of the Orange Order.

It was inevitable that an administration conducted on these liberal principles should be fiercely attacked by the conservatives, and especially by the Irish conservatives. The latter viewed with resentment and suspicion the promotion of Roman Catholics to positions of influence; and they asserted that the persistence of agrarian crime, which had by no means been eliminated, called for a sterner, not a milder, system of administration. When a Tipperary landlord was murdered in 1838 the magistrates of the county, as a body, demanded that strong measures should be taken, by special legislation if necessary, for the protection of life and property. In his reply Drummond refused to admit that the existing law was inadequate, and by connecting agrarian crime with the eviction of tenants from their holdings he laid the responsibility on the landlords. He reminded them that 'property has its duties as well as its rights', and went on: 'to the neglect of these duties in times past is mainly to be attributed that diseased state of society in which such crimes can take their rise'. But though Drummond had little sympathy with landlords, he had none with assassins; and the police force, as re-organized under his régime, was more successful than ever before in bringing criminals to justice. A house of lords committee, appointed in 1839 to inquire into the state of Ireland, was expected by its promoters to provide material for an attack upon the government; but its report showed that though crimes of violence were very widespread, the situation was much better than it had been when Mulgrave took office.[1]

(5)

O'Connell's informal alliance with the whigs involved, on his side, something more than a merely temporary suspension of the demand for repeal. He declared himself willing to give up the demand altogether, provided Ireland was treated on an equality with Great Britain:

'The people of Ireland are ready to become a portion of the empire, provided they be made so in reality and not in name alone; they are ready to become a kind of West Britons if made so in benefits and in justice; but if not, we are Irishmen again.'

[1] The conservative *Quarterly review*, though obviously eager to condemn Mulgrave's administration, found this report so little to its purpose that the article in which it is nominally discussed is devoted mainly to an attack on the influence of the Jesuits in Ireland. (*Quarterly review*, lxvii, 117 ff. (Dec. 1840)).

This apparently complete change of front was accepted with remarkable docility by his followers in parliament and in the country. But the change was perhaps greater in appearance than in reality. The qualifying clause — 'if not, we are Irishmen again' — was of essential significance. O'Connell was, to use his own term, 'testing' the union, not renouncing the right to reject it. The whigs were to be given a chance of showing that the union could ensure 'perfect equality of rights, laws and liberties' between Ireland and Great Britain; if they succeeded, well and good; if they failed, the union must go: 'We desire no more, we will not take less: a real effectual union or no union — such is the alternative'.

So far as the general conduct of administration was concerned, O'Connell had good reason to be satisfied with his allies, the more so as his influence carried great weight in the making of appointments. But he had looked also for substantial measures of legislative reform, and in this respect he met with delay and disappointment. The ministry was not entirely to blame. Its freedom of action was limited by the heterogeneous character of its majority in the house of commons; and the house of lords proved an insuperable barrier to any but the most moderate proposals for reform. In a less obvious but hardly less important way the ministry was also restricted by the prevailing temper of the times, which was opposed to state intervention in economic matters; for without such intervention it was almost hopeless to expect any permanent improvement in the condition of Ireland; and though British opinion was ready to admit that in the political sphere Ireland might require special treatment, it was less willing to accept the same necessity in the economic sphere also.

O'Connell's first great disappointment with the whigs was over tithe. In April 1835, while still in opposition, Russell had revived his proposal for diverting part of the Irish ecclesiastical revenues to secular purposes; and it was his success in carrying a resolution to this effect through the house of commons that had finally decided Peel to resign. The new ministry was thus committed to a policy of appropriation, which it proposed to combine with a reform of the tithe system. A bill for this double purpose passed through the commons in the summer of 1835; but the lords insisted on separating the two issues, and, while accepting tithe-reform, rejected any measure of appropriation. The government then dropped the bill, and decided, after long delay, to abandon appropriation altogether. It was not until 1838 that a tithe act was at length passed, and it was concerned only with the method of assessment and collection. Tithe was to be converted into a fixed rent-charge, calculated at 75 per cent of the nominal value of the tithe, and responsibility for payment was to be transferred from tenant to landlord. The consequent elimination of the tithe-proctor and tithe-farmer made an enormous improvement in the situation, and tithe ceased to be a popular grievance. But, in fact, the act of 1838 contained nothing that Peel would not have been willing to concede three years earlier; O'Connell supported it only because he realized that the ministry was now too feeble to carry any more radical reform; and the fundamental Roman Catholic complaint, that the church of the minority was supported at the public expense, remained.

The establishment of an Irish poor-law, in the same year as the passage of the tithe act, was even less satisfactory to O'Connell. Hitherto, Ireland had had no poor-law system of any kind, and with the increasing pressure of population the need for some such provision had become more and more obvious. Even before the union, the importance of the question had been recognized; by the 1820s it had a place in almost every discussion of the state of Ireland. Selfish as well as philanthropic motives were at work: the existence of some provision for the poor would make it easier for landlords to clear their estates, and effect the consolidation of holdings that was generally recognized as essential to any improvement in agriculture; and it might check the flow of destitute Irish into England, where they tended to depress the rate of wages, and where many of them became a charge upon the rates. But though the problem was recognized, action was delayed; partly because of the seemingly greater urgency of political issues, partly because of difference of opinion about the solution to be applied. In 1833, however, when the reform of the English poor-law was being considered, the government appointed a commission under the chairmanship of Richard Whately, archbishop of Dublin, to inquire into the need for a system of poor-relief in Ireland. The commissioners instituted a vigorous and exhaustive investigation into almost every aspect of Irish economic life; but by the time they presented their final report, in the spring of 1836, the ministry had already decided that the new English poor-law, which had come into operation in 1834, should be extended to Ireland. It was felt necessary to postpone formal action until the commissioners should have completed their task; but they were given (as Whately recorded later) 'a pretty broad hint, once or twice while the inquiry was going on, what government expected us to report'. These hints were ignored; the commissioners reported that the English system, with its 'workhouse test' was wholly unsuitable for Ireland; that the root cause of Irish poverty was lack of employment, and that this could be remedied only by an extensive scheme of public works, directed towards the development of natural resources.

Proposals so completely at variance with government policy had no chance of being accepted, and were, indeed, hardly even considered.

Instead, a new inquiry was entrusted to George Nicholls, one of the English poor-law commissioners, who was sent over to Ireland in August 1836 to report on the suitability of the workhouse system for Irish conditions. The inquiry was little more than a matter of form. Not only had the ministry already decided on the policy it meant to follow, but that decision had been strongly influenced by a memorandum presented to Russell, in January 1836, by Nicholls himself, though at that time, as he frankly admitted, 'he did not pretend to any personal knowledge of the state of Ireland'. A hasty tour of barely nine weeks did nothing to alter his opinion; and he reported, as was expected, in favour of extending the English poor-law to Ireland. A bill for the purpose was introduced in the house of commons in February 1837, and received the royal assent in July 1838.[1] As in England, the country was to be divided into poor-law districts, each with its workhouse under the control of a board of guardians, consisting of *ex officio* and elected members; and a poor-rate was to be levied, half to be paid by the landlord, half by the tenant.

Irish opinion was sharply divided over the measure; for though the great majority of the Irish members opposed it, they did so for various reasons. Some feared that the burden of poor-rate would ruin the country; some objected, on economic grounds, to relief for the able-bodied, and wished it to be confined to the aged and the sick; some denounced the whole idea of state charity. O'Connell's attitude was a rather confused one. The extent of the destitution revealed in the commissioners' report compelled him to admit, though reluctantly, that some system of poor-relief was necessary, and at first he supported the government scheme; but he distrusted the economic principles on which it was based, and asserted that it would impoverish the country; and he feared that the very existence of state relief would weaken the charitable instincts of the people. In the end, he voted against the bill, urging instead state aid for emigration and public works, and the imposition of a tax upon absentee landlords.

It is almost impossible to assess the justice of the arguments employed for or against the poor law of 1838 by reference to its results. Nicholls had been careful to point out that no rapid transformation of Irish conditions was to be looked for, and that a famine was a contingency 'altogether above the power of a poor-law to provide for'. But even he could not have foreseen the extent of the catastrophe that was to fall upon Ireland in 1845,

---

[1] The passage of the bill was delayed by the death of William IV, and the consequent dissolution of parliament.

when the system for which he was so largely responsible had barely come into operation. No matter what system of relief or scheme of development had been established, it must have been swamped by the Great Famine.

O'Connell's opposition to the poor-law, though due mainly to other causes, was also a reflection of his growing discontent with the fruits of the whig alliance. The promised appropriation of ecclesiastical revenue had been abandoned in 1838, and another measure to which he had confidently looked forward, the reform of the municipal corporations, still hung fire. The history of this measure illustrates at once the difficulties of the ministry and the reasons for O'Connell's dissatisfaction. The municipal corporations of England and Scotland had been reformed in 1834; and there were no grounds for leaving those of Ireland untouched, especially after the report of a commission of inquiry, published in 1835, had revealed a state of affairs that could hardly be defended. But reform was delayed for five years; and when it was eventually carried, the principles adopted were distinctly less liberal than those applied in Great Britain.

In 1835 there were in Ireland 68 corporate cities and boroughs; and though they had been nominally open to Roman Catholics since 1793, all but one were in protestant hands. Many of the corporations were self-perpetuating, commonly under the control of a patron; in none did the electoral body amount to more than a small fraction of the total number of householders. In those boroughs that had been disfranchised at the time of the union, the corporations had practically ceased to function, except where there was borough property to be administered; and many of them were so small that there was no reason why they should continue as separate municipalities. Even in the large boroughs, whether disfranchised or not, the corporations rarely took an active part in promoting the general welfare. In Belfast, for example, it was left to a voluntary society (founded in the 1750s) to establish a hospital, to care for the poor, to educate and apprentice pauper children, to bring water to the town, and to provide a new burial ground. Until the municipal corporations were given a more genuinely representative character they were hardly likely to fulfil functions of this sort.

In face of the evidence published in the report of 1835 it was universally admitted that reform was necessary; the object of conservative opposition in Ireland and at Westminster was to limit as narrowly as possible the element of popular control in whatever new system was established; and some conservatives even advocated the complete transference of municipal government to the crown. The strength of the opposition lay in the house of lords; and bill after bill sent up by the commons was so amended by the lords as to be wholly unacceptable to O'Connell and the whigs. The conflict continued for years; and it was not until 1840, when the ministry was so enfeebled that it had either to accept a compromise measure or abandon its proposals altogether, that an Irish municipal corporations act was at length passed. Fifty-eight corporations were dissolved, and the administration of the boroughs merged in that of the counties; the ten remaining corporations[1] were completely reconstructed, the old close bodies being replaced by elective councils. But whereas the English act of 1834 had granted the municipal franchise to all rate-payers, the Irish act of 1840 confined it to £10 householders; and the powers to be exercised by the councils were more restricted in Ireland than in England: they did not, for example, include control of the police; and the sheriff, instead of being elected by the council, as in England, was to be nominated by the lord lieutenant.

The act provided O'Connell with the opportunity for a spectacular triumph — in November 1841 he was elected lord mayor of Dublin, the first Roman Catholic to hold the office since the reign of James II. But in almost every other respect he was bitterly disappointed: by the long delay; by the sweeping away of so many corporations, which he had hoped, when once they were reformed, to bring under his own control; by the narrow franchise and restricted powers of those that remained. While municipal reform was still under discussion, he had declared that he would regard it as a test of the character of the union. If Ireland were genuinely incorporated in the United Kingdom, then Irish boroughs would be treated in the same way as English; if they were treated less favourably, then the union would be proved a sham. On the basis of this argument, the act of 1840 could certainly be used to support the case for repeal. And it was to a revival of the repeal campaign that O'Connell was now turning his thoughts.

The Melbourne ministry survived the passage of the corporations act by more than a year, but it carried no further Irish reforms; and the death of Thomas Drummond, in April 1840, removed the guiding spirit of its Irish administration. Drummond did a great deal for Ireland, but he was not in office long enough to make a permanent change in the character of the administration. Circumstances compelled him to follow a centralizing policy, for only thus could he counter the prevailing influence of the old ascendancy in every department of local government. He extended and strengthened the direct authority exercised by the Castle; but the liberal

---

[1] These were: Belfast, Clonmel, Cork, Drogheda, Dublin, Kilkenny, Limerick, Londonderry, Sligo, Waterford.

spirit that had informed this authority during his lifetime died with him. His death, rather than Melbourne's resignation sixteen months later, marks the end of a phase in Irish history.

(6)

In his decision to turn once more to repeal, O'Connell was influenced not only by dissatisfaction with the ministry but also by a well-founded conviction that it could not last much longer. Before the end of the 1830s it was already clear that Melbourne must soon be succeeded by Peel, with whom O'Connell neither would nor could co-operate. It is probable that he was influenced also by a consideration of a more personal character. The whig alliance, though highly acceptable to the bishops and the middle classes, had little appeal for the people at large; O'Connell found his popular prestige declining, and with it the income on which he depended to finance his political activities. The 'O'Connell tribute', under which name the 'Catholic rent' had been continued since 1829, had shrunk almost to nothing by the later 1830s. O'Connell could hardly fail to realize that if he were to recover and maintain the immense influence that he had once enjoyed it must be at the head of a popular campaign, and the obvious battle-cry for such a campaign was repeal. As early as 1838 he had taken the first step by establishing a society of 'Precursors' to prepare the way; in April 1840 he came into the open with the National Repeal Association, and published the first of a series of 'Addresses' to the people of Ireland, criticising government policy, and attacking the union.

It seemed at first as if O'Connell had misjudged the situation, for while his change of front alarmed the middle classes, it aroused little enthusiasm among the peasantry; the Repeal Association languished; and only a handful of repeal members were returned in the general election of 1841. But little more than a year later the position had changed completely. Archbishop MacHale of Tuam had declared himself in favour of repeal, and had been followed by many of the bishops and the bulk of the parochial clergy. This clerical lead naturally influenced the attitude of the peasantry; and the middle classes were won over, partly by O'Connell's skilful presentation of his case, partly by their general suspicion of the new ministry. Besides this, opinion among all classes, and in all parts of the country, was being profoundly influenced by the active propaganda of a group of journalists, soon to be known as 'Young Ireland', whose weekly newspaper, the *Nation*, began publication in October 1842. A 'repeal rent', established in place of the 'tribute' soon brought in an ample campaigning fund; and O'Connell found himself, before the end of 1842, at the head of a movement as widespread, as powerfully organized, and apparently as determined, as that which had forced Wellington and Peel to grant Catholic Emancipation a little more than a decade earlier.

This parallel was certainly in O'Connell's mind, and its influence appears in the assurance with which he foretold a speedy victory. But the parallel was not an exact one. In the first place, the disfranchisement of the forty-shilling freeholders had deprived O'Connell of a powerful weapon, for which his rather uncertain influence in the reformed borough constituencies was a very inadequate substitute.[1] Again, in 1829 he had had not only the unquestioning support of the entire Roman Catholic population, but the active sympathy of a large body of protestants; but in the 1840s, though he had a few enthusiastic protestant followers, protestant opinion in general was solidly against him. Among Roman Catholics, also, there were divisions of opinion that were no less weakening because concealed by the immense personal respect in which O'Connell was held. Popular enthusiasm for repeal had by no means destroyed the influence of the agrarian secret societies, which, loosely linked under the general name of 'Ribbonmen', existed in almost every part of the country; and O'Connell, alarmed at their strength and hostile to their methods, constantly endeavoured to outbid them for the support of the peasantry by fierce denunciations of the government and extravagant promises of good things to come. Language of this kind alarmed his more moderate supporters, who looked forward to an Irish parliament as opening a profitable political career to the middle classes, not as an instrument for upsetting the social structure. This alarm was probably needless, for O'Connell had as great a respect for property as any man in the country; and it may well be that his promises of future benefits, by fixing the attention of the peasantry on repeal as the immediate issue, helped to avert the danger of an agrarian war; but middle-class uneasiness remained, and inevitably tended to undermine the solidarity of the movement. Another, and more fundamental, rift — that between O'Connell and the Young Ireland group — though implicit from 1842 onwards, did not develop until some years later.

For the government also, the position in the early 1840s was very different from what it had been in 1829. British opinion had then been sharply divided on Catholic Emancipation; but its opponents were losing ground, and even without the crisis of the Clare election it could hardly

---

[1] But O'Connell's influence was often important and sometimes decisive: it was, for example, sufficient to secure the return of Joseph Hume for the borough of Kilkenny, in 1837, after his defeat in Middlesex.

have been delayed much longer. But on repeal there was no division at all; government, parliament, public opinion, all were firmly united in a resolve to maintain the union. Wellington had defended his surrender over Emancipation in 1829 on the ground that almost anything was to be endured for the sake of avoiding civil war; in May 1843 Peel, speaking in the house of commons, took exactly the opposite line with regard to the union: 'Deprecating as I do all war, but, above all, civil war, yet there is no alternative which I do not think preferable to the dismemberment of this empire'. In this determination, and secure in the knowledge that he would be supported by a majority in parliament, he could afford to defy any threat that O'Connell might make.

The essential strength of his position did not free Peel from immediate difficulties. O'Connell carried on his campaign in a series of monster meetings, which not only gave opportunity for the exercise of his splendid oratory,[1] but also demonstrated both the popularity of the movement and his power to control it. Though hundreds of thousands gathered to hear him, and though he used the most inflammatory language, there was never, at any of his meetings, any sign of disorder. All this was very damaging to the prestige of the government, not only at home but abroad; in France and the United States, especially, there was a good deal of public sympathy for the repeal cause, and O'Connell became a figure of international importance. Peel was naturally under strong pressure to restrain him in some way; the Irish conservatives, who were the only group in Ireland on whose support the government could in the long run rely, demanded that the whole repeal movement should be repressed as 'disloyal', and many British conservatives took the same view. But just at this time the

---

[1] Lord Lytton's description of one of O'Connell's meetings is worth quoting:

> *Once to my sight the giant thus was given:*
> *Walled by wide air, and roofed by boundless heaven,*
> *Beneath his feet the human ocean lay,*
> *And wave on wave flowed into space away.*
> *Methought no clarion could have sent its sound*
> *Even to the centre of the hosts around;*
> *But, as I thought, rose the sonorous swell,*
> *As from some church tower swings the silvery bell.*
> *Aloft and clear, from airy tide to tide*
> *It glided, easy as a bird may glide;*
> *To the last verge of that vast audience sent,*
> *It played with each wild passion as it went;*
> *Now stirred the uproar, now the murmur stilled,*
> *And sobs or laughter answered as it willed.*

Anti-Corn Law League was copying O'Connell's methods in England, and no one suggested that it was acting illegally. To advocate the repeal of an act of parliament was a perfectly legitimate proceeding, and it would have been invidious to have suppressed O'Connell's activities in Ireland, while tolerating those of Cobden and Bright in England.

O'Connell was more keenly aware of the government's immediate difficulties than of its underlying strength. In January 1843 he had announced that this was to be 'the repeal year'; and during the following months, at meeting after meeting, he assured his vast audiences that Britain must soon surrender. But there was no thought of surrender, either in London or in Dublin. De Grey, the lord lieutenant, urged on Peel the necessity of acting firmly, at all costs: 'Let whatever you do be strong enough . . . Let no morbid sensibility, or mawkish apprehension of invading the constitution, which might influence some hearts, or perhaps secure some trifling support, be allowed to weigh'. Peel's measures, though they did not reach this standard of ruthlessness, were yet firm enough. On 9 May he told the house of commons that he had been authorized by the queen to repeat, on her behalf, the royal declaration of support for the union made by William IV in 1834; and he announced that in defence of the union the government would use every means at its disposal, and would, if necessary, seek fresh powers from parliament. This announcement was followed up by the introduction of a stringent arms bill, and by a considerable expansion of the Irish military establishment. Even yet, O'Connell did not realize the strength of Peel's resolve, or the solidarity of British opinion. His language became more flamboyant, more aggressive, more confident; and though he constantly disowned any intention of beginning a civil war, he implied that if the government attempted to stop his campaign, war might follow — in the famous 'Mallow defiance' of 11 June 1843, when he defied the government to stop him, he warned his hearers: 'The time is coming when we must be doing. You may have the alternative to live as slaves or die as freemen'. But O'Connell mistook the temper of the government that he was trying to frighten with brave words; he never expected that his defiance would be put to the test; and when it was, he gave in.

The crisis came in the autumn of 1843. O'Connell had planned to hold his last great meeting of the year at Clontarf, on the outskirts of Dublin, the scene of Brian Boru's famous victory over the Danes in 1014. It was intended that this meeting should be even larger than those that had preceded it. For days in advance of the appointed date — Sunday, 8 October — parties from all over the country were converging on the capital; and 1500 Irish exiles returned from Britain to be present on the great occasion. But this time the government took up the challenge. The notices summoning the meeting and arranging for its organization had implied, though unintentionally, that it was to have a military character; and this was held to justify a proclamation, which was issued on 7 October, declaring it illegal. O'Connell submitted at once. He issued a proclamation of his own, cancelling the meeting; and he sent off messengers in all directions to turn back the approaching crowds. Next day, Clontarf was occupied by troops; but O'Connell's orders had been implicitly obeyed, there was no attempt to hold a meeting, and the episode passed off peacefully.

O'Connell's action in cancelling the meeting was entirely in accordance with his repeated declarations that he would act constitutionally; it was approved by his more moderate followers in Ireland; and it pleased those British whigs and radicals who, without conceding the necessity for repeal, yet sympathized with O'Connell's complaints about British administration in Ireland. But the rank and file of the repeal movement, who had been more impressed by O'Connell's defiance of the government than by his renunciation of physical force, were disappointed and puzzled by what seemed his tame surrender. From this time onwards, though he continued to agitate for repeal, he never again enjoyed the completely dominant position that he had held on the eve of the Clontarf meeting.

The decline of O'Connell's popular prestige might have been more sharply marked but for the action of the government, which almost immediately started a prosecution against him and some of his closest associates on charges of conspiring to excite disaffection. But this time the government had overshot the mark; for though the accused were found guilty and sentenced to imprisonment in May 1844, the whole proceedings were quashed by the house of lords, on appeal, in the following September. O'Connell and his friends had spent the interval pleasantly enough, the governor of the prison having received them as guests in his own house, where they had all the comforts and company they could desire. But though he was thus enabled to enjoy an easy martyrdom, this imprisonment, however mild, left its mark on O'Connell; it sapped his courage, and, combined with other circumstances, weakened his powers of leadership. He was now approaching seventy years of age; his energy and his judgement were failing; he was disappointed at the failure of the great campaign of 1843; his confidence was shaken by the vigorous and successful action of the government. He was still the central figure in Irish politics; but the old air of assurance was gone; and the later stages of his career were marked by hesitation, and by a barely-concealed readiness to compromise.

(7)

Peel's Irish policy did not begin and end with a determination to maintain the union. His earlier experience as chief secretary and at the home office enabled him to understand the problems of Irish government, and his correspondence between 1841 and 1846 shows that, as prime minister, he took a constant and informed interest in Irish affairs. He was convinced that 'mere force, however necessary the application of it, will do nothing as a permanent remedy for the social evils of Ireland'; and though prepared, on occasion, to act firmly, he was anxious to create an atmosphere of confidence, in which Ireland could be governed by the ordinary course of law. He saw the necessity for allaying the religious strife that had for so long bedevilled Irish politics, and to this end he attempted, in face of all difficulties, to maintain the non-sectarian character of the national system of education. He feared, above all, the dangers that must arise if the upper and middle classes among the Roman Catholics were thrown into permanent opposition to Great Britain, and he wished to attach them by a share of government patronage: 'Every avenue to *popular* favour is opened, and if every avenue to *royal* favour is closed, we have done nothing by the removal of disabilities but organize a band of mischievous demagogues'. De Grey, who had been appointed lord lieutenant at the opening of the administration, did not share these views; and his argument that the Roman Catholics, as a body, were so strongly united 'against the existing order of things' that nothing could win their support, seemed to Peel a counsel of despair: 'I know not how it will be possible in that case to conduct the government of Ireland, or to maintain the connection with this country'. It was in order to further a policy of conciliation that de Grey was removed from office in 1844, and replaced by Heytesbury, a man of more liberal outlook and more diplomatic temper.

Peel warned Heytesbury against yielding to the pressure of the Irish protestants, who claimed to be the only reliable friends of the British connection, and whose constant cry was, 'Support your friends, and they will support you'; and he insisted that Ireland would never be tranquil without 'a perfectly impartial, a perfectly just (I might with truth add), a kind and indulgent administration of civil government'. But he did not rely solely on such general methods of conciliation; and three measures, carried within the next few years, were specifically intended to win over at least a section of Roman Catholic opinion.

The first, in 1844, was the establishment of a board of charitable bequests, which replaced an almost exclusively protestant body set up in

1800; of the thirteen commissioners who were to constitute the new board at least five were to be Roman Catholics. The success of the measure was at first doubtful. O'Connell and MacHale opposed it strongly, asserting that it would bring church property under the control of the state; and though they failed to have it condemned by the Vatican, they did their best to ensure that no bishop should join the new board. The majority of the hierarchy supported them, either from conviction, or from fear of the popular clamour; and without some measure of episcopal support the government's purpose would be foiled. At length, however, three bishops consented to act; and the board came into operation in August 1844.[1] Peel regarded this as a considerable victory; and Heytesbury was delighted when Archbishop Murray of Dublin, one of the new commissioners, appeared at his levée — 'an event of some importance in Irish history, and certainly satisfactory at the present moment, as showing that Dr. Murray, at least, does not quail before the frowns of O'Connell'.

Peel's next measure of conciliation, in 1845, was to improve the position of St Patrick's College, Maynooth. The annual grant was increased from £9,000 to £26,000, and it was placed on the consolidated fund, so that it no longer had to be voted, and sometimes debated, every year; and at the same time a capital grant of £30,000 was made for the enlargement of the buildings. But this measure, though certainly popular, had no significant influence on the attitude of Roman Catholics to the government. Its political effects were, indeed, more marked in England than in Ireland. It aroused furious protestant opposition among some of Peel's own followers; and it was the occasion, though not on protestant grounds, of Gladstone's resignation from the cabinet.

While the Maynooth grant was still being debated Peel and his home secretary, Sir James Graham, were already at work on a much more important measure, designed to provide Ireland with a system of university education which should be equally acceptable to Roman Catholics, presbyterians and anglicans. The University of Dublin (Trinity College) was at this time the only university in Ireland; and though its degrees were open to all, its scholarships and fellowships were confined to members of the established church. Besides this, the strongly anglican atmosphere of the college made it unacceptable to Roman Catholics and presbyterians; and its expensiveness made it almost inaccessible to any but the well-to-do. The example of Scotland, which, with only one-quarter of Ireland's

[1] The three bishops were William Crolly, of Armagh, Daniel Murray, of Dublin, and Cornelius Denvir, of Down and Connor. The other Roman Catholic commissioners were laymen.

population, possessed five universities,[1] showed the benefits that a comparatively poor country might derive from a widely-diffused system of
higher education. But Peel was influenced by other considerations as well.
He believed that the development of a well-educated middle class would
be the best counter to the political influence of the clergy, and that the
prospects of professional advancement open to such a class would attach it
to the existing régime and thus weaken the power of popular agitators such
as O'Connell.

The scheme worked out by Peel and Graham was embodied in a bill
which passed through parliament during the summer of 1845; and at the
end of the year charters were issued, incorporating 'Queen's Colleges' in
Belfast, Cork and Galway. By 1849 the colleges were open for the reception of students; and in the following year the academic structure was
completed by the establishment of a federal university — the Queen's
University in Ireland — in which the three colleges were linked together.
The college fees were low, and the provision for scholarships generous,
so that university education was made more widely and generally acces-
sible in Ireland than it was in contemporary England. Yet few of the
advantages to which Peel had looked forward were attained; and the
foundation of the Queen's Colleges, which he had intended as a measure
of conciliation, proved instead to be a source of controversy and grievance.

The difficulty arose over religion. Peel was convinced that British
public opinion would not tolerate the state endowment of sectarian
colleges in Ireland; and, in any case, such colleges would not achieve the
purpose he had in mind. The seeming success of 'mixed education' under
the National Board misled him into supposing that the same principle
would be readily acceptable at university level; and the Queen's Colleges
were established as secular institutions, though arrangements were made,
comparable to those obtaining in the national schools, by which the
various denominations could provide for the pastoral care and religious
instruction of their own students. But no sooner had this scheme become
public than its 'godless' character was attacked on all sides. Anglican and
presbyterian criticism, though loud at first, soon died away; but Roman
Catholic opposition continued, and went far to stultify the whole scheme.
The lead was taken by Archbishop MacHale of Tuam, who had been a
consistent enemy of the National Board, and who had warned Peel in advance, even before the constitution of the proposed colleges had been made
public, that 'nothing but separate grants for separate education will ever

_____

[1] Until 1858 the two Aberdeen colleges. Marischal College and King's College,
were distinct universities.

give satisfaction to the Catholics of Ireland'. It was under his guidance that the bishops, without at first condemning the colleges outright, put forward conditions that would have undermined the whole system of joint education; they insisted that Roman Catholic students could not attend lectures in history, logic, metaphysics, moral philosophy, geology, or anatomy 'without exposing their faith and morals to imminent danger', unless those subjects were taught by Roman Catholic professors. Even after the government had rejected these conditions, a minority of the bishops still worked for a compromise settlement; but the influence of MacHale, who was against joint education on any terms, triumphed both at Rome and in Ireland. Papal rescripts of 1847 and 1848 called attention to the dangerous character of the colleges; and in August 1850 an episcopal synod, at Thurles, issued a formal condemnation, and warned the laity to shun the colleges as dangerous to faith and morals. This warning was not entirely effective; but the number of Roman Catholic students attending the Queen's Colleges was comparatively small; and it was only in Belfast, where the student body was predominantly presbyterian, that Peel's ambitious scheme attained any substantial measure of success. For more than half a century the 'university question' was to remain a standing grievance to Irish Roman Catholics, and a dangerous problem to successive British ministries.

In trying to promote higher education Peel had in mind the contribution that an educated middle class might make to Irish economic development: it is perhaps not without significance that the first president of Queen's College, Cork, was Sir Robert Kane, whose *Industrial resources of Ireland*, published in 1844, had attracted considerable attention. At the same time, however, Peel recognized that the basic essential for Irish prosperity was an improvement in agrarian conditions; but here the problems to be solved and the opposition to be overcome proved so serious as to make progress almost impossible. In 1843 he appointed a commission, under the earl of Devon, to inquire into relations between landlord and tenant; and after the commission had reported, in 1845, he brought in a bill to ensure that an outgoing tenant should receive some compensation for improvements that he had made to his holding. Even this modest reform aroused such strong criticism that it had to be withdrawn; and in the circumstances of 1845–6 Peel had no further opportunity to propose remedial legislation.

(8)

The conflict over the Queen's Colleges very nearly disrupted the Repeal

Association. O'Connell, though at one period he had advocated a system of joint university education, came out strongly against Peel's proposals, and threw the whole weight of his influence behind MacHale. But when he tried to commit the Repeal Association to this policy he found himself faced by a degree of opposition to which he was little accustomed. The centre of this opposition lay in the group of ardent young men associated with the *Nation* newspaper; and the feature of the Queen's Colleges that most appealed to these 'Young Irelanders' was that which MacHale had always detested, and which O'Connell had now joined him in denouncing — the provision for the education of Irishmen of different religious persuasions in the same institution.

The religious issue was one about which the Young Irelanders were particularly concerned. Some of them, including Thomas Davis, who was generally regarded as the leader of the group, were protestants; and all were insistent that if national unity were to be achieved sectarian differences must be kept out of politics, and religion treated as essentially a private matter. They were constantly on their guard against a tendency, common enough among O'Connell's closest associates, to identify the cause of Ireland with Roman Catholicism, and to regard with some suspicion even those protestants who supported the repeal movement: the 'positive and unmistakable' mark of distinction between Irish and English was, according to O'Connell's organ, the *Pilot*, 'the distinction created by religion'. The Young Irelanders were not anti-religious, or even anti-clerical; but in the atmosphere of mid-nineteenth-century Ireland it was hardly surprising that their insistence on the overriding claims of the nation against those of any group or section should expose them to accusations of being both.

The university question brought these latent differences to a head. The Young Irelanders were not entirely satisfied with the constitution of the new colleges; and they freely recognized the right of the bishops to seek safeguards for the spiritual welfare of their students; but they absolutely denied that such safeguards demanded the segregation of Roman Catholics and protestants in separate institutions. The reasons for separate education, wrote Davis, 'are reasons for separate life, for mutual animosity, for penal laws, for religious wars . . . Let those who insist on unqualified separate education follow out their principles — let them prohibit Catholic and protestant boys from playing, or talking, or walking together . . . let them establish a theological police — let them rail off each sect . . . into a separate quarter'. Between such views and those put forward by O'Connell no compromise was possible, and neither side was willing to retract. Davis and his friends, partly because of their unwillingness to weaken the repeal movement, partly because of their veneration for O'Connell, behaved with considerable restraint, and managed, though without surrendering their principles, to avert a split on this issue. But the tension and ill-feeling produced by difference of opinion over the new colleges in 1845 certainly contributed to the final breach between O'Connell and the Young Irelanders in the following year.

Such a breach was probably inevitable, sooner or later, for O'Connell and the Young Irelanders represented two different conceptions of national policy. O'Connell, despite all his talk about the national rights of Ireland, was essentially a pragmatic politician, ready to change his course according to the wind, and always more likely to be influenced by the prospect of immediate and material benefits than by slavish adherence to abstract principles. The Young Irelanders were typical doctrinaire nationalists of the Romantic era. Steeped in their own interpretation of Irish history, and inspired by a Mazzinian idealism, they looked forward to the achievement of national independence, not mainly for the sake of the material advantages to be gained, but as a means of raising the character and strengthening the self-respect of the people. They were not indifferent to reform, but they refused to accept it as a substitute for the establishment of full national rights; and they were impatient of O'Connell's constant anxiety to secure public appointments for his allies — to them it seemed unnatural that any patriotic Irishman should be willing to co-operate with the government.

There was much in the Young Irelanders' attitude that seemed to O'Connell ill-advised and even dangerous; but he might have tolerated them more easily had they not sometimes been critical of his own policy. He had for so long been surrounded by men who followed his lead without question that he found it hard to bear the free-spoken, though respectful, expression of independent views; and the Young Irelanders, on their side, resented the dictatorial lines on which he ran the Repeal Association. These differences first became acute in 1844. In that year, when the repeal movement was at a low ebb, a County Down landlord, William Sharman Crawford, came forward with an alternative scheme, which he called 'federalism': he advocated the establishment of an Irish parliament for purely local affairs, leaving final authority with the parliament at Westminster, where Irish representatives would continue as before. For a time it seemed that federalism might attract considerable support; and the Young Irelanders were not unwilling to give it a trial, though only as a step towards attaining their real object. But when O'Connell on his own responsibility suddenly issued a manifesto declaring that some form of federalism was to be preferred to repeal as a final settlement of Anglo-Irish relations, the Young Irelanders at once contradicted him in the *Nation*. The crisis did not last long. O'Connell, finding the federalists too weak to be useful, quickly returned to the policy of repeal; and the *Nation* gladly declared the incident closed. But on both sides some suspicion and resentment remained.

The difference of attitude to national rights revealed in this brief dispute came out more sharply over the question of physical force. The repeal movement was strictly constitutional, both in its aims and in its methods. But whereas this was a matter of principle with O'Connell, with the Young Irelanders it was simply a matter of expediency. They recognized that Ireland was in no condition to rebel, but they would not rule out the possibility of rebellion at some future date; and the poems and articles that they published, week by week, in the *Nation* constantly taught, at least by implication, that men must be ready to fight and die for national freedom. A critic who, on being asked to describe the 'tone' of the newspaper, answered 'Wolfe Tone' was not far wrong; the most famous of all its ballads begins with the significant line, 'Who fears to speak of Ninety-eight?' For all this, the question of using physical force was, at the time, merely an academic one, and it became important only because O'Connell found in it a convenient means of driving the Young Irelanders out of the Repeal Association when he finally decided to break with them. Thomas Davis, had he lived, might have been able to preserve harmony, for he was the most conciliatory and level-headed, as well as the ablest, of the group; but he died in September 1845, at the age of thirty-one; and thereafter their relations with O'Connell quickly deteriorated. It was, however, the impending change in British politics that provided the occasion of the final breach. Once the fall of Peel's government became probable, O'Connell started to angle for a renewal of his old alliance with the whigs; this was a policy which the Young Irelanders could never accept; and to get rid of them O'Connell brought forward, in the summer of 1846, a series of resolutions committing the Repeal Association to the doctrine that in no circumstances was a people justified in resorting to force to gain its independence. The Young Irelanders, though at the time they had no thought of rebellion, refused to accept such a sweeping declaration. Some of them withdrew voluntarily from the association, others were expelled; and, despite half-hearted attempts to patch up a compromise, no effective connection between Young Ireland and O'Connell could be re-established.

The activities of the Young Irelanders did not cease in 1846; but their influence in the country, now that they were separated from the main repeal movement, proved to be slight; and their efforts to establish a new organization met with little success. Though they continued to play a part in Irish affairs during the next four years, they were unable to work out a coherent policy, or even to maintain unity among themselves. The real importance of Young Ireland, however, depends less on its immediate political achievements than on its place in the development of modern Irish nationalism. Though it helped to revive and continue the revolutionary spirit of the United Irishmen, its appeal was to the history of Ireland rather than to the Rights of Man. It taught, implicitly if not directly, that the historic rights of Irish nationality justified recourse to violent revolution; and this was the doctrine that inspired the militant section of the nationalist movement from the mid-nineteenth century onwards and that forced itself on the attention of the world in Easter Week 1916.

The breach between O'Connell and the Young Irelanders took place under the shadow of national calamity. In September 1845, while Thomas Davis lay dying, came the first reports that the Irish potato crop was threatened with destruction. A few months later, the country was in the grip of famine.

XVII

The Great Famine

(1)

The famine of 1845–9 is a major dividing-line in the history of modern Ireland. Politically, economically and socially, the period that followed it appears sharply distinct from the period that preceded it. In some ways this appearance is misleading: one effect of the famine was to concentrate in a few brief years changes that would otherwise have been spread over generations, and thus to disguise the real continuity between the two periods. But the very rapidity of these changes affected their character; and the immense burden of human suffering by which they were accompanied left an indelible mark on the popular memory. The historical importance of the Great Famine lies not only in the physical results that followed from it — the decline in population, the transfer of property, the changes in agriculture — but in the attitude to the government and to the ruling class that it engendered in the great majority of the people.

From one point of view, there was nothing exceptional about the Great Famine save its extent and its intensity. Every year, a large section of the population was, for a period of two or three months, practically destitute; and on several occasions during the earlier nineteenth century, notably in 1817 and 1822, this destitution had amounted to absolute famine in some parts of the country. This state of affairs seemed to be the inevitable result of social and economic conditions. Ireland in the 1840s, with over 8,000,000 inhabitants, of whom more than four-fifths lived on the land, was one of the most densely populated countries in Europe. Even in some rural areas the population was as high as 400 per square mile, and over the country as a whole it averaged 335 per square mile of arable land. About half this population depended for its subsistence on the potato, and it was local and partial failures of the potato crop that had produced the earlier famines. What gave its special character to the Great Famine was that the crop failed over the whole country, and that the failure was repeated in successive years.

Though the dangers inherent in the Irish situation had long been recognized, no government had proved capable of working out any means of ameliorating it; and with the increase of population the margin of safety, always precarious, had grown narrower. Yet no one had foreseen a catastrophe such as actually occurred; and the very fact that there had been earlier potato failures and earlier famines made it natural to suppose, at first, that this was no more than a repetition of a familiar phenomenon. When the 'blight' on the potato crop was first reported, from the south of England, in August 1845, a few people quickly realized that if it should spread to Ireland its effect on the whole country would be infinitely more disastrous than in Great Britain; but even when the blight did appear in Ireland, in the following month, there was considerable divergence of view about its significance. And for a time this divergence was sustained by conflicting reports: some areas had escaped the blight altogether, and in others its effect was not immediately apparent — the potatoes seemed perfectly healthy when dug, only to putrefy later on.

Difference of opinion about the seriousness of the potato failure did not arise solely from variation in the reports; there was a political reason also. For some years Peel had been moving slowly towards the belief that the corn laws ought to be repealed, and events in Ireland convinced him that he must act at once. For the irreconcilable protectionists, who comprised a great part of Peel's own party, it was, therefore, a matter of policy to minimize the danger of famine. They seized on every favourable report, they declared that the others were exaggerated, and they discouraged the preparation of relief schemes as unnecessary. It was a misfortune for Ireland that the reality of the famine should have become a political question, and that the preparation of remedial measures should have become entangled in one of the bitterest parliamentary conflicts of the nineteenth century.

It is to Peel's credit that he did not allow personal or party interests to interfere with his plans for relief. Early in November 1845 he arranged, on his own responsibility, for the purchase by the government of £100,000's worth of Indian corn in the United States, and for its shipment to Cork. It was not his intention that the government should undertake responsibility for feeding the people; but he believed that by selling this grain cheaply it would be possible to keep down the general price of food, and prevent profiteering. He placed his main reliance, however, on local efforts by the gentry and professional classes; and a relief commission set

up by the government in November had, as its first main task, the organization of local committees, which were to raise funds and distribute food.
At the same time, the board of works was to undertake the construction of
new roads, a traditional method of providing employment in hard seasons.

Though Peel took the initiative in these measures, their direction fell
largely into the hands of Charles Trevelyan, assistant secretary to the
treasury, and one of the new generation that was transforming the
character of the British civil service. Trevelyan worked day and night at
his task; but his outlook was dominated by the prevailing *laissez-faire*
philosophy, and at times he gave the impression that he was more
alarmed lest the Irish should be demoralized by receiving too much help
from the government than lest they should die of starvation through not
receiving enough. 'You cannot', one of his agents in Ireland reminded
him, 'answer the cry of want by a quotation from political economy'; but
the warning had little effect. Nevertheless, during the first season of
famine, from the autumn of 1845 to the summer of 1846, the government's measures were substantially successful. And this success was due
mainly to Peel's foresight, promptness and determination. Even the
Freeman's Journal, an O'Connellite newspaper that rarely found much
good to say about any conservative, and Peel least of all, could pay him a
retrospective tribute in 1847: 'No man died of famine during his administration, and it is a boast of which he might well be proud'.

The real test, however, was still to come. The failure of 1845, though
widespread, had not been complete; and even in the affected areas the
people, save the very poorest, had still some reserves, something left that
they could pawn for food; and they were buoyed up by the hope that the
next year's harvest would be plentiful. It was when the blight struck
again, in August 1846, that despair became absolute. But by this time Peel
was no longer prime minister. His break with the protectionists of his own
party had compelled him to rely on the support of the whigs and radicals.
With their help he carried the repeal of the corn laws, in June 1846; but
almost at the same time he was defeated over an Irish coercion bill, which
outbreaks of agrarian disturbance, not unnaturally provoked by the
famine, had induced him to bring forward. In ordinary circumstances the
protectionists would have welcomed such a measure; but they were so
anxious for revenge on Peel that they readily joined forces with whigs and
radicals, and even with repealers; and this 'blackguard combination', as
Wellington called it, was strong enough to turn Peel out. In July, a whig
ministry was formed under Lord John Russell; and it was this ministry
that had to face the renewed crisis in Ireland.

When Russell took office there seemed to be some prospect of better times in Ireland; the weather in May and June had been warm, and the potatoes were flourishing. But the hopes thus raised were soon to be disappointed. 'On the 27th of last month', wrote Father Theobald Mathew early in August, 'I passed from Cork to Dublin, and this doomed plant bloomed in all the luxuriance of an abundant harvest. Returning on the 3rd instant, I beheld with sorrow one wide waste of putrefying vegetation. In many places the wretched people were seated on the fences of their decaying gardens, wringing their hands, and wailing bitterly the destruction that had left them foodless'. Similar tales of destruction and despair came from all over Ireland, for this time the failure was general. Weakened already by a season of unparalleled scarcity, and with all their resources gone, four million people faced the prospect of starvation.

This fresh disaster brought no immediate change in government policy. Trevelyan was still in charge of relief, and both the new prime minister and the new chancellor of the exchequer, Sir Charles Wood,[1] shared his outlook. 'It must be thoroughly understood', wrote Russell in October 1846, 'that we cannot feed the people'. The government was prepared to promote public works, to help with the organization of relief committees, and to make some financial contribution; but its basic thesis was that Irish poverty must be supported by Irish property. Such assistance as the government did give was, at first, made almost useless by the supposed necessity for conforming with the laws of political economy, as then understood. Thus, for example, no public money was to be spent on relief works that might be profitable to private individuals; and land reclamation and drainage, the improvements most likely to bring immediate benefit to the country, were thus excluded.[2] Again, relief committees were instructed not to sell food below the prices prevailing in their districts, lest the profits of normal traders should be endangered; and Peel's sensible, and partly successful, method of keeping down prices was abandoned.

The ineffective character of government action in Ireland, though resulting mainly from the economic principles on which it was based, had other causes also. Russell's parliamentary majority was precarious, depending as it did on the continued co-operation of inharmonious elements,

[1] Afterwards first Viscount Halifax.

[2] In 1847 this policy was modified; but the amounts of money actually advanced for reclamation and drainage were small.

originally brought together only by their antagonism to Peel; and even
within the ministry there was divergence of view over Irish policy. In
these circumstances, it might well seem that the safest course was to do
as little as possible. And apart altogether from its political difficulties, the
government suffered from an ignorance of Irish conditions so great that
it might, by itself, almost justify the repealers' contention that Ireland
could never be satisfactorily ruled from Westminster. What Russell,
Wood and Trevelyan all alike failed to realize was that the economy of
rural Ireland, especially in the areas most severely affected by the famine,
was totally different from that of England. The peasant in these areas
rarely handled money, and even more rarely used it for the purchase of
food. He paid his rent by his labour; and he and his family lived on the
potatoes that he grew himself. When the potatoes failed, he was helpless;
and there was little use in paying him a money wage for his labour on
relief works, without at the same time improvising a system of retail
distribution that would enable him to turn his wage into food.

The notion that Irish poverty, in the crisis created by the famine, should
be made a charge on Irish property displayed an equal ignorance of prevailing conditions. The government's readiness to criticize the landlords
was understandable. Some landlords simply disowned responsibility for
the welfare of their tenants; some took advantage of the situation to clear
their estates by wholesale evictions. But, whatever their attitude to the
famine, they were not, as a body, able to bear the burden that the government wished to place upon them. Very many, perhaps a majority,
habitually lived beyond their incomes; their estates were heavily mort-
gaged, and a large part of their rents was absorbed in the payment of
interest. When, as naturally happened at this time, income from rents
shrank, or disappeared altogether, they were faced with bankruptcy. To
saddle them with the cost of famine relief might complete their ruin, but
could bring little immediate benefit to their starving tenantry. What the
landlords demanded (and on this point they were in unaccustomed harmony with the leaders of popular opinion) was that the cost of famine relief
should be made a direct charge on the imperial exchequer: if Ireland was
indeed an integral part of the United Kingdom, then the United Kingdom
as a whole should be financially responsible for Ireland. It was a reasonable argument, but one that neither government nor house of commons
would accept. The average British politician, however he might talk of the
sanctity of the union, persisted in regarding Ireland as a distinct entity,
and he looked with jealous caution on every proposal for the expenditure
of 'the British taxpayers' money' on Irish objects.

If the people of Ireland had been left, during the bitter winter of

1846–7, to depend entirely on the cautious assistance of the government and the doubtful benevolence of their landlords, they would have fared even worse than they did. But a great deal was also done for them by voluntary effort. Societies, committees and individuals raised funds for the establishment of soup-kitchens, which for many months provided a large section of the population, especially in the west, with almost their only regular means of subsistence. A leading part in this work was taken by the Society of Friends — the Quakers — who set up central relief committees in London and Dublin in November 1846. These committees not only organized relief, but were careful to collect accurate information about the state of affairs: it was the reports sent in by Quaker agents in every part of the country that helped to enlighten British public opinion and the government about the true character of the situation in Ireland.

By January 1847 the cabinet at last began to realize that the measures so far taken were ineffective, and that a radical change of policy was needed; even Trevelyan was converted to the view that the provision of employment on relief works was no adequate answer to the problem, that the people must be fed, and that the cost of feeding them, now far beyond the range of voluntary effort, must be borne out of the public purse. The principle of local responsibility was not, however, to be abandoned; the provision and distribution of food was to be a charge on the rates; though the government would, where necessary, advance funds to start the new scheme, these advances were to be repaid, and running costs met, by the rate-payers. This new policy could only gradually be brought into operation, but by August over 3,000,000 people were being fed daily at the public expense. The burden was naturally heaviest in the poorer unions, many of which were now virtually bankrupt; for the collection of rates — difficult enough, especially in the west, even before the famine — had become almost impossible. By far the greatest part of the cost had therefore to be borne, in the first place, by the treasury; and though boards of guardians were made legally liable for the sums so advanced, most of this liability had, in the long run, to be cancelled.

In adapting the poor-law system to the situation created by the famine the government had had to abandon the 'workhouse test'; for though the workhouses were over-crowded, and though additional accommodation had been provided, they could not contain more than a tithe of those now dependent on public support. But the system of outdoor relief, reluctantly adopted, was intended as an emergency measure; its continuation throughout 1848, and until the late autumn of 1849, reflected the continuing pressure of famine. The potato did, indeed, escape the blight in 1847; but the area sown had been very small, and the crop, though particularly good, did little to relieve the situation. In one way, the absence of blight in 1847 had even an unfortunate effect. It revived popular faith in the potato, which was extensively sown in the following season, to the exclusion of almost anything else; so that when blight reappeared in the summer of 1848, and the crop was destroyed, conditions were as bad as they had been in 1846. By the end of 1849, however, though there had been a partial failure of the potato crop, the worst was over; and, for those who had survived, conditions gradually improved during the following decade.

(3)

In the gloomy picture of Irish society between 1845 and 1849 disease is an element no less important than hunger. The two had always been associated: typhus and relapsing fever[1] had long been endemic in Ireland; in any period of famine they spread with frightening rapidity; in the famine of the 1840s, more severe, more general and more prolonged than any that had preceded it, they ravaged the whole country. Both diseases are carried by the body-louse (though this fact was not recognized at the time), and in the crowded and filthy conditions generally prevailing in cabins, workhouses and hospitals a population whose resistance was already undermined by famine was fatally exposed to infection. Though these two were the most widespread and most deadly of the diseases that accompanied the famine, they were not the only ones: dysentery, for which Ireland had formerly been notorious, re-appeared in epidemic form; scurvy, unknown while potatoes formed a staple article of diet, became common on their disappearance; famine dropsy resulted from extreme malnutrition, and occurred only among those who were actually starving.

The fever epidemics that marked these years began, as might be expected, among the famine-stricken poor, especially in the hard-hit western areas; but it was impossible to confine them within social or geographical boundaries. Typhus, in particular, attacked all sections of the population, and even proved more deadly among the middle and upper classes than among the peasantry. The swarms of beggars that patrolled the roads and flocked into the towns, driven from their homes by hunger or eviction, carried the seeds of fever wherever they went. It was, for

[1] Down to the nineteenth century the term 'fever' was commonly applied, without discrimination, to various diseases later differentiated by medical science. By the time of the famine the distinction between typhus and relapsing fever was well established; but even medical observers sometimes used the general term 'fever', or 'famine fever', without any more specific description.

example, an influx of such refugees that started an epidemic in Belfast, in September 1846, at a time when provisions in the town were still plentiful and cheap, and when there was sufficient employment for the labouring classes.

Despite earlier experience of epidemics on a national scale (typhus in 1817–18, cholera in 1832), the medical services of the country were ill-prepared for the crisis resulting from the Great Famine. Each county possessed, or was supposed to possess, a county infirmary and a fever hospital; there was an infirmary attached to each workhouse; in most of the larger cities and towns there were hospitals founded by voluntary effort. Besides this, every part of the country had dispensaries, established and partly maintained by private subscription, and intended, in the first place, to provide free medical attention for the tenants and servants of subscribers. But this system, quite inadequate even in normal times, was completely overwhelmed during the famine. Hospitals were soon crowded to suffocation, for it was impossible to refuse the wretches who clamoured for admittance; and patients were packed into emergency accommodation in tents and 'fever sheds', outside the hospital walls, where they commonly lay on the bare ground, unable to obtain even a supply of water. Local officials and voluntary workers coped as best they could with these desperate conditions; and a specially-constituted Central Board of Health attempted, between 1846 and 1849, to improvise a national system of temporary fever hospitals. The attempt came too late to avert a major disaster, but it did something to mitigate the effect of the epidemics; and the high death-rate among hospital and dispensary doctors is evidence that, whatever the shortcomings of the medical services as a whole, individual medical practitioners did not shirk their duties.

It is impossible to calculate, with even approximate accuracy, the number of deaths from disease during the famine years. Hospital and workhouse records were often imperfectly kept; and even if they were complete, it would still be necessary to take into account the unknown thousands who perished in their own homes, or by the wayside, untended and almost unnoticed. It is equally impossible to calculate how many died from actual starvation; the number officially recorded, between 1846 and 1851, is 21,770; but it is certain that a very high proportion, and perhaps even a majority, of those who died from disease would not have contracted it in the first place, or would have survived it, had they been properly nourished. Taking into account all the available evidence, we may reasonably assume that between 1845 and 1850 not far short of 1,000,000 people died, either of disease or of hunger, as a result of the Great Famine.

The loss of population from the high mortality of the famine years was more than equalled by the loss through emigration. For thirty years before the famine emigration had been put forward, time and again, as the most obvious solution to the agrarian problem; but despite encouragement, and sometimes even pressure, from their landlords, Irish tenants had shown a strong reluctance to leave the country; and though a regular emigrant traffic had developed, the numbers were comparatively small: between 1841 and 1844 they averaged about 50,000 a year. The potato failure of 1845 hardly affected the situation, for there was a confident hope that the next season would be a good one; but the second failure, in 1846, produced a revolutionary change of attitude among the peasantry. Emigration, formerly a last desperate remedy, was now the first thing thought of; and there was an almost hysterical rush to leave the country, to escape, at all costs, from 'the doomed and starving island', and find safety elsewhere. In earlier years, emigrant sailings had been confined to spring and summer; and intending emigrants had made their preparations carefully. But, from the latter half of 1846 onwards, the panic-stricken crowds were clamorous to be off without delay; the traffic continued throughout the year; and thousands of helpless refugees put to sea with only the scantiest supply of provisions for the voyage, and without either means of subsistence or prospect of employment on their arrival. In 1846 they numbered 106,000, in the following year 215,000, and in 1851 the figure rose to a quarter of a million; though there was some decline after this, the volume of emigration remained very heavy during the rest of the century. Not all of this vast number could pay their own way: some were assisted by landlords anxious to clear their estates, some by the government; and, from 1849 onwards, remittances were coming in from earlier emigrants who had saved enough to enable them to pay the fares of relations they had left behind.

During the period 1846–51 about three-quarters of the emigrants went to the United States, the remainder to British North America,[1] and the strain imposed on trans-Atlantic shipping by this sudden tide of emigration had disastrous results. Even if government, landlords and shipping companies had combined to render the transfer of population from Ireland to America as safe and as comfortable as they could, the emigrants would still have had to face considerable hardship; as it was, in the competitive conditions of a *laissez-faire* age, their sufferings exceed description. Hungry, verminous, fever-ridden, they were herded together on

[1] There was some emigration to Australia during these years, but the total number (19,000) was insignificant.

cargo ships hastily and imperfectly adapted to carry this human freight; and they were for the most part too ignorant and too apathetic even to attempt the most elementary precautions against infection. Inevitably, the rate of mortality was high — of emigrants sailing from Liverpool to Canada in 1847, one in fourteen died at sea, of those sailing from Cork, one in nine; and the bitter memory of the 'coffin ships' is firmly entrenched in the folk-tradition of the famine.[1]

The emigrants found that the end of the voyage was by no means the end of their troubles. Neither Canada nor the United States welcomed the mass influx of Irish, whose arrival was marked by fever epidemics which no quarantine regulations could prevent, whose innumerable sick and poor were an immediate burden on the public, and whose low standard of living threatened the security of the working class. But though generations were to pass before the Irish element in the North American population was to become fully assimilated, its cohesion and its rapidly growing numerical strength soon gave it, in the United States, a political importance that could not be ignored; and the rising influence of the Irish Americans had an important effect on the politics of Ireland.

The combined effect of disease and emigration was a sudden and catastrophic fall in population: in 1841 it had stood at 8,175,000 and the natural increase might have been expected to raise it to about 8,500,000 by 1851; in fact, the census of that year showed a population of 6,552,000. And the famine not only halted the process of growth, but completely reversed it: the decline continued steadily, and by the beginning of the twentieth century the population of Ireland was only about half what it had been on the eve of the famine.

(4)

Though the Great Famine was to have, in the long run, a revolutionary influence on Irish politics, the immediate effect of its onset was comparatively slight. During the winter of 1845–6 political life continued to be dominated by the question of O'Connell's relations with the whigs, by the growing breach between Young Ireland and the Repeal Association, and by public controversy over the Queen's Colleges. In parliament, the repeal members showed less concern about famine relief than about Peel's coercion bill, to defeat which they were even prepared to jeopardize the repeal of the corn laws. The second failure of the potato crop, in 1846,

---

[1] The philanthropist and educational reformer, Vere Foster, made the crossing as an ordinary emigrant in order to collect authoritative information about the condition and treatment of passengers.

brought a new sense of urgency; but even this hardly disturbed the existing political relationships. O'Connell, deeply moved by the sufferings he had witnessed, denounced Russell's relief measures as misguided and inadequate; but he did not break off relations with the ministry, to which he acted as a sort of unofficial adviser on Irish affairs. Both O'Connell and the Young Irelanders proclaimed the necessity for re-uniting the repeal movement in face of a national calamity; but though their public utterances sounded magnanimous, in private negotiation neither side would give way to the other; the breach remained unhealed; and in January 1847 the Young Irelanders set up a rival organization of their own, the Irish Confederation, under William Smith O'Brien, a protestant landlord, and one of the few members of the group who had a seat in parliament.

For a brief period it seemed just possible that this very rivalry between the two branches of the repeal movement would lead to a new and wider union. Both sides were anxious to enlist landlord support; for the idea of a national movement embracing all social classes, and drawing its leadership from the aristocracy and gentry, was still strong. And just at this time most Irish landlords were politically adrift. The dispute over the corn laws and the consequent break-up of the conservative party had temporarily weakened the link between Irish and British conservatives. And landlords in general, whatever their political allegiance, were uneasy about the government's policy towards the famine; they objected to the principle that Ireland should bear the financial responsibility for famine relief; and they demanded that public works undertaken in order to provide employment should be directed towards increasing the productivity of the land. On this latter point they were in substantial agreement with both groups of repealers; and members of both groups, eager for landlord co-operation, were very ready to join them. A meeting of peers, gentry and M.P.s of all parties was held in Dublin in January 1847, and called for a radical change in the government's policy towards Ireland. But if it seemed for a moment that a united Irish party was about to emerge, it soon became clear that the basis of union was too narrow; the conservatives were still conservative, and most repealers still clung to the idea of a whig alliance.

The political activity of this period, seen in retrospect, seems almost completely detached from reality. Irish society was in course of disintegration, and the grouping or re-grouping of parties meant nothing to the thousands who were dying of starvation or fever. The maintenance of any kind of political organization on a national scale had become impossible; and though a general election in the summer of 1847 resulted in the return of thirty-nine repealers, the repeal movement had by this time virtually ceased to count; the 'repeal rent' had dried up; and O'Connell himself was dead. In February 1847 he spoke for the last time in the house of commons, where his appeal for generosity towards Ireland was heard in respectful silence, though it had no effect on government policy; then, his mind occupied almost exclusively with thoughts of his approaching decease, he set off for Italy, resolved to spend his last hours in Rome; but death overtook him at Genoa, on 15 May.

O'Connell's great contribution to the development of modern Ireland was that he called into being, and organized for political action, the force of mass opinion; he taught the Roman Catholic majority to regard itself as the Irish nation; and all succeeding nationalist leaders, even when they have disagreed most strongly with his policy, have had to build on the foundations that he laid. It is easy to pick holes in his character. He loved power, and was not always scrupulous in his methods of gaining and keeping it; his policy seemed often to be guided by expediency rather than by principle; he was indefatigable in pushing the interests of his family and his friends, and he had an eighteenth-century tolerance of jobbery. But when all this has been said, he remains a man of transcendent genius, which he devoted to the service of his native land; no other single person has left such an unmistakable mark on the history of Ireland. And his influence was hardly less important on those who opposed than on those who followed him. The character of the revolutionary tradition, which he detested, and the political development of the protestant minority, which he attempted in vain to win over to repeal, were both affected profoundly, though in different ways, by the career and achievement of O'Connell.

O'Connell's death marked the end of a period in Irish politics; but the continuing activity of the Young Irelanders was to provide a postscript. During 1847 and the early months of 1848 they conducted intermittent negotiations with O'Connell's son, John — 'the Young Liberator' — who now led what remained of the Repeal Association, with the idea of re-uniting the two branches of the movement. But during the same period many of them were moving in a more revolutionary direction. John Mitchel, an Ulster protestant and the most militant member of the group, established in 1847 a new journal, significantly named the *United Irishman*. He had come under the influence of Fintan Lalor, a reformer who saw in the existing landlord system the root of Ireland's distress; and it was to the propagation of radical ideas on agrarian reform, and to preparation for an armed rising, that Mitchel now devoted himself. At first, most of the Young Ireland leaders were alarmed at Mitchel's violent radicalism; but the easy success of the French revolution of February 1848 and the apparent strength of Chartism in Britain, combined with a growing conviction that no peaceful persuasion would ever induce the government to modify its policy in Ireland, made them think more favourably of rebellion. Mitchel himself was arrested on a charge of sedition, and condemned to transportation in May 1848; but almost immediately afterwards other Young Irelanders began preparations for a rising. They had neither the means nor the ability for the task; and they were too much out of touch with the temper of the country to realize that the famine had left the people in no mood for fighting. Their abortive attempt at rebellion, in the first week of August, ended in a brief skirmish with the police. Of the three principal leaders, one, John Blake Dillon, escaped to America; the others, Smith O'Brien and Thomas Francis Meagher, were taken prisoner. The government was too prudent to make martyrs; and though O'Brien was charged with high treason and condemned to death, both he and Meagher were, in fact, transported to Australia. But though the whole affair has about it an air of tragi-comedy, it is a not unimportant link in the tradition that stretches from the United Irishmen of 1798 to the Irish Volunteers of 1916.

While the Young Irelanders were planning impossible rebellions, a far more significant movement had made its appearance: in February 1847 a 'tenant-right association' had been formed in County Cork. The Irish tenant farmers had lost their enthusiasm for repeal, and they were not prepared to fight for a republic; but they were beginning to see the value of open and legal combination for the furtherance of their own social and economic interests.[1]

(5)

The decisive influence of the Great Famine on the economic and social life of Ireland arose directly from the sudden and continuing decline in the population: it was an effective, though terrible, solution to the problem of rural over-crowding. And yet, paradoxically, land became scarcer, not more plentiful; for though there were fewer people, there were also fewer holdings. Subdivision gave way to consolidation. In 1841 only one-fifth of the holdings had exceeded fifteen acres, by 1851 the proportion had risen to one half; but the total number of holdings had sunk from 690,000 to 570,000;[2] and in most parts of the country the process was a continuing

[1] Below, pp. 354–5.

[2] The change between 1841 and 1851 appears from the following table:

Holdings		1841	1851
1–5	acres	310,436	88,083
5–15	acres	252,799	191,854
15–30	acres	79,342	141,311
above 30 acres		48,625	149,090

one. The change was due partly to the landlords, who were anxious to clear their estates, and who were helped by the relief legislation of 1847, which had denied public assistance to any person holding more than a quarter-acre of land, so that many small-holders were forced to give up their land in order to escape starvation. But the continuation of the process reflected a change in the character of Irish agriculture; from the 1850s onwards there was a fairly steady decline in tillage, with a corresponding concentration on cattle-raising, and in an agrarian economy based on cattle there was little place for the very small farm. Only along the western seaboard did conditions at all resembling those before the famine continue to exist; elsewhere, the multitude of tiny holdings was replaced by farms of economic size, and the ultimate establishment of a peasant proprietary in place of a landlord system was made possible.

The change in the distribution of land had important social consequence. In pre-famine Ireland, early marriage had been easy and common: subdivision of the family farm could provide each son with a potato-patch, and since he had no prospect of improving his position, he had no inducement to delay marriage. But in the altered conditions of the later nineteenth century, when it was considered essential to keep the farm intact, only one son could inherit, and he normally had to postpone marriage until his father died, or was ready to hand over the farm; for the other sons, and often for unmarried daughters also, emigration was the obvious resource. One consequence of this state of affairs is seen in a falling birth-rate; its general effect on the character of rural society, though it cannot be so easily assessed, was hardly less important.

Politically, as well as economically and socially, the famine had a profound influence on later developments. It left in the popular mind a feeling of resentment against the whole system of government in Ireland; and from this time onwards Irish nationalism takes on a new bitterness, particularly among the emigrants in America. O'Connell had paid tribute to the generosity and humanity shown by thousands of English people during the famine: 'If the exhibition of these qualities by individuals', he wrote, 'could save Ireland in her present misery, we should be saved'. But, among Irishmen in general, gratitude for the aid afforded by English charity was overborne by a conviction that government policy had displayed a callous disregard for Irish suffering. Probably nothing did more to create and sustain this conviction than the government's refusal to impose an embargo on the export of food; and even at the height of the famine grain was being steadily exported from Ireland. Whether or not the imposition of an embargo would, by itself, have had much effect on the situation is open to some question. Those most in need of food had no

money to buy it, however plentiful the supply — the very reason why
Irish grain was being exported was that it had no market at home; and an
embargo would have upset the whole economy. But no one could doubt
that if a comparable crisis had arisen in England the government would
have ensured adequate supplies of food, at whatever cost to the economy;
or that an independent government in Ireland would have done the same.
The Great Famine killed the repeal movement; but to succeeding generations of Irishmen it stood as a clear condemnation of the parliamentary
union.

The British attitude to Ireland, as well as the Irish attitude to Britain,
was affected by the famine. The widespread sympathy with the sufferings
of the Irish poor was not unmingled with impatience, and sometimes with
contempt. Even well-intentioned people so little understood the situation
as to resent as folly or mere ingratitude the continuance of any Irish
demand for self-government; and many would have accepted Trevelyan's
verdict that 'the great evil' was not the famine itself but 'the selfish,
perverse and turbulent character of the people'. The abortive insurrection
of 1848 went far towards making this view general; and during the
following winter, when the famine was as severe as it had been in 1846–7,
there was a noticeable falling-off in voluntary contributions for relief. The
anti-Irish feeling that had existed all through the famine in some quarters
(it is reflected, for example, in the pages of *Punch*) now became stronger.
Public opinion in Britain was coming to regard the Irish as irresponsible,
ungrateful and treacherous, unfit to govern themselves, or even to enjoy
the same constitutional rights as the rest of the United Kingdom.

When, in August 1849, the queen made her first visit to Ireland she
was welcomed with enormous popular enthusiasm; but it would be a
mistake to regard this enthusiasm as a true indication of Irish feelings
towards Britain, and it certainly had no lasting effect on British feelings
towards Ireland. As the two countries approached the end of a half-
century of parliamentary union, they were, perhaps, more completely
estranged from one another than they had ever been before.

XVIII

Land and Politics, 1850–1870

---

(1)

The Great Famine had undermined the entire social system, and Ireland did not quickly recover from the shock. Mass emigration, though it affected mainly the tenant-farmers and agricultural labourers, was symptomatic of a sense of hopelessness and frustration that ran through all classes. For half a generation or more, every attempt to revive a popular political movement was to prove short-lived, lacking in discipline and leadership, and to all appearance ineffective. But though little might seem to be accomplished, the period was one of readjustment rather than stagnation. The more active political life of the 1870s derived much of its character from the ideas and events of the preceding twenty years; for it was during these years that the land question acquired a central importance in the public mind, and that the connection between land and politics, implicit in the Irish situation for centuries, came to be generally recognized.

The ghastly and unmistakable terms in which the Great Famine had posed the land question lost their urgency when the immediate crisis was past; but the question itself remained and could not be indefinitely postponed: how was Irish agriculture to be improved to a point at which it could provide adequate support for the population dependent upon it? For the next half-century this question, in various forms, occupied a central position in Irish politics, both in Ireland itself and at Westminster. Irish popular leaders demanded government action, and few British statesmen were prepared to deny that some such action was necessary; but the inevitable conflict of interest between landlord and tenant raised an almost insuperable barrier; and it was not until 1870 that the first decisive step was taken.

What Irish agriculture needed, above all else, was an infusion of capital. But though some public money had been advanced, reluctantly, for drainage and reclamation schemes during the famine, no government of the period was likely to continue such investment as a matter of permanent policy. 'The more I see of government interference', wrote Charles Wood, chancellor of the exchequer, in 1848, 'the less I am disposed to trust to it, and I have no faith in anything but private capital employed under individual charge'. This reflected pretty accurately the outlook of all his colleagues; and in so far as Russell's ministry could be said to have had any Irish land policy it was to encourage improvement by private enterprise. One obvious step would have been to strengthen the security of the tenant, so that he could put money and labour into improving his farm without risking loss by an increase of rent or by eviction. But though several bills were brought forward for this purpose, the landed interest at Westminster was able to defeat them. There was not, perhaps, much sympathy for the Irish landlords; but there was a strong feeling for the 'just rights of property', and a lurking fear that any legislation in favour of Irish tenants would be followed by a demand for similar legislation in Great Britain. 'The same interests exist on both sides of the channel', said *The Times*, in reference to one of these bills, 'and those who are prepared to invade the landlord's property in one country will speedily be called upon for a similar violation of principle in the other'.

But though the landed interest was successful in resisting the demands of the tenants, the Irish landlords were, as a body, too poor, too incompetent, too selfish, to initiate any general improvement themselves. 'The land', wrote an English economist in 1849, 'is in the hands of nominal and embarrassed proprietors, who either cannot or will not improve their estates, or allow such terms of tenure as will induce others to improve them'. The obvious solution, it seemed to many people, was to clear out these shiftless proprietors, and establish in their place new and efficient landlords, who would provide the capital and skill needed to transform the agricultural system: 'Foolish Irish peasants', declared Thomas Carlyle, 'must have wise Irish landlords to command them'. But the legal transfer of landed property was slow, cumbersome and expensive; the process of establishing title was often difficult and complicated; and many estates were bound by entail, limited by family settlements, and encumbered by mortgages. Those who placed their hopes in a general change in the landlord class demanded that the way should be opened by the establishment of 'free trade in land', that 'the principle of commercial freedom' should be fully extended, and the sale of land made as easy as the sale of any other commodity.

A demand so closely in accord with the prevailing spirit met little serious resistance. An act to facilitate the sale of land in Ireland was passed in 1848; and when this proved insufficient a second, more radical, act was passed in the following year. Under the terms of this 'encumbered estates act' of 1849, a commission, the 'encumbered estates court', was set up, empowered to sell estates on application either from owners or encumbrancers.[1] On completion of a sale, the court was to distribute the purchase-money among the various claimants, pay the residue to the vendor, and grant the new proprietor a clear and indefeasible title.

Great results were looked for from this measure. John Bright, who believed that the best chance for Irish agriculture lay in peasant proprietorship, hoped that many tenants would be able to purchase their holdings. Jonathan Pim, an Irish Quaker who had taken a prominent part in relief work during the famine, hoped that the tenants would be better off under landlords who would undertake the improvements hitherto left to the occupier. There was a widespread expectation that British purchasers would flock into the country, bringing new capital to invest in their estates, and peopling them with highly-skilled English and Scottish farmers: 'In a few years more', *The Times* prophesied, 'a Celtic Irishman will be as rare in Connemara as is the Red Indian on the shores of Manhattan'. Things turned out very differently. Between 1849 and 1857 over 3,000 estates were sold under the terms of the act. But there was no influx either of landlords or of capital: of some 7,200 purchasers only about 300 came from England or Scotland, and they contributed less than £3,000,000 out of the £20,000,000 paid in purchase-money.

The nationality of these new proprietors was, however, less important than their character. They were, for the most part, speculators. The decline in land values, due partly to the famine and partly to the throwing on the market of so many estates at once, had tempted them to invest in land; and their first object was to increase rents so as to get the best return they could on their money. Bad as the old landlords had often been, the new tended to be worse, and their conduct helped to embitter the agrarian struggle. A report on the relations between landlord and tenant, prepared for the chief secretary in 1869 by the poor-law inspectors, repeatedly draws attention to the hardship suffered by tenants on estates that had changed hands under the encumbered estates act. The act failed to introduce new capital, and failed to raise the standard of agriculture; but perhaps its most serious defect was that it established free trade in land without any regard to the effect that this might have on the interests of the occupying tenants.

[1] An encumbrancer is one who has a legal claim on an estate, e.g. by way of mortgage.

M   B.M.I.

(2)

Russell had intended that the encumbered estates act should be accompanied by a measure giving the tenant a right to compensation for his improvements; but this was dropped and, so far as the government was concerned, the solution of the land question was left to the operation of *laissez-faire* principles. Already, however, the tenants were beginning to work out a positive land policy of their own, and to put forward claims that threatened the whole basis of landlord power.

The distress resulting from the famine led, almost inevitably, to a recrudescence of agrarian crime; but it led also to a new kind of action on the part of the tenantry, the formation of open and legal 'tenant protection societies', often under the guidance of the local Roman Catholic clergy. The movement tentatively begun in 1847[1] spread during the next few years; by 1850 there were some twenty such societies in the south and west, and others soon followed; and though they had no organic connection, they had the same general aim — the fixing of fair rents by impartial valuation. The significance of this development was greatly increased by the fact that, at the same time, Ulster tenants also were preparing to defend their rights; and thus the way was open for a national tenant movement.

The activity among the northern tenants arose from a well-founded fear that the Ulster custom was in danger. Agricultural depression had reduced the price at which a tenant could hope to sell his right of occupancy, while rents remained, in general, as high as before; thus the tenant's position was weakened, and many landlords were taking advantage of the situation to curtail, as far as they could, the operation of the custom on their own estates. There was another, though less direct, threat to the Ulster custom in the attitude of government and parliament. The various compensation bills brought forward since 1845 had been intended to apply to the whole country; but the benefits they offered fell far short of those enjoyed in practice by tenants holding under the custom, and there was a natural suspicion that if such a bill should pass the custom would be superseded, a suspicion that was strengthened by criticism of the custom in the report of the Devon commission. The threat became more urgent in 1847, when a bill to legalize the custom, introduced by William Sharman Crawford, a County Down landlord and an old champion of the tenants' claims, was overwhelmingly defeated. It was in response to this defeat that Crawford and James McKnight, a prominent Ulster

[1] See above, p. 348.

journalist, founded, in the same year, the Ulster Tenant Right Association. Presbyterian ministers took a leading part in its affairs; and in 1850 the presbyterian general assembly, after some hesitation, resolved to petition parliament for legislation that would 'secure to the tenant-farmers of Ulster, in all its integrity, the prescriptive usage of that province, known by the name of tenant-right'.

This growing activity among the tenants, north and south, had been watched with great interest by three political journalists: John Gray, editor of the *Freeman's Journal*, the most important popular daily paper in the country, Gavan Duffy, editor of the *Nation*, and the only member of the Young Ireland group still active in politics in Ireland, and Frederick Lucas, editor of the *Tablet*, an English convert to Roman Catholicism, who had devoted himself and his paper to the cause of the Irish peasantry. Under their guidance, a national tenant-right conference met in Dublin in August 1850, and out of this arose the Irish Tenant League. The league adopted, as its basic policy, the legalizing of the Ulster custom, and its extension to the whole country; and it resolved to put up candidates for parliament at the next general election.

Because so many delegates from Ulster had been present at the conference of August 1851 the league was sometimes called, rather grandiloquently, the 'League of North and South'. But the part played by Ulster protestants, though considerable to begin with, soon declined in importance. Some became uneasy about their connection with a movement in which Roman Catholic clergy were so prominent, and this uneasiness was strengthened by the sectarian strife surrounding the ecclesiastical titles act of 1851, in which several members of the league, and particularly Lucas, were deeply involved. Some were suspicious that the league was being used for political purposes beyond its declared programme; and it is true that Gavan Duffy, at least, hoped to turn it into a national movement to secure self-government for Ireland. When the general election of 1852 gave the league a chance to test its strength in the constituencies, only one of the Ulster candidates was returned, Sharman Crawford himself being defeated in County Down.

Elsewhere, however, the league was more successful. An Irish franchise act of 1850 had increased the electorate from 61,000 to 165,000, of whom 135,000 were in the county constituencies, where the principles of the league made most appeal; and when the election was over some forty of the newly-elected members took a pledge to 'hold themselves perfectly independent of, and in opposition to, all governments which do not make it a part of their policy and a cabinet question to give to the tenantry of Ireland a measure embodying the principles of Mr Sharman

Crawford's bill'.[1] In the then existing state of politics such a party, if firmly united and skilfully led, might hope to carry great weight; and Derby's government was prepared to make important concessions. But the tenant-right members were unwilling to accept any compromise; they pressed on with a bill of their own; and when the government refused to accept it they joined with the whigs, radicals and Peelites to defeat Derby in December 1852.

So far from bringing them any advantage, the change almost ruined their party; for two of its leading members, John Sadleir and William Keogh, despite the pledge they had taken, accepted office in the new coalition ministry under Aberdeen. They defended their action on the ground that they could help the cause better in government than in opposition; but, though Aberdeen proved no more willing than Derby to accept the tenant-right programme, they remained in the ministry. This defection broke the unity of the party and dimmed its prestige. For a further six or seven years a declining group of members maintained the principle of independent opposition and upheld the tenant cause in parliament. But they had neither financial resources nor effective organization; their position was further weakened when Archbishop Cullen, from 1854 onwards, used his influence to deprive them of clerical support in the constituencies; and by 1859 the party was virtually extinct. Its example was more important than its achievement: its early success had shown that the grievances of the tenantry could be turned into a political channel; its disintegration and decline had shown the need for discipline and firm leadership. Twenty years later, in more favourable circumstances, another Irish party was to profit by these lessons.

The tenant-right movement, despite its weaknesses, did at least succeed in keeping the land question alive, not only in Ireland but at Westminster. Even after the final dissolution of the parliamentary party, there was always a handful of independent members who tried to maintain its principles; and a long series of land bills, some brought forward by private members, some sponsored by the government of the day, was introduced between 1852 and 1869. But landlord influence was strong enough to defeat any important concession to the tenants; and of all these bills, only two, both government measures, and both passed in 1860, became law; One of them provided that a tenant should be entitled to compensation for certain classes of improvements carried out at his own expense with the consent of the landlord; but it was so narrow in scope and so compli-

---

[1] The reference is to an unsuccessful bill, based on he principles of the league, introduced by Crawford early in 1852.

cated in operation that the tenant derived little real benefit from it. The other (generally known as 'Deasy's Act', from the name of its sponsor in the house of commons, Richard Deasy, attorney-general for Ireland) was wholly to the advantage of the landlord. It provided that in future the relationship between landlord and tenant was to be 'deemed to be founded on the express or implied contract of the parties and not upon tenure or service'. From a legal viewpoint this was a revolutionary measure, applying the nineteenth-century notion of free trade to the letting of land, in place of the long-established principles of feudal law; and, as a logical consequence, it simplified the process by which the landlord could recover possession of his property at the termination of a lease or yearly letting.

The purpose of the act was apparently to encourage the making of written contracts between owner and occupier, in which the rights of each should be expressly stated; and this might have been reasonable enough if both parties had stood on an equal footing. But the Irish peasant was so completely dependent on the occupation of land for a livelihood that he could hardly hope to make a fair bargain. The principle of 'free contract' applied to the letting of land might mean freedom for the landlord; for the tenant it could well mean slavery.

Deasy's act, despite its revolutionary character, does not seem, in practice, to have made much change in the situation: there is no evidence to suggest that the increased power given to the landlords led to any increase in the number of evictions. But the act was very alarming to the tenants, for the principle that it embodied destroyed the whole basis of tenant-right. So far from solving the land question, it increased the general uneasiness and discontent; and the most significant and most popular provisions of Gladstone's first land act, ten years later, were those that ran directly counter to the basic principle of the act of 1860.

(3)

With the disintegration of the tenant-right party at the end of 1852 Irish politics seemed to lose all sense of purpose. The national enthusiasm that had marked the general election of that year died away in disappointment, and could not be revived. The few members who still maintained an independent course at Westminster had little popular backing at home. Gavan Duffy's dream of a united national party was shattered, and in 1855 he left Ireland in despair, to make a new political career for himself in Australia. A. M. Sullivan, who later succeeded him as editor of the

Nation, describes the political atmosphere of the period, with some journalistic exaggeration, but with substantial truth:

'Repeal was buried. Disaffection had disappeared. Nationality was unmentioned. Not a shout was raised. Not even a village tenant-right club survived. The people no longer interested themselves in politics. Who went into or who went out of parliament concerned them not . . . All was silence.'

This political stagnation was not wholly due to the break-up of the tenant-right movement. Other causes contributed. There was, during the 1850s, a slow but marked economic improvement; if tillage declined, the cattle trade flourished; and over most of the country the standard of living was distinctly higher than it had been before the famine. At this time, also, the influence of the church, which had lent such weight to the repeal movement, was directed towards strengthening the link between Ireland and Great Britain. Archbishop Cullen, the most powerful member of the hierarchy, had brought from Rome, where he had lived for more than twenty years, an Italian ecclesiastic's horror of revolution — he regarded Gavan Duffy as 'an Irish Mazzini' — and he believed that the interests of the church could best be served by keeping Ireland firmly within the United Kingdom.

But the political apathy that A. M. Sullivan described did not, as he himself realized, spring from any general acceptance of the existing state of affairs. Tenant-right had failed as a national rallying-cry, and nothing else had so far taken its place; but there was a great mass of discontent, requiring only leadership and organization to weld it into a new national movement. Sullivan's own policy was to keep alive some flicker of nationalist feeling, and to await an opportunity for re-establishing a constitutional movement in the tradition of Grattan and O'Connell for the attainment of Irish self-government. Before the 1850s were out, this cautious attitude was to be challenged by a new, vigorous and aggressive organization, whose hero was not Grattan but Wolfe Tone.

This new organization took its rise among some of the younger refugees from the abortive insurrection of 1848. Two of them, James Stephens and John O'Mahony, had settled in Paris, where they mingled with the political exiles from many countries who made Paris their headquarters. They quickly conceived the idea of establishing a revolutionary society to work for the overthrow of British rule in Ireland; but it was not until 1858 that they took any positive action. By that time O'Mahony had removed to New York; the strong nationalist feeling that he found among the Irish Americans convinced him that their help could be enlisted for a new rebellion; and at his suggestion Stephens returned to Ireland, early in 1858, to survey the position and, if possible, prepare the way for revolutionary action. Shortly after his arrival, he established in Dublin the Fenian Brotherhood,[1] an oath-bound secret society; and for almost two years he toured the country, swearing in members.

The essential principles of Fenianism were that nothing could be achieved for Ireland by constitutional means; that British power must be overthrown by force; and that any delay in action would be dangerous — 'Soon or never' was an early Fenian watchword. Though it throve on social discontent, Fenianism had no programme of reform — it would be time enough to think of that when national independence had been won; and though its leaders often claimed to be acting on behalf of 'the Irish people', it was in no sense democratic. Stephens had insisted from the first that he himself should be given supreme control, and the organization that he devised was a military one. The Fenians did not set out, as the Young Irelanders had done, to educate popular opinion or win mass support; partly, perhaps, because they hoped that popular opinion was already, even if unconsciously, on their side; but also because they believed in the absolute divine right of nationality: it was their duty to make Ireland independent, whatever the majority of Irishmen might think. Nevertheless, Stephens soon realized the importance of propaganda, and in 1863 he established in Dublin a weekly newspaper, the *Irish People*. He himself had little skill with the pen, though he contributed a few articles to the early numbers; and the paper was mainly conducted by John O'Leary, Thomas Clarke Luby and Charles Kickham, all of whom had been involved in the 1848 rising.

During a precarious existence of barely two years, the *Irish People* was largely concerned in defending Fenianism against its Irish critics. Stephens had given the movement an elaborate secret organization, designed to protect it against spies and informers; but the fact that such a movement existed could not be wholly disguised; and Fenian attempts to infiltrate or break up every other movement of a nationalist character naturally alarmed and antagonized those who still aimed at establishing a party to win self-government by constitutional means. Though some of these constitutional nationalists would have accepted, in principle, the right of armed insurrection, they were absolutely convinced that in existing

---

[1] The name 'Fenian' (apparently suggested by John O'Mahony, who was an enthusiastic Gaelic scholar) was derived from 'Fianna', the military force led by Fionn MacCuchail (Finn MacCool), a heroic warrior of Celtic legend. The Fenians were also known as the Irish Republican Brotherhood (I.R.B.); but according to John O'Leary they themselves most commonly spoke simply of 'the Organization'.

circumstances it could lead only to useless bloodshed; and they strongly disapproved of the conspiratorial character of the Fenian organization: William Smith O'Brien, for example, who had returned to Ireland in 1858, published in the *Nation* a letter warning the people not to join secret societies. The *Irish People* denounced such caution as a cowardly betrayal of the national interest; but it was not, in fact, from the constitutional nationalists that Fenianism had most to fear. The hostility of the Roman Catholic church was infinitely more dangerous; and some of the bitterest attacks in the *Irish People* were those launched against the bishops. O'Leary and Luby kept clear of this controversy (the latter, perhaps, because he was a protestant), and left the work to Kickham, whose attitude is conveniently summed up in a couple of sentences from one of his articles: 'If the people were submissive to the clergy in politics there would be no Fenian Brotherhood. Ireland would be allowed to perish without a hand being raised to help her'.

In the hope of countering this Fenian propaganda Archbishop Cullen, supported by most of the other bishops, combined with a group of constitutional nationalists to found a new body, the National Association, in 1864. But the association's programme — land reform, disestablishment of the Church of Ireland, denominational education — contained nothing to attract those whose great aim was national independence; the association itself was weakened by internal divisions; and in the general election of 1865 its candidates made a poor show. The National Association survived for some years longer, and did something to sharpen popular hostility to the established church, but it had no effect on the position or prospects of Fenianism.

Despite all episcopal efforts, and despite the opposition of the *Nation*, Stephens was able to build up a considerable following, including some thousands of Irish soldiers serving in regiments stationed in Ireland. The movement also spread rapidly among the growing Irish population in Britain, and it acquired great strength in the United States. This expansion seemed to justify plans for an early rising, to which, indeed, the Fenian leaders had committed themselves. But they had counted on substantial help from the Irish Americans, and the outbreak of the American civil war virtually compelled them to postpone action. In other respects, however, the war offered prospects of advantage. On both sides were thousands of Irish soldiers, from whom it would be possible, when peace came, to recruit a force of trained men for service in Ireland; and Stephens seems to have hoped that the strained relations between the north and Britain would lead to a war in which the Fenians would have the full support of the Federal government. Though this hope was not fulfilled, the end of the war, in April 1865, seemed to provide the opportunity for which the Fenians had been waiting; some hundreds of experienced Irish officers from the American armies came over to Ireland; and Stephens decided that there should be an insurrection before the end of the year.

But by this time the authorities at Dublin Castle were on his trail. They had, of course, long been aware that there was a conspiracy on foot; but it was not until September 1865 that they had sufficient evidence to strike at its headquarters, which was, in fact, the editorial office of the *Irish People*. In that month the paper was suppressed; O'Leary, Luby and Kickham were arrested at once; and Stephens was tracked down a few weeks later. Stephens himself soon escaped; but the others were tried for treason-felony and sentenced to long terms of imprisonment. The trials, however, proved excellent propaganda for the Fenians; and the bearing of the prisoners helped to convert their counsel, a young tory barrister named Isaac Butt, to a belief in Irish self-government.

Most of the Fenian leaders still at large urged Stephens, after his escape, to call an immediate rising. But he insisted on postponement; and soon it was too late. The government took no chances: all over the country suspects were rounded up, arms were seized, regiments thought to be infected with Fenianism were removed from Ireland, and, early in 1866, the *habeas corpus* act was suspended. When at last, after Stephens had left the country, an insurrection was arranged for March 1867, it collapsed in a single night, almost without a blow. Stephens was widely blamed for his procrastination, and never recovered his prestige; but the fact that the movement survived the fiasco of 1867 is a tribute to the thoroughness with which he had laid the foundations. In America, in Ireland, and among the Irish in Great Britain, it remained a powerful political force, a rival and a spur to constitutional nationalism, and even, on occasion, its ally.

The influence of Fenianism on British opinion was, perhaps, hardly less important than its influence in Ireland. And this influence was more powerful than any that had been exercised by repealers or Young Irelanders, for the establishment since the famine of large Irish colonies in Great Britain made it easy for the Fenians to carry their hostilities into England itself. In 1866 they planned an attack on Chester Castle, which was frustrated only at the last moment; in September 1867 they rescued two Fenian prisoners in Manchester, killing a policeman in the process; in the following December an attempt to rescue another prisoner, at Clerkenwell, involved an explosion in which more than twenty people were killed. The immediate effect of these activities was to arouse a wave of anti-Irish fury; but, when this had subsided, public opinion was more ready than before to recognize that there must be something radically unhealthy in the political condition of Ireland, and to accept the view that the British government and British parliament could not escape responsibility for finding and applying a remedy. It is an error to suppose that it was Fenianism that first turned Gladstone's mind to Ireland; but it was Fenianism that disposed the British public to accept the remedial measures that he was shortly to put forward.

(4)

Apart altogether from the alarm caused by the Fenian disturbances, there was little in the condition of Ireland, social or economic, to justify complacency on the part of the government. The agricultural recovery of the years immediately after the famine was not maintained, and a series of bad harvests in the early 1860s caused widespread distress. As one land bill after another was defeated or abandoned, the farmers became more restive; and while the tenant-right movement lost its early prestige, agrarian secret societies flourished. The area under tillage continued to decline steadily; and between 1860 and 1870 it fell by 400,000 acres. There was, of course, a corresponding increase in livestock; and during the same period the export of cattle rose by about 50 per cent and that of sheep by about 75 per cent. But though this trade brought prosperity to the grazier and the cattle-dealer, the small farmer, who could make ends meet only by raising crops, was being forced out; and the agricultural labourer was being deprived of employment. A similar transformation was taking place in British agriculture also; but in Britain there were expanding manufactures to absorb labour thus displaced, while the Irish country-man, if he could not make a living on the land, had no resource but to emigrate. It was among small-holders and labourers that Fenianism made most headway in the rural areas.

The north-east provided a partial exception to these general conditions. In Ulster, as elsewhere, tillage was giving way to pasture; but a con-siderable proportion of the redundant rural population found employ-ment in the industrial area of the Lagan valley, and especially in Belfast. Here, as in Great Britain, manufacture was expanding. During the 1850s the linen industry suffered one of its periodical depressions; but the 'cotton famine' created by the civil war in America made it more pros-perous than ever. Between 1862 and 1864 the value of linen exports rose from £6¼ millions to £10¼ millions, and there was a rapid increase in the use of power-driven machinery. The demand for more machines en-couraged the expansion of the Belfast engineering industry, and this, in turn, contributed to the development of ship-building. By the 1860s, Belfast was not only the most prosperous and most rapidly-growing town in Ireland; it was also on the way to becoming one of the major industrial centres of the British Isles.

The economy of the north-east, based on textiles, engineering and ship-building, was closely assimilated to that of industrial Britain, and it benefited from the fiscal policy of the free-trade era. But for the rest of Ireland that policy was of very doubtful advantage. Manufactures, with the notable exceptions of brewing and distilling, continued to decline; and agricultural products had to face increasing foreign competition in the British market, and even in Ireland itself. It was, of course, true that cheap food and cheap manufactured goods brought some improvement in the standard of living. By the end of the century, all but the poorest families in the poorest districts of the west were much better-clothed, enjoyed a more varied diet, and had a far greater prospect of improvement than had been general before the famine. But, even then, Ireland lagged far behind Great Britain in this respect, and in the 1850s and 1860s the difference was still more marked. Yet it was in the 1850s, when the country might seem least able to bear it, that Irish taxation was suddenly and substantially increased.

The act of union had provided that, even after the exchequers of the two countries had been united, Ireland might be taxed more lightly than Great Britain, if the condition of the country seemed to warrant the distinction; and down to 1853 Ireland did, in fact, receive preferential treatment. But in that year Gladstone, then chancellor of the exchequer, extended income-tax to Ireland for the first time, and also increased the spirit duty, which was levied at a lower rate than in Great Britain. The policy of bringing Irish taxation into line with British was continued by Gladstone in his budgets of 1854 and 1855, and by Disraeli in his budget of 1858; and by the end of the decade Ireland had virtually lost the preference she had enjoyed during the first half-century of the union. In expounding the new fiscal policy towards Ireland in 1853, Gladstone had argued that the increase in the spirit duty was perfectly reasonable; that income-tax (which, in any case, he hoped to see abolished by 1859) would affect only the well-to-do; and that Ireland was being compensated by remission of debts accumulated on relief-works during the famine. But the net result was that Irish taxation rose by some £2,000,000 a year,[1] at a time when the only hope for the national economy was the investment of more private capital.

[1] The effect of the increase can be seen in the rate of taxation per head. In Great Britain, this rose from £2 7s. 8d. in 1850 to £2 10s. in 1860; in Ireland, during the same period, from 13s. 11d. to £2 5s. 4d. The Irish rate of increase was, however, exaggerated by the contemporary decline in population.

Though this change in fiscal policy aroused some protest from Irish members, their arguments went unheeded. British opinion was not disposed to pay much attention to Ireland; the country seemed reasonably quiet; and most of those who thought at all about Irish problems hoped that the continuing emigration would eventually solve them. Parliament and press found enough to occupy them in the Crimean War, in the Indian Mutiny, in the Italian question, and in the American civil war, with its repercussions on Anglo-American relations and on the Lancashire cotton industry. In the 1850s and early 1860s Ireland fell into the background; and the British public was surprised as well as indignant at the Fenian attempt to apply in Ireland those nationalist principles that it had so long and so loudly advocated for the Italians.

(5)

It might at first sight appear ironical that Gladstone, who was to devote so much of his later life to remedying Irish grievances, should have been responsible for increasing Irish taxation. But in 1853 his only concern had been to make a convenient financial adjustment in a manner that he considered fair to both countries; the time had not yet come for him to put Ireland in the forefront of his policy. And yet Ireland was already in his mind as a major problem; as early as 1845 he had seen the state of the country as the result of 'cruel, inveterate, and but half-atoned injustice' on the part of Great Britain, and he had even felt some sort of personal responsibility for helping to put things right. If he allowed more than twenty years to pass before he set about the task, he had developed his ideas during the interval; and by the 1860s he had in mind at least the outline of an Irish policy, based on disestablishment of the church and reform of the land system. Excitement over Fenian activities did much to prepare the British public to accept these measures, and they have often been regarded as hasty concessions exacted by fear; but, so far as their principal author was concerned, they were the logical outcome of convictions long held and deeply considered.[1]

Gladstone's choice of disestablishment as his first line of advance was dictated by circumstances. The very existence of the church establishment was a long-standing grievance among Roman Catholics and, though to a

[1] Isaac Butt, in a pamphlet published in 1870, attributed to Gladstone the statement that Fenianism was 'the justification and cause' of his Irish policy; in Gladstone's own copy of the pamphlet there is an emphatic 'no' in the margin at this point.

less extent, among presbyterians also. With the settlement of the 'tithe war' in the 1830s the question had fallen temporarily into the background; and the government's firm refusal to give the established church any privileged position either in the national schools or in the Queen's Colleges had tended to keep it there. In the 1850s, however, it revived; partly as a reaction against the exclusive claims embodied in the ecclesiastical titles act of 1851; partly because the Roman Catholic bishops were increasingly alarmed at missionary activity by some of the established clergy, which, especially in Connaught, had considerable, if temporary, success. But the real turning-point was the census of 1861, which provided, for the first time, reliable figures of denominational distribution. Out of a population of five and three quarter millions the Roman Catholics numbered four and a half millions, the members of the established church under 700,000, of whom well over half were concentrated in the province of Ulster: in Leinster they comprised only eleven per cent of the population, in Munster, five per cent, in Connaught, four per cent. These figures did not, of course, affect the defence of the establishment on grounds of principle, the grounds on which Gladstone himself had defended it in early life; but they provided useful ammunition for those already opposed to it, and helped to persuade those who took a detached or utilitarian view that the existing position was unreasonable.

Even so, the church question would hardly have come to a crisis when it did, but for the state of British politics. By 1845 Gladstone had already decided that he could no longer defend the establishment in principle; but it was not until 1865 that he stated his position publicly in parliament (a confession that contributed to his defeat at Oxford in the ensuing general election); and even then he did not think the time ripe for action: in the same year he wrote to a friend that the Irish church question was 'remote and apparently out of all bearing on the practical politics of the day'. Two years later, he had changed his mind, and before the end of 1867 he was putting forward the state of the Irish church as one of the most urgent problems facing parliament and the country. The explanation is to be found in the course of British politics during the interval. Palmerston had died; Russell's ministry had been split over the extension of the parliamentary franchise; the conservatives had come into office; Disraeli had 'educated' his party into accepting the second reform act; and now Gladstone, about to succeed Russell in the leadership of the liberals, had to find a line of attack that would unite all sections of the party, that would take the government at a disadvantage, and that would be likely to arouse popular support. Fenianism had turned public attention to Ireland; and of all the Irish questions that of the established church offered Gladstone the fairest prospects of victory. In March 1868 he took advantage of a motion on the state of Ireland, brought forward by an Irish member, to declare that the time had come when the connection between the Irish church and the state should be severed; and a few days later he gave notice of three resolutions embodying formal proposals for its disestablishment.

It seemed at first as if Gladstone might have miscalculated the temper of his party: 'Mr Gladstone's propositions', wrote Disraeli to the queen, 'were received with loud cheering by all those below the gangway: that is, by those whom we describe as radicals, Romanists, and especially voluntaries: but the great bulk of the gentlemen behind him, on well-filled benches, were cold and silent. These were the whigs.' When it came to a vote, however, Gladstone's judgement was shown to have been sound: on 3 April he carried by a majority of 56 a motion that the house should go into committee on the resolutions; and the resolutions themselves were subsequently carried by even larger majorities. Disraeli decided to appeal to the country; and in November[1] a general election, fought specifically on the church question, gave a majority of 112 in favour of disestablishment. Without waiting for the meeting of the new parliament, the government resigned, and Gladstone became prime minister. 'My mission is to pacify Ireland' was his first comment on receiving the expected summons from the queen; and it was to this task, above all others, that he devoted the next two years. The church act of 1869 was his own work in almost every detail; and though the land act of the following year owed a good deal to the advice of others, he alone could have carried such a revolutionary measure through parliament.

When, in December 1868, Gladstone set about framing his Irish church bill he had to face problems towards whose solution precedent offered little assistance. 'Disestablishment' had long been talked of, but no one had given much thought to its precise meaning in terms of legislative enactment; and though history could furnish examples of ecclesiastical institutions being violently overthrown, these had little relevance to Gladstone's purpose, which was the orderly separation of the age-old bonds between church and state, and the confiscation and redistribution of ecclesiastical property, with due regard both for individual rights and for the public interest. Even in the most peaceful political conditions the task would have been a formidable one. But Gladstone, in the aftermath of a bitterly-fought election, had to devise a measure that would at once

---

[1] The election was delayed by the necessity for completing arrangements consequent upon the extension of the parliamentary franchise in 1867.

satisfy all sections of his own party, leave the conservatives no vantage-ground for attack, and disarm in advance, as far as might be possible, the inevitable hostility of the house of lords. And he had little room for manoeuvre: 'Our mode of warfare', he wrote in December 1868, 'cannot but be influenced by the troops we lead. Our three *corps d'armée*, I may almost say, have been Scotch presbyterians, English and Welsh non-conformists, and Irish Roman Catholics.' But by the end of February 1869 his bill was ready, and on 1 March he introduced it in the house of commons.

Conservative opposition was loud and bitter; but the government majority in the commons was too strong to be shaken, and the bill passed its third reading on 31 May. The real struggle was in the lords, where the supporters of the bill seemed at first to be hopelessly outnumbered. But the conservative leaders feared the effect of a clash between the two houses, almost immediately after a wide extension of the franchise, over an issue on which the electorate had expressed a decisive opinion; and they were reluctant to risk so much for the sake of the Irish church. The queen shared their fears: much as she disliked the bill, mainly because it would deprive the crown of patronage, she used all her influence in favour of a settlement; and by the end of July the lords had been induced to accept the bill at the price of some trifling financial concessions to the Irish clergy.

From a constitutional point of view, the main effect of the Irish church act of 1869 was to sever completely the legal connection between church and state in Ireland — a breach of the act of union that some extreme opponents of the measure declared to be beyond the competence of parliament. As from 1 January 1871, the Church of Ireland would become a voluntary body; its ecclesiastical law, no longer part of the law of the land, would have merely contractual force; and its courts would cease to exercise coercive jurisdiction. But these provisions (though in fact they embodied the essence of disestablishment) attracted much less attention than those relating to ecclesiastical property. The public, indeed, was hardly concerned at all about disestablishment in the strictly legal sense, but only about the disendowment that was universally regarded as its necessary corollary. The property of the church consisted almost entirely of lands, buildings and tithe, the total value of which had been estimated by a royal commission, in 1867, at over £600,000 a year. All this property, except for churches and churchyards actually in use, was now to be confiscated, and vested in a body of 'commissioners for Irish church temporalities'. The commissioners were to provide for the life interests of clergy, schoolmasters and other ecclesiastical officials of the disestablished church; to make similar provision for presbyterian ministers in receipt of *regium donum*; to pay a lump sum to Maynooth in lieu of the annual grant;[1] and to compensate owners of advowsons for their loss of patronage. The remaining property was to be administered by the commissioners, and applied, under parliamentary direction, for the benefit of the people of Ireland, and especially for the relief of poverty; but none of it was to be used for the endowment of any form of religion.

The provisions of the act relating to clerical compensation were so framed as not only to secure individual interests but also to facilitate the reorganization of the disestablished church. The life-annuities to which the clergy were entitled might, with their consent, be commuted for a capital sum; this sum, together with a bonus to cover the cost of administration, would then be paid to a representative church body, provided for in the act, and this body would thenceforward be responsible for paying the clergy. The church took advantage of this scheme, which helped to strengthen its central authority; and though the sum paid by the commissioners did not constitute a permanent endowment, since it was so calculated that payment of the annuities should exhaust both principal and interest, it did provide the basis of a permanent financial system: the original capital was gradually paid out to the annuitants, but the amounts so paid were replaced by voluntary contributions from church members. Gladstone's disestablishment and disendowment of the Irish church exposed him to bitter abuse from churchmen both in Ireland and in England; but the process could hardly have been carried through with a more scrupulous regard for the interests both of individuals and of the church as a whole.

Though the Church of Ireland was, before disestablishment, a very wealthy body, almost the whole of its annual revenue was represented by the incomes of bishops, cathedral and parochial clergy, and various ecclesiastical officials. Inevitably, therefore, the buying out of life interests absorbed a large proportion of the confiscated property, and amounted in all to about £10 millions. The commutation of the Maynooth grant and of the *regium donum*, and the compensation to owners of advowsons, also paid out of church property, came to about £2 millions more. To make these payments, the commissioners of church temporalities had to find a large capital sum; they were able to raise part of it by the sale of property, but a great part had to be borrowed; and interest on the loans amounted eventually to over £4 millions. In all, then, the compensation paid under

---

[1] Both *regium donum* and the Maynooth grant had been charges on the exchequer of the United Kingdom. The payment of compensation from church funds was therefore a direct relief to the tax-payer, and was a deviation from the general principles of the act.

the act cost some £16 millions, and this probably represented more than half the capital value of the confiscated property. The remainder provided a fund to be used for the public benefit, and between 1871 and 1923 about £13 millions were applied to the relief of poverty, the encouragement of agriculture and fisheries, and the endowment of higher education.

These provisions relating to disestablishment, disendowment and compensation embodied the main purpose of the act. But it contained also provisions relating to landed property which, though merely incidental, were of great significance for the future. Tenants on church lands were to be given the option of buying their holdings, leaving three-quarters of the purchase money on mortgage at four per cent; and by 1880 over 6,000 tenants, out of some 8,400, had taken advantage of this opportunity. Thus, a beginning had been made with the policy of land purchase, which was eventually to provide at least a partial solution to the land question.

It was mainly as a symbol that the church act appealed to Irish popular opinion. To the great majority of the people it made little practical difference and brought no material advantage; disendowment did not mean that tithe was abolished, only that it was now paid to the state instead of to the clergy.[1] But as a symbol the act was very important; for it showed that the influence of the old protestant ascendancy, which had hitherto played such a large part in moulding government policy towards Ireland, was now in decline. This view of the significance of the act is confirmed by Gladstone's own attitude to it. In a memorandum presented to the queen in January 1869 he traced the history of the Irish church question, and explained the principle on which the government based its proposed measure:

'Only now, by a long, slow and painful process, have we arrived at the conclusion that Ireland is to be dealt with in all respects as a free country, and is to be governed like every other free country according to the sentiments of its majority and not of its minority; in subordination only to the general laws necessary for the three kingdoms as a whole.'

In 1869 he did not yet realize how far this principle was to carry him; but it was clear that the Irish church act was no more than the first step on the way.

(6)

The Irish policy that Gladstone put before the electorate in 1868 included land reform as well as disestablishment; and the church act had

---

[1] By subsequent legislation, the owner or occupier of land liable to tithe might redeem the annual charge by a capital payment.

hardly been passed before he turned his mind to this second problem. From September 1869 onwards he was busily collecting information, not only from Ireland but from the continent, on which to base a measure regulating relations between landlord and tenant. This relationship obviously lay at the root of the problem; and Gladstone set himself, in the first place, to understand as clearly as possible the actual state of affairs in Ireland, and then to consider how it might be modified by statute so as to meet the grievances of the tenantry. He got little help from his colleagues in the cabinet, some of whom were hostile and some indifferent. Bright was sympathetic; but he was too much attached to his own proposal that the state should buy out the Irish landlords to take an interest in any alternative scheme; and the only cabinet minister to whom Gladstone could confidently turn for assistance and support was Fortescue, the Irish chief secretary. It was Fortescue who put forward, in November 1869, a double proposal which was to become the core of the bill: that the Ulster custom should be protected by law, and that a tenant not enjoying the benefit of custom should be entitled, if evicted, to compensation from the landlord for 'disturbance'. Gladstone was convinced that this would meet the needs of the case: on all hands he was assured that the great demand of the tenants was for security; and here, he felt, was a means of establishing security without any startling infringement of the landlord's rights. For the next three months he elaborated and modified Fortescue's scheme; and on 15 February 1870 laid his land bill before the house of commons.

Well aware that his proposed reforms, which the cabinet had accepted with reluctance, were almost certain to arouse opposition among the whole landed interest, and perhaps also among the stricter disciples of *laissez-faire*, Gladstone had framed the bill very cautiously; and his speech in presenting it to the commons played down its revolutionary character: 'No one else in the country', Lord Dufferin, who heard the speech, afterwards assured him, 'could have recommended the provisions of such a bill ... with a slighter shock to the prejudices of the class whose interests are chiefly concerned'. So skilful was his management that the parliamentary struggle, even in the lords, turned mainly on points of detail; and the bill went through all its stages substantially unchanged. In achieving this success Gladstone was aided by circumstances. The influences likely to impede the bill were powerful: traditional respect for property, faith in free contract, alarm lest experiments in Ireland should be repeated in Britain — 'The fear that our land bill may cross the water', Gladstone wrote in April 1870, 'creates a sensitive state of mind among all tories, many whigs, and a few radicals'. But these influences were, for the

time being, outweighed by the conviction that something must be done
to pacify Ireland, and that nothing short of land reform could do it. Lord
Dufferin may have exaggerated when he wrote gloomily, in November
1869, that 'the great mass of the English people would sacrifice the Irish
landlords to-morrow, if they thought that by so doing they could tempt
the Irish populace into acquiescence in their rule'; but there can be no
doubt that the hope of countering Fenian influence by land reform made
parliament readier than it would otherwise have been to accept the act of
1870.

The most important provisions of the act were those relating to security
of tenure and compensation for improvements. The Ulster custom, and
other similar customs, were to be established by law wherever they already
existed. A tenant not enjoying the benefit of custom was to be protected
in two ways. First, his right to compensation for improvements, on giving
up his holding, was made more extensive than it had been under the act
of 1860; and whereas hitherto all improvements had been deemed the
work of the landlord, unless the tenant could establish the contrary, this
general presumption was now to be reversed, and the onus of proof was
to rest on the landlord. Secondly, if evicted, he was to be compensated by
the landlord for 'disturbance'—the amount of compensation, varying in-
versely with the value of the holding, to range from one to seven years' rent,
with a maximum payment of £250. A tenant evicted for non-payment of
rent was not to be entitled to compensation for disturbance, but if the
annual valuation of his holding did not exceed £25 the court might, in
special circumstances, order payment to be made. A lease-holder for a term
of thirty-one years or more was not to be entitled to compensation for
disturbance if his lease were not renewed, nor to compensation for
improvements other than permanent buildings.

As a concession to Bright, the act also included some provision for
land purchase. A tenant who purchased his holding might borrow up to
two-thirds of the price, on approved security, from the commissioners of
public works, and pay off both capital and interest in thirty-five years, at
the rate of £5 a year for every £100 borrowed.

The act failed, at almost every point, to achieve the purpose for which
it was intended. Even the legalization of the Ulster custom, in appearance
a very substantial concession, added little to the real security of the
tenant. So far from attempting to define either the custom itself, or
the areas within which it applied, the act referred in general terms to the
'usages' prevalent in the province of Ulster and elsewhere; and left it to
the courts to decide each particular case on its merits. A tenant claiming
at law benefit of custom had therefore to prove, in the first place, that his

tenancy was subject to custom, and, in the second place, that the rights he was seeking to establish were included in the custom under which he held. For more than twenty years many Ulster landlords had been trying, with some success, to minimize the force of the custom on their own estates, and, in particular, to limit the tenant's freedom of sale. Under the act of 1870 the courts were entitled, and indeed likely, to accept these restrictions as part of the custom on the estates where they had been enforced; and the tenant might find that what he had considered an infringement of long-established right was now confirmed by law. In the other three provinces custom had far less force. There is evidence to show that by 1870 a custom analogous to that of Ulster had spread fairly widely, and that in some areas it was actually gaining ground; but it lacked the long Ulster tradition of general acceptance by the landlords, and a tenant faced with the task of establishing his claim in a court of law found himself in a very vulnerable position. It was, in fact, a serious weakness in the measure as a whole that it left so much to be decided by the courts; the consequent litigation was expensive and vexatious to landlords and tenants alike, but it was the tenants who suffered most.

The provisions relating to custom affected only a minority of the 600,000 Irish tenant-farmers. It was the attempt to do something for the great mass of yearly tenants unprotected by any kind of recognized custom that formed the most important element in the act of 1870. The sections relating to compensation for improvements marked a great advance on earlier legislation. Their usefulness was somewhat weakened by the complicated nature of the arrangements for claiming and assessing compensation; but the general effect was to strengthen the tenant's position, especially by the presumption that all improvements were his work. The attempt to establish security of tenure was much less successful. Gladstone believed that the obligation to pay an evicted tenant not only compensation for his improvements but also compensation for disturbance would be sufficient to restrain the landlords. His object, he told Manning, was 'to prevent the landlord from using the terrible weapon of undue and unjust eviction, by so framing the handle that it shall cut his hands with the sharp edge of pecuniary damages ... Wanton eviction will, I hope, be extinguished by provisions like these'. This optimistic forecast was not fulfilled; partly because the 'pecuniary damages' proved an insufficient restraint; partly because, in the intense competition for land, a new tenant was often willing to reimburse the landlord for the expense of getting rid of the old; but above all because the landlord's power to increase the rent was untouched. And so long as the landlord could increase the rent at will, the tenant could never be secure;

for once he fell into arrears he virtually lost the protection afforded by the act.

By excluding leaseholders for a term of thirty-one years or more from the right to compensation for disturbance, Gladstone hoped to encourage the landlords to grant long leases; for he believed that if they did so the main grievances of the tenants would be met. But this belief, which was widely held in England, and not unknown even in Ireland, arose from an imperfect understanding of Irish rural conditions. The tenant-farmer, whatever might be his actual position, was convinced that he had a natural right to continue in occupation of his holding, subject only to payment of a rent; and a lease for any fixed term seemed to him a limitation upon this right. The kind of security that he wanted was not the temporary security of a lease, but the permanent security that could come only from the recognition of his co-ownership of the soil. Bright's strong advocacy of land-purchase showed that he understood this aspect of the agrarian problem more clearly than Gladstone. But the 'Bright clauses' in the act of 1870 accomplished very little: the landlords in general were not willing to sell; few tenants could raise the necessary one-third of the purchase-money; the transfer of landed property in small parcels was a complicated and costly legal process, which the act failed to simplify, and this was a deterrent to landlord and tenant alike. In the end only 877 tenants bought their holdings under this act.[1]

Though its practical results fell so far short of its purpose, the land act of 1870 marked a decisive advance towards a solution of the agrarian problem. The advance was very cautiously made, and Gladstone himself does not seem to have realized the full significance of what he was doing; but the principles of *laissez-faire* and free contract were, in fact, abandoned; and the state accepted the duty of regulating relations between landlord and tenant. The establishment of customary tenures on a legal basis might, perhaps, be regarded as no more than formal acceptance of an existing state of affairs. But compensation for disturbance meant, though Gladstone was very reluctant to admit it, the introduction of a new principle: implicit in it was the notion that the tenant had an interest in his holding independent of the expressed terms of his tenancy and distinct from the value of his improvements. And once this had been accepted, the whole landlord position, as it had stood for centuries, was fatally undermined. The revolution that was to be accomplished in the land act of

---

[1] The much greater success of the provision for land purchase in the Irish church act of 1869 (above, p. 369) may be attributed mainly to two facts: the commissioners were anxious to sell, and the terms offered were more favourable.

1881 simply extended a principle that was already present in the act of 1870.

There was another way also, in which the act of 1870 was significant for the future. Queen Victoria put her finger on it at once. After reading a draft of the bill, in January 1870, she wrote to Gladstone:

'The only thing the Queen would wish to remark is, the apparent want of sympathy with the landlords. It does not seem to her quite fair to impute to the landlord class the *entire* blame for the present state of things, and, as regards the tenant, it is scarcely right or expedient, she thinks, however real the grievance may, in many *instances*, be of which he complains, that he should be led to believe that the means by which he seeks redress for himself, are either excused or condoned.'

Though the passage of which the queen explicitly complained was in the preamble, and though she expressed the opinion that the measure itself was 'founded on the right principle', the whole tenor of the act did, in fact, bear out her objection. Its purpose was to settle relations between land-lord and tenant on an equitable basis; and since the intended effect of every proposed change was to limit the power of the landlords, it was impossible to overlook the implicit assumption that they, and they alone, were res-ponsible for every evil in the situation. It would hardly be surprising if the tenants should read into this a justification of agrarian outrage, or should feel that the government might be frightened into weakening the landlords still further.

(7)

The conciliatory policy to which Gladstone had committed himself did not produce in Ireland the effects for which he had hoped. The church act was popular with the great majority of the people, but it made no practical change in their condition. The land act, though much more important, fell so far short of the programme put forward, twenty years earlier, by the Irish Tenant League, that it could hardly fail to cause dis-appointment. In March 1870 Gladstone received, through Manning, a memorandum from the Irish bishops, setting out the view that nothing would satisfy the country save perpetuity of tenure. The continuation of agrarian disorder was an ominous indication that the bishops were right; and in the course of the spring, while the land bill was still under discus-sion, Gladstone felt obliged to pass a coercion act, in the hope of restoring order. Despite this, he still pinned his faith to conciliation, and at the end of the year persuaded a reluctant cabinet to approve the release of the Fenian prisoners. It was a well-meant gesture, but it produced little effect.

The church act and the land act were the first-fruits of Gladstone's resolve that Ireland should be governed according to Irish ideas; but they failed to convince the majority of Irishmen that their interests could safely be entrusted to a British parliament. 'Government of Ireland according to Irish ideas' had for them a very different interpretation, which Gladstone was not to accept for another fifteen years.

XIX

The Beginnings of the Home Rule Movement

---

(1)

Even during the period of apparent political stagnation that followed the break-up of the tenant-right party in the 1850s a few constitutional nationalists still kept alive, in the press and on the platform, the demand for Irish self-government; but they had neither party nor programme, and they attracted little popular support. The revival of the Italian question in 1859–60 helped to stimulate their activity: a petition, said to have been signed by half-a-million Irishmen, was presented to the queen, praying that the right of self-determination, which the government was so willing to recognize in Italy, should be extended to Ireland. The petition produced no result; and, rather paradoxically, some of those who helped to organize it were very active, about the same time, in support of an Irish Brigade, formed to defend the papal territories against the Italian nationalists. But this military adventure, though it did little for the pope, contributed something to the spread of national self-consciousness in Ireland. The growing activity of Fenianism had a far more important influence. Constitutional nationalists, though they distrusted its aims and detested its methods, were gradually forced into a cautious attitude towards it by the fear of seeming to support the British government against patriotic Irishmen. After the arrests of 1865 this fear grew stronger; and a demand for the release of the Fenian prisoners was almost automatically included in the programme of every popular politician. An Amnesty Association, founded by Isaac Butt in 1868, played an important part in preparing the way for a new, organized, nationalist movement.

Butt, the son of a Church of Ireland clergyman, was a prominent barrister who had started his political career as a conservative, and had first made his mark in public in a debate with O'Connell over repeal; he remained a conservative to the end of his life, and though he changed his mind about Anglo-Irish relations, it is not unreasonable to argue that he did so on conservative principles. His experience in parliament, where he sat from 1852 to 1865 as member first for Harwich and then for Youghal, had convinced him that Irish affairs were neglected and mismanaged at Westminster; but it seems to have been contact with the Fenian prisoners of 1865 that produced a decisive change in his outlook. He had not undertaken their defence out of sympathy with their principles; but he could not help recognizing their sincerity, or admitting that the state of the country gave some justification for their actions. At the same time, he remained firmly of opinion that a Fenian revolution would be a disaster; and he came to believe that the surest guarantee against it would be the government of Ireland by her natural rulers — the nobility, the gentry and the substantial middle classes. If they would take the lead, the people would follow; all that was good in Fenianism would be peacefully and safely achieved; and the stability of Ireland, of the constitution, and of the empire would be preserved: 'I have long since had the conviction forced upon me', he declared in 1870, 'that it is equally essential to the safety of England and to the happiness and tranquillity of Ireland, that the right of self-government should be restored to this country'. Not very consistently, perhaps, he put forward the further argument that the future of England was precarious; her power might be destroyed by foreign aggression, or 'broken up by an outbreak of the infidelity and socialism that are spreading throughout her own land'; and the time might come 'when every Irishman would wish that we had in Ireland a parliament and a government which an English revolution could not touch'. With all this in mind, be published in the *Nation*, in November 1869, a proposal for the formation of a united nationalist party.

The idea was not so chimerical as it might seem. Butt was not the only Irish protestant conservative to feel dissatisfied with the way in which the union was working. Many were disgruntled at the disestablishment of the church, and some even maintained that the church act had, *ipso facto*, dissolved the union; more were alarmed at the prospect of a land act. If the British parliament would not protect their interests, they might be better off with a parliament of their own. Despite the recent extension of the franchise, the landlords might still aspire, with an open ballot, to dominate the county constituencies, and middle class influence was still strong in the boroughs. It was not, therefore, altogether surprising that the meeting which Butt organized in Dublin, in May 1870, to consider his proposals, should include a strong protestant and conservative element, made up of clergymen, landlords, and representatives of the professional and business classes. Out of this meeting there developed, a few months later, a Home Government Association, formed to secure the establishment of a federal system, under which an Irish parliament would look after Irish affairs, leaving to the parliament at Westminster, in which Ireland would still be represented, responsibility for 'all questions affecting the imperial crown and government'.

The essential characteristic of the Home Government Association was its concentration on this single object: it had no policy beyond the establishment of an Irish parliament. It was, in principle at least, a non-party organization, and its membership included Roman Catholics and protestants, liberals and conservatives, Orangemen and repealers, survivors of the Young Ireland insurrection, and even a few Fenians. But this wide range could not disguise the fact that the association was a small self-constituted body, without any representative character; and popular opinion was inclined to suspect that it would not have attracted so much landlord support had its policy been genuinely intended for the benefit of the majority. Even apart from this, the very circumstances that had enabled Butt to enlist so many conservatives made the liberals very cautious about joining him. The election of 1868, fought mainly on the church question, had ranged the Roman Catholics solidly behind Gladstone: of some sixty liberal members returned for Irish constituencies all, save a handful from Ulster, were returned by their votes. Though they were disappointed with the terms of the land bill, announced in February 1870, they still looked to Gladstone for further reforms, especially in the field of education; and so long as this hope remained they were hardly likely to desert him for a new policy recommended by protestant landlords, a policy that the *Freeman's Journal* described as an 'insidious attempt made to seduce them from their allegiance to their country and drag them into the mire of toryism'. Within the next few years, however, both the character of Butt's movement and the attitude of Irish liberals towards it were to undergo essential change.

(2)

The Home Government Association had been formed to spread ideas, not to run a parliamentary campaign; but its objects could be achieved only by parliamentary action, and between 1870 and 1873 a series of by-elections was contested by members and friends of the association in support of 'home rule'.[1] The fate of these home rule candidates indicated

---

[1] The term 'home rule' seems to have appeared first in the 1860s; it was not until the 1870s that it passed into common use.

both the weakness and the strength of Butt's policy. It showed very clearly that home rule, by itself, was not enough to attract the voters. Conservatives who stood on the simple programme of the Home Government Association were either defeated or compelled, from lack of support, to withdraw. The successful home rule candidates won their seats not just on home rule, but also on local connection, personal reputation (two of them were old '48 men), and, above all, on their support for other causes with a strong popular appeal. Mitchell Henry, who was returned unopposed for Galway in February 1871, put denominational education and the independence of the pope in the forefront of his programme; Butt won Limerick, in the following September, mainly on the question of tenant-right. The lesson that emerged was that the home rule movement could certainly win elections, but that to do so it must broaden its programme and take in other issues of more immediate interest to the public. By the summer of 1872 this development was effectively, though informally, complete. The Home Government Association continued to exist as a non-party organization; but the six home rulers so far elected to parliament had all committed themselves to support for land reform and for denominational education. For more than a generation to come the home rule movement was to be identified with those causes hardly less closely than with the cause of Irish self-government.

Some such change in the character of the movement had probably been inevitable from the beginning. It was hardly to be expected that the Irish majority, in return for conservative support of home rule, would be prepared to abandon every other demand; if home rule was to become a popular cry it must be linked with other popular cries. But the change put conservative supporters of the movement in an awkward position. They had taken up home rule mainly because they disliked Gladstone's policy, and they were unwilling to see other policies that they liked even less tacked on to it. They complained, not without justice, that the original principles of the Home Government Association had been departed from; and by 1873 the bulk of them had withdrawn their support. Butt's own conduct was not very consistent; for, having launched the home rule cause on a non-party basis, he did more, perhaps, than anyone else to identify it with distinctly party issues. Yet it may well be that the inconsistency was more apparent than real, that in going along with popular opinion on such questions as land and education he felt that he was taking the best course to maintain upper-class leadership, and to preserve Ireland from revolution. Had any considerable body of Irish conservatives followed his lead the history of the next thirty years might have been very different.

Once it had acquired a popular, though informal, programme, the home rule movement made rapid headway; but it was not until the spring of 1873 that the main body of Irish liberals began to turn towards it. Their change of attitude, however, was due less to the character of the home rule programme than to their own disappointment with Gladstone's proposals for higher education, which had been announced in February. There had been a 'university question' in Irish politics ever since the Roman Catholic bishops had declared their opposition to the Queen's Colleges in the 1840s. In 1854 they had set up in Dublin, under papal authority, the Catholic University, with John Henry Newman as its first rector. But it had no endowments; its degrees were not recognized; and the bishops continued to demand that the government should provide, at the public expense, a university system that they could conscientiously accept. During the 1860s, half-hearted attempts had been made to meet their grievances; but these had come to nothing, and they now looked to Gladstone for a final settlement. But the English liberals were very unlikely to abandon the non-sectarian principle on which the Queen's Colleges had been founded, especially at a time when Trinity College, Dublin, was preparing to abolish all religious tests;[1] and Gladstone himself, having just severed the links between church and state in Ireland, was opposed to any form of new state endowment for denominational purposes. His university bill, though it proposed sweeping changes, offered no financial concessions to the bishops. The Queen's University was to be replaced by a new and enlarged University of Dublin, of which Trinity College, the three Queen's Colleges and the Catholic University were to be constituent institutions. But while Trinity College was to retain its endowments, and the Queen's Colleges their annual grants, there was to be no state aid for the Catholic University. From the bishops' point of view, this was a fatal defect; after brief consideration, and contrary to Manning's advice, they declared against it. This settled the fate of the bill. The bulk of Gladstone's Irish followers, under episcopal direction, voted against it; they were joined by some English liberals whose opposition, though on quite other grounds, was equally strong; and it was defeated on the second reading by three votes.

At Westminster, this episode led indirectly to the dissolution of parliament almost a year later. In Ireland, its effects were more immediate. The bishops, with nothing further to hope for from the government, were

---

[1] The abolition of these tests, approved by the college in 1869, was accomplished by statute (Fawcett's act) in 1873. The measure was strongly opposed in parliament by Irish Roman Catholic members.

more inclined to look favourably on home rule. Liberal M.P.s, with the next general election in mind, could not but reflect that support for Gladstone was not now likely to be a popular cry, and that home rule might serve their turn better. In these circumstances, the movement prospered, and its leaders were quick to seize their opportunity. In November, a great conference was held at the Rotunda, the scene of the Volunteer convention in 1783; the Home Government Association was dissolved, and a Home Rule League established in its place. Though the statement of policy adopted by the conference declared emphatically that 'the object, and the only object', of the league was to obtain self-government, the movement in its new phase was dominated by men who took the popular side on all important questions, and (as a conservative journal that had supported Butt's original proposals put it) arranged their policy 'in the significant order of denominational education, land without rent, and home rule'.

The first business of the Home Rule League was to prepare for the coming general election. But the sudden dissolution of parliament, in January 1874, interrupted these preparations before they had well begun; and the election had to be fought with an improvised organization and with such candidates as could be found at short notice. These disadvantages were balanced by other factors: home rule having, as it were, absorbed land and education, there was no alternative popular cause in the field; and the voters were now protected by the ballot act of 1872. Even so, the results were surprising; instead of the thirty seats they had hoped for, the home rulers won fifty-nine. But only two of these seats were in Ulster, in the border county of Cavan: Ulster protestants, as a body, were as strongly opposed to home rule as they had been to repeal.

The importance of this electoral success was greatly increased by the use made of it. Almost immediately after the election the home rule members met in Dublin, adopted resolutions constituting themselves 'a separate and distinct party in the house of commons', appointed an executive council, secretaries and whips, and agreed upon motions and measures to be introduced. 'Thus constituted, marshalled, and organized', wrote one who took part in these proceedings, 'the Irish home rulers took their seats in the imperial parliament' — stronger in numbers and in organization, and with a clearer and more comprehensive policy than any Irish party that had preceded them there.

For more than forty years this party continued, through various changes, to represent the majority of the Irish people at Westminster; but throughout this period it never wholly escaped the effect of a contradiction inherent in its character. Its professed policy was limited autonomy within a federal system, to be established by act of the British parliament; its popular appeal was to national sentiment — the Home Rule Conference of 1873 had set the tone by 'solemnly reasserting the inalienable right of the Irish people to self-government'; and home rule speakers were very apt to base their arguments on this claim of right, rather than on the law of the land. Again, in principle the home rule party was loyal to the crown and constitution; in practice, its favourite rôle was that of the champion of oppressed Ireland against English tyranny, of which the crown was often regarded as the symbol. Parnell was able to control this inner contradiction, and turn it into a source of strength; but it was more commonly a source of weakness. One might almost say that home rulers had the worst of both worlds: their readiness to accept something so much less than national sovereignty made it difficult for more thorough-going nationalists to support them fully; but it did nothing to reconcile the Irish unionists, who were just as ready to condemn federalism as Fenianism, and, indeed, often regarded them merely as variations of the same policy.

(3)

Events soon showed that the home rule party was not so strong as its more enthusiastic supporters had deemed it on the morrow of the general election. Many of the victorious home rule candidates had taken up the cause at the last minute in order to retain their seats, or win entry to parliament; and the Home Rule League lacked the organization necessary to impose an effective discipline. Butt himself proved an indifferent leader. Eloquent and earnest, he could sway a public meeting and inspire affection in his friends; but he lacked the concentrated energy, the single-mindedness of purpose, necessary to mould an embryonic party into an effective political instrument; and constant financial difficulties forced him to give up so much of his time to professional work that he had often to neglect his parliamentary duties. The electoral success of 1874 marked the height of his achievement, after which his influence, slowly at first and then more rapidly, declined.

The parliamentary position in 1874 was not altogether unfavourable to the new party. Had Gladstone's ministry survived, some home rulers would almost certainly have succumbed to the lure of office, and the collapse of 1852 might have been repeated. Had the gap between the two major British parties been narrower, the pressure on the home rule party to form an alliance with the liberals would have been very strong, and its separate identity would have been imperilled. As it was, the conservatives had an absolute majority, too strong to be endangered by any hostile combination; and the home rule party was given time to establish its independent traditions. There was, of course, danger as well as advantage in this situation. The party was not only independent but isolated; and unless it could work out some way of making its weight felt in the house of commons, it might sink into complete ineffectiveness. This was a danger that Butt seemed unable to avert. Despite his dissatisfaction with the way in which parliament had handled Irish affairs in the past, he had enormous respect for its traditions, and a rather naïve faith in its readiness to listen to reason and to be persuaded by argument. Early in the new session, on 30 June 1874, he presented the case for home rule in a powerful speech, which won some applause but no votes. During the next few years he returned to the attack again and again; but neither by oratory nor by argument could he make much impression on the stolid indifference of British M.P.s.

Even these repeated failures did not shake Butt's confidence in the power of peaceful persuasion. There were, however, a few members of his party who were unwilling to accept the continued neglect of Irish demands without attempting some effective protest. They set themselves deliberately to obstruct the business of the house of commons,[1] determined that if neither British party would take home rule seriously, then parliament should be prevented from getting on with the routine work of government and legislation. This policy of 'obstruction', initiated early in 1875 by J. G. Biggar, a Belfast provision-merchant and one of the members for Cavan, was gradually taken up by about half-a-dozen other Irish members, and most notably by Charles Stewart Parnell. Their activities did little or nothing towards converting parliament to a policy of home rule, but they had great influence on the development of the home rule movement itself. Irishmen, at home and abroad, could hardly help contrasting the aggressiveness of Biggar, Parnell, and their associates, with Butt's apparent acquiescence in parliament's continued neglect of Irish claims. The obstructionists soon became popular heroes, and Butt's abortive attempts to restrain them only increased their prestige and undermined his own; though he was still supported by the bulk of the home rule

---

[1] By 'obstruction' was meant the deliberate abuse of the rules of procedure for the purpose of holding up business. This was most easily done in committee, when each member had a right to make repeated motions for reporting progress. It was not until July 1877 that the obstructionists made their technique really effective. Obstruction was not entirely new; but in the past it had been employed only to hold up particular measures about which minority groups felt very strongly.

members, Irish public opinion, increasingly dissatisfied with his leadership, was now turning towards Parnell.

In 1875, when Parnell had been returned at a by-election for Meath, there had been little to suggest that he would quickly attain an influential position. He was a young man, without political experience, and he had none of Butt's easy eloquence or charm of manner; his selection for Meath, indeed, was due less to his personal qualities than to the fact that home rule candidates of any standing in the country were hard to find, and Parnell belonged to a distinguished Anglo-Irish landlord family. It was a family with a strong national tradition — both his grandfather and his great-grandfather had opposed the legislative union — but Parnell's own support for home rule may have owed more to the influence of his American mother, from whom he inherited the strong antipathy to England and the English that marked his whole career. But this anti-English feeling had in it something of the mingled jealousy and contempt with which the colonist is apt to regard the mother-country; Parnell's patriotism was not, at bottom, very different from that of Swift; and though he fought for a popular cause, he never forgot that he was an Anglo-Irish gentleman.

Parnell had in large measure the love of power that is perhaps inseparable from political genius. At least as early as 1877 he already had his eye on the leadership of the home rule party; and in taking up Biggar's obstructionist policy, and in expressing, even in parliament, his sympathy with Fenianism, he was deliberately seeking popular support. His aggressive attitude and his open contempt for English opinion made an immediate impression on the Irish in Great Britain, who were too much under Fenian influence to be satisfied with Butt's more gentlemanly methods. Since 1873, they had been organized in the Home Rule Confederation of Great Britain, of which Butt, as the acknowledged leader of the movement, had hitherto been president. It was Parnell's election in his place, in September 1877, that marked the first important stage in the transfer of power from one to the other. Parnell, however, moved very cautiously. He was now the accepted leader of the small obstructionist group; but the majority of the home rule members still adhered to Butt, and Parnell saw the danger of forcing a premature trial of strength. At home rule conferences, held in Dublin in January 1878 and February 1879, he made no attempt to assert his claims, and Butt was allowed to retain the formal leadership. But during these years Parnell's influence was steadily growing, and 1879 was to mark a decisive turning-point both in his own fortunes and in those of the home rule movement.

Two factors contributed to this development: a change of attitude among the Fenians, and the impact of agricultural depression on rural Ireland. Many Fenians had been impressed by the forceful character of Parnell's parliamentary obstructionism; some of their leaders, especially in the United States, began to think that a constitutional movement, under his leadership, might be worth supporting; and in 1878 John Devoy, one of the most prominent figures in American Fenianism, helped to draw up conditions on which such support might be given. One of these conditions, and in some ways the most significant, was that the parliamentary party should agitate vigorously for a settlement of the land question 'on the basis of a peasant proprietary'. This implicit suggestion that the constitutional and revolutionary wings of the national movement should combine to support the peasantry in its age-long struggle with the landlords came at a very opportune time. During the later 1870s economic depression in Britain, and the increasing competition of imported foodstuffs, had forced down agricultural prices, while rents remained unchanged; and a series of bad seasons, culminating in that of 1879, had brought matters to a crisis. Even in England, the position of the tenant-farmers was becoming precarious; in Ireland, they were threatened with absolute ruin. Thousands of them fell into arrears with their rent, thus losing the meagre protection afforded by 'disturbance money' under the act of 1870; and the number of evictions rose sharply. The tenants themselves were not the only sufferers; many of them had borrowed on the security of their 'disturbance money', and with this security gone, their creditors had no means of recovering their loans. The whole economy of rural Ireland seemed to be in danger of collapse; and Disraeli's government, deeply immersed in foreign affairs, could do nothing more effective than appoint a commission of inquiry. Thus the way was left open for the establishment of a national movement, linked closely to the immediate economic interests of the majority of the population.

The man who saw and seized this opportunity was Michael Davitt. When he was only four years old, his family had been forcibly evicted from its County Mayo holding, and had removed to Lancashire, where he was brought up. This early experience left him with a lasting hatred of the landlord system; and it was a desire for social justice, as much as doctrinaire nationalism, that led him to join the Fenians. A long spell in prison (1870–7) did nothing to shake his resolution; and a couple of years after his release he was back in Ireland, determined to bring the land question into the centre of Irish politics. During the summer of 1879 he had informal negotiations with Parnell and with John Devoy; the details of the transaction are obscure, but some sort of working agreement was reached; and from this time onwards both the parliamentary party and the

N

land agitation received considerable Fenian support, both moral and financial. This informal alliance, often called 'the new departure',[1] acquired fresh importance with the establishment by Davitt of a new agrarian organization, the Land League, in October 1879. At Davitt's invitation Parnell became president of the league; and an open connection was thus established between the land movement, in its new phase, and the most active section of the parliamentary party. Parnell had hesitated about accepting the presidency, partly because he feared that the aggressive character of the league might result in open defiance of the law, partly because he disliked Davitt's advocacy of land nationalization. But if he were to achieve the leadership at which he aimed, he could not allow the league to develop in complete independence of the home rule movement; and as president he might be able to exercise some control over its activities.

Earlier in 1879 one obstacle had been removed from Parnell's path: Isaac Butt had died in May. He had by that time lost effective control of the movement he had founded and of which he was still the nominal leader; and his career had closed amid wranglings and disappointments. Yet his contribution to the development of modern Ireland was much greater than might at first appear; for his policy of home rule, though it was ultimately to be rejected, played a vital part in the political education of the Irish people. Butt's death did not immediately open the leadership to Parnell. The bulk of the parliamentary party still regarded him as dangerous and irresponsible, and elected as chairman William Shaw, a protestant banker from Cork. But Shaw, a rather colourless politician, and more of a liberal than a determined home ruler, could do little to pull the party together. Parnell's influence in the country was growing all the time, and it was clear that he and his adherents now had a very wide measure of popular support. Their chance to show their strength came with the dissolution of parliament in March 1880. In the general election that followed, 61 home rule candidates were returned, many of them new men who owed their success mainly to Parnell's backing; and when the newly-elected members held a meeting in the Dublin City Hall, in May, to elect a party chairman, Parnell defeated Shaw by 23 votes to 18. This result led to a split in the party: the majority of those who had voted against Parnell refused to serve under him, and they were joined by some

[1] In October 1878, when the possibility of Fenian support for Parnell was being publicly discussed in America, the New York *Herald* published an article on the subject under the title 'A new departure in Irish politics'. The term 'new departure' was subsequently applied to the informal co-operation established in 1879.

of the members who had been absent from the meeting. But the dissidents did not form a new party of their own; some remained as independent home rulers, others became merged with the liberals; from May 1880 onwards the only effective 'home rule party' was that led by Parnell.[1] It is at this point that his career as the accredited leader of the Irish nationalist movement really begins.

(4)

The general election of 1880 brought Disraeli's second ministry to an end. Despite the appearance in parliament of a strong home rule party, the ministry had paid little attention to Ireland, and can scarcely be said to have had an Irish policy. It did, however, pass two important educational measures: an intermediate education act in 1878 and a university act in 1879. The act of 1878 did something to encourage secondary education by providing for the payment of government grants to secondary schools. The amount of grant paid to any school depended on the success of its pupils at examinations conducted by a Board of Intermediate Education, set up under the act; and for generations to come secondary education in Ireland was dominated (and, some would say, bedevilled) by these 'intermediate examinations'. The act of 1879 was an attempt to solve the long-standing university question. It provided for the dissolution of the Queen's University, and its replacement by the 'Royal University of Ireland', a purely examining body, empowered to grant degrees to all who passed the necessary examinations, no attendance at any college or institution being required, except for degrees in medicine. The main object of the act was to meet the claims of the Catholic University: its students were now given an opportunity to graduate; and the fellowships attached to the new Royal University were distributed in such a way that the Catholic University itself received an indirect government endowment of some £6,000 a year.[2] Neither of these measures was educationally satisfactory; and no one regarded the Royal University system as a final

---

[1] It is difficult to calculate precisely the numerical strength of this party in May 1880. During the next few years it was increased both by the conversion of former opponents among the home rulers and as a result of by-elections, and rose to between 35 and 40 during the life of this parliament.

[2] There were twenty-nine fellowships, which were distributed among the teaching staffs of certain 'approved colleges'. Of these fellowships, fifteen (each worth £400 a year) were regularly allotted to the Catholic University, which, from 1882 onwards, was known as University College, Dublin.

settlement of the university question, which continued to trouble Irish politics for another thirty years. In 1880, however, educational controversy was over-shadowed by the agrarian crisis; and it was this that provided the first great test of the new ministry's Irish policy.

XX

'The Uncrowned King'

(1)

In April 1880 Gladstone became prime minister for the second time, at the head of a large, enthusiastic and jubilant liberal party; just over five years later, its majority broken by internal disagreement, his government was defeated, and the conservatives returned to power. For Ireland, these were years of almost continuous agitation and coercion; but they were marked also by developments of great significance for the future: the land act of 1881, the firm consolidation of the home rule party, the extension of the franchise.

When Gladstone took office, a royal commission, appointed under his predecessor, was already at work examining the relations between landlord and tenant in Ireland, and the new government appointed another commission, charged with the specific task of investigating the operation of the land act of 1870. Gladstone had intended to postpone further action until these commissions should have reported; but strong pressure from Irish members compelled him to bring in an emergency measure, designed to protect tenants who were in arrears through no fault of their own from being evicted without compensation. Had this measure passed it might have quieted the country by meeting the most urgent grievance of the tenantry; but it was dropped after being defeated in the house of lords; there was an almost immediate increase in agrarian disturbance; and the Land League threw all its energy into a campaign for a much more radical reform. 'Depend upon it', Parnell told a meeting at Ennis, in September 1880, 'the measure of the land bill of next session will be the measure of your activity and energy this winter'; and he went on to advocate the policy that soon came to be known, from the name of its first prominent victim, as 'boycotting'. The organized ostracism of those who offended against the Land League's code proved a much more effective protection to the tenants than the more violent methods of the past, and the number of evictions fell sharply.

This demonstration of power was very alarming to the authorities. Cowper, the lord lieutenant, and Forster, the chief secretary, insisted that though in public the leaders of the Land League always advocated peaceful methods, their influence really depended on the threat of violence, and argued that though agrarian crime had declined, this was simply because no one had the courage to resist the orders of the league. During the autumn of 1880 they pressed hard for a strong measure of coercion as the only means of re-asserting the authority of the government. Very reluctantly, Gladstone gave way; and when the new session opened in January 1881 the cabinet's Irish policy presented the familiar combination of coercion and concession: a bill for the suspension of *habeas corpus* and a bill for the reform of the land system. The coercion bill, though unpalatable to many liberals and stubbornly resisted by Parnell and his followers,[1] was passed in February. It did little to quiet the country; and the bitterness that it aroused went far to negative the conciliatory effect of the land act that followed.

Early in 1881 the two royal commissions produced what Gladstone described as 'a litter of reports'; but beneath all variety of opinion there was a substantial measure of agreement that the power of the landlord must be restrained much more effectively than had been done by the act of 1870. Gladstone accepted this principle whole-heartedly, and the bill that he introduced in April virtually conceded the basic demands of the Land League agitation, popularly known as the 'three Fs': fair rent, to be assessed by arbitration; fixity of tenure, while the rent was paid; freedom for the tenant to sell his right of occupancy at the best market price. This sweeping measure, so much more radical than the unsuccessful bill of the previous year, went through both houses practically unchanged. Many liberals found it hard to swallow, and the duke of Argyll left the ministry in protest, but Gladstone's determination carried the great bulk of the party with him; and the conservative leaders, as in 1869, were afraid to provoke a conflict between the houses by defeating the bill in the lords. More important still, perhaps, was the general conviction that the state of Ireland called for extraordinary measures. When Gladstone, twelve years later, recorded his belief 'that without the Land League the act of 1881 would not now be upon the statute book', he did not mean that the league had changed his own conception of what was desirable, but that its influence on British opinion had made it politically possible for him to carry that conception into effect.

---

[1] It was during a debate on this bill that the Speaker first applied the closure, after the house had been in continuous session for forty-six hours.

Under the terms of the act, land courts were set up empowered to fix a 'judicial rent', on application from either landlord or tenant, and a rent so fixed was to stand for fifteen years; a rent voluntarily agreed on between landlord and tenant 'and registered in court was to stand for the same period. By these provisions, and by recognizing the permanent interest of the tenant in his holding, the act of 1881 established a system of dual ownership, and reduced the landlord to little more than a receiver of rent. This loss of independence made the landlords more ready to co-operate in a policy of land purchase; but the financial assistance offered by the act was insufficient to attract the tenants. The amount to be advanced by the state was increased from two-thirds to three-quarters of the purchase money, to be repaid over thirty-five years; but not many tenants could raise the necessary capital, and only a few hundred holdings were bought under the act.

Gladstone's expectation that these great concessions to the tenantry would be immediately welcomed in Ireland was not fulfilled, except in the province of Ulster. Here the political outlook was dominated by the strong protestant element in the population, and there was little of that hostility to government policy which in other parts of Ireland had been aroused or intensified by the coercion act, and the severity with which Forster enforced it. The agricultural depression had shown Ulster tenants that their customary rights had been very inadequately secured by the act of 1870; and they had campaigned so vigorously for its amendment that even conservative members for Ulster constituencies had felt obliged to support the measure of 1881. This seemed to give the Ulster tenants all that they had asked for; they received it with jubilation; and they made immediate use of the new procedure for adjusting rents. It is symptomatic of their attitude that at a by-election in Tyrone in 1881 a Land League candidate was defeated by a liberal. A few years' experience was to show that the act was by no means perfect; and land agitation in Ulster did not altogether die out. But the possibility, which had existed in 1880, of a firm alliance between the tenants of Ulster and those of the other provinces had practically disappeared.

Outside Ulster, the political situation was so unstable that the success of the act depended on its being supported by Parnell and the Land League; and their attitude was decidely hostile. Parnell himself was in an awkward position. On the one hand, he was threatened by extremist agitators, who would have ignored the act, defied the government, and waged direct war on the landlords — a development that might well destroy his hopes of achieving home rule. On the other hand was the possibility that the act, if generally accepted, might so far conciliate the tenants as to undermine their support for the home rule party. In the circumstances, Parnell played for time. He did not denounce the act completely; but he complained that it did little or nothing for tenants who were already in arrears, and that it excluded lease-holders from any immediate benefit; and he warned the tenants against making use of the new land courts until the league had satisfied itself about their character by a number of test cases. Parnell's attitude was determined by his reading of the political situation; but Forster believed that he was deliberately trying to wreck the act, and that if his influence were removed the tenants would accept it gladly. In October 1881, therefore, Parnell was arrested under the terms of the coercion act and imprisoned at Kilmainham.

The government soon found that it had miscalculated the situation. Parnell's arrest raised still higher his prestige in Ireland, and it strengthened his reputation among the American Fenians; but it did nothing to promote acceptance of the land act. Within a few days of the arrest, the Land League called on the people to withhold all rents until their grievances had been righted; and when the government seized on this 'no rent manifesto' as an occasion for suppressing the league, the only result was a wave of agrarian violence. But this increase in violence was a threat to Parnell as well as to the government; for the delicate combination on which the policy of the 'new departure' depended would be destroyed if the extremists were to get full control of the land agitation. By the spring of 1882 both sides had come to recognize the necessity for compromise, and in April they reached the informal agreement commonly known as the 'Kilmainham treaty': Parnell was to be released, coercion relaxed, the land act amended, and protection given to tenants in arrears; in return, Parnell was to use his influence to calm the country, and to secure general acceptance for the land act in its amended form.

Rather than acquiesce in this reversal of his policy Forster resigned office. By a dramatic coincidence, it was while he was making his explanatory speech in the commons that Parnell re-entered the house, and the speech was interrupted by the triumphant cheers with which the Irish members greeted their leader. But this parliamentary ovation did not represent the true state of affairs, for many of Parnell's allies regarded the 'Kilmainham treaty' as a surrender, even as a selfish surrender, to the government; and in America it was denounced as 'the sale of the Land League'. He might, indeed, have found it hard to maintain the national leadership that he had established in the previous year but that public attention was suddenly distracted by a startling event, an event which, though at first it threatened to drive him out of public life altogether, later enabled him to recover all the prestige that he had lost by coming to terms with the government. On 6 May, Lord Frederick Cavendish, Forster's newly-appointed successor, was murdered in the Phoenix Park, together with T. H. Burke, the under-secretary, who was the real object of the attack. The assassins, members of a band known as 'The Invincibles', had no connection with any organization in which Parnell was involved; but he was so horrified at the crime, and so deeply convinced that it would destroy his political influence, that his first resolve was to retire at once into private life. 'What is the use', he asked Davitt, 'of men striving as we have done . . . if we are to be struck at in this way by unknown men who can commit atrocious deeds of this kind?' It needed the combined persuasion not only of his parliamentary colleagues but of Chamberlain and Gladstone to make him change his mind.

In fact, however, the Phoenix Park murders turned to Parnell's advantage. The obvious sincerity with which he denounced the crime made a good impression in Britain; and in Ireland the whole question of the 'Kilmainham treaty' was completely overshadowed. Besides this, the introduction of a new coercion bill — an almost inevitable result of the murders — gave him an opportunity of opposing government policy in parliament and thus re-establishing his position as the champion of Irish rights. This did not prevent his practical co-operation with the government in making the land act effective, and a general reduction in rents led to a great decline in agrarian disturbance. But popular opinion gave the credit for this to Parnell rather than to the government, and his prestige stood so high that he was able to resist all demands for a revival of the Land League, and to set up instead, in October 1882, a new organization, the National League, which was closely linked to the parliamentary party and was, effectively, under his own control. Davitt declared, many years later, that the Phoenix Park murders saved Parnell from the perils involved in the 'Kilmainham treaty'; but they did more than this, for by the end of the year his position in Ireland was stronger than it had ever been before.

It was, however, only through a strong parliamentary party that Parnell could turn this position to full advantage; and at the end of 1882 the party still lacked effective discipline. But the foundation of the National League marked the beginning of a change; it provided the national political machinery that had hitherto been lacking, and enabled the party leaders to control the choice of candidates. The effect of this control on party discipline was reinforced, from 1884 onwards, by insistence on a 'pledge' by which the candidate bound himself, if elected, to 'sit, act and vote with the Irish parliamentary party', and to resign his seat if the party should decide that he had failed to fulfil this undertaking.

This strengthening of party organization came at a critical moment. The franchise act of 1884 and the redistribution act of 1885 — both of which included Ireland — completely altered the electoral outlook. The establishment of household franchise virtually handed over the counties, outside Ulster, to the home rulers; and most of the smaller boroughs, in which whig or liberal candidates had formerly had some chance of success, now ceased to be separately represented. It was important, also, that the redistribution act took no account of the fact that Ireland now contained a much smaller proportion of the total population of the United Kingdom than in 1800 or 1832, and the number of Irish members was left unchanged. In these circumstances the home rule party could confidently expect a great victory in the next general election; and even before the end of 1884 it was clear that a general election could not be far off.

(2)

During 1884–5 the political situation in Britain seemed to be developing to Parnell's advantage. With their eyes on the approaching general election both liberals and conservatives were increasingly anxious for his support; partly in the hope of gaining the powerful Irish vote in Great Britain, partly because they realized that with the extension of the franchise his following in the house of commons would be greatly enlarged. Parnell was inclined to think that for the time being he could get more out of the conservatives; and it was with his help that they were able to take advantage of disunity among the liberals and defeat the government in June 1885. As the administrative changes required by the franchise and re-distribution acts were not yet complete, a general election had to be postponed; and in the meantime the conservatives took office under Salisbury.

The result seemed to justify Parnell's choice. The new government dropped coercion immediately, and instituted a really effective scheme of land purchase. The 'Ashbourne act' (so called from the name of the Irish lord chancellor, who devised it) provided for the advance to a tenant of the whole sum necessary to purchase his holding, and this was to be repaid over forty-nine years, at the rate of four per cent per annum, covering both interest and repayment of capital. On these terms, a tenant could buy his holding at a terminable annual charge amounting only to about 70 per cent of what he had formerly paid in rent; and the act was so widely made use of that within three years the £5,000,000 voted to finance it had been exhausted, and a fresh grant had to be made.

Parnell's immediate interest, however, was not in land-purchase but in home rule; and here again it seemed that something might be gained by co-operation with the conservatives. The new viceroy was Lord Carnarvon, who had been largely responsible for the establishment of federal self-government in Canada in 1867, and had later tried to work out a similar system for South Africa. He was anxious to apply his experience to the problem of Anglo-Irish relations, and encouraged Parnell to believe that the government might grant Ireland a status within the United Kingdom similar to that of a Canadian province within the Dominion. Parnell treated these advances cautiously, and sounded Gladstone about the possibility of a counter-offer from the liberals;[1] but Gladstone refused to enter into any competition of the kind, with the result that in the general election (November 1885) the Irish vote in Great Britain was thrown on the conservative side.

The election made a great change in Parnell's position. Not only did home rule candidates carry 85 seats in Ireland, including 17 out of 33 in Ulster, but they now formed a solid and highly disciplined party under his unquestioned leadership; and they held a balance of power in the new house of commons. It was, however, an incomplete balance. There were 335 liberals, 249 conservatives, and the difference between them thus exactly equalled the total strength of Parnell's following:[2] though he could keep either party out of office, he could put in only the liberals. Before the new parliament met, in January 1886, the effect of this situation on the two British parties was to produce results of immense significance for the future not only of Ireland but of Great Britain.

Even before the election Gladstone had decided that the granting of home rule was inevitable. But realizing that the liberals were not yet prepared for such a change of front, and hoping that when the time was ripe the question might be settled on a non-party basis, he made no public pronouncement. Until mid-December only a few intimates were aware of his conversion, though he did let Salisbury know, indirectly, that he would support the government if it brought in a home rule measure. The conservative leaders, however, having made up their minds to throw over Carnarvon and his schemes, ignored this advance. Gladstone still intended to maintain silence until the government should have declared its policy; but his hand was forced by a premature and un-

---

[1] From 1882 onwards Parnell had maintained an indirect correspondence with Gladstone through Mrs O'Shea, whose husband was a member of the Irish party.

[2] In addition to the 85 home rule members for Ireland, T. P. O'Connor sat, as a home ruler, for the Scotland division of Liverpool — a seat which he held from 1885 to 1929.

authorized disclosure in the London press, on 17 December, of his new attitude towards home rule.[1] A junction of liberal and Parnellite forces followed almost as a matter of course; before the end of January the government had been turned out; and in February Gladstone became prime minister for the third time, committed in fact, if not formally, to a policy of home rule.

At first sight it might seem that the home rulers were now sure of victory: they had won the alliance of a great British party, under the most brilliant parliamentarian of the day; and the enactment of home rule could now be only a matter of time. The realities of the situation, however, were rather different. Gladstone had still to convert his own party; and his influence in the party, as well as in the country, was weakened by a strong suspicion, which (however unjustified by the facts) was not unnatural in the circumstances, that he had taken up home rule simply for the sake of office. British public opinion, which was likely to influence votes in parliament, still associated the Irish party with agrarian crime and Fenian conspiracy, an attitude which Parnell's open contempt for England and the English did nothing to modify. The conservatives might be in a minority in the commons; but in opposing home rule they could appeal to deep-seated prejudices — racial, religious, economic — of incalculable power. The cleavage thus introduced into British political life might have had no more than temporary significance if the home rule bill of 1886 had passed into law; the failure of the bill meant that the cleavage continued for another generation, growing ever more bitter as the years passed. And this cleavage affected Ireland no less than Britain, though in a different way. In 1885 the Irish party was still independent, and Parnell was free to choose between conservatives and liberals. But from 1886 onwards this freedom of choice was gone, for there was only one party which could help him. The conservatives were wont to twit the liberals with being the prisoners of the Irish; it was perhaps less obvious, but equally true and far more important, that the Irish were the prisoners of the liberals.

Between January and July 1886 the struggle over home rule was fought out in the liberal party, in the commons, and, finally, in the country. Within the liberal party opposition came mainly from the two wings. It was clear from the beginning that the whigs, under the guidance of Hartington, would have nothing to do with Gladstone's new policy; the radicals were suspicious and uneasy, but they did not immediately commit

[1] The disclosure was made by Gladstone's son, Herbert, who believed that he was acting in his father's best interests.

themselves, and Chamberlain, their principal leader, accepted a seat in the cabinet. But, as the full scope of Gladstone's intention was revealed, he became more and more dissatisfied; within two months he had resigned, and soon set himself to organize resistance among his followers in the party. Undeterred by this, Gladstone pressed on with his bill, which he presented to the commons in April. It provided for the government of Ireland by an executive in Dublin, responsible to an Irish parliament. But the union was not to be dissolved: the parliament at Westminster was still to have ultimate authority; it was to retain direct control in all matters affecting the crown, defence and foreign relations; and the fiscal independence of the Irish parliament was to be narrowly circumscribed. In the bill as originally presented Irish representation at Westminster was to cease; but it was strongly argued that in that case it would be difficult to justify the British parliament's retention of such extensive authority over Irish affairs, and Gladstone agreed that the question should be reconsidered. What this bill offered fell very far short of the national independence that Irish opinion had for so long demanded; but Parnell accepted it in principle, though he reserved the right to seek amendment in detail; and the Irish party supported the government throughout the parliamentary struggle. He took the common sense view that once an Irish parliament had been established its powers might be extended; and in the meantime his main concern was to have the financial relations between the two countries settled on the most favourable terms possible. Along with the home rule bill the government introduced a gigantic scheme of land purchase, by which virtually the whole landlord interest in Ireland would be bought out; but though Gladstone himself attached great importance to this, it was completely overshadowed by the question of home rule. With the defeat of home rule and the fall of the government it was abandoned; and the conservatives were left to continue their own more gradual land purchase policy.

The fate of the bill in the house of commons depended on the conduct of the dissident liberals. They were not numerous enough to defeat the government merely by abstention; and it was uncertain how many of them would carry their opposition to the point of voting with the conservatives, even against home rule. The issue remained in doubt until the last minute; but when the long-drawn-out debate on the second reading at length came to an end, and the house divided in the early hours of 8 June, 93 liberals voted against the bill, and it was defeated by 343 to 313. In his closing speech, before the vote was taken, Gladstone had urged his opponents to think 'not for the moment, but for the years that are to come', before rejecting the bill: however one may judge the motives of the majority on that fateful morning, their conduct was to have immense and unforeseen consequences for Great Britain as well as for Ireland.

Gladstone refused to accept defeat; he overcame, with some difficulty, the queen's reluctance to grant a dissolution; and the question was referred to the country in July. The result, in terms of seats, was a shattering rejection of home rule: the new house contained 316 conservatives and 78 anti-home rule liberals (soon to be known as 'liberal unionists') against 191 Gladstonian liberals and 85 Irish home rulers. An analysis of the popular vote shows that public opinion was much more evenly balanced than these figures would suggest; and it should be remarked that the opposition to home rule was distinctively English: three-fifths of the Scottish members and five-sixths of the Welsh supported Gladstone. But this made no difference to the parliamentary position. As soon as the election results were known Gladstone resigned; Salisbury resumed office; and for the next twenty years, with one brief interlude, the conservatives were responsible for the government of Ireland.

(3)

The announcement of Gladstone's conversion to home rule had come as a shock to the British public; but to Irish protestants it had seemed to threaten complete destruction. The character of the home rule movement had changed greatly since its first establishment by Butt, and the protestant attitude towards it had changed also; though there were still some protestant home rulers, and though the leader in 1885 was both a protestant and a landlord, protestants in general hated and feared the very idea of a separate Irish parliament. It is easy to find economic reasons for this attitude, especially among the upper classes: they saw the British connection as the best, if not the only, guarantee for their property; and in Britain and the empire they found a wide range of profitable careers — in the army, in the public service, in commerce — from which they might be shut out if the link between Ireland and Great Britain were weakened or severed. But there were other influences also, which affected the whole protestant population. Protestants of all classes still clung, even if sometimes half unconsciously, to the old notion of protestant ascendancy; and the establishment of an Irish parliament would not only bring what remained of that ascendancy to an end, but would establish a new Roman Catholic ascendancy in its place. The presence of a few protestants in the home rule party could not alter the fact that the party worked in close collaboration with the Roman Catholic clergy, and a pronouncement by the hierarchy in favour of home rule, in February 1886, seemed an ominous indication of things to come. The protestant Irishman was fond of asserting his loyalty to the crown; but he did not really regard home rule as an issue between Great Britain and Ireland; for him, it was a revival of the seventeenth-century struggle between Roman Catholics and protestants for ascendancy in Ireland, a struggle which his ancestors had twice fought to a victorious conclusion and which he was prepared, should the worst come to the worst, to fight again.

This protestant opposition to home rule was most intense and most formidable in Ulster. Elsewhere it derived its importance from the middle and upper classes, who formed the backbone of the protestant population; but in Ulster it was a popular movement, as widespread among farmers and farm labourers, among shopkeepers and artisans, as among landlords, professional men, merchants and industrialists. In the province as a whole, protestants and Roman Catholics were fairly evenly balanced numerically, but the balance of wealth was altogether on the protestant side. Among the lower classes there was, in some areas, a long tradition of sectarian rivalry — competition between Roman Catholic and protestant farmers for land, competition between Roman Catholic and protestant workmen for employment; but until 1885 well-to-do protestants generally had felt that their position of superiority was secure. The effect of the franchise act of 1884, as revealed in the general election, forced them to realize that this position was in danger of being undermined, and made their reaction to the home rule bill even more violent than it would in any case have been.

The acute sense of a common danger quickly brought the whole protestant population together. Conflicting interests and old rivalries were forgotten: churchmen and presbyterians, landlords and tenants, employers and employees, conservatives and liberals, readily combined in fierce determination to resist home rule. They found a useful instrument for maintaining this unity in the Orange Order, which had survived its formal dissolution in the 1830s, though it had lost almost entirely the support previously given to it by the upper and middle classes. Now they eagerly took it up again: the Orange lodges provided the basis of an effective political machine, while their tradition of fraternal equality between members tended to blur class distinctions, and helped to reconcile the protestant proletariat to the leadership of landlords and wealthy businessmen.

The part played by merchants and manufacturers in this Ulster movement was of great significance; for though they shared the outlook common to Irish protestants, they had also a special interest of their own. Their wealth depended on the industrial north-east, and they believed that its prosperity would decline under a Dublin parliament. In 1886 this concern for a particular area simply intensified their opposition to any form of home rule; but it soon came to dominate their policy, and in the long run they were ready to abandon all the rest of Ireland, including even part of Ulster itself, to safeguard their own position.

The opposition excited in Ulster by the home rule crisis took British statesmen by surprise, but the conservatives were quick to turn it to advantage. Their leaders saw in the Ulster situation an anti-home rule argument that could easily be made popular in Britain; and Lord Randolph Churchill, after a visit to Belfast, summed up his attitude in a phrase that soon gained wide currency — 'Ulster will fight; Ulster will be right'. The alliance thus formed was an enduring one. It yielded some electoral profit to the conservatives; but, in the end, they found it a dangerous embarrassment. To the Ulster protestants it proved an encouragement (which, perhaps, they hardly needed) to press their claims to the uttermost, even if it meant involving Ireland, and the whole United Kingdom, in a civil war.

(4)

The failure of Gladstone's home rule bill and the collapse of his following in the general election hardly affected Parnell's position or prestige; the home rule movement remained as strong as ever; and the alliance now established with the liberals seemed to make its ultimate success almost inevitable. The alliance, it is true, imposed a measure of caution on Parnell: he must now consider every move in the light of its probable effect on liberal opinion, yet without giving his Irish supporters any reason to suspect that he was ready to truckle to Britain. But this was the sort of situation that Parnell was well qualified to handle; and during the next few years his relations with the liberals became more cordial, without any damage to his reputation, in Ireland or America, as the champion of Irish rights against English tyranny.

Parnell's skill in maintaining this double policy was put sharply to the test before the end of 1886. A bad season had produced great hardship, especially in the poorer areas, and there was a demand that rents fixed under the act of 1881 should be reduced. But many landlords insisted on exacting the utmost of their legal dues, and the safeguards provided in the land act proved insufficient to protect from eviction those who fell into arrears. To meet this threat the National League organized the 'Plan of Campaign' — a scheme whereby tenants on particular estates were encouraged to act as a body, to offer the landlord a reduced rent, and, if this were refused, to pay the rent into a fund for the benefit of the evicted. Several members of the parliamentary party, especially John Dillon[1] and William O'Brien, were prominent in organizing this scheme, but Parnell, though he pressed the claims of the tenants in parliament, deliberately held himself aloof. Yet his actions and his speeches were so skilfully contrived that, while he did nothing to antagonize the British liberals, he still retained the full confidence of his followers at Westminster and in Ireland.

His position was made even stronger by the conservatives' reaction to the 'Plan of Campaign'. They recognized the need for further land reform; but they considered that their first task was to restore respect for the law, and this meant a return to coercion. Early in 1887 the execution of their policy was entrusted to Arthur James Balfour, whose recent experience as Scottish secretary might be thought a useful preparation, for at this time the western islands were the scene of a land agitation similar to that in Ireland, though less savage in its methods. Strengthened by a severe coercion act, the new chief secretary attempted to break up the National League and make the 'Plan of Campaign' unworkable; and the rigour with which he employed the special powers granted by the act, though it failed to achieve his purpose, not only aroused the strongest resentment in Ireland, but also exposed him to fierce criticism by British liberals, who were soon as ready as any home ruler to denounce 'Bloody Balfour' as an epitome of all that was cruel and tyrannical.

With liberal M.P.s appearing on Irish platforms, to support home rule and the 'Plan of Campaign' and to denounce the whole system of conservative administration, Parnell attained a new level of political respectability in the eyes of the British public; yet at the same time his prestige in Ireland and America had never stood higher. An accusation made by *The Times* in 1887 that he had privately condoned the Phoenix Park murders was dramatically refuted, two years later, by the discovery that the letters on which the newspaper relied had been forged by a journalist. The accusation and the subsequent inquiry had received great publicity; and with his vindication Parnell's reputation immediately soared. On his next appearance in the house of commons the entire opposition, including the front bench, gave him a standing ovation; he became the lion of liberal society; he received the freedom of Edinburgh; he was Gladstone's guest at Hawarden. This public demonstration of alliance between liberals and home rulers came at a time when the liberal party, having recovered its confidence after the collapse of 1886, seemed to be on the way back to power; the government had lost one by-election after another, and its

[1] Son of J. B. Dillon, the Young Irelander.

original majority of 188, made up of conservatives and liberal unionists, had sunk to 70 by 1890. The prospects for home rule had never seemed brighter; but before the year was out Parnell's career lay in ruins and his party had been shattered.

The circumstances that led to this sudden reversal arose out of Parnell's private life. A long-standing liaison with Mrs O'Shea, the wife of one of his followers, resulted in an action for divorce, in which Parnell was cited as the co-respondent. He offered no defence; and on 17 November 1890 the verdict was given against him. Victorian Britain could tolerate sexual immorality in its statesmen provided it was decently disguised; but on this open admission of guilt the liberals, and especially the powerful non-conformist element among them, demanded that Gladstone should repudiate all alliance with the Irish party so long as it was led by Parnell. The Irish reaction was quite different. A public meeting in Dublin enthusiastically re-affirmed confidence in his leadership; and on 25 November the members of the parliamentary party, meeting at West-minster, re-elected him as their chairman for the coming session. In making the election, however, they were not fully informed of Gladstone's attitude. He had no wish to act as censor of morals; but he was absolutely convinced that in the existing state of feeling among liberals it would be useless for him to continue his advocacy of home rule if Parnell were to remain at the head of the Irish party. When Gladstone's views were made public, on 26 November, there was a strong conviction among the Irish members that Parnell ought to resign; and on 1 December the party met, in committee room 15 at the house of commons, to re-consider the question of the leadership. The debate was protracted over several days; Parnell, who was still chairman, presided; and, realizing that there was a majority against him, he used all his ingenuity to prevent a decisive vote being taken. At last, in the afternoon of 6 December, the crisis came: Justin McCarthy, vice-chairman of the party and a con-vinced though temperate opponent of Parnell's continued leadership, called on those who agreed with him to leave the meeting; 43 members followed him, and Parnell, with 27 others, remained behind.

The debate that raged in committee room 15 during the first week of December 1890 may be said to have continued ever since. But two points, which were clear enough at the time, have survived all subsequent argument and investigation: the difficulties of the party arose, in the first place, from the liberal alliance; and it was Parnell's obstinacy that forced these difficulties to the point of splitting the party. Until Gladstone's views had been published no Irish leader, with the single exception of Davitt, took any stand against Parnell on account of the divorce action;

and when, on 26 November, there was a move among the Irish members to oust him from the chairmanship to which they had re-elected him the day before, it was on the purely political ground that they could not afford to sacrifice their alliance with the liberals. Once the controversy began, it was inevitable that the 'moral question' — as it was called — should be brought in, and in the popular mind it soon came to have a central position; but for the Irish members the basic issue was whether they should stand by Parnell and lose Gladstone's support, or abandon him and keep it. The only hope of preserving unity lay in compromise; and Parnell was urged to give up the chairmanship until the excitement should have died down, on the understanding that he would then be re-elected: 'Resign — marry — return' was the succinct advice cabled from South Africa by Cecil Rhodes;[1] and the same advice, in various forms, came from many quarters at home. But Parnell's obstinate determination to retain power made any compromise impossible. In a 'manifesto to the Irish people', published on 29 November, he had turned his back completely on his previous policy, denouncing Gladstone's home rule proposals as hopelessly inadequate, and repudiating the idea of alliance with any British party. The issue of the manifesto did not put an end to the search for a compromise; but it forced the Irish members to choose between loyalty to the political principles that Parnell had taught them, and loyalty to the man himself; and it was along this line that the split among his followers took place.

Though left with little more than one-third of the parliamentary party, Parnell still believed that he could carry the country; and he threw himself at once into a furious campaign of propaganda. Popular opinion in Ireland was deeply divided; but the whole weight of clerical influence was against Parnell, and it was his morality, rather than his policy, that seemed to be on trial. He now had to fight for a hearing where once he had been received like a king; and during a by-election tour in North Kilkenny he was pelted with mud. His health gave way under the strain of incessant travelling and speaking; but he drove himself relentlessly until, on 2 October 1891, he collapsed completely; four days later he was dead. He was just over forty-five years of age.

It is not easy to assess Parnell's place in Irish history. For more than a decade he held together, in an ill-defined but effective alliance, the constitutional and revolutionary wings of the nationalist movement; and this alliance added enormously to the importance of his most striking achieve-

---

[1] Rhodes supported home rule for Ireland because he believed that it would forward a system of 'imperial federation'.

ment — the creation of a strong and well-disciplined home rule party at Westminster. Yet by his own conduct he split both the party and the country; and though he did not openly appeal to the revolutionaries, he abandoned the policy that he had so skilfully pursued, and cast doubts upon the possibility of securing any satisfactory settlement by parliamentary action. The furious quarrel that he left behind him distracted and discredited the home rule movement for years after his death, and helped to prepare the way for its final collapse. But when that collapse came, Parnell's memory escaped the contempt with which a more militant generation regarded the whole concept of home rule: he was remembered, not as the skilful parliamentarian of 1886, but as the desperate fighter of 1891, the 'lost leader' who had turned his back on British party politics, and had tried in vain to rescue the nation from the fatal entanglement of the liberal alliance. This attitude to Parnell may have been based on a misunderstanding of his motives, but it showed a sound appreciation of his posthumous influence. The 'Parnellite' movement, which was far more widespread than its meagre representation in parliament would suggest, bred a suspicion of clerical influence, a contempt for majority opinion, a distaste for political manœuvre, that helped to create an atmosphere congenial to the growth of a more radical nationalism than the home rulers had ever dreamt of. Parnell's contribution to the making of modern Ireland must be judged by the power of his memory, no less than by the achievements of his prime or the disasters of his fall.

XXI

The Policy of Conciliation,
1891–1905

(1)

The fall of Parnell was a blow both to the home rule movement and to its liberal allies in Britain; and the consequent split of the Irish party into 'Parnellites' and 'anti-Parnellites' almost destroyed, for a time, its influence in parliament. All this worked to the advantage of the conservatives; and save for a brief period of ineffective liberal rule between 1892 and 1895 they remained in control of government until 1905. For Britain, this was a period of prosperity and expansion, a period during which foreign and colonial affairs filled the public mind; the problem of Ireland fell into the background; and even the liberals, once Gladstone had finally left the political scene, in 1894, ceased to make Irish reform the major element in their programme. In Ireland, the crisis of 1890–1 inaugurated a major transformation of political outlook; but for the time being this was obscured by the squabbling of the rival home rule parties, and its full significance did not appear until the second decade of the twentieth century. To many contemporaries in the 1890s and early 1900s it seemed that the social and economic developments then taking place were of far more importance for the future of the country than any change in its constitutional relations with Great Britain.

From the time of their return to office in the summer of 1886, the conservatives had determined to apply to Ireland a system of 'resolute government' accompanied by conciliation; and they had given an earnest of their readiness to undertake further land reform by an act of 1887 providing for a revision of the 'judicial rents' fixed under Gladstone's act of 1881. They were convinced that the home rule movement derived much of its strength from social discontent, and that if this discontent could be cured the movement would wither away. In order to preserve the parliamentary union unimpaired they were willing to outbid the liberals: Gladstone had curtailed the power of the landlords; the conservatives proposed to eliminate landlordism altogether. They had done something in this direction with the Ashbourne act of 1885; but it was A. J. Balfour who, as chief secretary, made land purchase the distinctive conservative policy for Ireland. In 1888 the operation of the Ashbourne act was extended by the advance of a further £5 millions; and in the following year Balfour set to work on a new and more ambitious measure. His own view was that land purchase should be made compulsory, for he regarded the existing Irish land system as 'essentially and radically rotten'; but he realized that parliament would not accept such a revolutionary proposal, and he had to satisfy himself with a more extended voluntary scheme for which the government was to guarantee an advance of £33 millions. The passage of his bill was delayed by strong opposition from liberals and home rulers; and the scheme did not come into operation until 1891. It proved less immediately successful than he had hoped. Tenants were discouraged from purchasing by the complicated nature of the new financial arrangements, and landlords from selling by the fact that they were now to be paid, not in cash, but in land stock, redeemable in thirty years, and liable to considerable fluctuation in market value. An amending act in 1896 offered somewhat more attractive terms; but the rate of land purchase remained relatively slow: between 1885 and 1891 an average of over 4,000 sales had been negotiated each year; after 1891 the average annual rate sank to a little over 3,000. Despite this, the act of 1891 marks an important turning-point; it put land purchase in the centre of the government's policy towards Ireland, and helped to prepare the way for its acceptance as the only practicable solution of the Irish land problem. In taking the next great step towards this solution, twelve years later, the conservatives were influenced by external forces; but they were, in fact, carrying Balfour's policy of 1891 to its logical conclusion; and it was Balfour himself who, as prime minister, presided over the opening of this final phase.

Landlords and tenants alike were dissatisfied with the acts of 1891 and 1896. The landlords had been deprived by earlier legislation of any real control over their estates; the ballot act of 1872 had destroyed their influence in parliamentary elections; the establishment of elective county councils in 1898 took away their control of local government. In these circumstances they were increasingly ready to sell; and the tenants were no less ready to buy. But both sides hoped for better terms, and in 1902 they combined to bring pressure on the government. In December of that year a conference representing landlord and tenant interests, and presided over by Lord Dunraven, a leading County Limerick landlord, produced an agreed plan; and the chief secretary, George Wyndham, accepted this, with Balfour's approval, as the basis of a new land purchase act. The Dunraven conference was not, however, the only influence that moved the government in this direction. There was a growing demand among tenants in Ulster that the sale of estates should be made universal and compulsory. In 1902 an independent candidate, standing on this programme, won a by-election in East Down, hitherto regarded as a safe conservative constituency; and the government was in no position to face any more such defeats. Besides all this, the home rule movement seemed in these years to have lost much of its impetus; and a bold measure of reform at this point might go far to weaken its hold on the popular imagination.

The new act ('Wyndham's act') was passed in 1903, and proved so satisfactory to both sides that without making the sale of estates compulsory it went far towards making it universal. The landlords found that the prices they received ruled substantially higher than those realized under the earlier acts; but any consequent disadvantage to the tenants was more than off-set by the reduction of the annual charge to $3\frac{1}{4}$ per cent with a corresponding extension of the period over which repayment was to be made; and besides this, the legal cost of transfer, formerly borne by the purchaser, was now to be met out of public funds. One distinctive feature of the act was that it encouraged the sale of entire estates. Where the landlord and three-quarters of the tenants agreed on a price acceptable to the commissioners appointed for the execution of the act, the sale could go through, the commissioners taking over the landlord's responsibilities towards those tenants who did not wish to purchase; and where a landlord parted with an entire estate he received a bonus payment equal to 12 per cent of the total sale price.

The success of Wyndham's act was immediate. At the time of its passage there were still more than half-a-million tenant-farmers. By 1909 some 270,000 purchases had been negotiated, and a further 46,000 were pending. Little more than a decade later, landlordism in rural Ireland had become a thing of the past.[1]

In their land purchase policy the conservatives were not, perhaps, actuated solely by a desire to weaken the influence of the home rule movement. A party in which the landed interest was still so powerful could hardly fail to be concerned about the future of the Irish landlords; and in the social and political conditions of the period a policy that enabled

[1] When the Irish Free State was established, in 1922, some 70,000 holdings were still unpurchased, about three-quarters of them in the Free State. In the following year both Irish governments passed legislation making sale of estates compulsory.

them to dispose advantageously of their estates must bear at least some appearance of having been designed with an eye to their benefit. But whatever the motives behind it, the policy of land purchase effected a transformation that has exercised a great and continuing influence on Irish life; and Balfour's claim, in the 1920s, hardly went beyond the limits of pardonable exaggeration: 'What was the Ireland the Free State took over? It was the Ireland that we made'.

The policy of land purchase proved a final solution to the long-standing problem of landlord-tenant relationships; but in fact, by the 1890s, this had ceased to be the dominant problem of rural Ireland. It was no longer landlord tyranny or excessive rent that threatened the farmer's security, but the growing competition of the overseas producer. Grain, meat, butter — agricultural produce of all kinds, were pouring into the British market; and there was a consequent depression of agriculture throughout the whole United Kingdom. This depression fell with particular severity on Ireland, where agriculture formed such a large element in the total economy, and where so much of the land was held by small farmers, who had neither the capital nor the skill necessary to adapt themselves to the new conditions. The export trade in cattle continued to prosper, and more and more land was given over to pasture; but on the average-sized farm it was difficult to make more than a bare subsistence out of raising cattle. If the rural population was to have a decent standard of living the whole agricultural system must be improved and developed; and how this was to be accomplished formed the real 'land problem' at the end of the nineteenth century.

The government was unlikely to accept responsibility for any major undertaking; but Balfour recognized that there were certain areas of exceptional poverty, which might be considered as having a legitimate claim to assistance from public funds; and in 1891 a new body of commissioners, the Congested Districts Board, was set up to administer this assistance. A 'congested district' was defined as one in which the rateable value was less than 30s per head of the population, and such districts were to be found in nine western counties, stretching from Donegal to Kerry. In 1901 these districts had between them a total population of about 500,000, who might be divided, according to the commissioners, into 'two classes, namely, the poor and the destitute'. The Congested Districts Board was financed mainly out of the funds of the disestablished church; and during the thirty years of its existence[1] it expended large sums in

---

[1] In 1923 the board was dissolved by the government of the newly-established Irish Free State.

building harbours, encouraging fisheries and fish-curing, introducing cottage industries, and trying to improve agricultural methods. But the board soon became convinced that any real improvement would require an enlargement of holdings, to be achieved by the taking over from land-lords of untenanted lands. Wyndham's act authorized it to acquire estates for this purpose, and in 1909 it was given compulsory powers. In all, the board bought and re-distributed almost 1,000 estates, containing some 2,000,000 acres; and this, rather than its attempts to diversify the economy and improve agriculture, was its lasting achievement.

The work of the Congested Districts Board was confined to a limited area; but, just before it was set up, a campaign had been launched for the improvement of Irish agriculture in general. In 1889 Horace Plunkett, an Irish landlord who had been farming in the American Middle West, returned to Ireland and began to spread the idea of co-operation. The essence of Plunkett's teaching was that the basic problem of Irish rural life was social and economic rather than political, that it should be approached without regard to political differences, and that it could be tackled at once, on a basis of self-help, without waiting for government direction or constitutional changes. Plunkett's doctrine was strongly criticized by many nationalist leaders. They distrusted him as a landlord and a unionist; and they feared that he might distract popular attention from the demand for home rule. There was, besides, an element of self-interest in this opposition: the shopkeeping and merchant class, which was very influential in the home rule movement, felt uneasy at the prospect of a strong co-operative system establishing itself throughout the country.

Despite all opposition, however, Plunkett's ideas spread rapidly; many local co-operative societies were founded, and by 1894 a central body, the Irish Agricultural Organization Society, had come into existence to co-ordinate their efforts and to encourage the expansion of the movement. Within ten years the co-operative system was at work in every depart-ment of the agricultural economy: the marketing of produce, the manu-facture of butter and bacon, the supplying of equipment and fertilizers, the provision of credit through land banks. All these activities, involving an annual turn-over of £3 millions, were handled by some 800 local co-operative societies. But though Plunkett based his movement on local and voluntary effort of this kind, he believed that there was a place for state action also, and it was at his instance that the government established, in 1899, a department of agriculture and technical instruction for Ireland, with Plunkett himself at its head.

These efforts of private and public enterprise helped to improve the standard of farming, though they did little to check the decline of tillage.

But the agricultural position had to be considered in relation to the whole economy, which suffered from over-concentration on a single source of wealth. To many people it seemed that Ireland could never be prosperous without a greater diversity of employment, and that this could only be attained by developing manufactures, which would require, at least to begin with, protection against British competition. Plunkett himself, though his primary interest was in agriculture, did what he could to encourage manufactures also; and when he abandoned his unionism and took up the cause of home rule, his main concern was to keep industrial Ulster within a self-governing Ireland.

(2)

The controversy arising from the O'Shea divorce had been a set-back for the liberals; but during 1891 they began to recover ground, and as the time for a general election drew near their spirits rose. This growing possibility of a liberal victory, with a second home rule bill as its inevitable sequel, was naturally alarming to Irish protestants; and those of Ulster were particularly loud in their denunciation of Gladstone's policy. In June 1892, on the eve of the dissolution of parliament, a unionist demonstration was held in Belfast, and the duke of Abercorn, who presided, summed up its whole purpose in a single sentence: 'We will not have home rule'. This blunt declaration was soon to be the watchword of the protestants of Ulster.

The result of the election in the following month raised the excitement in the province still higher. The conservatives were reduced to 268, the liberal unionists to 47; and the Irish members once more held a balance of power. When the new parliament met in August they joined with the liberals to turn Salisbury out; Gladstone, at the age of 83, formed his fourth ministry; and parliament was prorogued until January to give the government time to prepare its measures. Everyone knew that the most important of these would be a home rule bill; and Ulster unionist leaders were already declaring that even if it were to pass into law they would never submit to it: 'As a last resort', one of them had declared at the Belfast demonstration in June, 'we will be prepared to defend ourselves'; and it was not long before the means of defence were being seriously discussed.

Parliament reassembled in January 1893, and in February Gladstone introduced his second home rule bill. Unlike the first, it provided for continued Irish representation at Westminster; but this concession to the principle of parliamentary union between the two countries did nothing to placate the opposition; the bill was fiercely contested at every stage; and only a ruthless application of the closure enabled the government to force it through the commons by September. A week later, it was overwhelmingly rejected by the house of lords. Very reluctantly, Gladstone accepted this defeat; he neither went to the country, nor resigned, but simply allowed the bill to drop.

Throughout the whole course of the parliamentary struggle, the bitterest opposition came, as might be expected, from the Ulster unionist members. By this time, they were acting together as a distinct group within the conservative party, and they had found a dashing and single-minded leader in Edward Saunderson, member for North Armagh. Saunderson was in many ways a typical Ulster unionist of his time, whose whole outlook was dominated by intense protestant convictions. In private life his protestantism took the form of a sincere, if narrow, piety; in all public affairs it expressed itself in fear and hatred of Roman Catholic clerical influence. A whig in early life, he had broken with Gladstone over disestablishment. During the 1870s, as the home rule movement grew stronger, he became more and more convinced that Irish protestants must organize themselves for self-defence — it was this conviction that led him to join the Orange Order in 1882; and he was one of the first to suggest that it might be necessary to resist home rule by force of arms. The protestant workers of Belfast were not indisposed to violence; the home rule crisis of 1886 had produced an outbreak of sectarian rioting, and there was a similar outbreak in April 1893. But the force on which Saunderson proposed to rely was not that of the undisciplined mob; his plan was to raise, train and equip an Ulster protestant army. During the early months of 1893 he helped to establish an Ulster Defence Union, which collected funds and laid the groundwork for the organization of effective resistance to the government. British public opinion was not inclined to treat all this activity very seriously; and with the defeat of the home rule bill in September it naturally declined; but later events were to show that at least some Ulster protestants meant what they said.

Though Saunderson commonly acted as the spokesman of the Ulster protestants, he never forgot that he was an Irishman; and it was in the interests of Ireland, as he understood them, that he waged his long campaign against home rule. When it had been suggested, during a debate on the bill of 1886, that home rule might be more acceptable if special terms were made for Ulster, Saunderson had been emphatic in his reply: 'On the part of Ulster and every loyal man in that province, I repudiate that suggestion. We are prepared and determined to stand and fall, for weal or woe, with every loyal man who lives in Ireland'. If he habitually concentrated attention on the strength of Ulster resistance to home rule, it was because he felt that this was the ground on which the whole project could most readily be defeated. At this time, indeed, Irish unionist leaders, north and south, regarded themselves as patriotic defenders of their country against a revolutionary faction, bent on the destruction of property and the overthrow of the constitution. It was only slowly, and almost imperceptibly, that the notion of a distinct and self-centred Ulster interest came to dominate the scene.

With the failure of the home rule bill Gladstone's political career came to a close; and in March 1894 he resigned the premiership. He was the first major British statesman to consider seriously the implications of the parliamentary union between Great Britain and Ireland, and to realize that if Ireland were indeed an integral part of the United Kingdom, it must be governed on the same principles as the rest; and it was this realization that prepared him to accept the policy of home rule. His importance in the history of Anglo-Irish relations lies less in the measures that he actually carried, far-reaching though they were, than in the immense influence that his concern for Ireland had on British public opinion. It was he, more than anyone else, who made the state of Ireland an issue in British politics.

On Gladstone's resignation, Rosebery, who had been his foreign secretary, became prime minister. He was an imperialist, with little interest in home rule; and the Irish members, on whom he depended for his majority, gave him only reluctant and unreliable support. After struggling on for sixteen months, the government resigned in June 1895; and Salisbury resumed office, at the head of a coalition ministry of conservatives and liberal unionists.[1] At a general election in July the new government swept the country, securing a majority of 152 over the combined forces of the liberals and home rulers; and for a decade to come the unionists remained in control.

With the triumph of their British allies, the Irish unionists could feel safe once more; and many of them were inclined to believe that the policy of home rule was now dead and buried. But the more far-sighted realized that sooner or later the liberals would return to office, and that home rule would be revived; they did what they could to keep alive the defence organizations, and the spirit of resistance, created by the crisis of 1892–3; and when their forecast proved correct, they were ready to take the field once more.

---

[1] From this time onwards the term 'unionist' was commonly used to include both conservatives and liberal unionists.

(3)

The split in the Irish party had not been healed by the death of Parnell in October 1891. Negotiations for a settlement continued; but they were interrupted by the general election of 1892, and all the bitterness of committee room 15 was revived and intensified during the election campaign. The Parnellites were fighting a hopeless battle: not only had they all the weight of clerical influence against them; but with the prospect of a liberal victory and a second home rule bill, it was hardly likely that the electorate would endorse the Parnellite repudiation of the liberal alliance. In the event, only 9 Parnellites were returned; and the anti-Parnellites, who numbered 71, were now much less inclined to offer concessions to a group that appeared to have so little popular support, and attempts at reunion were not renewed for some years. In fact, however, Parnellite influence was much more important than the election results would suggest; and the rapidly-growing tradition of 'the lost leader' was to play a significant part in preparing the way for the final rejection of the whole parliamentary movement.

Of more immediate consequence was the fact that continuing division weakened Irish influence at Westminster; the old discipline was gone, and (to quote William O'Brien) 'one-man power was replaced by eighty-man powerlessness'. There were now two home rule parties. The Parnellites, led by John Redmond, were small in number; but, in the precarious balance of power at Westminster, their votes carried some weight; and their very existence placed the anti-Parnellites under a constant necessity of justifying their own policy and conduct before Irish opinion, not only in Ireland but in Great Britain and America. And the anti-Parnellites were not even united among themselves. Justin McCarthy, whom they had elected chairman in December 1890, exercised little effective authority, and his leadership was hardly more than nominal. He was assisted by a committee of eight, among whom John Dillon was by far the most important. But Dillon's supremacy was challenged by T. M. Healy, a man of infinite resource, who might, perhaps, have risen to political greatness had not his abilities been marred by defects of character. The rivalry between the two men was to prove of incalculable damage to the home rule movement.

Healy, by turn railway clerk, journalist and barrister, had at one time been secretary to Parnell; but he had become increasingly distrustful of his leader, and in the crisis of December 1890 had taken a prominent part in his overthrow. It might be unjust to Healy to suggest that his opposition to Parnell had had its origin in jealousy; but he was certainly unwilling to play second fiddle to Dillon. At every point he tried to secure the advancement of men on whose attachment to himself he could rely — in the election of the party committee, in the choice of parliamentary candidates, in the management of the new Irish National Federation, which had been established in 1891 to replace the National League, which had remained loyal to Parnell. The struggle came to a head during the general election of 1895, when Healy openly defied the authority of the party committee, on which Dillon's supporters had a majority. As a result, he was himself excluded from the committee, and, with some of his associates, expelled from the National Federation. But Healy was not to be so easily suppressed; and though Dillon was elected chairman of the party in February 1896, Healy was soon able to collect sufficient support throughout the country to enable him to establish, early in 1897, a new national organization of his own, the People's Rights Association. The association put the need for a united party in the forefront of its programme; but, in fact, its very existence threatened to deepen still further the existing divisions in the home rule movement.

The disruption of the parliamentary party, coupled with the failure of the bill of 1893, had a depressing effect on American supporters of home rule, and there was a considerable falling-off in their subscriptions to party funds. This was a serious matter, for many Irish M.P.s depended on regular allowances from the party to enable them to live in London; without American help these allowances could hardly be maintained, and the belief that this help would be more readily given to a reunited party had an important influence in stimulating new negotiations for peace. But the state of opinion in Ireland had an even stronger influence in the same direction. The Irish members at Westminster, resident for most of the year in England, hardly realized the effect of their divisions and squabbles on public opinion at home. The excitement and enthusiasm of Parnell's time had been succeeded by apathy and even cynicism. Home rule candidates still won elections; but popular belief in home rule as a policy was losing its force.

It was William O'Brien who first recognized the need to put new life into the home rule movement, and in 1898 he founded the United Irish League. The league started in Connaught, and its demand that estates should be broken up and re-distributed so as to provide larger holdings appealed in the first place to the poverty-stricken farmers of the west, who were far from satisfied with the early achievements of the Congested Districts Board. But O'Brien hoped that this policy of agrarian reform would provide a basis for reuniting the whole national movement; and though things did not work out exactly as he had intended, the propaganda of the United Irish League helped to bring the political leaders to the point of decision. During 1899 negotiations between Parnellites and anti-Parnellites were resumed; and early in 1900 the two groups merged in a single Irish party, of which Redmond was elected chairman in February. But it still remained to be seen whether the parliamentary movement, weakened by a decade of internal strife, could now recapture the popular imagination.

(4)

The decline of popular interest in home rule during the 1890s left a sort of gap, which was not immediately filled by any alternative policy or movement. But during this period the diverse and sometimes conflicting ideas that were later to come together in a new and more aggressive nationalism were already at work, though the apparent range of their influence was not wide.

Parnell's manifesto of November 1890, with its repudiation of the liberal alliance and denunciation of Gladstonian home rule, had seemed to justify, at least indirectly, those who had always been suspicious of con-stitutional methods. The informal co-operation between the parliamentary party and Fenianism, embodied in the 'new departure', was now virtually at an end; and though there was no overt revival of republican activity, Fenians were once more looking forward to an opportunity for violent revolution. The centenary of the insurrection of 1798 favoured their cause; for the celebrations were marked, naturally enough, by enthusiastic glorification of the men whose example they claimed to be following. 'Ninety-eight Clubs', founded to perpetuate 'the memory of the dead', occasionally masked Fenian activity; and in any case they fostered a militant anti-British spirit, far removed from that of the parliamentary party. Some indication of the strength of this spirit was given in 1900, when Arthur Lynch was elected M.P. for Galway, in his absence, and with no other recommendation than that he had fought for the Boers during the South African War.[1]

The attitude represented by Lynch and his supporters was almost entirely negative. One man at least wanted to turn the spirit of 'ninety-eight' to more positive purpose. Arthur Griffith, a Dublin printer, founded in 1898 the *United Irishman*, a weekly paper in which he preached the doctrine later to be known as *Sinn Féin* —'Ourselves'. Like

[1] Lynch was later tried for high treason, and condemned to death; but the sentence was commuted, and he was released after a brief imprisonment. He subsequently fought in the British army during the war of 1914–18.

Plunkett, he advocated self-reliance; but unlike Plunkett he was more concerned about industrial than agricultural development, and he applied his doctrine in the political as well as in the economic sphere. He was convinced that Ireland must be politically free, before it would be economically prosperous. But he did not believe that this freedom could be gained either by violent revolution or by action in parliament. He advocated instead a policy of non-co-operation. The Irish members should withdraw from Westminster, assemble in Dublin and set up an Irish government, which would simply take over the administration of the country, relying on its moral authority to ensure obedience. In this way, Griffith asserted, the continuance of British rule would be rendered impossible, and the British would peacefully withdraw. He claimed to have found a model in the policy of the Hungarian nationalist, Francis Deák; and he apparently hoped to achieve a kind of *Ausgleich* between Ireland and Great Britain. But for Griffith this was no more than the preliminary to a great economic expansion, which would turn Ireland into an industrial nation, with a population even greater than that before the Famine. Belfast, rather than Dublin, represented his idea of what an Irish city should be like.

Because of his concern about industrial development, Griffith's sympathies lay with capital rather than with labour. Despite his origins, he was essentially middle class in outlook, and deeply suspicious of trade unionism and socialism. But the vagaries of political life were later to bring him into alliance with the most active Irish socialist of the time, James Connolly, founder of the Irish Socialist Republican party, whose paper, the *Workers' Republic*, began publication almost at the same time as the *United Irishman*. Though Connolly's socialism prevented him from taking up a narrowly nationalistic outlook, he saw in contemporary Britain an embodiment of the capitalist imperialism that he hated, and he came to believe that only in an Ireland freed from British rule could the socialist society of which he dreamed come into being. In 1903, disappointed at the slender results of his propaganda, he left Ireland for the United States; but within a few years he was to return, and to take up again his unfinished task.

By the second decade of the twentieth century the ideas of the Fenians, of Griffith and of Connolly had been fused together in an outburst of revolutionary excitement. And by that time also they had been reinforced, and partly transformed, by the influence of another and more radical kind of nationalism, drawing its inspiration from concepts of race and culture rather than from politics or economics. In Ireland, as elsewhere, the nineteenth century saw the growth of a romantic interest in the past; and in

Ireland, as in other small and dependent countries, this was commonly associated with aspirations after a separate political existence. The Young Irelanders, for example, had encouraged the study of Irish history as a means of developing national self-consciousness. Such writers as Sir Samuel Ferguson, a Belfast-born barrister and poet, gave popular currency to the heroic tales of ancient Ireland; and though these writers might have no political purpose, they both reflected and stimulated an awareness of Irish tradition that could hardly fail to have political significance.

In the 1880s and 1890s this rather ill-defined historical and literary movement produced a band of enthusiasts who brought in a new note of exclusiveness, significantly indicated by the use of the term 'Gaelic' — all that was regarded as of English origin, however long established, however widely accepted, was now to be cast aside. The Gaelic Athletic Association, founded in 1884, not only encouraged traditional Irish sports, such as hurling, but placed a ban on all 'foreign' games, a term which its first patron, Archbishop Croke of Cashel, defined as including 'such foreign and fantastic field-sports as lawn tennis, polo, croquet, cricket and the like'. The Gaelic League, founded in 1893 by Douglas Hyde, son of a Church of Ireland clergyman, had as its aim the 'de-Anglicization of Ireland', mainly by reviving the general use of the Irish language. These movements were not in origin political; but it was inevitable that politically-minded nationalists should be attracted into them, and should try to use them for their own ends. Besides this, everything that tended to emphasize the distinctive character of Irish life strengthened the sense of national identity, and provided arguments in favour of breaking the union with Britain.

Hyde did his best to keep politics out of the Gaelic League. He was not himself greatly concerned about political independence, and he hoped that a common interest in the language might unite Irishmen of all parties and all creeds. But in fact the politicians captured the league in spite of him, and from it sprang the idea of an 'Irish Ireland' — 'Ireland not free only but Gaelic as well; not Gaelic only but free as well' — an Ireland, in short, in which the Ulster protestant could hardly be expected to feel at home. The Gaelic nationalism that developed during the last two decades of the nineteenth century helped to prepare the way for the partition of Ireland that was to be accomplished during the first two decades of the twentieth.

Stimulated by the Gaelic revival and by the growth of national self-consciousness, a group of Anglo-Irish writers tried to develop, through the medium of English, a distinctively national literature. The extent of

o

their success — even the possibility of their succeeding at all — may be open to question; but their work gave Dublin a new importance in the literary world, and especially (with the opening of the Abbey Theatre in 1904) in the world of drama. Most of these writers, whether or not they were politically active, sympathized with the demand for self-government; and the greatest of them, William Butler Yeats, was later on to express in his poems the spirit of nationalist Ireland on the morrow of the 1916 rising.

(5)

To most contemporary observers the new ideas that were stirring at the end of the nineteenth century had no great significance. Ireland as a whole appeared to be tolerably quiet and content. The parliamentary party, even after its reunion in 1900, showed little drive or initiative. The conservatives might not unreasonably feel that their policy of conciliation — of 'killing home rule with kindness' — had justified itself, a feeling that was strengthened by the immediate popularity of Wyndham's land purchase act of 1903. But this was their last success in Ireland; and it led indirectly to a serious set-back, which helped to bring down the government.

Lord Dunraven and Sir Anthony MacDonnell, the under-secretary at Dublin Castle, who had worked together on the land purchase measure, next turned their attention to a scheme of devolution, by which a central Irish council was to exercise a measure of local authority, within the framework of the existing constitution. The negotiations went on during 1904, and were meant to be confidential; but news of them leaked out; the Irish unionists were immediately up in arms; and Wyndham, though not directly involved, was obliged to resign in March 1905. The controversy surrounding his resignation weakened still further a government already declining in popularity and strained by internal dissension; Balfour resigned in the following December; and the liberals, under Sir Henry Campbell-Bannerman, took office after ten years in opposition. A general election in January 1906 confirmed them in power with an overwhelming majority; and all Ireland, nationalist and unionist alike, waited anxiously to see what the issue would be.

XXII

The Home Rule Crisis, 1906-14

(1)

When the liberal government was formed, in December 1905, the outlook for Ireland was not unhopeful. The reforms of the previous twenty years had removed many grievances; the country was increasingly prosperous; and at least on the surface the political situation was stable, for the more militant nationalists were not yet in a position to challenge the dominant parliamentary party: of the 81 members that it returned at the general election in January, 73 were unopposed. In the north, the protestants were loudly defiant; but no one outside Ulster took them very seriously. Within ten years the whole picture had changed. The Ulster unionists, with a well-equipped and disciplined volunteer army, 100,000 strong, were preparing to establish a government of their own. In the rest of Ireland, Redmond's authority was slipping from his grasp, and the revolutionary forces that he had hitherto held in check were threatening to capture the whole nationalist movement. They were no less willing to fight for independence than the protestants to fight for union; and in the summer of 1914 Ireland was on the edge of civil war.

The danger of a civil war was probably inherent in the situation from the point at which home rule first became a serious possibility. The Irish protestants had, perforce, acquiesced in one concession to the majority after another, until their privileged position had been almost wholly eaten away. But faced with a policy that would establish a Roman Catholic ascendancy in place of their own, they refused to acquiesce any longer; and though the fears that they expressed might seem fantastic to others, they were very real to those who felt them. Irish protestants of the 1660s had declared that they would not suffer the lands they had won by their swords to be filched from them by Ayes and Noes; their successors of the early 1900s were equally contemptuous of parliamentary procedure in a matter that, as they believed, affected not their property only, but their lives and their religion; and they made ready to receive a home rule act, if one should be passed, with rifles and machine-guns. Inevitably, protestant intransigence aroused equal determination among nationalists; and they too prepared for armed conflict. British statesmen found themselves faced by a problem to which their sober rules of give and take offered no solution.

In 1906, the liberals had no idea of any such startling developments. Elated by their triumph at the polls, and full of reforming zeal, they had little thought for Ireland. Home rule had played no part in their electoral campaign; and though it was still included in their programme, few of them considered it an urgent question. The king's speech at the opening of the new parliament contained only a vague and cautious reference to the ministry's consideration of plans for introducing into the government of Ireland 'means for associating the people with the conduct of Irish affairs'; and after many months' delay it was revealed that all this amounted to was a scheme of devolution, similar to that of 1904. There was to be an 'Irish council', partly elected and partly nominated, controlling certain Irish departments, and financed by a grant from the imperial exchequer. This was certainly not 'home rule' as traditionally understood; Redmond, after some hesitation, rejected it completely; and in the summer of 1907 the ministry abandoned the bill that had been introduced to give effect to the proposal. But it put forward no alternative; and home rule seemed to have been relegated to an indefinite future.

Redmond thus found himself in an awkward position. Many of his colleagues wished to throw over the liberal alliance as useless; and there were indications that the country, impatient of delay, might abandon home rule for other and more vigorous policies. Griffith's Sinn Féin movement, which had been organized as a political party in 1905, put up a candidate at a by-election in North Leitrim in 1908; and though Redmond's candidate carried the day, after a violent contest, the threat to the home rule party was already emerging: it must either produce results, or make way for those who could. It is very doubtful if Redmond himself realized how serious the threat was, for during his long attendance at Westminster he had lost touch with the people in whose name he spoke, and he hardly understood the new forces at work in Irish politics. To the electors of Wexford, or the Irish-Americans in Boston, he could use the language of revolution, eulogize the 'men of Ninety-eight', and proclaim his hatred of England. But at bottom he was an orthodox parliamentarian, who hardly suspected that people might take to fighting for what they could not get by votes. He did, however, realize that his own party was dissatisfied, and he pressed the cabinet for assurances that there would be a home rule bill in the near future. But, even when he got no satisfaction on this, he insisted on maintaining the liberal alliance, in the firm conviction that there was no other way in which home rule could be obtained. Though he succeeded in persuading the party, with a few exceptions, to acquiesce in this policy, the strain on his authority was considerable; and it was not to be relieved until the position at Westminster had been transformed by the general election of January 1910.

In defending the liberal alliance to his colleagues and to public opinion in Ireland, Redmond did not rely solely on the argument that the liberals would, sooner or later, grant home rule; he pointed also to the social reforms that they had actually carried. These, though less substantial than the conservative reforms of the previous twenty years, were not unimportant. Between 1906 and 1908 legislation was passed for the improvement of rural and urban housing, for the re-instatement of tenants formerly evicted from their holdings, and for the protection of tenants in towns; and, in 1909, the financial provisions of Wyndham's act, which experience had shown to be inadequate, were amended. Much of this legislation was the work of Augustine Birrell, who had become chief secretary in 1907. But Birrell's greatest achievement in Ireland was the universities act of 1908, which at long last put an end to the 'university question'. The Royal University was abolished, and two new universities established in its place: the National University of Ireland, with colleges at Dublin, Cork and Galway; and the Queen's University of Belfast. This was, essentially, a political solution. Birrell started with the conviction that he must satisfy the claims of the Roman Catholic bishops; he knew that they would not accept any system that did not give them a measure of effective control; and the new National University, though formally non-denominational, was so organized as to fulfil this condition. Protestant opinion could hardly be expected to regard such a system as satisfactory; and its establishment was made possible only by excluding Queen's College, Belfast, which was turned into an independent university — not because of a strong local demand, but because there was nothing else to do with it. The abandonment, after sixty years, of a university system embracing the whole country, and the recognition that north and south must be treated differently, were particularly significant at a time when home rule was once more a question of practical politics.

Many of these social measures were quite acceptable to the Ulster unionists; but they offered a resolute, though unsuccessful, opposition to the universities bill. Even the promise of an independent university of Belfast did nothing to placate them; for they regarded it merely as 'part of the scheme for satisfying the monstrous demands of the Roman hierarchy'. But no social legislation, whether they approved of it or disapproved, could distract their attention from the home rule issue; and neither the government's delay in bringing it forward, nor the failure of the council bill of 1907, could dull their sense of danger so long as the liberals were in power. As early as March 1905, when a change of ministry was still only in prospect, they had begun to organize themselves for defence by setting up an Ulster Unionist Council, a large representative body, with a permanent executive committee. During the next few years this executive committee co-operated with the Irish Unionist Alliance (an all-Ireland body with headquarters in Dublin) in presenting the Irish unionist case to the British electorate. But the committee's main work was in Ulster itself. Here the need was not for propaganda but for organization. Local unionist clubs, which had been established in many areas in the 1890s, were now revived, and linked in a network covering the whole province, so that a high proportion of the adult protestant population was brought into membership. The movement was not yet openly a military one, but in this way the machinery for enlisting and organizing a disciplined military force was provided. When political changes at Westminster made the passage of a home rule act virtually certain, the Ulster unionists were not slow to put this machinery into motion.

(2)

The government's delay in bringing forward a home rule bill had been due partly to its pre-occupation with other matters, but partly also to its independence of the Irish vote; the events of 1909–10, arising from a dispute between the lords and the commons, were to change this situation. Since 1906, the conservatives had regularly used their permanent majority in the upper house to delay, amend or defeat government measures, and the resulting tension between the two houses came to a crisis with the lords' rejection of the budget in November 1909. The fact that a general election was now inevitable put the Irish party in a much stronger bargaining position. Redmond was able to exact, as the price of his support, a promise that home rule would be included in the government's election programme: Asquith, who had become prime minister on the death of Campbell-Bannerman in 1908, gave a public assurance that the liberals regarded home rule as the only solution to the Irish question. The Irish party did not, indeed, like the disputed budget, for it threatened the interests of distillers and publicans, who carried great weight in the party organization; but it liked the house of lords even less, and hoped that a government victory in the election would mean the end of the lords' veto on legislation.

From Redmond's point of view, the result of the election, in January 1910, could hardly have been better. It was true that the Irish party had once more been split—partly over the question of supporting the budget —and that 11 independent nationalists had been elected, reducing his own following to 70. But this was more than compensated for by the fact that he now held the balance of power at Westminster. The liberals had fallen to 275, the unionists had risen to 273: even with the support of the 40 labour members, the government could do nothing without Redmond's consent. It was under this hampering condition that Asquith had to face the great constitutional issues of the next four years. Liberal attachment to home rule was undoubtedly genuine; and it had been strengthened by the successful grant of self-government to the Transvaal in 1906: Redmond, it was said, would turn out an 'Irish Botha'. But the government's dependence on the Irish vote certainly weakened its moral authority in Great Britain, and lent some colour to unionist jibes that it was acting under duress.

The first major question to which the new parliament turned its attention was the future of the house of lords, and the ensuing conflict lasted for more than eighteen months. The death of Edward VII, in May 1910, brought a temporary easing of tension, and the liberal and conservative leaders combined in an effort to find an agreed solution. But neither side could forget that behind the immediate question lay the prospect of a new home rule bill: the conservatives would not surrender, and the liberals would not tolerate, the lords' power to veto it. Negotiations broke down in November, and the lords then rejected the measure in which the government had embodied its proposals. A new general election followed in December. This left the state of the parties almost unchanged, and the government, with its majority intact, was able to get its way; though it was not until August 1911 that the upper house, under threat of a mass creation of liberal peers, finally gave in. By the terms of the new act (the 'parliament act') the lords lost their absolute veto on legislation; they might hold up a bill for two years, but at the end of that time it could pass into law without their consent.

All Ireland, nationalist and unionist alike, had watched the struggle with intense interest. The house of lords had defeated the home rule bill of 1893, and was certain to reject any other measure of the same sort; but with the power of the lords broken, with a liberal government in office, and with Redmond the arbiter of the house of commons, the passage of a home rule act would be almost inevitable. The new situation thus created contained both advantages and dangers for the two Irish parties.

For the nationalists, the advantages were more immediately obvious than the dangers. Home rule now seemed within their grasp, and Redmond's prestige accordingly rose. Even those who had been contemptuous of the parliamentary party, who had scorned home rule as an unworthy substitute for true national independence, now began to take a rather different view. The establishment of an Irish parliament, even with restricted powers, would be a step in the right direction; and the party that could secure it immediately ought not to be hampered by opposition. But the higher expectation rose, the more impatient the country would become; and herein lay the danger to Redmond. In the two years that must inevitably elapse between the introduction of a home rule bill and its enactment, there would be time for criticism of its shortcomings to gather weight, for the sense of triumph to fade away, and for a reaction to set in; and in such a period of reaction all the forces that had been slowly undermining the prestige of the parliamentary party during the previous two decades were likely to grow stronger.

For the unionists, the passing of the parliament act meant that their strongest constitutional bulwark had been destroyed; but those of Ulster, who had already expressed their readiness to defy the constitution if necessary, simply continued with their preparations. And they now had the advantage that the British conservatives were committed to their cause. In the general election of December 1910 Balfour and his colleagues had deliberately decided to make opposition to home rule the main plank in their platform; and now, in rancorous disappointment at the liberal victory over the house of lords, they would go to almost any lengths for the sake of revenge. Like Lord Randolph Churchill in 1886, they believed that 'the Orange card was the one to play'.

The Ulster unionists, however, were too much in earnest to be safely used by any constitutional party. They had a policy and an organization of their own; and in 1910 they had found a leader of national reputation in Sir Edward Carson,[1] one of the most prominent advocates at the English bar, who had been a member of the conservative ministry, as solicitor-general, from 1900 to 1905. It was, at first sight, a strange choice. Carson was a Dubliner, an M.P. for Dublin University, who knew little or nothing of Ulster; and he certainly did not share the typical Ulster protestant's hatred of 'popery' — he had been a consistent supporter of Roman

[1] Saunderson had died in 1906. Walter Long, at that time member for South Dublin, had succeeded him as leader of the Irish unionists at Westminster; but in January 1910 Long had been returned for an English constituency.

Catholic claims in the controversy over university education. His main concern, as a member of parliament, was for the welfare of Ireland as a whole, which, he was convinced, depended on the maintenance of the union. 'It's only for Ireland that I'm in politics', he had told Arthur Balfour in 1900; and, when he accepted the leadership of the Irish unionist party ten years later, he regarded Ulster opposition to home rule simply as a means of saving all Ireland for the union. But for the Ulster unionists it was an enormous advantage to have the prestige of Carson's name; they knew him as a man of courage and sincerity; and even if his viewpoint was rather different from theirs, they still believed that they could trust him to support their cause.

Carson realized from the first that his task was not merely to lead a parliamentary party, but to act as spokesman for a popular movement that might easily overstep the limits of the constitution, and he accepted the risk with open eyes. During the struggle over the house of lords, his main work was at Westminster. But with the passage of the parliament act the situation changed. To most people, home rule now seemed inevitable; and the Ulster unionists determined to show the government that in this matter they would not be bound by a parliamentary decision. In September 1911 Carson was at Belfast; and though this was not his first visit, he now, for the first time, appeared as leader of an organized popular movement. It was a rôle in which he was immediately successful. As an orator he lacked the emotional power of a Redmond or a Lloyd George; but his tall grim figure, with its touch of menacing flamboyance, appealed to the mood of his followers; and, above all, he told his tightly-packed audience of 100,000 unionists just what they wanted to hear: 'We will yet defeat the most nefarious conspiracy that has ever been hatched against a free people'. The plan of resistance that he put forward was an uncompromising one: if a home rule act should pass, the unionists would ignore it, and would set up a government of their own for the province of Ulster. This might seem a startling proposal from a parliamentary politician, but it was seriously intended; and a few days later the Ulster Unionist Council set up a commission to draft a constitution, and to prepare the way for taking over control of the civil administration.

Carson himself does not seem to have recognised the importance of this decision. He still hoped to defeat any measure of Irish home rule; he was convinced that Redmond would not accept home rule with Ulster excluded; if, therefore, it could be shown that Ulster would fight rather than submit, the whole scheme would have to be dropped. But the Ulster unionists themselves took a narrower, and perhaps more realistic, view. The commission set up to prepare a constitution for Ulster was instructed to have 'due regard for the interests of loyalists [i.e. unionists] in other parts of Ireland'; but this was little more than a face-saving formula; the Ulstermen, determined to defend their own cause, were not going to encumber themselves with responsibility for the politically powerless protestant minority in the rest of the country. Carson, the Dublin lawyer, was their spokesman in Britain and their popular hero at home; but the man who most fully embodied their fears, their prejudices, their arrogance, their courage and their stubborn self-regard was one of themselves — James Craig, member for East Down, and a typical representative of the wealthy middle class that controlled the economic and political life of the province.

(3)

Neither liberals nor nationalists took the situation in Ulster seriously; but the conservatives were anxious to make the most of it, partly because they were divided on tariff reform, and home rule was an issue on which they could stand firmly together. They were, however, following a dangerous policy; and it was not long before they found themselves more deeply committed to Carson and Craig than they had foreseen. Balfour, had he retained the leadership, might have attempted to curb the more violent element in the party; but he resigned in November 1911, and his successor, Bonar Law, was much more disposed to encourage it. Influenced, perhaps, by the fact that he was himself of Ulster presbyterian stock, he showed a reckless determination to support the northern unionists: in April 1912, on the eve of the parliamentary session, he was present with Carson at a great semi-military demonstration in Belfast, and there assured his hearers that the conservative party regarded their cause as its own and 'as the cause of the empire'. In July, addressing a conservative rally at Blenheim, he went much further. 'I can imagine', he said, 'no length of resistance to which Ulster will go which I shall not be ready to support'.

Two days after Bonar Law's visit to Belfast, on 11 April, Asquith introduced his home rule bill. It offered only a narrow measure of autonomy — even control of the police force was not immediately to pass to the new Irish government, and the supreme authority of the United Kingdom parliament 'over all persons, matters, and things in Ireland' was specifically retained. But the nationalists were, for the time being, in a mood to be easily satisfied; and a convention in Dublin expressed its 'solemn conviction' that home rule on these terms would 'link the people of Ireland to the people of Great Britain by a union infinitely closer than that which now exists and by so doing add immeasurably to the strength of the empire'. The Sinn Féin leaders, it is true, condemned the bill as hopelessly inadequate: 'If this is liberty the lexicographers have deceived us', wrote Arthur Griffith. But popular opinion, long taught to regard 'home rule' as the panacea for Ireland's ills, was untroubled by constitutional detail, and gave Redmond uncritical support.

The moderate character of Asquith's proposals did nothing to conciliate the unionists; they contested the bill fiercely at every stage; and despite a relentless use of the 'guillotine', the third reading was not carried until January 1913. A fortnight later, the bill received its expected defeat in the house of lords; and the conflicting parties were left to make what use they could of the interval that must elapse, under the terms of the parliament act, before it could become law.

The parliamentary struggle, though bitterly—even violently—conducted, had about it an air of unreality. The ultimate passage of the bill was a foregone conclusion, and the government steadily rejected all proposals for compromise. Had the liberals and conservatives been free agents they might well have found an agreed solution, but they were, in fact, acting under pressure. Lloyd George, on one occasion, failing to get a reply from Bonar Law, accused him of being afraid to speak, and, pointing to Carson, exclaimed, 'There sits his master'; whereupon a conservative member pointed to Redmond, and shouted out in reply, 'And there sits yours'. It is, indeed, hardly an exaggeration to say that both British parties were prisoners of their Irish allies: the government dared not resist Redmond's demand that the bill should go through unchanged; and the conservatives, though less obviously under pressure, had surrendered themselves to the Ulster unionists. The legislative union forced upon an unwilling Ireland a century earlier had brought its Nemesis.

While the bill dragged its way through the house of commons the Ulster unionists went ahead with their preparations. In January 1912 they had already begun openly to raise and train a military force,[1] soon to be styled, from some confused recollection of the 1780s, the 'Ulster Volunteers'; and great efforts were made to increase the size and efficiency of this force, and to supply it with arms. The unionist leaders had a double purpose in view: the 'provisional government', if it were ever to come into operation, would need an army to support its authority; and in the meantime it was necessary to impose some discipline on the protestant population, lest the rising political excitement should result in uncontrollable disorder. Sectarian rioting in Belfast, in July 1912, warned

[1] By applying for and obtaining the sanction of the local magistrates they kept within the letter of the law.

Carson and Craig how easily their followers might get out of hand; they tightened up their organization; and in September they staged an impressive public demonstration, to serve as a safety-valve for popular emotion and at the same time to convince the world of the solidarity, determination and self-discipline of the Ulster protestants. A brief statement of policy was drawn up and published; copies were distributed throughout the province; and on 28 September, which the Unionist Council decreed should be a public holiday, it was signed by more than 200,000 men, Carson himself leading the way at a ceremony in the Belfast City Hall.

The ceremonial signing of this document — 'Ulster's solemn league and covenant'[1]— was conducted in an atmosphere of religious devotion, and blessed by clergy and ministers of the Church of Ireland, the presbyterian church and other protestant denominations. But the document itself, despite its invocation of divine aid and expression of loyalty to the crown, clearly foreshadowed rebellion against constitutional authority. The signatories bound themselves to use 'all means which may be found necessary to defeat the present conspiracy to set up a home rule parliament in Ireland', and further pledged themselves to reject the authority of such a parliament if it should be set up. The military preparations of the previous nine months left no room for doubt that 'all means' included the use of armed force to resist the execution of a British act of parliament.

The circumstances surrounding the preparation and signature of the 'covenant' demonstrate in a striking way one characteristic of the Ulster unionist movement at this period. It was a movement supported by all sections of the protestant community: landlords, manufacturers, merchants, professional men, farmers, industrial workers, all displayed the same enthusiasm. Looking back after an interval of half a century it is easy to suggest that the employing class was here exploiting sectarian prejudices for its own selfish ends; and had the movement stopped short at the limits of constitutional action, this might seem a reasonable diagnosis. But the leaders who, against all the traditions of their upbringing, organized armed rebellion were not influenced solely by class interest; and those who followed them included a high proportion of men not likely to be hoodwinked by a trick. What protestants of all ranks were preparing to fight for, though they might not have admitted it, was the maintenance, in some form, of the threatened protestant ascendancy in Ireland.

Whatever their motives might be, the obvious determination of the

---

[1] The term 'covenant' was chosen by the unionist leaders in imitation of the very different Scottish covenant of 1580.

Ulster unionists, and their persistent propaganda in Great Britain, began to have some effect on liberal opinion, even while the home rule bill was being debated in the house of commons; and it was a liberal member who first formally proposed that part of Ulster should be excluded from the scope of the bill. The government rejected his amendment, but there was some division of opinion in the party and in the cabinet; and from this time onwards the policy of exclusion was never wholly lost sight of, as a possible basis of compromise. It presented obvious difficulties, which few people were at first prepared to face. Redmond could hardly be expected to acquiesce in a settlement that would virtually deny the national identity of Ireland, nor could he lightly abandon the northern nationalists. His own attitude was that the 'Ulster question' was largely artificial. He assured Asquith that the Ulster unionists were playing a 'gigantic game of bluff and blackmail', and that once home rule had been established Irishmen would quickly learn to live peaceably together. Asquith, whether convinced by these arguments or not, refused to risk his adminis-tration by an open breach with Redmond, and decided simply to wait on the course of events. It was for the Ulster unionists that the policy of exclusion raised the most acute problems. Carson himself viewed the situation as an Irishman; and though he brought forward an amendment, in January 1913, for the exclusion of the whole province of Ulster, this was no more than a tactical move: he still believed that home rule without Ulster would be impossible, and his object was to wreck the bill altogether. But Craig and his colleagues on the Ulster Unionist Council took the question more seriously. They were not, at bottom, very much concerned about the protestant minority in the other three provinces; but they were uneasy about the possible effect of exclusion on themselves. Though they commonly spoke as if the province of Ulster were solidly protestant and unionist, they knew very well that Roman Catholics formed almost half the total population, that in three of the nine counties they were over-whelmingly predominant, and that in two more (Fermanagh and Tyrone) they had a small, but distinct, majority. If the unionists were to bargain for the exclusion of all Ulster, could they, in fact, keep control of it? If they were to surrender a part, for the sake of dominating the rest, would they not be breaking their 'covenant'?

By the beginning of 1913, then, the basis for the solution that was eventually to be adopted had already been foreshadowed. But at the time its difficulties seemed greater than its advantages: ten years were to pass before an Ireland exhausted and demoralized by civil strife came reluc-tantly to accept it.

(4)

The introduction of a home rule bill by a government strong enough to pass it into law opened for Redmond a brief period of triumph. Congratulations flowed in from the self-governing dominions — from Botha and Smuts in South Africa, from Sir Wilfred Laurier in Canada, from the prime minister and the leader of the opposition in the Commonwealth of Australia. He appeared now as the herald of a new and happier era in Anglo-Irish relations; and he could point to the enthusiastic welcome given to the king and queen on their visit to Dublin in the summer of 1911 as evidence that the Irish were fundamentally loyal to the crown. But the long-drawn-out struggle over the bill in the house of commons, and the delay resulting from its rejection by the lords, imposed a period of waiting that was full of danger to Redmond and his party. It gave time for Sinn Féin propaganda to take effect; and people began more and more to realize that the home rule for which they were told to wait patiently did not, in fact, amount to very much.

One of the most significant developments during this period was the rise of a militant spirit throughout nationalist Ireland. The Ulster Volunteers had set an example that other Irishmen, of a very different political outlook, regarded less with hostility than with admiration and envy. Patrick Pearse, one of the leaders of the Gaelic League, and a convinced republican, expressed the feelings of many when he declared: 'Personally, I think the Orangeman with the rifle a much less ridiculous figure than the nationalist without a rifle'. By the summer of 1913 members of the Irish Republican Brotherhood were already considering how best they could encourage the formation of a volunteer movement in the south.

The first move in this direction, however, was taken in circumstances that were only indirectly connected with the home rule controversy. During 1913 James Larkin, of the Irish Transport Workers' Union, had organized the Dublin tramwaymen, and other poorly-paid labourers in the city and its neighbourhood, in a demand for higher wages; strikes were followed by a lock-out; and the struggle continued for five months, until it ended in victory for the employers in January 1914. The strikes were accompanied by numerous demonstrations, during which there were some serious clashes with the police; and in October 1913 the strikers and their supporters, claiming that the police had acted in an aggressively brutal manner, organized a military force, the Irish Citizen Army, for their own defence. Its first leaders were J. R. White, an Ulster protestant nationalist, who had served with distinction in the British army, and James Connolly, who had returned from America in 1910, and had been trying in vain to convert the Belfast workers to socialism until he was called to assist Larkin in Dublin. The spirit of the Citizen Army was that of revolutionary socialism; in March 1914 it adopted as its 'first and last principle' that 'the ownership of Ireland, moral and material, is vested of right in the people of Ireland'. But its leaders regarded the establishment of political independence as the necessary first step towards a workers' republic; and its example, which was more influential than its principles, did much to stimulate militarist activity throughout the national movement.

Very shortly after the establishment of the Citizen Army, in November 1913, an informal committee launched a movement for the organization of a volunteer force similar to that in the north. This met with an eager response, especially among young men who had lost faith in the middle-aged and elderly politicians of the parliamentary party, who were tired of waiting for home rule, and who were anxious to be doing something for Ireland themselves. Hundreds of recruits came from the Gaelic Athletic Association, and the Gaelic League provided many of the leaders, including Patrick Pearse and Eoin MacNeill, professor of early Irish history at University College, Dublin. It is, perhaps, worth noting that two important officials of the movement were protestant nationalists from Ulster: Bulmer Hobson was secretary and Sir Roger Casement (who had had a brilliant career in the British consular service) was treasurer.

This new force, the 'Irish Volunteers', had no clearly-defined policy or purpose. It had certainly not been formed to fight against the Volunteers of Ulster — both MacNeill and Pearse were emphatic on that point; but neither was it intended to fight for home rule, whose supporters meant to gain their ends by political and not by military means, and about which, in fact, few of the Volunteer leaders really cared. Probably the most important influence in the central direction of the Volunteers was that of the Irish Republican Brotherhood, whose members held many of the key posts. Though they had not, at this stage, worked out any definite project for an insurrection, they saw in the Volunteer movement a useful means of educating public opinion, and also a potential weapon to be used if an opportunity for insurrection should occur.

From Redmond's point of view the very existence of the Volunteers was an embarrassment; and their independence was a menace to his authority. For a time, he tried to ignore them; but by March 1914 he realized that the movement had grown so strong that the only safe course was to bring it under his own control, and he demanded that the existing committee should be enlarged by the addition of twenty-five members nominated by the parliamentary party. Though many of the Volunteer leaders resented this demand, they knew that open rejection would result in a split, for Redmond's influence was still powerful; and in June the committee was reconstructed on his plan. But the republican element, though now outnumbered, still kept its place, and waited for an opportunity to assert itself.

Meanwhile, the northern unionists had been strengthening their organization. In the summer of 1913 they had appointed a retired British general,[1] selected for them by Field-Marshal Roberts, to command the Volunteers. In September, the Ulster Unionist Council had formally turned itself into a provisional government, ready to take over the administration of the province as soon as the home rule bill should become law. A £1,000,000 guarantee fund had been established and fully subscribed. Preparations had been made for the evacuation of women and children to England in the event of hostilities in Ulster.

Neither in their actions nor in their language did the unionists show much regard for the law, and Carson repeatedly challenged the government to arrest him. But Asquith was convinced that to do so would only precipitate a crisis that might otherwise be averted; and Redmond, who already saw himself as first prime minister of Ireland, and who had no wish to take up office against a background of British coercion in Ulster, encouraged him in this attitude.

This apparent weakness on the part of the government, and the repeated assurances of support given them by the British conservatives, made it less and less likely that Carson and Craig would give ground. Redmond, on his side, was acutely aware that nationalist opinion would not tolerate any substantial concession. But, for Asquith, the only hope lay in effecting a compromise. Early in March 1914 he induced Redmond to accept, very reluctantly, a proposal that any Ulster county might, by a vote of its parliamentary electors, exclude itself from the operation of the home rule act for a period of six years, after which it would be brought in automatically; and an amending bill embodying this proposal was shortly afterwards introduced in the house of commons. But Carson rejected it outright. 'We do not', he said, 'want sentence of death with a stay of execution for six years'.

Despite this rebuff, Asquith went on with the bill. He believed that the prospect of six years' delay would weaken the sense of urgency among the Ulster unionists, and that if they persisted in threats of violence after the offer of such a concession they would lose the support of their friends in

[1] Lieut.-General Sir George Richardson, who had served in the army in India. Though not an Irishman, he had settled in Ireland.

Britain. Meanwhile, the government resolved on making a show of force; and during the third week in March orders were given for naval and military movements that would strengthen the position of the crown forces in Ulster. The result was to show that claims often made by the unionists that they had support in the army were not without foundation. The commander-in-chief in Ireland, Sir Arthur Paget, acting on authority from the war office, took the unprecedented step of asking officers likely to be involved in the proposed operation in Ulster for an assurance that they were willing to serve, warning them that if they refused they would be dismissed. Fifty-eight of the cavalry officers stationed at the Curragh, the Irish military headquarters, indicated that they would prefer dismissal to the risk of being ordered to take aggressive action against the Ulster Volunteers; and the press was soon filled with controversy over this 'mutiny', as the officers' action was misleadingly called. The whole business was quickly patched up, and the officers retained their commissions; but the shock to public confidence in the army had been severe, and the prestige of the government suffered accordingly.

The Ulster unionists, however, continued on their course with renewed confidence. Their main object now was to complete the arming of the Volunteers; for though they had been smuggling rifles and ammunition for years, the quantities so far imported were relatively small, and only a minority of the force was fully equipped. Much of this smuggling had been organized by F. H. Crawford, a Belfast businessman with a taste for adventure; but early in 1914 he embarked on a much larger project, which he brought to a successful conclusion on the night of 24–25 April, when 25,000 rifles and 3,000,000 rounds of ammunition were landed, most of them at Larne and Donaghadee, so efficiently that the whole operation had been completed before police or military could interfere. The Irish Volunteers, following this example, carried out a similar landing at Howth on 24 July, though on a much smaller scale. The Howth landing, unlike that at Larne, was conducted publicly in broad day; and the Castle authorities, as soon as they knew what was happening, sent troops to seize the arms. This attempt failed; and the soldiers, marching back through a jeering, stone-throwing mob, forgot their discipline and opened fire; with the result that three civilians were killed. The episode had an enormous effect on public opinion, raising the prestige of the Volunteers, and making it more dangerous than ever for Redmond to show any sign of weakness in negotiations with the government.

By this time, indeed, the chance of a negotiated settlement seemed to have vanished. The king, who had made various unobtrusive efforts at mediation, had finally called a conference of the opposing leaders to meet at Buckingham Palace on 21 July, under the chairmanship of the Speaker. The question before the conference was whether or not Ulster, or a part of Ulster, should be permanently excluded from the home rule bill. This was an issue on which neither Carson and Craig, who represented the Ulster unionists, nor Redmond and Dillon, who represented the nationalists, could afford to yield; and it was with them, rather than with the liberals and conservatives, that the decision lay. On 24 July the conference broke up, having failed to reach agreement 'either in principle or in detail'. Within a few weeks the home rule bill must pass into law, despite the house of lords; and it was hard to see how the government could then avoid a clash with one or other of the rival armies established in Ireland.

At the last minute, the crisis was deferred, and its character changed, by the outbreak of war in Europe.

XXIII

The Revolution in Ireland,
1914-23

(1)

The outbreak of war between the United Kingdom and Germany in August 1914 meant, almost inevitably, the postponement of home rule, for the government shrank from giving effect to such a controversial measure in a crisis that demanded, above all else, national unity. Fortunately for Asquith, the leaders of the two main Irish parties accepted this view of the situation; both Carson and Redmond promised full support for the war effort, and accepted a compromise by which the home rule bill was to pass into law, accompanied by a suspensory act, postponing its operation until the return of peace. To some optimistic observers this agreement opened a prospect of future harmony between north and south; but such hopes had only a slender foundation. Among unionists and nationalists alike there was, no doubt, some element of generous enthusiasm for the Allied cause; but each side felt that it was establishing a claim on the gratitude of Great Britain, and that its services during the war would entitle it to full satisfaction when victory had been won. The struggle between them had been deferred, not averted.

But for the time being things went smoothly. Redmond's support of the government was well received by nationalists in general, and recruits for the British army came forward by the thousand. The fact that Belgium was a Roman Catholic country made it easy to arouse sympathy; and the stress laid by Allied propaganda on the rights of small nations had considerable effect. Besides this, war quickly stimulated the Irish economy: there was soon plenty of money in circulation, and the farmers had never been so prosperous. Nationalist Ireland as a whole seemed quite happy to wait for peace to bring home rule, and in the meantime to enjoy the profits of war.

The more militant nationalists, who had always been suspicious of the parliamentary party, viewed the situation very differently. Many of them had been ready to accept home rule as an interim measure; but their real aim was the separation, more or less complete, of Ireland from Great Britain, and they regarded the war as an opportunity to forward this end. They were altogether opposed to Redmond's policy of co-operation with the government, and they did what they could to hinder recruiting for the British army. Those who held these views, and who may conveniently be described as 'separatists' to distinguish them from the home rule nationalists, were not linked together in a single body, nor had they arrived at an agreed policy. They worked through a variety of organizations, of which the I.R.B. was the most influential, and even within the I.R.B. there was some difference of opinion about the best course to pursue. But the leading separatists maintained close personal contacts, and they had a common field of activity in the Volunteer movement, with which most of them were associated, and which they had, in fact, created. Even among the Volunteers, however, their popular following at this time was small; when they seceded from the main body, in September 1914, as a protest against Redmond's recruiting policy, only about 11,000 men, out of a total of 180,000 followed them, and formed a distinct force, with Eoin MacNeill as chief of staff.[1] But they made up in ability, enthusiasm and determination what they lacked in numbers; and it was from their ranks that the leaders of a new Ireland were to emerge.

In their attitude to the situation created by the war the separatists fell into two main groups. One group, of which MacNeill and Bulmer Hobson were leading representatives, wished to follow a cautious and defensive policy, and reserve their strength until the end of the war, when they hoped that the outcome, whatever it might be, would provide an opportunity for asserting Irish independence. In the meantime, they were opposed to aggressive action, unless the government should force their hand by attempting to suppress or disarm the Volunteers, or by imposing conscription on Ireland. In MacNeill's opinion, this defensive policy was the only one that could be morally justified in the circumstances; for the government was so strong that no insurrection could have any reasonable prospect of success. 'Without that prospect', he wrote in February 1916, 'military action (not military preparation) would in the first place be morally wrong ... To enter deliberately on a course of action which is morally wrong is to incur the guilt not only of that action itself but of all

---

[1] The minority that followed MacNeill retained the name 'Irish Volunteers'; the Redmondite majority became known as 'National Volunteers'.

its direct consequences. For example, to kill any person in carrying out such a course of action is murder'. And he went on to argue that a hopeless insurrection could not be justified by the prospect of 'some future moral or political advantage which may be hoped for as the result of non-success'.

The other main group of separatists took a radically different view. Within a few weeks of the outbreak of war, they had resolved that before it ended the independence of Ireland should be asserted in arms; and, in making their resolve, they were moved less by any calculation of the prospects of success than by a feeling that, if such an opportunity were allowed to pass, the reality of Irish national aspirations might be called in question. The group that made this decision, composed mainly though not exclusively of members of the I.R.B., included Arthur Griffith, founder of Sinn Féin, and Thomas James Clarke, a veteran of the Fenian movement; but the most characteristic representative of its viewpoint was Patrick Pearse. Pearse had been influenced, though perhaps not consciously, by the cult of bloodshed and violence that had spread through Europe during the previous two decades. He seems to have regarded war as good in itself; and he certainly welcomed the outbreak in Europe for its own sake, quite apart from any advantage that it might bring to Ireland — the heart of the world, he proclaimed, would be refreshed by the 'red wine of the battlefields'. He believed that the 'heart of Ireland 'needed to be refreshed in the same way. 'There has been nothing more terrible in Irish history', he wrote, 'than the failure of the last generation'; and nothing but a 'blood-sacrifice' could redeem this failure.

Connolly stood apart from both these groups. Like Pearse, he was resolved on insurrection; but he believed that a military success was possible, for though his Citizen Army was barely 300 strong, he was convinced that once the first blow had been struck the whole country would rise in support. Pearse and his colleagues were continually alarmed lest Connolly should ruin their plans by a premature move, until at last, in January 1916, they persuaded him to accept a scheme of combined action.

Though few of those who were planning insurrection counted on military success, they realized that, if they were to gain the moral and political ends they had in mind, the threat to the government must be a serious one: another fiasco such as had occurred in 1867 would be fatal. They prepared, therefore, to use their meagre resources to the best effect, and to expand them if possible. They did what they could to get arms and ammunition from Germany, with which they were able to maintain contact by way of the United States; and Sir Roger Casement, who had reached Berlin from New York in October 1914, acted as their agent with the German government. But though the possibility of German help had some propaganda value, and may have influenced a few waverers, the real instigators of rebellion relied, in the long run, on themselves, and were determined to go ahead, with or without foreign intervention.

Preparations for rebellion could not be conducted with complete secrecy, and the government was tolerably well informed about what was going on. But Birrell, the chief secretary, maintained the pre-war attitude of *laissez-faire* towards Irish political activities. From time to time separatist newspapers were suppressed, when they were particularly outspoken in their attacks on recruiting or in their advocacy of insurrection; but Sinn Féin, the I.R.B., and similar bodies were left alone; and the Irish Volunteers and the Citizen Army paraded openly with their rifles, and even carried out sham attacks on strongholds in Dublin, without any interference. The government took the view that the country as a whole was content, that the separatist bodies were too weak to be dangerous, and that it would be foolish to provoke them to violence by direct suppression. During the early months of 1916, the authorities began to regard the situation more seriously; but they still believed that they had it under control. Their failure was a failure of understanding. They had most of the external facts — they even knew the details of the negotiations with Germany — but the spirit of deliberate self-sacrifice that animated Pearse and his colleagues lay beyond their calculations; and the events of Easter Monday were to take them completely by surprise.

(2)

Many movements and influences contributed to the insurrection of April 1916; but the planning and direction of the final stages was the work of the I.R.B., which, in the previous January, had settled the date in collaboration with Connolly, and had arranged for a cargo of German arms to be landed on the coast of Kerry a day or two before the insurrection was due to begin. But though the I.R.B. might plan a rising, it must depend on the Irish Volunteers to provide the men; and the Volunteers were officially committed to the defensive policy of MacNeill, their chief of staff, and Bulmer Hobson, their secretary. There were, it is true, some Volunteers who rejected this policy: Pearse himself, who was Volunteer director of operations, and Thomas MacDonagh, who was commandant of the Dublin brigade, were also members of the I.R.B. military council, which was secretly preparing for insurrection. For a long time they succeeded in deceiving MacNeill about their intentions; but it is hard to see how, in the long run, they could have hoped to bring the whole force of the Volunteers into action without his knowledge and approval; and their attempt to get round the difficulty produced, at the last minute, a great deal of confusion and misunderstanding.

The date fixed for the insurrection was Easter Sunday, 23 April; and early in the month Pearse, in his capacity as director of operations, gave orders for Volunteer field-manœuvres to begin on that day. This was meant to appear as a routine arrangement, and only a very small inner group knew that anything more was intended. MacNeill, whose suspicions had already been aroused, showed signs of uneasiness; but Pearse and MacDonagh reassured him that no aggressive move was being planned. It was not until late on 20 April (Maundy Thursday) that he learnt the truth, and then only by accident. His first thought was to avert the insurrection by appealing to Pearse and the other I.R.B. leaders, and by issuing instructions to the Volunteers. Then, on Good Friday, he was persuaded that things had gone so far that the government was bound to strike, and he agreed to collaborate in what he now considered a defensive action. But on Saturday he received fresh information about the government's attitude; hope of saving the situation returned; and that night he issued an order, which was distributed over the country by special messengers and published in the press next day, countermanding Sunday's manœuvres.

In all this, MacNeill acted in strict accordance with his principles, which were well known to the leaders of the I.R.B.; and any apparent inconsistency in his conduct on the eve of the insurrection arose directly from the deception that had been practised on him. Nothing that he could have done would have prevented an outbreak; but his countermanding order ensured that it would be confined to the capital. However his action may be judged, it did at least help to prevent bloodshed.

The confusion arising from MacNeill's discovery of the truth was not the only last-minute difficulty that the I.R.B. leaders had to face. On 20 April a German ship, the *Aud*, had arrived on the coast of Kerry with a cargo of arms. But there had been a misunderstanding about dates: the *Aud* found no one to meet her; and next day she was captured by the British and brought into Queenstown harbour, where her captain scuttled her. Almost at the same time, Casement, who had been put ashore from a German submarine, was taken prisoner near Tralee. It was with this news before them, and with the knowledge that MacNeill's countermanding order would almost certainly neutralize the Volunteers in the provinces, that the I.R.B. military council met on the morning of Easter Day, and resolved, in spite of all, to strike at noon on Monday. The one thing in their favour was that the capture of the *Aud* had dulled the fears of the Castle authorities, who had suspected for some time that a rebellion was brewing. Now they believed that the danger had been scotched; and MacNeill's cancellation of manœuvres, though they did not fully understand its background, confirmed this belief. There were only some 1,200 troops in Dublin, and no arrangements had been made to reinforce them; many of the officers had been given leave to attend a local race-meeting on Easter Monday; and the Castle itself was garrisoned by half-a-dozen men with blank cartridges.

Dublin was so accustomed to Volunteer parades that the holiday crowds paid no special attention to the columns that marched through the streets on Easter Monday morning. Without opposition they took possession of the General Post Office, where they set up their headquarters; and from the steps in front of the building Pearse read a proclamation declaring the establishment of a republic. It began with an appeal to Irishmen and Irishwomen to support the struggle for the independence of their country 'in the name of God and of the dead generations from which she receives her old tradition of nationhood'. It went on to declare that the right to independence could not be extinguished by 'the long usurpation of that right by a foreign nation and government', and it constituted a provisional government of the Irish Republic, with a claim on the allegiance of all citizens.[1] It was only by degrees that the people, or indeed the authorities, came to realize that this was something more than a mere demonstration; and by that time the insurgents had already established themselves in well-selected strongholds. Before nightfall, almost the whole of the centre of the city was in their hands and they had a cordon of fortified posts in the suburbs.

There had been little serious fighting on this first day, for the government forces were too weak to attack. But on Tuesday reinforcements began to arrive, artillery was brought into play, and the hopelessness of the insurgents' position soon appeared. They maintained resistance as long as they could, but they were almost helpless in face of artillery fire; they had no prospect of reinforcements; their strongholds were isolated from one another; on Friday, the General Post Office caught fire and had to be evacuated. On Saturday, at half past three o'clock in the afternoon Pearse surrendered unconditionally, and wrote out an order to the commandants of other posts to do the same. The insurrection was at an end.

In its immediate effect, the insurrection seemed likely to disappoint the expectations of those who had organized it. Though they had held out

[1] The proclamation was signed by Thomas J. Clarke, Sean MacDiarmada, P. H. Pearse, James Connolly, Thomas MacDonagh, Eamonn Ceannt [Kent], Joseph Plunkett. Pearse was both head of the provisional government and 'commandant general' of its forces.

for a week with less than 2,000 men against all the forces that the government could bring against them, their appeal to the country had fallen flat. Here and there, especially in Galway and Wexford, some Volunteers had turned out, despite MacNeill's order; but their action had had no influence on the course of events. And public opinion was utterly hostile. The Dublin mob, while eagerly seizing the opportunity to loot, had cheered the government troops, many of them Irish, as they moved in to the attack. In some areas the National Volunteers had come to the assistance of the police and the military. Redmond denounced the insurgents in parliament. The *Freeman's Journal*, the most widely-read newspaper in the country, summed up the general feeling when it declared, on 5 May, 'The insurrection was not more an insurrection against the connection with the Empire, than it was an armed assault against the will and decision of the Irish nation itself constitutionally ascertained through its proper representatives'. The insurgents had been prepared for a military defeat, but they seemed to have suffered a moral defeat also.

It was the action of the government that transformed this situation. The policy of *laissez-faire* seemed condemned by its result; Birrell resigned office; and the cabinet, overburdened by the conduct of the war in Europe, left Ireland for the time being to the military. Martial law had been proclaimed at the outbreak of the insurrection, and the captured insurgent leaders were tried by court martial: between 3 May and 12 May fifteen of them, including all the signatories of the republican proclamation, were executed. It is unlikely that any European government of the period, faced with a similar situation, would have acted less harshly. But Irish opinion was horrified; and as one day after another brought its curt official announcement, giving the names of those who had been tried, found guilty and shot, horror turned to anger against the government and admiration for the insurgents. The British authorities were, as Bernard Shaw warned them at the time, 'canonizing their prisoners'. Before the middle of May executions had ceased, and Asquith himself had come to Dublin in an effort to establish confidence and goodwill. But it was already too late. Ireland was quickly passing under the most dangerous of all tyrannies — the tyranny of the dead.

(3)

The insurrection convinced the cabinet that some new settlement of affairs in Ireland must be worked out; and the necessity for placating public opinion in the United States, where Irish influence was still very powerful, made the task an urgent one. It was entrusted to Lloyd George;

but, despite his energy and ingenuity, the negotiations that he initiated in May 1916 dragged on for almost two years, and in the end achieved no results. These negotiations have about them, at least in retrospect, an air of unreality; for the surviving leaders of the revolutionary movement took no part, and it was they, rather than Redmond, who now presented the dominant force in Irish politics.

The negotiations, however, were not entirely without effect: it was in them that the policy of partition, vaguely adumbrated in 1914, took definite form. Lloyd George proposed that the home rule act should come into operation, without waiting for the end of the war, but that six Ulster counties, which had between them a clear unionist majority, should remain outside its operation.[1] The proposal came to nothing, for though Redmond and Carson both reluctantly accepted it, they understood it in different senses: Redmond supposed that the exclusion was to be temporary, Carson that it was to be permanent — 'a clean cut'. Once the difference was revealed, neither would give way. But whereas the Ulster unionists had established themselves in what proved to be a strong and defensible position, Redmond's willingness to accept partition on any terms damaged his prestige still further.

The entry of the United States into the war on the Allied side, in April 1917, did not abate the government's desire for a settlement: President Wilson himself urged its necessity if American opinion were to be firmly united behind the war effort. In May, Lloyd George, now prime minister, set about preparations for a new move — an 'Irish Convention', representative of all the principal interests in the country, to draw up a scheme of government. He had already, as a gesture of good will, released some hundreds of internees who had been rounded up after the insurrection and held for several months without trial; and in June 1917 those who had been sentenced to terms of imprisonment were released also. The only effect of those concessions was to reinforce the surviving revolutionary organizations, which had been temporarily shaken by the collapse of the rising. During the early months of 1917 the I.R.B. was making plans to re-form the Volunteers; and Sinn Féin re-emerged as the political wing of the revolutionary movement. Two by-elections showed that this revival was winning popular support: in Roscommon in February, in Longford in May, Sinn Féin candidates were successful in face of all the strength that the home rule party could muster in what it had long regarded as perfectly safe constituencies. Perhaps the most significant

---

[1] The counties to be excluded were Antrim, Armagh, Down, Fermanagh, Londonderry, Tyrone.

item in their election propaganda was a promise not to take their seats at Westminster.

It was against this background that the Irish Convention met in July, under the chairmanship of Sir Horace Plunkett. The refusal of Sinn Féin to take part, and the intransigent attitude of the unionist delegates from Ulster, foredoomed it to failure; for these were now the only political parties exercising effective power. Most members of the Convention were out of sympathy with the new mood of the country, or represented groups, such as the southern unionists, which were politically impotent. Though in the following April it agreed, by a majority, to recommend the establishment of a home rule parliament for all Ireland, its decision was irrelevant to the situation that had by that time developed, and the government did not even attempt to give effect to it.

While the Irish Convention pursued its hopeless way Sinn Féin had been extending and strengthening its organization. At a national conference (*ard féis*), held in Dublin in October 1917, it passed under new leadership, Griffith standing aside in favour of Eamon de Valera, who had been returned for East Clare, with a huge majority, in July. When, in November, de Valera was also elected president of the Irish Volunteers, both the political and military wings of the revolutionary movement were brought under the control of one man. De Valera owed his position, in the first place, to the fact that he was the only survivor among the Volunteer commandants who had taken part in the insurrection;[1] but that position was quickly confirmed by his power to win confidence and admiration. A scholar and an enthusiast, he was also a competent man of affairs and a shrewd, if occasionally over-subtle, politician. The main source of his strength lay in a firm tenancity of purpose, combined with a flexibility of method; his weakness, in an unwillingness to work with those who would not subordinate their own views to his. Though the leadership that he established in 1917 was to be broken less than five years later, he was destined to occupy a central place in Irish politics until well beyond the middle of the century.

Another leader who emerged at almost the same time as de Valera was Michael Collins. Interned after the insurrection, he had quickly established an influential position among his fellow-prisoners; and in November 1917, when the Volunteers were re-constituted, he was appointed director of organization. Efficient, straightforward and ruthless, he

[1] De Valera was tried by court martial and condemned to death; but in deference to American opinion the sentence was commuted to one of imprisonment. Though not an American citizen, he had been born in the United States. Like the other Sinn Féin prisoners he was released in June 1917.

quickly established discipline, and prepared the way for guerrilla warfare against the government forces. In politics, he had little of de Valera's subtlety, but was guided by what he took to be the common-sense view of the facts; and having formed his opinion, he acted on it courageously. More, perhaps, than any other man he has a claim to be regarded as the creator of the Irish Free State.

During the winter of 1917–18 Ireland was in a strange condition of mingled excitement, foreboding and suspense. The government, waiting for the Convention to report, hardly knew what to do. It was unwilling to provoke disorder by a serious attempt to break the Sinn Féin and Volunteer organizations; but scores of known or suspected republicans were arrested, republican newspapers were from time to time suppressed, and there were frequent searches for arms. But all this activity only served to exacerbate public feeling. Over much of the country the moral authority of the government was rapidly breaking down, and Sinn Féin, resurgent and confident, was preparing to take its place. Volunteer numbers constantly expanded; for republican propaganda appealed particularly to the young, and the number of young men in the country was swollen by the wartime closing of emigration to America and by the deterrent effect of conscription on emigration to Britain. The home rule party, though it still dominated Irish representation at Westminster, had almost lost its hold on the Irish people; and John Redmond's death, in March 1918, hardly affected the political situation. The policy to which he had devoted his life was already out of date; and though his Waterford constituency returned his son, a captain in the British army, with a comfortable majority over a Sinn Féin opponent, this was rather a tribute to past service than an expression of contemporary support for home rule.

It was the action of the government itself, in proposing to apply military conscription to Ireland, that finally confirmed the popular influence of Sinn Féin. Ireland had been excluded from the conscription act of 1916; but the pressure on man-power was constantly rising, and a new act, passed in the spring of 1918, not only raised the age of exemption, but empowered the government to extend the operation of the act to Ireland by order in council. All nationalist Ireland at once united in protest. A conference called by the lord mayor of Dublin asserted that the proposal was 'a declaration of war on the Irish nation'; the home rule party withdrew from the house of commons; the Roman Catholic bishops issued a statement condemning the government's policy, and affirming that 'the Irish have a right to resist by every means that are consonant with the law of God'; a one-day strike, effective everywhere except in the north-east, was a clear indication of national solidarity. In the end, conscription was not extended to Ireland, and public opinion gave the credit to Sinn Féin; the home rulers, indeed, by their withdrawal from Westminster, had virtually admitted their own impotence, and accepted the Sinn Féin argument against constitutional co-operation with the British.

Alarmed at this exhibition of national feeling, the government made a belated attempt to break the revolutionary movement. In May 1918, de Valera, Griffith and other leaders were arrested; Sinn Féin and the Volunteers were proclaimed as illegal; and a ban was placed on public meetings. But the organization built up during the previous twelve months could not so easily be destroyed; and before the end of the year Sinn Féin was given an opportunity to show the extent of its hold on the country. The armistice in November was followed by a general election in December; Sinn Féin candidates contested every constituency, and 73 of them were successful; the unionists, with 26 members returned, somewhat strengthened their position; the old parliamentary party was reduced to 6. This victory was less sweeping than it seemed; for though Sinn Féin secured unopposed returns in 26 constituencies, it received less than half the votes cast in the remainder, and it is very probable that a good many of those votes reflected anger against the government and contempt for the home rule party, rather than convinced support for a full republican programme. But all this did not alter the fact that Sinn Féin could now claim, with justice, to represent majority opinion in Ireland.

In accordance with the principles long ago laid down by Arthur Griffith, the Sinn Féin members ignored Westminster. Instead, they met in Dublin in January 1919, proclaimed themselves the parliament of the Irish Republic (*Dáil Eireann* — the Assembly of Ireland), re-affirmed the declaration of independence of 1916, adopted a provisional constitution, and appointed delegates to attend the peace conference of the Allied powers in Paris.[1] The government, nervous of American opinion and uncertain how to act, made no immediate attempt to check these proceedings, and the republicans were given time to strengthen their organization. De Valera, who had escaped from prison in England in February, was elected president of the Dáil in April, and he appointed a ministry of eight members, which claimed henceforth to be the legitimate government of Ireland. It was, in fact, eventually able to make its authority effective over

[1] There were 69 Sinn Féin members, some having been elected for more than one constituency. Of these, only 25 were present at the first public meeting of the Dáil on 21 January 1919; 2 were ill, 7 were absent on Sinn Féin business; 1 had been deported; 34 were in prison.

much of the country, partly through the normal organs of local administration, many of which were dominated by republicans, partly through arbitration courts, which in some areas virtually superseded the courts of the crown. With two rival governments in operation, a clash was inevitable.

(4)

Though Ireland in 1919 was slipping into a state of war, neither side was in a hurry to precipitate the conflict. Government policy, stumbling between ineffective repression and half-hearted attempts at conciliation, seemed to lack all direction. Sinn Féin was proclaimed as an illegal organization in August, the Dáil in September; but even after this the government hesitated between a determined effort to restore its authority and a settlement by negotiation. The republicans awaited hopefully the outcome of their negotiations in the United States, where de Valera received an enthusiastic welcome in June. They had, so far, failed to secure a hearing in the peace conference at Paris; but there was at least some prospect that American influence might bring about a change in the situation, and that Britain would be forced, by external pressure, to yield to Irish demands. This prospect was not to be fulfilled; but in the autumn of 1919 the republican leaders were still sanguine of success; and in the meantime they were content to strengthen their organization and build up their military resources, for which purpose large sums of money were being raised both at home and in the United States. Some clashes between republican forces and the police and military occurred throughout the year, and became more frequent towards its close; but they were isolated episodes, due for the most part to the initiative of local republican commandants, and did not form part of a coherent scheme of attack.

In 1920, however, the issue became more clear-cut, and before the middle of the year the long-threatened war was in full flood. The republicans did not follow the example of open assault set by the insurgents of 1916, nor did they attempt to occupy and hold any clearly-defined area. The Irish Volunteers had been reconstituted, early in 1919, as the army of the republic — the Irish Republican Army (I.R.A.); but it was an army of guerrillas, operating in flying columns, fifteen to thirty strong, and conducting a war of raids and ambushes. Members of the I.R.A. rarely wore uniform, so that even in daylight they could easily achieve an element of surprise that baffled the ingenuity of the crown forces and shook their morale. But it was unlikely that a war waged in this way could achieve military victory, in the normal sense of the term; and the republicans fought with the more limited aim of making regular government impossible, and the cost of holding the country so great that the British would be compelled to withdraw.

The government's response to the tactics of the I.R.A. was dictated as much by political conditions in Britain as by military conditions in Ireland. Lloyd George's coalition ministry, despite its electoral victory in 1918, was not in a strong position, and its conduct of Irish affairs was under constant attack in parliament and in the press; it dared not admit that Ireland was in a state of war, and insisted that the I.R.A. was supported by only a small section of the population, and could be dealt with by police action. Though the number of troops in the country was steadily increased, and though some areas were later put under martial law, it was on the police that the government placed its main reliance. The Royal Irish Constabulary had borne the brunt of the republican attacks in 1919; but the casualties that it suffered, and even more, perhaps, the social ostracism to which its members and their families were subjected by order of the republican government, weakened its will to resist; there were many resignations, and it was impossible to find fresh recruits in Ireland. To meet this situation, the government raised men in England, mainly among ex-soldiers; and since there was no immediately available supply of police uniforms, they wore khaki, with police caps and belts; it was from this mixed dress that they received their nickname — the 'Black-and-Tans'.[1] About the same time the government raised another force also, the 'Auxiliary Division' of the constabulary, consisting for the most part of young ex-officers, and commonly known as 'Auxiliaries'. It was the Black-and-Tans and the Auxiliaries who formed the spearhead of the government's attempt to break the I.R.A. during the later months of 1920 and the first half of 1921.

The character of the war was largely determined by the forces engaged in it, for on neither side were the politicians in effective control. The Dáil, meeting with difficulty and at uncertain intervals, was in no position to direct military policy; and the I.R.A., which had inherited from the Volunteers the sense of being a distinct and independent organization, acted throughout on its own responsibility. Two of its principal commanders were members of the Dáil cabinet, Cathal Brugha (Charles Burgess) as minister of defence, and Michael Collins as minister of finance; but it was not the cabinet that controlled the conduct of the war. On the British side the politicians exercised much more direct influence; but Sir Hamar Greenwood, who was appointed chief secretary in the summer of 1920, was convinced that the police and the military should

[1] This was the name of a well-known pack of hounds in County Limerick.

be given a free hand, and he consistently defended them against all criticism.

In effect, then, the struggle was fought between two largely irresponsible military organizations, in circumstances where the normal laws of war could hardly be said to apply, and the main object of each side was to break the morale of the other by a system of terrorism — an object that was pursued with increasing ferocity as the war went on. It was inevitable that civilians should suffer heavily. The I.R.A. claimed that the whole population owed allegiance to the republic, and that anyone giving aid to the crown forces deserved to be executed as a traitor; and on this principle they shot, without regard to age or sex, dozens of persons suspected of having supplied information to the police or military. Probably most people were, in any case, at least passively sympathetic towards the republican cause; the ruthless efficiency of the I.R.A. kept the rest quiet; and the British found themselves operating in what was, in reality, a hostile country, against an enemy undistinguished by badge or uniform: at any moment a group of loungers in a village street might spring into action as a detachment of the I.R.A. In such circumstances, even regular troops were liable to break discipline and avenge themselves on the civilian population; but the Black-and-Tans and the Auxiliaries, whose discipline was never very effective, carried out reprisals of this sort as a matter of course. These reprisals were generally condoned, and sometimes encouraged, by those in command; but it was not until the beginning of 1921 that a regular policy of reprisal, under certain restrictions, was officially authorized. It is doubtful if this formal change of policy made much practical difference: after it came into operation the Black-and-Tans continued, as before, to follow their own course.

The system of 'authorized reprisals' was only part of a sterner policy towards which the government had been moving during the latter half of 1920: by January 1921, eight southern counties were under martial law; and the I.R.A. met this threat by intensifying its attacks. But already the conviction was gaining ground that a military decision was impracticable. The I.R.A. had succeeded in making normal government impossible, but it could do no more; it could not force the withdrawal of the British forces while the government was prepared to face the cost, in men, money and prestige, of maintaining them. For Britain, the choice now lay between a systematic conquest of Ireland, which British public opinion would never tolerate, and the offer of terms that the republican leaders might reasonably be expected to accept. More than two years of bloodshed had, at last, opened the way for compromise.

(5)

The Irish republicans and the British government were not the only parties involved in the conflict in Ireland — the unionists of Ulster were no less deeply concerned in the outcome. Ever since the insurrection of 1916 they had been watching the course of events with growing anxiety, and with growing distrust in the government's ability, or even willingness, to protect their interests. The Dáil claimed authority over Ulster, as over the rest of Ireland, and this claim was backed by the activities of the I.R.A. throughout the province. The rising sense of danger thus created among the protestant population stirred up the sectarian passions which were never far below the surface of Ulster life; and these passions were further stimulated by reports, sometimes no doubt distorted or exaggerated, of the ill-treatment suffered by the scattered protestants of the south and west. The home rule crisis of the pre-war years had strengthened still further the religious element in the cleavage between unionist and nationalist, and in the circumstances of 1920 it was easy for the protestant workman of the north-east to identify 'Roman Catholic' with 'republican' (or, as he would have said, 'rebel'), and to feel that the very presence of a large Roman Catholic minority was a threat to his own safety. It was this fear of being overwhelmed in a rising tide of republicanism that lay behind the fierce riots that broke out in Belfast in the summer of 1920, and recurred from time to time, both there and in other parts of Ulster, during the next twelve months. Sometimes the rioting was occasioned by a particular action of the I.R.A. — as at Lisburn in August 1920, when it followed the shooting of a police inspector as he left church on a Sunday morning; sometimes it was, apparently, planned in advance. But whether spontaneous or planned, the riots always took the form of indiscriminate attack on the Roman Catholic population of the neighbourhood: thousands of families, who had no connection and often little sympathy with the I.R.A., were driven from their homes, not without immense damage to property and some loss of life; and the government seemed as powerless to protect the Roman Catholics of the north as the unionists of the south.

The unionist leaders viewed these developments with mixed feelings. They shared, at least in some measure, the fears of their more violent followers, and tried to excuse their actions on the ground of extreme provocation; but they could not help realizing that the character of the riots must weaken their case in the eyes of the British public. At the same time they were forced to recognize, with some natural resentment,

P   B.M.I.

that the conservatives' pre-war enthusiasm for the cause of the Ulster protestants had almost withered away. Their best hope, therefore, lay in a speedy settlement; and when the government proposed terms they accepted them, though reluctantly, as the best they were likely to get.

The terms of the settlement were embodied in a new home rule bill, decided on by the cabinet in September 1920 and passed into law in the following December. This measure (the government of Ireland act) divided the country in two: 'Northern Ireland', consisting of the six Ulster counties whose exclusion from home rule had been proposed in 1916, and 'Southern Ireland', consisting of the remaining twenty-six counties. Each was to have its own parliament, made up of a house of commons and a senate, and a responsible ministry. The powers granted to these parliaments were very similar to those granted by the home rule act of 1914, and the supremacy of the imperial parliament, in which both parts of Ireland were still to be represented, was explicitly preserved. The partition effected by this act was not meant to be complete or, necessarily, permanent: certain matters of concern to the whole country were to be controlled by a 'council of Ireland' whose powers might be enlarged by agreement between the two parliaments; and the re-union of the country could be brought about at any time by the merging of the two parliaments in one, if both should so desire.

Ulster unionists saw two disadvantages in this settlement: it involved the abandonment of all their fellow-unionists outside the six-county area; and it weakened that link with the rest of the United Kingdom which they had for so long striven to maintain. But they were won over by the fact that, in the six counties left to them, they would be in a permanent majority; and with their constitutional position safeguarded by an act of parliament they need no longer fear, as they had feared in the past, that their interests would be sacrificed by a British government seeking to conciliate Irish nationalist opinion. When the first election for a Northern Ireland parliament was held, in May 1921, the unionists secured 40 out of the 52 seats in the house of commons; and a cabinet was shortly afterwards formed. Carson had by this time given up the unionist leadership, on grounds of age and ill-health, and it was Sir James Craig[1] who, as prime minister, undertook the complicated and dangerous task of getting the new government into working order.

The unionists' acceptance of the government of Ireland act was, in the long run, to prepare the way for a general settlement; but its immediate

---

[1] Created a baronet in 1918.

effect was to intensify the opposition of the republicans. They rejected with scorn the very idea of home rule, declared implacable hostility to partition, and set themselves, by every means, to destroy the new government in the north, almost before it had come into existence. They did, however, make use of the election for a Southern Ireland parliament, held under the terms of the act in May 1921, as a means both of demonstrating their strength and of securing the election of a new Dáil. Of the 128 members elected to the house of commons, 124 were Sinn Féin candidates who had been returned unopposed, for no one had dared to appear against them. The remaining 4 were the representatives of Trinity College, Dublin; and they alone appeared when the parliament was formally opened in June. It adjourned almost at once: 'Southern Ireland' as a political entity was still-born.

The British government did not limit its search for a settlement to this experiment in home rule; it also made a series of informal approaches to the republican leaders, and though one effort after another proved abortive, at least the line of communication was kept open. This anxiety for peace reflected not only the growing difficulty of the military situation in Ireland but, even more, the state of public opinion in Britain. An influential section of the British press consistently maintained the necessity for compromise; and through every medium of communication—in newspapers, books, pamphlets, public meetings — an incessant attack was kept up on the conduct of the crown forces in Ireland. And this was no matter of party politics: the attack was made from all quarters; and it became almost irresistible when the king, in private, and the archbishop of Canterbury, in public, expressed their uneasiness. With the general feeling of the country in this state, the government dared not employ its military resources to the full, nor could the army be counted on to wage an unpopular war. Sir Henry Wilson, chief of the imperial general staff, though an Irish unionist and violently anti-republican, had the common sense to recognize the realities of the situation: 'Unless England was on our side', he wrote in June 1921, 'we would fail, and if we failed we would break the army . . . unless England was on our side . . . it would be madness to try and flatten out the rebels'. Lloyd George knew very well that 'England' would not support any attempt to 'flatten out the rebels'. Though he had occasionally made bellicose statements, he had never committed himself wholly to a settlement by force; it was lack of direction in the coalition ministry, rather than any deliberate decision on policy, that had allowed the conflict to proceed so far; and when an opportunity of opening formal peace negotiations occurred, he was easily persuaded to take it.

The opportunity came in the summer of 1921, when King George, speaking at the opening of the newly-elected Northern Ireland parliament in Belfast, on 22 June, made a moving appeal for reconciliation:[1]

'I appeal to all Irishmen to pause, to stretch out the hand of forbearance and conciliation, and to join in making for the land which they love a new era of peace, contentment, and goodwill.'

The expressions of hope and relief with which the appeal was received, in Ireland as well as in Britain, showed clearly enough that, whatever die-hards and doctrinaires on either side might feel, the overwhelming desire of most people was to bring the struggle to an end. On 24 June, Lloyd George invited de Valera and Craig to a conference; a truce, on which the republicans insisted as a preliminary to negotiation, came into operation on 10 July; and two days later de Valera was in London. The search for peace had begun.

Though the negotiations initiated in July dragged on for almost five months, the issue was clearly defined from the beginning. During the first round of talks in London, the British cabinet laid down two conditions on which it was resolved to stand: that Ireland must remain within the empire, and that Northern Ireland must not be coerced; but, subject to these limitations, Ireland would be granted the fullest possible measure of self-government. In all that followed, the British never departed from these terms; and they formed the basis of the treaty ultimately signed in December.

The long delay before the Irish accepted these terms, and the fact that they did accept them in the end, both resulted from the Dáil cabinet's failure to agree on a settled line of policy. At first, it refused the terms completely; but this was not regarded as final, and negotiations, though suspended, were not broken off. During the summer, Arthur Griffith, always more concerned about the substance of independence than about its form, became increasingly disposed to compromise, and many of his colleagues supported this view; others, especially Cathal Brugha and Austin Stack, were utterly opposed to it, and de Valera, though uncommitted, inclined to their side. But the matter was never pushed to a decisive vote; and, when the London talks were resumed in October, the cabinet gave the delegation that it appointed no guidance at all as to what might or might not be conceded. Left to itself, the delegation could probably have reached a settlement fairly quickly; for it was headed by Griffith and

---

[1] The decision to take this opportunity of appealing for peace was due partly to the king himself, partly to General Smuts, who also used his influence with de Valera to promote a settlement.

made up of men in general sympathy with his views, though some of them, and notably Collins, were not at first prepared to go as far as Griffith himself in meeting the British demands. But though the delegates were formally invested with plenipotentiary powers, they were, somewhat inconsistently, told not to sign any treaty until the terms had been approved in Dublin; and de Valera, though he refused to go to London, tried to keep control of the negotiations in his own hands.

This unresolved conflict among the Irish threatened to postpone a settlement, one way or the other, indefinitely. Had they openly insisted, as an essential condition of agreement, that Britain should recognise the republic, then (as Griffith said later) the whole negotiation would have been over in five minutes. But de Valera, now almost completely under the influence of Brugha and Stack, preferred to play for time by securing the rejection in Dublin of any proposal that fell short of this ideal. It proved a mistaken policy, for time was not on his side. With every week that passed the delegates in London came nearer and nearer to accepting the British view. Despite constant control from Dublin, they could not forget that they were plenipotentiaries; they felt that the issue of peace or war was in their hands: and Collins, in particular, was convinced that the I.R.A. could not renew the struggle with any prospect of success. Lloyd George played skilfully on their doubts and fears, and on their hopes of ending partition. By a subtle combination of persuasion and threat he led them from one concession to another; and in the end, by a well-timed and dramatic ultimatum, delivered with all the force of a commanding personality, he induced them to sign a treaty without reference to Dublin.

This treaty,[1] signed at 2.30 a.m. on Tuesday, 6 December 1921, embodied the settlement proposed by the British cabinet in July. Ireland, under the style of the 'Irish Free State', was to become a self-governing dominion within the empire, enjoying the same constitutional status as Canada; and members of the Irish parliament were to take an oath of allegiance to the crown 'in virtue of the common citizenship of Ireland with Great Britain and her adherence to and membership of the group of nations forming the British Commonwealth of Nations'. Britain was to remain, for the time being, responsible for coastal defence, and was to be allowed to maintain naval establishments in certain Irish ports. Other

---

[1] The instrument itself bears the title 'Articles of agreement for a treaty between Great Britain and Ireland', but it is almost invariably spoken of as 'the treaty'.

articles settled the basis of future financial relations between the two countries, and arranged for the setting up of a provisional government. The treaty applied formally to the whole of Ireland; but the position of Northern Ireland was specifically safeguarded: if the Northern Ireland parliament should, by an address of both houses to the crown, request to be excluded from the authority of the government and parliament of the Irish Free State, then Northern Ireland should retain the constitutional status within the United Kingdom accorded to it by the act of 1920. But in that event, the boundary between the two parts of Ireland was to be re-adjusted by a commission representing the Irish Free State, Northern Ireland and Great Britain. This provision was of the utmost importance; for Lloyd George had led the Irish delegates to believe that the revision of the boundary would so reduce the area of Northern Ireland that its continued existence as a political unit would become impossible. They signed the treaty in the conviction that they had, at least, secured the ending of partition.[1]

Two days later the delegates were back in Dublin: it remained to be seen whether they had brought peace, or a sword.

(6)

The signing of the treaty at last forced the long-standing division of opinion in the Dáil cabinet into the open. At a meeting on 8 December it was contended, on one side, that the delegates had had no authority to sign any treaty; on the other, that they had acted within their rights as plenipotentiaries, and that the terms were the best that could be hoped for in the circumstances. A vote taken after hours of argument showed a majority in favour of the delegates; but de Valera refused to accept this as binding. When the Dáil met on 14 December the cabinet had no agreed policy to lay before it: the Dáil itself must decide between Griffith, Collins and their supporters, on the one hand, and de Valera, Brugha and Stack, on the other.

The debate in the Dáil continued until 7 January, and every member was called on to speak; but on both sides the same arguments were repeated again and again, and the essential points can be compressed into

---

[1] The appointment of a boundary commission was delayed until 1924. Its report (which has never been published) was not acted upon. Instead, the governments of the United Kingdom, the Irish Free State and Northern Ireland signed a tripartite agreement in 1925, confirming the boundary as established in 1920.

a small space. Those who advocated acceptance of the treaty admitted that it was not an ideal document; but they claimed that it gave Ireland the substance of independence immediately, and did not bar the way to further progress — 'It has', said Griffith, 'no more finality than that we are the final generation on the face of the earth'. But perhaps their strongest argument was simply that the terms were the best that could be got, and that their rejection meant a renewal of war. To this argument the opponents of the treaty made no effective answer. They denied that the delegates had had any right to sign it, and accused them of having betrayed the republic; they rejected the notion of dominion status, and, in particular, they attacked the oath of allegiance to the crown. But they did not offer any practicable alternative policy. Some of them, indeed, declared their readiness to 'go another round with England'; but many, including de Valera himself, spoke as if better terms could be had for the asking: 'The sad part of it', he said, 'is that a grand treaty could at this moment be made'. But he did not explain how, at this stage, the British government could have been induced to re-open negotiations on the basis of recognizing the republic. When a vote was at last taken, on the evening of 7 January, the treaty was ratified by 64 votes to 57. De Valera at once resigned the presidency, and next day Griffith was elected in his place.

The Dáil's decision was certainly in accordance with popular feeling. When the treaty was first published the country was delighted at the prospect of a lasting peace, and most people thought the terms very good. De Valera's declared opposition, and the subsequent debates, caused many to change their minds; but opinion in general, though less jubilant than at first, remained firmly behind Griffith and Collins. Even in de Valera's own constituency of Clare the county council passed, by an overwhelming majority, a resolution advising acceptance of the treaty. Perhaps the most ominous feature of the Dáil debate was that some of the anti-treaty members, conscious that public opinion was against them, denied in advance the right of the people to disown the republic. From this it was but a short step to resisting the popular decision by force. And the means of doing so lay at hand; for on this issue the I.R.A. was more sharply and more evenly divided than the country as a whole, and its members were not accustomed to subordinate themselves to any civil authority. In the first weeks of 1922 the shadow of approaching civil war already lay over Ireland.

Meanwhile, as the opposing parties took shape, the provisions of the treaty, which had already been ratified by the British parliament on 16 December, were being rapidly put into effect. A provisional government was formed on 14 January,[1] headed by Michael Collins and containing two men who were soon to bear the main burden of building up the new state — W. T. Cosgrave and Kevin O'Higgins. It was to this government that Viscount Fitzalan of Derwent, last of a long line of viceroys, formally handed over power on 16 January; and Dublin Castle, for centuries the symbol of British rule in Ireland, passed into Irish keeping. The evacuation of British troops began almost immediately; and the I.R.A., now regarded by the British as the army of the provisional government, took over their barracks, their depots, and much of their equipment.

But by this time the I.R.A. was breaking into pro-treaty and anti-treaty sections. Almost immediately after the Dáil had ratified the treaty a large and influential body of officers repudiated its authority, claiming that their allegiance was due only to the republic; and for a time it seemed possible that they might get control of the whole army, and establish a military dictatorship. The provisional government rallied sufficient support to prevent this; but the army was irretrievably split; and in March 1922 those opposed to the treaty organized themselves as a separate force. During this confused period the evacuation of British troops was in progress; and it not infrequently happened that posts and equipment abandoned by the British fell into the hands of the anti-treaty party, to be used later in war against the provisional government. Both those who supported and those who opposed the treaty claimed to represent the true I.R.A.; but the ordinary citizen found new terms for a new situation, and distinguished the opposing forces in the coming conflict as 'National' or 'Free State' troops, and 'Irregulars'.

During the spring and early summer, tension between the two sides, both in the army and in the country, mounted steadily. De Valera organized his supporters in a new republican party, and embarked on a propaganda campaign that seemed designed to encourage resistance to the new régime by force of arms; and the anti-treaty section of the I.R.A. was openly defiant. But the provisional government, still uncertain of its strength, hesitated to provoke a conflict by attempting to assert its authority; and even when Irregular forces occupied the Four Courts, the Dublin headquarters of the Irish judiciary, in April, they were left in

---

[1] The treaty required that the provisional government should be set up by the parliament of 'Southern Ireland', elected under the terms of the government of Ireland act of 1920, and this parliament was briefly resurrected for the purpose. A Dáil cabinet, presided over by Griffith, continued for some time to function side by side with the provisional government, and there was some overlap in membership; but only the provisional government was recognized by the British.

peaceable possession. Many, especially on the government side, hoped that the general election, which was to take place in June, would open the way for a peaceful settlement. But a powerful section of the anti-treaty party, unwilling to wait and distrustful of popular opinion, saw in a renewal of war with Britain the best chance of restoring unity and reviving the republican cause; and the state of affairs in Northern Ireland, where the I.R.A. was still united in an effort to wreck the unionist government, seemed to offer a fair prospect of achieving this end.

Craig and his colleagues were having a tough fight in their effort to weld the six-county area into an administrative unit under effective government control. Stability could not be achieved unless some *modus vivendi* could be worked out both between Northern Ireland and the rest of the country, and between the majority and the minority within Northern Ireland itself; and there seemed little prospect of success in either sphere. Since the summer of 1920 northern goods had been subjected throughout most of Ireland to a boycott, enforced by the I.R.A., in retaliation for the attacks on Roman Catholics during the riots in Belfast. The main effect of this was to confirm the Ulster protestant in his belief that he was regarded by republicans as an unwanted foreigner; and the activities of the I.R.A. seemed to him but a more violent way of saying the same thing: by the beginning of 1922, relations between the protestant north-east and the rest of the country were worse than they had ever been before. So far as the internal situation was concerned, the setting up of a separate Northern Ireland government had helped to exacerbate rather than assuage ill-feeling. The Roman Catholic and nationalist minority not unreasonably regarded it as designed to perpetuate a protestant ascendancy; and any inclination to try to come to terms with it were more than counterbalanced by the belief that its career would be short-lived, and that partition would soon be ended. The minority's consequent refusal to co-operate with the new government, together with the fact that I.R.A. activity was almost invariably based on predominantly Roman Catholic areas, strengthened the unionist tendency to regard all Roman Catholics as 'rebels'; and the rift between the two groups became even wider. Craig's task was not made any easier by the attitude and conduct of his more violent followers. A large force of special constabulary had been raised and armed in an effort to restore order; and, as was perhaps inevitable in the circumstances, it was manned exclusively by protestants.[1] Such a force, at such a time, could not be kept under effective discipline; and its

[1] This constabulary was in fact, though not in name, a revival of the pre-war Ulster Volunteer Force, and it was armed with the rifles landed at Larne in 1914.

campaign against the I.R.A. often took on the character of a sectarian war. For a time, the government's authority seemed to be in hardly less danger from its friends than from its foes.

In this state of affairs, an intensification of I.R.A. activity against Northern Ireland could be counted on to make a wide appeal, as an effort not only to end partition but also to rescue fellow Irishmen from oppression; and, in the likely event of a clash with British forces along the border, a renewal of war might be expected. Some of the pro-treaty party were, in fact, inclined to fall in with this plan. But Collins, having chosen the constitutional road, was determined to follow it. At the end of March he met Craig, in London, and promised to call off the boycott and end hostile action by the I.R.A., in return for a promise that the Northern Ireland government would protect the interest of the nationalist minority. Collins's control over the I.R.A. forces operating in the north was far from complete; but the agreement had some effect; the increasingly severe measures adopted by the government had more; and within twelve months Northern Ireland had achieved a degree of tranquillity that at one time might have seemed almost beyond hoping for.

Another factor that contributed to this pacification of the north was the outbreak of civil war in the south: from June 1922 onwards, the anti-treaty section of the I.R.A. was concentrating its efforts on a struggle with the provisional government. The general election, on 16 June, instead of opening the way to peace, proved to be a prelude to war. Of the 128 seats the government secured 58, and de Valera's republican party 35. Since the smaller parties and independent members who divided the remaining seats between them were all prepared to accept the treaty, the government interpreted the result as a popular endorsement of the treaty settlement. It was now less willing to seek for a compromise with the republicans; and if it still delayed to take measures against the anti-treaty section of the I.R.A. this was, in part at least, because it was under strong pressure from Britain to do so, and did not wish to have the appearance of acting at British dictation. But it was no longer prepared to be patient; and when, on 27 June, the republican garrison in the Four Courts kidnapped a government general, Collins quickly resolved to take firm action. Early the following morning, after the republicans had rejected an ultimatum, government troops opened the attack, using artillery borrowed from the small British force still remaining in Dublin. Two days later the garrison surrendered, mining and firing the building before they left, and destroying in the process the public record office, with its irreplaceable collection of historical documents.

The attack on the Four Courts was the signal for a general engagement between pro-treaty and anti-treaty forces throughout the country; and though both sides had been reluctant to begin war, they waged it, once begun, with increasing fury and bitterness until it ended the following spring. The Irregulars used once more the tactics that had proved so successful against the British; but now they could no longer count on the solid support of the civilian population; they were facing an enemy who had learnt his trade in the same school as themselves; above all, they had to deal with a government that was not hampered, as the British had been, by the restraining influence of a hostile public opinion. During the last six months of the civil war almost twice as many republican prisoners were executed by the Free State authorities as had been executed by the British during the whole course of the struggle from 1916 to 1921.

The war had a political as well as a military aspect. Almost immediately on its outbreak de Valera and his party formed a junction with the Irregulars, and in October 1922 they set up, under de Valera's presidency, a government that claimed to represent the legitimate authority of the republic. But they had little chance of attracting popular support: the overwhelming desire of the country was for peace; and the Roman Catholic hierarchy threw the weight of its immense influence behind the Free State government, stigmatizing the republican campaign as 'a system of murder and assassination of the National forces'. With the people apathetic or hostile, and with the Irregulars' power of resistance being steadily undermined by the growing efficiency of the Free State army, de Valera saw that the struggle must be abandoned. But he still hoped to gain something by negotiation. At the end of April 1923, having with some difficulty secured the approval of the Irregulars' army council, he announced that the republican forces would suspend hostilities, so that terms might be discussed. The government, however, were in no mood to make concessions; and after three weeks of futile negotiations de Valera accepted the inevitable. On 24 May he proclaimed a definitive cease fire, and told his followers that 'military victory must be allowed to rest for the moment with those who have destroyed the republic'.

The Free State emerged from the war under new leadership. Griffith had died on 12 August 1922, and Collins had been killed in an ambush ten days later. The main strength of Griffith's character lay in a courageous persistence and in a firm grasp of political essentials. He had begun his career at a time when most nationalists aimed at no more than a modest degree of self-government, and for half a generation his propaganda had produced little visible effect. But he had lived to see Ireland attain something like the constitutional status that he had long advocated, and free to follow the economic policies that he thought essential to her well-being.

Collins, young, handsome, daring, had been the popular hero of the war against Britain; but it was the ruthless efficiency with which he had organized and used his forces that had made him such a formidable opponent. Griffith and Collins form, in some ways, an oddly-assorted couple; but history has linked them inseparably together, for it was their joint decision, first to accept the treaty, and then to enforce it, that made the establishment of the Irish Free State possible. With the removal of Griffith and Collins the main burden of responsibility passed to W. T. Cosgrave, who became head of the government, and Kevin O'Higgins, the minister for home affairs. It was they who directed government policy during the remainder of the civil war, and initiated the stern measures that brought it to a successful conclusion.

While the war was still in progress the last formal steps necessary to give effect to the treaty were being taken. A constitution for the Irish Free State, published on the eve of the general election in June 1922, was approved by the Dáil and by the British parliament, and came into force on 6 December. Next day, the parliament of Northern Ireland, acting under article 12 of the treaty, voted an address to the crown, praying to be excluded from the jurisdiction of the Free State: when, in the spring of 1923, Ireland, north and south, settled down in weary but welcome peace, it was under two separate and mutually suspicious governments.

The constitutional settlement, formally completed in December 1922, and made fully effective by the cessation of armed resistance a few months later, was not the result of any deliberate plan, nor did it represent the policy of any party. The Ulster unionists had set out to defeat home rule for Ireland as a whole; and when, later on, they agreed to a compromise based on their own exclusion, it was on the assumption that the excluded counties would retain their then existing relationship to the rest of the United Kingdom. They had not wanted the constitution of 'Northern Ireland', imposed on them in 1920, and regarded their acceptance of it as an act of self-sacrifice in the interests of peace. For nationalists, of all shades of opinion, the settlement was, at best, an unattractive compromise, acceptable less for its own sake than for the prospect it offered of gaining more in future, and, in particular, of ending partition by re-uniting Northern Ireland with the rest of the country. The third party to the settlement, the British government, might, perhaps, be called its architect, but that the term implies some deliberate purpose, some preconception of design. In fact, between 1912 and 1921 successive governments stumbled from one expedient to another, without having either the courage to enforce their authority, or the insight to apprehend the essential conditions of peace. The problem that faced them might well have frightened braver men, and puzzled wiser ones; and the solution at which they finally arrived was not without its merits. But it was a solution that they adopted rather than created; and their influence was decisive only because they, and they alone, were in a position to insist on its acceptance.

In 1923 it might well have seemed that Ireland was quiet only from exhaustion; and that a settlement thus arrived at, thus enforced, thus accepted, must soon turn out to be a source of renewed strife. But the event proved otherwise. Though the settlement left a legacy of bitterness, issuing occasionally in local and sporadic disturbances, it inaugurated for Ireland a longer period of general tranquillity than she had known since the first half of the eighteenth century.

Select Bibliography

THE purpose of this bibliography is to give some help to the general reader in search of further information, and to provide initial guidance for the more serious student. No account has been given of unpublished material; but some of the more important printed collections of documents have been included, as well as a considerable number of specialist papers, and those who wish to examine the evidence for themselves can at least make a start. The inclusion of all the important secondary authorities would have swollen the bibliography to unwieldy dimensions; but it is hoped that the selection given is reasonably comprehensive, and that the descriptive and critical notes will prove of some value. A list of some of the more important local histories is given at the end. Many works primarily concerned with Great Britain are also of considerable importance for Ireland; but these, with a very few exceptions, have been excluded from the following lists.

The division into sections, necessarily imprecise, is intended only as a general guide. Items included in one section are not repeated in another, and the bibliography must therefore be used as a whole.

The following abbreviations have been used:

E.H.R. *English historical review*
H.M.C. Historical Manuscripts Commission (London)
I.H.S. *Irish historical studies* (Dublin, 1938–)
I.M.C. Irish Manuscripts Commission (Dublin)

BIBLIOGRAPHIES AND GUIDES

C. Maxwell, *Short bibliography of Irish history* (London 1921) may be consulted for older works. Publications since 1936 appear in the annual list of 'Writings on Irish history' published in *I.H.S.* by the Irish Committee of Historical Sciences. The following deal with particular periods and topics: K. Povey, 'The sources for a bibliography of Irish history, 1500–1700' (*I.H.S.*, i. 393–403); R. H. Murray, *Ireland, 1603–1714* (London, 1921); P. L. Prendeville, 'A select bibliography of Irish

economic history: Part 2, The seventeenth and eighteenth centuries'
(*Economic history review*, iii. 402–16); S. Simms, 'A select bibliography of
the United Irishmen, 1791–8' (*I.H.S.*, i. 158–80); J. Carty, *Bibliography
of Irish history, 1870–1911* (Dublin 1940) and *Bibliography of Irish
history, 1912–21* (Dublin, 1936). There are important sections on
Ireland in G. Davies, *Bibliography of British history: Stuart period*
(Oxford, 1928) and S. M. Pargellis and D. J. Medley, *Bibliography of
British history: the eighteenth century, 1714–89* (Oxford, 1951).

For the great body of Irish material included in the publications of the
Historical Manuscripts Commission (of which only a few of the more
important volumes are noticed below) see *Guide to the reports . . . Part I
Topographical* (London, 1914) and *Guide to the reports . . . 1870–1911.
Part II Index of persons* (2 vols. London, 1935, 1938).

WORKS OF REFERENCE

The Annual Register and the *Dictionary of national biography* are hardly
less important for Irish than for British history. On the succession in
offices of state there is a mass of ill-arranged, and not always reliable,
information in R. Lascelles, *Liber munerum publicorum Hiberniae* (2 vols.
London, 1852; index in *Ninth Report of the Deputy Keeper of the Records,
Ireland*). F. M. Powicke and E. B. Fryde (ed.), *Handbook of British
chronology* (2nd ed. London, 1961) contains detailed lists of chief governors
and chief secretaries (but see also J. L. J. Hughes, 'The chief secretaries
in Ireland, 1566–1921', in *I.H.S.*, viii. 59–72). F. E. Ball, *The judges in
Ireland, 1121–1921* (2 vols. London, 1926) contains biographical information and comments on the organization of the judiciary as well as
succession lists. J. Lodge, *Peerage of Ireland* (ed. M. Archdall, 7 vols.
Dublin, 1789) is important for family history and connections. S. Lewis,
Topographical dictionary of Ireland (2 vols. London, 1850) provides a
handy means of identifying places. E. Curtis and R. B. McDowell (ed.)
Irish historical documents, 1172–1922 (London, 1943) contains a useful
selection of source material, mainly, though not exclusively, of constitutional interest.

PARLIAMENTARY RECORDS, DEBATES, ETC.

The records and debates of the parliaments of England, of Great
Britain and of the United Kingdom are of direct importance for Irish
history, but need not be listed in detail here. There is no complete guide
to the mass of nineteenth-century parliamentary papers relating to
Ireland; but convenient lists of the more important of them will be found

in R. B. McDowell, *Government policy and public opinion in Ireland,*
1801–1846 (London, 1952) and *The Irish administration, 1801–1914*
(London, 1964).

For Irish legislation see *Statutes at large passed in the parliaments held*
in Ireland (20 vols. Dublin, 1786–1801). *Journals of the house of lords of*
the kingdom of Ireland (8 vols. Dublin, 1779–1800) and *Journals of the*
house of commons of the kingdom of Ireland (20 vols. Dublin, 1796–1800)
are, basically, formal records of business transacted; but in the *Journals of*
the house of commons there are many reports and other papers of great
importance, particularly on financial and economic matters. The commons'
debates for the period 1781–97 are reported in *The parliamentary register,*
or the history of the proceedings and debates of the house of commons in
Ireland (17 vols. Dublin, 1782–1801); but see *H.M.C. 2nd report* appendix,
pp. 99–100 (1871). W. W. Seward, *Collectanea politica* (3 vols. Dublin,
1801–4), though it contains other matter, is essentially a record of parliamentary proceedings from 1760 to 1800.

Though they are not strictly records of parliament, five contemporary
annotated lists of members may conveniently be noted here: D. Large
(ed.), 'The Irish house of commons in 1769' (*I.H.S.*, xi. 18–45); M. Bodkin
(ed.), 'Notes on the Irish parliament in 1773' (*Proceedings of the Royal*
Irish Academy, vols. 48–9, C, pp. 145–232); W. Hunt (ed.), *The Irish*
parliament, 1775 (London, 1907); G. O. Sayles (ed.), 'Contemporary
sketches of members of the Irish parliament in 1782' (*Proceedings of the*
Royal Irish Academy, vol. 56, C, pp. 227–86); Edith M. Johnston (ed.),
'The state of the Irish house of commons in 1791' (*ibid.*, vol. 59, C, pp.
1–56).

GENERAL HISTORIES

E. Curtis, *History of Ireland* (6th ed. London, 1951) is the standard
work. Shorter histories include R. Dunlop, *Ireland from the earliest times*
to the present day (Oxford, 1922); B. Inglis, *Story of Ireland* (London,
1956); J. C. Beckett, *Short history of Ireland* (revised ed. London, 1958).
Chapters by R. Dunlop in the [old] *Cambridge modern history*, iv–vi, cover
the seventeenth and eighteenth centuries. R. Bagwell, *Ireland under the*
Stuarts [1603–91] (3 vols. London, 1909–16) is mainly a narrative of
political events, with comparatively little attention to economic and social
developments; but it is firmly based on the sources, and remains absolutely
indispensable. J. A. Froude, *The English in Ireland in the eighteenth*
century (new ed. 3 vols. London, 1881) is strongly marked by the author's
prejudices; but it is vigorously and vividly written. W. E. H. Lecky,
Ireland in the eighteenth century (new ed. 5 vols. London 1892), a kind

of counterblast to Froude, is the most authoritative work on the period; it should be noted, however, that four-fifths of the space is devoted to the years 1780–1800. There is no equally satisfactory work on the nineteenth century. G. Locker Lampson, *A consideration of the state of Ireland in the nineteenth century* (London, 1907) is a series of loosely connected chapters, mainly on social and economic questions, rather than a coherent history. J. O'Connor, *History of Ireland, 1798–1924* (2 vols. London, 1928) is a rather pedestrian narrative, written from a moderate nationalist view-point. P. S. O'Hegarty, *Ireland under the union* (London, 1952), described by the author as 'the story of a people coming out of bondage', is a highly subjective commentary on political events; but it contains a mass of factual information, and it is studded with apposite quotations from contemporary sources.

ECCLESIASTICAL HISTORY

Most works on Irish ecclesiastical history, if not written explicitly from a denominational standpoint, are directly concerned with one or other of the major denominations. W. A. Phillips (ed.), *History of the Church of Ireland* (3 vols. Oxford, 1933–4) is the standard work on its subject; but R. Mant, *History of the Church of Ireland* (2 vols. London, 1840), though old-fashioned and uncritical, still has some value, especially for biographical details and for the documents that it includes. Two papers by J. C. Beckett deal with church-state relations during the generation following the Revolution: 'The government and the Church of Ireland under William III and Anne' (*I.H.S.*, ii. 280–302); 'Swift as an ecclesiastical statesman' (in *Discussions of Jonathan Swift*, ed. J. Traugott, Boston, 1963). Olive J. Brose, 'The Irish precedent for English church reform: the church temporalities act of 1833' (*Journal of ecclesiastical history*, vii. 204–25), though not exclusively concerned with Ireland, throws light on the background of the agitation for disestablishment. Contemporary views on the disestablishment question may be found in William Shee, *The Irish church, its history and statistics* (2nd ed. London, 1863), for the attack; and in *Essays on the Irish church, by clergymen of the established church in Ireland* (Oxford and London, 1868), for the defence. The organization of the campaign for disestablishment is traced in P. J. Corish, 'Cardinal Cullen and the National Association of Ireland' (*Reportorium novum*, iii. 13–61, Dublin, 1962).

There is no full history of the Roman Catholic church in Ireland; but much relevant source material is to be found in *Spicilegium Ossoriense* (ed. P. F. Moran, 3 vols. Dublin, 1874–84), a collection of documents for the period from the reformation to 1800; it is of particular value for the seventeenth century. M. J. Brenan, *Ecclesiastical history of Ireland . . . to the year 1829* (2 vols. Dublin, 1840) is very sketchy. J. MacCaffrey, *History of the Catholic church in the nineteenth century* (2 vols. Dublin, 1909) is a general work, but gives considerable space to Ireland. M. Wall, *The penal laws, 1691–1760* (Dublin, 1961) gives a brief but carefully-balanced statement of the position during the penal period. J. G. Simms examines one aspect of this in 'Irish catholics and the parliamentary franchise' (*I.H.S.*, xii. 28–37). Kennedy F. Roche, 'The relations of the Catholic church and the state in England and Ireland, 1800–52' (in *Historical studies III*, ed. J. Hogan, Cambridge, 1961) is an illuminating survey. Part of the same theme is treated in more detail in J. F. Broderick, *The Holy See and the Irish movement for the repeal of the union with England, 1829–47* (Rome, 1951). E. R. Norman, *The Catholic church and Ireland in the age of rebellion* (London, 1965) is a detailed analysis (based largely on material from the Vatican archives) of the interaction of ecclesiastical and political affairs in the period 1859–73.

There are important biographies of three leading bishops, who played an influential part in secular as well as in ecclesiastical affairs: Bishop Doyle of Kildare and Leighlin (*Life, times, and correspondence*, by W. J. Fitzpatrick, 3rd ed. 2 vols. Dublin, 1890); Archbishop MacHale of Tuam (*Life and correspondence*, by B. O'Reilly, 2 vols. New York, 1890); Cardinal Cullen (*Paul Cullen and his contemporaries, with their letters*, by P. Mac Suibhne, 2 vols. Naas, 1961, 1962). W. McDonald, *Reminiscences of a Maynooth professor* (ed. D. Gwynn, London, 1925) reveals the inter-action of ecclesiastical, social and political questions in the early twentieth century.

J. S. Reid, *History of the presbyterian church in Ireland* (ed. W. D. Killen, 3 vols. Belfast, 1867), though betraying some denominational bias, is in many ways a model of its kind. J. M. Barkley's much slighter *Short history of the presbyterian church in Ireland* (Belfast, 1959) is particularly useful for its well-documented account of church life in the eighteenth and nineteenth centuries. An important source for the early history of Irish presbyterianism is P. Adair, *True narrative of the rise and progress of the presbyterian church in Ireland, 1623–70* (ed. W. D. Killen, Belfast, 1866); and, for the later period, *Records of the general synod of Ulster, 1691–1820* (3 vols. Belfast, 1890–8). T. Witherow, *Historical and literary memorials of presbyterianism in Ireland* (2 vols. London, 1879–80) contains selections from the writings of Irish presbyterian authors from the mid-seventeenth century to the end of the eighteenth, with biographical notices. St J. D. Seymour, *The puritans in Ireland, 1647–61* (Oxford, 1921) examines the ecclesiastical policy of the Commonwealth, and its effects. J. C. Beckett, *Protestant dissent in Ireland, 1687–1780* (London, 1948) is mainly concerned with presbyterianism, but deals briefly with the minor sects. T. Wight and J. Rutty, *Rise and progress of the people called Quakers, in Ireland* (4th ed. London, 1811) covers the period 1653–1751. G. L. Lee, *Huguenot settlements in Ireland* (London, 1936) and A. Carré, *L'influence des Huguenots français en Irlande* (Paris, 1937) are important contributions to social and economic as well as to ecclesiastical history.

ECONOMIC AND SOCIAL HISTORY

T. W. Freeman, *Ireland: its physical, historical, social and economic geography* (London, 1950) provides a good basis for further study. The first serious examination of the Irish economy was made in the seventeenth century by Sir William Petty (see *Economic writings of Sir William Petty*, ed. C. H. Hull, 2 vols. Cambridge, 1899; *The Petty papers*, ed. Marquis of Lansdowne, 2 vols. London, 1927). The most influential writers on the subject in the eighteenth century were Arthur Dobbs (*Essay on the trade and improvement of Ireland*, 2 vols. Dublin, 1729–31); Jonathan Swift, whose Irish tracts may best be studied in *Prose writings of Jonathan Swift*, ed. H. Davis, vols. ix, xi, xii (Oxford, 1948, 1941, 1955); and John Hely-Hutchinson (*Commercial restraints of Ireland*, Dublin, 1779). For a contemporary view of the position at the end of the eighteenth century and beginning of the nineteenth see E. Wakefield, *Account of Ireland, statistical and political* (2 vols. Dublin, 1812). R. M. Martin, in *Ireland before and after the union* (London, 1843), tried to demonstrate that the legislative union with Great Britain had benefited Ireland economically; but most Irish writers have taken the opposite view.

There is no satisfactory economic history of the whole period. D. A. Chart, *Economic history of Ireland* (Dublin, 1920) is a brief general outline. J. F. Burke, *Outlines of the industrial history of Ireland* (revised ed. Dublin, [1928]) contains much statistical information, but gives no reference to sources. For the greater part of the period the best guide is still G. O'Brien, *Economic history of Ireland in the seventeenth century* (Dublin, 1919), *Economic history of Ireland in the eighteenth century* (Dublin, 1918), *Economic history of Ireland from the union to the famine* (London, 1921). O'Brien, however, is sometimes uncritical in his use of evidence, especially that of contemporary pamphlets; and the same may be said of A. E. Murray, *Commercial and financial relations between England and Ireland from the period of the Restoration* (London, 1903). Older views of the state of Irish trade in the eighteenth century are corrected in T. M. O'Connor, 'The embargo on the export of Irish provisions, 1776–9' (*I.H.S.*, ii. 3–11); F. G. James, 'Irish smuggling in the eighteenth century' (*I.H.S.*, xii. 299–317) and 'Irish colonial trade in the eighteenth century' (*William and Mary quarterly*, 3rd series, xx. 574–84). M. Wall, 'The rise of a catholic middle class in eighteenth-century Ireland' (*I.H.S.*, xi. 91–115) is a re-assessment of the part played by Roman Catholics in commercial life. K. H. Connell, *The population of Ireland, 1750–1845* (Oxford, 1950) is an admirable study, ranging far more widely than the title might at first suggest. (But cf. M. Drake, 'Marriage and population growth in Ireland, 1750–1845' in *Economic history review*, 2nd series, xvi. 301–13).

For industrial development C. Gill, *Rise of the Irish linen industry* (Oxford, 1925) is a standard work. E. R. R. Green, *The Lagan valley, 1800–1850* (London, 1949) deals with the industrial revolution in the north-east. These should be supplemented by W. Cunningham, 'The suppression of the woollen manufacture in Ireland' (*E.H.R.*, i. 277–94); J. J. Monaghan, 'The rise and fall of the Belfast cotton industry' (*I.H.S.*, iii. 1–17); D. L. Armstrong, 'Social and economic conditions in the Belfast linen industry, 1850–1900' (*I.H.S.*, vii. 235–69); J. Conroy, *A history of railways in Ireland* (London, 1928). P. Lynch and J. Vaizey, *Guinness's brewery in the Irish economy, 1759–1876* (Cambridge, 1960) is important for its treatment of general economic problems as well as for its special theme.

T. J. Kiernan, *The financial administration of Ireland to 1817* (London, 1930) is the only modern book on its subject, but is by no means exhaustive. R. V. Clarendon, *A sketch of the revenue and finances of Ireland* (London, 1791) gives tables of income and expenditure for the eighteenth century. More specialized studies include: V. Treadwell, 'The Irish court of wards under James I' (*I.H.S.*, xii. 1–27); H. F. Kearney, 'The court of wards and liveries in Ireland, 1622–4' (*Proceedings of the Royal Irish Academy*, lvii, C, no. 2, pp. 29–68); F. G. Hall, *The Bank of Ireland* (Dublin, 1949); F. W. Fetter (ed.) *The Irish pound, 1797–1826* (London, 1955).

During the period of the union Ireland attracted the attention of many British and continental economists, e.g. Gustave de Beaumont, *L'Irlande, sociale, politique et religieuse* (2 vols. Paris, 1839) and W. Nassau Senior, *Journals, conversations and essays relating to Ireland* (2nd ed. 2 vols. London, 1868). For a comprehensive survey of contemporary opinion, with an excellent bibliography, see R. D. C. Black, *Economic thought and the Irish question, 1817–1870* (Cambridge, 1960).

The land question, as it developed in the eighteenth and nineteenth centuries, was closely linked with the confiscations and plantations of

Tudor and Stuart times. A good introduction to the subject can be found in W. F. T. Butler, *Confiscation in Irish history* (2nd ed. Dublin, 1918) and J. P. Prendergast, *The Cromwellian settlement in Ireland* (2nd ed. London, 1870, reprinted Dublin, 1922). These should be supplemented and corrected by more modern studies, notably T. W. Moody, *The Londonderry plantation, 1609–41* (Belfast, 1939) and 'The treatment of the native population in the scheme for the plantation in Ulster' (*I.H.S.*, i. 59–63); S. R. Gardiner, 'The transplantation to Connaught' (*E.H.R.*, xiv. 700–734); J. G. Simms, *The Williamite confiscation in Ireland, 1690–1703* (London, 1956).

For agrarian conditions in the eighteenth century the best-known authority is Arthur Young, *Tour in Ireland, 1776–9* (ed. A. W. Hutton, 2 vols. London, 1892). There is an earlier contemporary view, in much more general terms, in *Reflections and resolutions proper for the gentlemen of Ireland* (attributed to Samuel Madden, one of the founders of the Dublin Society, Dublin, 1738, reprinted Dublin, 1816). See also J. G. Alger, 'An Irish absentee and his tenants: 1768–92' (*E.H.R.*, x. 663–74); K. H. Connell, 'The colonization of waste land in Ireland, 1780–1845' (*Economic history review*, 2nd series, iii. 44–71).

The standard source of information about early nineteenth-century conditions is the report of the Devon commission; the evidence has been conveniently arranged and summarized in *Digest of evidence taken before her majesty's commissioners of inquiry into . . . the occupation of land in Ireland* ([ed. J. P. Kennedy], Dublin, 1847). T. W. Freeman, *Pre-famine Ireland* (London, 1957), based largely on the census returns of 1841, gives the best modern critical account of the state of the country. W. S. Trench, *Realities of Irish life* (London, 1869) is a vivid contemporary picture by a well-intentioned land-agent. For two special aspects of rural economy see D. McCourt, 'Infield and outfield in Ireland' (*Economic history review*, 2nd series, vii. 369–76) and K. H. Connell, 'The potato in Ireland' (*Past and present*, no. 23 (Nov. 1962), pp. 57–71).

The conflict between landlord and tenant is clearly and competently traced in J. E. Pomfret, *The struggle for the land in Ireland* (Princeton, 1930), and more vigorously, if less dispassionately, in Michael Davitt, *The fall of feudalism in Ireland* (London, 1904). R. B. O'Brien, *Parliamentary history of the Irish land question* (London, 1880) is useful for the details of actual and proposed legislation.

The literature of the famine period is enormous. Here it will be sufficient to mention two books, each of which affords ample guidance for further study: R. D. Edwards and T. D. Williams (ed.), *The Great Famine* (Dublin, 1956) and C. Woodham-Smith, *The Great Hunger* (London, 1962).

Conditions at the turn of the century are described in: *Ireland, industrial and agricultural* ([ed. W. P. Coyne], Dublin, 1902), which contains some account of the work of the Congested Districts Board; M. J. Bonn, *Modern Ireland and her agrarian problem* (Eng. trans. Dublin, 1906); L. Paul-Dubois, *Contemporary Ireland* (Eng. trans. Dublin, 1908). For the co-operative movement see H. Plunkett, *Ireland in the new century* (London, 1904) and M. Digby, *Horace Plunkett, an Anglo-American Irishman* (Oxford, 1949).

C. Maxwell, *The stranger in Ireland* (London, 1954), a series of essays on foreign visitors, provides, incidentally, a popular outline of social history. There are contemporary accounts of the country and its inhabitants in H. Morley (ed.), *Ireland under Elizabeth and James I* (London, 1890) and C. L. Falkiner, *Illustrations of Irish history and topography* (London, 1904). E. MacLysaght, *Irish life in the seventeenth century* (2nd ed. Cork, 1950) is a well-documented study of post-Cromwellian conditions. C. Maxwell, *Dublin under the Georges* (London, 1936) and *Country and town in Ireland under the Georges* (revised ed. Dundalk, 1949) are descriptive rather than analytical in approach; but they contain much information, pleasantly presented, and they have extensive bibliographies, particularly useful for contemporary travel-books. D. Corkery, *The hidden Ireland* (Dublin, 1925), a study of Gaelic Munster in the eighteenth century, deals with the continuing influence of the native tradition. Another survey of a single province, briefer and more general, is J. G. Simms, 'Connacht in the eighteenth century' (*I.H.S.*, xi. 116–33).

Among the numerous collections of correspondence and papers illustrating eighteenth-century social life the following may be noted: *Correspondence of Jonathan Swift* (ed. F. E. Ball, 6 vols. London, 1910–14; ed. H. Williams, vols. i–iii, Oxford, 1963 (in progress)); *Correspondence of Emily, Duchess of Leinster* (ed. B. FitzGerald, 3 vols. I.M.S., 1949–57); *The Orrery papers* (ed. Countess of Cork and Orrery, 2 vols. London, 1903); *Inchiquin manuscripts* (ed. J. Ainsworth, I.M.S., 1961); *Kenmare manuscripts* (ed. E. MacLysaght, I.M.S., 1942). Sir Jonah Barrington, *Personal sketches of his own times* (3rd ed. London, 1869) gives a somewhat highly-coloured picture of Irish life in the closing years of the century.

D. A. Chart, *Ireland from the union to Catholic Emancipation* (London, 1910) is a wide-ranging account of social conditions. R. B. McDowell (ed.) *Social life in Ireland, 1800–45* (Dublin, 1957) is a collection of brief but very competent essays. T. W. Moody and J. C. Beckett (ed.), *Ulster since 1800, second series: a social survey* (revised ed. London, 1958) is a similar, but more extended and more substantial, survey of the north. Two papers by K. H. Connell deal with aspects of rural life: 'Peasant marriage in Ireland after the Great Famine' (*Past and present*, no. 12, pp. 76–91); 'Illicit distillation: an Irish peasant industry' (in *Historical studies, III*, ed. J. Hogan, Cambridge, 1961).

J. J. Auchmuty, *Irish education: a historical survey* (Dublin, 1937) is a brief general outline. H. Kingsmill Moore, *An unwritten chapter in the history of education* (London, 1904) is an account of the Kildare Place Society, 1811–31, and describes the background of the national system. On the early operation of this system see T. ÓRaifeartaigh, 'Mixed education and the synod of Ulster, 1831–40' (*I.H.S.*, ix. 281–99). On the university question see [W. Walsh], *The Irish university question: the catholic case* (Dublin, 1897); D. Gwynn, *O'Connell, Davis, and the colleges bill* (Cork, 1948); T. W. Moody, 'The Irish university question of the nineteenth century' (*History*, xlii. 90–109).

POLITICAL AND CONSTITUTIONAL HISTORY

Seventeenth century: *The Calendars of state papers* provide the most important source covering the whole century. Down to 1670 the Irish papers are calendared separately (13 vols. London, 1872–1910); thereafter they are included in the Domestic series (82 vols. London, 1857–1924), which also contains material of Irish interest for the earlier period. State papers for the period 1603–24 are also to be found in the *Calendar of Carew manuscripts*, vi (ed. J. S. Brewer and W. Bullen, London, 1873).

The *Lismore papers* (ed. A. B. Grosart, 10 vols. London, 1886–8) comprise letters and diaries of Richard Boyle, first earl of Cork, and are invaluable for the first part of the century. D. Townshend, *The great earl of Cork* (London, 1904) is a good biography, based largely on these papers. H. F. Kearney, *Strafford in Ireland* (Manchester, 1959) supersedes earlier works on its subject, and has a comprehensive bibliography.

There are numerous collections of documents dealing with the insurrection of 1641 and the subsequent wars. *Letters and papers relating to the Irish rebellion, 1642–46* (ed. J. Hogan, I.M.S., 1936) is mainly important for the year 1642. *Commentarius Rinuccinianus* (ed. S. Kavanagh, 6 vols. I.M.S., 1932–49) contains a contemporary memoir of Rinuccini's career in Ireland, embodying a great mass of documentary material; vol. vi contains an English synopsis of the whole work. J. T. Gilbert edited two contemporary accounts of the Confederate wars: *A contemporary history of affairs in Ireland, 1641–1652* (6 vols. Dublin, 1879–80) and *History of the Confederation and the war in Ireland, 1641–48* (6 vols. Dublin, 1882–90); both contain very extensive appendices of documents from

Irish, English and continental sources. T. Carte, *Life of James, first duke of Ormonde* (3 vols. London, 1735–6; 6 vols. Oxford, 1851) and Lady Burghclere (Winifred Gardner), *Life of James, first duke of Ormonde* (2 vols. London, 1912) are both based on the duke's vast collection of papers, of which Carte prints over 700, mostly of the 1640s, in his appendices. The *Ormonde manuscripts* (10 vols. H.M.C., 1895–1920), though containing some important material for the 1640s and 1650s, are of much greater value for the Restoration period.

D. Coffey, *O'Neill and Ormond* (Dublin, 1914) is a readable account of the Confederate period. T. L. Coonan, *The Irish Catholic Confederacy and the puritan revolution* (Dublin, London, New York, 1952) must be used with extreme caution; see *I.H.S.*, xi. 52–5. P. J. Corish, 'Bishop Nicholas French and the second Ormond peace, 1648–9' (*I.H.S.*, vi. 83–100), J. R. MacCormack, 'The Irish adventurers and the English civil war' (*I.H.S.*, x. 21–58) and J. Lowe, 'Charles I and the confederation of Kilkenny, 1643–9' (*I.H.S.*, xiv. 1–19) are important specialist studies. For a recent general survey see J. C. Beckett, 'The Confederation of Kilkenny reviewed' (in *Historical studies II*, ed. M. Roberts, Cambridge, 1959).

R. Dunlop, *Ireland under the Commonwealth* (2 vols. Manchester, 1913), a collection of state papers of the period 1651–9, with a valuable introduction, is indispensable for the Cromwellian settlement and administration. The details of the settlement may be traced in the *Civil survey, 1654–56* (ed. R. C. Simington, 10 vols. I.M.S., 1931–61) and *Books of survey and distribution* (ed. R. C. Simington, 3 vols. I.M.S., 1949–62). For the general effect of the land changes see Y. M. Goblet, *La transformation de la géographie politique de l'Irlande au XVII siècle* (Paris, 1930). The anger of the dispossessed Irish at their failure to recover their estates at the Restoration is reflected in Nicholas French, *Narrative of the earl of Clarendon's settlement and sale of Ireland* (1668; in his *Historical works*, 2 vols. Dublin, 1846).

Apart from the *Ormonde Manuscripts* (see above) the most important collections for the Restoration period are: *Letters written by the earl of Essex . . . in the year 1675* (Dublin, 1770); *Essex papers, 1672–5* (ed. O. Airy, London, 1890); *Essex papers, 1675–7* (ed. C. E. Pike, London, 1913); *State letters of the earl of Orrery* (ed. T. Morrice, 2 vols. London, 1743); *Calendar of Orrery papers* (ed. E. MacLysaght, I.M.C., 1941); *State letters of Henry, second earl of Clarendon* (ed. S. W. Singer, 2 vols. London, 1828).

The Williamite wars and their immediate aftermath are competently treated in R. H. Murray, *Revolutionary Ireland and its settlement* (London, 1911). P. W. Sergeant, *Little Jennings and Fighting Dick Talbot* (2 v

London, 1913) is a biography of Richard Talbot, earl of Tyrconnell, and covers much of the. same ground from a rather different viewpoint. J. G. Simms, *The treaty of Limerick* (Dublin, 1961) is a judicious study of one of the most controversial topics in Irish history. W. King, *The state of the protestants of Ireland under the late King James's government* (London, 1691) expresses the contemporary protestant view of the Revolution. C. Leslie, *An answer to a book intituled The state of the protestants of Ireland* (London, 1692) is a reply to King by an Irish protestant non-juror.

On the question of Irish parliamentary independence, raised in the 1640s and revived in the 1690s, see P. Darcy, *An argument delivered . . . . by the express order of the house of commons in the parliament of Ireland, 9 Junii 1641* (Waterford, 1643; reprinted Dublin, 1764); W. Molyneux, *The case of Ireland's being bound by acts of parliament in England stated* (Dublin, 1698).

Eighteenth century: The political life of the early part of the century has attracted little attention from historians. J. G. Simms, 'The making of a penal law, 1703–4' (*I.H.S.*, xii. 105–118) and 'The Irish parliament of 1713' (in *Historical studies IV*, ed. G. A. Hayes-McCoy, Cambridge, 1963), and J. L. McCracken 'Irish parliamentary elections, 1727–68' (*I.H.S.*, v. 209–30) illustrate the working of the parliamentary system. The struggle over Wood's patent has aroused interest mainly because of Swift's intervention. One of the best accounts of the affair is in H. Davis's introduction to the Oxford edition (1935) of the *Drapier's letters*; but reference should also be made to O. Ferguson, *Jonathan Swift and Ireland* (University of Illinois press, 1962), where Swift's Irish pamphlets are conveniently summarized and discussed. For the politics of the 1720s and 1730s Archbishop Boulter's *Letters* (2 vols. Dublin, 1770) is an indispensable source-book. For the early 1750s see 'Correspondence of Archbishop Stone and the duke of Newcastle' (ed. C. L. Falkiner, *E.H.R.*, xx. 508–42, 735–63). There is an important essay on Stone in C. L. Falkiner, *Studies in Irish history and biography* (London, 1902); other essays in the same volume, notably that on Lord Clare (John Fitzgibbon), deal with the politics of the later part of the century. J. L. McCracken, 'The conflict between the Irish administration and parliament, 1753–6' (*I.H.S.*, iii. 159–79) is essential for an understanding of the 'undertaker system'.

The *Calendar of home office papers, 1760–75* (4 vols. London, 1878–99) contains valuable material on Irish administrative and parliamentary affairs. E. Burke, *Letters, speeches and tracts on Irish affairs* (ed. M.

Arnold, London, 1881) is important for contemporary opinion in the later eighteenth century. W. E. H. Lecky, *Leaders of public opinion in Ireland*, i (new ed. London, 1912) contains brief but authoritative biographies of Flood and Grattan. W. Flood, *Memoirs of . . . Henry Flood* (London, 1838) is unsatisfactory; but there is no full-length modern biography. H. Grattan (the younger) *Memoirs of . . . Henry Grattan* (5 vols. Dublin, 1839–46), though chaotic in arrangement, contains a mass of valuable material. S. Gwynn, *Henry Grattan and his times* (London, 1939) is directed to the general reader, but is based on extensive study of the sources. M. J. Craig, *The Volunteer earl* (London, 1948) is a very readable biography of James Caulfield, first earl of Charlemont; but for a proper understanding of Charlemont's political career it is necessary to use the *Charlemont manuscripts* (2 vols. *H.M.C.*, 1891, 1894). There is also some very important source material for the same period in the *Stopford–Sackville manuscripts*, i (*H.M.C.*, 1904) which includes correspondence of John Hobart, earl of Buckinghamshire.

The constitutional history of the period is treated in detail in Edith M. Johnston, *Great Britain and Ireland, 1760–1800* (Edinburgh, 1963); for a much briefer survey see J. C. Beckett, 'Anglo-Irish constitutional relations in the later eighteenth century' (*I.H.S.*, xiv. 20–38). There is an older, but still valuable, discussion of the constitutional position in J. T. Ball, *Legislative systems operative in Ireland* (revised ed. London, 1889). For the early working of the 'constitution of 1782' reference should be made to the *Rutland manuscripts*, iii (H.M.C., 1894), which contains correspondence of the third duke of Rutland during his viceroyalty, 1784–7, and to *Correspondence of Pitt and Rutland, 1781–7* (London, 1890).

R. Jacob, *The rise of the United Irishmen* (London, 1937) is the best modern work on the revolutionary movement at the close of the century; but R. R. Madden, *The United Irishmen, their lives and times* (7 vols. London, 1842–6) is useful for biographical detail. Wolfe Tone's *Autobiography* (ed. R. B. O'Brien, 2 vols. London, 1892) helps to re-create the atmosphere of the period; D. Ireland, *Patriot adventurer* (London, 1936) is a convenient collection of extracts, with linking narrative.

The history of the legislative union is traced in J. R. Fisher, *The end of the Irish parliament* (London, 1911). H. M. Hyde, *The rise of Castlereagh* (London, 1933), a detailed and authoritative study, is largely concerned with Castlereagh's share in bringing the union about. Sir Jonah Barrington, *Rise and fall of the Irish nation* (Paris, 1833) is a vigorous but unreliable account of the last two decades of the century by a contemporary politician; it prints lists of those who voted for and against union in 1799 and 1800. *Correspondence of the Right Hon. John Beresford* (ed. W. Beresford, 2 vols. London, 1854) stretches from 1775 to 1804; it is of great importance for the whole period, and particularly for the years immediately preceding the union.

The period of the union: R. B. McDowell, *Public opinion and government policy in Ireland, 1801–1846* (London, 1952) is a comprehensive study of the political 'atmosphere' in the pre-famine period. *The Irish administration, 1801–1914* (London, 1964) by the same author, is a detailed examination of the machinery of government. Both books have excellent bibliographies. N. Gash, *Mr. Secretary Peel* (London, 1960) includes the period of Peel's chief secretaryship, and gives a brilliant analysis of the social, economic and political problems facing government at the time. D. Gwynn, *The struggle for Catholic Emancipation* (London, 1928) conveniently summarizes the main political theme of the early nineteenth century. For O'Connell's share in the Emancipation campaign, as well as for his later career, the best introduction is still W. E. H. Lecky, *Leaders of public opinion in Ireland*, ii (new ed. London, 1912). S. Ó Faolain, *King of the beggars* (London, 1938) is perhaps the best modern biography. A selection of O'Connell's correspondence was edited by W. J. Fitzpatrick (2 vols. London, 1888).

A. H. Graham, 'The Lichfield House compact' (*I.H.S.*, xii. 209–25) is a careful re-examination of O'Connell's alliance with the whigs in 1835. The effects of the alliance on the Irish administration may be studied in J. F. McLennan, *Memoir of Thomas Drummond* (Edinburgh, 1867) and R. B. O'Brien, *Thomas Drummond: his life and letters* (London, 1889). The Young Ireland movement and its aftermath provide the theme for three books by C. G. Duffy, which have attained almost the status of classics: *Four years of Irish history, 1845–9* (London, 1883); *The league of north and south* (London, 1886); *Thomas Davis* (London, 1890). These must be supplemented and corrected by more recent studies: R. Clarke, 'The relations between O'Connell and the Young Irelanders' (*I.H.S.*, iii. 18–30); T. W. Moody, *Thomas Davis* (Dublin, 1945); D. Gwynn, *Young Ireland and 1848* (Cork, 1949); J. W. Whyte, 'Daniel O'Connell and the repeal party' (*I.H.S.*, xi. 297–316) and *The Independent Irish Party, 1850–9* (Oxford, 1958); K. B. Nowlan, 'The meaning of repeal in Irish history' (in *Historical studies IV*, ed. G. A. Hayes-McCoy, Cambridge, 1963) and *The politics of repeal ... 1841–50* (London, 1965). L. Fogarty (ed.), *James Fintan Lalor* (revised ed. Dublin, 1947) is a collection of writings by the most radical social reformer among the Young Ireland group, with an introductory essay.

D. Ryan, *The phoenix flame* (London, 1937) gives an account, in popular form, of the Fenian movement. For more serious study the following provide essential source material: J. O'Leary, *Recollections of Fenians and Fenianism* (2 vols. London, 1896), for the period before 1870; J. Devoy, *Recollections of an Irish rebel* (London, 1929); W. O'Brien and D. Ryan (ed.), *Devoy's postbag* (2 vols. Dublin, 1948, 1953), a collection of correspondence, particularly important for Fenianism in America.

E. Strauss, *Irish nationalism and British democracy* (London, 1951) traces the background and development of the home rule movement, with strong emphasis on economic factors. With this should be compared N. Mansergh, *Ireland in the age of reform and revolution* (London, 1940), a brief but pregnant commentary on nineteenth-century Irish problems, in the light of contemporary British, European and American opinion. A. M. Sullivan, *New Ireland* (2 vols. London, 1877) is a contemporary view of Irish politics during the thirty years after the famine, by one of the early home rulers. D. Thornley, *Isaac Butt* (London, 1964) gives a definitive account of the formation and early history of the home rule party; but see also L. J. McCaffrey, 'Home rule and the general election of 1874 in Ireland' (*I.H.S.*, ix. 190–212); D. Thornley, 'The Irish home rule party and parliamentary obstruction, 1874–87' (*I.H.S.*, xii. 38–57); and, for the later history of the party, F. H. O'Donnell, *History of the Irish parliamentary party* (2 vols. London, 1910). R. B. O'Brien, *Life of Charles Stewart Parnell* (2 vols. London, 1899) remains the best full biography of Parnell, but on certain aspects of his career has been superseded by later studies. C. Cruise O'Brien, *Parnell and his party, 1880–90* (Oxford, 1957) is a detailed examination of the membership and organization of the home rule party under Parnell's leadership. F. S. L. Lyons, *The fall of Parnell* (London, 1964) is a brilliant analysis of the struggle in 1890–91; for British attitudes see also J. F. Glaser, 'Parnell's fall and the non-conformist conscience' (*I.H.S.*, xii. 119–38) and L. P. Curtis, Jr., 'Government policy and the Irish party crisis, 1890–92' (*I.H.S.*, xiii. 295–315). Some important contemporary correspondence is presented in T. W. Moody, 'Parnell and the Galway election of 1886' (*I.H.S.*, ix. 319–28) and C. H. D. Howard, 'Joseph Chamberlain, W. H. O'Shea, and Parnell, 1884, 1891–2' (*I.H.S.*, xiii. 33–7). F. S. L. Lyons, 'The economic ideas of Parnell' (in *Historical studies II*, ed. M. Roberts, Cambridge, 1959) collects and examines the scattered evidence on its subject.

For British policy in Ireland during this period J. L. Hammond, *Gladstone and the Irish nation* (London, 1938) is a standard authority; but it has not wholly superseded an older and briefer book by Lord Eversley

(Charles Shaw-Lefevre), *Gladstone and Ireland* (London, 1912). An indispensable complement to these is L. P. Curtis, Jr., *Coercion and conciliation in Ireland, 1880–92: a study in conservative unionism* (Princeton, 1963). A. V. Dicey, *England's case against home rule* (London, 1887) is a forceful statement of views widely held at the time.

The history of the home rule party during the two decades after the Parnellite split can best be followed in F. S. L. Lyons, *The Irish parliamentary party, 1890–1910* (London, 1951); but see also H. W. McCready, 'Home rule and the liberal party, 1899–1906' (*I.H.S.*, xiii. 316–48); and, for an almost forgotten episode, M. A. Banks, *Edward Blake, Irish nationalist: a Canadian statesman in Irish politics, 1892–1907* (University of Toronto Press, 1957). The following are among the most notable biographies and memoirs of leading home rulers: W. O'Brien, *An olive branch in Ireland* (London, 1910); T. M. Healy, *Letters and leaders of my day* (2 vols. London, 1928); T. P. O'Connor, *Memoirs of an old parliamentarian* (2 vols. London, 1929); M. Sullivan, *No man's man* (Dublin, 1943) a biography of T. M. Healy; D. Gwynn, *John Redmond* (London, 1932), which contains numerous extracts from Redmond's papers.

There is no adequate treatment of Irish unionism or of the 'Ulster question'. R. Lucas, *Colonel Saunderson, M.P.* (London, 1908) throws some light on the formation of an Irish unionist group at Westminster. T. W. Moody and J. C. Beckett (ed.) *Ulster since 1800: a political and economic survey* (revised ed. London, 1957) is a collection of brief essays. D. C. Savage, 'The origins of the Ulster unionist party, 1885–6' (*I.H.S.*, xii. 185–208) and F. S. L. Lyons, 'The Irish unionist party and the devolution crisis of 1904–5' (*I.H.S.*, vi. 1–22) deal competently with particular topics. R. McNeill, *Ulster's stand for union* (London, 1922), though strongly partisan, is important, especially for the negotiations over exclusion. There are good biographies of Carson by E. Marjoribanks and I. Colvin (3 vols. London, 1932–6) and H. M. Hyde (London, 1953); but neither gives an adequate account of the unionist movement in Ulster. H. Shearman, *Not an inch: a study of Northern Ireland and Lord Craigavon* (London, 1943) is slight but well-written. The official biography by St John Ervine, *Craigavon: Ulsterman* (London, 1949), is uncritical, but is based on the sources and contains some valuable material. F. H. Crawford, *Guns for Ulster* (Belfast, 1947) is a vivid, if ill-constructed, account of the 'gun-running' exploit of 1914 by the man who conducted it. W. S. Armour, *Armour of Ballymoney* (London, 1934) is worth noting as the biography of a prominent Ulster protestant home ruler.

R. M. Henry, *The evolution of Sinn Fein* (Dublin, 1920) is a brief but illuminating analysis of the revolutionary movement from the later nineteenth century onwards. C. Cruise O'Brien (ed.) *The shaping of modern Ireland* (London, 1960) is a series of short studies of leading personalities from the Fenians to Pearse. A. P. Ryan, *Mutiny at the Curragh* (London, 1956) treats its subject in the general setting of the home rule controversy. Sir James Fergusson of Kilkerran, *The Curragh incident* (London, 1964) concentrates on the events of a single week, and is based on detailed research.

For an understanding of the immediate background to the Dublin insurrection of 1916 F. X. Martin, 'Eoin MacNeill on the 1916 rising' (*I.H.S.*, xii. 226–71) is essential. M. Caulfield, *The Easter rebellion* (London, 1964) gives a detailed account of the fighting in Dublin, but has nothing of importance to say about the general political situation. For events from 1916 to 1923 by far the best guide is E. Holt, *Protest in arms* (London, 1960). W. A. Phillips, *The revolution in Ireland, 1906–1923* (2nd ed. London, 1926), though written from an Irish unionist standpoint, is not uncritical, and remains important for its detail. D. Macardle, *The Irish republic* (4th ed. Dublin, 1951) is coloured by firm adherence to the republican side on the treaty issue. For the making of the treaty see F. Pakenham, *Peace by ordeal* (London, 1935); and for a clear and balanced account of the first Dáil and of the general election of 1922 see the early chapters of J. L. McCracken, *Representative government in Ireland* (Oxford, 1958). Some of the leading figures of the period still lack satisfactory biographies; but the following should be noted: P. Beaslai, *Michael Collins and the making of a new Ireland* (London, 1926); F. O'Connor, *The big fellow: a life of Michael Collins* (London, 1937); R. Taylor, *Michael Collins* (London, 1958); S. Ó Faolain, *De Valera* (London, 1939); R. M. Fox, *James Connolly* (Tralee, 1946); T. de V. White, *Kevin O'Higgins* (London, 1948); R. McColl, *Roger Casement* (London, 1956). C. E. Calwell, *Sir Henry Wilson* (2 vols. London, 1927), though not primarily of Irish interest, contains material of vital importance for an understanding of the situation in Ireland.

SELECT LIST OF WORKS ON LOCAL HISTORY

Armagh: J. Stuart, *Historical memoirs of the city of Armagh* (Newry, 1819. A 'revised edition' by A. Coleman, Dublin, 1890, is virtually a new work).

Belfast: G. Benn, *History of the town of Belfast* (London, 1877).
H. Joy, *Historical collections relative to the town of Belfast* (Belfast, 1817).
R. W. M. Strain, *Belfast and its Charitable Society* (Oxford, 1961).

R. M. Young, *Historical notices of old Belfast* (Belfast, 1896); (ed.), *The town book of the corporation of Belfast* (Belfast, 1892).

Carrickfergus: S. McSkimin, *History and antiquities of Carrickfergus* (ed. E. J. McCrum, Belfast, 1909).

Cork: R. Caulfield (ed.), *Council book of the corporation of Cork* (Guildford, 1876).

C. Smith, *Ancient and present state of the county and city of Cork* (2 vols. Dublin, 1774; later ed., Cork, 1893–4).

W. O'Sullivan, *Economic history of Cork city from the earliest times to the act of union* (Cork, 1937).

Down: E. R. R. Green, *The industrial archaeology of County Down* (Belfast, 1963).

J. Stevenson, *Two centuries of life in Down, 1600–1800* (Belfast, 1920).

Drogheda: J. D'Alton, *History of Drogheda* (2 vols. Dublin, 1844).

Dublin: F. E. Ball, *History of the county of Dublin* (4 vols. Dublin, 1902–6).

D. A. Chart, *The story of Dublin* (London, 1907).

M. J. Craig, *Dublin, 1660–1860* (Dublin, 1952).

J. T. Gilbert, *History of the city of Dublin*, (3 vols. Dublin, 1854–9); (ed.), *Ancient records of Dublin* (13 vols. Dublin, 1889–1907).

J. J. Webb, *Industrial Dublin since 1698, and the silk industry in Dublin* (Dublin, 1913).

Dundalk: J. D'Alton and J. R. O'Flanagan, *History of Dundalk* (Dublin, 1864).

Dungannon: W. Hutchison, *Tyrone precinct* (Belfast, 1951).

Galway: J. Hardiman, *History of the town and county of Galway* (Dublin, 1820).

M. D. O'Sullivan, *Old Galway* (Cambridge, 1942).

Limerick: M. Lenihan, *Limerick: its history and antiquities* (Dublin, 1866).

Sligo: W. G. Wood-Martin, *History of Sligo, county and town* (Dublin, 1889).

Waterford: S. Pender (ed.), *Council books of the corporation of Waterford, 1662–1700* (Dublin, I.M.C., 1964).

C. Smith, *Ancient and present state of the county and city of Waterford* (2 vols. Dublin, 1774).

Wexford: P. H. Hore, *History of the town and county of Wexford* (5 vols. London, 1900–11).

Index

Abbey Theatre, 418

Abbot, Charles, 297 n.

Abercorn, James Hamilton, 2nd duke of, 410

Abercrombie, Sir Ralph, 262

Aberdeen, George Hamilton Gordon, 4th earl of, 356

Absentees, 167–8, 171, 241 and n., 290; proposal to tax, 203

Adair, Patrick, 124

Addington, Henry (1st Viscount Sidmouth), 288

Adventurers, claims of, 87, 106; grants to, 107, 109; position of, after Restoration, 119, 120

Africa, 218

Agrarian unrest (18th century), 176–9, 245, 273; (19th century), 291–2, 354, 374. *See* Hearts of Oak, Hearts of Steel, Land League, Ribbonmen, Tithe, Whiteboys

Agriculture, 15, 26; (18th century), 167–8, 171, 172–6, 243–5; (19th century), 292–3, 348–9, 351–2, 362, 385–6, 408–10

Albemarle, George Monck, 1st duke of, 100, 116, 117

Algerine pirates, 62–3

American civil war, 360, 364

American colonies, trade with, 131, 218, 242; emigration to, 178, 180, 181; political influence of, 203, 205, 206–7. *See* United States of America

Amnesty Association, 376

Anabaptists, 124, 126

Anglesey, Arthur Annesley, 1st earl of, 129

Anglo-Irish, 15 n. *See* Old English

Anne, Queen, 157, 160, 161

Annesley, Francis (Baron Mount-
morris and 1st Viscount Valentia), 63, 68 and n., 69

Anti-Corn-Law League, 326

Anti-Parnellites, 405, 413, 415

Antrim (county), Scottish settlements in, 22, 47, 114; agrarian unrest in, 178; insurrection in (1798), 264, 265; 88, 112, 170, 175

Antrim, Randal MacDonnell, 2nd earl and 1st marquis of, 79, 80

Argyll, George Douglas Campbell, 8th duke of, 390

Armagh (city), 28, 98, 221; (county), 45, 52, 71, 112, 253

Army, under James I, 36, 52, 56; under Charles I, 58–9, 60, 63, 69, 75–7, 79, 84; under Commonwealth, 110; at Restoration, 115–17; under Charles II, 127, 128, 134; under James II, 139–40, 141, 145; after Revolution, 154, 200, 201–2, 208, 219–20

Ashbourne Act (1885), 394, 406

Asquith, Henry Herbert, 422, 423, 427, 429, 432, 435

Athlone, 23, 147, 148

Aud, 439

Aughrim, 148

'Auxiliaries', 447, 448

Ayrshire, 47

Bacon, Francis, 55

Baker, Henry, 143

Balfour, Arthur James, 401, 406, 408, 418, 424, 426

Ballinamuck, 266

Ballinasloe, 148

Ballot Act (1872), 381, 406

Ballycastle, 175

Ballynahinch, 185, 264–5

Baltimore, 62

TORY ISLAND

INISHOW

LOUGH
SWILLY

Lond

LC

D O N E G A L

FO
LE

Strabane

T Y

LEITRIM

Enniskillen

Sligo

FERMANAGH

N

C A V

The counties included in the
plantation of James I

Area settled by Montgomerys
and Hamiltons in the reign of
James I

25 Miles

LONGFORD

MULL
OF
KINTYRE

NORTH CHANNEL

Coleraine

NDERRY

ANTRIM

BANN

Draperstown

Salterstown

Antrim

LOUGH

Larne

Carrickfergus

BELFAST LOUGH

Bangor
Clandeboye

Belfast

Newtownards

NE

Mountjoy

NEAGH

Dungannon

LAGAN

Lisburn

Saintfield

Charlemont
Benburb

Ballynahinch

Armagh

BANN

DOWN

ARMAGH

AGHAN

Newry

LOUTH

N

MEATH

EVENTEENTH CENTURY

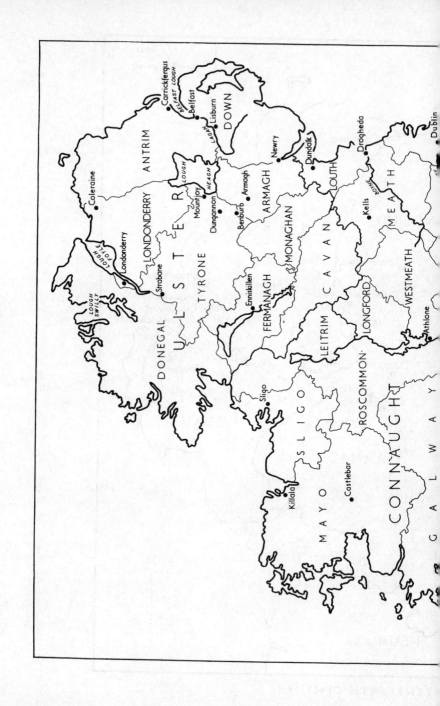

IRELAND

25 Miles

N

SHANNON

CLARE

LEINSTER

KILDARE

LEIX

WICKLOW

CARLOW

WEXFORD

Enniscorthy

Wexford

KILKENNY

Kilkenny

New Ross

Waterford

TIPPERARY

Cashel

Clonmel

WATERFORD

Dungarvan

Youghal

LIMERICK

Limerick

MUNSTER

Kanturk

CORK

Cork

KERRY

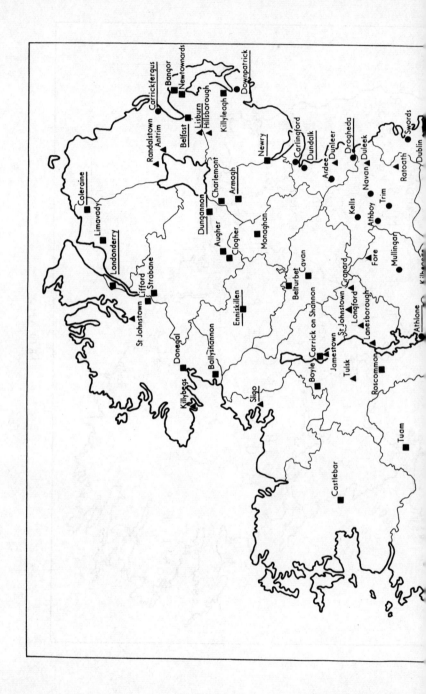

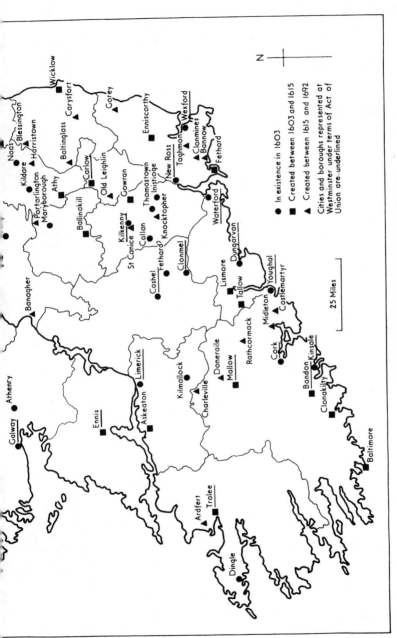

In existence in 1603 ●

Created between 1603 and 1615 ■

Created between 1615 and 1692 ▲

Cities and boroughs represented at
Westminster under terms of Act of
Union are underlined

25 Miles

PARLIAMENTARY CITIES AND BOROUGHS